THE CHILDREN OF THE SUN

MARCIENNE ROCARD

THE CHILDREN OF THE SUN

Mexican-Americans in the Literature of the United States

Translated by
Edward G. Brown, Jr.

THE UNIVERSITY OF ARIZONA PRESS   TUCSON

Publication of this book was made possible in part by a grant from the Southwest Center of the University of Arizona.

THE UNIVERSITY OF ARIZONA PRESS

This book was set in 10/12 Linotron 202 Bembo.
∞ This book is printed on acid-free, archival-quality paper.
Manufactured in the U.S.A.

94 93 92 91 90 89   5   4   3   2   1

Library of Congress Cataloging-in-Publication Data

Rocard, Marcienne.
   [Fils du soleil. English]
   The children of the Sun : Mexican-Americans in the
literature of the United States / Marcienne Rocard :
translated by Edward G. Brown, Jr.
      p.   cm.
   Translation of: Les fils du soleil.
   Bibliography: p.
   Includes index.
   ISBN 0-8165-0992-1 (alk. paper)
      1. American literature–History and criticism.
2. Mexican Americans in literature.
3. American literature–Mexican American authors–
History and criticism.   I. Title.
PS173.M39R613 1989
810'.9'352036872–dc 19   88-39772
                                CIP

British Library Cataloguing in Publication data are available.

Contents

Translator's Note   vii
Introduction   ix

PART ONE: 1848–1940
THE CONQUERED: THE YOKE OF THE STEREOTYPE

  The Anglo-American Point of View
    1848–1930: The Placing of the Yoke   3
Chapter 1. Ethnocentrism: The Myth of Anglo Superiority   11
Chapter 2. Romanticism: The California Myth   24
Chapter 3. Realism: The Mexican-American Faces Anglo Society   40
    1930–1940: The Yoke of the Stereotype Loosens   51
Chapter 4. Admiration for a Different People   53
Chapter 5. The Defenders of the Oppressed   62

  The Mexican-American Point of View
    Early Modes of Expression   67
Chapter 6. Mexicans Take Refuge in Their Myths   72
Chapter 7. Mexican-Americans Confront the Present   82

PART TWO: 1940–1965
THE INVISIBLE BUT INVINCIBLE MINORITY

The Anglo-American Point of View
  Introduction to the Period   109
Chapter 8. Flight Into the Past: The Children of Nature   113
Chapter 9. The Barrio: Refuge and Trap   129

The Mexican-American Point of View
  The First Literary Spokesmen   153
Chapter 10. In the Traditional Framework of the Barrio   155
Chapter 11. The Pocho's Dilemma   171

PART THREE: 1965–1974
CHICANOS PRESENT THEIR OWN IMAGE

The Anglo-American Point of View
  Confronting the Chicano Phenomenon   189
Chapter 12. One Last Beautiful Dream   191
Chapter 13. Marginality and Difference   193
Chapter 14. Mexican-Americans Confront the Debacle   201

The Mexican-American Point of View
Chapter 15. The Chicano Movement: Sociopolitical and Literary
  Awareness   207
Chapter 16. Strangers in Their Own Land   217
Chapter 17. Enough! The Chicanos in a Rage   246
Chapter 18. I Am Joaquín / Yo Soy Joaquín: Chicanos Affirm
  Their Identity   266
Chapter 19. The Children of the Sun: Chicanos as Precursors of a
  New World   281

Conclusion   293
Notes   297
Bibliography   359
Index   385

Translator's Note

In the interest of readability, and in consultation with the University of Arizona Press, this translation is slightly abridged from the original manuscript. Also, the preface to the original edition does not appear here. Notes and bibliographical references have been restructured to agree with the 1985 edition of the *MLA Style Manual*.

I have observed the following procedures in rendering Professor Rocard's *Les Fils du soleil* into English:

1. Historical Present. A good 80 percent of the French verbs in Professor Rocard's book are in the present tense. I have retained the present tense in some cases and have rendered others into the past, depending upon the context. The choices were not always simple ones.

2. Semicolons. The author has used the semicolon quite liberally. I have observed her stylistic use of this punctuation mark except when its use would have made the English translation awkward.

3. Accents. I have followed the use of Spanish accents in the original manuscript. As Professor Rocard notes, some Anglo-American writers were not well versed in the use of Spanish diacritical marks, and direct quotes from their works often reflect this. The author of this book has also used the names of many characters exactly as they appear in the works cited.

4. Quotations in Spanish. Wherever possible, I have gone to the bibliographical sources cited to find existing translations of quotations in Spanish. Such translations are denoted by asterisks. Where existing translations are not available, I have used the author's own translations (into French) as a guide. The passages from Octavio Paz's "*El laberinto de la soledad*" were taken from the

English translation by Lysander Kemp (New York: Grove, 1961); the lengthy translation of the *Corrido de Gregorio Cortez* was taken from Américo Paredes's *With His Pistol in His Hand* (Austin: U of Texas P, 1958); the passages from Tomás Rivera's ". . . *y no se lo tragó la tierra*" were taken from Herminio Ríos's translation in the bilingual edition (Berkeley: Quinto Sol, 1971).

I would like to acknowledge the assistance of my good friend and colleague, Professor Jean F. Goetinck, with respect to some particularly problematic passages. His invaluable suggestions are sincerely appreciated.

E.G.B.

Mexican-American, Chicano, Hispano, Latino-americano, Boy, Latin American, Legless war vet, Spanish-surnamed, Spanish American, Spanish-speaking American. People who refuse to go back to where they came from, namely, Texas, New Mexico, Arizona, Colorado, California, etc.[1]

Introduction

The Mexican-American was born in 1848, the date of the annexation of the Southwest by the United States. This vast territory, which stretches along the border with Mexico from Brownsville, Texas, on the Gulf of Mexico to Tijuana on the Pacific, includes the five states of Texas, New Mexico, Colorado, Arizona, and California. For almost four centuries, this land was the homeland of the Mexican-Americans' ancestors. Only the Indians were there before them. The history of Mexican-Americans goes back to the Spanish *conquistadores* and, even further, to the Aztecs. In 1519, Hernán Cortés captured the Aztec capital of Tenochtitlán; two years later, after the surrender of Emperor Cuauhtémoc, twenty million Indians came under Spanish dominion. The almost systematic interracial crossbreeding practiced by the Spanish, unlike the British colonists, gave their enterprise a unique character.[2] From the coupling of Aztec and Spaniard was born the *mestizo*, the ancestor of today's Mexican-American.

After gradually establishing the Vice-Kingdom of New Spain at the end of the sixteenth century, the colonizers moved north of the Rio Grande. In 1598, they founded the first capital of New Mexico, San Juan de Caballeros, nine years before the birth of Jamestown, the oldest English settlement in the New World.[3] The founding of the second capital, Santa Fe, in 1609, preceded by eleven years the Pilgrims' landing of the *Mayflower* in Plymouth Bay. The wife of Juan de Oñate, the founder of this new kingdom in New Mexico, was the great-granddaughter of the Aztec emperor Montezuma; many who accompanied the Spanish colonist were either of mixed or Indian blood. Similar groups established the Indo-Hispanic civilizations of Arizona, Texas, and California.

The attitude of the indigenous populations, and their level of development, affected the method of settlement. In Arizona, the expansion movement was plagued by Indian hostility. New Mexico was colonized before the end of the seventeenth century, however, and Spaniards and Mexicans assimilated and profited from a native culture that they judged to be equal, if not superior, to their own. In Texas and California, by contrast, where the colonists encountered only the political maneuverings of foreign powers[4] and not the hostility of the Indians, the settlers did not adopt the Indian culture. They arrived almost two centuries after New Mexico was explored, and they found the Indian society archaic. Of the three provinces in the Southwest, only New Mexico, the first Spanish and Mexican outpost, was able to achieve the "Indo-Hispanic synthesis"[5] that Spanish colonial policy attempted to establish.

Isolated from one another and shaped by differing geographic and economic conditions, *Nuevo Mexicanos*, *Tejanos*, and *Californios* quickly formed three distinct communities that were nonetheless linked by a common Hispano-Mexican cultural heritage. But these communities were also different from the Mexican society they sprang from. Although they shared a semifeudal system with Mexico, their socioeconomic structures were simplified by the absence of Spanish bureaucrats (*gachupines*). Nothing prevented the *ricos* (the "rich"), from gaining absolute power over the *peones* ("laborers"), the *mestizos* who were more Indian than Mexican, and the Indians, especially in New Mexico. There reigned an oligarchy of some twenty loosely allied families, who claimed to be descendants of the first pioneers. They controlled the territory's economy and politics. In Texas, the absence of democratic traditions was just as flagrant. California had a seemingly more flexible caste system, with three classes: the *gente de razón*, the great landowners of Spanish ancestry who comprised 10 percent of the population; the *cholo*, poor illiterates, for the most part *mestizo* or mulatto, who were usually cowherds, shepherds, artisans, or small landowners; and, at the lower end of the social scale, the Indians, subjected to the most menial labor.

In New Mexico, as in California, the mission system only reinforced this stratification. By proselytizing, the priests extended their control over the Indians, and, like the *patrones* ("bosses"), used their labor to develop a prosperous system of stock-raising and mixed-crop farms. The missions of the Southwest, like those in Mexico, received land grants; parcels were also granted to private citizens for services rendered to the crown. The number of grants increased after Independence in 1821.[6] During the secularization of the missions in California, the *hacendados*, or landowners, also were given domains confiscated from the Franciscans. Cattle-raising and diversified agriculture on these vast *ranchos* made California the wealthiest province of the Mexican Southwest. Texas specialized in raising longhorn steers, and New Mexico continued its traditional seminomadic sheep-raising while developing copper and gold mining.

The first Anglo-American immigrants from the United States found not an arid desert, but a flourishing economy with irrigated land and opulent *rancherías*

("settlements"), where food and lodging were generously offered to the passing traveler. Each locality, even the most remote mountain village, had its *plaza*
("town square"), the center of an active social life. The frequent fiestas drew
upon all of the musical and artistic resources of the Hispanic-Mexican people, and permitted them for a time to forget their arduous labors. The Anglo
colonists' fascination with this way of life is too well documented in the literature for us to dwell on it here. They also profited from Hispanic-American
achievements: the *hacienda* would serve as a model for the future ranches of the
American West; the *vaquero* was the prototype of the cowboy;[7] and American
gold prospectors would rely upon Mexican mining techniques.

In a sense, this first Anglo immigration paved the way for the future conquerors. What were individual enterprises in the beginning slowly took on
national and political importance; the arrival of foreigners ended up destroying
the precarious balance that had been established between metropolitan Mexico
and the provinces north of the Rio Grande. Lured by adventure and commerce,
the first Anglo colonists gained the confidence of the native population. Mixed
marriages sealed friendships between the American trappers and the *gente de
razón* in California, between Eastern merchants, who came after the opening
of the commercial Santa Fe Trail, and the *ricos* ("rich") in New Mexico.[8] In
Texas, ironically, the Mexican government itself called for Anglo colonization
to enlarge the population and to prevent meddling by France and England.
The good will was nonetheless illusory. Cordial relations existed only within
limited circles; most Anglo colonists displayed open contempt for the Mexican
culture, so different from their own. The distance between these two ethnic
groups widened after 1840 with the arrival of a new type of immigrant who
was proud of belonging to an American nation convinced of its "Manifest Destiny,"[9] of its right to possess the entire continent, and of its duty to regenerate
it. Negative stereotypes of Mexicans prevailed even before the United States
waged war against Mexico; the accounts of travelers during this period are
filled with them.[10] The Mexican-American War, in a sense, was no more than
one episode in a continuing conflict between two incompatible cultures.

The war was precipitated both by the American desire for expansion and by
the American residents' skillful exploitation of the growing irritation of Mexican provincials toward an overly centralized government. Mexico's centralizing
policy, begun in 1834 by Antonio López de Santa Anna, paradoxically, was to
serve the American expansionist objectives. The final repression of California's
independence movement and the restoration of order in Santa Fe following
the assassination of New Mexico's governor, Albino Pérez, in 1835 reflect the
unstable dependence of these far-flung provinces with regard to metropolitan
Mexico. Even more precarious was the situation in Texas, where the overwhelming numerical superiority of the Anglos (25,000, as opposed to 4,000
Tejanos) could only result in secession. The independence of Texas, exacted
in 1836 after a fierce struggle and a bloody, long-remembered defeat suffered
at the Alamo,[11] lasted nine years, until its annexation by the United States.

This was followed by a complete, rapid, and nearly bloodless conquest of the Mexican Southwest. From 1846 on, Americans encountered no resistance from New Mexico, whose leaders were seduced by the promises of the invaders. The following year, after the revolt of southern California was swiftly crushed (the only serious engagement of the campaign), the American flag was flying over what is now the state of California.

On February 2, 1848, in the village of Guadalupe Hidalgo, the treaty that officially ended the Mexican-American War was signed. The United States forced Mexico to recognize the right of Texas to enter the Union and to cede the two immense provinces of New Mexico and California;[12] in compensation, Mexico received $15 million. Clause IX guaranteed former Mexican citizens the exercise of their civil and political rights, freedom of religion, property rights, and cultural autonomy.[13] Article 2 of the protocol attached to the treaty guaranteed the retention of Spanish and Mexican land grants and property titles recognized by Mexican law. The fact that the American government did not live up to these clauses would strain forever the relations between the vanquished people and their conquerors.

How many Mexicans were affected by this treaty? Very few, despite the area of these ceded provinces, which represented 50 percent of the national Mexican territory but less than one-hundredth of its population. There were no more than 23,000 in 1790. The troubles following Mexican Independence set off the first large migration northward. Of the some 80,000 Mexicans who resided in the Southwest on the eve of the annexation, about 2,000 went back across the Rio Grande in order to retain their Mexican citizenship; those who remained automatically became American citizens after one year. After the annexation, by a reverse process, a certain number of Mexicans chose to move "north of Mexico"; they "emigrated,"[14] trusting the terms of the treaty and hoping to find better living conditions and a more liberal society. The wave of immigration intensified between 1890 and 1930, and again after World War II.

It has always been difficult to determine the exact number of Mexican-Americans in the United States (increased annually by several thousand illegal immigrants). Which criterion should be used—place of origin, language, or surname? After the census of 1940, they were no longer classified as Mexicans, but rather, among whites, as "Spanish-Speaking Whites" (1940), then as "Spanish-Surnamed Whites" (1950, 1960, 1970).[15] The term "Mexican-American," which acknowledges both their Mexican cultural heritage and their participation in the American nation, would have been more appropriate; it should have been made official in the treaty of 1848, which made the Mexicans of the Southwest American citizens. Indeed:

> Seventy years ago there were no "Mexican Americans." There were people in the Southwest who were somehow both from Mexico and natives of the United States. But in the view of the regular Americans who knew them best, the transplanted Easterners, Midwesterners, Southerners, Irish, Italians, Jews, and Chinese busy Americanizing the Southwest, and the

Negroes serving them, these people did not belong there as Americans. They were "Spaniards" if they were prosperous and pale, and "greasers"[16] or "Spics"[17] or "Mexicans" if they were poor or brown.[18]

For a long time, the terms "Mexican" and "Spaniard" (including its variants, "Hispanic-American" and "Hispanic") prevailed. Both are improper. Formerly used by Anglo-Americans and by Mexican-Americans themselves to designate two different social classes, they still retain this original meaning. The great landowners prided themselves on their Spanish ancestry. But with the exception of a handful of families in isolated villages of New Mexico, few could really substantiate a direct line of descent from Spanish colonists and *conquistadores*. The *Hispanos* rejected the term "Mexican" as an insult. It was reserved for the "mixed-blood" lower classes and has been geographically incorrect since 1848. The term "Hispanic-American" survived the collapse of the grand "Spanish" families and has enjoyed a resurgence each time the affluent, assimilating middle class wanted to dissociate itself from the foreign-born and poor. This was the case during the 1920s in New Mexico, where increasing immigration created a rift between long-established Mexican-Americans and newly arrived Mexicans.[19] During the same era, another euphemistic label was adopted in Texas, New Mexico, and Colorado: "Latin-American." It is found in the title of the first association of leading Mexican-Americans, the League of United Latin American Citizens (LULAC), created in 1929. The middle class considered itself either "Hispanic-American" or "Latin-American."

In the years after 1960, the militant residents of the barrio, or Mexican neighborhood, introduced the term "Mexican-American," especially in Southern California. They refused to disguise their ethnic origin in vague terminology. The title of the association they founded in 1960, the Mexican American Political Association (MAPA), is eloquent. This straightforward name was too direct for those who moved in circles outside the barrio, among Anglos. They preferred "American of Mexican origin," which highlighted their American citizenship. However, "Mexican-American" was little used outside California and was considered insulting by the *Hispanos* of New Mexico and elsewhere.

The hyphen was rejected by many as a humiliating sign of Mexican-Americans' "minority," or second-class, status. The activists sought a more specific name. As playwright Luis Valdez put it:

> Our insistence on calling ourselves Chicanos stems from a realization that we are not just one more minority in the United States. We reject the semantic games of sociologists and whitewashed Mexicans who frantically identify us as Mexican-Americans, Spanish-Americans, Spanish-Surnamed, Americans of Mexican descent, etc. We further reject efforts to make us disappear into the white melting pot. . . .[20]

The term "Chicano" was used officially for the first time by Rodolfo ("Corky") Gonzales at the Chicano Youth Liberation Conference in Denver in

1969. He revived a word that had been in use previously and gave it a new meaning by applying it to young Mexican-American activists. The origin of the word is obscure and it is difficult to define. The interpretation of Professor Philip D. Ortego of the University of Texas at El Paso, that Chicano is derived from the Nahuatl *meshicano*, seems to be generally accepted.[21] It may also come from the Nahuatl word *mexicanoob*, which designated the god Quetzalcoatl; as appealing as this explanation is, it appears rather implausible. On a more prosaic level, *Chicano* might be nothing more than a slang expression, an abbreviated form of *Mexicano* or a compound word composed of two elements: *Chihuahua* (a Mexican state that borders the United States) plus *Texano*; or from *chico* ("young boy") plus -*ano*. A Chicano would therefore be a Mexican-American who acts childishly. A link to the word *chicazo*, which designates an uneducated young street urchin, is interesting, if not conclusive. In other inventive hypotheses, Chicano is a deformation of *chinaco*, a nickname given by the French to the Mexicans, or from *Chichimeca*, an Indian tribe.[22] Some people have likely confused Chicano with the almost identical *chicana* and *chicanero*, which, respectively, mean "ruse" and "scoundrel" in Spanish. It may be that the discredit heaped upon this term derives in part from this unfortunate confusion.[23] The word *Chicano* is generally unknown in Mexico.[24]

The meaning of the word has varied depending upon the period. It appeared for the first time, in a variant spelling, in the early 1930s in the works of sociologist Manuel Gamio, to designate newly arrived immigrants whose status was not yet well defined and whom the local people had named *cholos* or *chicamos*.[25] It is these Chicanos of whom union leader Ernesto Galarza wrote, forty years later, in his autobiography. He arrived at the same definition as his predecessor: the "name by which we called an unskilled worker born in Mexico and just arrived in the United States."[26] It was no more than "a nickname given in sympathy and exasperation. . . ."[27]

The word was used once again in the forties during the Zoot Suit race riots, then, in the same period, used for the first time in a literary work, a short story by Mario Suárez. The author describes a Tucson barrio, whose inhabitants, the Chicanos,

> . . . raise hell on Saturday night and listen to Padre Estanislao on Sunday morning. While the term chicano is the short way of saying Mexicano, it is not restricted to the paisanos who came from old Mexico with the territory or the last famine to work for the railroad, labor, sing, and go on relief. Chicano is the easy way of referring to everybody.[28]

At the end of the 1960s, under the influence of student groups in Southern California and the Raza Unida party,[29] the term took on a specifically political connotation. The Mexican-American Law Students Association of the University of California at Los Angeles renamed itself the Chicano Law Students Association. Richard Vásquez published the novel *Chicano* in 1970; the barrio newspaper in San Bernardino, California, was named *El Chicano*, and so forth.

The term became more and more common, without dethroning "Mexican-American," even among militants (while Black activists completely rejected "Negro" in favor of "Black"). The literary review *El Grito* [The Cry], for example, was subtitled *A Journal of Contemporary Mexican-American Thought*,[30] and it was founded by Berkeley professors who ardently defended *chicanismo*.

The fortunes of the term generally were tied to its political, social, and economic context. While Republicans remained resolutely faithful to "Mexican-American," and even to "Hispanic" and "Spanish-Speaking," Democrats quickly established a semantic equivalency between "Mexican-American" and "Chicano," the latter becoming a synonym for "*La Raza*," and for "brown" or "bronzed." There was a parallel with Black Americans, among whom "Negro" (Mexican) slowly gave way to "Afro-American" (Mexican-American), and then to Black (Chicano). Brown Power and the Brown Berets of the 1970s evoked Black Power and the Black Panthers of the preceding decade.[31]

In the strictest sense, Chicanos subscribe to Brown Power; they represent no more than a "minority within a minority," [32] and not the entirety of Mexican-Americans. They are usually from the barrio.

The word "Chicano" has thus undergone many transformations in meaning since the 1930s. Formerly a term of derision, it now stands for *La Raza*. It is more difficult than ever to define, as indefinable as the "soul" of Blacks.[33]

What image of this minority is projected by Anglo-American literature and the literature of the Mexican minority itself?

Anglo literature now treats this subject less often than it used to, while Mexican-American literature, now in full flower, appeared to have been non-existent for decades. In an anthology, for example, Edward Simmen ascribes the first Mexican-American literary work to the year 1947,[34] while critics generally discuss only the militant Chicano literature of the past few years. Were there really no literary works earlier? Not a single literary history mentions any intellectual activity within the Mexican minority, and the earliest Mexican-American works, with rare exceptions, are not to be found in American libraries.

Yet, a body of literature derived from a long Spanish and Mexican tradition persisted long after 1848 but never became popular, for several reasons. The difficult situation of Mexicans just after the annexation, their ambiguous position toward both Mexico and the United States,[35] hardly created a climate favorable to literary development.

Some works of the years immediately following annexation were probably burned,[36] others lost; written in Spanish, they were published in Mexico, where they were studied in universities, then forgotten. Mexican-Americans were in no position to publish their own literature. Works that conformed to neither the linguistic nor literary standards prevailing in the rest of the country could hardly expect to receive a favorable reception from Eastern publishers or from the Anglo public; so they were sent instead to Mexico. Mexican-American newspapers became more and more numerous and published short pieces, poems, essays, and short stories, as well as news reports, but the majority of these newspapers were short-lived.[37]

Apart from these publication difficulties, there was a cultural problem: ties to Mexico remained very strong. After 1848, the children of the affluent continued to go south of the Rio Grande for their studies. For the rest, the family was the school. It carefully safeguarded the language and the inexhaustible reservoir of songs, poems, and legends, which were passed on orally from generation to generation. But those who made a career of writing found themselves in a dilemma: if they published in Mexico, they had to follow Mexican models to please the Mexican public and, consequently, disregard their experiences as Mexican-Americans. To succeed in the United States, they would have had to abandon their language and consequently a certain intellectual orientation.

Thus oral literature predominated.[38] To a certain degree, the conquered people, living in isolation on ranches or distant farms, locked into their language, limited in opportunities to publish, lost interest in a higher literature. The literary impulse had such difficulty in blossoming that it ended up flowering only in oral and folkloric form. However, the abundant folklore did not obscure the beauty of the *corridos*, whose form was inherited from Mexico but whose content reflected the personal experience of the author. There still exists an entire body of this literature, which is either in need of publication or, neglected, in need of resurrection.[39]

This was the task undertaken from 1967 to 1974 by a team from the Berkeley literary review *El Grito*, under the direction of Octavio Romano;[40] it sought out unpublished works in the hands of private citizens,[41] it cataloged old newspapers,[42] and it searched through private collections.

Mexican-American literature was not born during the Chicano movement. Like its authors, it was shaped by annexation, immigration, the struggle for survival in a hostile society, difficult socioeconomic conditions, and, finally, a long period of intellectual and literary maturation.

I propose here to study the image of the Mexican-American in Anglo-American literature and both the oral and written literature of the Mexican minority. By "Mexican-American," I mean the American of Mexican origin as well as any Mexican worker residing in the United States. I will examine how the image of the Mexican-American was formed and transformed by its historical, social, and political context, from the annexation in 1848 to 1974. By the latter date, the young Chicano literature had become abundant and varied enough to evaluate.

Two types of presentation were possible: one thematic and diachronic, the other synchronic. The first possibility was tempting; indeed, some major themes were discernible: the primitivism of Mexican-Americans, acculturation, rebellion, the alienation of the worker, the barrio, and so forth. But this method did not account for the problems posed by the language; in Mexican-American literature, the choice of linguistic vehicle is a function of the sociohistorical context. With few exceptions, Spanish, the native language, remained the favored form of expression during the problematic period of adaptation to American culture; the assimilation phase, on the other hand, was marked by the predominance of the majority society's language. Most recently, with the return toward ethnicity, the vernacular language has reestablished its rights: while some Chicanos write in English, others have returned to Spanish. An original mode of expression has also appeared in which the two languages are used alternately within the same work, especially in poetry; this internal bilingualism is not only a literary form of expression but, as we shall see, a political act as well.

The division I have chosen for the study corresponds to the three traditional phases through which most minorities pass in the United States and elsewhere. In the case of the Mexican minority, the first and longest phase covers the period extending from the annexation to World War II. In the postwar years, the second period, acculturation definitely took hold. Beginning in 1965, the year of the strike in Delano, there is a veritable sociopolitical and literary explosion, accompanied by an impassioned rediscovery of the past.

The sociohistorical perspective unifies this study, even though it risks introducing a disconcerting segmentation. This method also raises the problem of fragmentation and repetition. I have tried to remedy this by comparing the two perspectives, Anglo-American and Mexican-American, in each period, and to clarify the evolution of each distinct epoch.

Anglo-American writers at first conformed to fixed ideas without really "seeing" the Other, writing of this person only in stereotypes that originated before the annexation, stereotypes that would long persist in the collective memory of Americans. For their part, Mexicans first gave themselves a static image that fully corresponded to their role as the Other. Once they had cut the umbilical cord and gone beyond the folkloric stage, they regained their literary and intellectual autonomy. Turning inward, they defined themselves as Mexican-Americans confronting Anglo-American society—instead of allowing themselves to be defined by the Other, they made themselves "visible." Gradually, a more objective image took shape in the mind of the Anglo-American and a more personal one in the mind of the Mexican-American.

PART ONE
1848–1940

The Conquered: The Yoke of the Stereotype

Who am I? In reality,
I am who you want me to be. [1]

The Anglo-American
Point of View

1848-1930: The Placing of the Yoke

Anglo-Americans showed an intense interest in the Southwest in the first years following annexation. There were, of course, already Anglo pioneers in Texas as early as 1821. The first Anglo settlements in California were also established before annexation; the region's fabulous riches were just beginning to be discovered, and from 1826 on, it attracted trappers, hunters, and merchants, some of whom stayed on to become Mexican citizens and land-grant holders.[2] Their numbers increased with the outbreak of the war with Mexico in 1846. This war was to be waged under the influence of the expansionist ardor of the 1840s, by a nation convinced of its Manifest Destiny, which in 1848 meant the conquest of the Mexican Southwest. The Anglos wanted to regenerate this region economically, politically, and morally. The United States annexed the rather sparsely populated territories of California, New Mexico, and Arizona in order to satisfy its thirst for new land.

Speculators rushed to the empty territories captured by the Army during the first years of occupation, and gold prospectors followed as early as 1849. It was also necessary to establish the Mexican-American boundary line, survey the new lands, and pacify the borderlands, which remained volatile until the end of the second decade of the twentieth century.[3] The federal government dispatched various experts, geologists, and military men, and curious adventurers set out on their own. The conquest was not only military, commercial, and administrative, but literary as well. Officials and travelers alike began writing on what they found. Such gold prospectors and traders as George Evans, Alonso Delano, W. L. Manly, and Louise Amelia Knapp Clappe described their experiences in mining camps,[4] while agents of the federal government added personal observations on the native population to their official reports. Among these writers were John Russell Bartlett, a member of the commission charged with drawing up the borders; William Brewer, who worked four years with the Geological Service of the State of California; and J. Ross Browne, who, in 1849, was the official recorder of the commission charged with drafting the first Constitution of the State of California. In their diaries, travelers recorded their first encounters with the people of the Southwest, from whom they differed in appearance, language, and customs. William Davis, who spent two and a half years in New Mexico, naturalist John W. Audubon, who set off with a group of emigrants, J. Ross Browne, the indefatigable explorer, and the historian Francis Parkman all wrote accounts of their travels. These chroniclers were, for the most part, "Yankees," strangers to the Southwest. Most often, they crossed it without tarrying.

Out of the U.S. victory was born another genre, the pseudoliterature of the patriotic Dime Novels. A veritable literary offensive from the East, it was launched in 1859 by the Beadle and Adams publishing house, whose head was businessman and staunch patriot Erasmus Beadle.[5] His presses flooded the country with third-rate romantic writings, whose patent nationalism inflamed an entire generation. True "mercenaries of the pen," the authors he hired were selected primarily for their knowledge of the Southwest. Most were military men who had been in the war or served in the borderlands, former mountain men delighted to supplement their meager incomes. Among them were Lieutenants James Magoon and Henry L. Boone, Major Sam S. Hall, and others.

Thus it was through the eyes of the soldier, the mountain man, the peddler, the explorer, and the border surveyor that Anglos first saw the early Mexican-Americans.

But these fledgling authors quickly disappeared from the literary scene (or continued to exist only in certain Dime Novels). The war had left behind a bitterness, and interest in the Southwest waned. Instead, the nation turned toward the East, which was enjoying a golden age of industrial expansion. Then, in the 1880s, the Southwest, particularly California, was rediscovered. This renewed interest, even infatuation, can be explained only partially by the construction of the transcontinental railroad.[6] The flood of European immigrants into the United States had destroyed the racial and cultural homogeneity of the thirteen colonies, creating a sense of rootlessness among Americans and an unmistakable nostalgia for tradition. Distinguished by neither its past nor its culture, the American cultural landscape was desolate. The yearning for a golden age had not been fulfilled. Americans were no longer attracted by the conquest of new territory but rather by the rediscovery of the past.

"The 'Spaniards' went into apotheosis; Spanish California became a cult."[7] The historians of the period encouraged this devotion. Hubert H. Bancroft, in his four volumes on California before its conquest, exalted Spanish virtues and deplored the aggressiveness of the Yankee conquerors.[8] Josiah Royce, although slightly condescending toward Hispanics, presented a rather attractive image of the Mexican.[9] Many journeyed to the Southwest as "health seekers."[10] A partially paralyzed Charles F. Lummis went to New Mexico to regain use of his limbs; Helen Hunt Jackson, having come to prepare a series of articles, spent the entire winter of 1872 in California, recovering from bronchitis; she also gathered material for some of her novels.[11] Everyone, the sick and the healthy alike, counted upon the regenerating power of Spanish California to provide moral rejuvenation. The American hero of Gertrude Atherton's novel *Los Cerritos*, disillusioned by San Francisco's money-oriented society, weary of a cold and calculating wife who symbolizes the mercantile civilization imported from the East, feels threatened by "spiritual suffocation."[12] "A piece of driftwood on the stream of Circumstance," he arrives at the ranch of Los Cerritos, hidden away in the heartland of Spanish California, as if "to an island of peace and security."[13]

Hispanomania often was somewhat artificial and snobbish. Many, like Mrs. Tremaine, the wife in Atherton's novel, wished to play at being a *don* or *doña* and dreamed of entertaining at a ranch in the manner of the Spanish grandees.[14] The desperate efforts "to graft a Spanish past on an Anglo-Saxon Stock,"[15] to create a Spanish soul as if by hydroponic culture,[16] without first establishing roots in the soil of the country, led to eccentricities. Dressed in a *rebozo*, the shawl worn by Mexican women, Mary Austin went from door to door gathering the text of her *Pastorals* from the mouths of natives.[17] Lummis dressed and ate in the Spanish manner and ordered an entire Spanish liturgy for his civil funeral. The literary pseudonym for the very Anglo-Saxon Major Horace Bell was Don Guillamo Embustero y Mentiroso ("charlatan and liar"). A few years earlier, poet Cincinnatus Hiner Miller adopted the first name of the Mexican bandit-hero Joaquín Murrieta[18] and wore the outfit of a Spanish cowboy, as if the sombrero and wide red silk belt alone sufficed to make him a *vaquero*.

These eccentricities demonstrated a desire to adopt not only the costumes but the mentality of the Hispanic people. It was no longer a question of conquering them, but rather allowing oneself to be won over by their charm. To accomplish this, and describe the culture all the better, it was essential to settle in the region. The writers of this period no longer came only for the duration of a specific mission; certain authors, such as Atherton, were born there.[19] Others, like Charles Warren Stoddard and Austin, arrived as youngsters with their families.[20] An entire literary society was formed around the review *The Land of Sunshine*,[21] which featured translations of Spanish documents, regional news, and poems. Among the regular and well-known Hispanophile contributors were Joaquín Miller and Eugene Manlove Rhodes, and several women, including Grace Ellery Channing, Yda Addis, Mrs. Charles Stewart Daggett, Marah Ellis Ryan, and Austin. Their short stories and novels reflected their interest in Mexicans.[22]

The feminist movement was perhaps not unrelated to this "feminization" of letters. Indeed, literature at that time seemed to be the special province of women;[23] masculine energies were more likely to be channeled into the construction of highways and railroads or the restoration of missions. Women, in particular Atherton and Hunt Jackson, played a major role in the literary group of the eighties. The earlier chroniclers of the Southwest, with the exception of "Dame Shirley,"[24] were men, unpolished for the most part, and lacking the refinement with which the female intelligentsia took pride in the California of the 1880s. This change influenced the way Mexican-Americans were portrayed.

The passionate interest in Mexican-Americans continued until the Mexican Revolution (1910-1917), although its context changed. The depressions of 1893 and 1907, the beginnings of Populism in 1891, and the start of the second wave of Mexican immigration in 1890 all affected writers at the end of the nineteenth century: Bret Harte, who drew upon his California experience in short stories and poems; Jack London, the California proletarian; Stephen Crane, who spent most of his twenty-third year in the Far West and Mexico; and Hamlin Garland, the Midwestern frontier specialist who turned his interest toward the New Mexico Territory.

After 1910, Mexican-Americans became "a forgotten people."[25] Ironically, the long history of these people on American soil, surpassed only by that of the American Indians, was so old it was forgotten. The term "forgotten people" was to be revived by sociologists in future years.[26]

The Mexican was also the "forgotten man"[27] of American letters. How are we to explain this literary oblivion, which so struck Edward Simmen, author of an anthology of short stories on the Mexican-American? According to Simmen, the revolution that overthrew the dictatorial regime of Díaz in 1911 was strongly anti-American; one of the revolutionaries' first objectives was to put an end to foreign exploitation of Mexico, especially by American industrialists. Quite naturally, the American writer and the reading public came to associate Mexican-Americans negatively with Mexico and reacted toward them as Americans would later react toward Japanese-Americans during World War II. It is not surprising that Mexican-Americans did not figure in novels, except in the role of villain; this did not change until the 1930s.[28] The anti-American demonstrations of 1912 and 1913 in Mexico,[29] and the belief, from 1914 onward, that Mexican-Americans were spies working for the Kaiser,[30] only augmented their unpopularity among Anglo-Americans.

They were neglected on the literary level because they could not be ignored on either the diplomatic or social levels. Increasing immigration provoked an outbreak of nativism. In the case of Mexican-Americans, the nativism was all the more virulent because it was directed against immigrants who were Catholics; anti-Catholicism once again became fashionable with the founding of the new Ku Klux Klan in 1915. Lothrop Stoddard's racist book, *The Rising Tide of Color: Against White World-Supremacy* (1920), exploited the white American's fear of seeing "the rising tide" of people of color "threaten" white supremacy in the world. The immigration quota law of 1924, designed to stem this flood of "coloreds," echoed the themes of Stoddard's book, in which the

Klan mentality of the 1920s found its most perfect expression.[31] According to Stoddard, the racial war in Mexico, which pitted *mestizos* against whites and pure-blooded Indians against both ethnic groups, was a real menace to civilization, since its objective was the triumph of the brown race.[32]

North of the border, the people of this "brown race," the Mexican-Americans, elicited the interest of only a few isolated writers: Willa Cather, Eugene Manlove Rhodes, Robinson Jeffers, Harvey Fergusson, Robert Herrick. These writers profited, in a way, from the literary triumphs of their predecessors by reworking old themes and mining the same literary veins. This lode eventually became exhausted, just as the California mines had. The economic changes engendered by the Great Depression also brought about a change in perspective, and a different view of Mexican-Americans began to appear.

From the very start, the image of Mexican-Americans differed according to the writer. Between 1848 and 1910, a period in which they evoked lively interest, there were three clearly discernible conceptions of Mexican-Americans. But the attitude of the American writer should not be oversimplified. The relationship between Anglos and Mexican-Americans has been complex ever since the first contacts took place well before 1846 and the start of the war with Mexico. In California, Arizona, and New Mexico, there were efforts to integrate the two cultures. In Texas, there was hostility and conflict. The Anglo-American colonists of the 1820s and 1830s merged easily with California society; after 1848, frequent marriages between young American Navy officers and rich heiresses (whose families had not yet been dispossessed of their property by the occupiers) also facilitated relations between the conquerors and the defeated. *The Splendid Idle Forties*, a novel by Atherton,[33] depicts the mutual infatuation of suitors and *señoritas* in courtships conducted under the sympathetic and complicitous eye of matrons. The parents initially found these matches convenient and suitable for their daughters. Assisted by love and a taste for money, the handsome officers of the American garrison were quickly won over by the feminine members of this Jane Austen-style society, whose lives were marked by leisure, pretty dresses, amorous intrigues—and substantial dowries. With the less privileged, however, relations were less cordial. Highway robbery became rampant in the years following the war; cattle rustling occurred daily on the ranches. Joaquín Murrieta[34] and Tuburcio Vásquez, the Robin Hoods of California, were the terror not so much of the natives as they were of colonists, of the police and vigilantes in San Francisco, and of the Rangers, a volunteer police force created in 1853 to combat increasing lawlessness.

Order was, more or less, finally established in California, but in Texas it was not accomplished until the end of the 1920s. There, the Rangers exacerbated already existing conflicts.[35] The situation was more complicated because in the early years Texas was a slave state, and the first American settlers were originally from the South. If there was intermarriage after 1848 between Anglo-Americans and native Texans of the affluent classes, there was still discrimination against those accused of helping slaves escape across the Mexican border. The Anglos seemed to transfer their prejudices, inflicting upon Mexicans the same racial bias they held against Blacks.

To these conflicts was added the bitterness left by a war that for ten years had pitted Mexico against Texas, until the latter was annexed by the United States in 1846. Anglo-Texan history held painful memories, not the least of which was the Battle of the Alamo, where, people liked to say, so many valiant Americans perished, victims of Mexican cruelty.[36]

It is no surprise, then, that the first Anglo-Americans to write about the conquered people had an essentially unfavorable attitude. The "pioneer-writers," "missionaries"[37] of a new order, bearers of Manifest Destiny, believed they were called upon to bring the benefits of American civilization to the Mexican barbarians. They took up their mission with all the exuberant optimism that charged the first half of the nineteenth century in America. It was the optimism of a young nation and contained a great deal of naiveté. Were they not, after all, Anglo-American, members of the "chosen race,"[38] with a monopoly on intellectual and moral values? Wasn't the degenerate Mexican race manifestly inferior, biologically speaking? Americans coined a new word, nativism, for their own version of racism. Nativism was, by definition, opposition to all minorities and foreigners. Since Mexican-Americans were not "American," Anglo opposition to them was justified. Their Catholicism rekindled the American hatred of Rome, which had so marked the years preceding the Civil War that people often considered "nativism and anti-Catholicism as more or less synonymous."[39] The Mexicans' feudal and highly stratified conception of the church and society shocked the Protestant Anglos, who favored political and social liberalism and individual liberty. Mexican-Americans were quite different from the Puritan pioneers, who placed more emphasis on the value of work than on the enjoyment of life. Finally, the bourgeois Anglos were baffled by a society that had no middle class.

Everything about Mexican-Americans went against the American mentality; everything thus reinforced the pioneer-writers' sense of superiority and encouraged them to look down upon the Other and see him as nothing more than a "greaser."[40] The exaggeration of the writer's own self-image engendered, as if by some compensating mechanism, a reduction of the image of the Other. Even though a clear dichotomy had been established on the social level between the *rancheros*, the large landowners who fought alongside the Rangers, and the lower-class "Mexicans,"[41] the writer still felt some ambivalence toward the ranchers. This ambivalence, along with an overriding ethnocentrism, appeared in the earliest chronicles and the Dime Novels of the Mexican Southwest.

The mountain men, who saw every foreigner as an enemy to be run through with a sword, were followed by a group of writers who were less certain of themselves and the virtues of American civilization. Denouncing the principles of Manifest Destiny, they glorified the Mexican world, so different from their own. In it, they found what they had thought to be forever lost: tradition, romance, the poetry of dreams. They contrasted these "flowers of our lost idylls" [42] to the flashiness of the modern industrialized world and to the Puritan sterility of New England; to the "unromantic" conquest of New England by the Puritans, they compared the discovery of the New World by the Spaniards, which provided "four centuries of uninterrupted and infinitely varied Romance." [43] In their longing for the past and the picturesque, the New World romantics of the nineteenth century created the "California Myth," [44] rich in color and tradition. In reverse compensation, these writers, conscious of their own deficiencies, looked at the Mexican-American through a distorted lens and no longer saw anything but the *don* or *doña*.

Toward the end of the century, however, writers no longer sought to portray only the ridiculous or the picturesque; a more realistic literary movement began. Mexican-Americans depicted during this time took on more human proportions; they were described as facing problems that continue to trouble them to this day. Here again we must avoid generalization: there was still a great deal of romanticism and caricature in the works of Harte and London, a lack of verisimilitude in Garland. Nevertheless, these writers tried to provide a more objective image of Mexican-Americans and of their situation in American society.

Three attitudes, then, characterized the beginnings of literature focused on the Mexican-American. The first was ethnocentric and based upon a belief in Anglo superiority. The second was romantic and inspired by nostalgia for a bygone and different world. The third was realistic and sprang from a desire for objectivity and a sincere sympathy for an oppressed and defeated people. These three attitudes were to continue until 1930 and beyond; for a long time, there were vestiges of Manifest Destiny. The yearning for the past intensified with the erosion of traditional values after World War I and the advent of a materialistic world increasingly oriented toward money and progress. The economic instability the nation experienced beginning in the 1890s, along with the Mexican Revolution, was to furnish the historical setting for the realistic writers.

He was a Mexican, and that was it. [1]

CHAPTER I

Ethnocentrism: The Myth of Anglo Superiority

The origin of the word "greaser" is uncertain. If we are to believe Jeremiah Clemens, the author of Texas Romances, [2] the term was originally applied to Mexican *rancheros* by the first American settlers. Later, the American Army reportedly adopted it. The explanation that Clemens gives for the origin of the word is offensively simple-minded but typical of his era: "The people look greasy, their houses are greasy—everywhere grease and filth hold divided dominion. . . ." [3] Willa Cather, in her early short story "The Dance at Chevalier's," which is heavily tainted by ethnocentrism, used the term "greasy" to describe a Mexican's hand. [4] In his satirical poem "Tamales," O. Henry used the word literally. The revenge of a tamale vendor [5] whose ancestor was killed by the Texans is to be the "greaser" of the American nation, in a literal and figurative sense:

> This is your deep revenge,
> You have greased us all,
> Greased an entire nation
> With your Tamales. [6]

Clemens's etymology is still accepted today, if only by the make-up artists of Hollywood. More than a century later, Duncan Emrich gave the term "greaser" a more plausible and less biased interpretation. He argued that a greaser was a worker who ran alongside ox carts and other wagons with a grease bucket to lubricate dry and squeaky wheels. Anglos were unfamiliar with the procedure and ended up applying this now-pejorative word to all Mexicans. [7] McWilliams adopted this version, but added two variants: a Mexican grease vendor greased the ox carts on the Santa Fe Trail[8] in Raton Pass before they descended into the New Mexico plateau. In the California hide-and-grease trade, McWilliams said, American sailors gave the name greaser to the Indians and Mexicans who loaded the greasy and tick-laden hides onto clipper ships.[9] Authors of the postannexation period and later seemed to have adopted the term in preference to "oiler."[10] "Greaser" soon developed a pejorative meaning, often accentuated by the denigrating adjective "dirty."[11]

Who was this "dirty greaser"? After the annexation, there were but two classes in Mexican-American society: a rich landed aristocracy of Spanish ancestry and a mass of mixed-blood and destitute *mestizo* workers. It was the *mestizo* who inevitably became the "greaser." Later, after the Revolution of 1910, the Mexican refugee replaced the *mestizo* as the "greaser" upon whom Anglo-Americans heaped contempt and animosity.[12] The term "greaser" was sometimes used as a synonym for "Mexican."

In what context does this "greaser" appear? How is he portrayed? Let's follow John William DeForest to Santa Fe as described in *Overland*:

> In those days, Santa Fe, New Mexico, was an undergrown, decrepit, out at-elbows ancient hidalgo of a town, with not a scintillation of prosperity or grandeur about it, except the name of a capital . . . it consisted of a few narrow, irregular streets, lined by one-story houses built of sun-baked bricks. Owing to the fine climate, it was difficult to die there, but owing to many things not fine, it was almost equally difficult to live. Even the fact that Santa Fe had been for a period under the fostering wings of the American eagle did not make it grow much. . . . Nobody seemed to want to stay in Santa Fe, except for the aforesaid less than five thousand inhabitants, who were able to endure the place because they had never seen any other, and who had become a part of its gray, dirty, lazy lifelessness and despondency.[13]

For this author, the renowned style of the city center holds little attraction. He concentrates instead on the dilapidated, the run-down, and the pitiful, accentuating the "gray" and "dirty" color of the city—not the warm pink shades of its adobe. Ethnocentric writers such as DeForest presented only an unfavorable image, in which filth predominated, of the Mexican quarter in the cities they traveled through. J. O. Borthwick recalls only the "greasy looking Mexican fondas [inns]" in the Mexican section of San Francisco.[14] The "filthy buildings of the Mexican suburbs" of San Antonio quickly erase the favorable impression Bartlett had when he viewed the town from a distance.[15] In San Antonio de Bexar, Sidney Lanier complains that Mexican washerwomen squatting in the most graceless positions destroyed the poetic qualities of the San Pedro River.[16]

Not only were the Mexican quarters gray and sordid, the authors implied, but threatening as well. In Santa Fe, there were "many things which were not excellent," which DeForest does not elaborate upon, allowing the reader to imagine the worst. This troubled and sinister setting is the background for Dime Novels with often suggestive titles. Their plots invariably lead to a conflict between the Rangers, the defenders of the settlers, and Mexican bandits, a "conflict which must end only in death."[17] The bandits either "sell out" to white desperadoes, or, under the orders of their leaders, Cortina in Texas (in the novels of Hall), Joaquín Murrieta in California (in those of Joseph E. Badger), attack ranches or wagon trains heading for Santa Fe and San Antonio, laden with government arms or merchandise. To enhance the tragedy, Hall adds to his cast of settlers beautiful young ladies who are inevitably kidnapped by American or Mexican outlaws. These novelistic abductions are often organized by Americans and carried out by Mexican hired killers, who are more than equal to the bloody task. These hackneyed plots, more melodramatic than tragic, stress the villainy of the Mexican bandits, whose dastardliness surpasses that of their American counterparts. The theme of the pretty young Anglo-American orphan who receives an unexpected inheritance in California—an inheritance the California heir feels cheated of—appears in a Dime Novel by Edward Willet[18] and also, more elaborately, in the novel *Overland* by DeForest. In these two works, the heroine undertakes a long and perilous journey to the West, escorted by trustworthy friends (the Americans who will help her gain her inheritance) and by others with dishonorable intentions (the Mexicans who attempt to steal it from her). And what natural background could be better suited to these terrifying adventures than the dark chaparral thickets and forbidding canyons of the Sierra Nevada?

The Mexican setting, repulsive in its dirtiness, was also bathed in blood. Life is anything but pleasant in the filthy streets of Santa Fe; the squalid shacks of Greaser Flat, the Mexican quarter of a California mining town described by Badger, are nesting places for murderers.[19] Later, at the turn of the twentieth century, O. Henry made no distinction between the squalor and the danger of the Mexican environment into which he placed his tamale vendor. These qualities explain quite naturally the strangeness of his behavior. He is from the "Land of the bull fight, / Fleas, and revolution."[20]

The reader, therefore, was predisposed toward antipathy and contempt. DeForest [see note 13] spoke of the Mexican pejoratively. He gave a negative image of Santa Fe and its inhabitants through an abundant use of negative or semi-negative adjectives and adverbs: "out at-elbows" ("out" denoting privation), "with not," "a few" (not numerous), "undergrown" (not having reached normal development), "irregular," "one-story houses" (signs of destitution). The town had never prospered. "Nobody" wants to live there. The population is significantly "lower" in number than it should be. The natives have never tried to enlarge their horizons. One should note, finally, the privative prefix and suffix of the last two nouns, "lifelessness" and "despondency." The capital of New Mexico lacks vital substance; it is no longer anything but a name. Similarly, the words used to describe Greaser Flat all had negative connotations: "Dingy canvas tents, and rickety, tumble-down slab shanties, . . ."[21]

The only positive thing that DeForest cannot deny Sante Fe, the excellence of its climate, is canceled out by the very manner in which he expressed it. Death snuffs out life. Irony, negative and deadly, sets the tone from the very first lines of DeForest's novel. With mordant bitterness, he compares the decay of the city with the decline of the Spanish nobility, and signals his ethnocentrism, in which not even Hispanic-American high society is spared. I will return to this point later.

Irony is thinly disguised in Badger's passage on Greaser Flat:

> It is very quiet, now, under the warm rays of the afternoon sun. A few men, an occasional woman or child may be seen, lying prone in the grateful shadow, or lazily passing to and fro. But all is still. This is but the hour before dawn with the inhabitants of Greaser Flat.[22]

The afternoon is the calm before the storm of the noisy evening disturbances, because, for the Mexican, dawn breaks just before nightfall. The Mexican siesta would long remain the object of Anglo-American sarcasm.

In most cases, the sarcastic tone gave way to the comic, even the farcical and the ludicrous. The Mexican became the object of mocking derision. Scenes depicting the cowardice of Mexicans were always treated humorously. Mexicans became associated with the animals they tended: they "stampeded"[23] or fled "like frightened sheep."[24] O. Henry's parody of the greaser, "Tamales," is pure farce; the vile tamale vendor undergoes a mock-heroic transformation into a high priest, not a priest who blesses crowds, but one who "greases" Americans.

From bantering sarcasm to direct attack is a very short distance. It's a step more often taken in folklore than in authentically literary works, where invective is rare. Folklore is often exaggerated in the extreme, and in one tale the "law west of the Pecos River" was particularly harsh. Take, for example, the sentence imposed on the accused, Carlos Robles, by Roy Bean, a famous judge in folklore: ". . . it's the order of this court that you be took to the nearest tree and hanged by the neck till you're dead, dead, dead, you olive-colored son-of-a-billy-goat!"[25] One can find the same rhetoric in the mouths of other judges of folklore, notably, Judges Parker of Fort Smith and Benedict of Santa Fe.[26]

Ethnocentric authors generally proceeded in a more subtle, less openly aggressive manner, by using what is called the parallel technique. They established a parallel between the American of Mexican descent and the American of Anglo origin, the comparison, of course, always being to the Anglo's advantage. DeForest, for example, contrasted Mexican backwardness to American creative power (note the magnifying value of the metonym "American eagle" in the passage quoted earlier). In the passage by Badger, the existence of a run-down and unsafe Spanish quarter implies the presence of other clean and well-constructed sections of town; here, the parallel is implicit. This was not always the case. Each time that ethnocentric writers described San Antonio, whose population at that time was ethnically diverse, they stressed the attractive arrangement of the German and American neighborhoods, in comparison to what they saw as the sordid decrepitude of the Mexican part of town. Thus we read in the work of Frederick Law Olmsted:

> The singular composite character of the town is palpable at the entrance. For five minutes, the houses were evidently German . . . neat, and thoroughly roofed and finished. . . . From these we enter the square of the Alamo. This is all Mexican. Windowless cabins of stakes, plastered with mud and roofed with river-grass . . .[27]

DeForest's novel *Overland* is partially constructed on a parallel: the heroine is escorted during her perilous journey to California by an Anglo and two Mexicans, and the author frequently compares the courage and seriousness of the former with the cowardice and shallowness of the latter.

The work of these writers was infused with a simplistic, irritating, and unconvincing Manichaeism, an idea of two contending forces of good and evil. To Henry Llewellyn Williams (whose pseudonym was Boone, the famous pioneer of the late eighteenth century), the Yankee had all the virtues. This author even systematically considered all the good qualities historically granted to Mexicans, but only to demonstrate their seamy underside: he found their generosity calculated, their hospitality suspect, their horsemanship inferior (New Englanders, excellent riders all, he claimed, could give pointers to the *vaqueros*). Politeness was more an attribute of Americans; the Mexican gift for music was also questioned; humor was too foreign to soldier-writers like Williams for them to believe Mexican humor could be a subtle form of self-criticism.[28] This Manichaeism gave rise to exaggerated situations, particularly in the Dime Novels and folklore, in which Mexican villainy reinforced the American pioneer's "epic sense of life,"[29] and the desire for good to triumph over evil.

This use of the parallel had another negative effect. Mexican-Americans were judged according to Anglo standards that inevitably established their inferiority, and not according to their own system of values.

The Half-Caste and the Peon

The "greaser" was a "Mexican" or "Mex," a half-caste, more Indian than Spanish. The term "Mexican" often alternated with "greaser" or was used alone by some authors, such as Bartlett. But a distinction was established between the sexes. Men were often called "Mexican" while women, especially attractive ones, were not. Parkman used the adjective "Spanish" to describe the women he met, even though their undiluted Spanish heritage was certainly questionable.

The ethnocentric writer judged people according to the color of their skin. This biological determinism governed the hierarchy of merit established by Parkman during his stay in Colorado:

> The human race in this part of the world is separated into three main divisions, arranged in the order of their merits: white men, Indians, and Mexicans; to the latter of whom the honorable title of "whites" is by no means conceded.[30]

Here is an "intellectual competition" imagined by Alfred Lewis's storyteller: "An intellectual competition—whites barred—mules will stand at the head. The list should come out mules, coyotes, Injuns, Mexicans, ponies. . . ."[31]

The hero of Harvey Fergusson's novel *The Blood of the Conquerors* is a Mexican defeated by superior forces. Although the blood of Spanish conquerors still flows in his veins, Ramón, a "barbarian" and "weakling" (these terms recur endlessly in this writer's work), cannot escape the consequences of his ancestors' miscegenation. Thus, "Ramón knew that he must be beaten."[32] The book's entire thesis may be summed up in this one line.

The undeniable respect that real-life bandits Joaquín Murrieta and Juan N. Cortina enjoyed among Anglos was due, in part, to their Spanish origin and, consequently, to their intellectual and social superiority. Hall specifies that Cortina's complexion is "more Castilian than Mexican."[33] He also declares that Cortina has the aura of a conqueror. His followers, on the other hand, recruited from among the peasantry, the most mixed-blooded of all Mexicans, inspire nothing but contempt. They are "swarthy, serpent-eyed, low-browed ruffians. . . ."[34] While Cortina's eyes have the proud glare of the eagle, the eyes of his men invariably have the vile look of the snake. If the degree of morality was truly proportional to the degree of interbreeding, as Anglos commonly believed, then it was among the lower classes of Mexican society that the worst vices abounded. In his trilogy devoted to Murrieta, Badger pleads on behalf of this man, forced by circumstance to resort to banditry and crime.[35] Bartlett concludes that the Mexican masses are inferior to Castilians because they are a "mixed breed, possessing none of the virtues of their European ancestors, but all their vices, with those of the aborigines superadded."[36]

While the upper classes of Mexican-American society claimed pure bloodlines and freedom from all Mexican influence, half-castes were strongly marked by their native country. Although a resident of Austin, O. Henry's tamale vendor remains "the Mexican." Once on the other side of the Rio Grande, poor immigrants were still "Mexicans." They could no more deny their origin than could the tamale vendor wash away the grease that clung to his hands like the indelible stain of original sin. Nor could they remove the smell of chili peppers, which lingered even in death. This tenacious odor, nauseating to Anglos, was long considered an attribute of the poor Mexican-American. Folklore exaggerated the use of this seasoning, which even made of the dead Mexican an inedible dish: "A coyote won't eat dead Mexican because the Mexican eats chili."[37] The buzzard and the crow, scavengers both, would not touch a Mexican corpse either. The body of an Indian, Negro, or Anglo, however, would be attacked immediately by these birds of prey.[38] In Texas, the heat of Mexican spices was a greater hell than the heat of battles waged against Mexico. According to one song: "Just dine with a Greaser and you will shout, / 'I've hell on the inside as well as the out.'"[39]

The Traitor's Knife

It was this ill-smelling peon that the ethnocentric writer attacked. How could one do anything but continue the subjugation of these primitive beings, governed entirely by instinct and emotion? They were believed incapable of keeping their hands off their knives: Alonzo Delano's mule driver, enraged by the offensive attitude of an interpreter, quickly went for his weapon.[40] To William Davis, there were two categories of people in New Mexico, the "elite" and the "primitive people." The latter were ignorant of the proper manners so essential to real self-discipline.[41]

The memory of the Mexican war of independence, coupled with the Reform in the 1880s and the conflicts that followed that social revolution[42] only made landed Hispanic-American aristocrats and Anglo-Americans more antagonistic toward Mexicans in the United States. The Mexican *mestizos*, held responsible for their nation's political instability, were associated with half-breed "greasers," whom Anglos inevitably considered troublemakers, especially after the revolution of 1910. This supposition was borne out more than once, by actual border incidents. All immigrants from the country of "murderers,"[43] bullfights, and revolutions represented a threat because they were believed to carry a legacy of violence. We have already seen the subversive tendencies that O. Henry ascribed to his tamale vendor. Since his grandfather was killed by Texan soldiers, the vendor takes revenge by selling the people of Austin tamales filled with dog and cat meat. Although obviously intended to be humorous, the poem reveals the author's attitude. In the works of Lewis, every "greaser" is, a priori, a bandit deserving of a lynching.

But was the Mexican bandit genuinely cruel? Historians and sociologists persist in seeing cruelty as a trait inherent to the Mexican character, attributing it either to Indian[44] or Latin[45] ancestry. The cruelty of Mexican-Americans struck Davis, who blamed the Spaniards, their "spiritual masters," for never teaching them "that beautiful doctrine which teaches us to love our neighbors as ourselves."[46] The vengeance in Cather's short story "The Dance at Chevalier's" is lethal: the Mexican does not hesitate to poison his Anglo rival, who dies before the eyes of the beautiful Severine. Accustomed to such violent sports as bullfighting and the rodeo, the Mexican-American quickly gained a reputation for liking blood. In point of fact, the real-life victims were more often Mexican than American and their killer was generally a "bad man," Billy the Kid or one of his cohorts; folklore made little effort to justify their cruelty. On the contrary, Billy the Kid

> . . . was always after Greasers
> And kept 'em on the run.
> He shot one every morning
> For to make his morning meal.[47]

Such acts were considered justifiable reprisals for the atrocities committed by Mexicans during the war with Texas.[48] However, authors in the years following the war saw the Mexican-American as more devious and treacherous than cruel and bloodthirsty. Bartlett denounced the "acts of treachery of the grossest and cruelest description" committed by Mexicans against Indians.[49] The Mexican was portrayed as a born traitor, a villain who could not be trusted, "a back-stabber" in confrontations with the Rangers.[50] In Hall's Dime Novels, every Mexican was "villainous-looking" and "serpent-eyed."[51] Belief in Mexican cowardice was a legacy of the war; Davis attributed the cruelty of Mexicans to a lack of self-confidence and to incompetent leaders rather than to a lack of personal courage: "with American Officers to lead them, they will make excellent troops,"[52] he declared. The writers of this period took pleasure in stressing Mexican cowardice; it was a way of ridiculing the newly defeated people, while making the contemporary reader laugh at their expense. Thus, comic settings and backgrounds abound. Typically, in these works, a Mexican of ludicrous cowardice flees in the face of Anglo-American military power or courage. During one of the expeditions conducted by Audubon, Lieutenant Browning finds himself confronted by a crowd of Mexicans. But:

> He drew his revolver and ordered the (Mexican) crowd off, and in an instant the ground was clear, and the fear that characterizes these miserable creatures was shown as they hurried off, holding their hats to shield the back of their heads.[53]

In the duel that pits the mule driver against Delano's interpreter, that is, the knife against the revolver, it is the Mexican knife-wielder who takes to his heels, "deeming 'discretion the better part of valor.' "[54] Compare this definition of courage to the more facetious one given by the narrator of *Wolfville Days*, a tale about a Mexican who kills a bear without realizing the risk he is incurring. "Courage is sometimes knowledge, sometimes ignorance, sometimes courage is desp'ration, an' then ag'in it's innocence."[55] Whether they were discerning or ignorant, Mexicans lacked nobility, while Americans were eminently heroic. In folklore, heroism is conferred on the Ranger, the dragon slayer, like the *beau sabreur* [swordsman] of France, "He's first in the hour of peril."[56]

In this American epic, the hero was the Ranger, the fearless and irreproachable knight; the villain was the "greaser." The Mexican's knife was a weapon less noble than the pistol of his American adversary. In the Southwest, the knife was considered vile and its use a sign of cowardice. Mexicans did not have the right to carry firearms—their use was reserved for Americans and the landed aristocracy—so Mexicans were reduced to the knife out of necessity.[57]

Neither courageous nor bold, but rather stealthy and distrustful, Anglos wrote, Mexicans fled at the approach of strangers;[58] on occasion, they resorted to theft. Bartlett noted "the thievish propensities of the lower class of Mexicans" and complained of their stealing baggage.[59] But Anglos considered the Mexican specialty to be horse stealing, one of the recurring themes of Texas folklore. Listen, for example, to Juan Murray, the repentant horse thief exiled to Mexico. His lament fails to impress the Rangers and makes him appear ridiculous: "Don't never be a cow-thief, don't never ride a stray." "It is better to be honest and let other's stock alone / than to leave your native country and seek a Mexican home."[60] Throughout the Southwest, the Mexican-American was considered a thief of livestock, just as in the South, the black man was portrayed as the rapist of white women.

The Siesta

Anglos believed the vile deeds committed by Mexicans were a natural consequence of a deep-seated immorality, a Mediterranean legacy that they could not deny.[61] In the eyes of Davis, a lawyer, these new members of the American nation "[did] . . . not bring with them all the virtues and wisdom possessed by our own people, who have been reared under a purer code of morals and a wiser system of law."[62] This immorality manifested itself, in particular, in a love of gambling. The game of chance was "considered a gentlemanly and respectable calling"[63] by Mexicans but shameful by the Anglo Protestants, who believed in a more ordered life, one less centered on profit than on work itself. The game of monte[64] was favored by many Mexican-Americans.

A relaxation of customs and discipline was perceived in the Catholic church of the mid-nineteenth century. Davis, the unshakeable Protestant, was shocked by the concubinage that belied official priestly celibacy, and other abuses. He praised Monsignor Lamy for restoring law and order in the anarchical diocese of Santa Fe.[65]

Nineteenth-century Americans such as Davis, Browne, who drafted the California constitution, and the military writers were proud of having initiated an age of reason and a well-ordered society from which they believed all excess and violence had been excluded. They could only react negatively to the rampant chaos—psychological, moral, and religious—that in their eyes was the very foundation of the Mexican character. They saw a direct connection between this chaos and laziness, the mother of all Mexican-American vices. When a Mexican was not wielding a knife or sitting at a noisy monte table, it was because he was taking "the siesta to which that race are addicted,"[66] a wide-brimmed hat protecting him from the sun. If he walked, his pace was listless. American authors continually used the words "lazy" and "lazily" to describe any activity. They intentionally exaggerated the squalor and disorder of the setting in order to make the "greaser's" laziness all the more reprehensible. Here, for example, are the natives of Colorado as depicted by Parkman: "Two or three squalid Mexicans, with their broad hats, and their vile faces overgrown with hair, were lounging about the bank of the river. . . ." Further on: "A few Squaws and Spanish women, and a few Mexicans, as mean and miserable as the place itself, were lazily sauntering about."[67] Browne did not back away from sordid details: he twice described carcasses being devoured by buzzards and coyotes in front of *rancheros* or a sleeping *vaquero* "too lazy" to throw them farther away.[68]

There was nothing in common between this sluggard, who felt no shame at begging, and the American, who owed success only to hard work. The pioneer-writers never wearied of contrasting the Anglo-American, the man of action, builder of the future, to the passive and backward Mexican-American, handicapped by technical incompetency, living, like the Indian, on past glories. In San Antonio, Bartlett noted:

> Mexican indolence cannot stand by the side of the energy and industry of the Americans and Europeans. . . . Some few of the Mexicans have the good sense to fall in with the spirit of progress; but the great majority draw back before it, and live upon the outskirts of the town in the primitive style of their forefathers.[69]

There was "no contest" between the Anglo-American and the Mexican-American. Anglos used "draft carriages," Mexicans "heavy wooden-wheeled carts" and the farm equipment of "the agriculturists of ancient times, without the addition of a single point of improvement."[70] Anglos owned businesses, Mexicans were mere mule drivers—the recognized profession of the "greaser" and symbol of his technological backwardness. Give a ranch to a Mexican-American and it would soon be in ruins.[71] Entrust it to an American and he would make it prosper. To the Puritan, work was sacred, indeed, a spiritual end in itself. Profit-seeking was not immoral and was certainly superior to shiftlessness.

Mexican Catholicism

Who should be held accountable for Mexican laziness, Anglos wondered, if not the Catholic religion? It was tempting to infer from the proverb "Either eat well or sleep well" that it was the Protestant who preferred to eat well and the Catholic who wished to sleep undisturbed.[72] To the first chroniclers of the Southwest, Protestants all, Mexican-Americans seemed to expect everything from heaven, from their saints, and especially from the Holy Virgin. Davis rejected the cult of the saints, which he called "a blind adoration of these insensible objects."[73] He especially attacked the Virgin of Guadalupe, whose cult he believed bordered on fetishism.[74] Mexicans seemed to allow priests to lead them about like children. Fergusson emphasized the hold of a priest on his parishioners:

> Father Lugaria was a man of imagination and the special home of his imagination was hell. For thirty years he had held despotic sway over the poor Mexicans who made up most of his flock, and had gathered much money for the church, by painting word-pictures of hell. He was a veritable artist of hell.[75]

Anglo-American Protestants, whose religion addressed the mind rather than the heart or the senses,[76] judged Catholicism strictly from the point of view of ethics; the aesthetic side escaped them completely. They tended to view Catholicism as the sum of exterior forms and hollow phrases. O. Henry ordained his tamale vendor high priest of the Mexican religion. With holy oil dripping from his Tamales (spelled with a capital T, since they are henceforth invested with a supernatural quality), the vendor anoints the American congregation in the name of the Holy Ghost and all the saints, whether real or imaginary, of the Mexican calendar:

> Santos Esperitos
> Vicente Camillo
> Quintana de Rios,
> De Rosa y Ribera.[77]

While they did not go so far as O. Henry, the other writers also were disturbed by the minutely detailed ritual and colorful aspects of Mexican Catholicism, so heavily influenced by Indian traditions.

They remained equally insensitive to the colors and forms of the national costume, which to them seemed a mark of social inferiority. Davis rejoiced at seeing the aristocracy abandon it in favor of the American style of dress.[78] The Mexican outfit appeared ridiculous to Henry L. Boone; the American in *Yankee Jim* sneers at the hunting clothes of Don Alberto. Every detail of the costume is treated with derision; he is "amused at the idea of Don Alberto stalking a puma, in his equestrian costume of short chaqueta ["jacket"], and calzoneras ["pants"], adorned with silver buttons . . ."[79]

This sartorial splendor was all the more artificial since it clothed nothing admirable, the conservatively dressed American seemed to insinuate: it showed nothing more than vanity, bravado, and braggadocio, traits that were also reflected in the language. The Mexican love of words, accentuated with gestures, was suspect and irritating to Anglo-Americans. While Cristobal of *Yankee Jim* "poured forth his flowing tale with copious verbiage and much gesticulation," the American "gravely unyoked the oxen. . . ."[80] Lewis found excessive hyperbole in the song of an old *guitarrero* ("guitar player") hired for the wedding of Don Anton and Doña Inez.[81]

These writers showed little interest in the missions of the Southwest and the art they housed. Bartlett retrospectively shared the sadistic pleasure with which soldiers had destroyed the hands and faces of statues in the San José Mission, near San Antonio. The soldiers had used them as "convenient marks for rifle and pistol shots," proudly "showing at the same time their skill in arms and their contempt for the Mexican belief."[82]

In the period after the Mexican defeat, the portrait of the Mexican-American painted by Anglo writers, those "glandular haters of the 'greasers,' "[83] resembled a bullet-ridden target more than a work of art. The weapons that writers often wore while wielding their pens reminded them of their real profession, the military. How seriously could Major Hall have pretended that "for a brief space" he had "laid aside our rifle and revolver to grasp the pen"?[84] Seen in the light of the "superior mind"[85] of the Anglo-American, the portrait of the Mexican-American was dimly lit indeed. It was an incomplete picture, whose characteristics were invariably the same. This portrait was too heavily marked by overt racism, belligerent chauvinism, and impassioned puritanism to avoid approaching caricature.

It was this "distortion"[86] in the ethnocentric literature that later critics attacked. In the writings of all the early visitors to the Southwest, the prototype of the "greaser" abounds. The set phrases they used were hollow—just as hollow as those to which they reduced the entire religion of the defeated people— but they were faithfully transmitted from generation to generation as a national and literary legacy, if not a religious one. These early stereotyped impressions, "national currency"[87] during the war against Mexico, stayed in circulation for a long time. Alongside the negative stereotypes of Mexicans, Anglo writers created positive stereotypes that glorified Anglo-Americans.

It is not surprising that Chicano critics of today protest against this "army of blond-haired and blue-eyed argonauts for whom no obstacle is too great. . . ."[88] They attack the first chroniclers, mountain man James O. Pattie and journalist George W. Kendall, whose works were influential long before the annexation,[89] and they criticize Texas literature and folklore, which purposely fostered contempt for Mexicans before and after the war.[90] The Texas romances, those of Charles W. Webber and Clemens in particular, have come under attack.[91] These romantic writings and popular legends passed on defamatory images of Mexican-Americans to posterity.

Chicano critics also reproach sociologists for classifying these stereotypes and giving them scientific definitions, because "the words have changed but the meaning is still the same."[92] For example, the "lazy" Mexican-Americans of old have become "non–goal oriented," "underachievers," "retarded," "fatalistic," or "resigned to their lot."[93] In a seminal essay, Octavio I. Romano-V. held sociologists William Madsen, Celia S. Heller, Ruth Tuck, Murro S. Edmondson, Lyle Saunders, and Carey McWilliams, among others, responsible for the "distortion of Mexican-American history."[94]

Just as the ethnocentric writers saw laziness as the source of Mexican vice, sociologists later used passivity—religious, political, and social—to explain every aspect of Mexican-American behavior. Out of this idea emerged the popular image of the "Mexican lazily asleep under the cactus."[95] The Anglo sociologist took every opportunity to contrast this fatalistic and passive culture to the "activist" Anglo culture,[96] thus reinforcing Anglo stereotypes, as well as Mexican-American ones. This phenomenon led Nick Vaca to formulate a paradigm of the two value systems, as presented by American sociologists. In the column marked "Mexican-American value system," he places the terms "non-intellectual," "fatalistic," "emotional," "superstitious," "traditional," and so forth; on the opposite side, respectively, "intellectual," "non-fatalistic," "rational," "non-superstitious," "progressive," and so forth.[97]

Mexican-Americans were henceforth judged by a cultural determinism that justified, in the eyes of Anglo-Americans, existing social, political, and economic relations between the two cultural groups. This error equates "economic determinism with cultural determinism. This is the modern version of the Protestant Ethic as described by Max Weber many years ago."[98] These damaging sociological theories originated around the year 1912. Chicano critics hold them responsible in large part for the negative opinion present-day Anglo-Americans have of Mexican-Americans and for the low status of Mexican-Americans in many areas.

The ethnocentrism of the early authors sprang from the Mexican-American War, which also made a "gringo"[99] of the American. One of the first to denounce the gringo's xenophobia was a soldier and writer of the succeeding generation, Major Horace Bell, who wrote:

> Gringo, in its literal signification, means *ignoramus*. For instance: An American who has not yet learned to eat chili peppers stewed in grease, throw the lasso, contemplate the beauties of nature from the sunny side of an adobe wall. . . ."[100]

This colorful irony reveals the changes taking place in many minds. The myth of gringo superiority was to be followed by the myth of the splendor of the old California families.

The lands of the sun expand the soul.
SPANISH PROVERB[1]

CHAPTER 2

Romanticism: The California Myth

It was in splendid and sun-bathed California that the aristocrats of Spanish descent lived an endless idyll. Their land was a veritable Arcadia "with perpetual
blue skies and floods of yellow light."[2] New Mexico, where all was "sun,
silence, and adobe,"[3] was no less a land of enchantment, one that impressed,
among others, Lummis and Austin. But California dominated the works of
this era. A gay pastoralism prevailed in Atherton's collection of short stories
significantly titled *The Splendid Idle Forties.* The countryside around Monterey
is the ideal place for picnics and amorous adventures between blooming young
California *señoritas* and handsome American officers:

> Girls in gay muslins and silk rebosos were sitting beneath the arches
> of the corridor or flitting under the trees where the yellow apricots hung
> among the green leaves. Languid and sparkling faces coquetted with ca-
> balleros in bright calico jackets. . . . The water rilled in the winding creek,
> the birds carolled in the trees; but above all rose the sound of laughter and
> sweet strong voices.[4]

The flowers of the San Luis Obispo Mission, musk in particular, lent their fra-
grances to *Ramona*, the novel by Helen Hunt Jackson. In Mrs. Mary Daggett's
novel *Mariposilla*, Ophir Gold, the rose of the San Gabriel Valley, symbolizes
the beauty of both the young Mexican woman and the natural setting. In the
poems of Joaquín Miller and Robinson Jeffers, the landscapes were grandiose.
Before nature's splendor, the heroine of Atherton's novel *The Californians* "had
wondered occasionally if all people were not happy in such a country."[5]

George Evans extolled the beauty of California to the preceding generation
but spoke of it as if it were uninhabited. The writers of this period, by contrast,

peopled it with natives who lived in harmony with their natural setting. The authors were tempted to see the exterior natural beauty as a reflection of inner beauty, and the natives as good, pure individuals in love with life. California was idealized and celebrated as a virgin land despoiled by civilization.[6] The lost paradise of the Spanish past was gradually disappearing, slowly eroded by the American present. Pastoral idylls gave way to commercial transactions as the wave of prosperity of the eighties ushered in a rapid Americanization of Southern California. Because of its geographic isolation, New Mexico continued to resist the encroachments of the present. But in California, the dissolution of land grants sounded the death knell for the great families.[7] Fiestas of that era attempted, if only momentarily, to recapture the past. Thus, during the Pasadena Rose Festival described by Daggett: "from secluded Spanish gardens, flourishing now only in the imagination of the aliens who destroyed them, came the dark, happy, historic señoritas."[8] Later, at the turn of the twentieth century, in the California heartland ravaged by bitter struggles between farmers and the railroad company, Frank Norris, a romantic in spite of himself, created an idyllic oasis of peace and poetry. In the "moribund"[9] town of Guadalajara, Presly, one of his heroes, finds the substance of an epic poem. From the pages of these American writers emerged an entire world in the process of disappearing. Thus, in *Mariposilla*:

> Close to the old church are the houses and stores of the once thriving village, now, alas! dusky with memories of the Señora, the captivating Señorita, the valiant Don, and the watchful Padre. . . . When the old Spanish bells call to the early Sabbath mass, if one is observing, he may find among the weather-beaten countenances of the Mexicans, often marked with the high cheek bone of the Indian, true descendants of the early aristocracy, holding aloof from the horde, absorbed in prayers, that alone are the same since the ranches were ruthlessly divided and railroads allowed to invade. Yet the Spanish homes that remain in the valley are mere echoes of former times, but tiny specks upon the map of the real estate dealer, which have miraculously escaped the clutches of strangers. Although humble, a few of these homes are strikingly picturesque.[10]

The author is a woman of sensitivity; the setting is the luxuriant San Gabriel Valley; the heroine is the graceful Mariposilla, the "little butterfly." Let's go back for a moment, as if in a dream, to that bygone era.

In this romantic literature, the past and present are in constant conflict. "Long ago" alternates with "nowadays." Everything that existed before, "alas!" is slowly fading away. The present is represented by the decay of the village; the ruthless breaking-up of ranches, which shattered the power of the *dons*; the construction of the railroad, which put an end to the region's cultural homogeneity; and the rapaciousness of the real-estate agent. Standing for the past are the prosperous village of long ago, a society of handsome and refined people, the mission, and "Spanish" residences. But the memories live on, and the old mission bells still ring. The present, despite its considerable achievements, cannot overshadow the picturesque charm of the past, no matter how humble it might have been.

This juxtaposition of past and present was to be found in two forms in these works. In the first, an American of Mexican origin, with a value system inherited from the past, is face to face with an Anglo-American who represents a new order; in the second, a younger generation feels both the weight of tradition and the fascination of modern American life. In each, the forces of the past prevail, as if to indicate that traditional Mexican values outweigh Yankee money. In Atherton's novel *The Californians*, two young women, Magdalena Yorba and Helena Belmont, each seek the heart of the Yankee Trennahan. Yielding to the spell of the past, he weds the young Mexican woman, telling her: "You don't belong to the present at all. No wonder you bewitched me. I am beginning to feel quite out of place in the present myself. It is a novel and delightful sensation." [11]

These are the "true descendants of the old aristocracy" who assured the preservation of the past; "the only ones who escaped change." "Absorbed in their prayers," taking refuge in another world, they "escaped" the dominion of the Anglo-American "foreigners." The proud señora of *Ramona*,[12] widow of General Moreno, one of the twelve founders of the city of Los Angeles, passes on to her son Felipe her hatred of the Yankee invader and her respect for the Spanish past. In the novel *For the Soul of Rafael*, by Mrs. [Marah Ellis] Ryan, Don Rafael's mother insists that he seek a Mexican wife, who will watch over Rafael's soul, which is too easily tempted by American life.[13] The vigilant Spanish old guard refused to surrender.

This elite stood out clearly from the "horde" of Mexicans. Pure of blood, they had higher social status and more education. A pejorative attitude toward the lower classes of Mexican-American society, however, was uncharacteristic of this period. The Anglo authors, while admitting their distaste for inter-marriage, made every effort to look beyond this biological "imperfection" of mixed race and see the real qualities of the *mestizo*, whom they seldom called a "greaser." In the rest of *Mariposilla*, the few "Mexicans" provoke no ungracious comments on the author's part. At the funeral of a young Mexican lady, she refers to the pallbearers as "six swarthy young Mexicans"[14] and nothing more. Skin color in itself does not elicit a single insulting remark. The ethnocentrism and racism of the preceding generation, directed mainly toward the "greaser," had not spared the higher levels of Mexican-American society. Similarly, the later period's glorification of the old order, of the "Spanish" elite, often trickled down to the world of the more humble "Mexicans."

Exaltation of the past manifested itself in the adjectives, all positive, with which Daggett describes the *señora*, the *señorita*, the *don*, the *padre*. These people, the symbols of the past, all virtue and beauty, were immortal. To the young Mariposilla, who weeps at not being American and thus not able to marry the Yankee Sanderson, the female narrator responds: "You are very beautiful, dear child! . . . more beautiful than any American girl I ever knew." [15] Why try to change? Writers tried to perpetuate that past beauty, just as, in a few residences, the splendors of the Spanish past had "miraculously" survived.

The *Don*

Why, in the view of the romantic generation of the eighties, was the Mexican-American world so beautiful? They saw it as a once-grand world of nobility, now fallen into decline but which still retained the importance of name and lineage. Intermarriage, especially with the Indian, was considered an ignominious flaw, a sign of physical and moral weakness. All half-castes, whatever their bloodlines, were repugnant to these aristocrats. Señora Moreno would have preferred her adopted daughter Ramona, born of an Anglo father and an Indian mother, to be a pure-blooded Indian, for, said she, in these mixed marriages, "it is the worst and not the best of each, that remains."[16]

This repugnance accounts for the distance the aristocrats created between themselves and lower-class "Mexicans." The daughter of Don Yorba is insulted, for instance, at being called a "greaser" by an Anglo policeman who is of the same class as her father's coachman.[17] Mexican servants were mistreated, suffering the contempt the master of the house had previously shown toward Indians. Thus, "Don Roberto regarded servants, in spite of the heavy wage they commanded, as he had the Indians of his early manhood."[18] Racial pride existed at all levels of society. The "Mexican," in turn, felt superior to the Indian. Juan Canito looks down on Alessandro, the son of the Indian chief Pablo, because: "To Juan, an Indian was an Indian, and that was the end of it."[19]

This pride conferred an undeniable sense of nobility upon even the humblest of Mexicans. The dignity of the Mexican-American's demeanor impressed Anglo-Americans. In Fergusson's novel *In Those Days*, young Aragon, heir of a great New Mexican family, intimidates Yankee pioneer Robert Jayson by his bearing on horseback: he "rode furiously a black lathered stallion and did all this with an air of high-nosed all-spurning pride, he contrived to seem superior without doing a thing to prove that he was."[20] Dismounted, the Mexican maintains the same haughty posture.

The defeated Mexicans faced their conquerors with dignity. What were these invaders if not lowly "tradesmen," unworthy of speaking to Señora Moreno as equals?[21] Young Aragon, from astride his mount, refuses even a glance at Jayson, who came west after the Civil War to trade along the Santa Fe Trail. In the Lummis short story "Bravo's Day Off," an American doctor, who came to New Mexico only grudgingly, is attacked by a Mexican dog during a walk. Terrorized, he climbs a tree to escape and a passer-by, Santiago, extricates him by chasing the dog away. To reward him, the "Conquerin' Saxon"[22] flips a dollar at the young Mexican, who refuses to pick it up. *Waste*, a novel about the 1820s, relates a similar incident: Maria, whose son was killed by a young American, refuses the money the murderer's mother offers her for her silence.[23]

We find a similar refusal in the works of ethnocentric writer Browne; however, when Browne reports that a *vaquero* rejected a watch offered him, he immediately attributes it to pettiness.[24] In Lummis, to the contrary, though the doctor sees Santiago's gesture as impudence, the author presents it as a noble act by a Mexican who has been defeated but who has not abandoned his pride.

The Noble Savage

Not even America's dollar-oriented civilization could debase this nobility. Mexican-Americans were portrayed as living in a state of primal innocence, untouched by the evils of over-industrialization. In the midst of the century of scientific progress, Mexican-Americans prized the qualities of the heart, the primitive virtues, above all else. To Atherton, the California ranch of Los Cerritos, cut off from the outside world, is the land of blissful ignorance.[25] To Austin, the New Mexico town of Las Uvas is a sort of paradise: "There is not much villainy among them. What incentive to thieving or killing can there be when there is little wealth . . ."[26] Blessed are the poor: the same idea was repeated, twenty years later, by Robert Herrick.

Writers stressed the pastoral rather than the feudal nature of Mexican-American society, especially when the action was set in New Mexico. The short stories of Lummis and Austin are filled with shepherds, *vaqueros*, and *rancheros*, all by nature tranquil and uncomplicated. Characters inhabiting Cebolleta around 1860 are presented this way: "In his young manhood Pablo married a pretty Mexican girl. . . . They lived together happily. Pablo tended his little flock of sheep while Juanita carded the wool. . . ."[27] This simplicity fascinated the Anglo authors. Austin compared it to the simplicity of the Indians.

Like the Indian, the Mexican-American is "nature's own child,"[28] and fully understands all her secrets. Carmelita, the young heroine of Atherton's novel *Los Cerritos*, understands the language of the birds and confides her troubles and joys to a sequoia tree. To George Emery, the sorcerer is not a charlatan but a "sage," a "mystic" who draws his knowledge from an intimate union with the earth.[29] To Jeffers, the romantic poet of the primitive and the irrational, this intimacy was precious. Enchanted by the California territory, he believed that only Mexican women could achieve a perfect union with the earth, which they came to symbolize. The love of his hero, Cawdor, for his beloved, Concha Rivas, is more than a physical bond; in spirit, he would remain faithful to her all his life.[30]

The earth was the source of true richness, altogether different from the richness of the gold fields. "You do not understand in this country, you are progressive,"[31] explains Willa Cather's Mexican-American heroine, Mrs. Tellamantez, whose own source of knowledge is a conch shell. In the Lummis short story "Bravo's Day Off" the doctor seeks out Miss Parker, the schoolteacher, after his misadventure with the dog, to complain, falsely, that his clothes were torn in an attack by desperadoes. He fulminates against the barbarism of Mexicans. The schoolteacher replies that, despite their ignorance, she has learned much from the Mexican schoolchildren, for they possess a wealth of generosity.[32] Young Santiago could have laughed at the doctor's cowardice on seeing him perched in a tree, but he did nothing of the sort.

All these writers emphasized the often ostentatious hospitality of the *dons* and the simpler but no less warm hospitality of the peasants. Years later, Cather often pointed out the generosity of the poor Mexican. Father Vaillant, in her novel *Death Comes for the Archbishop*, knows that he can count on contributions from poor Mexicans but not from Americans: "Down among the Mexicans, who owned nothing but a mud house and a burro, he could always raise money. If they had anything at all, they gave."[33] Mexican-Americans were also generous with one another, treating fellow villagers like members of the family. This strong sense of community is highlighted in Atherton's *Los Cerritos*. Tragic problems afflict both white and Mexican squatters who settled on former land grants and are now threatened with eviction by the new proprietors. The *rancheros* as a group pay lawyers' fees while Carmelita does her part by doing needlework.

Unburdened by material possessions, the Mexican-American was free: the rider in full gallop was a symbol of freedom in the alienating age of the machine. Seeing Carmelita mounted on an "unprincipled mustang," Mr. Tremaine muses: "She was never born for clothes at all. . . . She might be the primitive woman."[34] Why would Mariposilla abandon "her mountains and her unconventional life,"[35] for a society rife with taboos? Like the rose she resembles, she would wither away. Mexican-Americans were no longer seen as misfits, rebels against progress; rather, they were glorified as people who could live without conforming to the promethean ideal of progress. The beautiful allegorical poem by Jeffers, "The Dead Man's Child," was a challenge hurled at the American spirit of progress. The scene is the California desert, where several Mexican workers have died of thirst. The rest have departed. Only Rosaria Rivas, one of the camp girls, remains, carrying within her a child conceived under mysterious circumstances. To her, only "the dust of the deceased" and the ashes of the now-dead fire, before which she had lifted her skirt and warmed her knees, could have placed within her the seed of life. What would become of this "dead man's child," born of the past?

> his life
> Ran smooth because he had nothing *future* about him.
> Men do not stumble on bones mostly but on seeds,
> And this young man was not of the sad race of Prometheus,
> To waste himself in favor of the future.[36]

Conquering the universe is pointless if people lose themselves in the process. Mexican-Americans found in the enduring values of the past the best guarantee against the uncertainties of the future.

But could these values be preserved from contamination? As early as 1880, Horace Bell sounded the alarm:

> . . . there is an old adage which is . . . that "the gringo spoils all other peoples with whom he is brought in contact." The noble race of California Spaniards has greatly deteriorated by its association with the conquering gringo.[37]

The writers saw the gringo as a civilized man governed by inflexible conventions and as the man of the dollar. The Mexican-American's warm dark eyes, a reflection of inner richness, constantly met the American businessman's cold blue eyes. Mexicans judged Americans according to their true value. In Atherton's short story "A Ramble with Eulogia," young Eulogia sees Abel Hudson, a bandit, as the prototype of the American: "His heart is like the Sacramento Valley, veined with gold instead of blood!"[38] The gringo attitude toward money both intrigued and puzzled young Californians, for they had a completely different set of values.

Later on, in reaction to the moral breakdown of the "dollar civilization," authors again stressed this characteristic of Mexicans, "whose minds are not upon gain and worldly advancement,"[39] as Cather said in *Death Comes for the Archbishop*. In another novel, *The Professor's House*,[40] she emphasizes the preeminence of spiritual and moral values over material ones. This theme was also treated by Robert Herrick, a writer of the same era. His hero, Thornton, who takes refuge in a small New Mexico town, cannot avoid comparing the two lifestyles and praising the primitive virtues of the natives:

> Thornton felt that Tia, including Maria and Tranquilino, was in many essentials the most urbane, the most civilized American community in which he had ever lived, poor and primitive as it was by ordinary standards.[41]

These unsophisticated creatures, these savages, the Anglo writers declared, possessed true riches and held the secret to superior civilization.

Mexican Hedonism

According to these writers, money had no intrinsic worth to Mexican-Americans, who valued it only as a source of enjoyment. In Daggett's novel, Doña Maria, who previously was wealthy, knows that the love of gold can be expressed in two different ways:

> . . . we, too, had gold in abundance, but we loved not our gold as the Americans love theirs, to keep in the bank. We loved gold because it gave us joy to buy lands, and cattle, and jewels, and lace.[42]

For Mexican-Americans, pleasure took precedence over utilitarianism and enjoyment over money; their values were more epicurean than practical. This hedonistic conception of life fascinated the writers of the eighties and beyond.

The natives of Guadalajara interest Presly, the poet in Norris's novel, because he sees them as "relics of a former generation, standing for a different order of things, absolutely idle, living God knew how, happy with their cigarette, their guitar, their glass of mescal, and their siesta."[43] To Austin, life for the humble people is a perpetual amusement. Thus, at Las Uvas:

> ... they keep up all the good customs brought out of old Mexico ... ; drink and are merry and look out for something to eat afterward; ... have cockfights, keep the siesta, smoke cigarettes and wait for the sun to go down. And always, they dance.[44]

In the case of the great families of California or New Mexico, writers dwelt on the way of life made possible by the income derived from the vast land grants. Atherton introduces Don Roberto Yorba and his peers this way:

> Living a life of Arcadian magnificence, troubled by few cares, a life of riding over vast estates ... eating, drinking, serenading at the gratings of beautiful women, gambling, horseracing. ...[45]

Even though she loses part of her holdings and is forced to reduce her staff of servants, Señora Moreno remains faithful to the lifestyle of the past.

The Mexican-American was no longer portrayed as a knife-wielding killer but rather as a guitar player; ambushes in chaparral thickets gave way to leisurely picnics in the mission garden under the watchful eye of the good Padre.[46] The Mexican-American was no longer vilified for rustling livestock but praised for his prowess with the lasso and as a bullfighter. Instead of fighting, he indulged in the pleasures of love. Weddings and related festivities replaced the border incidents and the reprisals they used to provoke. The Mexican capacity for getting the most out of life, like the Anglo ability to get the most from a dollar, fascinated nineteenth-century writers, who were obsessed by "the chilling despair at not having lived at all."[47]

Enjoyment of life presupposed leisure time, for haste was the enemy of pleasure. The Mexican-American took the time to enjoy life. To Lummis, this was New Mexico:

> ... the land of *poco tiempo*—the home of "Pretty Soon"—Why hurry with the hurrying world? The "Pretty Soon" of New Spain is better than the "Now, Now" of the haggard states. ... Let us not hasten. *Mañana* [tomorrow]. ... Still better, *pasado mañana* [the day after tomorrow].[48]

Shameful laziness became nothing more than indolence, fully justified by the climate (the term "lazy" tended to disappear in favor of "indolent"). Under the warm California sky, even Anglo energy melted away. New arrivals to New Mexico were warned that "Such unprecedented energy can never last in this Vale of Sleep; that before a month is over [we] shall all have settled down to a chronic state of somnolence from which [we] shall awaken from Saturday till Monday only."[49] This indolence and nonchalance confuses Polk, one of the heroes of *The Californians* and the prototype of the American whose entire life has been governed by the Puritan work ethic. During the thirty years he has spent in California, not once has he taken a day's vacation nor ever gone to see either Yosemite or Sequoia park.[50]

What counted for Mexican-Americans was the immediate moment. Life was meant to be lived today, but their concept of time was not rigid. The present spread itself out langorously and spilled over into an almost nonexistent future. In a charming short story by Grace Ellery Channing, "The Basket of Anita," Manuelo falls in love with a young Englishwoman who has come to a small Southern California town for her health. She can't understand how he can remain in a place where everything seems to induce sleep: he should leave. When he responds, " 'Perhaps—some day,' " she retorts, " 'Some day is no good . . . you should make up your mind to go at once.' " " 'Señorita,' " he replies, " 'it is good here too.' "[51]

It was good to live in a world where pleasure was not proscribed by work or moral austerity, where one could savor life as time flowed on. Fergusson's Yankee hero, Robert Jayson, thus recalls the little town of Socorro as it was before the construction of the railroad:

> An atmosphere he knew and loved . . . lazy, quiet, but with a note of music about it, a throb of passion. . . . A life of indolent men who yet could fight, of sleepy women waiting for the night and lovers. . . . He knew that life had given him something that he needed, set something in him free.[52]

Free at last from the constraints of his Puritan upbringing, he allows himself to be seduced by this life where all is calm, leisure, and sensuality.

The Beautiful *Señorita* and the *Macho*

Anglo writers were fascinated by a world they saw filled with men capable of both fighting and loving, and with women made to be loved. In the Mexican-American society that they depicted, the two sexes were clearly differentiated.

The woman was expected to be supremely "feminine" and completely submissive to male authority. Physical beauty was indispensable. Young Magdalena Yorba's problem is precisely that she is more intellectual than beautiful. Her father "deeply resented Magdalena's lack of beauty; all the women of his house had been famous throughout the Californias for their beauty. It was the duty of a Yorba to be beautiful."[53] Magdalena disappoints her father further for she also lacks the usual feminine talents and prefers reading to playing the piano. Don Roberto's ideas on women's education are strict: it is out of the question for his daughter to accompany her friend Helena Belmont to England to study, she who cannot even go about the streets unescorted! One can imagine the father's fury on learning of his daughter's ambition to be a writer: " 'The ladies never write,' announced that grand son of old Spain, 'Nor the gentlemens.' "[54] Mexican-American women remained far removed from the feminist movement of the latter nineteenth century.

As a sex object, the woman had to be feminine in both dress and demeanor. Magdalena Yorba does not wear men's clothing as Helena Belmont does; she would have to abandon her Spanish dignity to climb a balcony as her friend does. In *The Splendid Idle Forties*, Atherton introduces a gallery of pretty *señoritas*. Dancing shows their beauty and grace to best advantage: "As they whirled in the dance, their full bright gowns looked like an agitated flowerbed suddenly possessed by a wandering tribe of dusky goddesses."[55] Atherton sometimes endows nature with a sensual femininity; a perfect symbiosis seems to exist between the setting and the characters:

> The air was *mad* with melody and intoxicating with perfume. The sun sent waves of *delicious* warmth to the very hearts of the *joyous* flowers. The earth lay wrapped in her newly woven *garment, sensuous* and *dreamy*. (Emphasis added)[56]

When he meets Carmelita for the first time in such a setting, Mr. Tremaine, intoxicated himself, exclaims: " 'And who is she?' . . . 'Probably the daughter of one of these squatters. But she might be a young goddess.' "[57] A veritable cult honoring the Mexican-American "goddess" was established; *caballeros* addressed passionate letters to her. Her flashing dark eyes fascinated the Anglo-American observer: "Lend me the loan of a light, Juanita, / Matches? Never! Your eyes will do!" exclaims the suitor described by Lummis.[58]

Anglo writers have always presented the Mexican-American woman in a better light than her male counterpart. Writers of the preceding generation found her beautiful and desirable. This bias can be partly accounted for by the fact that the writers belonged to a society that was dominated by women and shackled by a rigid puritanism, a society not only anti-erotic but anti-aesthetic as well. Trennahan, the Yankee bachelor of *The Californians*, for example, marries Magdalena Yorba and not Helena Belmont, the young American "feminist."

But from this time on, the writers also began to show admiration for the strength and virility of the Mexican-American "*macho*." The entire collection of stories by Lummis, *A New Mexico David*, offers homage to the physical prowess of some young Mexicans in New Mexico, each of whom, in his own way, re-enacts the Biblical David's feat. In the first story, "Pablo Apodaca's Bear," for example, Pablo, endowed with herculean strength, wrestles a bear and succeeds in throwing him (the Mexican-American would long be portrayed as a born wrestler). In "The Box S Round-Up,"[59] young Santiago dazzles two strapping Texans with his skill at the lasso during the annual cattle roundup —in the preceding generation, the roles would have been reversed. In the last story, the moving "On the Pay-Streak," young Rodolfo, to put an end to his family's poverty, searches desperately for a vein of gold, even at the risk of being buried alive in a rock slide.

As a horse-breaker and rodeo performer, the mounted *vaquero* was the supreme symbol of virility [60] and the Mexican *macho* par excellence. He placed great importance on the details of his costume, especially his sombrero, which emphasized his masculinity. [61] Joaquin Miller devoted a poem to the *vaquero*; the following is the first of the three stanzas:

> His broad-brimmed hat pushed back with careless air,
> The proud vaquero sits his steed as free
> As winds that toss his black abundant hair.
> No rover ever swept a lawless sea
> With such a haught and heedless air as he,
> Who scorns the path, and bounds with swift disdain
> Away, a peon born, yet born to be
> A splendid king; behold him ride, and reign. [62]

The poet's pen transforms bandit Joaquín Murrieta into a superhorseman, no longer pursued by the Rangers but by some invisible enemy; his splendid ride across the Sierras ends in a manly and sublime death. [63] In a book devoted solely to the *vaquero*, Frederic Remington treated all aspects of his trade, [64] while Mark Twain particularly admired his equestrian talents. [65]

The intrepid *vaquero* was also a dashing lover. Bret Harte gives an amusing version of the Mexican in love. In his short story "The Devotion of Enríquez," [66] a gallant *caballero*'s courtship of the daughter of a Congregational pastor is strongly laced with eroticism. Serenades and feats of bullfighting and horsemanship are brought into play to soften Miss Mannersley, an American woman locked into rigid "good manners" (her name is undoubtedly symbolic). He finally persuades this puritan and intellectual New Englander to run off with him. Thus the Mexican male approached his mate with assurance and a strong sense of possession, and the woman expected no less. California, the sexually unfulfilled heroine of "Roan Stallion," admires the virility and strength of a beautiful roan horse for she has an unsatisfying marriage with an Anglo-American "emasculated" by machine-age civilization. [67] All of Jeffers's heroines are passionate creatures. Although sometimes shocked by the audacious dress and sensuality of some Mexican-American women, the Anglo was finally won over by the warmth of their passion and by the Mexican-American society's seeming lack of sexual taboos.

A novel by Fergusson, *In Those Days*, relates the career of Jayson, a Connecticut Yankee who arrives in New Mexico after the Civil War, and his psychological and emotional development during a time span of fifty years. Jayson envies the young aristocrat Aragon for his reckless ease with women. The way Aragon grasps the "so-virginal Nina" astounds him; he "smacked loud kisses on her flushed cheeks while she averted his mouth. Robert blushed painfully, feeling as though he saw a child ravished before his eyes."[68] But Jayson feels no more at ease with the two Doxey girls, Baptists for whom life in New Mexico is a real ordeal;[69] he is happy to leave them and return to the plaza. There, the sight of two Mexican sweethearts kissing in public without the slightest embarrassment gives him a curious sensation. He rejects the none-too-subtle advances of his young servant Maria, but gradually he becomes bolder and seeks out the lovely Nina. Later, when he reflects on times gone by, his thoughts go back nostalgically, not to Elizabeth, his friend from New England, but to Maria, Nina, Cucaracha, and all the "brown girls hugged in a tipsy whirl."[70]

The full acceptance of the human body by these handsome and sensual people was considered a thing of beauty by the Anglo-American writer.

The Cult of Beauty

For the Anglo-American, whose aesthetic sensitivity was anesthetized by the utilitarianism and ugliness of an industrial and commercial society, the Mexican world was a haven of beauty. Its landscapes, inhabitants, and language were all beautiful. Even when Anglicized, Mariposilla's Spanish loses none of its sweetness and picturesqueness. Eugene Rhodes found undeniable charm in the English of Monte, a Mexican-American:

> The unslurred vowels stressed and piquant, the crisp consonants, the tongue-tip accents—these things combined to make the slow caressing words into something rich and colorful and strange, all unlike our own smudged and neutral speech.[71]

Mexican-Americans, with an innate sense of the aesthetic, gave their language both form and soul. Nothing better expresses this sense of form than their exquisite politeness, which has so impressed authors since the days of the annexation. Even when impassioned, Mexican-Americans never departed from their customary politeness, the outsiders said. Altimira, although bested by his American rival in his quest for the beautiful Benicia, succeeds in controlling his rage.[72] Anglo writers, who previously treated this attachment to appearances as nothing more than vanity, braggadocio, and bad taste, now considered it the foundation of an aesthetic and nonutilitarian conception of life. Every Mexican was an artist. The women paid attention to dress and interior decoration; the bright colors they preferred seemed borrowed from nature. Of her young heroine Carmelita, Atherton writes: "She loved color with all the sensuous ardor of a nature steeped from birth in the riotous hues of the most colored country two hemispheres can show."[73] The house of Don Yorba's sister is arranged more artistically than his own for his wife is a native of New England. Though his work was demanding, the *vaquero* did not neglect his dress, whose splendor struck even the early chroniclers of the Southwest. The details of his sumptuous costume appeared with more frequency and elaboration, however, in the writings of the romantic authors, so attracted to local color: the *vaquero* typically wore a wide-brimmed sombrero on his head, a red serape around his waist, high leather boots, often tied at the knee by a white silk cord, short pants, sometimes decorated with lace, and spurs, often encrusted with gold and silver. His saddle was of embossed leather.

Anglo-Americans relished the work of Mexican artisans; McWilliams detected a double influence in art objects, which he called "Indian in feeling, Spanish in plan."[74] The Mexican-American's appreciation of music was attributed to the Indian. The Mexican-American drew from his guitar the most melodious music imaginable; no serenade or homage to feminine beauty was complete without the guitar. Every novel had its musician: the hero of Cather's *The Song of the Lark* is a talented singer and guitarist. In the Mexican barrio of a small Colorado town, a group of art-conscious people gravitates about him. Young Thea, raised in a strict religious environment devoid of aesthetic sensitivity, is attracted to this world as if to the source of life itself. Those who did not play the guitar danced, and much better than the Anglos, who, young Californians said, "hop like puppies."[75]

All the writers noted these artistic talents, and the authors of the eighties and later praised them. However, the taste for traditional form in the Catholic religion drew jeers rather than praise. Earlier authors showed little interest in the missions, and Catholic religious rites had provoked sarcasm. Well before the missions were returned to the Church[76] they had recovered their congregations. From that point on, not a single novel failed to include a mission: the San Gabriel Mission, for example, was treated in both *Mariposilla* and *The Splendid Idle Forties. In the Footprints of the Padres*[77] traced the travels of Spanish priests. For Presly, the romantic poet of Norris's novel *The Octopus*, the sight of an old mission brings to mind a marvelous past worthy of an epic poem.[78] The missions had picturesqueness and grandeur. In *Ramona*, Señora Moreno helps to safeguard the San Luis Rey Mission. Her house and private chapel are filled with madonnas and saints, rescued by the sacristan from pillaging. The figures allow her to perpetuate the old customs: the Franciscan Father Salvierderra of the Santa Barbara mission[79] celebrates Mass there, and the churchgoers, for the most part, are Indians. The priest quite correctly sees the Moreno home as "the last stronghold of the catholic faith left in the country."[80] The novelist, a Protestant herself, stresses the goodness of the padres, the salubrious effect of the missions on the Indians (she makes no mention of the brutal way the Spanish church converted them).[81] Even the padre's name, Salvierderra, means "he who gives salvation."[82]

The Anglo-American, accustomed to the austerity of Protestantism, was fascinated not only by the serene beauty of the mission buildings, but by the colorful rites of Mexican Catholicism as well. What to the preceding generation was superstition became picturesqueness. The cult of the Virgin ceased to elicit sarcasm. The author of *Mariposilla*, for example, admires Doña Maria for her simple devotion. The holy image "whispered something to the simple, aching heart that a stern theology could never say."[83] Young Magdalena Yorba, once she loses her faith, regrets being torn away from "the sensuous embrace of the Church of Rome."[84] For the late-nineteenth-century Anglo-American, Catholicism appealed to the senses, offering equal measures of devotion to both God and beauty.

The nostalgia of American writers at the end of the nineteenth century caused them to see Mexican-Americans essentially as symbols of beauty and the past. American women cannot see Mariposilla otherwise: as she prepares to play her guitar, Mrs. Sanderson rushes to cover the young lady's head with a mantilla so that she can be truly beautiful and Spanish:

> "She must have a mantilla for her head," Mrs. Sanderson cried.... "There! Is she not a divine Señorita?" She exclaimed ... "Is she not exquisite?" ... "See how easily we have caught the loveliest butterfly in all old Spain! . . ."[85]

The romantic writers transfigured Mexican-American reality. They assigned positive values to things that the early chroniclers of the Southwest had seen as negative: "Where as the original Yankee travelers had carped on the retrograde tendencies of the old order, the new writers vaunted its solid virtues."[86] But the virtues that so enthused these authors were restricted to a little world of grand old Spanish families and the humble ones that gravitated about them, an "old regime" that was fast disappearing. Around this world writers built the "California myth,"[87] "a vision from a lost century, playing upon the credulity of the present."[88]

This idealized vision of the past, focusing on one segment of the society, was sharply attacked. As a perfect illustration of this cult of the past, Hunt Jackson's novel *Ramona* quite naturally became a target. Franklin Walker reproved "the Helen Hunt Jackson formula for sugar candy."[89] The damaging effects of *Ramona*'s enormous success were noted with alarm. With the perspective of hindsight, Austin, herself guilty of a number of romantic literary excesses in her youth, judged harshly this "second-rate romance very popular at the time. . . ."[90] She considered "factitious" the efforts of all those, like Hunt Jackson, who sought "to re-create a sense of the past out of sentiment for the old missions. . . ."[91] To Walker, a similar false re-creation of the past made Marah Ellis Ryan's Spanish characters "hothouse Spaniards."[92]

The cult of the past was not only artificial but unhealthy to the extent that it caused the "split-personality"[93] from which present-day California still suffers. Californians' attitude toward their Mexican heritage was contradictory: they revered the Spanish past while despising its living representatives. To McWilliams, nothing better illustrates this continuing contradiction than the holiday parades that featured *"dons"* as well as those who choose to live in the present: "When one examines how deeply this fantasy heritage has permeated the social and cultural life of the border-lands, the dichotomy begins to assume the proportion of a schizophrenic mania."[94]

Infatuation with the past led to excess. Chicano critics have reproached this school of writers for having "embellished and romanticized the Hispanic-American experience in California."[95] Hunt Jackson, no doubt, embellished the role the Franciscans played in the missions; in tying the fate of the Indians to the great dispossessed Spanish families, she made the Indians the victims of gringo imperialism rather than of Spanish clericalism and feudalism. McWilliams deplored the fact that this image of the Indians of Southern California was "firmly implanted in the mythology of the region."[96] To John Houghton Allen, idealization was a distortion of the truth. It was in the person of the *vaquero* that he found the deformation most evident. Born in the harsh and violent border region of south Texas, the author of *Southwest* was well acquainted with the rough trade of the *vaqueros*. His book is a genuine work of demythification. His *vaquero* sat on a much less ornate saddle:

> This is something, this is no idyll of the Californias, no be-sashed, singing and laughing vaqueros with long flapping toe-fenders to their stirrups or silver-mounted harness of jackets embroidered, but this is a tale of the violent and untamed, of the old times. . . .[97]

The romanticizing of the outlaw Joaquín Murrieta made him quasi-legendary, took away his historical character, and neutralized him by denying any deep political meaning to his rebellion.[98] Sociologists added their own criticism. In his book on the decline of the Californians, Pitt appears to see their grandeur as nothing more than the seeds of their decay.[99] In a study devoted to the images that Anglo-Americans and Mexican-Americans hold of one another, Ozzie G. Simmons demonstrates that the most flattering images the Anglos hold end up being turned against the Mexicans. For example, the idea that Mexicans love music, fiestas, and flowers tends "to reinforce Anglo-American images of Mexicans as child-like and irresponsible," and to "support the notion that Mexicans are capable only of subordinate status."[100]

The Anglo-American writers glossed over less colorful and more troublesome aspects of Mexican-American reality. It was easier to describe the idylls of the Spanish aristocracy than the bitter struggle of the *mestizo*: "The restored mission is a much better, a less embarassing, symbol of the past, than the Mexican field worker . . . ,"[101] McWilliams said of *Ramona*.

Indeed, shouldn't *mestizos* arouse the same degree of interest as descendants of the great Spanish families? And who could legitimately claim to be of purely Spanish blood? As Ruth Tuck declared:

> The most robust Castilian gene, in such a situation, could hardly be expected to survive, unchanged, to populate Texas, New Mexico, Arizona, and California with descendants of "pure Spanish ancestry." But such is the fiction the romantic tradition likes to maintain.[102]

With the same sort of irony, McWilliams questioned the purity of blood of the founding fathers of Los Angeles (one of whom was José Moreno, the illustrious husband of the proud Señora Moreno in *Ramona*).[103]

Among the half-castes were some eminent settlers and true pioneers. Ruth Tuck asked, why not write a history of these *mestizos*?

> ... such stories would not make such fine escapist reading as the sentimentalized version. They would connect "old Spanish culture" with present-day Latin-American culture in the Southwest. It would be impossible to maintain the fiction that the "old Spanish" were so superior, of such a different strain, and of such exalted background that any comparison between them and the immigrant Mexican is out of the question.[104]

A more realistic school of writers would take interest in this *mestizo* who was struggling for existence and belonging to a contemporary reality rather than a mythic past. A truer image of the Mexican-American would be depicted for us at the end of the nineteenth century.

If in olden days the dominant Mexican culture had transformed some Yankees into "Mexicanized gringos," now the new culture created a class of "gringoized Mexicans." This did not, however, represent a true blending of two cultures, but rather a triumph of the most aggressive and a defeat of the most recessive cultural characteristics. [1]

Realism: The Mexican–American Faces Anglo Society

At the end of the nineteenth century, the realistic writers made every effort to depict Mexican-Americans as real human beings, not as static, outdated stereotypes. Mexican-American reality was no longer fixed by the conventions of a literary school. It changed with the times; neither ignominious nor inspiring, it was dynamic, contemporary, Mexican *and* American. Nor were the images any longer limited to a particular social class.

Mexican-Americans were confronted by an Anglo-American society that forced them to live between two worlds. It was this conflict, rather than any fanciful contrast between the past and the present, that the realistic writers accentuated. All the classes felt this conflict: neither the *peones* nor the *dons* nor the *mestizos*, the future Mexican-American middle class, experienced it exclusively. The difficulties of Mexican-Americans, brand-new citizens of the United States, in integrating into Anglo society came to the forefront in literature. The awakening of a social consciousness in the last decade of the nineteenth century also marked its literature. [2] Authors began to depict Mexican-Americans as the victims of an exploitative social and economic system, and they tried to show Mexican-Americans' real, though still unsuccessful, efforts to combat this exploitation. Two forces were now present, as indicated in the following passage by Hamlin Garland:

> In the eyes of these cattle barons and their retainers the greaser was a nuisance. He was given to cultivating the soil along the river-beds, and might be seen any day wading like a snipe in the red mud of his irrigating ditches. They were getting too plenty anyhow and needed to be discouraged. They interfered with the water-rights, and were coming to be so

infernal sharp as to argue their rights, saying, "We have as good a claim to the government range as you cattlemen."

The Mexicans, as a matter of fact, knew very little about American politics or any other kind, but they were "agin' the government," so far as they knew it. They collected, therefore, under the Republican banner, and made persistent but ineffectual efforts to gain their rights in the county. Numerically, they were considerably in the lead, but as the cattlemen controlled all the election machinery, numbers did not count. At the time when Delmar crossed the river and became a citizen of Felipe, the cattlemen were calm and complacent in despotic control of the county.

Delmar at once lined up with the Mexicans. He was half-Spanish, and spoke the Mexican dialect perfectly; but was also a shrewd trader and ambitious to rule.[3]

The little New Mexico town of San Felipe was torn apart by the rivalry between the Anglo-American cattle ranchers and the Mexican sheepherders. Such rivalry was common in this territory, where traditional sheep-raising dominated until the turn of the twentieth century. The conflict over grazing rights too often degenerated into bloody confrontations between cowboys, the cattlemen's "hired hands," and the sheepmen.[4] The situation described in the passage above dates back to the 1870s, the heyday of cattle-raising in New Mexico. The fight over water rights was added to this struggle. The victims were clearly poor Mexican-Americans, who were politically powerless to defend their interests and protect their rights.

Conflict is at the very heart of the passage: between the two types of livestock raisers; between the two ethnic groups; between the two political parties (the lower classes "rallied around the Republican banner" while the upper levels of Mexican-American society and the big cattle owners belonged to the Democratic party);[5] between the two languages, English and the "Mexican dialect"; "against" and "agin'." This duality is symbolized by the dual ancestry of the hero himself, both Anglo and Mexican. This adversarial situation was the basis of all the works that attempted to depict Mexican-American reality objectively. The theme of two towns, the Old One (Mexican) and the New One (American), in Fergusson's novel *The Blood of the Conquerors* illustrates this fundamental opposition. This theme would reappear after 1930.

The writers also denounced an Anglo-American society that inevitably destroyed whatever preceded it. The cattlemen, hungry for more pasture land, find the sheepmen "too numerous"; they try everything possible to "discourage" them from continuing their sheep-raising. Little by little, the old world is destroyed, here by intensive cattle ranching, elsewhere by the construction of the railroad (*The Blood of the Conquerors*), by the reorganization of the Diocese of Santa Fe (*Death Comes for the Archbishop*), and so forth. In the new society, Mexican-Americans had no place, even though they were American citizens. They had no adequate political representation.

Garland's short story describes actual facts. Though the characters are fictional, the circumstances are not imagined; rather, it is a concrete situation conveyed in precise terms (the "red" earth of New Mexico, the scarcity of water, the electoral fraud). The heroes are ordinary, neither "greasers" nor descendants of rich Hispanos.[6] Delmar is a trader. The same is true in other works. Jack London's Mexican character[7] is a young proletarian, while one of the most important personages in *Death Comes for the Archbishop*[8] is Father Martinez, a *mestizo*; in his short stories, Stephen Crane[9] often portrays shepherds. Garland makes every effort to present the Mexicans of his banal story straightforwardly and accurately. The usual stereotypes are absent: the term "greaser" is used only to designate the poorer Mexicans. While the word would have immediately elicited the epithets "lazy" or "dirty" or both from the ethnocentric writer's pen, here the term loses its pejorative meaning. When confronted with systematic exploitation, Garland's Mexican-Americans do not remain passive. The blind resistance, caused by their political naiveté, with which they oppose the American government is certainly ludicrous. But they "made persistent but ineffectual efforts to obtain their rights." These are no longer beings frozen into conventional attitudes, but rather people reacting in a historical present to a specific situation and beginning to fight for recognition as full-fledged citizens.

Garland, like Delmar, their future leader, enlisted on the side of the oppressed Mexican sheepherders. London would later side entirely with his Mexican character. In the last two novels of Fergusson's trilogy on racial conflict in the Southwest, the author acknowledged having taken the point of view of the "Conquering Yankee"; in the first book, he made Ramón, the defeated Mexican, the central character.[10] Garland did not hesitate to denounce electoral tampering (the elections of San Felipe were rigged by Anglo-American politicians who "regulated the entire electoral machinery," in collusion with the great cattle barons). Thus he highlighted the Mexican majority's inability to shake off the social and political yoke imposed by the Anglo minority ("numbers did not count"!). The note of protest in London, Herrick, and Crane was just as clear.

Cultural Conflict

In the view of the early realistic writers, the conflict was, above all, cultural. When couples from the two groups married, a clash was almost inevitable. In the area of religion, the coexistence of two divergent strains within Catholicism also seemed precarious.

Harte's short story "The Passing of Enríquez" recounts the failure of the marriage between Enríquez Saltello and Rainie Mannersley. In the story "The Devotion of Enríquez,"[11] discussed earlier, the author presents his *caballero* nimbly overcoming the barriers of language and social tradition; everything is depicted comically. The tone of the sequel[12] is more serious; the hero dies, the victim of a graver conflict deep within himself. In many respects, this story marks a turning point, presenting both a romantic and realistic image of the *dons*. There is more than just a linguistic barrier between Enríquez and the Anglo-American world he is obliged to frequent after marrying. The author's intention is not so much to make the reader laugh at his hero's strongly Hispanicized English as it is to demonstrate the incompatibility of two value systems. Enríquez and the landed nobility he came from represent a system based essentially upon honor, while the American system is governed by the profit motive. The clash is inevitable. Enríquez discovers a gold deposit on one of his properties and arranges for Yankee capital to develop the new mine. The geologist hired by the company discovers an obstruction in the vein, but, bowing to pressure from the management, agrees not to make the matter public in order to avoid discouraging possible investors. Enríquez, for his part, refuses to condone this fraud; to the members of the administrative council, he declares:

> "I say that for three hundred year my family have held the land of thees mine; that it pass from father to son, and from son to son; it pass by gift, it pass by grant but that nevarre there pass a lie with it!" [13]

Unable to comprehend his quarrels with the company, his wife leaves him. Enríquez then sells his stock; some time later, while on a horseback ride with his son, he and the boy disappear into a crevasse during an earthquake. The possibility of suicide is strongly suggested.

We are far removed from the ridiculous Americanomania of Don Roberto Yorba, the hero of *The Californians*, a pitiful Mexican who abandons all his dignity in his desperate efforts to Americanize himself. He ends up hanging himself with an American flag for his failure to achieve the lifestyle and mentality of the conqueror. Fergusson's hero Ramon Delcasar, in *The Blood of the Conquerors*, is more complex; the author evokes here his inner conflict, even though the deck is stacked against him from the start. This young lawyer is caught between two women, symbols of the two worlds that divide his life. Indeed:

> He was the product of a transition, and two beings warred in him. In town he was dominated by the desire to be like the Americans and to gain a foothold in their life of law, greed and respectability; in the mountains he relapsed unconsciously into the easy barbarous ways of his fathers. [14]

He is in love with Julia Roth, whom he meets in the town's business circles but whose family opposes their marriage. At the same time, he is attracted to Catalina, the daughter of a Mexican-American peasant, a now-ruined former nobleman. In the end, it is Catalina who consoles him after his disillusionment with American society.

Two lifestyles and ways of thinking were also reflected in the Anglo and Mexican versions of Catholicism. When American priests succeeded Mexican clergymen in the Southwest, they found a native, and quite different, church.

The natives, in turn, found the new arrivals disturbing. The newcomers believed that the Indian influence that so strongly flavored Mexican Catholicism brought out the religion's "sensual" aspect and introduced irrationalism.
Cather's real contribution was the objective exposé of the conflict in the Catholic church in New Mexico. Her book *Death Comes for the Archbishop* is a novelized biography of Jean-Baptiste Lamy, who established a new diocese in Santa
Fe, which had been the jurisdiction of the bishop of Durango.[15] The prelate's
French origin added a new novelistic dimension; in her prologue, the author
writes that the French missionaries "have a sense of proportion and rational
adjustment. They are always trying to discover the logical relation of things.
It is a passion with them."[16] This Cartesian passion for logic could not escape
conflict with the irrational character of Mexican religion, as the confrontation
between Monsignor Latour and the local Catholic representative, Father Martinez of Taos,[17] demonstrates. The Mexican priest lectures the man he refuses
to recognize as his bishop:

> And you know nothing about Indians or Mexicans. If you try to intro-
> duce European civilization here and change our old ways, to interfere with
> the secret dances of the Indians, let us say, or abolish the bloody rites of the
> Penitentes, I foretell an early death for you. I advise you to study our native
> traditions before you begin your reforms. You are among barbarous peo-
> ple, my Frenchman, between two savage races. The dark things forbidden
> by your Church are a part of Indian religion.[18]

In undertaking his reforms, the archbishop bears this advice in mind and attempts to reconcile the Indian and Catholic elements, but he dies before the
conflict is resolved.

The Oppressed "Greaser" in Search of a Leader

This fundamental cultural conflict partly explains the difficulties Mexican-
Americans had in integrating into Anglo society. But the Anglo attitude was a
problem in itself. Toward the end of the nineteenth century, the most realistic
writers began to denounce the aggressiveness of the conquering Yankee. They
emphasized three things: the dispossessing of the *hacendados*, the great Mexican
land barons; the arbitrary nature of the justice system; and, in a general way, the
overall intolerable situation of Mexican-Americans throughout the Southwest.

The earlier writers alluded to the dispossession of the Californios by American usurpers: Bartlett and Brewer were sincerely outraged by that plundering,[19]
while Bell[20] sought to exonerate the American government. Olmsted held
Mexican ignorance more or less responsible for the expropriations and apparently excused the Yankees.[21] Hunt Jackson's novel describes the hatred Señora
Moreno feels for those who took her land; the numerous problems the squatters cause on the abandoned ranch of Los Cerritos; and their expulsion after an

Anglo-American capitalist buys the former Moreno domain from the federal government. But Hunt Jackson and Atherton fail to convince the reader of the seriousness of the problem. One is not easily moved by the financial difficulties of the outraged señora, who is still quite well off. Presenting Los Cerritos as an innocent little island cut off from the outside world, almost a place of fantasy, was hardly realistic. Not until Fergusson's novel *The Blood of the Conquerors* did one find the matter of the land grants treated with breadth and accuracy by a writer who knew the Southwest well. The treatment of the land grants is the most interesting aspect of the book and confers upon it undeniable documentary value. The story is based, in part, on the struggle between gringos and Mexicans whose lands were expropriated by the federal government during construction of the railroad in New Mexico. This project caused endless problems for the native population and eventually became a major literary theme. In the novel, James MacDougall, a crafty and unscrupulous speculator, becomes associated with Don Diego, Ramon's uncle, who dies before the American has a chance to steal all of his land. MacDougall becomes the major creditor in the entire area and demands the property of his Mexican debtors in payment.

Appeals to the law were pointless, because at that time the courts rarely sided with the weak and the dispossessed. In San Felipe, and everywhere else, "To kill a Mexican was reprehensible, but not criminal." [22] This sad truth became almost an adage in the Southwest. Anglo writer Herrick, for one, rebelled against the corruption of New Mexico's justice system; the incident he relates is certainly not unique in that state's annals. In Tia, young Tranquilino is killed by a rifle shot fired by Gordie Lane. Cynthia, Lane's mother, easily buys the silence of the Mexican sheriff and the affair is promptly quashed. Justice is mainly in the hands of corruptible Mexicans, and, with the tacit complicity of local American authorities, immunity is accorded only to the rich. Thornton, the hero, bitterly concludes that

> Justice . . . in this thinly settled country, with traditions of lawless violence, was largely in the hands of Mexicans and was quite venal. One of the superior caste who had means and friends rarely if ever paid the full penalty for his misdeeds, and he had never doubted that the Lane boy would escape without any serious consequence. . . . [23]

Corruption apparently was the rule in all parts of New Mexico, and electoral fraud was more flagrant than elsewhere. Anglo politicians' tampering with Mexican votes sadly resembles the manipulation of black ballots in the South. Garland's short story stresses the disastrous consequences of electoral fraud for the Mexican population of San Felipe and shows how Delmar finally turns it to his own benefit. In an unlikely victory, he is elected sheriff.

Mexican-Americans were considered of negligible importance; they suffered the contempt, if not the outright aggression, of Anglos. Jack London's Mexican character, the short and half-starved young boxer Rivera, fights against the champion, Danny Ward. What makes this spectacle intolerable is not so much the mismatch in size and strength of the participants as the hatred of the Anglo capitalists crowded around the ring, furious at seeing the American boxer beaten by a puny little Mexican, despite the referee's bias in Ward's favor. Although somewhat exaggerated, this scene is indicative of a certain mentality. The "Kill'm, Danny, kill'm" of the crowd in Los Angeles[24] could well have been heard anywhere in the Southwest, in Warpost, Arizona, or on the California express headed toward Yellow Sky. Two stories by Stephen Crane give us a view of the true situation of the Mexican-American in the Southwest. The inhabitants of Warpost, the unpleasant little town in "Moonlight on the Snow," decide to change things in order to attract Eastern capital. They decree that anyone caught carrying a firearm will be hanged. Of course

> Everybody was enthusiastic, save a few Mexicans, who did not quite understand; but as they were more than likely to be victims of any affray in which they were engaged, their silence was not considered ominous.[25]

Among the six men drinking in the bar of the California express are "two Mexican sheepherders, who did not talk as a general practice in the Weary Gentlemen saloon. . . ."[26] A drunken gentleman arrives. Foreseeing a possibly dangerous situation, "the two Mexicans at once set down their glasses and faded out of the rear entrance of the saloon."[27]

Wisdom is achieved through experience; experience also made Mexican-Americans feel the intolerable nature of their inferior status. The early chroniclers of the frontier randomly depicted nothing but petty vendettas and saw the rebellious acts of Murrieta or Cortina as nothing more than pure banditry; the romantics obscured any attempts at revolt by making the bandit leaders demigods who moved in the unreal world of myth; the realistic writers presented ordinary people becoming aware of their status and demonstrating the will to escape it. They described this awakening with sympathy—perhaps too much sympathy, which sometimes took them beyond the facts.

The recent Mexican Revolution is the background for London's short story. On both sides of the border, people are working for the cause of the revolution, including the boxer Felipe Rivera. A climate of suspicion long reigned in the United States; every Mexican refugee was suspected of subversive activities:

> Too many of the comrades were in civil and military prisons scattered over the United States, and others of them, in irons, were even then being taken across the border to be lined up against adobe walls and shot.[28]

The young revolutionary goes hungry and risks death in the ring against a fearsome opponent in order to buy rifles. Garland's hero Delmar, a more mature man, organizes the resistance against the Anglo-American minority and quickly becomes a leader to the Mexican population of San Felipe.

Another hotbed of resistance was the lodges of the Hermanos Penitentes ("penitent brothers")—the lay brotherhoods native to the Rio Abajo region of New Mexico, as well as Santa Fe and Taos. The members of these sects reenacted the crucifixion of Christ each year; one of their number was crucified and sometimes even died during the rites, which were preceded by bloody flagellations. These practices were forbidden by the Church.

In their defiance of the established church, which was subservient to the wealthy, these dissidents recalled the Methodists and Anabaptists of the English lower classes. The lodges also enjoyed a political power whose importance in the nineteenth and early twentieth centuries should not be underestimated. Just as they proclaimed their separation from the Catholic hierarchy, they also often opposed the political establishment and attracted the opponents of the new Anglo regime.[29]

The early chroniclers of the annexation and the writers of the decades that followed were virtually unaware of the *penitentes* and their practices; otherwise, they would surely have described them with repulsion, if we can judge by the writings of Anthony Ganilh prior to 1848[30] and Josiah Gregg, a frequent traveler on the Santa Fe Trail.[31] The romantic authors barely mentioned them in their novels, though the savage beauty of the rites could not have failed to fascinate them. The more realistic writers were conscious of the important role the *penitentes* played in New Mexico; they stressed the political aspects of the associations, whose religious demonstrations were often subordinated to less spiritual aims. In Cather's novel *Death Comes for the Archbishop*, the threat Father Martinez issues to Monsignor Latour is a double one.[32] The prelate is threatened as a representative both of Catholic orthodoxy and of European civilization. The close ties between the lodges and local political groups are particularly evident in Fergusson's novel *The Blood of the Conquerors*. Ramón Delcasar knows only too well that to get Mexican votes he must not only be initiated into the secret rites of the Penitentes, but take an active part in the flagellation and crucifixion as well. Hadn't he heard it said that to secure power and prestige certain gringos had submitted themselves to these tortures? Would he follow, then, the advice of his friends?

> All those little *rancheros* are penitentes. It's the strongest *penitente* county in the state, and you know none of the *penitentes* like gringos. . . . You could give a few *bailes*. You are Mexican; your family is well-known. If you were a *penitente*, too . . .[33]

The ceremonies of the *morada*, the *penitentes'* lodge, are repugnant to Delcasar. He refuses to take part in the crucifixion, and the final victory goes to the gringos. Fergusson analyzes the disgust of his hero, a young lawyer already overly influenced by the Anglo world he frequents. The author intimates that if Mexican-Americans are to assert themselves in Anglo society, they will have to find a more effective means than the outmoded brotherhoods.

The first realistic writers made a real contribution by revealing some of the predicaments Mexican-Americans faced in Anglo-American society, by evoking their problems and struggles, by suggesting their inner psychological dramas, and by telling the truth with courage.

Their testimony, nevertheless, was too often distorted by a romanticism still greatly influenced by certain racial prejudices. Character study remained superficial, and even though they had taken a step toward social realism, their view of the society they portrayed was still incomplete. An exploited proletarian himself, obsessed by the notion of a racial revolution, London identified too strongly with his young hero to avoid making him a romantic revolutionary. Like Victor Hugo's Enfant Grec, who seeks powder and ammunition, London's Mexican youngster seeks powder and rifles. He has to win in the ring, for only then "the guns were his. The revolution could go on." [34] Rivera is less a militant than a fanatic, and, in spite of his youth and small stature, he is a sort of superman; his prowess as a boxer recalls Fergusson's wrestlers, those Davids of New Mexico. In Garland's work, picturesqueness predominates over verisimilitude. Delmar is too much like the sheriff of the typical western. The "greaser sheriff" wins a victory over the cattlemen's clan gathered at "Charley's Place" with an ease bordering on improbability: "Every man in the room was his enemy and everyone was armed but himself." [35] This short story by Garland, its realism tempered by fancy, contrasts to some degree with the bitter realism of his other stories about the borderlands. In Bret Harte, the search for picturesqueness and local color is more conscious. In Harte's story, the strongly Hispanicized English spoken by all members of the Enríquez family, a "marvelous combination of Spanish precision and Californian slang," [36] seems meant to be more comic than realistic.

Fergusson, by contrast, is not guilty of excessive romanticism. His intention to write a realistic work and espouse the cause of the defeated people emerges clearly in the introduction to his trilogy. [37] But his premise that the blood of the Spanish *conquistadores* had weakened since their conquest of the natives influences his perspective and casts his hero in an unfavorable light. He glosses over the character's inner conflict, and the rather hasty and irritating psychological portrait he paints depicts him as basically weak. In spite of himself, Fergusson once more became the "conquering Yankee" that he had determined to be no longer.

The vision offered by the early realistic writers was sometimes fanciful and shallow; it was also incomplete. The laborer is notoriously absent in these works. Josiah Royce justifiably reproached Bret Harte's passion for the picturesque and declared his realism less profound than that of Mrs. L. A. Knapp Clappe, and his presentation of life in California mines less accurate. [38] To her credit, Dame Shirley, beginning in the mid-nineteenth century, also took an interest in the fate of the miners. Although most of the stories on the gold rush —those of Evans, Delano, and Manly, for example—accentuate the hardships of the journey more than the situation of the workers themselves, Shirley was not afraid to reveal scandals. [39] But, in these realistically oriented works of the late nineteenth and early twentieth centuries, where are the immigrants who each day crossed the border in search of work and who posed serious problems for American authorities and the Mexicans long since settled in the Southwest? Where are the strikes that ravaged California, Arizona, and Texas from the end of the nineteenth century onward?[40] There is not a single reference to the mass movements of the Mexican-American proletariat. It is significant that most of the works discussed here are set in New Mexico. Long closed off to outside influences because of its geographical isolation and its essentially agricultural economy, New Mexico had a static character.

Other, more moving aspects of the Mexican-American world remained to be explored, and the realistic writers would perhaps have gained objectivity from such an exploration.

This first period was characterized by three different approaches to Mexican-American reality. The early writers, whether ethnocentric or romantic, made Mexican-Americans eminently static individuals, either turned toward a past in decline or a pastoral era, within an essentially dynamic Anglo-American society. With little concern for psychological and social verities, they painted, with large brush strokes, two-dimensional characters closer to "motion picture characters of the worst sort"[41] than to real people. They created stock characters, like those of the commedia dell'arte; whether the stereotypes were of the "greaser" or the "noble savage," they were oversimplifications; whether the images were reduced or magnified, there was always "unrealization."[42] The Anglo-American writers saw Mexican-Americans as they wanted them to be, in order to justify their attitude toward them, to give themselves a more flattering self-image (projection is one of the dynamics of racism), or to find in Mexican-Americans what they themselves wanted to be, but were incapable of becoming, "something lacking in himself."[43]

A more objective view of Mexican-American reality emerged at the turn of the century; though somewhat compromised by a tendency toward sentimentality, comedy, and farce, the authors of these first attempts at realism are to be applauded for their genuine concern for objectivity. This objective tendency would continue during the troubled period of the Depression, but it failed to dull an increasingly acute sense of immediacy and awareness of the burning issues facing Mexican-Americans.

The Anglo-American
Point of View

1930-1940: The Yoke of the Stereotype Loosens

In many respects, the climate of the thirties resembled that of the twenties. Madison Grant's book *The Alien in Our Midst*[2] set the tone; at the transition point between the two decades, it summed up a state of mind that boded ill for the "foreigner" in American territory. Beginning in 1930, legal immigration of Mexicans diminished rapidly; restrictive measures were passed, in part, because of pressure from mining and farming unions. Social unrest reflected a deep uneasiness in Americans. In 1922, T. S. Eliot's poem "The Wasteland" sounded the death knell of spiritual values in Western civilization, which was reduced to a "wasteland" haunted by "empty souls." This moral depression was compounded by the economic depression; the sense of insecurity it engendered provoked a resurgence of nativism.[3] The breakdown of the social system reawakened a feeling of superiority in the Anglo majority. The era of disillusionment was followed by one of suspicion.

Doubt was also spreading among writers to whom American civilization in general and the social system in particular appeared increasingly suspect. They would continue to see the Mexican-American as the representative of a different civilization while at the same time perceiving him more and more clearly as the victim of Anglo-American society. Thus, in certain writers there persisted, in the face of this world in disintegration, a romantic nostalgia for the past, for a people of unchanging values, while in others a more realistic tone of indictment and accents of pity would prevail. In all of them one finds the same sincere sympathy for the Mexican-American, a more or less explicit anger directed at the economic system, and in all a common effort at objectivity. The seeds sown by the early realistic writers had taken root. Frank Harris acknowledged, with the hindsight of the years (he wrote his recollections of the 1870s at age seventy-five, in 1930), that the term "greaser" betrayed in the Anglo nothing less than ". . . the full-flavored contempt of complete ignorance."[4] Not only had the era of contempt run its course, but public apologies were offered. Self-criticism began to cut through the self-delusion. Certain stereotypes were questioned; what had previously been nothing more than a two-dimensional puppet gradually took on human proportions and became the complete individual with whom the Anglo would henceforth have to reckon.

CHAPTER 4

Admiration for a Different People

With the apparent failure of American civilization, a failure capped off by the Depression, some writers turned to people with a different system of values.

Just like Presley, Norris's turn-of-the-century romantic poet,[1] Paul Horgan's poet and musician, David and Edmund Abbey respectively, find their inspiration in the Mexican people. David writes poems about them while Edmund, in his symphony titled *Mexicana*, attempts to capture the Mexican soul.[2] This soul once more began to stimulate poetry, dreams, and the imagination. In some writers, a yearning for a bygone Spanish world predominated, while others found the Mexican-American's immediate situation a source of inspiration. In his collection of short stories and essays, *Figures in a Landscape*, Horgan, that great admirer of the Southwest, deplores the changes in the familiar "figures" in the Mexican "landscape." To him, "the end of an occupation" means the disappearance of picturesqueness from the "landscape" and the abandonment by the younger generation of the colorful traditions of the past, which have been, alas, appropriated by Hollywood's commercial enterprises.[3] The only one of his generation of writers to do so, he chose a descendant of New Mexico Hispanos as a hero, in a short story with the significant title "The Hacienda."[4] Born in the time of the annexation, Don Elizardo, the former owner of the *hacienda*, is now in his sixties, living not in the new part of town transformed by the arrival of the railroad but rather in the old town, in the past. This confrontation between past and present is reflected in the vertical structure of the story, whose first part is devoted to the present time (the tragedy of the dispossessed *don*), the second to the past (Don Elizardo recounts his memories of yesteryear), and the third, once again, to the present. The same insistence on

the contrast between past and present figures in the chronicle of New Mexico
by Horgan and Maurice Fulton; the first of the two sections is called "The
New Beside the Old."[5] A short story by Philip Stevenson, "The Shepherd,"[6]
takes us back to the distant time of sheepherders at the beginning of the Anglo
occupation of New Mexico.

These writers placed the Mexican world wholly within the past; they bemoaned the encroachment of the present and the inevitable process of assimilation. Other authors remained in the present and varied the location of their
stories. Their characters were ordinary Mexican-Americans, whose existence,
however humble, reflected an appealing philosophy of life. Like writers in the
preceding century, they preferred an attractive natural setting that contrasted
extraordinarily with contemporary American life, made even uglier by the Depression; "in the world of roots and clouds and wings and leaves there exists
no Depression," declared economist/ecologist Calvin Ross in his study on the
Southwest, *Sky Determines*.[7] Heaven once more became important. In his epi-
sodic novel *The Pastures of Heaven*,[8] Californian John Steinbeck takes us back to
a pleasant valley hidden away in central California, which, to the tourists in
the final chapter, seems the ideal retreat from the world's ugliness. This Eden-
like setting of gardens and orchards, of course, has little to do with the lettuce
fields and fruit farms for which Salinas is famous. And the two Mexican-
American families of the "pastures of heaven" know none of the difficulties
of the Depression. The "Long Valley,"[9] in Steinbeck's collection of stories of
the same name, also deals little with the effects of the Depression. In the two
stories about Mexican-Americans, the scene is shifted from the valley to the
foot of the mountains; the coast range into which the young hero of "Flight"
disappears becomes a barrier between him and other people; Gitano, the old
Mexican of "The Red Pony," takes refuge in the somber and mysterious Santa
Lucia Mountains. These mountains impart a fairy-tale atmosphere not unlike
that of Tortilla Flat in Steinbeck's novel of the same name. Tortilla Flat is situated outside the city of Monterey, in a "no-man's land," "on the hill where the
forest and the town intermingle, where the streets are innocent of asphalt and
the corners free of street lights. . . ."[10] A similar return to a more primitive era
occurs in the fanciful tale by Austin, "The Politeness of Cuesta la Plata."[11] This
little New Mexico town is so far removed that in 1917 its inhabitants know
nothing of the war.

A novel by Richard Summers, *Dark Madonna*,[12] has a more urban setting,
but the sense of displacement remains, even though Little Mexico is a section
of the American city of Tucson. Although the Depression did indeed affect the
Mexican section, the author dwells less on the poverty of this *colonia*, or colony
(which was no different from any other *colonia* in the Southwest at that time),
than on the life and imagination emanating from this microcosm of Mexico.

In these works by Steinbeck and in "The Gambler, the Nun and the Radio,"[13]
a short story by Hemingway, the Depression is not a factor. Not until *The
Grapes of Wrath* in 1939 did Steinbeck deal with seasonal farm workers, who

were not Mexicans[14] but Anglos from Oklahoma and neighboring states. Hemingway's work is less a short story than a morality play; the plot is of less importance than the lesson. One of the three characters is a Mexican beet-picker, but Hemingway tells us nothing of his work situation. Just as in works of the preceding century, the essential message is that this American of Mexican descent is different.

The *Paisano*

These Mexican-Americans—so appealing because they were so different—were presented in essentially two forms: as the *paisano* and the *macho*. Steinbeck defined the *paisano* in *Tortilla Flat*, the first book of real value devoted to Americans of Mexican origin. It was Hemingway, in the story "The Gambler, the Nun and the Radio," who paid homage to the *macho*, the virile man par excellence.

Paisanos were people of the soil, children of nature. In the midst of a civilization in crisis, the myth of the primitive man was revived. Indeed, for Steinbeck: "The paisanos are clean of commercialism, free of the complicated systems of American business, and, having nothing that can be stolen, exploited or mortgaged, that system has not attacked them very vigorously."[15] Other contemporary writers—Saroyan, Summers, Horgan—presented similar images, although with less verve and literary talent than Steinbeck.

"Embattled as the Ancient Britons are embattled in Wales,"[16] the *paisanos* of Tortilla Flat struggle against twentieth-century civilization; as marginal people in a society intent upon acquiring material goods, they neither know nor wish to know dependence upon property. *Tortilla Flat* is a eulogy to poverty, accepted willingly with a sense of brotherhood and joy. After returning from the war, Danny finds himself the owner of two houses and feels "a little weighed down by the responsibility of ownership."[17] At first he drinks to forget, then eagerly rents one of the houses to his friend Pilon but never demands rent. When the house catches fire, he makes little effort to determine the cause. Gitano, the *paisano* in the poetic Steinbeck short story "The Red Pony," is happy to possess nothing at all; this "light traveler" comes from the mountains to the civilized world of the valley and finds nothing but misunderstanding from adults and the rich. The society of Tortilla Flat reposes not upon "the complicated systems of American business" but rather on a spontaneous harmony among all people and the universe. The *paisanos* are "people who merge successfully with their habitat";[18] Danny's humble house, transfigured, becomes the symbol of their world of "sweetness," "joy, philanthropy. . . ."[19]

The only social contract linking Steinbeck's "buddies" is their friendship; it attracts them all to Danny, like a "talisman,"[20] and also transfigures them into knights gathered together in Danny's house as if at the Round Table. The refined language, including the archaic familiar form "thou" that Steinbeck uses, symbolizes their nobility. Witness this passage, in which Pilon, on learning that Danny is now a proprietor, cautions him:

> When one is poor, one thinks, If I had money I would share it with my good friends. But let that money come and charity flies away. So it is with thee, my once-friend. Thou art lifted above thy friends. Thou art a man of property. Thou wilt forget thy friends who shared everything with thee, even their brandy.[21]

In Danny's house, sharing is the rule, sharing whatever its inhabitants possess, or more often, what they do not possess. It is no surprise that, attaching so little importance to what belongs to them, they also come to place little value on what belongs to others. In the moving episode about the foundling Tularecito in *The Pastures of Heaven*, Steinbeck had already emphasized the generosity of the *paisano*—of Franklin Gomez, who insists upon keeping an abnormal little creature dangerous to society and who, despite all the evidence to the contrary, insists on believing in the fundamental goodness of his nature. This generosity, no doubt, contains the naiveté typical of these simple people, whom the author contrasts to the petty Miss Martin, the American schoolteacher.[22] In the same tone, Horgan presents the Mexican's qualities of the heart. Only one episode in his novel *Main Line West* is devoted to Mexican-Americans, but its drama makes it one of the book's most striking. The scene is a train headed for Los Angeles. An American woman, Irma, the novel's heroine, dies while with her husband and young son. Some humble Mexican-American travelers offer a wealth of sympathy to the two mourners, a sympathy that contrasts with the callousness of the conductor and the indifference of the other travelers, who relieve their consciences by taking up a collection for the child.[23] In a charming short story by William Saroyan, "The Mexicans," gardener Juan Cabral, whose riches consist of a large family and four dogs, seeks employment in the wine region. The nephew of the vintner (who is also the author) attempts to soften his uncle, who sees every Mexican-American as a potential thief and prefers Japanese laborers. The nephew stresses Juan's affection for his family ("His heart is full of love") and, finally, to convince his uncle, adds: "The stealing they do never amounts to anything."[24] Indeed, what do a few minor thefts matter, in view of the graciousness of the *paisano*? Saroyan, like Steinbeck, attached little importance to them.

The *paisanos* themselves see such thefts as nothing but minor transgressions. After all, isn't a self-confessed error already half-pardoned? In Tortilla Flat, in the Pastures of Heaven, or in Little Mexico, people yield successively to pleasure and repentance. Confession has a cathartic effect. Steinbeck and Summers described both their propensity for pleasure and the naive simplicity that accompanied their revelries. The essential thing was not that they partook fully of the pleasures of the table and the flesh, but rather the healthy and unrestrained way in which they let themselves go. In *Dark Madonna*, after struggling for a time against obesity, the Lopez sisters allow nature to take its course, while the men take every opportunity to eat and especially to drink. *Paisanos* and *paisanas* all yield to the call of the flesh. Teresina, in Tortilla Flat, and Maria Delgado, in Little Mexico, are perpetually pregnant. The Lopez sisters, enchilada vendors by trade, don't hesitate to consort with their clients to supplement their income. A man would pay for the *enchilada*, then dally with one of the vendors.

How can this *joie de vivre*, this feeling of harmony with the universe, be reconciled with the concept of sin, which is a breakdown of the innate harmony between man and God? *Paisanos* needed divine complicity; they enlisted the aid of the heavens by burning candles to the saints and especially to the Virgin Mary—thus making them accomplices in their ventures and responsible for failure. Danny's gang sets off to steal only after duly making the sign of the cross; Pilon searches for the Pirate's treasure with a cross in his hand; the Lopez sisters sin, then throw themselves at the feet of the Virgin, whom they hold responsible for their errant ways.[25] In all of these superstitious practices is an intimacy with the sacred, which might shock some people as it did the early chroniclers. For the *paisanos*, such rites were a way to recapture inner peace and harmony with the hidden forces that govern the universe, with the Godhead. The Catholic Paul Horgan arrived at this conclusion in his novel *No Quarter Given*; touched by the simple and naive faith of the people of Santa Fe, the heroine believes that this faith is the solution to the problem of human existence, "the grandest wisdom in the world": "Nothing is without its solution because everything has the same big solution. For the Mexicans it's living as you must, and talking about it afterwards to God." [26]

That Mexican-Americans were innately wise was an idea that had been suggested in the preceding century; it was now reiterated with great insistence. The sack belonging to Gitano, the knight errant of "The Red Pony," contains nothing but a gold rapier—a useless object in a utilitarian society but a symbol of the inner richness accessible only to the young, the child Jody and the farmhand Billy Buck. The treasure hunt by Pilon and Big Joe Portagee, however unsuccessful financially, is fruitful since it leads Pilon to recognize that, after all, "happiness is better than riches" and that "to make Danny happy" is "a better thing than to give him money." [27] This is the essence of Steinbeck's message.

But the readers of *Tortilla Flat* saw nothing but a comical treasure hunt and laughed. The book was enormously popular, and its success was crowned by Hollywood's acquisition of screen rights soon after its publication.[28] This laughter throughout America troubled the author; he was upset by the superficial interpretation of the work. He felt obliged to explain his true intentions and justify himself. In the foreword of the second edition, published in 1937 by the Modern Library, the author says in a clearly defensive tone that he never considered the *paisanos* "curious or quaint, dispossessed or underdoggish" [29] and never wished to provoke laughter by showing the picturesque side of poverty. That "the *decent* people" believed that that was his intention and had been shocked was regrettable; that the *paisanos*, "these good people of laughter and kindness, of honest lusts and direct eyes, of courtesy beyond politeness," [30] had suffered because of this book's success was infinitely more regrettable. Later, Chicano essayist Francisco A. Ríos lamented this undeserved success earned at the expense of Mexican-Americans. He granted Steinbeck's good faith but believed that

> ... to sentimentalize about people in poverty, to give them exaggerated speech and manners, is not to praise them; especially when these same people are also portrayed as a drunken lot, inundated in cheap wine, sleeping in ditches, fighting for the enjoyment of it, stealing at every turn, and living in rampant promiscuity. [31]

Let there be no mistake, Steinbeck was not laughing at the *paisanos* but rather with them at American society. To do this, he chose the allegory. If he contrasted the "complicated system of American business" to the "strong but different philosophic-moral system" [32] of the *paisanos*, it was to demonstrate the aberrations of the former. If he maintained that the *paisanos'* social structure was "beautiful and wise," [33] it was because he saw it infused with a wisdom that might appear to be madness to others. Austin was also amused by the American sense of self-importance. [34] In her humorous short story "The Politeness of Cuesta la Plata," she imagines that the federal government decides to make this little New Mexico town the national center for the manufacture of goat cheese. The government, however, is unaware that this city is famous both for its goat cheese and for its extreme politeness. An American dietitian is assigned to teach the inhabitants the recipe for the cheese—their own recipe. One can imagine the dietitian's consternation had they departed from their legendary politeness and denounced the hoax! In a more serious vein, Horgan praised the simple faith of the Mexican-American. Simplicity, the ultimate form of wisdom, becomes synonymous with the Mexican soul; the American heroine of his novel comes to consider herself Mexican, exclaiming: "We're all Mexicans. You and I and David . . . I suppose we all have the same simplicity." [35] The contrast between the Anglo and Mexican-American ways of life is more marked, the criticism more explicit, in *Dark Madonna*. Summers takes us alternately from Little Mexico, the Mexican neighborhood that his young heroine, Lupe Salcido, leaves each morning, to the American part of town, where she works as a servant; the vibrancy and laughter in Little Mexico accentuate the drab, prosaic nature of Anglo life. In the way of life personified by the *paisanos*, the children of nature, Anglo-Americans saw a condemnation of their own system.

The *Macho*

The *macho*, the symbol of virility, is presented in Hemingway's tale "The Gambler, the Nun and the Radio" and in Steinbeck's short story "Flight."

Hemingway's *macho* awaits death with dignity and stoicism; Steinbeck's adolescent prepares himself for manhood. Machismo has undeniably exercised great fascination for American writers, but in the nineteenth century they primarily glorified the attitude of the Mexican-American man toward women. In making the *vaquero* the epitome of virility, they emphasized the elegance of his bearing and dress, which provoked the vehement criticism of John Houghton Allen.[36] In a little collection of poems, devoted in part to the *vaqueros* of Randado, Allen stresses the *vaqueros'* capacity for endurance: "men of deed and men of brawn used to the monte, heat and grime."[37] Their work requires strength above all else. Hemingway depicts his Mexican *macho* in a Montana hospital, in a world of "men without women."[38] The only woman is a nun whose thoughts are turned entirely toward heaven. The author emphasizes the stoicism of the injured man as he confronts the prospect of physical suffering and death. Steinbeck's young hero, whose invalid father can no longer act as head of the family, must become a man before assuming his father's place. The importance of *machismo* in the Hispanic world is well established. Hemingway himself was strongly influenced by his Spanish experiences, by the Civil War, and by the bullfight arena. He strove toward the ideal of virile stoicism his whole life. More a poet, Steinbeck chose not the world of adults and consummate heroes, but that of childhood and of initiation into manhood. His story has a fairy-tale quality, not unlike the dreams and fantasies from which the adolescent slowly emerges.

Machismo was also associated with death, the ultimate consecration. By confronting physical suffering and death, the gravely injured Cayetano Ruiz demonstrates his full measure of manhood. The initiation of Pepe Torres is achieved through death; by killing a man during a barroom quarrel, the adolescent becomes a man. His solitary and dignified death, at the end of the story,[39] is the ultimate confirmation of this initial baptism in blood. The weapon, the instrument of death, is of utmost importance to the *macho*; Pepe refuses to give up his father's knife (Gitano's rapier was also handed down from his father). When his mother sends him alone for the first time to Monterey, he insists on wearing his father's black hat with the embossed leather band and using his father's saddle on his horse. The hat and the horse are the two quintessentially male attributes. The Mexican mother also plays a role in the child's initiation; since her husband's accident, she acts as the head of the family until the oldest son can reestablish male preeminence in the household. (Later, we shall reexamine the subject of paternal dominance and maternal abnegation in the Mexican-American family.) "He is nearly a man now. . . . It will be a nice thing to have a man in the house again,"[40] the mother says as she thinks about Pepe. Because he has killed and is now a man, he has to flee to avoid being "caught like a chicken."[41] Later on, he stoically accepts his inevitable death. Cayetano accepts his paralysis just as he accepted losing when he gambled: as a gambler, he attributes his fatal wound entirely to bad luck: "I am completely without luck,"[42] he says simply. It was probably not by chance that Hemingway chose to make his hero a gambler; he knew that for the Spaniard life was like a game with inflexible rules. The Mexican, as a descendant also of the Indian, was also aware of the implacable nature of fate.

Steinbeck and Hemingway introduce us to two stages of *machismo,* the initiation and the trial (physical suffering and death), but each author tends to make his characters exceptional and unrealistic, of purposely vague dimensions. Pepe takes refuge in the mountains where no man has ever set foot. His death has an artificial quality. Cayetano's hands are too fine, the nun thinks to herself, for a common beet-picker; he retains an aura of mystery.

This romanticizing masks more serious intentions on the part of the two writers. Steinbeck's young *macho* dies alone, in a primitive and virgin world where the mountain lion observing him has not yet learned to fear humans; he dies after abandoning his horse, hat, and rifle, outward signs of the world he has fled. Indirectly, the author returns to one of his basic themes, that one does not require the advantages of civilization in order to be a man; *machismo* is not beyond the reach of the *paisano.*

Hemingway's story presents three different attitudes toward life and death: the nun prays, drawing all her strength from her faith; the Mexican gambler accepts his fate, drawing all his strength from within himself; the American, Frazer, another injured patient, draws strength from songs he hears on the radio (his absence from the title, "The Gambler, the Nun and the Radio" is noteworthy); he lacks the Mexican's courage. Was Hemingway portraying himself in the character Frazer? After an automobile accident in 1931, Hemingway, indeed, was hospitalized in Billings, Montana, for a compound fracture of the arm. The Mexican gambler probably personifies the ideal of stoic virility to which he aspired at the time. But the story is more than autobiographical; Frazer is not only Hemingway but the American male in general, emasculated by a progress-oriented civilization that rejects suffering and avoids contemplating the implacability of death. Hemingway contrasts the Mexican's stoical silence to Frazer's unmanly behavior; the latter sobs in the night and uses drink and the radio as opiates to avoid thinking. The comparison of the two is clearly to the Mexican's advantage. They speak in front of the nun watching them:

> "She tells me you never made a sound," Mr. Frazer said.
> "So many people in the ward," the Mexican said deprecatingly. "What class of pain do you have?"
> "Big enough. Clearly not as bad as yours. When the nurse goes out I cry an hour, two hours. It rests me. My nerves are bad now."
> "You have the radio. If I had a private room and a radio I would be crying and yelling all night long."
> "I doubt it."[43]

Both admiration and shame are discernible in Frazer's words.

Hemingway, Steinbeck, and their contemporaries expressed their fascination with a wholly different people by using traditional stereotypes. The *paisano* was a descendant of the noble savage, the *macho* in the direct lineage of the *vaquero*. Chicano critics would later condemn this lack of realistic Mexican-American characters in Anglo-American literature.[44] We have already seen how the *paisanos* of *Tortilla Flat* were open to criticism. The *macho*, frozen into his inspiring exploits, also lost his reality. But while the stereotypes of the romantics of the past constituted an escape from reality, the stereotypes of the Steinbeck era represented a return to reality, an American one, and a criticism of that reality. In certain writers of the thirties, nevertheless, this turning inward gave way to a more objective vision of the Other. They became interested in Mexican-American reality for its own sake.

CHAPTER 5

The Defenders of the Oppressed

The general conflicts of Mexican-Americans were first outlined in the early realistic works toward the end of the nineteenth century. The writers of the thirties were more specific, taking readers directly to the places where the Mexican-American tragedy unfolded, describing the difficulties of the wet-back,[1] or illegal worker, and the itinerant laborer. Without a contract, the wetback was exploited, the seasonal worker under contract scarcely less so. These two Mexican workers appeared for the first time on the literary scene. William Saroyan, Paul Horgan, and John McGinnis, in particular, went directly to the heart of the problem, taking an interest in the Mexican-Americans who suffered most under the economic system introduced by Americans into the Southwest. The *hacendados*, of course, had lost land during the construction of the railroad, but those who labored on the railway suffered much more. Horgan's short story "The Surgeon and the Nun"[2] depicts Mexican laborers at work on the railroad in the Pecos Valley in 1905.[3] The rapid development of agriculture in the Southwest required cheap labor; Mexican-Americans thus became agricultural workers, in most cases forced to adjust to the fluctuations of temporary and seasonal work. Saroyan's short story "With a Hey Nonny Nonny"[4] and McGinnis's story "The Tomato Can"[5] both portray Mexican-American cotton-pickers during an unspecified era. The exploitation of the Mexican-American seasonal agricultural laborer by agribusiness, the large-scale agricultural industry, remained a theme in succeeding years.

Contempt for the poor and for sheepherders had already been denounced in literature, but the role it played in the exploitation of Mexican-American agricultural workers had never been exposed. The details of agricultural workers' lives were revealed for the first time, varying little from one story to the next: the merciless summer sun, the stifling dust, the inhospitable shanties, the hostile foreman. The agricultural worker lived in a "summer universe"[6] of work and overwhelming heat. Summer was physically oppressive in the three stories by Horgan, Saroyan, and McGinnis. Horgan's story is set in parts of New Mexico and Texas where there is "nothing but dust to breathe," where "the heat swam on the ground."[7] The situation concerns a Mexican laborer who is stricken with appendicitis, in the midst of the heat and dust. The California sun makes the labor of Saroyan's cotton-pickers even more arduous; the sun loses its past splendor and becomes the symbol of the work itself.

Horgan dwells at length on relations between the American foreman and the Mexican workers, while McGinnis takes more interest in the seasonal farm worker's living conditions. Horgan's foreman, "a big American," takes advantage of his stature and nationality to reign despotically over his Mexican hands, most of whom are short. He refuses to take seriously a worker's incapacitating injury: "They all do it. Nothin' matter with him. He's just play-actin',"[8] he says as he pushes the prostrate Mexican with his big, dusty shoe. The tone is less impassioned but the situation just as dramatic in the McGinnis story; the narrative's apparent simplicity in no way diminishes the significance of the author's brief but moving message. A Chicago journalist has come to write a series of articles on a small Texas border town. During his stay, a grudge fight between two cotton-pickers ends in bloodshed. After discovering that the real cause of the quarrel is an empty tomato can, the reporter decides to sensationalize the incident. His editor refuses to take the explanation seriously and devotes only a brief, vaguely phrased paragraph to it. The story that the journalist wanted to publish—McGinnis's story—was the sad and all-too-common tale of two families of seasonal farm workers living in wretched camp conditions:

> Two tents, both nearly new, had been pitched just inside the barbed-wire fence. . . . In the twenty-foot space between tents was a black iron kettle, and under it a smouldering fire. Hanging on the fence were pieces of wash, perhaps two dozen in all.[9]

Each family owns two tomato cans, which, because of their destitution, they use as drinking glasses. The quarrel between the two families erupted over another, larger tomato can. One of the fathers is killed, the other flees, so that now in the tents remain ". . . two families destitute by the death of one father and the flight of the other."[10] The depression of the thirties struck Mexican-Americans with particular harshness. The poverty of transient Mexican-Americans, sketched out by McGinnis in 1931, was the same as that of the Oklahoma emigrants of whom Steinbeck would so masterfully write in *The Grapes of Wrath* at the end of the decade.

How did Mexican-Americans react? Horgan's wetbacks withdraw into distrust, their traditional behavior pattern, but one the author makes every effort to explain objectively. Faced with their foreman's cruelty and the unexpected kindness of the surgeon and the nun, how can the Mexicans adopt anything other than a prudent distrust? Saroyan gives a more positive image of Mexican-American attitudes. By making the Mexican-American labor strike a theme in his story, he demonstrates that Mexican-Americans, whose first strikes dated back to the nineteenth century, do not accept their fate with the submissiveness traditionally attributed to them. The public could no longer ignore the strikes. McWilliams wrote, in all sincerity: ". . . by 1930 the myth of the docility of Mexican labor had been thoroughly exploded. . . ."[11] It was an illusory disappearance, according to Romano, who argues that this myth of docility, thanks to the semantic subtleties of sociology, lives on in another form, that of the Mexican-American who is "fatalistic and non-goal oriented."[12] In Saroyan's story, cotton-pickers organize a strike that is quickly and brutally quashed by the American company. In a sense, Saroyan brings up the theme of American repression raised by Garland in "Delmar of Pima," but the later story has a social and psychological realism missing in the earlier work. Garland's leader triumphs too easily while Rivas, Saroyan's young hero, is killed by the company's bullies. The Mexican-American worker would face many setbacks for a long time to come.

The revolt depicted by Saroyan was a revolt of the Mexican-American proletariat, of the "have-nots" against the "haves," the Anglo-American capitalists. The struggle of the Mexican-American is also a class struggle: "[strike organizer] Agunaga says we must not work to make them rich,"[13] young Rivas repeats to himself. Since the Mexican Revolution, a whole body of anarchist propaganda had crossed the border and spread among Mexicans working in the United States.[14] By 1934, when Saroyan wrote his short story, more than one revolt, like that of the cotton-pickers, had failed for lack of union support.[15] The social and economic demands of the Mexican workers had led only to a "ghastly frustration."[16]

Saroyan's story, however, is more than the recounting of a strike and its failure. The bitterness experienced by young Rivas, who is also in love, is complex. He takes part in the strike, of course, but he tries in vain to convince himself that it will be effective: he leaves for the battle already beaten. His death at the end of the story is meaningful. Deep within him reigns a sense of frustration, caused by the impossibility of being himself, of understanding "the meaning of himself,"[17] in an absurd world. The absurdity of American society, of technological civilization, is symbolized by an incoherent, "jangling"[18] pianola song, whose stupid words "With a Hey Nonny Nonny" haunt the youngster in the streets, in the fields, and all the way to his grave. This music, "nervous, fidgety as men had been made fidgety by the feverishness of the time,"[19] drowns out another music that arises within him, a muted and ineffable music of the earth, of the sun, of love, of beauty. "With a Hey Nonny Nonny" drowns out a third kind of music, with more serious sounds: Agunaga's words. The story, interlaced with three different leitmotifs, should be

listened to as a song for a trio, the triumph of the discordant notes foreshadowing the victory of the company over the workers, of death over love, of ugliness
over beauty. The nonsense words "With a Hey Nonny Nonny" give meaning
to the story, but it's the music in the heart of the young Mexican that gives the
tale its moving poetry. Through the musicality of the words, Saroyan suggests
to the reader the inner turmoil of his young hero and the dilemma from which,
finally, death is the only escape.

In a less contemporary and realistic context (the setting is New Mexico),
Philip Stevenson's symbolic short story evokes the distressing situation of a
young Mexican-American "At the Crossroads."[20] What route would Transito
finally take? The one to Santa Fe, where he worked among gringos he detested
but was dependent upon? The one to his native village, to which he returned
on the day before Easter, where his brother Jesús still lived, his name symbolic
of an attachment to the religious traditions of the past? Transito wished to
become the leader of his people; but it was Jesús who had been chosen to
play Christ in the annual procession of the Penitents. As the procession was
taking place, a gringo truck, skidding on the snow, bore down at full speed
on Jesús; Transito rushed forward to save his brother; the truck, a symbol of
American civilization, crushed them both. The slightly contrived short story
is not quite convincing but gives testimony, nonetheless, to Stevenson's efforts
at expressing the malaise of the Mexican-American.

The particular interest of Saroyan's story comes from the new element
that he introduces: the Mexican-American situating himself in relation to the
Anglo-American. American civilization appeared absurd to Rivas because he
himself felt out of step with it, because as a Mexican, he was obliged to live
in a society dominated by American culture. Saroyan, himself an American of
foreign ancestry, may well have experienced this cultural uneasiness. To Rivas,
English was nothing more than the instrument for his social existence; the
language of his heart was Spanish, which alone was capable of expressing his
innermost being. Thus, as he thought about Maria:

> Saying her name over and over again, breathing the bitterness of a vio-
> lent and unknown frustration, his blood foolishly remarking with a hey
> nonny nonny, doing it in English, while the rest of it, more deeply inward,
> spoke in Mexican. . . .[21]

It remained to be seen to what degree the Anglo writer, issuing from an English
cultural and linguistic background, could speak authentically about the heart
of the Mexican.

As a result of all of this probing, a more intimate and moving image of
the Mexican-American took shape. Authors tried for more objectivity in character study, and stereotypes gave way to the imperatives of realism. Social
authenticity was more rigorously observed: the heroes of the Revolution were

replaced by more obscure heroes of class struggle. However, alongside this realistic movement, an indomitable romanticism persisted. Writers continued to situate themselves in relation to Mexican-Americans rather than portraying Mexican-Americans as they situated themselves in relation to Anglos. The decline of romanticism, which never completely died out, was balanced by a progressive rise of realism.

To Leave a Remembrance

Must I go as flowers winters leave?
One day will there be nothing of my name?
Behind me is it nothing I must leave?
At least flowers, at least my songs' fame!
How shall my heart achieve?
Maybe we come to bloom on earth, to live in vain?
NAHUATL SONG[1]

The Mexican–American
Point of View

Early Modes of Expression

Very little information has been passed on to us by Anglo-American writers on the literary activities of the newly conquered Mexican-Americans. Chronicler Harris Newmark[2] limited himself to a brief reference to Francisco Ramírez, the director of the literary review *El Clamor Público*; Royce's brief sketch of the California intelligentsia conformed to the poor opinion he held of it.[3] It seems that Mexican-Americans were known principally for singing and poetry; as guitar players and poets, they went from fair to festival, from village to village like the troubadours of old. Novelist Alfred Lewis criticized the taste for hyperbole of the *guitarrero* hired for the wedding of his two young heroes,[4] while Fergusson nostalgically evoked the sad and melancholy beauty of Mexican ballads.[5] Only Atherton made note of a theatrical tradition in the Spanish-speaking Southwest, by describing briefly in a short story the performance of the pastoral "Los Pastores."[6]

The literary and folkloric efforts of early Mexican-Americans[7] were long relegated to oblivion. On the order of Governor Pico, records were burned in California. Animosity toward Mexicans after the war fostered a lack of interest in their traditions. In the nineteenth-century Southwest, Anglo-Americans were primarily interested in economic development; in literature, they turned toward the Indians. Not until the first decade of the twentieth century did folklorists begin to reveal Mexican-American modes of expression at the time of annexation; this folkloric form of expression remained very active until 1910. Among the specialists in Texas folklore are two great names, Frank Dobie,[8] a longtime active member of the Texas Folklore Society,[9] and Américo Paredes, currently director of the Center for Intercultural Studies in Folklore and

Oral History at the University of Texas at Austin. We should also mention Mody Boatright, Frank Goodwyn, and Jovita González, among others; in New Mexico there were Arthur Campa, a specialist in religious theater and folkloric poetry, Charles Lummis, Mary Austin, and Frank Applegate. Research on the folklore of California and New Mexico became a veritable family enterprise for the Espinosas. Aurelio Manuel Espinosa, a professor at Stanford University, collected New Mexico ballads; under his direction, his son, José Manuel, spent the summer of 1931 gathering stories from the inhabitants of the northern part of the state. Professor Juan Bautista Rael, a former student of Aurelio Espinosa, did the same in Colorado and New Mexico, and so forth. The work was doubly difficult in the case of folklorists for whom English was a first language; despite the accuracy of their translations, some of the original flavor of the item sung or narrated was necessarily lost.

Mexican-American thought and creativity surpassed the primitive folkloric level. Octavio Romano, who founded the literary review *El Grito: A Journal of Contemporary Mexican-American Thought* in 1969, accused Professor Edward Simmen of lending credence to the fable that Mexican-Americans could not write literature until recent years, thereby condemning their early literary production to be "permanently entombed in that sterile academic cemetery called folklore."[10] From 1969 until 1974, when the Quinto Sol publishing company was dissolved, a team of researchers gathered at Berkeley with Romano actively worked to prove that a genuine Mexican-American literature took shape after the annexation. This same effort is still being pursued, though on a smaller scale, by Mexican-American studies centers created since the 1960s, especially in southwestern universities. Anthologies are published frequently, often in collaboration with Anglo-Americans.

Was there really a climate suitable for literature in 1848? The Californians had lived in a Spanish environment since the eighteenth century; they had few literary ambitions, if we are to believe Richard Henry Dana's chronicle, *Two Years Before the Mast*,[11] or Royce. Royce, however, found in these Californians qualities he believed inherent to Mediterranean people, that is, wittiness and vivacity, and he recognized in their writings a certain facileness and vigor; the women, in his view, lacked culture but not piquancy in conversation.[12] The intelligentsia in California struggled desperately to express itself,[13] but literary newspapers written in Spanish were short-lived because of a lack of both subsidies and a sufficiently literate Spanish-speaking public. To expatriate Mexican poet Aurelio L. Gallardo (1831–1869), who lived in San Francisco, the publication of sensuous poetry in a country where Spanish letters hardly flourished seemed rather daring.[14] The Hispanos of New Mexico took refuge in their isolated mountain villages, withdrawn into the traditions and language of the past. Their way of life was pastoral; they expressed themselves in a folkloric "literature" that had no need of publication. Transmitted orally, it had all the drawbacks that such transmission entails. Folklore was also the means of expression of the Texas *vaquero*.

In the literary field, poetry predominated. Poets favored such themes as love and death and rarely concerned themselves with contemporary events. In California, particularly, the neoclassic poetry typical of nineteenth-century Latin America, known to us only through fragments, appeared in the newspapers of the period: *El Nuevo Mundo, La Gaceta,* and especially *El Clamor Público.* The latter's ambitious editor, Ramírez, later added the words *Literario e Independiente* [15] to the title to make it sound more literary. Gallardo's poetry, on the other hand, was published in book form. [16] To our knowledge, the only novel ("*novela*") published at this time was one by Gallardo; [17] a chronicle by an anonymous author, "La Vida y Aventura de Joaquín Murrieta," published in *La Gaceta* in 1881, resembled reportage more than fiction. Other works remained to be discovered. The publication of works by León Calvillo-Ponce, whose first known writings date from 1891, was held back because of a disagreement among his heirs. The poetic works of Gabriel Dela Riva, who wrote in the twenties, have yet to be studied.

Spanish remained the literary language until about 1940. However, Miguel A. Otero's memoirs and his study of Billy the Kid [18] were written in English. The author, then governor of the New Mexico Territory, handled the language perfectly. The narratives of Jovita González [19] display a similar command of English. On the eve of World War II, brief stories and poems written by Mexican-Americans began to appear in journals of the Southwest and in the *Lulac News.* [20]

The folklore of New Mexico (from the plateau to the north of Santa Fe, in particular) and Texas, remained profoundly Hispanic; there was little Indian involvement. The strength and tenacity of the Spanish influence stemmed from the fact that the acculturation of Mexican-Americans was considerably hindered by their isolation, by their exclusion from Anglo-American unions, and especially by the contact they maintained with Mexico through immigrants. The language and the genres were Spanish, and the subjects, in general, were traditional. Gradually, however, works of originality began to appear that distinguished the Mexican living and working on American soil from the Mexican *peón* ("laborer"). To the Aztec and Spanish components of this folklore was added a third, American.

The most popular of the *pastorelas* ("pastorals") in the Southwest at the time of the defeat was, incontestably, *Los Pastores* (The shepherds); [21] it was theater, music, dance, singing, and celebration all rolled into one. The story of Christ was relegated to the background while the antics of the shepherds and the devil took center stage. Performances were generally given in the open by shepherds or laborers, foreshadowing early Chicano theater, performed in California by farm workers themselves on the site of their labors.

Unfortunately, I have been unable to find the text of the only play that, to my knowledge, was of secular and satirical inspiration: *La Lluvia de los Ingleses* (The showers of the Englishmen), mentioned by Ruth Laughlin Barker. [22] It deals with the burning issue of the arrival of the first Americans.

Cuentos ("tales") were, for the most part, of European or Middle Eastern origin, while others were Aztec. Added to these stories were such staples of the Mexican Southwest as corrals, *vaqueros*, priests, Indians, fiestas, *brujas* ("witches"), and *curanderos* ("healers"). Ever since the annexation, allusions to American life and bilingual jokes had brought a different tone to the traditional narrative, revealing a different civilization to the isolated populations of Texas and New Mexico. It would have been preferable if more liberties had been taken with the original texts as they were transmitted from one generation to the next; the stories would have better reflected contemporary life.

The *corrido* ("ballad") was genuinely innovative; it adopted a more modern structure and more current themes, and became a uniquely Mexican form. At the end of the nineteenth century, in northern Mexico and Texas, the *corrido* replaced the traditional ballad or *romance* of Spanish origin, and the *décima*, a type of poetry;[23] the isolated northern part of New Mexico, on the other hand, long remained faithful to the older genres and their universal themes. The *corrido* resembled the English ballad of the seventeenth century; both addressed the illiterate masses and recounted an item of current interest, often satirically. But while the ballad was first printed and then transmitted orally, the *corrido* was sung by *cantadores* (professional street singers) on public squares, in *cantinas* ("saloons"), and at fiestas, or was recited by poets to the accompaniment of the guitar; it was sometimes printed and sold for one or two *centavos* ("cents") in Mexico or a nickel in the United States. As indicated by its name, taken from the verb *correr*, "to run" or "to flow," the *corrido* related a story "simply and swiftly, without embellishments."[24] The *corrido*, containing both reportage and satire, needed a more flexible form than that of the traditional ballad; a succession of *coplas*—eight-syllable couplets of four lines—added to one another at will by the narrator, became the standard form.

In the isolated parts of New Mexico and Texas where people took little interest in the outside world, the *corrido* reported news of a more personal nature, such as a wedding or a funeral. Thus, troubadour Próspero Baca related the tragedy of little Alfonso Sedillos, who froze to death in the snow in 1929 near Bernalillo, New Mexico, and the heroic deeds of his dog Fido;[25] Baca's daughter, Andrellita Baca de Martínez, described the calamity that struck this same little village the same year, when it was flooded yet again by the Rio Grande.[26] But the *corrido* is not merely a gazette of purely local interest or a simple sentimental ballad. Manuel Gamio, the Mexican anthropologist who has studied all aspects of immigration—its oral expression in particular—makes a distinction between the *canción*, a poem of a lyrical and autobiographical nature, and the *corrido*. The latter, also called a ballad, usually celebrates extraordinary men, "types that catch the popular imagination: swaggering bandits who boldly defy the rest of the world, brave men foully assassinated, or men who 'kill for love.'"[27] Américo Paredes, a specialist in the *corridos* of the border, also subscribes to this definition. However, the term tends to be used indiscriminately and less to designate the content of the poem than its form.

The *corrido* (both *corrido* and *canción*) brought the experience of Mexicans in American territory to light: their initial demonstrations against the hated occupier in the border regions, the labor of the *vaqueros*, the vicissitudes of the immigrants, and their reactions to a new civilization.

It is difficult to determine which of the *romances*, *décimas*, *cuandos*,[28] and *corridos* of the nineteenth century were composed by Mexican-Americans, for relations between *México de Afuera* ("outer Mexico") and the Republic of Mexico remained close; many poems popular in the Southwest undoubtedly originated in Mexico. In addition, the names of the authors in most cases were lost; the poet was not a professional but a simple worker who remained anonymous. Occasionally, however, like artists who paint themselves into a picture by way of signature, they revealed their names in the last stanza.[29] In New Mexico, only a few such authors are remembered: Vilmas, renowned for his *Trovos* (tender *romances*), Chicoria, for his love of the epigram, and, especially, Jesús Gonzales, the poet-shepherd nicknamed El Pelón ("the Bald One"), born near Santa Fe in 1844. His manuscripts, written on animal skins, were discovered in a cavern sometime around the 1930s. The best known in our time is Próspero Baca of Bernalillo, born at the end of the nineteenth century. Except for a few poems containing the date of composition in the first few lines, we must be content with approximate dates. This poetry was sung, transmitted orally before being transcribed from memory, and the versions varied from one village to another, from one storyteller to the next. However, thanks to Aurelio Espinosa, we have a nearly complete collection of the folkloric poetry in New Mexico following annexation.[30] During the 1920s, throughout the Southwest, sociologists Manuel Gamio and Paul Taylor did extensive research, collecting a number of *corridos* concerning immigration; in the aggregate, they comprise a collective autobiography of the immigration.[31] In the same era, Frank Dobie and Frank Goodwyn went from ranch to ranch, gathering the *vaqueros'* favorite songs directly from them.[32] During the fifties, folklorist Américo Paredes began to inventory the *corridos* of the borderlands.[33]

From the folklore and literary works through which the Mexican-American people had expressed themselves since 1848, there emerged a double image of this group, the first one "static," a legacy of tradition, and the second "dynamic," a reflection of the present.

CHAPTER 6

Mexicans Take Refuge in Their Myths

In 1864, poet Juan B. Hijar y Jaro sang of the sadness of exile: "Y dije adiós a mis benditos lares" (And I bid adieu to my blessed home).[2] The line recurs like a leitmotif throughout his long poem, which recounts his heartrending departure from his native land and his arrival in the United States on a ship. The exile remained forever a child of Mexico:

El pan en tierra extraña es desabrido, *Y el vino en hiel y lágrimas fecundo;* *¡Ay es tan triste sin la patria el mundo* *Que muere de orfandad el corazón!*[3]	[The bread in foreign lands is without taste, The wine rich in bitterness and tears; How sad the world without a homeland How the heart for being orphaned pines away!]

J. M. Vigil laments "the bitterness of an inhuman fate" "on a foreign shore," on an "indifferent soil."[4] In the preface of his poetic autobiography, Gallardo bemoans the fate of "those who live in the bitterness of exile and cast upon foreign shores . . .";[5] he was intent on giving expression, in his collection of poetry, to "that blessed and far-off country," to "its national traditions and customs," to "the sweet peacefulness of the family home and that sublime ostentation of Christian belief."[6]

Like the expatriate writers, the Mexican-Americans remained attached to the land of their ancestors and to a way of thinking that isolated them from a world so different that it made them uneasy. Writers locked themselves into their myths and into a stasis reflected in their language (contact with English had not yet bastardized their Spanish) and in the themes they explored. Their poetry emphasized traditional Mexican attitudes about love and death, while short stories revealed an ethnic community faithful to ancestral beliefs and hostile toward a foreign culture and civilization. Art constituted a romantic escape into the past, reflecting an essentially Mexican reality and experience. The self-portrait provided by early Mexican-Americans resembled, in certain ways, the picture painted by the "mountain men" or the romantics at the end of the nineteenth century. Transposed into Spanish are some of the stereotypes developed by Americans.

Love

What is striking in the literary works of the early Mexican-Americans is their lyricism and their sensual and elegiac nature. The closely related obsessions of love and death cast both light and shadow upon Mexican-American lyric poetry.

A considerable number of love poems, often anonymous, appeared in the Mexican-American press of the nineteenth century and the early decades of the twentieth century. Unrequited love was also one of the favorite subjects of folklore, dominated by the figure of the love-struck *vaquero*.

The love poetry revealed an excessive cult of form and a certain conception of women, both uniquely Mexican. For Mexican-Americans, love was a delicate balance between passion and formalism, between intrigue and conventions. Every step in courtship was rigorously defined; this set ritual is reflected in the poet's formulaic expressions. José Elías González addressed himself to an anonymous beauty in 1856:

Es tu semblante divino:	[Your visage is devine,
Tu sien, como el lirio, pura;	Your temple as pure as the iris,
Al verte, hermosa, imagino	At your sight, my beauty, I imagine
Que eres ángel de ternura.[7]	That you're an angel of tenderness.]

A similar attention to form and the same fidelity to the rites of courtly love appears in the dithyrambic quatrains of F. N. Gutiérrez, composed in 1880:

Tú eres la fuente de amor,	[You are the fountain of love
Eres del diamante el fulgor,	You are the brilliance of the diamond
Del cielo el astro superior,	The sky's most shining star
De la tierra un ser, el mejor.[8]	The Earth's most perfect creature.]

Flowers are often cited in the discourse of the love-struck poet: the rose; the iris, a symbol of purity; the palm tree, whose shade is comforting in the desert of life; and so on. This grandiloquence, sarcastically noted by Anglo-American writers, was not unrelated to the competitively embellished flowers "of rhetoric" in the verses of professional village poets; they were often hired by various suitors of the same beauty to help capture her heart:

Piedra preciosa de mil colores	[The thousand-hued precious stone
Que con las flores junto de ti	Along with the flowers by your side
Yo las contemplo una por una	I contemplate one by one
Y no hay ninguna que iguale a ti.[9]	And there is not one that rivals you.]

The same love of form was reflected in Mexican-American poets' adherence to the rigid structures of neoclassic poetry (quatrains and *décima*) and rhyme. These structures gave the poetry a cold rhetorical character that conflicted with the warmth of the sentiments.

In traditional Mexican courtship, the woman waited passively to be conquered; the man took the initiative toward this conquest, whose difficulty sometimes required feats of prowess in the medieval tradition; Mexican love had an undeniably combative quality.[10] Thus, the lover in the *corrido* "Los Amados" [The sweethearts] searches beyond the seas for his beloved, a young lady whose parents have spirited her away, against her wishes, from her suitor's constant attention:

Amado es muy valiente	[Very valiant is the beloved man
Que a amada fué a traer	Who left to seek his lady love
Se la trajo para acá	He brought her back here
Porque ya es su mujer.[11]	For she is now his wife.]

In a *corrido* about Juanita Alvarado, which takes place in 1882, the parents give their daughter orders to reject a young man whose marriage proposal has been duly presented by *portadores* ("messengers"); on horseback and rifle in hand the young man finally carries out his intentions.[12] His action is typical of the love-struck hero in numerous *corridos*.

Love often led to violence. Two news items illustrating passion's fatal consequences engendered two Mexican-American *corridos* collected by Gamio and probably dating back to the early years of the nineteenth century. In a concise narrative of a dance hall quarrel, Jesús Cadena faces his rival, ready to fire his pistol to win the heart of his beloved:

Decía este Jesús Cadena:	*[Said that Jesús Cadena:
"Mi pistola no la enfundo	"I will not put away my pistol
"Ora los hago a mi ley	Now I shall make you do as I please
O los separo del mundo."	Or I shall send you away from this
Decía este Jesús Cadena:	world."
"Voy a ver a mi querida."[13]	Said that Jesús Cadena:
	"I'm going to see my sweetheart."]

Frank Cadena, "a criminal because of love," frustrated in his passion, is condemned to death by a San Antonio court for shooting to death his beautiful sister-in-law, Paulita Jiménez:

Su mente ciega por el cariño.	*[His mind blinded by passion
Siniestra impuso su decisión	Impelled his actions to evil

Sacó el revolver de su bolsillo	He took out his revolver from his holster
Matando luego a su adoración.[14]	And immediately killed his adored one.]

The Mexican woman did not try to attract the man; her sensuality passively waited to be awakened by him, a detail little noted by Anglos, who were fascinated by the open paganism of Mexican-Americans in sexual matters. In the neoclassic poetry, the woman is the immutable goddess, the "goddess here among the beautiful women,"[15] an "angel of love," an "enchanting nymph," "an idolized object."[16] "Eres mi bien, mi tesoro / El ídolo que venero," (You are my riches, my treasure / The idol I adore),[17] cried José González, emphasizing the intensity of his fervor through a progression of terms and, perhaps, through strict observance of the same rhyme throughout the quatrain, the seriousness of the goddess cult. This idol of hieratic calmness possesses a magnetic power; like a distant, mysterious, motionless sun, she exercises an irresistible attraction on men; she is: "del cielo el astro superior" ("the most magnificent star in the sky"). José E. Gutiérrez expresses this feminine magnetism in cosmic or scientific terms. The following lines, of doubtful poetic quality, were perhaps justified by the then recent discovery of electricity:

Tus ojos llenos de fluido,	[Your eyes filled with fluid
Con pilas de electricidad . . .	With electrical batteries . . .
Tus pasos forman las planetas,	Your footsteps form the planets
Tus voces expiden estrellas . . .	Your cries send out the stars . . .
Tú eres el sol aquí en la tierra,	You are the sun here on Earth
Que con tus rayos magnetisas . . .[18]	Which with your rays you magnetize . . .

Death

The most beautiful lyric poems of Mexican-Americans were perhaps the most desperate. In a subtle mixture of narcissism and masochism, lovers took pleasure in seeing love as nothing but illusion and torment, and in showing both to themselves and the beloved the wounds of their aching heart. Their lust for life, their eagerness to enjoy the immediate moment, which had particularly struck the Anglos, actually concealed an innate sense of the tragic and transitory nature of life. Life was both "Tears and Perfume," the meaningful title of Gallardo's second book of poetic reflections on human existence.[19] Sadness was inherent; it was this people's "inseparable companion, its older sister, fiery at times, tragic upon occasions."[20] The themes of ill-fated love and the ephemeral nature of life introduced into Mexican-American poetry a melancholy and plaintive note generally absent from the Spanish *romances*.

The "Corrido of Macario Romero," a cuckolded husband, composed in Mexico around 1878, appeared in the Southwest around 1892 in many variants. One of them relates the marital difficulties of the soldier Macario, who is ready to desert and risk his life to see his unfaithful wife.[21] At least five ballads, one of which, "El Vaquero,"[22] became very popular, sang of the seldom-happy loves of the *vaqueros*, who were more than skilled horsemen who could break broncos or rope balky cattle. In contrast to the American cowboy, the *vaquero* of Mexican folklore was generally a melancholy and suicidal lover, in the image of the Spanish Don Juan; his repertoire consisted almost entirely of love songs;[23] he often gave way to the languor and laments of the abandoned lover:

Me abandonastes, mujer, porque soy muy pobre	*[You abandon me, woman, because I am very poor;
Y la desgracia es ser hombre apasionado	The misfortune is to be a man of passionate devotion.
Pues ¿qué he de hacer, si yo soy el abandonado?	Then, what am I to do if I'm the abandoned one?
Pues, qué he de hacer, será por el amor de Dios.	Well, whatever I am to do will be done by the will of God.
Tres vicios tengo, los tres tengo adoptados	Three vices I have cultivated:
El ser borracho, jugador, y enamorado	Gambling, drunkenness and love.
Pues . . .	Then . . .
Pero ando ingrato si con mi amor no quedo;	I go unhappy if with my love I cannot remain
Tal vez otro hombre con su amor se habrá jugado	Perhaps another man has toyed with her love
Pues . . .[24]	Then . . .]

Nicolas, the hero of the famous ballad "El Vaquero," confides his lovesickness to his foreman while sitting melancholically in the corral; on learning that the woman he loves is actually the foreman's wife, he despairs and sees no other recourse but suicide.

In non-folkloric poetry, the trials of love, or the loss of the loved one, give rise to more general reflections on life and death. On earth, everything is pain and illusion; the only possible attitude is resignation: "Pain and resignation are brothers,"[25] wrote Gallardo at the beginning of his novel *Adah; o, El Amor de un Angel* [Adah; or, The love of an angel]. This book is less a work of fiction than a long lyrical outpouring on the woman who inspired it. The corpus of his poetry reveals a bitter outlook on life:

Y los años vendrán, y tras los años	[And the years will pass, and after the years
La variedad inmensa de ilusiones;	The immense variety of illusions
Del efímero amor los desengaños,	And the disappointment of ephemeral love
Y el hastío letal de las pasiones.[26]	And the deathly loathing of passions.]

The words "disappointment" and "illusions" were used often by poet-journalist Francisco Ramírez:

Yo tambien sufrí un engaño! . . .	[I also suffered a deception
También yo tuve ambiciones	I also had ambitions
Y en el mar del desengaño	And in the sea of disappointment
Se ahogaron mis ilusiones. [27]	My illusions perished.]

While one of his contemporaries lamented:

Todo es aflicción: no hay alma	[Everything is sorrow: there is no soul
Sin quebranto: no hay mejillas	Without pain: no cheeks
Que las lágrimas no bañen;	Not bathed in tears
No hay corazón que no gima. [28]	No heart that does not moan.]

One must watch "with indolent calm"[29] as illusions vanish; one must resign oneself to the trials of human existence: *"Resignate y padece en tu quebranto / Que algún día en la tumba descansado / Alivio encontrará tu triste llanto."* ("Resign yourself to your sorrow and suffer / One day, in the tomb, your sad tears / Will find restful deliverance.")[30] The flooding of Bernalillo by the Rio Grande brought no bitterness to the lips of Andrellita Baca de Martínez, who saw this disaster as the will of God: *"Hemos de tener consuelo / Porque Dios lo permitió."* ("We must console ourselves / For it was the will of God.")[31] This Christian resignation was laced with a strong dose of fatalism:

Todo es ya polvo, No alcanza	[All is now but dust. Neither knowledge
Ni saber, ni fuerza invicta,	Nor invincible strength, nor beauty, nor
Ni la hermosura, ni el cetro	scepter
A evitar la ley precisa.[32]	Can succeed in avoiding
	The irresistible law.]

More than 300 years before, an Aztec poet had sung of his sadness at the illusory and ephemeral nature of life:

> Oh friends, this earth is but lent to us.
> One day we must abandon the lovely poems,
> One day we must abandon the lovely flowers,
> And that is why I am sad in singing for the sun.[33]

The Supernatural

Like their attitudes toward love and death, Mexican–Americans' religious beliefs were also in the mainstream of Mexican tradition. They integrated the sacred into daily life through activities in which the secular elements, such as music, dance, and other amusements, played a preponderant role. The spirit of "Los Matachines" [The buffoons], a sacred drama of the sixteenth century strongly marked by both Spanish Catholicism and Indian paganism, survived until the twentieth century. As late as 1925, the feast of San Lorenzo, patron saint of Bernalillo, was celebrated elaborately; the extent of the festivities is reflected in the interminable length of Próspero Baca's *corrido*:

La danza sigue adelante	[The dancers continue to advance
Va guiando la procesión,	They guide the procession,
Toda la gente le sigue	Everyone follows them
Rezando su devoción.	Reciting prayers.
Vuelven de la procesión	They return from the procession
Todos llenos de confianza,	All filled with enthusiasm
Porque quieren ver bailar	Because they wish to see
De matachines la danza. [34]	The dance of the *matachines*.]

The famous José Apodaca, the *monarca* ("leader") of the *matachine* dancers, performed right inside the church, before the statue of San Antonio, with Malinche[35] at his side. A *corrido* was written in his honor during the twenties in the little New Mexico village of San Antonio:

Con su guajito y su palma	*[With his rattle and his *palme*
Y aquel cupil de diamantes	["sculptured baton"]
Se enfrentava de San Antonio	And his headdress of diamonds
Con un grupo de danzantes. . . .	He presented himself before San Antonio
	With a group of dancers. . . .
Vestido de mil colores	
En nuestra iglesia se alegraba,	In vestments of a thousand colors
Y el pueblo lleno de gusto	In our church he danced
Cuando Apodaca bailaba. [36]	And the entire village rejoiced
	When Apodaca danced.]

The Mexican Virgin of Guadalupe stood at the center of the religious universe of the Mexican-American, who made a distinction between her and the Virgin Mary of Roman Catholicism. For example, when Próspero Baca described the interior of the church of Bernalillo, he first mentioned the "Virgen María," then, separately:

. . . en el templo sagrado	[. . . in the sacred temple
La Virgen Guadalupana	The Virgin of Guadalupe
Echando su benedeción. [37]	Giving her benediction.]

At the painful moment of departure, the emigrant instinctively joined together in a single thought the Mexican Virgin and the land of which she was the patron saint:

¡Adiós! mi madre querida	*[Goodbye, my beloved mother
La Virgen Guadalupana,	The Virgin of Guadalupe
Adiós! mi patria amorosa,	Goodbye, my beloved land
Republica Mexicana. [38]	My Mexican Republic.]

Quite naturally, young María in the *corrido* "Vida, Proceso, y Muerte de Aurelio Pompa" (The life, trial, and death of Aurelio Pompa) commends her friend Aurelio to the Virgin's guardianship: *"Cuídalo mucho, Virgen María, / Que yo presiento no volverá."* ("Look after him, Virgin Mary / I feel a forboding he won't return.")[39]

The Virgin was the mediator between people and the world of the supernatural. Folklore, in its naive way, transformed her into a "good fairy," sometimes armed with a magic wand, as in the tales "Estrella de Oro" [Gold star], the Mexican version of "Cinderella," and "El Violincito" [The little violin], the story of a young shepherd and his magic violin, both collected by J. M. Espinosa.[40] Jovita González retrieved the legend of the "Vine of Guadalupe": a *vaquero* has been thrown and seriously injured by his bronco; as he sits in a daze, a beautiful lady, dressed in a blue cloak sprinkled with stars, approaches with a small red berry in her hand. She tells the *vaquero* to soak it in some mescal and apply it to his wound. He does, and it heals instantly. Since that time, it is said, the seeds bear the image of the Virgin of Guadalupe's face.[41]

This naive interpretation of the Virgin of Guadalupe as a fairy tale lost favor as folklore declined, but her quintessentially Mexican image persisted in Mexican-American literature. For Chicano activists, she became a rallying sign, like the black eagle on the red flag of the Aztecs.

Many of the supernatural beliefs originated among shepherds and *vaqueros*, who applauded and participated in the pastorals and composed songs and poems in the solitude of their pastures. On village squares and in adobe houses, before attentive and unsophisticated audiences, they tirelessly repeated the same stories about people like themselves. Thus, on a ranch in the Rio Grande region, Jovita González writes, the entire community gathers together for the shelling of corn:

> All came: Tío Julianito, the pastor, with his brood of sunburned half-starved children, ever eager for food; Alejo the fiddler; Juanito the idiot, called the Innocent, because the Lord was keeping his mind in heaven; Pedro the hunter, who had seen the world and spoke English; the vaqueros; and, on rare occasions, Tío Esteban, the mail carrier. Even the women came, for on such occasions supper was served.
>
> A big canvas was spread outside, in front of the kitchen. In the center of this canvas, ears of corn were piled in pyramids for the shellers, who sat about in a circle. . . .
>
> It was then, under the moonlit sky, that we heard stories of witches, buried treasures, and ghosts.[42]

These folkloric tales followed a typical format and contained the same basic elements, all derived from the prevailing culture and religion. Mexican folklore abounded in stories of devils, sorcery, hidden treasures that only "the seventh son of a seventh son born on a Friday, the day obscured by the sun,"[43] was supposed to find, and of the "*tatema*," a buried treasure whose location could be revealed only by supernatural intervention,[44] and so forth. Catholic religious practices inspired certain superstitions: people held to the Catholic belief that those who died without confessing their sins or receiving extreme unction went to purgatory or hell, but they also believed that some souls continued to wander on earth as penance. Those who had departed without repaying their debts, carrying out their promises, or revealing certain secrets seemed to be held to earth by particularly strong bonds. These souls had to seek the aid of living people to be delivered of whatever retained them on earth.[45] Among the wandering spirits who prowled through the Mexican imagination, the most terrifying was, without a doubt, the *Llorona*, the wailing woman, who roamed the streets at night in search of her children. The source of this myth is uncertain, but it is likely more Aztec than Catholic. The *Llorona* was reputedly the Aztec goddess Matlaciuatl (the woman with the net), a sort of vampire who devoured human beings, or perhaps Ciuapipiltin, the goddess who went out at midnight bearing an empty crib and wailing over the loss of her child; Ciuapipiltin also possessed certain attributes of Ciuacoatl, the goddess of the earth. For many, she became Malinche, Cortés's Indian mistress, who moaned over the betrayal of her people.[46] Later, the myth was often blended with real-life tragic stories, generally about infanticide. In the folklore of the Southwest, there were many variants,[47] but the woman appeared in two principal forms, either as a beautiful, weeping woman of awesome seductive powers (a version corresponding to her original vampirism) or as a wailing mother in search of her children (whom she herself had often killed). In certain Texas legends, she attracted men like a siren, with a softly plaintive voice, and led them to destruction.[48] The following is a different version, also collected in Texas, by Soledad Pérez:

> A long time ago there was a woman who had two children. She did not love them; so she mistreated and neglected them. The children were always hungry and cold because their mother was too busy going to parties and dances to take care of them.
> Finally one of the children died and later the other died too. The woman felt no remorse. She continued to lead a very gay life. When she died, she had not confessed her sins or repented of her ill-treatment of the children. Now she appears in the east and southeast parts of Austin grieving for her children. Her soul is doing penance for her sins.[49]

The figure of the *Llorona*, representing the Mexican mother,[50] was taken up by modern Chicano writers and sometimes given a new symbolic dimension: the mother weeps for her children, who are caught up in modern society and uncertain of their identity. As they increasingly withdraw from her, she no longer represents anything to them.[51]

Orientation Toward the Past

Mexican-Americans' essentially melancholy love poetry and their folklore created a perception of a static people oriented to the past. Their self-image on the linguistic and cultural levels had not changed since 1848. Their forms of expression remained unchanged; their vocabulary, traditional and strictly Spanish; their images, fixed; their poetic tone, conventional. The audience for this poetry, the people who developed the folklore, remained cut off from the Anglo-American world, isolated on a cultural island. Art was limited to the glorification and the perpetuation of the past, finding its highest expression in the conjuring of a famous *matachine* dancer who dated back to the sixteenth century, and in the nostalgic lament of the expatriate poet.

The treatment of the theme of exile, by J. B. Hijar y Jaro and others, was a typically romantic attempt at escapism.[52] The exaltation with which Hijar y Jaro describes his departure from Mexico in 1864 would be suspect to the Chicano critic of today. The nostalgic love the exile held for his native land does not prevent him from adopting the American flag upon his arrival in the United States. This contradictory attitude was shared by many of his contemporaries:

¡Tierra! gritaron todos, y al instante	[Land, they all shouted, and in an instant
Tronó el cañón, que saludaba el puerto,	The cannon which saluted the port
Y el espléndido sol, en el levante,	roared,
Alumbró de concierto	And the splendid sun, in the East,
La ciudad, las montañas y el desierto.	Lit up as if by agreement
Tremoló el pabellón de las estrellas . . .	The city, the mountains and the desert.
	I unfurled the star-spangled flag . . .
Y dije adiós a mis benditos lares![53]	
	And I bid adieu to my blessed home!]

To this weakness of the nineteenth-century poet, later critics contrasted the independence of Chicanos who rallied around the Aztec flag, with neither stars nor stripes, as celebrated in the verses of Elizondo:

Tengo una bandera Apá,	*[I have a flag, Apá,
Colorada sin rayitas,	Red, without a stripe,
ni estrellas, ni tiritas,	No stars, no borders
de oro robado, por acá.	Of stolen gold right here.
Tiene una aguila negra,	It has a black eagle,
alas iguales	Its wings are even
hecha de puro algodón.[54]	made all of cotton.]

The neoclassic poetry and certain folklore tended to intensify Mexican-Americans' passivity and unwavering fidelity to tradition. Like the poet, they resignedly accepted their status as "orphans" and their sad lot, without trying to change the course of history or integrate into a different society. Submissive and outmoded like the burro, the donkey of folklore who was duped by the coyote, then whipped by his master,[55] they were party to their own exploitation. They themselves helped forge the stereotypes which would later be used against them.

Para decir diez reales
Dicen dolen ecuaora;
Para decir mañana
También dicen tumora.[1]

CHAPTER 7

Mexican–Americans Confront
the Present

In the years before the Second World War, Mexican-Americans developed a different self-image; no longer a legacy of the past, the image was a new one of Mexican-Americans confronting their current situation on American soil. It appeared in such issues of burning timeliness as border disputes, the exploitation of Mexican laborers, and cultural conflict. Resistance to the invader had been celebrated in the *corridos* of the border region between 1848 and the late 1930s; the quasi-heroic labor of the *vaquero*, the more modest and pathetic adventures of the Mexican *peones*, forced into emigration by poverty, as they wandered from one state to another, were evoked in many *corridos*. Mexican-Americans resisted the foreign culture; their language remained Spanish, but they sometimes made ironic use of English and criticized the occupier more overtly; both actions were a form of revolt, a way of asserting themselves without recourse to arms. While neoclassic poetry symbolized a certain immutability of Mexican-Americans, the *corrido*, a vehicle of resistance, represented the dynamic and living side.

The Rebel *"con su pistola en la mano"*

From the early years following the annexation, a cry of revolt was sounded from Francisco Ramírez's newspaper, *El Clamor Público*, which launched the first crusade for Hispanic-American civil rights:

> Everyone is convinced that California is lost to all Hispanic-Americans; and here in Los Angeles, because of the last revolution (?), if they formerly

asked for favors, they will now ask on their knees for *justice and liberty* in carrying out their activities.[2]

During this same era, Pablo de la Guerra, a senator, judge, and member of the "Spanish class," was becoming the spokesman for the great landowners:

> They are foreigners in their own land. They have no voice in this senate with the exception of the person now speaking with so little effect on their behalf. . . . We should be shown some measure of consideration . . . We are forced to pay taxes which exceed a million pesos, and in order to pay them, have been compelled to sell our personal property and part of our land . . . after having suffered all these injustices and experienced all sorts of prejudice, now we find the legislature anxious to take away our last cent because the squatters are more numerous than the native Californians.[3]

For the Mexican masses, liberty was inseparable from social equality. Witness the following hymn to liberty from a Texas poet, Santiago de la Hoz. In 1904, he was still writing in the neoclassic tradition, but he echoed the fundamental protests of the oppressed:

Que si esta sociedad estulta y vana
Hoy se halla dividida
En el hombre de arriba y el de abajo,
Cuando fúlgure tu cabeza erguida
Y a Nerón y al burgués lleves al tajo,
Medidos con la vara del trabajo
Todos serán iquales en la vida![4]

[If this stupid and vain society
Now finds itself divided
Between oppressor and oppressed,
When your high-held head begins to
  shine
And you take both Nero and the
  bourgeois to the executioner.
If measured by the yardstick of his labor
Everyone will be equal in life!]

The protesting spirit was fostered by continual border incidents up to the year 1930. Ballads and songs, probably lost forever, undoubtedly were composed on this subject well before the appearance of full-fledged *corridos*. Juan Nepomuceno Cortina[5] was the first border hero whose exploits were celebrated, in a *corrido* between 1880 and 1890. A *corrido* of the borderlands, about the famous rebel Gregorio Cortez became very popular between 1901 and 1905, after his capture. The *corrido* rapidly became taboo on the northern side of the Rio Grande: whoever sang it ran the risk, it was said, of getting arrested or losing a job.[6] Américo Paredes has cataloged eleven Mexican-American variants. Between 1913, the date of Cortez's release, and 1920, this *corrido* enjoyed a renaissance; its hero was hailed as the symbol of the border dispute. It was still being sung in 1940, regaining favor for the last time in the heat of emotions inspired by World War II, although this time borderland Mexicans fought alongside their former adversaries. The revolt of Aniceto Pizaña[7] in 1915 gave the border *corrido* a final impetus.

The border *corrido*, as its name implies, reflected the border conflicts that long ravaged the Southwest; thus it was in the tradition of the ballad, according to

Paredes. Born of conflict, it was like the Russian *bylini*, which was engendered by the battles between Russians and the steppe nomads, and like the Spanish *romance*, which appeared in Castille when the native people were fighting to recapture Spain from the Moors.

That the border regions of Texas were troubled zones controlled only with difficulty is attested to by the vendettas that were the subject of many *corridos*. I will not dwell on conflicts between Mexican-Americans, sometimes settled by a Mexican sheriff, as in "Versos de Montalgo" [Verses of Montalgo],[8] and usually limited to saloon brawls, as in the *corridos* of "Gregorio Doff," "Agustín Jaime," and others.[9] The true border conflict always implied a confrontation with American authorities, the Anglo serving as a "reacting agent."[10] The conflicts took three forms: smuggling, banditry, and, especially, the struggle of those forced to kill in defense of their rights. Like its Mexican counterpart, the *corrido* of the Mexican-American border was based upon certain conventions, which conferred upon it the characteristics of a heroic epic and treated the subject with nobility. "The Corrido of Gregorio Cortez," which follows, is the purest example of the genre:

En el condado de Carnes	★[In the county of Karnes
miren lo que ha sucedido,	Look at what has happened
murió el Cherife Mayor	The Major Sheriff died
quedando Román herido.	Leaving Román badly wounded.
Serían las dos de la tarde	It must have been two in the afternoon
Cuando la gente llegó	When people arrived.
unos a los otros dicen:	They said to one another:
"No saben quien lo mató."	"It is not known who killed him."
Decía Gregorio Cortez	Then said Gregorio Cortez
con su pistola en la mano:	With his pistol in his hand,
"No siento haberlo matado,	"I don't regret that I killed him,
lo que siento es a mi hermano."	I regret what happened to my brother."
Decía Gregorio Cortez	Then said Gregorio Cortez
con su alma muy encendida	And his soul was all aflame
"No siento haberlo matado,	"I don't regret that I killed him,
la defensa es permitida."	A man must defend himself."
Venían los americanos	The Americans were coming,
más blancos que una paloma	They were whiter than a dove,
de miedo que le tenían	From the fear that they had
a Cortez y a su pistola.	Of Cortez and his pistol.
Tiró con rumbo a Gonzales	He struck out for Gonzales
sin ningúna timidez:	Without showing any fear
"Síganme, rinches cobardes,	"Follow me, cowardly rangers,
yo soy Gregorio Cortez."	I am Gregorio Cortez."

Cuando rodearon la casa	When they surrounded the house
Cortez se les presentó:	Cortez suddenly appeared before them,
"Por la buena sí me llevan	"You'll take me if I'm willing,
porque de otro modo no."	But not any other way."
Decía el Cherife Mayor	Then the Major Sheriff said,
como queriendo llorar:	As if he was going to cry,
"Cortez, entrega tus armas,	"Cortez, hand over your weapons;
no te vamos a matar."	We are not going to kill you."
Decía Gregorio Cortez	Then said Gregorio Cortez,
decía en su voz divina,	He said in his godly voice,
"Mis armas no entrego	"I won't surrender my arms
hasta estar en bartolina."	Until I'm inside a jail."
Ya agarraron a Cortez,	Now they have taken Cortez,
ya terminó la cuestión,	Now matters are at an end
la pobre de su familia	His poor family
lo lleva en el corazón.	Are suffering in their hearts.
Ya con ésta me despido	Now with this I say farewell,
a la sombra de un ciprés,	In the shade of a cypress tree;
aquí se acaba cantando	This is the end of the singing
el corrido de Cortez.[11]	Of the ballad of Cortez.]

Typically, in a *corrido*, the place and dates are facts recounted, along with a synopsis of the poem, at the beginning. It usually ends with a conventional stanza, the *despedida* ("farewell"), in which the troubadour takes leave of the audience in the first line and repeats the title or subject in the last.

The structure is invariable: once his exploit is carried out, the hero takes flight, pursued by the numerically superior *rinches* ("Rangers"), against whom he wages a heated battle. His defeat is inevitable; he sometimes escapes death by crossing the border, but most often he is killed or captured.

The hero is never a common criminal; he enjoys undeniable prestige among his people; the deeds of "that General Cortinas" described below would forever remain in the popular imagination. The demonstrative "that" quite possibly is laudatory.[12]

The hero is depicted through several characteristic traits: *con su pistola en la mano* ("pistol in hand") he defies the *rinches*, crying out his name, "yo soy . . ." ("I am . . ."), in the heat of battle, like the Spanish warrior of old.[13] It is curious that there is no reference to Cortez's horse in his *corrido*.[14] The hero's valor is heightened by the cowardice of one of his companions, or opponents, who is invariably presented *como queriendo llorar* ("as if he wanted to cry").

The true hero of the borderlands, personified by Juan Nepomuceno Cortina, Gregorio Cortez, and Jacinto Treviño, was a peaceful man provoked into violence by the Anglo-Texan *rinches*. He was not a Robin Hood engaged in class struggle, giving to the poor the money he took from the rich, like Joaquín

Murrieta of the Mexican *corrido*.[15] On 13 July 1859, Cortina killed Sheriff Robert Shears, who had arrested one of his former servants. Then he freed the Mexican, fled Brownsville on horseback, and reached Mexico:

Ese general Cortinas	[That General Cortinas
es libre y muy soberano,	Is very sovereign and free
han subido sus honores	His honor has increased
porque salvó a un mexicano . . .	Because he saved a Mexican . . .
Los americanos hicieron huelga,	The Americans celebrated
borracheras en las cantinas,	And with drunken sprees in the saloons
de gusto que había muerto	They rejoiced at the death
ese general Cortinas.[16]	Of that General Cortinas.]

On 12 June 1901, Cortez shot down W. T. Morris, a sheriff who had come to arrest him for a horse theft he had not committed. According to one of the variants, the sheriff had wounded his brother Román for refusing to allow his carriage to be searched.

In 1910, Jacinto Treviño killed a rich ranch owner's son who had beaten his brother; he succeeded in fleeing to Mexico.[17] During the same era, Ignacio Treviño was peaceably sitting with a whiskey in a Brownsville bar when a detachment of Rangers, charged with "cleaning up" the police in this border town controlled by Mexican-Americans, arrived. Seeing his boss killed by a shot in the back, Ignacio leaped up and drove off the assailants, but his victory was short-lived. Along with the other survivors, he was forced to take refuge south of the border.

The deeds of the hero elevate him above his peers and above those who wish to defeat him. It is significant that the Major Sheriff, rather than one of his companions, plays the role of anti-hero to Cortez. In the *corrido* "Ignacio Treviño," the one-armed Cesario quite naturally fulfills this function:

Gritaba el manco Cesario,	[The one-armed Cesario shouted
Como queriendo llorar:	As if he wanted to cry
"Ignacio ya no les tires,	"Ignacio, stop shooting at them,
No te vayan a matar."[18]	Or they will kill you."]

Contempt was added to hatred for American lawmen; faced with disreputable authorities, the Mexican-American was not afraid to assert himself:

Entrenle rinches cobardes	["Come into the fight, cowardly Rangers,
que el juego no es con un niño,	You're not playing with a child,
soy purito mexicano,	I'm a real Mexican,
me llamo Ignacio Treviño.[19]	My name is Ignacio Treviño."]

Although less noble, the smuggler and the bandit were also praised, though in a less elevated epic style, because they defied the established order. Along the banks of the Rio Grande, the smuggler enjoyed a certain prestige; in Mexican *corridos*[20] smugglers are never taken prisoner; they die in gun battles. The songs stress not their smuggling activities but their battle with the *guardas* ("border guards"). This is also the case in the Mexican-American "Corrido de Laredo," whose heroes are dreaded by the border police:

Este puerto de Laredo	[This border station of Laredo
es un puerto muy mentado;	Is a very famous station
los agentes de la ley	The agents of the law
andan siempre con cuidado.[21]	Are always on their guard.]

The valiant conduct of the Laredo contingent during World War I earned them a certain respect from the American authorities:

Debemos de recordar	[We should remember
que muchos jamás volvieron	That many never returned
por cumplir con su deber	In carrying out their duty
en esa lucha murieron . . .	Many died in battle . . .
por eso en Laredo, Texas,	And that is why in Laredo, Texas,
aprecian los mexicanos.[22]	Mexicans are respected.]

The lighthearted *despedida* makes it difficult to believe that a sad fate awaits these kings of contraband:

Ya con ésta me despido,	[Now with these lines I bid adieu
tomándome un anisado;	As I drink my anisette;
adiós lindas morenitas	Goodbye you dark-haired beauties
de ese Laredo afamado.[23]	Of this renowned Laredo.]

The sniveling tone and the craftsmanship of the *corrido* "El Contrabando del Paso" [Smuggling in El Paso], on the other hand, are not at all in the tradition of the border *corrido*, nor is the smuggler it presents. We see only the least glorious aspects of his adventure, the smuggling itself and its unfortunate consequences:

El contrabando es muy bueno,	*[Smuggling is very good,
se gana muy buen dinero	One makes good money
pero lo que no me gusta	But what I don't like
es que me lleven prisionero.[24]	Is that they take me prisoner.]

On the train to the federal prison at Leavenworth, Kansas, the young prisoner bitterly regrets having been lured to *el charco seco* ("the dry marsh"), the hotbed of smuggling on the Rio Grande,[25] and swears never to be caught there again. He puts his personal experience into verse to serve as a lesson to his comrades.

The "Versos de los Bandidos" [The bandits' verses] and "Los Sediciosos" [The rebels], which relate the attack on the Las Norias ranch[26] by Aniceto

Pizaña and his gang, offer a dual image of the bandit. This divergence is reflected in the terms for criminals: *bandidos* are common outlaws, *sediciosos* are
rebels against the established order. The author of "Versos de los Bandidos"
(often called "Versos del Rancho de las Norias" by Mexicans) is a *Kiñena*, a
resident of the King Ranch. This fact is disavowed in the fourth stanza, but,
according to the annotator, the disavowal may be purely conventional:

El que compuso esos versos	*[The man that made those verses
No sabía lo que decía.	Did not know what he was saying.
Esos versos van compuestos	Those verses have been composed by
Por los rinches y bandidos.[27]	The rangers and the bandits.]

The *Kiñena* knows through experience that the principal victims of the raid
will be Texas Mexicans; like the other *rancheros*, he gives his unconditional
support to the Rangers attached to the King Ranch and to "Maestro César"
(Mr. Caesar Kleberg), its general manager. The author of "Los Sediciosos" was
probably a Mexican–American less comfortable financially than the preceding
one and less concerned, consequently, about the assistance and sympathy of
the Rangers. The last two stanzas, full of malicious insinuations, lead us to
believe that the idea of insurrection does not displease him. The poet does not
wish his audience to believe that the dreaded bandit has departed permanently;
while identifying with the rebel, he refuses to give the traditional farewell:

Ya se van los sediciosos,	[Now the rebels ride off
y quedaron de volver	Vowing to return
pero no dijeron cuando	But they did not say when
porque no podían saber.	For they could not know for sure.
Despedida no la doy	I do not give my farewell
porque no la traigo aquí,	For I do not have it here
se la llevó Luis de la Rosa	It was taken by Luis de la Rosa
para San Luis Potosí.[28]	To San Luis Potosí.]

By contrast, the rancher celebrates the formidable power of the Rangers: *"A
qué susto les han dao / Los rinches de la Kiñena!"* ("What a scare / The King Ranch
rangers gave them!")[29] He ridicules and casts doubt on Pizaña's well-known
valor. Pizaña, born right on the King Ranch, by an irony of fate, is afraid
to come near it; the "valiant" Pizaña "is afraid to die."[30] This timid rancher
lacks the verve of the singers of the Scottish ballads; his story is of primarily
documentary interest. Lifeless and rather pedestrian, it describes in detail the
movements of the bandits from one place to another; it does not pretend to be
an epic, not even an epic of the Rangers of the King Ranch.

The *corrido* "Los Sediciosos" has a facetious conclusion; the author is evidently amusing himself. In turn, he uses traditional elements of the epic and
some farcical images, which produce a reverse magnification. He parades the
bandits stanza by stanza. Aniceto Pizaña, first of all, duly "mounted on a
horse," hurls the traditional challenge to the *rinches* but "while singing": "en

su caballo cantando: / 'Donde estan por ahí los rinches? / que los vengo vis-
itando' " ("on his horse singing: / 'Where are the rangers? / For I'm coming
to pay them a visit.' ").[31] Then, portrayed in the conventional way, Teodoro
Fuentes, while "buttoning a shoe,"[32] taunts the Rangers of the *Kiñena* (King
Ranch). In the following stanza the contrast adds a grotesque element:

Decía Vicente el Giro	[Vicente the braggart then said
en su chico caballazo:	Mounted on his little old nag
"Echenme ese gringo grande,	"Send me this big gringo
pa'pos llevármelo de brazo."[33]	And I'll carry him off in my arms."]

In the epic tradition, inordinate importance was accorded to the coward.
The usual expression *como queriendo llorar* is missing here, but the idea is present
and is developed by a series of variations:

En ese punto de Norias	[From that place known as Norias
se oía la peloteria,	One could hear the noise of gunfire,
del señor Luis de la Rosa	But from señor Luis de la Rosa
nomás el llanto se oía.	Nothing but the sound of crying.
El señor Luis de la Rosa	Señor Luis de la Rosa
se tenía por hombrecito,	Who thought himself quite a young man,
a la hora de los balazos	At the hour of the gunfight
lloraba como un chiquito.[34]	He cried like a little child.]

Further on, he "stained the flag" with his tears and shame.[35] Luis de la Rosa
was an instigator of the 1915 uprising, but here his reputation is sacrificed to
conform to tradition, as it is in other *corridos* dealing with the same theme.

The poet's attitude is disconcerting. Whose side is he on? The *rinches*? Certainly not; through the rebels of his poem, he takes malicious pleasure in de-
fying the Rangers, the symbol of gringo power. Is he for the bandits? Hardly;
his Pizaña does not have the stature of a Jesse James or of a José Mosqueda,[36]
even though Pizaña equals their exploits by conducting the armed robbery of a
train. The author pokes fun at everyone, the *mexicotejanos* and himself as well;
let's listen:

Ya la mecha está encendida,	[Now the fuse is lit
muy bonita y colorada,	It is pretty and red in color
y la vamos a pagar	We are going to pay for it
los que no debemos nada.[37]	Even though we've done nothing.]

His *corrido* is a mock-heroic epic, a parody of the border *corrido*, its conventions
and characters.

Only one *corrido* celebrates a borderer whose penchant for law and order
proved fatal. José Lozano was a policeman for the International Great Northern
railroad company in San Antonio. He had all the characteristics of a Gregorio
Cortez save one: he inspired fear because of "his gigantic size." With his shoot-

ing skill, he "fought like a lion," but he was also a "peaceful man with a good heart."[38] However,

Dicen que tenía enemigos   *[They say that he had enemies
pues a la ley ayudó   Because he helped the law
cuando el Cuerpo de los Rangers   When the company of Rangers
en San Antonio operó.[39]   Was active in San Antonio.]

The tone of the poem, more edifying than laudatory, distinguishes it from the true border *corrido*, which it does not particularly resemble in structure. "José Lozano" would never enjoy the same popularity as "Gregorio Cortez" among Mexican-Americans.

Those who collaborated with the power structure undoubtedly enjoyed less prestige than the rebel; it is not surprising that the rebel in the folkloric border epic was somewhat romanticized. Here, it was not the Ranger who was the hero, as he was in the Anglo-American press and literature. Rather, the rebel was the hero as he confronted the *rinches* and became the symbol of resistance against the occupier. Nevertheless, the border epic was based on reality. It was one of the earliest manifestations of the Mexican-American revolt.

The Mexican Worker in American Territory

Though less inspiring than the borderer's revolt, the worker's tribulations were no less fruitful as material for folklore, and eventually for literature. The work of the *vaquero* and the sheepherder was still prestigious, although destined to disappear, but it was less popular as a theme than the Mexican *peón*'s migration and movements through the United States.

The Mexican cowboy became a folkloric hero, yet in a different way from the border rebel. His virile bearing, which so fascinated the Anglos, also attracted the authors of the *romances*. In the "Reunión de los Vaqueros" [The gathering of the *vaqueros*], the poet nostalgically recalls the annual gathering of New Mexico's elegant horsemen:

Con espuelas y frenos de cobre   [With copper spurs and bits
Con sillas muy elegantes   With very elegant saddles
Recuerdos de lo pasado   Memories of the past
De un país incivilizado.[40]   Of an untamed country.]

He also brought to mind:

. . . su agileza en montar   [. . . their skill in riding
Aquinos mansos y broncos   Horses both tamed and unbroken
Bovinos bravos y roncos.[41]   Cattle both fearsome and wild.]

The *vaquero*'s heroic activities were shown to particular advantage in the *corridos* written on the King Ranch, some of which were practically interminable. They celebrated the thrilling work of the Texas *vaqueros*, such as the dangerous search for *ladinos* ("unbranded cattle"); "El Toro Moro" [The purple bull] describes the *vaqueros* of Las Norias (a subdivision of the famous ranch) searching for a certain purplish bull, which is finally roped by Euvence García, the *caporal* ("foreman"). He is famous for having rounded up more cattle than anyone else in Texas:

Señores voy a cantar	★[Sirs, I'm going to sing
Con muchísimo decoro.	With a lot of decorum.
Estos versos son compuestos	These verses are composed
Al mentado Toro Moro.	About the famous Purple Bull.
Es un torito moro	He is a little purple bull
Tiene el espinazo bayo.	He has a dun (tan) back.
No lo han podido lazar,	They have not been able to rope him,
Y hechan la culpa al caballo.[42]	And they blame it on the horse.]

The passage "Sirs, I'm going to sing" is the introductory verse common to many *corridos*. Directed at the audience, whose admiration the singer desired, the "I" does not necessarily refer to the story's protagonist.

The shepherd's hazardous life seems to have inspired the troubadours less than the *vaquero*'s. There is only one *corrido*, to my knowledge, on the subject. On the plains of New Mexico, the lone tender of a flock is at the mercy of a winter *revilión* ("sudden snowstorm"). The poet, speaking from experience, maintains a tragic tone. The squall that corners David González and Tiofilo Vigil occurs on a Friday, which seems a bad omen:

Año de mil ochocientos	[In the year eighteen
Noventa y cinco es decir,	Ninety-five, that is,
Vean lo que sucedió, ¡Ay!	Look at what took place, alas,
El día cinco de abril . . .	On the fifth day of April . . .
Estos eran dos pastores	It was to these two shepherds
Lo que así les sucedió;	That it happened this way;
Era viernes de dolores, ¡Ay!	It was a fateful Friday, alas,
Cuando el revilión llegó.[43]	When the snowstorm arrived.]

The risks taken by *vaqueros* were great, but not one in the *corridos* backs away from the work, except a certain Texan from the Rancho de Los Olmos. Afraid of swimming, he dreads crossing the rain-swollen Nueces River with a herd of cattle; he simply returns to camp, claiming to have a liver ailment. Thus was born "La Canción del Rancho de Los Olmos," begun by the *anti-vaquero* but finished collectively by his courageous comrades on their return, each one singing about himself in a separate stanza. The song attests to the difficulty of the task accomplished:

Lupe no carga chivarras	[Lupe is not wearing goat-skin breeches
Anda muy bien abrigado	But he is well protected

Y de tanto que se mojó	And has gotten so wet
se le desbarrató el calzado.	That his shoes have fallen apart.
Lupe cargaba su capa,	Lupe was wearing his cloak,
Que era un purito rajón,	Which was totally in shreds
Y se quedó en el Camerón,	And he stayed in Camerón
Secando su pantalón.[44]	Drying out his pants.]

"El Corrido de Kiansis," whose epic style ties it to the *corridos* of the border region, is certainly the most famous of the *vaquero* ballads. The story dates back to about 1870, soon after the opening of the Chisholm Trail linking Texas to Kansas. Anglo literature often evoked the exploits of cowboys on this famous trail, making no mention of the Mexican *vaqueros*. The *corrido* rectified this oversight, in a tone more ironic than protesting, by emphasizing the danger of the *vaquero*'s work: one man is killed by a bull. The difficulty of handling untamed livestock is complicated by unfavorable weather; "a heavy rainstorm" surprises the drive. Sudden downpours cause stampedes. *Vaqueros* have to cut in front of the herd and try to make the lead steer turn and bring the others along with it, an extremely perilous task. They often have to fire a shot near the lead steer and, if it does not turn back, shoot it down and try to make the cattle behind turn. The stampede on the Chisholm Trail was impressive enough that José Gómez remembered it years later, despite his failing memory. A former King Ranch *vaquero*, Gómez was also the author of a shorter version of the "Corrido de Kiansis:"

Cuando dimos visto a Kansas	*[When we came within sight of Kansas
Se vino un fuerte aguacero,	There was a heavy rain-shower,
No los podíamos reparar	We couldn't keep them herded
Ni formar un tiroteo.[45]	Nor get a shooting started.]

This *corrido* would serve as a model, fifty years later in the 1920s, for the "Corrido de la Pensilvania," whose heroes are not *vaqueros* but Texas workers going by train to Pennsylvania to build a railroad.

With malicious pleasure, the author of the "Corrido de Kiansis" shows the *vaquero* demonstrating his superiority over the cowboy at the *corrida* ("bull-fight"):

Llegaron diez mejicanos	*[Ten Mexicans arrived
Y al punto los embarcaron	And immediately controlled the steers
Y los treinta americanos	And the thirty Americans
Se quedaron azorados.[46]	Were left completely astounded.]

Both pride and sarcasm can be detected in the singer's words. Crossing the Salado River does not worry the Mexicans, and for good reason:

Pues qué pensaría ese gringo	*[What did this gringo think
Que venimos a esprimintar	That we were yearlings
si somos del Río Grande,	Why, we are from the Rio Grande,
de los buenos pa' nadar.[47]	And know how to swim.]

Still, they valiantly tend their employers' herds. All things considered, the image of the *vaqueros* in the *corridos* and songs was rather conservative; not a word was said about their low wages or social status. Celebrating their deeds helped Mexican-Americans build up their self-image; *corridos* were a sort of challenge to the gringo, though not yet a cry of protest. It was, however, under the conditions described in these poems that Juan Gómez organized, in the 1880s, the first strike by *vaqueros*.

> My life is a real story, especially here in the United States where they drive one crazy from working so much. They squeeze one here until one is left useless, and then one has to go back to Mexico to be a burden to one's countrymen. But the trouble is that it is true not only here but over there also.[48]

The story of immigrant Elías Garza collected by Gamio is fairly typical. The same tale is told in many songs and *corridos*, all with the same elements: emigration, exploitation, deportation, and, despite everything, continued attraction to the United States.

Just like the early immigrants from the "Old World,"[49] Mexican emigrants sang of the sadness of farewell:

¡Adiós! mi Patria querida	*[Goodbye, my beloved country,
Yo ya me voy a ausentar,	Now I am going away;
me voy para Estados Unidos	I go to the United States,
donde pienso trabajar.	Where I intend to work.
¡Adiós! mi Madre querida	Goodbye, my beloved mother
la Virgen Guadalupana,	The Virgin of Guadalupe;
adiós! mi patria amorosa,	Goodbye, my beloved land,
República Mexicana.[50]	My Mexican Republic.]

The same sort of filial devotion that tied them to the Mexican Virgin Mary tied them to their native land. Emigrants tried to justify their departure, to relieve the guilt they felt:

Pues yo no tengo la culpa	*[For I am not to blame
Que abandone así mi tierra,	That I leave my country thus;
la culpa es de la pobreza	The fault is that of poverty,
Que nos tiene en la miseria.[51]	Which keeps us all in want.]

The *corrido* "Defensa de los Norteños" is a long defense by the "people of the North," who are accused of being unpatriotic by those remaining south of the Rio Grande:

Mucha gente así lo ha dicho:	*[Many people have said
dizque no somos patriotas	That we are unpatriotic
porque les vamos a servir	Because we go to serve
a los infames patotas.[52]	For the accursed *patotas* ("big feet").]

For their departure, they blame "pure necessity";[53] the Mexican regime: "esos ingratos patrones/que no les dan a su gente / ni aun cuando porte chaqueta" ("Those unkind employers / Who don't give their people / Enough to buy a jacket");[54] and flagrant social inequality:

Siempre el peón es agobiado,	*[The peon is always burdened,
tratándole con fiereza,	Is treated with cruelty
donde le miran los pies	The rich would like to see his head
quieren verle la cabeza.[55]	Where they see his feet.]

The emigrant always departs for the North, ". . . con gran gusto y afán" ("with high hopes and eagerness").[56] Young Aurelio, hero of the corrido, finally convinces his mother to go with him to California because of the riches there: "Vámonos, madre, que allá está el dollar / y mucho, juro, que he de ganar" ("Let's go, Mother, for that's where the dollar is / and I swear I'll earn a lot of them").[57]

The immigrants' dreams crumbled, alas, as soon as they arrived in the United States. If they chose to enter legally, they were treated inconsiderately by immigration officials. The author of the corrido "Deportados" [The deported] was told he did not have enough money to cross the border. The officials put him through the ritual test: "Su dinero nada vale, / Su dinero nada vale / te tenemos que bañar" (Your money is worthless, / Your money is worthless/We'll have to give you a bath").[58] If they got through, immigrants' hopes for a happy and easy life were dashed by harsh working conditions. The reenganchista, the labor contractor, moved them from one state to another like pawns on a chessboard; a man might have to leave his family in Texas to go to Kansas or Pennsylvania to build a railroad, to Michigan to pick beets, or to the industrial cities of the North to avoid the cotton harvest. Migration always followed the same pattern, mirrored by the structure of the corridos. One finds almost identical passages in the corridos, an inevitable plagiarizing caused by the similarity of circumstances, the workers' as-yet limited means of expression, and the popularity of these constantly repeated poems. (I will therefore offer fewer quotations here.) The best-known migrant corrido, "La Pennsylvania," patterned after the "Corrido de Kiansis," has an equally epic structure that transforms the worker's humble migration into a moving adventure. Herewith a few significant passages:

El día veintiocho de abril	[On the twenty-eighth of April,
a la seis de la mañana,	At six o'clock in the morning,
salimos en un enganche	We left under contract
para el estado de Pensilvania . . .	For the state of Pennsylvania . . .
Y el enganchista nos dice:	And the labor contractor said to us:
"No se lleven la familia,	"Don't take your family along
para no pasar trabajos	So as to avoid difficulties
en el estado de West Virginia . . .	In the state of West Virginia" . . .

Adiós Foro West y Dalas	Goodbye Fort Worth and Dallas,
pueblos de mucha importancia;	Cities of great importance;
ya me voy pa' Pensilvania	I'm going to Pennsylvania
por no andar en la vagancia.	And put an end to my wandering.
Adiós estado de Texas,	Goodbye state of Texas,
con toda su plantación;	With all your plantations;
ya me voy pa' Pensilvania	I'm going to Pennsylvania
por no pizcar algodón."[59]	So as not to pick cotton."]

Two points are emphasized: the early-morning departure without wife or family and the itinerant life imposed upon the Mexican worker by his aversion to cotton-picking (some Blacks deserted the South for the same reason). These facts are repeated, with slight variations, by other migration *corridos*. In "Los Inmigrantes" [The immigrants], the departure hour was even earlier and the destination unknown:

Cuando salimos de El Paso	★[When we left El Paso
A las dos de la mañana	At two in the morning
Le preguntó al reenganchista,	I asked the boss contracter
Si vamos para Louisiana.[60]	If we were going to Louisiana.]

The labor contractor of the "Corrido de Texas" considers it preferable to separate married couples;

El enganchista nos dice	★[The contracter tells us
que no llevemos mujer	Not to take a woman along
para no pasar trabajos	So as to avoid difficulties
y poder pronto volver.[61]	And so as to return soon.]

The repetition of the word *adiós* throughout certain *corridos* symbolizes the migratory life of the farm worker who fled from Texas and its cotton fields.

The author of the "Corrido de Robestown" was an exception; he was happy picking cotton in Nueces County, Texas, at the end of the 1920s. His long poem is a lively one:

Estos bersos son bonitos	★[These verses are pleasing
son del pueblo de Robestown	They are about Robestown
pues el que quiera aprenderlo	So he who wants to learn them
pues tiene que ir a piscar.[62]	Must go there to the picking.]

Newly arrived from Mexico, he is impressed by the wealth of the planters and the international labor force; not yet discouraged by the work's harshness, he is still in the first stage of emigration.

By the end of the second "emigration," to the North, the worker was usually more bitter. Thus in 1923, the author of "Los Betabeleros" [The beetpickers] bemoaned the Michigan beetpickers' situation and complained of being deceived:

Aquí vienen y les cuentan	*[Here they come and tell you
Que se vayan para allá,	That you ought to go up there
Porque allá les tiene todo	Because there you will have everything
Que no van a batallar,	Without having to fight for it.
Pero son puras mentiras . . .⁶³	But these are nothing but lies . . .]

The tone of the *corrido* "El Enganchado" [The contract laborer] is just as bitter:

Pues me decían que aquí los dólars	[For they would tell me that here the
se pepenaban y de a montón	dollars
que las muchachas y que los teatros	Could be picked up by the bundle
y que aquí todo era vacilón.	And about the girls and the theaters
	And how great everything was here.
Y ahora me encuentro ya sin resuello	
soy zapatero de profesión	And now here I am all out of breath
pero aquí dicen que soy camello	I'm a shoemaker by trade
y a pura pala y puro azodón.⁶⁴	But here they tell me I'm a camel
	And good only for a pick and shovel.]

In Spanish, through an irony of semantics, *enganchado* means both "hooked" or "caught," and "recruited"; the Mexican who crossed the Rio Grande fell victim to the American system.

The *enganchado* is undernourished:

Cuando llegamos a Houston	*[When we arrived at Houston
Trabajando noche y día	Working all night and all day
No nos daban de comer	They didn't give us anything to eat
No más que pura sandía.⁶⁵	Nothing more than just watermelon.]

He has to "camellar,"⁶⁶ to work hard, his back arched like a camel's. The harsh work makes him yearn for Texas or Mexico:

Decía Jesús el Coyote	*[Said Jesús, "El Coyote,"
Como queriendo llorar	As if he wanted to weep,
"Valí más estar en Juárez	"It would be better to be in Juárez
Aunque sea sin trabajar."⁶⁷	Even if we were without work."]

He raises a timid protest, which is not taken seriously:

Unos descargaban rieles	*[Some unloaded the rails,
Otros descargaban "tallas"	And others unloaded ties
Y otros de los compañeros	And others of my companions,
Echaban de mil malallas.⁶⁸	Threw out thousands of curses.]

Mexican workers, whether they entered legally or illegally, were isolated. They often refused to join unions, knowing that American unions wanted only to increase their membership and were unable to secure social benefits for members who were not citizens. Such was the case of the laborers hired to build the Kansas railroad. An illegal immigrant who worked on the project composed

"Los Reenganchados a Kansas" [Contracted to Kansas], set at the end of the nineteenth century:

Decían los americanos	*[The Americans said
Con muchísimo valor:	With a great deal of bravery:
"Júntense a los mexicanos	"Round up the Mexicans
Para meterlos en la unión."	So as to put them in the union."
Nosotros le respondimos:	We replied to them:
"Lo que es la unión	"We will not join this thing
No entramos,	Called a union,
Esta no es nuestra bandera.	This is not our flag.
Porque somos mexicanos."[69]	Because we are Mexicans."]

The immigrant also had no recourse before the law. The *corrido* "Vida, Proceso, y Muerte de Aurelio Pompa" recounts the life, trial, and death of young Aurelio. Victim of a travesty of justice in the early twentieth century, he was found guilty in California for defending himself against his American assailant.

The constant threat of deportation intensified the difficulty of the alien's itinerant life and lack of legal rights. The massive repatriations of the 1930s are described at length in the *corrido* "Efectos de la Crisis" [Effects of the Depression]; it is the only "literary" testimony on the poverty of the Mexican minority in that era. The scene is Globe, Arizona:

En este tiempo fatal	*[In these unhappy times
la crisis ya nos persigue;	Depression still pursues us;
se come mucho nopal,	Lots of prickly pear is eaten
lo demás no se consigue . . .	For lack of other food . . .
Se pierden casas algunas	Some lose their houses
porque los pisos no pagan;	Because they can't pay rent;
han muerto varias fortunas,	The fortunes have collapsed,
de algunas que las poblaban . . .	Of some who live in them. . . .
Divorcios han aumentado	Divorces have increased
en estos últimos años . . .[70]	in these late years . . .]

The "Corrido de la Emigración" [immigration officials] takes us to Miami, a little Arizona mining town where Mexicans often received visits from the *emigración*. The officials' methods, as well as those Mexicans used to avert suspicion, are related with a light humor that gives the poem, in addition to its documentary value, an appealing tone, softening the brutality of the police procedures:

Con la mano en la cintura	*[With hand on belt they pause
se paran a investigar	To make investigation
como si fueran el cura,	As though it were the priest,
cuando te va a confesar.	About to hear confession.

Yo voy a dar un consejo	I am going to give advice
a todo joven soltero	To every young bachelor;
que se mire en este espejo	Let him look in this mirror,
aquí en suelo extranjero.	Here on foreign soil.
Que arregle su pasaporte.	Have your passport in order
no viva amancebado . . .	Do not live with a mistress . . .
Si antes has hecho cerveza	If you used to make beer
y has vivido de alambique,	And operate a still,
hoy te rascas la cabeza	Just scratch your head
no tienes ni que te explique.[71]	And don't admit anything.]

The playful tone here is in contrast to the open indignation in the *corrido* "Deportados"; a young Mexican is shocked by the animal-like treatment of deported workers by American immigration agents:

Hoy traen la gran polvadera	*[Today they are rounding them up
hoy traen la gran polvadera	Today they are rounding them up
y sin consideración,	And without consideration,
mujeres, niños y ancianos,	Women, children and old folks,
los echan de esa nación	Are taken to the border.
los llevan a la frontera.[72]	And expelled from that country.]

The repetition of certain lines adds weight to the deported laborer's accusation.

Emigrants are severely criticized by their compatriots, immigrants rudely mistreated by the Americans:

Los corren, los maltratan	*[They're insulted and mistreated
los gringos desgraciados,	By those gringo wretches,
no tienen vergüenza	They have no shame
siempre allá están pegados.[73]	They are always beaten there.]

The deported win little pity from Mexicans who think it wiser to stay home. The Mexican *peón* has two cruel alternatives: starvation wages or unemployment in Mexico; or hard labor and continual harassment in the United States in exchange for relative security. Most do not hesitate to choose the lesser of two evils:

Allí se va a trabajar	*[One has to work there,
macizo, a lo Americano,	Hard, in the American fashion,
pero alcanza uno a ganar	But one succeeds in earning
más que cualesquier paisano.	More than any of our countrymen.
Aquí se trabaja un año	Here one works for a year
sin comprarse una camisa . . .[74]	Without earning enough for a shirt . . .]

This chronicle of the Mexican worker in American territory is composed in a simple style that suits both its humble heroes and its audience. It is of interest because it describes not only the American but the Mexican view of those who emigrate to the United States.

The poet tries to touch the audience by recounting the misfortunes of Mexican laborers. The opening lines leave no doubt about his purpose: "Voy a contarles la triste historia / de un mexicano que allá emigró . . ." ("I'm going to tell you the sad story / of a Mexican who emigrated there . . .").[75] This is the way the narrator begins the tragedy of young Aurelio Pompa; the first stanza of another *corrido*, "Deportados," sets the tone:

Voy a contarles, señores,	*[I'm going to sing you, señores,
voy a contarles, señores,	I'm going to tell you, señores,
todo lo que yo sufrí,	All about my suffering,
cuando dejé yo a mi patria,	When I left my native land,
cuando dejé yo a mi patria,	When I left my native land,
por venir a ese país.[76]	In order to see that country.]

The poet's lament, unpolished but touching, is one of the first protests by Mexican immigrants against the gringo:

Estos versos son compuestos	*[These verses were composed
Por un pobre mexicano	By a poor Mexican
Pa' ponerlos al corriente	To spread the word about
Del sistema americano.[77]	The American system.]

It was an early step toward the Chicano literature of protest.

The Clash of Two Cultures

Cultural conflict was also treated in the *romances* and *corridos* during the century after the defeat in 1848. Culture shock provoked many Mexicans to reject the foreign culture clearly and somewhat simplistically. Others, however, became belligerent and leveled criticisms, sometimes amusing and sometimes caustic, at the occupier. These barbs are found in the earliest songs and *romances* inspired by the annexation.

The grievances of the immigrant, who had rural and traditional roots, against American civilization are illustrated in the *corrido* "El Enganchado," which details the American experience of the contract laborer. The time is the 1930s, and industrialization is threatening the Mexican artisan. A shoemaker is forced to abandon his work; his small-scale trade is no longer viable. He takes refuge in withdrawal and suffers at the reactions of other Mexicans to similar problems: many of his countrymen give in to racial prejudice and "pass" for Spaniards, giving up their native language and shamelessly becoming Americanized. His own children become contaminated by the foreign culture: they speak "perfeck Eengleesh," call him "fader" and are "crazy about the Charleston"; but it is the emancipation of Mexican women that provokes the greatest censure. The girls walk around "half-naked" and call the *tienda* ("shop") "estor" (or "store"); and doesn't his own wife go out "all painted up" like a *piñata* and go to dances at night? Weary of "these absurdities," he returns to Michoacán alone.[78]

The immigrants' resistance to progress and their yearning for their old rural homes are depicted in the *corrido* "El Rancho donde yo nací" [The farm where I was born]. The ballad is structured by the opposition of American and Mexican elements, as shown in these two stanzas (out of five):

no me gusta la pistola escuadra	★[I don't care for your automatic pistols
como al estilo de por aquí	That you have here
a mí me gusta carabina negra	What I want is a black rifle
como en el rancho donde yo nací. . . .	Like on the farm where I was born. . . .
No me gusta coche ni automóvil	I don't care for your carriages and
como al estilo de por aquí	automobiles
a mí me gusta carreta de bueyes	That you have here
como en el rancho donde yo nací.[79]	What I want is a cart with oxen
	Like on the farm where I was born.]

The song "El Ferrocarril" [The railroad] was probably composed at the end of the nineteenth century, when the rail line arrived in Victoria; the inhabitants of this little Texas town dread "el que lleva a los hombres / y nunca los vuelve a traer" ("the one that carries men away / and never brings them back").[80] Those who assimilated easily and rapidly were suspect to Mexican-Americans who had not yet adapted. "El Renegado," the social climber who "denies his race" to advance more rapidly, provokes only contempt and censure:

Andas por hay luciendo	★[You go along showing off
gran automóvil	In a big automobile
me llamas desgraciado,	You call me a pauper
y muerto de hambre	And dead with hunger
y es que ya no te acuerdas	And what you don't remember is
cuando en mi rancho	That on my farm
andabas casi en cueros	You went around almost naked
y sin huaraches.	And without sandals.
Así pasa a muchos	This happens to many
que aquí conozco.[81]	That I know here.]

Generational conflict was inevitable, even though the second generation of Mexican-Americans, born in the United States, was not yet sizable. In the *corrido* "El Padre del Charro Vargas" [The father of Vargas the charro], the life led by a former *vaquero* who now associates with writers is an enigma to his father: ". . . yo, tu padre, 'hora quiero / de tu vida explicación; / aquí en el extranjero" ("I, your father, now wish / An explanation of your life / Here in a strange land").[82]

Nothing was more offensive than the sight of young Mexican women imitating the Americans, displaying a freedom of behavior so different from the reserve expected of women in the past. *Las pelonas* ("the bobbed-haired ones"), who cut their hair short like the flappers, were a favorite theme of the songs and *corridos* of Texas:

Las muchachas de San Antonio	*[The girls of San Antonio
Son flojas pa'l metate	Are lazy at the *metate* ("grinding bowl")
Quieren andar pelonas	They want to go out bobbed-haired
Con sombreros de petate.[83]	With a straw hat on.]

"La Vida Moderna" [Modern life] is a savagely comic indictment of Mexican women:

Las mujeres se pelaron	[The women had their hair bobbed
señores ya bien lo ven	As you can see, gentlemen,
se levantaron la falda	They've lifted their skirts
para enseñarnos el pie.[84]	To show us their feet.]

Then the author warns men about these "lionesses"[85] anxious to rule, to marry and divorce at their pleasure; knowing that the vehemence and truth of his allegations cannot fail to offend his female listeners, he concludes by begging their pardon.

The dominant language gradually began to take precedence over Spanish; a growing number of common English words, usually deformed, slipped into the Mexican-American's vocabulary. The soldier of the *corrido* "La Guerra Mundial" [The world war] speaks of *nodrizas* ("nurses") who *tritiaban* ("treated") soldiers during an epidemic of "American flu" at the barracks. Later on, he explains that in New York his outfit has to take a "*hike a pié*," a long hike, before arriving at the port, and so forth.[86] The usage is sometimes purposely humorous, as if the poet, instead of rebelling against inevitable linguistic osmosis, is laughing both at himself and his countrymen. The *corrido* "Un Picnic" is a parody of New Mexico Hispanos confronting American civilization, symbolized by words that were becoming common: *bill*, *daime* ("dime"), *troca* ("truck"), *flate* ("flat tire"), *flatió* "(had a flat tire").[87] The author scores twice; through the language, he indirectly pokes fun at both Mexican-Americans' technical ineptness when cars break down and at the way they are adjusting to American culture. His objective, and his technique of sprinkling Hispanicized English terms throughout his verses, recall "Sánchez and the Víbora,"[88] a humorous short story by the Anglo-American Robert Granat.

But in general, the tone is more serious. The fear that an entire culture would disappear along with its language was quite real. The author of the *corrido* "Los Mexicanos que Hablan Inglés" [The Mexicans who speak English] bitterly deplores the linguistic "revolution"[89] taking place in Texas. Speak to people in Spanish and they will respond in English:

> *Y hau-dididú mai fren*
> *en ayl sí yu tumora*
> *para decir "diez reales"*
> *dicen dola yene cuora.*[90]

(How do you do, my friend? and I'll see you to-morrow; for "ten reales" they say a dollar and a quarter.) In California, those who clung to traditions and Spanish had little respect for the *pochis* ("faded ones") and their hybrid language and behavior:

Los pochis de California	[The *pochis* of California
No saben comer tortilla	Don't know how to eat tortillas
Porque sólo en la mesa	Because at the table
Usan pan con mantequilla.	All they use is bread and butter.
Me casé con una pochi	I married a *pochi*
Para aprender inglés	In order to learn English
Y a los tres días de casado	And three days after the marriage
Yo ya decía yes.[91]	I was already saying "yes."]

Through the language, often deformed for satire, the poet attacks the society it represents; through the "Americanized" Mexican woman he attacks the gringos; indeed, the English he attributes to the *agringada* (the "gringoized woman") is purposely deformed: ". . . me no like Mexican men."[92] Describing the feverish activity of Anglo politicians in the barrios in election years, the poet sarcastically cites the friendly terms they use to obtain Mexican votes but quickly forget after the election:

Y en tiempos de elección	[And at election time
Y hay aló y hay mai fren;	There are *aló* (hello) and *mai fren*;
Ya pasada la elección	And once the election is over
Ya no hay mai fren ni hay aló.[93]	There is no more *mai fren* or *aló*.]

It may well be that the term *inglear* ("to speak English") used in the "Corrido Pensilvanio" was intended to be lightly mocking.[94]

In certain folkloric stories, English is used to attack the way of thinking that the language represents; in one story, for using "yes" and "no" incorrectly, a Mexican-American is twice beaten up by Anglos.[95] In another, a man confused by English (and a bit simpleminded as well) is incapable of making himself understood by a store salesman who knows no Spanish. Here is the dialogue of these two "deaf persons":

> "What do you want?"
> "*Sí, guante*" *le dice él* (Yes, gloves, he tells him.)
> "What do you say?" *le dice* (he says to him).
> "*Sí, pa José*". (Yes, for José)
> "Oh, you fool!"
> "*Sí, de ésos de la correita azul*" (Yes, those with the little blue laces.)
> "Oh, you go to hell," *le dice* (he says to him).
> "*Sí, de ésos me mandó él*." (Yes, those are the ones that he asked me for.)[96]

At a deeper level, these misunderstandings reflect the incompatibility of two ways of thinking.

English was also the primary vehicle of Anglo-American hostility toward the Mexican-American. In one story, a *paisano* returns to Mexico disgusted; even the animals in the United States speak English and seem to want him out of the country: a rooster chases him, saying "Get out of here"; a sow followed by her piglet tells him, "Go on, go on" and a duck followed by a flock of ducklings quacks, "Quick, quick."[97]

Elsewhere, the poet goes directly on the attack. In the malicious sketch "La Americanita," he compares the habits of the Mexicans to those of the new Anglo arrivals, imagining a dialogue between a "little American woman" and a "little Mexican woman." Each time that the American boasts of her civilization the other counters with a turnabout:

Nosotras Americanas	[We American women
en bogue nomás paseamos.	Only go about in buggies.
Nosotras, las mejicanas	We Mexican women
hasta en burrito nos vamos.[98]	Even go about on burros.]

The Mexican woman's ripostes become more insulting:

Y ustedes, las mejicanas,	[And you Mexican women
no se ponen ropa fina.	Never wear fine clothes.
Y ustedes americanas	And you American women
se embocan a la cantina	Drink your fill at the saloon
y salen cacaraqueando	And leave cackling
lo mismo que una gallina.[99]	Just like a chicken.]

The song ends with a final salvo at the American:

Adiós, americanita,	[Good-bye little American lady,
ya te puedes retirar:	You can go away now;
las mulas que te trajeron	The mules which brought you
que te vuelvan a llevar.[100]	Can now take you away.]

The tone is less playful in the *cuando* "Los Americanos," composed in 1909, which denounces the foreigners' encroachment and their materialistic values: the Mexicans have been dispossessed of their lands by the American imperialists:

Vienen a echarnos del país	[They've come to throw us out of the
Y a hacerse de nuestra tierra.	country
A todo el mundo abarcaron	And to take away our land.
Y se hacen del bien ajeno.[101]	They've taken over the entire world
	And seized the property of others.]

They have made "slaves" of the Mexicans. Nevertheless, the author, a humble shepherd, has ambivalent feelings; he admires the hardworking nation, renowned in agriculture, medicine, and science, but he has only contempt for their cult of mammon.

Su creencia *es en el dinero,*	[They place their *faith* in money,
en la vaca, en el caballo,	In cows and horses,
y ponen todo su haber	And stake all their worldly goods
en la gallina y el gallo.[102]	On the hen and the rooster.]

Once the clash between the two cultures subsided somewhat, criticism in the songs and *corridos* of recent years has changed directions from the strictly cultural to the social. The intrusion of a foreign civilization is decried less than the actual malfeasance of Anglo-American capitalism.

The *Corrido*: An Emotional Safety Valve

¡Pueblo, piensa y combate! el pueblo debe	[People, think and fight! the people must
Combatir y pensar; el pensamiento	Fight and think; thinking
Siempre ha de ser un ala que lo eleve;	Should always be a wing that uplifts
Y si sabe luchar a todo viento	them;
Con la pluma y la espada y el rugido . . .[103]	And if they can fight against all odds
	With the pen, with the sword, and with a
	roar . . .]

Santiago de la Hoz wrote these lines in 1904. Mexican-Americans had adopted the poet's words even before they were written: the borderer defended himself "with a gun in his hand" against the often arbitrary authority of the Rangers; immigrant workers expressed their early demands, if not with a roar, at least explicitly; the Mexican-Americans refused to endure harassment from the occupiers or to accept their civilization indiscriminately. Obscure shepherds and laborers put into verse, then set to music, the struggles of their compatriots; through their poems a dynamic image emerged of the people who fought for liberty and equality.

The *corrido* was born from a people's poverty and suffering; it became their favored means of expression. It fulfilled the same function for Mexican-Americans that the blues had for Blacks, and humor had for the Jews. Like the blues and like humor, the *corrido* was not only a means of protest for an oppressed and powerless minority but also a way to transcend a painful experience and survive.[104] It expressed both the comedy and tragedy of the human condition.

Que dice, mi reenganchista,	*[What do you say, my contractor,
No le dije que volvía	Didn't I tell you I'd be back
Mándeme par 'onde quiera'	Send me wherever you will,
Que ya traigo compañía.[105]	Because now I bring someone with me.]

This the wetback sang as he returned yet again to the United States, knowing what awaited him there; like the blues, the *corrido* was a "sort of emotional escape-valve."[106]

The Anglo-American and the Mexican-American were both prisoners of a myth. The first looked upon the other as he would like him to be in order to justify his attitude toward him and to give himself a more flattering and confident self-image, or in order to find in the Mexican-American what he himself would have preferred to be but was not; in both cases he situated himself in relation to the Other and to himself in the "unreal" mode. The conqueror needed to impose the yoke of the stereotype to strengthen his sense of superiority or to overcome a personal shortcoming. For his part, the Mexican-American, through the image he often offered of himself, tended to justify the use of the yoke, the status of inferiority, the literary subordination in which he was kept by the Anglo-American writer; he did not set himself up as an object to be defined; he unconsciously accepted the image imposed upon him by the Other. At the turn of the century, however, there appeared a true concern for objectivity in the Anglo-American writer, although a clear tendency toward sentimentality, humor, and caricature somewhat compromised these first attempts at realism. They were, nonetheless, encouraged by the climate of the 1930s, a period of change that shook the foundations of society; the yoke of the stereotype itself also gave way before the clearsighted enthusiasm of Anglo-American writers and their denunciation of social injustices.

As society evolved, certain stereotypes disappeared—for example, the "cowardice" of the Mexican-American fostered by works on the war with Mexico. Other stereotypes changed with the circumstances: the "bandit" was reincarnated as a hero; fatalism led to the myth of docility. Mexican-Americans' withdrawal into themselves and resistance to all attempts to approach them justified, in the eyes of the Anglo-Americans, their "invisibility" in the years to come.

Despite the static image they tended to project, Mexican-Americans became combative on the social level; they began to "see" themselves in relation to the foreigner. Mexican-American writers progressively began to question the traditional self-image that had been imposed on them, and to cast off its yoke. The English language also became a means of demanding their rights, of making themselves heard by the Anglo majority, of making themselves "visible."

PART TWO
1940–1965

The Invisible but
Invincible Minority

The Anglo-American
Point of View

Introduction to the Period

The Depression was followed by a period of wealth and relative self-satisfaction. The return of prosperity gave back to America a self-confidence that even the war had not stimulated; rather, the war reinforced self-confidence, as it revived national pride. But the optimism rising out the nation's successful foreign policy and the dizzying increase in economic activity could not hide a certain uneasiness to which McCarthyism gave a tangible form in the 1950s. The racial conflicts of the next decade intensified the sense of disorientation in Americans, who were plunged into an increasingly absurd society and cut off from their past. Just as they had at the end of the nineteenth century, Americans turned toward the past, out of both pride and a need for reassurance. Regionalistic literature experienced renewed favor; the South and the Civil War enjoyed a revival of interest while the Southwest became the object of numerous studies: George Evans's manuscript, *Mexican Gold Trail, the Journal of a 49er,* was published in 1945; Charles Goldfinch set out to rehabilitate the image of Juan Cortina;[2] the Texas Folklore Society pursued its work.

In literature, just as in preceding eras, two orientations emerged—romantic and realistic—which could often be found co-existing in a single work. For the many writers who were trapped in a romantic literary tradition, writing about the Southwest continued to be a form of escapism. They sometimes exulted in its past and, at other times, saw its present untouched by the upheavals of the postwar era. They expressed their enthusiasm for a time past by glorifying the past or by using a sympathetic humor not unlike that found in *Tortilla Flat.* They presented a traditional image of the Mexican-American, living in a land of dreams. The universe into which they relegated the Mexican-American was closed, situated outside history, far removed from the struggle for survival. It was governed by the laws of stereotypes and by a language that evoked timeless values, expressed in familial, social, and religious traditions. The social context was generally vague and the prevailing atmosphere either pastoral or comic. While the present exercised progressively insistent pressure on the real-life Mexican Southwest, the Anglo-American writer withdrew into the past, into myth, into humor.

In the face of this romantic and waggish literary current, from which a rather engaging Mexican-American emerged, there appeared a literature more profoundly committed to the present time. A growing number of sociological studies were now devoted to the Mexican minority, while the decade before the war had been primarily distinguished by the work of folklorists. These folklore specialists had unearthed the Mexican of the past, who was more inclined to avoid conflicts. Sociologists, by contrast, investigated the problem of the Mexican minority's integration into postwar Anglo-American society. Short-story writers and novelists writing on behalf of Mexican-Americans victimized by the social and economic system sharpened both their commitment and their criticism of Anglo-American society. The distance between the romantic and realistic extremes of the literary spectrum was greater than before the war. The committed writer did not relegate the Mexican-Americans to a static, ahistoric universe, but rather showed their evolution, that is, everything that made them progressively more visible to the Anglo majority.

Mexican-Americans were gradually emerging from isolation; in the border-lands the chaparral gave way to fruit orchards; the general exodus toward the cities, triggered by the Depression, increased after the war. With the accelerating urbanization, Mexican-Americans found themselves suddenly plunged into a society dominated by Anglo-Americans. It was increasingly urgent for them to define and assert their identity. The war was a catalyst; although it brought to light inequality of the races through massive conscription of Mexican-Americans, it made the Mexican-American conscious of belonging to the nation. To the peoples of Europe and the Pacific, the Mexican-American soldier was an American just like the Anglo with whom he fought a common enemy. From then on, it was a matter of securing his rightful place in his own country, a demand all the more justified because of his often distinguished service under the American flag.[3] But the war also brought setbacks. The attack on Pearl Harbor automatically increased nativism; certain groups of foreign ancestry, like the Japanese, found themselves considered subversive. Racism directed at the Mexican minority reached its zenith during racial disorders in June 1943; the Zoot Suit Riots,[4] a veritable hunting down of Mexican-Americans, were evoked in a contemporary short story as reminiscent of Hitler's pogroms.[5] Those singled out were young men with "duck-tail" hairstyles dressed in zoot suits—baggy pants pegged at the ankles and over-sized jackets. This uniform sported by the *pachucos*, or zoot-suiters, like some Blacks and Filipinos, actually was a sort of challenge to the world. As Octavio Paz noted:

> By means of their grotesque dandyism and anarchic behavior, they brought to light not so much the injustice and incapacity of a society that failed to assimilate them as their personal desire to continue being different.[6]

The origin of the term *pachuco* is uncertain. According to the most widely accepted version, the older generation applied it to the young people because their baggy, narrow-cuffed pants resembled the costume worn in the Mexican city of Pachuca. It was also a colloquial term for the inhabitants of El Paso, the Texas city where the term first became popular and where a jargon called *pachuco* or *pachuquismo* developed in the early thirties. Composed of English, Spanish, and elements of *caló*, the slang of Mexican thieves,[7] this hip language spread to California in the 1940s, where many Mexican-Americans from Texas had settled.[8] Los Angeles thus became the capital of the *pachucos* and of a movement that really was born ten years earlier in the El Segundo barrio of El Paso. The riots of 1943 familiarized the public with the term and the phenomenon it represented.

The *pachucos* were usually from poor immigrant families who had not integrated into Anglo society. They felt this failure deeply and chose to live it out in a negative defiance. The Mexican writer Octavio Paz, who lived in the United States from 1943 to 1945, defined *pachuquismo*:

> They don't try to defend their race or the nationality of their ancestors. Their attitude reveals an obstinate, and almost fanatic will-to-be, but this will affirms nothing except their intention—ambiguous as we shall see—to be different from those around them. The *pachuco* does not wish to return to his Mexican origin; at the same time he refuses, in appearance at least, to blend into American life.[9]

A rift developed between the generations at the same time that the middle class began to separate from the lower classes of the Mexican minority. The new middle class yielded to the power of the majority without challenging it and reproached the *pachucos*. Similarly, the upper classes of Mexican-American society during the preceding century had rejected the "greaser" as undesirable. More tormented than the greaser, who remained close to his origins, the *pachuco* of the 1940s felt doubly estranged; neither the family nor Anglo society could provide the security he needed. He began to seek it among his peers, in the gangs in the heart of the barrio.

The minority as a whole pursued acculturation more or less successfully. The gap widened between the middle class, assimilated or in the process of assimilating, and the proletariat, excluded from the melting pot. After 1942, the *braceros* ("day-laborers") were added to the latter group; these semi-itinerant Mexican laborers were brought in to overcome the worker shortage created by the exodus of American farm workers to defense factories during the war. Not only were they exploited—despite agreements between the Mexican and American governments guaranteeing freedom from discrimination, decent working conditions, and salaries—they also were despised by Mexican-American and Anglo agricultural workers because they accepted wages lower than those of unionized workers.[10] Additionally, uninterrupted influx of illegal immigrants—the *mojados*, or wetbacks—fostered tension in the barrios where they took refuge, especially after 1950.[11]

The barrios, Mexican neighborhoods, were truly cohesive for the Mexican minority in United States, and the importance of their communal life should not be underestimated. In the barrio, some groups purposely remained "invisible" while others remained so in spite of themselves. The barrio generated the ferment that would rouse the masses; at the end of the 1950s a political consciousness, which had been germinating since World War II, would finally be born in the Mexican-American.[12]

Single-language and bilingual newspapers continued to appear and to publish poems in Spanish directed at Spanish speakers, while in the predominantly Anglo literary journals of the Southwest, the first short stories that we know of by Mexican-Americans began to appear. These literary activities reflected the historical situation of the Mexican-American people, faithful to the Mexican past but immersed in spite of itself in American society. The short stories, and the first novel by a Mexican-American, in 1959,[13] all in English, were an attempt to make the Mexican minority visible through the use of the pen. The language of this period of acculturation was English. The Mexican-American public spoke a progressively more Americanized Spanish, and bilingualism had not yet been accepted in the public schools. This second period, 1940 to 1965, was characterized at the linguistic level by a definite effort toward assimilation. At the level of content, however, the degree of assimilation remained to be seen. Mexican-American thought would one day be uncomfortable within this English mold: it would break out and return to its original modes of expression.

The historical process is irreversible. Although Mexican-Americans still remained "invisible" to those who persisted in seeing them through the obscurity of myth, in exotic backgrounds, or in comic situations, their painful and real struggles attracted increasing public attention and provoked a bolder stance on the part of Anglo-American writers.

CHAPTER 8

Flight Into the Past: The Children of Nature

The cult of primitivism did not die. Rather, it was reborn, increasingly vigorous, at every new leap forward of civilization. In an America more and more governed by reason, science, and technology, a nostalgia for nature and the primal human state persisted. Faulkner was obsessed with the virgin land of the Mississippi delta;[1] others escaped into the villages of New Mexico perched high in the Sangre de Cristo mountains or became enamored of the wild beauty of California. The primitives—Indian, Black, or Mexican-American—were rare beings who lived in tune with the rhythms of nature, remaining unspoiled by machine-age civilization, which neither broke their internal fiber nor killed the spontaneity of their emotions. It was this purity and simplicity that the romantics of the postwar era accentuated in the Mexican-American.

The *campesinos* ("peasants") drew inner strength from the land that provided their sustenance. Certain writers, still haunted by nostalgia for an idyllic past, saw only an idealized, pastoral environment.

Mexican-Americans were also considered children of nature in their rejection of all forms of deviousness and constraint. This view was certainly no newer than the pastoral ideal; it dated back to the nineteenth century and the early decades of the twentieth. Steinbeck gave a masterfully humorous rendition of it when he immortalized the *paisanos* of Monterey in *Tortilla Flat*. The originality of Kerouac's novel *On the Road*,[2] published twenty years later, was its mystical orientation. The hero sets off in search of truth, life, and love; his long journey, of which the California episode is but one stage, finally leads him to Mexico, where he immerses himself in the sources of life and truth. Some contemporaries of the Beat writer Kerouac, without delving into mysticism, presented a similar image of the Mexican-American.

The Mexican-American's primitivism ultimately gave way to less romantic and mystical interpretations; some writers transformed Mexican provincialism into buffoonery; others turned the Mexican-American into a bizarre individual, indeed, a stranger in the world of normal people.

The *Campesino*: The Earth

"Who speaks of conquering? To endure is everything."
                              RILKE[3]

The era of the pastoral was far from over. Some romantics preferred New Mexico settings; they took pleasure in imagining the Mexican-American living on the fringes of culture, in this part of the Southwest so long protected from civilization by its geographic isolation. Oliver LaFarge shielded this region "behind the mountains" of the Sangre de Cristo range, whose ramparts were even higher than those of California's Coast Range in Steinbeck's novels;[4] LaFarge wrote that the region "consists of fertile watered valleys *guarded* by rugged, *masculine, protective* hills" (emphasis added).[5] The entire life of Little Jo, the young peasant created by Robert Bright,[6] takes place in an isolated village. Frank Waters's anonymous valley, *"muy retirado, muy cerrado . . .* grew more isolated, more closed within its mountain walls."[7] No matter how hidden away, alas, the valley was inexorably doomed to destruction. The words purposely left in Spanish in the text are a way of expressing the *campesino*'s resistance toward gringo civilization. The novel by Waters, which takes place in the mid-nineteenth century, is the story of María del Valle, who symbolizes resistance to "the maquina (machine) of progress,"[8] a dam designed to prevent the floods that continually ravage the valley. The people cling to tradition just as Tonita, Helen Stevens's heroine, clings to her black shawl.[9] They remain faithful to their beliefs and to a traditional interpretation of life and the universe, and continue to believe in evil spirits. In her memoirs, Agnes Morley Cleaveland relates that, after the procession of the Penitentes (the only thing she recalls about New Mexico at the end of the nineteenth century) candles were lit ". . . to frighten away the evil spirits who might be hovering about the holy preparations for celebrating the breaking of Easter morn."[10] In the midst of the atomic age, in the Nambé Valley, dominated by the nuclear facilities of Los Alamos (alias "The Hill"), José de la Rosa, the peasant in Roy Rosen's short story "Music for the Night," holds the Evil Eye responsible for the pitiful yields of his harvests.[11] To reverse a drought, he ignores scientific methods and calls on the patron saint of farmers, San Ysidro, whose statue he places in a tree overlooking his fields. In Tonita's village, house doors were painted blue because this "sun color" brought good luck and "kept out the evil spirits."[12] LaFarge devotes an entire chapter to Sena Delfina, the specialist of the supernatural in the village of Rociada. Indeed, wasn't it common knowledge that "mountain country, like the sea coast, is enemy to incredulity?"[13] The author hastens to add that "such families as Baca y Pendaries, educated, traveled, *gente de razón* ('enlightened people'), of course took no stock in the superstitions of the ignorant. . . ."[14] But what these enlightened minds considered superstition were for believers the secret codes of nature that only they could decipher.

For believers, progress was sacrilege because it destroyed the original harmony of humankind, nature, and the sacred. This emerges most strongly in "Music for the Night," perhaps because the author contrasts two extremes: modern progress and the ageless common sense of the peasant.

> California, yes, if he had to, but not the Hill. The Hill was anathema. It was anathema. It was a curse on the Valley.[15]

To José, progress means the powerful explosions that threaten to damage the china and pictures on the wall; at a deeper level, progress, which he associates with townspeople, destroys the original harmony of the universe by tearing people away from nature and the *campesino* from the fields: "The Hill was *malo*, bad. It bred unhappiness, made *borrachos*, drunkards, out of once good *campesinos*."[16]

And so it was that in a period of massive urbanization and assimilation of the middle class, the public held an image of the *campesino* who remained resolutely faithful to an ancestral way of life and thought. As late as 1963, this image still fascinated Alvin Gordon, writer and educational book producer, whose *Inherit the Earth: Stories from Mexican Ranch Life*,[17] a book on rural New Mexico, accentuated the positive aspects of paternalism. The singular and anachronistic character of the Mexican-American peasant touched all these works with the exotic, and judging from the success of LaFarge's book, exoticism still sold well.[18] The "exotic characteristics of the Spanish South-West,"[19] lovingly extolled by LaFarge, also made novels about the grand Hispanic-American families popular.[20] We encounter yet again the well-known names of Fergusson and Horgan. The principal interest of these works is the nostalgic evocation of a bygone feudal era, with an essentially rural economy and wealth concentrated in the hands of a few landed proprietors and tied to a primitive conception of the Mexican-American. In the series of sketches that make up *Behind the Mountains*, LaFarge recounts the recollections of his wife, a member of the Baca family.[21] She remembered an immense ranch in the 1920s, from fifteen to twenty thousand head of sheep and cattle, and the little village of Rociada, a dependency of the ranch; in brief: ". . . a *Seigneurie* that was more like something out of past time than like anything one would expect to find in the United States of the prohibition era."[22] A symbiosis existed between the ranch and the village: the latter furnished a labor force to Don José, who provided many services in return; the ranch staff often tended to the needs of the poor village families, just as plantation staffs ministered to Blacks in the South. But the idyllic world of the Bacas (and the white Southern planter) gradually felt the encroachments of the outside world and became a dream of the past.[23]

Until this time, the decline of the great ranches elicited more interest than the difficulties of *campesinos* forced to sell or leave their land. For this reason, Waters's novel *People of the Valley* and Rosen's tale "Music for the Night," despite their literary mediocrity and sometimes irritating affectations, are worthy of scrutiny. They depict two aspects of the peasant's problem: expropriation of land and harsh working conditions in a country of endemic drought. Waters goes back to the nineteenth century: "the people of the valley" are threatened with expropriation by a gringo businessman who is constructing a dam. María del Valle tries to rally the *paisanos* by appealing to their love for the land; she harangues them in the street, creating crowds that block traffic; she is even arrested. The final attempts at resistance are quashed both by the federal government and gringo money, which the *paisanos* squander in town. And then, an exodus. Rosen's hero, José, a farmer and father of eight, is caught in a dilemma: he must either stay on his land and deal with the drought, or, an apparently more appealing possibility, leave to work in a nuclear research center, which offers higher pay and better working conditions. Before the center was built, the alternative would have been to leave for California, where José worked as a seasonal laborer the year before his marriage. But José would no more leave his valley than would María.

In his novel of the same period, *The Lady*,[24] Conrad Richter dwells at length on the distress of Doña Ellen, owner of the immense Johnson y Campo ranch, who is forced to sell out after the drought of 1893. The divergence between this work and the two preceding ones is interesting sociologically and psychologically. Richter's grande dame yearns for the lifestyle and celebrations of yesteryear, made possible by enormous profits from sheep-raising. The *campesino*, on the other hand, has a filial devotion for the land similar to the Indian's; any separation from the earth mother is tragic: "We have never sold our land. It is not the custom. The land is our mother. It has suckled our fathers, our fathers' fathers. What would we do without the land? Even with a dam?"[25] shouts María del Valle. The theme of the earth mother would later be amply treated in Mexican-American literature. José refuses to leave his valley because he "loved his land, all of the earth";[26] his affection for the things of the earth is emphasized by the author's animistic terms: "Here the chilis grew sweet and *hot* like *young love*, the corn in ripeness, moist as a *baby's kiss*, the alfalfa *tender* as the *licking*, of a *new-born calf*" (emphasis added).[27] The *campesino*'s love for the land was meditative and detached, while the Anglo peasant had a conqueror's lust to extract maximum profit from the soil.

True peasants do not try to change life by transforming nature scientifically. They accept life as it is, with a patience inherited from the earth, which supports their existence both literally and figuratively. Earlier writers had been struck by the physical and moral courage of Mexican-Americans; the term "enduring" appeared frequently in their writings, but often submerged in long lists of not-always-flattering adjectives. Is this capacity to endure nothing more than an "attribute of the oppressed in American culture," as suggested by Pierre Dommergues, who inferred it from Faulkner's admiration for the endurance of Blacks?[28] Mexican-American endurance was highlighted again in the fifties and sixties; it is not surprising in a period marked by the instability of urban populations, insecurity fostered by McCarthyism, and, in a general way, an increasing sense of the absurdity of life. One thing is striking: in all the writers mentioned in this period, patience is a feminine trait characterized by a serene acceptance of life and death. Only one work, *The Ox-Bow Incident* by Walter Van Tilburg Clark (situated in Nevada in 1885), relates an example of masculine courage. A Mexican-American cattle rustler's indifference to pain elicits admiration from the other men. They shudder as they watch him pull a bullet from his thigh after he is wounded while trying to escape from a lynching.[29] Patience is a virtue of all the women in the preceding works: Sabina, the wife of José and mother of eight, encourages her husband to remain on his land; Tonita, the peasant woman with the black shawl, endures for years being kept from her daughter by her son-in-law, a hardhearted Dutchman; María del Valle, who refuses to leave the valley, at age ninety presents "the aspect of a citadel still beleaguered but still impregnable."[30] Finally, in the short story by Robert Granat, whose title, "To Endure," and epigraph[31] are both laden with meaning, the unexpected pathos makes the conclusion even more moving. Indeed, who could anticipate such a capacity for suffering in a mother who had just learned of the death of her very young daughter?

> Mama comes to the door. 'Abrán, hurry, eat your supper' she says and I come. I want to kiss Mama but I was scared. The beans was in the plates, Mama sit down in the corner under the picture of the Virgin next to the one of Jesus opening his chest to show us his beautiful heart. She was talking to the Virgin. '*Ay María Santísima . . . perdí mi hijita . . . Ay . . .*' ["Holiest Mary, I lost my little daughter."]
> And underneath she hold Ubaldo up so he could suck his milk.[32]

Life goes on. As a mother, her duty is to care for the family.

Woman, like the earth, gives life; it is from the earth that she gets her stability and strength. It is fitting that the terms that describe her are also derived from the earth: the features of María del Valle's face are "powerful and primitive . . . timeless with sorrow and fecundity . . . savage and enduring as if cut out of rock. . . ."[33] Just as the earth represents the stable feminine element of the universe in primitive philosophies, so the *campesina* is the hub of the family. Kerouac saw this maternal stability as a characteristic of all the "fellah" peoples, the peasants of the world.[34]

One aspect of Mexican-American primitivism, then, was personified by *campesinos*. Distrustful of changes brought about by the city, they are passionately attached to the earth, from which they draw their physical and moral sustenance. Their fundamental simplicity is reflected in the purposely spare and concrete style of the Anglo writer of this period. It is unfortunate that the literary representation of this simplicity too often resembled children's stories, such as those of Florence Crannel Means,[35] and contributed to the portrayal of the Mexican-American as naive and excessively childlike, as yet uncorrupted by urbanization and progress.

A Return to the Roots

Sam knew things that had been tamed out of our blood
so long ago that we have not only forgotten them, we
have to live together in herds to protect ourselves from
our own sources. [36]

While on the road, Kerouac's hero, Sal Paradise, enthusiastically discovers the California and Texas barrios; he gets a foretaste of Mexico and its "fellah" people,[37] whose basic simplicity brings them close to truth. Steinbeck, in the course of his long journey to discover America, joyfully returns to Monterey, the land of his friends, the *paisanos*.[38] Juan Chicoy, Steinbeck's half-Mexican, half-Irish fictional hero, married to an American, dreams of running off to Mexico in his bus.[39] These three journeys, each in its own way symbolic, return to the source, to the authentic person, to humanity's original natural state. Sal Paradise rejects the artificiality of postwar America; his encounter with Teresita on the bus from Los Angeles marks a decisive point in his life. Steinbeck, a native Californian with a Mexican soul, knows what he is returning to: the spirit of the *paisanos* of yesteryear lives on in Johnny García's bar. Juan Chicoy feels caught in a "damned trap"[40] amid the comfort and stylish furnishings of his home; he tries to escape from his bus and his passengers— a microcosm of America, all branded by Anglo civilization and puritanism— and return home to the land of his birth.

But this return to the source has to be realized through nature. As a cotton-picker, Sal Paradise bows down before the earth and attempts to blend into it, for its simplicity brings him closer to "the little people"[41] of Mexican origin and to the old Black couple working alongside him. His back bothers him. No matter: ". . . it was beautiful kneeling and hiding in that earth. If I felt like resting I did, with my face on the pillow of brown moist earth."[42]

Steinbeck evokes the Monterey of another time, to which he returns in spirit, an era when there were, as yet, no swimming pools, "where frogs and crayfish used to wait for us."[43] Juan leaves the bus under the false pretext of going for help; he really feels the need to escape. To elude Pimples, his suspicious mechanic assistant who is following him, he takes refuge in a cave, as if withdrawing from the world and returning to a state of primordial innocence.[44] His steps carry him instinctively toward nature, toward its most primitive and time-distant elements. He prefers to sleep on hay in an old abandoned barn ("I like old places,"[45] he later confesses to Mildred Pritchard, the young passenger who comes to join him there). He finally falls asleep after recalling moments of pure happiness from his past and having gone back to the sources of true joy, so different from the artificial happiness of his current life:

... little pictures came into his mind. There was a very early morning with chill air and the sun was coming up behind the mountains and in a muddy road little gray birds were hopping. There wasn't any reason for joy, but it had been there.[46]

Contact with nature gave authenticity and freshness to the affective life of Mexican-Americans; instinctively hostile to the artificial and conventional, they created a world free of the constraints imposed by a society of rigid institutions and inflexible moral codes. In literature, the splendid region of New Mexico remained an austere and impregnable citadel, while California, the land of abundance, symbolized the perpetual fountainhead of life. Kerouac and Steinbeck, in particular, wanted not so much to demonstrate the resistance of Mexican-Americans to the encroachments of Anglo society[47] as to depict them still living in tune with the rhythms of an untamed and luxuriant nature.

Mexican-Americans appear as people who love life and live it fully; their vitality and enjoyment of people and things are spontaneous and intense; their special province is not subtle abstractions but immediate and basic emotions. The warm and unaffected Monterey of Pilón, Jesús María Corcoran, and Joe Portagee[48] seems concentrated in Johnny García's bar. Back in his favorite city, the reunions, accompanied by "tears and embraces, speeches and endearments,"[49] touched Steinbeck deeply. This Mexican exuberance, brought out by Steinbeck with sympathetic humor, intoxicates Kerouac; the Beat author characterizes himself as "mad" and sees everything Mexican-American as frenetic: each day is followed by "another wild day";[50] the streets of the barrio in Fresno were "wild";[51] San Antonio, 150 miles from the Mexican border, offers America's best in terms of madness:

> We stopped at a mad gas station . . . there were shacks . . . and a wild cinnamon smell in the air. Frantic teenage Mexican girls came by with boys. . . . Music was coming from all sides, and all kinds of music. . . . We were already almost out of America and yet definitely in it and in the middle of where it's maddest.[52]

Mexican-Americans' lust for life appeared inexhaustible. The *paisanos* of *Tortilla Flat* are ready to celebrate at the slightest provocation. In *Travels with Charley*, the now-aged and disillusioned author believes himself irrevocably changed since the time long past when he wrote *Tortilla Flat*. But Johnny García reassures him: "You still love wine, you still love girls."[53] Nothing is lost, therefore! Unlike his Anglo wife, Juan, the hero of *The Wayward Bus*, "could enjoy people. Alice could only love, like, dislike, and hate."[54]

Goodwyn and Fergusson emphasized the importance Mexican-Americans accorded to the pleasures of life. Goodwyn's novel *The Black Bull* recaptures the Texas of his childhood, and the King Ranch in particular, where he spent the better part of his youth. The only memories he retained of the *vaqueros*, the book's principal characters, were of men so in love with life that even the most exhausting daytime work could not prevent them from celebrating at night. Thus Timoteo Nieto

> . . . could work all day in the dust and sun, dance all night with little in his stomach except wine. . . . He ate sparingly and spasmodically but dearly enjoyed what he did eat. Being gifted with high sensitivity, he felt pleasures keenly and lingered long over the thought of them. . . .[55]

To Fergusson, the ability to enjoy life was not the prerogative of any social class. In his last novel, *The Conquest of Don Pedro*, a traditional romantic work, he wrote of the rich Hispanos of the Rio Grande Valley of the 1880s and lamented the end of a lifestyle that saw life as an art. He dwelt nostalgically on the festivities of the aristocracy, which contributed to a general gaiety; thus, at Cebal:

> Everyone laughed and clapped more and more as the evening lengthened and the crowd madness of music and rhythm seized them all. Leo was again impressed by the great capacity these people had to enjoy themselves, to seize and devour the moment . . .[56]

To seize the moment and wring all possible happiness from it was the essential thing for Kerouac. His characters' constant use of the present tense to express the future is a grammatical peculiarity indicative of the Hispanic mentality.[57] The word *mañana*, repeated like a refrain in all the Mexican quarters of Colorado, California, and Texas, literally casts a spell on Sal Paradise: " 'Sure, baby, *mañana*.' It was always *mañana*. For the next week that was all I heard —*mañana*, a lovely word and one that probably means heaven."[58] In the barrios where life explodes amid the shouts and rhythms of the mambo, Sal seems to find an outlet for his rage to live.

The constraints of American middle-class society were viewed as alien to Mexican-Americans' primitive vitality. In Kerouac's works, Mexican-Americans lead a bohemian life outside traditional society; other writers also describe their rejection of puritan sexual morality.

The California episode of *On the Road* contains the implicit criticisms that are formulated allegorically and humorously in *Tortilla Flat*. Danny's gang in the Steinbeck novel is a world unto itself, governed by its own laws; Kerouac has a similar view of the barrio as an autonomous little island within Anglo-American society. The dominant society is loosely represented by its cotton fields and vineyards, the starvation wages it pays, the uncomfortable tents it rents to workers, in brief, by Anglo-American capitalism, personified by "the big fat woman who owned the camp."[59] The Beat writer offers an alternative to this hostile society based upon the exploitation of workers and the profit motive. By means of his Mexican-American characters, Kerouac depicts a lifestyle based upon solidarity and freedom, on the outer fringes of society.

For Ricky and Ponzo, the essential thing is to be "together": " 'We're all in this together!' yelled Ponzo. I saw that was so—everywhere I went, everybody was in it together." [60] The constant use of the word "us" by the narrator and his companions is revealing. No one suffers ostracism. Sal Paradise, though not Mexican, finds refuge in the barrio of Sabinal for two weeks. This Mexican sense of hospitality and sharing has often been praised; Kerouac sees it as a manifestation of a mystic brotherhood, a stop on the path to transcendence.

That path also included a stage of liberation. In Kerouac's view, the beatnik, like the Mexican-American, refused to settle down or establish ties. Ponzo has no attachments whatsoever; "he had no place to sleep." When asked by Sal where he lives, he answers "nowhere." [61] Sal and Terry practically sleep in the open, in a rented tent. The Mexican-Americans whom Sal meets never allow themselves to be enslaved by materialism. Their first concern is pleasure and immediate pleasure at that: a beer with friends, picking up girls in the barrios of Fresno and Madera. *Mañana* and the struggle for survival in a capitalist society are no more than hazy notions in an uncertain future: "Today we drink, tomorrow we work," [62] Ricky says. "Tomorrow we make a lot of money; tonight we don't worry," [63] adds Ponzo, going him one better. Both refuse to bow before a rigid, austere work ethic.

In these works, Mexican-Americans reject everything in the middle-class and puritan mentality that inhibits their natural penchant for pleasures, especially those of the flesh. Some Anglo-American writers brought up yet again the wellworn theme of Mexican sensuality. Their approach was hardly different from that of their predecessors. They all praised the sensuality cultivated by Mexican-Americans; they all more or less explicitly condemned puritanism. Steinbeck took up the traditional theme of masculine virility, and Fergusson, the woman's expertise in the art of love. Horgan approached the subject as a converted Catholic. Goodwyn admired the natural sexuality of his Texas *vaqueros*, while Kerouac, contributing a new note, projected love against a background of nocturnal Dionysian revelry.

A major part of the allegorical novel *The Wayward Bus* concerns sexuality. Lisca offers an interesting interpretation. He distinguishes three categories of characters: among the "damned" and the "souls in Purgatory," he numbers the conformist zealot Mr. Pritchard and his prudish, hypocritical wife; Norma, the sexually frustrated servant of the Chicoys; Louie, the falsely virile first bus driver; and Alice Chicoy, who, despite her sexual desires, is too insensitive to know true love. On the other side are the "elect": Ernest Horton, who is direct in love; Camille Oaks, the blond stripteaser; and, in particular, Juan Chicoy. [64] For this group, the bus trip is crowned with success. The new driver symbolically changes the name of the bus, "The Great Power of Jesus," to "Chérie." The author feminizes and sexualizes the countryside through which Juan is driving the "bus named desire": "rounded woman-like hills, soft and sexual as flesh." [65] Juan's manliness has always fascinated Alice: "Mrs. Chicoy was insanely in love with him and a little afraid of him too, because he was a man and there aren't very many of them. . . ." [66] For Mildred Pritchard, who watches him in the rear-view mirror, he is the total man, the macho: "This was the kind of man that a pure woman would want to have because he wouldn't even want to be part woman." [67] His open and straightforward sexuality requires none of the deception used by the intellectual and hypocritical Mildred before she begs Juan to make love to her in the barn:

> "I don't want you to think that I followed you in here," she said.
> "You don't want me to think it, but you did," said Juan.
> . . . His hand came out again and rested on her covered knee . . . [68]

It is by means of two women that Fergusson depicts love Mexican style. The writer, who knew the Southwest well, could not resist emphasizing, with amusement, the ambiguity of the Mexican sexual code. The central character in his novel *The Conquest of Don Pedro*, Leo Mendes, the outside observer in Don Pedro's village, can never completely win over the little town until he makes a conquest of Doña Lupe, the *patrón*'s wife; he later marries this lady's niece, Magdalena Vierra. The Mexican-American woman, as she appears in Leo's eyes, is an "artist of love" and gives herself without shame to the pleasures of the flesh, whether legitimate or not. Here, for example, is Lupe:

> Lupe came out of a class and race of women for whom sex had been their whole profession . . . for centuries, and they had made an art of it and of every phase of it, from the first faint smile of flirtation to the final spasm. . . . She was truly an artist of love. . . . Sin she accepted as a necessary part of human life on earth. For her every act of passion was both a fall and a redemption, leaving her pure and pacified. [69]

In spite of her American-style education, young Magdalena never loses her taste for love affairs. This feminine licentiousness, however, should not make us overlook the rigorous constraints placed upon the Mexican-American woman:

> Unmarried girls were guarded with firearms and sometimes locked up for safe keeping with ferocious dogs, but the boys and girls of a village nevertheless contrived to explore the wonders of love at an early age as Leo had the opportunity to observe. Men were always ready to fight for the purity and fidelity of their wives, yet adultery had almost the status of an institution. Husbands had to be much away from home and wives were sly and cunning.
> Desire was not to be denied, and without sin how could there be repentance and divine forgiveness? [70]

This permissiveness enchanted Horgan, who was attracted to Latin Catholicism precisely because of its liberalism, so different from the Irish austerity of the American Catholic church. His novel *The Common Heart* was, like preceding ones, a nostalgic evocation of the New Mexico of yesteryear, notably its religious context. It offers a number of provocative scenes: in the Albuquerque of long ago, Doña Catalina's bordello carries on a rivalry with the church of San

Felipe de Neri; from the pulpit on Sundays, the priests rebuke the activities of this lady, who expressed agreement in the church; but once outside: ". . . they bowed to her, blessing her and thanking her for the offerings she made, and in general recognizing her humanity without condoning the expression of its failures." [71]

Kerouac's novel is bathed in darkness—there is no shame or damnation in this "underground" world where sensual ecstasy flourishes. No matter how intense it is, sexual gratification among Goodwyn's *vaqueros* is down to earth; Timoteo is happily married to Cristina: "She had a beautiful body built for copious enjoyment and the production of numerous babies." [72] In Kerouac, pleasure is more complex; it is the path that leads to self-knowledge and knowledge of others. Sal Paradise arrives at this stage only through orgiastic stimulation and the liberation of the dark forces within him. After passing through the city's Black and Mexican sections, he considers himself a Denver Black or Mexican, so disturbed does he feel in the white world, which cannot offer him ". . . enough ecstasy, not enough life, joy, kicks, darkness, music, not enough night." [73] On the bus from Los Angeles, Terry, a young Mexican-American woman, spontaneously responds to Sal's embrace—though she has just met him. She shouts: "I love love," [74] expressing through repetition of the word all the intensity of her feeling. This first meeting occurs at night, and it is partly at night that various Mexican episodes of the book take place. Kerouac's road ends at nightfall, in Mexico City, "the great and final wild uninhibited Fellahin-childlike city that we knew we would find at the end of the road." [75]

For Steinbeck, to return to the Mexican Southwest, the midpoint on the road to Mexico City, is to return to ". . . a place of sweet and sentimental violence, and a wise innocence as yet unknown and therefore undirtied by undiapered minds." [76]

Mexican Slapstick

I force myself to laugh at everything for fear of having to weep. [77]

A less romantic view of Mexican-American primitivism was offered by certain humorists and fanciers of the fantastic. Although their work resembled Steinbeck's sympathetic humor in *Tortilla Flat* more than the derisive caricature of O. Henry, it encompassed the entire spectrum of comedy, from vaudeville to the tragicomic, or it took flight into the unreal. Some Mexican-American problems were lightly touched upon in the stories of Ray Bradbury, William E. Barrett, Larry Harris, Alice Marriott, and Goodwyn's fablelike novel, but these writers intended not to denounce social injustice but rather to accentuate the unexpected and the bizarre. [78]

Forgoing the extended narrative, they generally preferred brief sketches of

Mexican-American life, painted with large, rapid brushstrokes. The situations were always ludicrous or strange, and bordered on the improbable. While certain aspects of Mexican-American primitivism lent themselves to fantastic interpretations, others were exploited for humor, reinforced by a comical use of Spanish. Bradbury, the well-known science-fiction author, presents an extreme image of the Mexican's resistance to progress, as if to better delineate the flaws of the Anglo system. In the works of Alice Marriott, Harris, and Goodwyn, the Mexican-American's familiarity with death and the supernatural takes the reader into the realm of the imaginary, while the themes of the happy-go-lucky, childlike Mexican-American (in Barrett and Bradbury) and hardy peasant (in Granat) embody a more direct and commonplace humor.

The Bradbury short story "The Little Mice" sketches a world of the bizarre, right in the midst of twentieth-century America. The narrator has rented part of his house to a married working couple from Mexico who intrigue him:

> Where were they from? Mexico, yes. What part? A farm, a small village, somewhere by a river? Certainly no city or town. But a place where there were stars and the normal lights and darknesses, the goings and comings of the moon and the sun they had known the better part of their lives. Yet here they were, far faraway from home, in an impossible city, he sweating out the hell of blast furnaces all day, she bent to jittering needles in a sewing loft. They came home then to this block, through a loud city, avoided clanging streetcars and saloons that screamed like red parrots along their way. Through a million shriekings they ran back to their parlour, their blue light, their comfortable chairs, and their silence.[79]

These mysterious tenants live in absolute silence and almost total darkness; not the slightest sound from a radio, television, telephone, or kitchen appliance, not even a conversation, emanates from their quarters, illuminated by a single twenty-five-watt bulb, their only concession to civilization. The pale blue glimmer of the light bulb reflects on hundreds of bottles scattered about the floor and on bookshelves, thus becoming a source of natural light. They have neither paper nor books and burn the magazines lent to them by their Anglo-American neighbors without reading them. Like two "little mice," they scurry around furtively in a noisy and demoniac world. They avoid their landlord, paying their rent three months in advance to reduce contact to the minimum. One day, the Mexican man breaks out of his usual silence, shouting: "I don't like you. Too much *noise*. I don't like you. You're too crazy."[80] The contrast of two parallel worlds, nature and super-industrialized society, is one of the recurring elements of Bradbury's works.[81] This is a fantastic but moving variant, an improbable story of two *campesinos* transplanted to the city, the very heart of civilization, unable to settle there.

The theme of Mexican-Americans' familiarity with death and the supernatural, and their belief that they live in a world peopled with spirits, is taken up in a partially folkloric, partially fantastic manner in one novel and two short stories discussed here. Goodwyn's fablelike novel *The Magic of Limping John*[82] centers on John Luna, a crippled itinerant violinist who has become a sorcerer in spite of himself. To convince him of his magic powers, one of his friends, taking advantage of his momentary absence, substitutes a live baby for the dead infant just brought to him by a distraught father. Thus manipulated by Don Fabian, a real scoundrel, he becomes a *curandero* ("healer") and rapidly makes his fortune. He becomes so corrupted by success that not even the discovery of the original hoax shakes him, until finally, overcome with remorse, he smashes his violin while playing at his own wedding. In the last scene, he tries in vain to use sorcery to repair his instrument. In a setting not remotely pastoral, with characters who are swindlers and innocents rather than sages, the author, in a tragicomic tone, laughs at human ignorance and its exploitation. In the only stories that they devote to Mexican-Americans, both Harris and Marriott depict a retarded youth. The brief story by Harris, "Mex," is included in an anthology of science fiction; it takes place, the author informs us, "near the Mexican border, where men are closer than we are to ancestral memories and to the ancient things which dwell in the shadows. . . ."[83] "El Zopilote," Marriott's human vulture, gorges himself at funerals; the story is a parody of the *velorio*, the Mexican wake. The young hero, himself a living skeleton, lies in wait for funeral processions; on the public square he is: ". . . a skeleton figure of grotesque, ragged movement. With a swirl of arms and coat-tails, the boy swooped upon the funeral procession, establishing himself in a place just behind the bier and the eight men who carried it."[84]

Let's leave the macabre and proceed to a few humorous interpretations of Mexican-American primitivism. Bradbury and Barrett sketch out three playlets on the order of *Tortilla Flat*: joyous children of nature, unconcerned about tomorrow, imbued with a deep sense of camaraderie, their characters are often short of money but never of imagination or craftiness. The three jobless men in Bradbury's story "The Wonderful Ice Cream Suit," Vamenos, Martínez and Villanazul, see a handsome Mexican-American in an elegant white summer suit pass by with a woman on each arm. Attributing his success to the suit, they chip in, along with three other cronies, to raise the sixty dollars needed for the purchase of "this marvelous suit as white as ice cream," as white as Quetzalcoatl, "the Great White God come from the East."[85] They agree that each will have the right to wear it for a half-hour at night. This zany story, punctuated with "*madre mía*," "*compadres*," and "*caramba*," ends in an homage to poverty and friendship. Martínez curses "this suit which belonged to them but which owned them all,"[86] adding: "If we ever get rich . . . it'll be kind of sad. Then we'll all have suits. And there won't be no more nights like tonight. It'll break up the old gang. It'll never be the same after that."[87] It's as though Danny of *Tortilla Flat* were speaking. The hilarious Bradbury story "En la Noche"[88] emphasizes the Mexican sense of solidarity: which man will sacrifice himself to console Mrs. Navárrez, the lonely woman whose husband has enlisted in the army and whose sobbing keeps everyone in the barrio awake at night?

Among Barrett's workers,[89] we find the two character traits illustrated in the Bradbury stories: lightheartedness and camaraderie. The workers make plans among themselves to enjoy the money that they do not yet possess; time and again, they ask for salary advances on false pretexts; they do not hesitate to quit their jobs once "Señor Payroll," the paymaster, tries to put a stop to these abuses. Since regulations prohibit rehiring them for at least thirty days, they reapply under assumed names and, as a result, some of the most famous names in Latin American history turn up on the payroll. Their cunning gets the best of Señor Payroll.

Right alongside Bradbury and Barrett's merry Mexicans, spiritual brothers of Steinbeck's *paisanos*, we find Granat's *campesina*, so different from the tragic image of feminine stoicism he conveys in the story "To Endure." In "Sánchez and the Víbora: A New Mexican Tale," he portrays Doña Agneda Herrera, the mother of thirteen, as a peasant as solid as the earth she labors on for Perfecto M. Sánchez. Granat begins by duly praising the physical robustness and moral strength of the *peona*. He uses images taken from nature, as did others who nostalgically celebrated the virtues of the *campesina*, but the resemblance stops there. He initially compares her to a Mexican pyramid ("a handsome square adobe-brown face and a shape as square and solid as a block quarried for a pyramid to Quetzalcoatl");[90] however, humor surfaces in this eulogy and soon transforms the *campesina* into a mock-heroic character. This robust woman, like the mountain who is afraid of the mouse, trembles at the sight of a snake:

> When sickness, birth, death, catastrophe struck, she stood as a rock among the weaker souls. She could work as hard as a man, ten or twelve hours in the sun. And yet, small reptiles of any kind, snakes, toads . . . would send her screaming like a little girl. A beautiful combination of femininity and strength, like the great pink breasty mountains of New Mexico.[91]

Later on, this mountain of strength melts away in the sun: "Arroyos ran down the slopes of her face, over the hillocks of her collarbones and disappeared in a torrent down the canyon of her chest."[92] Sánchez is well aware of Doña Agneda's physical endurance, which he exploits, and her weakness, which he ridicules. But one day he mistakes a tractor tread fallen in the grass for a snake, is overcome by fright, and calls for help from the *peona*; then in an outburst of magnanimity, she sufficiently overcomes her fear to think of the life of her irascible boss. Granat once again depicts, but in here in a comic mode, the strength of the *campesina* and her superiority over her male counterpart.

The Spanish in these stories is no longer used for exoticism, but rather to accentuate the humor of certain primitive traits in the characters. For example, when Granat uses the words "marinated in Spanish," it's not to evoke our pity on the problem of assimilation but to make us laugh at the misadventures of the Mexican-American Sánchez and his ineptness with anything mechanical.

His truck remains an enigma and provides him daily with unpleasant surprises, which he greets with loud but ineffectual shouts of "*cabrón*," or "*sanamagán*."[93] Sánchez considers *sanamagán* stronger and more vulgar than *cabrón* because it's an English swear word! This does not prevent him from then piously murmuring "*La voluntad de Dios* [God's will]" as he makes the sign of the cross. One day the brakes give out ("*brecas fregadas* [damned brakes]," the little man shouts); another morning it is a breakdown that he attributes to a "*chorte* [short circuit]." The author explains, as if to justify the driver's incompetence: "automotive terms were always English words (the Conquistadores were not motorized) marinated in Spanish."[94] He is then seen "*monkeyando* [monkeying]," vainly fiddling around with the motor, and so forth. The terms *brecas*, *chorte*, and *monkeyando*, are *pochismos*, Hispanicized English words, such as those used by all Mexican-Americans regardless of age. The *pochismo* is different from the *pachuco* dialect, which contains a strong dose of American slang, is spoken exclusively by young lower-class people, and is incomprehensible to the rest of the minority to which Sánchez belongs.

Purely Spanish words, along with English words "marinated in Spanish," thrown in here and there in certain works, also contribute to the exaggeration technique sought by the writers studied previously and designed to offer an image of Mexican-American primitivism capable of disarming, of making the "civilized" reader smile or even laugh out loud.

The henceforth familiar image of the Mexican-American as a child of nature therefore, seemed still to prevail in a certain category of writers of the postwar period; this modern romantic vision responded to the same need as in the past and also elicited the same reservations.

The same sense of identification may be observed in the Anglo-American. Nothing would have given Sal Paradise (alias Jack Kerouac)—who finally realized his dream of being "a man of the earth" during his time with Terry in a squalid camp—greater pleasure than to be mistaken for a Mexican by the neighbors in the next tent: "They thought I was Mexican, of course; and in a way I am."[95]

As always, this eulogy to the noble savage contained an implicit criticism of the industrialized and commercialized society of the United States; also as always, the need to fill a void within himself induced the writer to idealize reality and, by the same token, to situate the Mexican-American problem in the realm of the unreal. Life in Rociada, as described by LaFarge through the recollections of his wife, was so idyllic that it is impossible to avoid suspecting an unconscious embellishment of the facts. The writer himself, in his preface, seems to anticipate such criticism:

> One of the aims of this book is to record a fair picture of a way of life that has ceased to exist. Left-wingers will immediately object that the relations between the *patrones* and the workers cannot have been as idyllic as they appear here, to which part of my answer is that one must stick to his data, which in this case is the memory of the *patrones*, gilded by time.[96]

Enraptured by the life radiating from the barrios, Kerouac remained blind to the ugliness of the tent camps: "There were a bed, a stove, and a cracked mirror hanging from a pole; it was delightful."[97]

What we receive, then, from these idealists who could not resist the happiness of a lost paradise or the temptations of a utopia, is the image of a world on the periphery of the real one, crystallized and just as resistant to change as Rociada, "a clear pool into which the stream of time trickled and then stood still."[98] As attested to by the tenacious survival of the stereotypes, these writers retreated into an attitude that venerated the past; they could not envision the Mexican minority as a people on the march toward a problematic future, struggling to make itself visible in the eyes of the majority and to assume this visibility in relation both to Anglo-American society and to the Mexican community. Primitivism, no matter what its virtues, was no solution.

. . . A timid, sensitive, confused fellow, trying to hold his own in two worlds and not succeeding in either. [1]

CHAPTER 9

The Barrio: Refuge and Trap

In the postwar period, more Anglo-American literature was devoted to the Mexican problem than during the preceding decade. In general, it was timely, containing more specific details and a less subtle irony; it was directed at a majority of the population, which preferred to ignore it. The writers took an interest in the turmoil, covert struggle, and slow maturation of Mexican-Americans that took place in the confused period between World War II and the beginning of the 1960s. Some confusion also afflicted the Anglos: even though liberalism had made advances since the Depression and the Democrats' rise to power, racism persisted and was given new life during the 1950s by the specter of communism. If not actually hostile to minority groups, the general public remained at least indifferent to their problems. This was especially true of Mexican-Americans, who were even less visible at that time than Blacks.

Writers of good will, often clumsy in their desire to uncover the truth, ran into hostility or indifference from the public, just as in many novels the "peon-lover" [2] was thwarted by his racist adversaries. The reception given the realistic works of this period is significant. Let us look at "A Fistful of Alamo Heroes" (1950), a story by Sylvan Karchmer, and Edna Ferber's well-known novel *Giant* (1952). Karchmer's tale is the fictional story of a novel that should be published but is not; an editor rejects it because its hero is Mexican-American. The clever narrator of the story succeeds in relating the substance of the unwritten novel by describing the disillusionments he has suffered as a novelist. The hero of his would-be novel is a soldier, De León, whose exemplary behavior during the war he admired. The displeased publisher "in no uncertain terms" advises the fictional author "to relegate him to a subordinate place in the novel";

but the author cannot bring himself to present a less "visible" and less trouble-some "phony De León, modeled in large part on the Mexican characters in other writers."[3] He prefers instead to remain silent, a prudent silence that will protect him from the wrath of the dominant society. Perhaps one day, as his publisher advises him, he will write of the "handful of Anglo-Saxon heroes" who distinguished themselves at the Alamo.

Determined to write a best seller, novelist Edna Ferber traveled to Texas in search of something sensational. Similarly, her heroine, Leslie Lynnton of Virginia, after marrying a Texas cattle baron, Jordan Benedict, sets off to discover Texas. The young muckraker is intent on getting involved in matters that don't concern her. "You ain't supposed to be in there,"[4] she is constantly reminded. In this epic of the great white cattle barons, the novelist tried to expose an empire based in part on the exploitation of Mexican labor.[5] The book caused a scandal in Texas and provoked the anger of this "giant," but it delighted the rest of the nation. However, the meanness of the giant and the poverty of the Mexican-Americans went unnoticed,[6] according to the critics.[7]

In the majority of works of this period about the Mexican problem, the point of view is American. In *Trial*, the 1955 novel by Don Mankiewicz, the hero is an Anglo intern breaking into the justice system during the trial of a young Mexican-American. *Border City* (1945), by Hart Stilwell, relates the in-surmountable difficulties of Dave Atwood, a young journalist who undertakes the defense of a Mexican-American woman seduced by a powerful Anglo politician in a Texas border town. In William Barrett's *The Shadows of the Images* (1954), Tom Logan, police commissioner in a large city in Colorado, alias Denver, is torn between the racial prejudice toward Mexican-Americans endemic to people in his position and more humanitarian feelings. Four writers, however, tried to describe Mexican reality from the point of view of Mexican-Americans themselves. The Claud Garner novel *Wetback* (1942) relates the difficulties young Dionisio Jesus Molina encounters on both sides of the Rio Grande. After many trying experiences, he finally realizes his dream of obtaining American citizenship. In *The Naked and the Dead* (1948), Norman Mailer records the personal drama of soldier Julio Martinez in a vast literary fresco that examines eight Americans, all from different ethnic groups. In their diversity, they symbolize the United States and all of humanity. Each of these potential war fatalities has his own approach to life and is the product of his environment. The Irving Shulman novel *The Square Trap* (1953) takes us inside a Mexican family. But it is the psychologist and sociologist Beatrice Griffith who best grasps intimate Mexican-American reality in "In the Flow of Time" (1949) and "American Me" (1948), two brief narratives that are more reportage than creative writing. "American Me" appears in *Literatura Chicana*, an anthology of literary statements on Mexican-Americans.

These works show no interest in the acculturated Mexican-American middle class, concerning themselves only with the proletariat, those generally perceived to be incapable of assimilating. We will dwell neither on LaFarge's memoirs, *Behind the Mountains*, about a family perfectly integrated into Anglo society, nor on Fergusson's novel *The Conquest of Don Pedro*. Set at the end of the nineteenth century, this work describes, in overly idealized fashion, the emancipation of Magdalena Vierra, niece of an eminent villager. Under the influence of a wandering Jew, Leo Mendes, the young Mexican–American woman acquires a perfect command of English and thereby achieves a synthesis of two cultures, the synthesis that the author dreamed of seeing in the American Southwest.

The realistic literature of the postwar period, by contrast, emphasized everything that went against this desired symbiosis. It stressed the growing impossibility of barrio Mexican-Americans' ever integrating into the existing social structures. Caught between two cultures, each of which rejected them, they resembled the real De León, whom Karchmer's luckless novelist would have liked to depict, "a timid, sensitive, confused fellow, trying to hold his own in two worlds and not succeeding in either."[8] Their broken English, which writers attempted to render as faithfully as possible, gave testimony to their precarious situation. In spite of more liberal legislation, they faced discrimination in housing, education, employment, and legal matters, which made them marginal in the dominant society. Inhibited by an inferiority complex and a language handicap, they often gave up trying to overcome their alienation and took refuge in the barrio. Many, however, sought to escape from the barrio and blend into the Anglo population. Others felt deeply disturbed by an increasingly acute identity problem; they expressed their sad dilemma in the anarchical form of *pachuquismo*. Still others, who shared a common conception of *la Raza* ("the people"), were shaping a protest movement, as yet covert. These diverse behavior patterns caused estrangement not only within the Mexican-American community but within individual families as well.

Alienated from the Anglo World: Invisible in the Barrio

"Where are the Mexicans? It's all about Spain, and Mexico and old Texas. Where are they?"[9] asks Leslie Benedict in "Giant" after attending the Fiesta de Vientecito. Mexicans take part in the parade only as "props"; the real participants are all Anglos. They lend their prestigious names, such as Hernando de Soto and Coronado, to sumptuous hotels, in which they themselves are forbidden to stay; to Edna Ferber, Texas is like a gigantic parade, a dazzling conjuring away of half of reality: ". . . the lush new hotels and the anachronistic white-pillared mansions; the race horses in rich pasture, the swimming pools . . . the cattle herds . . . cotton fields and Martian chemical plants" draw the attention of the billionaires flying to fellow billionaire Jett Rink's party more than "the grey dust-bitten shanties of the Mexican barrios."[10]

Mexican-Americans are "invisible," living in segregation. Though slightly less dark-skinned than Blacks, they are treated the same way. When the indiscreet Leslie insists upon seeing Nopal, the Mexican shantytown on the outskirts of Benedict, the Anglo city, Jett Rink informs her what awaits her:

> "Nothing. Only Mexicans. It's Benedict only they call it Nopal like it's another town. It's like real Mexico, I don't guess there's two white people living there."
> "White. You mean—but the Mexicans aren't—"
> "They sure ain't white, for my money. Two Americans, then. Maybe you like that better."[11]

The Black ghetto, especially after the war, was rarely as shabby as the Mexican barrio, swollen as it was by a flood of penniless and jobless immigrants. The novel by Barrett clearly establishes that Mexican-Americans had a lower social status than Blacks. Their neighborhoods indicate this difference in status: Gin Hill, the Black section of fictional State City, is more attractive than the Second Ward, where the most underprivileged Hispanic-Americans have replaced other minority groups who fled after becoming more affluent.

The war brought little change in attitude; despite laws prohibiting discrimination in housing, *de facto* residential segregation persisted. This is one cause of the dramatic problem of Angel Chávez, the young Mexican-American in Mankiewicz's novel *Trial*, set in a small Northern California town in 1947. Angel attends San Juno High School, but lives in Juno Flats, the area tacitly reserved for those of his race. The beach is reserved solely for the village residents and is thus off-limits to him, though he runs the risk of going there to meet a young white girl. Seasonal workers from the southern part of the state are often incapable of reading the warning sign at the beach. Each time they dare to challenge the regulation, they are duly ejected; though their sufferings are more moral than physical, for

> The worst that might befall a Mexican caught on Village Beach, in cold fact, was that while he was being ejected, chivied back to the sea wall, and up the steps to the road, he might hear an occasional insult.[12]

Mexican-Americans were sometimes denied access to white neighborhoods because they lacked political power, but more often because they were ignorant of the law. Angel is unaware that no law prohibits him from living in the village; he doesn't know that neither white homeowners nor real estate agents can legally prevent him from acquiring a house in the white section, nor that they regularly take advantage of Mexicans' inability to stand up for their rights to keep them locked into the barrio.

Trauma at the Schoolhouse

Less pervasive than housing discrimination, but perhaps more damaging, educational segregation and indifference to the problems of Mexican-American schoolchildren also delayed integration into American society.[13] These educational problems, a burning issue in Mexican-American literature in the 1940s and 1950s,[14] were considered only briefly and superficially by Anglo-American writers. However, the fight for school integration was foremost among the postwar activities of Karchmer's hero, De León. In her novel, contemporaneous with Karchmer's short story, Ferber took issue with the segregation still rampant in Texas schools after the war, and with the harshness of Anglo-American teachers toward Mexican-American students. Her heroine, Leslie Benedict, includes the educational situation in her Texas probings and visits the ranch school reserved for the children of Mexican workers. The enrollment in the single class is too large and diverse (students from ages four to fifteen) and the teacher speaks only English. Later, after the war, when Leslie tries to establish a ranch school open to both races, she meets nothing but incomprehension from her acquaintances. The author dwells at length on the behavior of the teacher, whom she depicts very unfavorably: in Texas against her wishes and in a Mexican school to boot, she carries out her duties with little enthusiasm. (Teaching positions in the barrio, as in the Black ghetto, were often given to those in disfavor.) She has a disagreeable air: ". . . a thin sallow woman in a drab dark dress. A fretful-looking woman with fine black eyes whose heavy brows met over her nose in a dark forbidding brush."[15] The strictness of Miss Cora Dart is reflected in the very sounds of her names; her last name, like the "look of pure hate" cast by this woman's eyes, makes one think of "the red darting flash of a snake's tongue."[16] When Leslie inquires about the number of years she has taught at Reata, Miss Dart responds venomously: "Too long for my own good. . . . They've had about a million teachers here, first and last."[17] This picture, drawn with broad brushstrokes and obviously designed to strike the imagination, nevertheless gives us a view of the atmosphere coloring a barrio child's first contact with Anglo society. Children also were shuttled about from one place to another because of their parents' itinerant work; this additional handicap is mentioned briefly by Barrett when he describes the seasonal work of beet-pickers in Colorado. In 1954, when Barrett wrote his novel, child-labor and mandatory school-attendance laws apparently were not enforced for migrant workers; rural schools simply turned away this flood of young nomads. Many Americans, concluding that young Mexicans were intellectually inferior, blamed their educational failures on racial characteristics, rather than on wretched environmental conditions and culturally disadvantaged families. Tom Logan, Barrett's hero, constantly faces the problems of barrio youngsters unable to acquire occupational training. He arrives at the same conclusion: ". . . they were the people of the deserts, of the herds, of the sun crops, bewildered by the requirements of a civilization that despised them."[18] One can understand why the myth of the Mexican-American's suitability only for agricultural work died hard.

The Exploited Worker: The Vaquero, the Seasonal Farm Worker, the Wetback

Thrown into life and American society with insufficient intellectual skills, young Mexican-Americans from the barrio were relegated to menial jobs formerly reserved for Blacks. Two types of workers appear in postwar literature: the traditional *vaquero* and the seasonal farm worker, who arrived either legally or illegally as a wetback. The image of the fruit or vegetable picker, back bent over in the sun, began to replace that of the laborer working on railroad construction.

Ferber praised the manliness and proud elegance of the *vaqueros* of Reata, whom she saw as the descendants of the "Mexican horsemen whose land this Texas had been little more than a century ago." [19] Fascinated by the artfulness of their work, which tempered its harshness, she describes them "working in this inferno of heaving flesh and choking dust and noise and movement and daring and danger and brutal beauty." [20] But the novelist's real objective was to reveal the "smallness" of this "giant," the ugliness hidden beneath so much beauty. The beauty of the *vaqueros*, like everything else in Texas, was nothing more than a mask. While J. H. Allen, intent on demythologizing the *vaqueros* in his own way, emphasized the prosaic roughness of their tasks,[21] Ferber uncovered the sordid side of their lives; these people whose forebears had been dispossessed were still experiencing the effects of this plundering of long ago. In her novel, the *vaqueros* live with their families right on the Benedict ranch, where quasi-feudal relations still exist between employers and employees. Their primitive living quarters are even more comfortless than the huts of Black sharecroppers of the same period. *Vaquero* Angel Obregon's shanty is decrepit and lacks basic conveniences: "The floor of the little wood and adobe hut was broken so that you actually could see the earth over which it stood." [22] His sick wife and ailing newborn make the place seem even more desolate. The novelist concludes, ironically: "So this splintered shanty was the house of one of those splendid bronze gods on horseback." [23] These contrasting tableaux illuminate the positive and negative sides of the *vaquero*'s life, including his scandalous exploitation.

The fate of the migrant worker, who, unlike the *vaquero*, did not enjoy the advantages of a regular job and residence, was even more pitiful. Edna Ferber vehemently denounced the ugliness, dilapidation, and unhealthfulness of the shacks in migrant camps: ". . . the open latrines, fly-covered, an abomination beneath the noonday sun." [24] The father of Tomas Cantanios, the hero of Shulman's novel *The Square Trap*, emigrates to the United States in 1919 and for many years knows only the life of the work camp: his children are all born in camps and two of them die there, one of dysentery and the other for lack of medical care.

American employers took advantage of these seasonal laborers, whom they did not have to feed once the harvest was over.[25] This capitalistic exploitation was denounced by Barrett, who was shocked by the situation of sugar beet-pickers in Colorado, where he was living:

> The working peon was not a very great problem, but when the short beet season was over, he was nobody's responsibility. The farmer paid him off, the sugar company refused to become involved with him, the labor contractor was elsewhere, and the small towns would not let him linger, loiter, or look for work.[26]

Vicky Leighton, Tom Logan's liberal friend, empathizes with the migrant workers, whom she compares to the "displaced persons"[27] of Europe. She believes the sugar companies should be forced to provide year-round jobs for them. Tom replies that any legal suit would be fruitless, since the guilty party is uncertain—is it the sugar company, the beet farmer, or the labor contractor?

In Shulman's novel, the problems of the immigrant worker are personified by the moving figure of old Vidal Cantanios, the hero's father. In 1919, he leaves Mexico to escape poverty, the persecution to which the followers of Zapata were subjected, and the harassment of the *federales*;[28] the picture painted by the author is exceedingly dark. Cantanios finds even more precarious living and working conditions in the United States:

> In California he was not exploited and abused by soldiers, but by farmers, foremen, storekeepers, labor contractors, sheriffs and their deputies, and armed guards who kept him in his place, terrorized him if he wished to protest an injustice, and enslaved him because he did not know the laws, the language, or the customs. And very often the law, the language and the customs were changed to keep him in his place as a ten-cents-an-hour transient stoop laborer.[29]

His years in the United States are nothing more than a long series of disappointments and humiliations:

> He heard himself promised one wage and saw himself paid another. Several times he was thrown into jail and was beaten by deputies because he complained. Once his sentence was suspended and he was paroled in the custody of the farmer, who made him work out the season; when the season was over the farmer ordered him out of the camp and paid him nothing.[30]

The immigrant worker's situation prior to the 1930s justified the severity of Shulman's indictment.[31] When the story begins, just after World War II, Vidal is unemployed; he drinks to forget his free time, which weighs heavily on him, and the shame of not being able to support his family adequately. Handicapped by age, deprived, as in the past, of any union support, losing out to wetbacks and "border jumpers,"[32] he despairs of ever again finding a job. The aging, jobless laborer, like so many others, ends up leaving his home because it is impossible to live up to his family responsibilities or maintain his dignity before his children. We experience this drama, and the reactions it provokes in the son, from the viewpoint of the characters themselves, not through an outside observer, as in Ferber's book. This intimacy is one of the book's major achievements.

The wetbacks (*mojados*), or the "border jumpers," worked for practically nothing if a rancher promised to hide them and help them remain in California or Texas. Their illegality gave them an even lower status than the contracted seasonal workers. The tragedy of these "illegals," the most destitute of the immigrants, invariably unfolded in the same way: Act I, the economic conditions in Mexico are so bad that "whatever they're paid it's more than they'd get home in Mexico starving to death."[33] Act II, the passage:

> About fifty, sixty thousand of these wetbacks slip out of Mexico every year, swim or wade the Rio Grande where it's shallow, travel by night and hole up by day. The Border Patrol and the immigration boys and Rangers, and all, they can't keep all of them out. Sometimes they make it, a lot of 'em are caught and thrown back. Sometimes they're shot by mistake, sometimes they wander around and starve . . .[34]

Uncle Bawley explains to a horrified Leslie. Garner, the author of *Wetback*, also describes these rites of passage. On the banks of the Rio Grande, where some children are swimming about, young Chepe explains to his companion, Dionisio Molina, the procedures to follow for the crossing:

> ". . . each time I cross I take some clothes, and if the law don't stop me, I hide them over there on the Texas side; and if they see me I pretend I'm just swimming and come back across."
> "Sounds very simple, but what if they catch you after you are on the other side?"
> "Do just as they tell you; don't never run away . . .
> "They will only take you back to the river and tell you to vamoose back across to Mexico; but if you run, they will shoot you like a snake."[35]

Act III, a sinister character arrives on stage:

> . . . [he] lives off of them; he sneaks them across the border from Mexico to work as pickers and then when they're here, by the time he's through with them they don't have nothing left when they get through working in the Valley crops.[36]

He's the "coyote," the recruiter of wetbacks, the twentieth-century slave trafficker whose treachery Ferber denounces in Chapter 14 of her novel.

Act IV, the boss takes over from the labor contractor in exploiting this vulnerable labor force. He can threaten them with blackmail at the slightest sign of rebellion: "Do you want me to turn you in? . . . and back to Chihuahua with you?"[37]

Act V, after the harvest; what to do with the seasonal worker? ". . . kick them back across the border where they belong."[38] Resident Mexican-Americans also showed hostility toward wetbacks who tried to settle in the barrio, to stay in the United States.

Giving in yet again to her penchant for richly colored literary portraits, Ferber in Chapter 19 dwells once more on the tragedy of the wetbacks. She describes a young boy who crosses the Rio Grande and covers a hundred or so miles on foot, then hides away in the armory of Uncle Bawley's ranch. Here Leslie discovers him half-dead of fatigue and starvation. The pathos is heightened both by the fugitive's youth and the cavalier reaction of Leslie's uncle to this routine problem:

> "This skin-and-bones says he's been eating rats." ["No!" She was stiff with horror.]
> . . . "But he ought to have come in with the regular Mexican labor lot."[39]

Bawley reflects a general indifference toward the problems of the lower-class Mexican. The author does not miss the opportunity to present a grim image: "A boy, dark ragged shaking, was flattened against the white-washed wall, the palms of his hands were spread against it like one crucified. . . ."[40]

The illegal immigrant never completely escaped the specter of deportation, which recurs like an obsession throughout Garner's novel. The novel is set around 1920, when deportation already was a fact of life for the undocumented worker but well before the massive repatriations of the 1950s. Young Dionisio is constantly threatened with discovery while he is hiding in the cactus and mesquite thickets, or being tracked to his workplace by the Ranger, his worst enemy. The lawman's attitude toward this new "outlaw" reflects the contempt that long prevailed against the "Mexican" in the borderlands. The arrested wetback had but two options, as the prison guard explains to Dionisio:

> V R means voluntary return. They book you as wanting to go back home, and no bad charge is filed against you; so you can swim the river again the next night and be back here for work . . . but if they file charges and you are deported, then that's something serious. You can't come back for two years, and if you do, and they catch you, it will be tough because most likely you'll get a fine and a prison sentence.[41]

Garner's young wetback overcomes every obstacle with such ease that the book provoked serious criticism among Chicanos.[42] These critics reproached the Anglo-American writer for presenting the United States in an overly favorable light; the hero, who always meets with success, is too much like a Horatio Alger hero. His case is exceptional and unconvincing; he has an American father, who endowed him with tall stature and red hair, so he is never penalized for his physical features. As the critics noted, racism is minimized; Dionisio does have several misadventures; he is sent away by the father of the young

American girl he loves, an officer of the Border Patrol mistreats him for not using the ritual "Sir," and so forth. However, the two cattlemen who successively hire and exploit him (they obtain not just cheap but free labor by having the wetbacks deported just before payday) are themselves of Mexican origin.

However, in a period when the country was not yet genuinely sensitive to the problems of minorities, the author honestly tried to rouse public opinion, even at the risk of sinking into melodrama or affectation.

A more convincing work, James K. Bowman's short story "El Patrón," deserves closer scrutiny, not for its documentary value, but for its psychological dimension and atmosphere, which the author succeeded in creating in just a few pages. The story's brevity, the style's density, and the denouement's moderate tone make the drama that occurs between El Patrón ("the Boss"), Matthew Fennel, and Chapo infinitely more tragic than anything Ferber's vehement pen could ever have written. The plot has a classic simplicity. El Patrón and the Mexican have been working together in total silence for several months, ever since Chapo was hired to make adobe; he is to be paid and taken back to the river whenever the other chooses. Threatened with denunciation to the immigration authorities for the slightest lapse, the wetback bends his back in labor without ever giving a hint of his hatred for his boss: "There was no answer. Chapo looked down at his feet, like a dog being punished."[43] One day Matthew falls into his cistern; in anguish, he listens for his employee's footsteps, hoping that the Mexican will hand down the ladder leaning against the tank. Chapo finally arrives:

> The ladder creaked as Chapo climbed. The familiar black sombrero with brown leather band came up, a silhouette against the sky. Grimy hair hid the ears and made the head appear large and rectangular. The face showed teeth but had no expression.
> "Drop the ladder down inside," Matthew ordered, lifting his head slightly. "Did you bring water?"
> But the dark face was no longer there, and as he strained to locate it, he saw the two knobs of the ladder disappear. He heard it fall on the sand with a dry rattle of old wood.[44]

Without departing from his usual silence, Chapo, the wetback, takes his revenge. Only a long series of humiliations could have provoked such a savage act from this defenseless man.

The plight of unskilled migrant Mexican workers was pitiful. With the exception of a few people of good will, who were indignant but powerless, the majority of the population seemed oblivious. Barrett mentions the role El Socorrido ("relief") had played[45] since the Depression; public welfare programs indeed alleviated suffering but were nothing more than stopgap measures. We will return to this issue later.

The Partiality of American Justice

The poor people jammed together in the barrio aroused the wariness of the police even more than Blacks did; in the judicial system, the Mexican-American was also the victim of prejudice. Writers did not present a totally negative image of the police; not a single scene of police repression appears in any of the works discussed. However, in her brief narrative on the Los Angeles race riots of 1943, Beatrice Griffith stresses the inaction of the police and the evident pleasure with which they watched American sailors beat up young Mexican-Americans from the barrio, in particular those dressed in *pachuco* zoot suits.[46] Tom Logan, entrusted with maintaining order in the barrio of Denver, alias State City, is torn between his racism and more charitable sentiments. Shulman's *pachucos* win the pity of one police officer: called by a Beverly Hills restaurant that refuses to serve them, he soon realizes that he is not dealing with troublemakers. Moved by their situation, he demands that the restaurant serve the young men, and even eats with them and pays the check. His attitude is an exception, as clearly shown by Barrett's novel *The Shadows of the Images*. The contempt and mistrust police have for the "Mexican" is aggravated by rumors about barrio youth, that, for example, most of them carry knives as soon as they are able to walk or that they have razor blades hidden in the soles of their shoes. By and large, to the contemporary policeman the Mexican-American man was what he had been to the frontier vigilante: the man with the knife. Tom Logan maintains that his work in the barrio is more difficult than his colleague's in Gin Hill, the Black neighborhood, and that the city no longer considered Blacks to be troublemakers. The low social status of Mexican-Americans contributed to their low standing with the police, who were additionally irritated by constraints placed on them by civil rights advocates.

Automatically suspect in the eyes of the police, Mexican-Americans were less likely than whites to get a fair trial. Three novels, *Border City* by Stilwell,[47] *Trial* by Mankiewicz, and *The Shadows of the Images* by Barrett, deal with this judicial inequality, caused in large part by the pressure placed on judges and juries by the local Anglo majority. A judge's dependence on the voters often made him a representative of racism; Mexican plaintiffs or defendants, who lived on the fringes of political life or whose votes were bought by corrupt and opportunistic *políticos* ("politicians"), found themselves deprived of legal protection. In each of the three novels, an idealistic Anglo-American who tries to defend the oppressed is unable to win his case.

In his dedication, Stilwell ironically quoted Jefferson on the basic equality of all men; he set his novel in Border City, Texas, along the border, where racial conflicts were particularly acute; the time is the beginning of the Second World War. A Mexican-American woman has been seduced by a white man who is the most influential politician in town; his position prevents her from normal recourse to the judicial system. Young journalist Dave Atwood learns of the scandal, but the politician's clever maneuvers doom his naive, idealistic efforts to failure.

Mankiewicz's novel centers on the 1947 trial of a young Mexican condemned for an imaginary crime. A young white woman has died of a heart attack. Though she was not raped, Angel Chavez is accused of this crime, a violation of the supreme racial taboo. The case, which causes great excitement in the little northern California town of San Juno, is exploited by various Anglo groups. The forces of the Establishment, upholders of certain racial, social, and moral standards, make their views known through a newspaper called, significantly, *The Standard*. The liberal, even radical, elements, rally around young lawyer David Blake and Consuelo Chavez, mother of the accused. The People's party tries to turn the trial into another Sacco and Vanzetti affair. Some details are reminiscent of racially charged trials in the South, in particular the Scottsboro case in Alabama, in which the Communist party became involved.[48] In a rather improbable scene, the town population, thirsting for a lynching, gathers around the prison, singing to the tune of "John Brown's Body," with new words adapted for the occasion. Everyone from the United Daughters of Pacific America to the Unitarian church conspires against David and his young client; the choice of a Black judge adds a disquieting note to the case. Angel is convicted without possibility of appeal because David is easily outmaneuvered by more experienced attorneys.

Barrett takes pains to demonstrate the arbitrariness of the justice system and the legal inequality between white Americans and Mexican-Americans. At the beginning of the novel, set around 1950, three Mexican-Americans—Tony Pelado and the two Garra brothers—are accused of raping Teresita Rojas. They are acquitted thanks to Frank Zancudo, the all-powerful *político* whose influence in the barrio is well known to the district attorney, himself intent upon securing Zancudo's support during the forthcoming gubernatorial election. This rape, however, is exploited by Beverly Colter, the future sister-in-law of police commissioner Tom Logan. In an attempt to secure a hospital abortion for herself, the Anglo woman falsely accuses the same three men of sexually assaulting her and succeeds in having Tom imprison them. Later, Tom is overcome with remorse and tries to reopen the case. His friends, the future governor of the state among them, try to dissuade him; a clergyman, Father Brennan, finally convinces him to cover up the affair in order to spare his brother. Later on, the tragic murder of little Carmelita García, strangled by her abductor, Luke Taler, is remarkably similar to the Rojas case; the criminal, without evidence, manages to concoct a story implicating some Mexican-Americans. He protests his innocence, though the police no more believe him than they did Beverly Colter. In the end, the guilty man is sent to a psychiatric hospital, a loophole that never would have been available to a Mexican-American.

The documentary values of these three novels exceed their artistic ones. Psychological analysis and style are sacrificed somewhat to the demands of thesis. Three pessimistic novels, brimming with good intentions, show an overly candid liberalism inevitably doomed to failure: three testimonies to Anglo guilt over inequality before the law.

The Mexican-Americans Confront Their Alienation

How did Mexican-Americans react in the face of continued discrimination, even after the war? Three attitudes may be distinguished: silence, the attempt to assimilate, and the rejection of assimilation. The drive to succeed in the Anglo world sometimes led Mexican-Americans to deny their brothers and sisters, estranging themselves from their own community. The drama of alienation also took place within the family itself. The older generation remained faithful to traditional culture while the new generation no longer considered it an effective means of dealing with Anglo-American society.

Refuge in the Barrio

"Why were they so stern and silent? They hardly looked at us,"[49] exclaims Ferber's young heroine after meeting the *vaqueros* of the ranch.

> It was curious, their manner, not unfriendly but withdrawn . . . as though they wished to be as unnoticeable as possible. They moved silently . . .[50]

To Leslie, the servants also seem difficult to approach. Faithful to their old tactic of withdrawal, as noted by Parkman[51] and later by London,[52] the Mexican-Americans withdraw into silence as though it were a mask that makes them invisible. Their perpetually unsmiling faces, their fleeting glances are disconcerting. Leslie thinks nostalgically of "the submissive masks of the Negroes" in her native Virginia,[53] and also, perhaps, of their joyfulness, reassuring to whites. According to Octavio Paz, a Mexican's silence is a mask hiding a deep sense of inferiority, but one that may fall away unpredictably.[54] This tendency to explode without warning is the subject of two short stories. We already know of the terrible fate that Bowman's wetback has in reserve for his employer. Helen Stevens creates a pathetic old woman, Tonita, who bears in silence the separation from her daughter, imposed by her son-in-law, until she finds traces of violence on the young woman's body. Then one day,

> Tonita slowly unwound her shawl, turning its silken length into a loose rope. With one swift movement of arms made powerful by a lifetime of heavy labor she threw it over his head, tightening it around his neck . . .[55]

Besides these spectacular outbursts, there are attempts at protest, such as the one by Vidal Cantanios, the migrant worker in Shulman's novel. However, job insecurity, the roughness of working conditions, and the uncertainty of the future elicit in him feelings of insecurity and helplessness that reduce him to inertia. "Fear" characterizes old Cantanios, he is "afraid to take risks," "his hands were stigmata of defeat,"[56] he is "afraid" to leave the Los Angeles barrio of Chavez Ravine to live elsewhere. In the warm and familiar atmosphere of the barrio, near his blood brothers, the worker forgets his struggles and failures and relaxes. The same is true of the inhabitants of the Mexican town of Nopal, Jett explains to Leslie in *Giant*:

> "They stick together and can't even talk English, half of 'em. Go around solemn-looking on the outside, but boy! when they get together! Dancing and singing their corridos telling about everything they do, like a bunch of kids."[57]

Childlike qualities and a total lack of political awareness characterize most people in Nopal, Chavez Ravine, and the barrio in State City. Shamelessly manipulated and dominated, they leave everything to a *político* (often an Anglo-American) instead of taking charge of their own cause. Barrett, in particular, stresses this point. The *político* is Zancudo, a petty political tyrant descended from a long line of corrupt Mexican bureaucrats, more concerned with their own interests than those of their constituents. The literature of the preceding decades amply describes them. Zancudo obtains the acquittal of the young Mexicans guilty of the rape of a Mexican, Teresita Rojas, but to avoid alienating his white political allies, he abandons them when they are falsely accused of raping an Anglo-American woman. The *político* could be a man of good will, whether a communist or not,[58] influenced by the spirit of the New Deal; in *The Square Trap* he plays a major role in the life of Diego Seboso, a former beet-picker; after a lifetime of arduous labor, Seboso now lives out his life in saloons, with women, and in a dirty house filled with children. What is the use of putting up a fight? He is taken care of by the *político*: this man of influence intervenes when he is threatened with eviction, or in trouble with the police, or with the social worker who brings the welfare check.

Anglo writers made no mention of the strikes; they stressed that the inertia of the Mexican minority might also encourage white America's own inaction. The barrio, which offered refuge, could also become a trap.

Attempts at Assimilation: The Boxer and the Soldier

Many young barrio Mexicans did not resign themselves to the fringes of American society; they overcame their alienation through extraordinary acts that made them visible to Anglos and gave them access to a better life. The younger generation of the postwar years rejected the abject lives into which their parents, often recent immigrants, had settled. However, in spite of their knowledge of English, these youths remained handicapped by lack of education and inadequate occupational training; the only avenues of social mobility were boxing, the traditional path of the Mexican-American, and the military.

Boxing did not so much permit minorities to assert themselves physically as give them a new sense of value. Barrett's novel presents matches in which most of the boxers are of Mexican origin; Tom Logan explains the reason to his girlfriend:

> He told her about the first decade of the century when the Irish were the despised minority and fighters were nearly all Irish, of the second and third decades when the Jews and Italians were hungry and when Jewish and Italian boys dominated boxing, of the coloured boys, who were always hungry. . . . The history of the prize ring was a study in sociology . . .[59]

London's young hero boxes in order to buy cannons for the revolution; Paco Seboso and Tomas Cantanios see the ring as a rung up the social ladder and a way to improve their families' lot. If the two fathers are "losers," their two sons are fighters in both senses of the word. "Up 'til tonight I was just a *pachuco* kid to the people on the outside. A greaser, a spic, a goddam Mexican and they wanted me to be one forever . . . ,"[60] explains Shulman's young hero to his father after his first victory. He dreams of seeing his family leave the Los Angeles barrio and of finding his father a suitable job. He refuses to let him play a traditional Mexican for tourists, dozing on the ground with a *serape* ("blanket") on his shoulders and a sombrero pushed down over his forehead: "You're not gonna go back to Olvera Street and have those goddam Anglos think you're lazy and stupid."[61] Old Diego Seboso's situation is equally repugnant to his son Paco; when Paco returns from the Army after three years of discipline and cleanliness, he decides to change everything at home by becoming a boxer. A splendid Pontiac bearing his monogram in gold letters is the symbol of his success; in his desire to integrate, he has, like some Blacks, adopted one of the most quintessentially American characteristics, a love of flashy cars.

Shulman's novel concludes on a note of defeat: Tomas gets a stomach injury that cuts short his career as a boxer. Had he been able to continue, his efforts would probably have been in vain anyway, for he is permanently marked by his ethnic origin, despite the Anglicizing of his name to Tommy Kansas. The need for new avenues becomes obvious; when his younger brother, itching to follow in his footsteps, has to give up boxing for lack of ability, Tomas wonders: ". . . what would he be? Another *pachuco* fighter? That wasn't enough."[62] The career of Barrett's hero is also short; Paco believes he will never make a name for himself in boxing, but his brief moment of glory in the ring prevents him from ever again accepting the menial jobs reserved for the uneducated. Just like old Diego, he abandons his ambitions and, like him, he begins to drink. He wanted to be so different from his father, but will he end up in the barrio like him? The novel does not say so explicitly, but the implication is there.

Was the Army a better means of escape and integration? Not one writer offered a positive answer. They emphasized the heroism of Mexican–American soldiers who tried to overcome their ethnic origin through exemplary conduct during World War II, and, conversely, the futility of their efforts. Camaraderie under the flag was a myth. Karchmer writes that his Lieutenant De León was prepared to do anything, that he "was willing to learn anything if it meant acceptance. . . ."[63] Four years of war transform this little lieutenant into a super-man whose heroism in the Italian and French campaigns contrasts with the defeatism of other combat veterans. The author takes pleasure in dwelling on this subject, for it is the central theme of his narrator's unpublishable novel. Mailer's position in The Naked and the Dead was more radical. The social mobility seemingly offered by the Army to the underprivileged with neither jobs nor occupational training was a false hope; human relationships in military life were hindered by the same racial and class barriers that existed on the outside. Among the eight heroes, each from a different ethnic group, Julio Martinez is a Mexican-American from the poor and boisterous barrio of San Antonio. Would the Army make him worthy of white, blond, Protestant women, the private preserve and symbol of the Establishment, whose image obsessed him as a youth?

> Little Mexican boys also breathe the American fables. If they cannot be aviators or financiers or officers they can still be heroes. . . .
> Only that does not make you a white protestant, firm and aloof.[64]

He enlisted in 1937 but soon discovered the disillusionments of military life; he did not allow himself, however, to be discouraged by his slow advancement or the difficult tasks usually given to him alone; he even redoubled his effort to comply: "He would have been perfectly willing to declare the task beyond his strength and give up, but there was a part of his mind that drove him to do things he feared and detested."[65]

Those who foresaw the war as a means of assimilation were soon disappointed. The Zoot Suit Riots in July 1943 occurred a year after the victory over the Japanese at Bataan, a battle marked by fierce fighting and the valiant conduct of Mexican-Americans. But on the home front, the hostility did not let up. Karchmer and Beatrice Griffith, the author of the story "In the Flow of Time," demonstrate that America was being torn apart by war and by internal discord. Finding his little Texas border town divided by racial conflict, Lieutenant De León throws himself into the fight for school integration and is killed by a gang of racist hoodlums. Beatrice Griffith imagined two young Mexican servicemen on leave in Los Angeles at the time of the race riots in 1943. One of them is outraged: "Oh, so you have to wear a goddam uniform before you can be a brother to a man, is that it?"[66] As a result, he wishes to return to Mexico and fight, no longer alongside the gabachos ("whites") but the Mexicans, his blood brothers. His more moderate friend tries to reason with him, extolling the advantages of the Army: "In the Army it's different with the Mexicans."[67] He vainly cites examples of camaraderie between Mexican and American soldiers; Mingo is shocked that Mexican-Americans can be subjected to racial violence at home while others are fighting overseas.

Ferber also noted that the American army constituted a world apart, governed by different values. Seeking, as always, to strike the imagination and the conscience of the reader, she sketches a picture of the glory and downfall of young Angel Obregon. Here, first of all, is a military citation attesting to the heroism of this soldier, who died on the field of honor:

> ... conspicuous gallantry and intrepidity, above and beyond the call of duty ... undaunted ... miraculously reaching the position ... climbed to the top ... heroic conduct ... saved the lives of many comrades ... overwhelming odds ....[68]

The honor is canceled out by the curt refusal of Benedict's funeral director, who says he "naturally ... could not handle the funeral of a Mexican."[69]

Mailer is cynical: although Julio Martinez has not found perfect equality, he cannot imagine any career other than the Army after the war. Griffith concludes on an optimistic note: "in the flow of time"[70] all men will be brothers, even without uniforms. The facts she recounts, however, do not support such optimism. The barrio was a trap; all hope of escaping it and blending into American society was still futile.

Rejection of Assimilation: Pachuquismo and La Raza

If the war brought a hope of brotherhood and equality for some, for Mexican youths it was also a period of turmoil that would continue beyond 1945. This anxiety expressed itself in *pachuquismo*. The anarchical behavior of the *pachucos*, the "angry young men" of the Mexican minority, masked a profound alienation, for they could no more escape their own ethnic and cultural identity than they could avoid the influence of Anglo civilization. Griffith makes a brief reference to this schizophrenia of the 1940s in the short story "American Me." The daughter of migrant agricultural workers is the narrator. She reports an incident that makes her conscious of her double "self": a young American insults a friend of hers, calling him a "dirty Mexican" and hitting him. When the boy asks his assailant who he was to insult him, the American answers: "Well, I'm me, American me. That's who I am!" To which the other responds, as he strikes back: "Yeah? Well, I'm American me too. American inside, but Mexican on top!"[71]

This identity crisis is implicit in Shulman's novel *The Square Trap*, but the author is more interested in the outward manifestation of the *pachuco*'s schizophrenia. School, rather than helping to acculturate Mexican children, is almost always traumatic and negative. The turmoil and instability of Mexican youngsters, the heart of the book, probably derive partly from an education that does not address their needs: "School's not for us guys. The teachers don't care. We're not missed,"[72] explains an habitual school truant.

Young Tomas Cantanios considers his life pointless:

> ... he wasn't different from most of the boys in Chavez who graduated from public school and spit on the school walls after they received their diplomas and then didn't do anything but wait around for the army to take or reject them. ...[73]

The idleness of Tomas and the Ravine Cats gang is a rejection of the surround-ing reality. They are on the fringes of both the barrio and the dominant society; their affected style of dress is a way of affirming their double and self-imposed alienation. Tomas wears the uniform of the *pachuco*: long, straight, dark hair, combed into a "duck-tail" at the neck,

> . . . dark blue sharply pegged pants with deep pleats, a tooled cowboy belt decorated with large and small colored stones and a large buckle, a light-tan zelancloth wind breaker, candy-striped socks, and rugged cordovan-colored shoes . . .[74]

The *pachuco*'s language also proclaims his difference; it is an "almost secret language of Spanish and English, understandable only to the sharps, the rights, the real gones, kids who never chickened."[75] The only genuinely *pachuco* term in the novel is "*tinto* (black)."[76]

The anarchical behavior of Tomas causes a growing discord with his father, to whom he remains, nonetheless, attached. It makes him suspect to the police, symbol of the Anglo world. The young *pachuco* has frequent run-ins with the police in the course of some tumultuous street battles.

This Anglo author is to be commended for portraying *pachuquismo* from within rather than entirely from its ludicrous outward appearances, and for intending his book as a plea on behalf of Mexican youth of the 1940s.

Alongside the negative revolt of *pachuquismo*, after the war a more realis-tic, active protest movement developed, inspired by the common bond of "la Raza." Conscious and proud of their ethnic and cultural community, the mili-tants fought to have it accepted as part of the American nation. Previously nothing more than a synonym for "Mexican,"[77] "la Raza" began to take on a broader meaning. For old Angel Obregon, the word has only a racial con-notation, while for Pete Genusa it implies ethnic solidarity that goes beyond mere emotional attachment. As he says to Tomas Cantanios, whose misdi-rected physical strength he wished to channel for worthier ends: "Remember, Tommy, I'm *la raza*."[78]

The activities of some within la Raza appeared both senseless and suspect to the Anglo racist. Ferber, who does not otherwise dwell on the politicization of la Raza, gives a glimpse of its manifestations and how they were greeted by the Establishment. A rich Texan speaks:

> . . . since the war's over . . . they've been rabble-rousing, shooting their mouths off, getting together saying they're American citizens without rights and that kind of stuff. They want to be called Latin Americans, not Mexicans any more. I hear they're getting up organizations, the boys who fought in the war, and so on. Spreading all over, they say. Got some fancy names for their outfits with America in it to show how American they are.[79]

Although Shulman does not provide specific details, he implies the presence of a new and active force within the Los Angeles barrio. Genusa is a man in contact with both the outside world and working-class Mexicans whose young talent he seeks to promote. It is he who helps Tomas during a quarrel with some Anglos and introduces him to a trainer, who, for the moment, gives Tomas a sense of purpose. Since the novel is set just after the war, *pachuquismo* is prominent. Barrett develops the theme of political activism in the 1950s within the framework of the virulent anticommunism of the all-powerful Senator McCarthy. Certain *políticos* in the barrio of State City are militant members of la Raza; they form "organisms," or groups, that try to inform Mexican-Americans of their social welfare and political rights, and especially to assist them in court and in their dealings with the police. Juan Gola tenaciously defends the rights of prisoners, particularly their right to counsel. Every Mexican-American receives a booklet for use in case of arrest:

> The title of the booklet was, "*Sus derechos en caso de arresto*" (Your rights in case of arrest). In content it was a veritable manual of crime, explaining exactly what the police had to prove in court in rape cases, burglary cases, hold-ups, sluggings, etc., and emphasizing the difficulty confronting the police when a suspect refuses to talk. Again and again the booklet repeated its most solemn message: "*No hable con ningún policía*" (do not talk to any policeman), and its secondary message: "*No se dí culpable*" (Plead not guilty).[80]

When some young Mexican-Americans vandalize an apartment building, Mrs. Leighton, the owner, complains to police commissioner Tom Logan. He answers that any intervention on his part would be useless, since an "organism" would immediately hire a lawyer and "clear" the guilty parties.

Are we to regard these organisms, as Tom Logan does, as an outgrowth of communism and Juan Gola as a "commie"[81] engaging in subversive activities? Logan's attitude is dictated by his era (which constitutes the documentary interest of the book), but the role played by communists among minority groups during the Depression is well documented.[82] Whatever the case, the true spokesman for the barrio of State City can never be Francisco Zancudo or his crony, Luis Capinaro, the opportunistic politicians who ultimately make a mockery of the system, but rather Juan Gola. The Mexican minority needed leaders like Juan Gola to help them emerge from silence and invisibility. For him the barrio is neither a refuge nor a trap but a springboard.

The Vendido

The Mexican minority is not composed entirely of heroes and of people who try to escape oppression while retaining their dignity as human beings and Mexicans. It also has its renegades, people who seek material benefits within the system at any cost. The *vendido* ("the one who sells out") is the Uncle Tom of Mexican-Americans,[83] and appears in three forms. The *jefe político* is the petty political tyrant whose local influence has always been very powerful; the *coyote* transports illegal immigrants across the border for a fee; the third is the Mexican–American frustrated by attempts at assimilation who turns to accumulating money as the only way of succeeding in a profit-oriented society.

It is curious that Anglo literature showed little interest in the often shady *jefe político*. In Barrett's novel *The Shadows of the Images*, two men control State City's Second Ward, composed essentially of migrant farm workers whose ignorance and poverty they exploit for their own purposes. They are Francisco Zancudo, who pulls the strings behind the scenes, and his confederate, city councilman Luis Capinaro, who is better known to the public. These two cunning politicians maneuver on the matter of the rape of the young Mexican-American woman, not hesitating to corrupt the police but careful above all not to alienate the Mexican voters or lose the support of Anglo political leaders. Nothing could be more foreign to them than the generosity of a Delmar, Garland's hero, who dedicates himself to the cause of the Mexican sheepherders in Pima. Rather, their corruptness recalls some self-serving bureaucrats of New Mexico, as depicted in certain novels.

The *vendido* appears in Ferber's novel in his vilest form, that of the *coyote*. In the person of the wetback, the profit-oriented society furnishes the parvenu with the ideal opportunity to become rich and to "arrive." He resembles both the scavenging coyote and Judas. Fond of sensational details, as always, the novelist bluntly describes the person who procures a complement of foreign workers for citrus growers in the Benedict Ranch area. He is a man low enough to become rich at the expense of the less fortunate members of the Mexican community while claiming to be their friend. Here is Fidel Gomez, better known as coyote, as described to Leslie Benedict by Jett Rink:

> . . . he runs the Mexicans, he's the richest man in town. He's got a nice
> house . . . no 'dobe stuff but concrete white-washed and a tree in front
> and a bathroom and a living-room set and a bedroom set and a parlor set
> and a Chevy and he married the swellest-looking Mexican girl in town.
> . . . Everybody in the county knows Gomez. He makes out he's the poor
> Mexicans' friend.[84]

Since the author wishes to provoke a scandal, the coyote's shocking activities are vividly described. Nothing of this sinister character's inner nature is revealed, apart from a certain anxiety visible in his face. On both of the occasions that Leslie Benedict runs across him, she is struck by his worried air: ". . . his eyes and mouth were ovals of apprehension."[85] Only grudgingly does he agree to drive the curious young woman to the camp of the farm workers.

By contrast, Shulman notes the condemnation of the *vendido* by his own community. This contempt gives "Mr. Iscariot," the melancholy hero of the short story by Richard G. Brown,[86] a guilty conscience destined to prove fatal. The *vendido* denies the values of la Raza by adopting the materialism of America; others consider his attitude an insult to their dignity. The *vendido* wins both laughter and contempt: in the only humorous passage in Shulman's novel, the *pachucos* of Chavez Ravine ridicule one youth's uncle. The affluent life of the apparently unemployed Uncle Leo intrigues the young men, who are jobless and broke. Gogo, one of the gang, mockingly imitates the Blacks' Uncle Tom, of whom this servile Mexican-American reminds them:

> the kinda nigger they show in the movies with white hair and wearin' a butler's uniform with lotsa brass buttons on it and carryin' a tray with drinks and if you kick him in the ass he says, 'Yassah, Massah, Yassah' . . .[87]

The tone is more bitter in Brown's short story. The author dwells, first of all, on the universal disgust Mario Alejandro de Valera y Guerrero, "Mr. Iscariot," provokes in the barrio of his small border town. He is a drunkard who works for an Anglo finance company, earning his living by repossessing goods from Mexican-Americans behind on their monthly payments. The second part of the story illustrates the tragic way in which he finally perceives his own moral prostitution. After seizing the car of local gangster John Sánchez, a particularly delicate task, he is greeted at the *cantina* ("bar") by the caustic jeers of his unemployed friends: by sacrificing his dignity to his security, Mario has lost his manhood. He is called a *monstruo* ("monster") in his own home: "Why don't you get a job and be a decent man?"[88] his mother asks him. His situation becomes unbearable. The *vendido* goes to a hill where the Gumuchil tree stands. The obsessions of the emasculated, banished Mario crystallize around the tree, which he imagines to be "masculine, like the word *árbol*" (which is masculine in Spanish). From the top, he can see Mexico, this great "masculine" land, from which he and his father came so many years ago. Just as Judas hanged himself, Mario hangs himself from the Gumuchil tree out of self-loathing.

The problem of the *vendido*, the person who plays the game according to the system, is common to all minority groups; the problem became more acute among Mexican-Americans as a militant faction mounted opposition to a middle class "co-opted" by Anglo society. The *vendido*, rejected by the barrio he had betrayed, was often caught in his own trap.

Generational Conflict

The family, long the nucleus of Mexican society, was threatened both by the inadaptability of the father and by a generation gap which often resulted from the father's problem. More so than the mother, who maintained the family's stability, the father represented to the son exactly what he did not want to be: an exploited, unemployed failure. The father's inability to provide for the family's needs contributed to the decline of his personal status and to a decrease in filial respect.[89] Lower-class Blacks also experienced a breakdown of family structure and an increase of maternal authority caused by the desertion of the father, but among Mexican-Americans the inevitable generational conflict was exacerbated by the pressures placed upon the young by a different cultural world. The father, like the mother, remained close to his original culture;

convinced that the Mexican–American would only degrade himself through contact with the gringo civilization, he ridiculed his son's efforts at assimilation. He reproved the servile imitation of the American lifestyle, speech, and way of thinking, which, sooner or later, would lead the younger generation into a cultural no-man's-land. In another context, Allen, harking back nostalgically to the old *vaqueros* on the Texas border, lamented the "schizophrenic" behavior[90] of their successors.

Ferber and especially Shulman treated this generational conflict. To their sons Angel and Tomas, the trades and halting English of former *vaquero* Angel Obregon and migrant farm worker Vidal Cantanios are the very symbols of the past and of failure. To old Obregon, the traditional values are personified by the language of his ancestors, by the ranch, and by la Raza, which to him has a purely cultural connotation. Seeing his son affect a bizarre style of dress and "a bastard dialect" as he tries at all costs to convert himself into an Anglo both saddens and irritates the father:

> At seventeen he spurned Reata with all of its years of Obregon family loyalty. He took a job as a bellboy at the Hake in Vientecito and on his visits to the ranch he swaggered the streets of Benedict in side-burns, fifty-dollar boots, silk shirt, his hair pomaded the luster of black oil-cloth. He and his friends affected a bastard dialect made up of Mexican jargon, American slang, Spanish patois . . . The Reata vaqueros said of him in Spanish "He's trying to change the color of his eyes to blue" . . .
>
> His father, Angel Obregon the Caporal, his mother Deluvina, were by turns furious and sad at this metamorphosis. He was a disgrace to the raza —the proud race of Mexican people. They were ashamed. . . .
>
> Almost tearfully Angel Obregon said, "He is a good boy, Angel. It is as if some bruja, some evil witch, had him under a spell. He is without respect for the things of life."[91]

Vidal Cantanios has had a certain image of the family and of Mexican society, engraved indelibly in his mind since his emigration: ". . . a world where families meant much, where each member of the family knew his proper place, and fathers and mothers were revered and respected by their children."[92] His refusal to allow his children to call him "Pop" is in itself eloquent. During the novel, basically a series of flashbacks on Mexico and stormy confrontations between father and son, Vidal painfully realizes that his son and daughter Helen correspond less and less to his idealized image; the word "corrupted" comes several times to his lips as a description of his children and those of his neighbors.

Young Angel and young Tomas take views opposed to their fathers'; Angel, the *vaquero*'s son, rejects the traditional occupation of the Mexican:

> "Vaquero with twenny or twenny-five dollars a month," Angel said, and laughed scornfully . . . "Vaquero like my father and his father and his father, not me! I want to marry with Marita Rivas . . . But I don't want my

kid to be a vaquero, and his kid and his kid. Now who does that is a borlo [an imbecile]."[93]

Despite the steadfast opposition and cutting remarks of his father, Tomas continues his training as a boxer. Just as young Obregon will have no part of the ranch, Vidal's son aspires to leave the Chavez Ravine barrio and establish a different kind of life elsewhere.

More so than Ferber, Shulman concentrates on the conflict within the family created by growing discord between father and son. Communication between them becomes more difficult day by day, to the extent that Vidal insists that his children speak to him in Spanish, while they are increasingly reluctant to express themselves in their native language, since they use English constantly. Tomas is no more at ease at home than his sister Helen is; if it were not for his pity for his father and affection for his mother, he would leave the family home.

Although there is no formal break, father and son become strangers. Tommy makes a sort of transfer to Pete Genusa, his mentor, whom he sees as the ideal father:

> Tommy stared at his father. They were really strangers, so how was he expected to know and understand this stranger—his father? . . . he also thought of what it would be like to have a father like Pete Genusa, a father who could read, write, drive a car and knew all about contracts. Someone who knew all about politics . . . someone who knew all about movie stars and other important people.[94]

The father ". . . looked at this son—this unruly and antagonistic stranger in his house—who stood with his hands in his pockets and defied him."[95] The word "stranger" returns obsessively throughout the story. This estrangement at the heart of the family is the book's most moving aspect. By trying to keep his son in the barrio, the father is caught in his own trap.

All of the postwar Anglo-American works written with a concern for realism denounced the most flagrant injustices that victimized barrio Mexican-Americans. They also brought to light how Mexican-Americans reacted to this oppression, depending upon their generation. A triple image of the Mexican minority emerged—that of a people still invisible and divided, but in full ferment.

Assimilation: A rough translation is the exchange of
one set of problems for another, oftentimes bigger. [1]

The Mexican-American
Point of View

The First Literary Spokesmen

The first generation of writers, mostly sons of poor immigrants and former migrant workers themselves, emerged from the barrio after the war; this is the case of short-story writers Mario Suárez and Arnulfo Trejo, novelist José Antonio Villarreal, and sociologist Ernesto Galarza.[2] They transcribed their experiences and those of their parents into English. Born in the barrio of a Mexican mother, John Rechy "penetrated the literary iron curtain"[3] on talent alone; a politically uncommitted writer, he created a world of forbidden beauty, that of homosexuality, which went beyond the confines of the ethnic group to which he half belonged. The experience related in his *City of Night* is no more solely Mexican-American than is the one depicted in James Baldwin's *Giovanni's Room* a uniquely Black experience. *City of Night* (1963) and Rechy's other novels have an originality and aesthetic value lacking in Villarreal's *Pocho.* Nonetheless, *Pocho* draws our attention despite its modest literary value and open didacticism for it is the testimony of a writer who fully accepts himself as a Mexican-American. I will discuss a few passages from *City of Night* and two brief narratives, "Mardi Gras" and "El Paso del Norte,"[4] in which Rechy recalls childhood incidents from which he could never completely free himself. He would forever be haunted by the memory of an admirable mother, whom he loved passionately but with overbearing affection, and of his father, a violent and misunderstood artist who detested him and for whom he felt a hatred tempered by affection. The ambiguous position he adopted toward the barrio, midway between love and rejection, reflects these impassioned and complex family relationships. He portrays the barrio, in turn, with warmth and an ironic detachment that never reaches outright denial.

Living on the periphery of the barrio, Franciscan Fray Angélico Chávez[5] wrote religious poems remarkable for their formal perfection and universality of theme; they harked back to the work of seventeenth-century Black poet Phillis Wheatley. We will set aside this poetry in favor of his short stories, set in faraway New Mexico, which was heavily influenced by the unsophisticated brand of Catholicism that still characterized postwar Mexican-Americans. Differing from the preceding writers is Chester Seltzer, or Amado Muro, who became a child of the barrio through an elaborate hoax.[6] The Mexican Southwest exerted a strong attraction on this young Anglo journalist from a middle-class Ohio family; in the Southwest he met and married Amada Muro, who was originally from Chihuahua. In addition to his pseudonym, which led to a curious sort of transsexualism, he concocted a Mexican-American biography[7] and personality, to such a point that many people, including some well-known ones, were deceived.[8] I will categorize Chester Seltzer, alias Amado Muro, among those he so wished to be like and of whom he spoke in illusory terms.

Alongside the short story and the novel, *corridos* told in Spanish persisted. They remained the unsophisticated and spontaneous oral expression of those not yet acculturated. Like the Anglo writers, the Mexican-Americans have a dual interest: the past, *their* past, and the anguishing present, leading to an uncertain future. The literature of this period of assimilation, however, clearly attempts to reconcile the two value systems; the tone is often bitter in Villarreal, sarcastic in Rechy, but never aggressive. The barrio, home of ancestral traditions, is in the foreground in these short stories; it is peopled with happy individuals whose aspirations are limited by the narrow confines in which they live. The broader framework of the novel allows Villarreal to explore fully the problems of the Mexican minority; he stresses the difficulties Mexican immigrants, still prisoners of their past, experienced in integrating, and the dangers of assimilation. This period was dominated by the *pocho*, a derogatory name given to assimilationists. But their desire to integrate led these hybrid, pathetic characters to an awareness of their tragic ambivalence and to a search for their real identity. Mexican-Americans still had a long road to travel before they would be able to resolve this internal conflict and more effectively confront the dominant society.

CHAPTER 10

In the Traditional Framework
of the Barrio

Born of the urbanization of Mexican–Americans, the barrio is less a geographic reality than a symbol that gathers together all the "spiritual sons of Mexico."[2] It is El Hoyo, the hollow, nestling within the heart of the great American city, where Mexican-Americans feel secure and return to their roots after their long day in a world that's still foreign. Thus it is that "barrios" spring up in the migrant labor camps, as if by spontaneous generation, for the duration of the harvest. The barrio is the urban equivalent of the isolated villages in the New Mexico mountains. Each barrio has its own face, its own heroes, sometimes its own dialect, its traditions, its culinary specialties, but a common spirit vibrates under this apparent variety.

The narrow framework of the short story does not permit Mario Suárez, Amado Muro, or Arnulfo Trejo to give detailed descriptions of the barrios of Tucson, El Paso, or Santa Monica respectively. In the course of his novel, Villarreal has the luxury of dwelling at length on the California barrio of Santa Clara; but he limits himself, for reasons I will explain later, to two Mexican-American homes. In his stories "El Hoyo" and "Southside Run," both of which resemble reportage more than the traditional short story, Suárez sketches a picture of the Mexican section of Tucson that is not without humor:

> Except for some tall trees which nobody has ever cared to identify, nurse, or destroy, the main things known to grow in the general area are weeds, garbage piles, dark-eyed chavalos ["lads"], and dogs.[3]

Since the architecture of houses is a function of the inhabitants' resources, "Spanishizing them, Mexicanizing them, Colonializing them, or Puebloizing them"[4] is financially impossible. This absence of style deprives their shabbiness of any picturesqueness:

> They are simply houses with sometimes plastered but usually unplas-
> tered exteriors. With rickety wood porches which seem about to fall the
> instant one's foot is set on the decaying wood.[5]

Muro and Rechy are even more succinct on housing in the El Paso barrio, but they emphasize the same characteristics: poor construction, neglect, and overcrowding, especially with children. Here is Muro on "Little Chihuahua" (whose nickname allows him to remind us that his adopted family was from Chihuahua, the Mexican state bordering Texas): "a broken-down Mexican quarter honeycombed with tenements; . . . with howling children running in its streets. . . ."[6] Rechy retains a similar memory of the El Paso barrio, where he spent his youth: ". . . the torn clothes just laundered waving on rickety bal-conies. . . . Row after row of identical boxhouses speckled with dozens and dozens of children."[7] Suárez adds a touch of color to his picture: the "inevi-table Chinese stores"[8] (the Mexican-American was not a merchant at heart) were always better patronized than the most splendid American supermarkets, which had no future in the barrio. During depressions and lean years it was these stores and the bean harvests that kept Mexican-Americans from starving to death.

The short-story writer must go directly to the essentials, but in the barrio the setting is less important than the people who give it life, the *Chicanos*. This term had not yet acquired a political connotation; for Suárez it represents nothing more than an "easy way of referring to everybody"[9] in the barrio. In spite of their diversity, they had a common heritage; like Chicanos, the *capirotada*, a Mexican dish, varies from one family to the next but always has certain basic ingredients. "While being divided from within and from without, like the capirotada, they remain chicanos."[10]

The accent is placed not on material living conditions but on the barrio's spiritual dimension; it was a guardian of traditional values and a home full of life and human warmth.

Like the isolated mountain village of New Mexico, the barrio still lived on "Mexican time." The little town in the story "Sunday in Little Chihua-hua,"[11] where Chester Seltzer-Amado Muro claimed to have spent his child-hood, well deserved its nickname, so heavily was it steeped in Mexican culture. The heroes it venerated during the 1920s were Mexicans. Poet-journalist Don Ignacio Olvera did not dare write or recite poems on the matadors in any lan-guage but Spanish, for he would otherwise be neither read nor listened to; if he wished to compare a champion of bullfighting to another hero, he used two celebrities from south of the Rio Grande—novelist Mariano Azuela and painter Rafael de Urbino. The residents of the El Paso barrio spoke only Span-

ish and ". . . when they say the Capital, they mean Mexico, D.F.,"[12] wrote
Rechy in 1958. El Paso is an extreme case, since it is right on the border; in
barrios throughout the Southwest, however, people retained the values, traditions, and language of the past. Innately conservative, Mexican-Americans of
the barrio were suspicious of anything that threatened their traditional institutions. Because both *pachuquismo* and women's liberation represented, in their
own ways, attacks upon the integrity and ethics of the Mexican community,
they incurred unanimous disapproval. I will return to these two phenomena
later but limit this discussion to the hostile reactions they provoked. The Suárez
short story "Kid Zopilote" relates the tribulations of young Pepe García on
returning to Tucson after a summer in Los Angeles, where he associated with
pachucos and adopted their clothes, lifestyle, and dialect. In his native barrio,
he meets only mockery and rejection. The girls refuse to dance with him; his
mother criticizes his vocabulary; his uncle calls him a "cursed *pachuco*" and "a
no-good zoot-suiter,"[13] and even rejoices when the police arrest him and shave
off his hair. Pepe becomes "Kid Zopilote," the buzzard, to everyone; like the
buzzards who "eat puke even when better things are available a little farther
away from their beaten runways and dead trees,"[14] the *pachuco* rejects Mexican
values in favor of less reliable ones.

The same rejection mechanism operated against the liberated woman; witness the satirical *corrido* "El Siglo Pasado" [The past century], sung after the
war in the barrios of the Southwest, where trousers and freedom were still
the prerogatives of men:

Dicen que el siglo pasado	[They say that the past century
Siglo de las luces fué;	Was the century of enlightenment.
Ora será el de las sombras,	Now it must be the one of shadows
Porque todo anda al revés.	For everything is going backwards.
Antes eran las mujeres,	Women used to be women,
Mujeres y nada más,	And nothing else,
Y los hombres eran hombres	And men were men
Y iba la cuenta cabal.	And everything was fine.
Hoy tienen las mujeres	Women now seem more
De hombre más que de mujer,	Like men than they do women,
Los instintos varoniles,	They have masculine instincts
Y la libertad también.	And freedom as well.
Quien nos pudiera decir	And who could have told us
Al ver estas del ujo fuerte badlon	On seeing these women's figures
Quién pudiera pensar	Who would have thought
Que eran mujeres con pantalones.[15]	That they were women in long pants.]

When the barrio refuses to absorb the dominant culture, reverse contamination sometimes occurs, as in the amusing story by Suárez, "Mexican Heaven."
The author stresses Mexican-American inflexibility in such sensitive areas as
religion and implicitly questions any policy aimed at rigidly systematic assimi-

lation. The religion of the barrio remained a reflection of the Spanish tempera-
ment, essentially affective, more "colored" than rigorous. Anglo priests, whose
training emphasized theory and internal coherence over ways of teaching the
flock, fail with the inhabitants of El Hoyo in Suárez's story. The people much
prefer the "near comic eloquence" of a priest of Spanish or Latin American
origin to church rituals presented "too methodically" and to sermons delivered
"insipidly." [16] Father Raymond soon sees that he will never reach the hearts of
his parishioners unless he changes his own; little by little he adapts to their
way of life and way of thinking. He begins to enjoy their spicy food (adding
piquancy to his homilies) and their music (patterning his speech on it). He
becomes so completely Mexican that the faithful forget his real name and call
him Padre Ramon, "one of the parish's permanent fixtures." [17]

The "past century" continued as a frame of reference. Nineteenth-century
history remained alive in the barrio; each year, on September 16, Mexican Independence Day, a queen was elected, the streets were decorated with flags and
bunting, and ". . . more than one flag is sworn allegiance to amid cheers for the
queen";[18] celebrating the heroes of Mexico was a way to express sentimental
allegiance to their country of origin. The more recent memory of the revolution, provoked by a long series of social and economic quarrels, also persisted.
Juan, the father of the Rubio family in Villarreal's novel *Pocho*, remains marked
by his combat service in Pancho Villa's forces; "the loss of his god" [19] in 1923
profoundly affects him a few years later in Los Angeles. Villarreal devotes most
of his introductory chapter to Juan's revolutionary period to illustrating the
impact of this Mexican past on the exile's life and on the emotional context in
which the exile's son would spend his youth. As an officer in the rebel army
and distant cousin of Zapata as well, Juan escapes the purges of the Obregón
government. Obregón's coming to power provokes a counteroffensive in the
border barrios, particularly in El Paso, which rallies together former *villistas*
prepared to assassinate the new president. In the eyes of Juan's wife, Consuelo,
the revolution is a failure: too much blood spilled in vain and thousands of
Mexicans, themselves included, forced by poverty to emigrate to the United
States. As the wife of a militant, she lives through these troubled years in
solitude and fear of reprisal. Juan recalls the revolution as a series of richly
colored paintings, an event of historic and sentimental value. For his apolitical son Richard, it is a dead issue; he is indifferent to its ideology. In general,
the revolution left traces in the barrios and was discussed in newspapers and
schools, but postwar Mexican-Americans were not sufficiently politicized to
use its ideology as a political weapon.

During this period of assimilation, the revolution and its heroes became like
figures in a museum, frozen in wax, or, like the old revolutionaries of Little
Chihuahua, "sunning themselves on its curbs like iguanas." [20] But Mexico's
cultural influence remained strong in religion, family, and social life.

Relationship with the Sacred

Faith was still very much alive in the barrio. According to Suárez, there were very few who did not attend church on Sundays and holy days of obligation. Rechy recalls his pious childhood: "I was very religious then. I went to Mass regularly, to confession. I prayed nightly." [21]

Christmas in the barrio of El Paso was celebrated with particular warmth and richness before the splendid *nacimientos* ("mangers"). In the Rechy home, Christmas Eve had an essentially family and religious character:

> My mother led the rosary. We all knelt. Someone had been chosen to be the padrino—the god-father—of the Christ-child to be born that night. He carried the Child in his hands, everyone kissed it ("adored" it), and then finally He was put into the manger, in the hay. We prayed some more. Dios te salve, María, llena eres de Gracia ["Hail Mary, full of grace"]. . . . At the stroke of midnight, the Child was born. Then there was a party—tamales, buñuelos ["fritters"], liquor.[22]

Rechy, an atheist who remained obsessed by God and tormented by his admittedly sinful pleasure, yearned for the confession of his Catholic youth; after a period of abject debauchery he desperately sought a priest by telephone: ". . . I longed for innocence more than anything else, and I would have given away all the frantic knowing for a return to Grace. . . ." [23] Julien Green, another repentant homosexual, might well have endorsed these lines.

For some, religion was still a synonym for magic; precise details provided by Villarreal and Rechy confirm the survival of witchcraft in the Southwest. In the 1920s, there were still some witches among immigrants to the Imperial Valley of California; when one was murdered, Villarreal tells us, "she was committed to the earth, and the English-speaking population knew nothing of her death, if, indeed, they had known of her existence." [24] According to Rechy, neither the number of witches nor the consideration they enjoyed in El Paso had at all diminished; they had virtually the same status as priests. Witches had a sort of hierarchy; Don Ben acted as "pope" and universal counselor. Rechy did not forget the *"espíritu maligno,"* the evil spirit of his childhood who constantly moved his father's glasses about, nor a device of his aunt, who long kept a photograph of her husband behind her bedroom door. She had inverted the picture in a glass containing a strange liquid, in hopes of securing the return of the man who had deserted her forty years earlier.[25] The author, who takes diabolical pleasure in recalling ludicrous childhood incidents, concludes in a turnabout: "And why should devout Mexican Catholics (as they are) consult witches (as they do)? For the same reason that a man with a sick ear goes to an ear specialist. . . ." [26]

The essentially Mexican character of Catholicism in the barrio emerged in the writings of the postwar period. The fortuitous and spontaneous relationship of Mexican-Americans with the sacred was the foundation both of their religion and their conception of human existence:

> Mexican religion is a very real thing, not lukewarm at all, nor forbidding
> and awesome. Mexican Catholics (and this, again, includes the Priests)
> believe in a God with two hands, two feet, eyes—the works. The Devil
> has horns, a tail, and he is most certainly red.[27]

The Virgin and the saints, in particular, are beings of flesh and blood incorporated into daily life, not semi-imaginary inhabitants of an inaccessible and
fearsome beyond. As both the good fairy of folklore and the patron saint of
the immigrants of the *corridos*, the dark Virgin of Guadalupe remained the protective mother figure; closer to Mexican-Americans than the white Virgin of
Anglo and European Catholicism, she still occupies a central position in their
religious universe. Thus, in María Tepache's cramped room in San Antonio,
there is room "on a tiny shelf in a corner" for a gilt-framed picture of María
Guadalupana and a crucified Christ.[28] Grasping an image of the dark Virgin,
the dying young man in Suárez's short story "Mexican Heaven" is reassured
as he departs for the Mexican-style heaven Padre Ramon has described. Fray
Angélico Chávez dedicates the third panel ("Hunchback Madonna") of his literary triptych on traditional New Mexico to the Virgin Mary;[29] in an extremely
spare style well suited to the simplicity of its subject, and offering a contrast to
the neoclassic bombast of his poems, he revives an old legend. Although the
action seems to be set in a relatively distant era, the atmosphere that emerges
still prevailed in the northern mountains of the state after World War II. Old
Mana Seda undertakes the task of propagating devotion to the Virgin Mary in
her village: each day in May, little girls dressed as maids of honor offer flowers
to the Virgin. The old woman constantly bemoans the fact that the statue of
the Virgin of Guadalupe ordered from Mexico has either been lost en route
or destroyed by the Apaches. Caught by surprise one day by a rainstorm in
the forest where she usually gathers flowers, she takes refuge in the cabin of
a young artist. Recreating the act of the Virgin herself, who imprinted her
image on the shawl of young Juan Diego in order to convince unbelievers of
her presence, the artist paints a hunchback Virgin resembling Mana Seda on
her shawl, which she later donates to the church. Legend has it that the tomb
of the "Hunchback Madonna," on which daisies and tufts of verbena flower
each May, became a place of pilgrimage. Rechy sees the Virgin of Guadalupe,
above all, as the image of the mother; he identifies the mother of the Mexicans
with his own mother, who in turn becomes the symbol of Mexico for him.
Thus, his evocation of the Virgin has an impassioned exaggeration unusual for
him:

> Oh, how tenderly they believe in the Virgin Guadalupe (*even the priests*),
> and how they love Her, the Mother of all Mexico.
> How they Respect the mother because of it. Mothers are a Grand Mexi-
> can thing. They belong sacredly in Mexico and the Mexican Southwest.[30]

The dark Virgin of Guadalupe linked Mexican-Americans to their land of origin, but the bond, like that created by the revolution, was still emotional, not yet political.

Each church had its patron saint, whose feast day was duly celebrated once a year. On this occasion, as the *corridos* showed, the sounds, colors, and fiestas of the barrio entered right into the church. Conversely, crucifixes and religious images also decorated the walls of private homes. A sort of fortuitous natural syncretism of mixed sacred and secular elements abolished the separation between genres; this was yet another characteristic of religion and life in the barrio. Rechy's ironic and nostalgic pen depicts the long procession of the faithful slowly climbing the Cristo Rey [Christ the King] mountain overlooking El Paso to the sound of church canticles and a pagan brass band:

> . . . carrying placards of the Virgin, Saints in colors. Small bands jazz solemnly, crying dissonant sounds. The shawled ladies of the order of Saint Something grip rosaries and mumble and feel—as rightly so as anyone in the world—Holy . . . the musicians wiping the sweat off their dark faces, and drinking cool limonada and mingling with the sellers of coca-cola, religious medals.[31]

In the second panel of his triptych, "The Penitente Thief," Fray Angélico Chávez evokes the brotherhoods of the Penitentes and their bloody celebrations during Holy Week (lodges continue to operate secretly in isolated parts of New Mexico to this day). In the style of Steinbeck, he blends some humorous elements into his religious tale, as if to show better the fusion of the sacred and the obviously secular, and to demonstrate that there is no inconsistency in the illegal swindling activities of Lucero and Maldonado and their membership in the Penitente brotherhood. Through an irony of fate, Lucero is even chosen to play the role of the Good Thief. Indeed, didn't the ceremonies at the *morada* ("lodge") implicitly demand that the participants be first-class sinners? Thus, the amused but by no means shocked author adds, the two friends ". . . entered whole-heartedly into the spirit of the brotherhood, hoping to atone the better for their sins the more they crisscrossed their backs with scarlet welts."[32]

The life of Mexican-Americans was somewhere between the secular and the sacred, with no clear sense of demarcation. Suárez is amused by the residents of El Hoyo who "raise hell on Saturday night and listen to Padre Estanislao on Sunday morning."[33] The sacred permeated the language of the barrio. The expression "It's the will of God" implied a life of many tribulations accepted in a spirit of fatalism and serene submissiveness. The words were uttered frequently:

> You . . . must fulfill the destiny of your God. . . . That is God's will. . . . It is God's will that we live as we do. That we raise our children and they, in turn raise their children. . . . That is how God wants it . . .[34]

Juan Rubio never wearies of repeating these sentiments to his son. Apparently, women more often than men made religious supplications, especially to the

Virgin. The speech of old María Tepache is punctuated by such expressions as "Señora Madre de San Juan," "Válgame San Crispin [Heavens!]" and "May the Indian Virgin who spoke with Juan Diego, protect you and cover you with her mantle."[35] Muro also attributes this last expression to his imaginary Mexican grandmother, who uses it each time she refers to her father, a pushcart vendor of vegetables.[36] The Mexican Virgin, who was close and familiar, gave Mexican-Americans of the barrio a sense of security; in the shelter of her ample cloak, they forgot the outside world.

The Family: Pitfall of Machismo

Although it was weakened when transplanted onto American soil, the family remained Mexican in many respects because it reposed on a traditional conception of man and woman. According to some sociologists in Mexico, a false notion of masculinity and femininity prevented the man from being "candid and humane" and the woman from being "dignified and independent";[37] Chicano sociologists are concerned that this overly simplistic theory has created a false myth about the Mexican-American family.[38] It is erroneous to attribute all problems to machismo, the cult of virility, that is, to a peculiarity of the Mexican psyche. External problems, such as the difficulty of integrating into a foreign society and job dissatisfaction, must be taken into account.

Two complementary principles provided an internal balance in the Mexican-American family, namely, paternal dominance and maternal abnegation. The barrio wife, placed under the husband's domination, ceased to be a goddess, the distant idol of classical or folkloric poetry whom the male won in a hard-earned conquest, out of a need to exceed himself. Instead, she was a domestic slave whose alienation confirmed the authority of the male. In the novel *Pocho*, Consuelo Rubio ". . . wished that once, only once, she could sit to dinner with her family, but she could not. She must wait on them until they were finished, and not until then could she sit down."[39] Self-sacrifice was the only ideal available to the woman.

With rare exceptions, she depended totally on her husband for subsistence; restricted to the home, she was cut off from the world outside the barrio. Her principal task was raising the invariably numerous children; the theories of Malthus had not yet reached the strongly Catholic Mexican minority. Even if women had resisted the Church's prohibition of contraception, they still would have had to battle the aversion of men, who considered birth control an attack on virility. The barrio swarmed with children; the barber of El Hoyo is the youngest of seven; at thirty-four years of age, Consuelo Rubio already has eight daughters and one son, and so forth.

Every male child was privileged; the mother, as the keeper of traditions, initiated him into his role as a man, paying particular attention to the eldest or only son. Like Mama Torres in Steinbeck's short story "Flight," Consuelo

Rubio inculcates both a sense of authority and a taste for it into her son Richard and wants him to marry a woman of his own race "because only a Mexican woman can appreciate the fact that her husband is a man."[40] For Richard's father, Juan, a "virility fanatic," manliness is an end in itself. When the boy reaches puberty his father tells him proudly: ". . . you are a man, and it is good, because to a Mexican being that is the most important thing. If you are a man, your life is half lived; what follows does not really matter."[41] Juan wants to give his son riding lessons. The boy loves his father "because he was a man and was trying to make a man of him."[42]

The sometimes tyrannical domination that a man wielded over his family compensated for his humiliation outside the barrio; he transformed his weak and impotent public self into a private, triumphant self. In many of these men, the more or less sublimated image of the matador lived on. When Cuco Martinez imitates the passes of the great bullfighter Armellita during a drinking bout in an El Hoyo bar, his pantomime is more than just an amusing spectacle; for this man, whose life borders on failure, it is a pathetic way of identifying with a "superman." If he goes back to Mexico, abandoning his wife and children, it would be in the hope of finding once more a social structure geared toward manliness.[43] The situation is similar, the identification process only slightly different, in "Sunday in Little Chihuahua," the short story by Muro, who knew only too well that for the Mexican, the royal road of virility passed right by the bullfight arena. On Sundays, in a barrio saloon, the poet-journalist recreates through his prose or poetry the exploits of the great matadors who were "impregnated with the odor of greatness."[44] Each of his listeners, transfigured by the theatrical interpretation, is swept away from his own mediocrity, at least for a moment. Childishly and violently, the head of the household would often vent on his family, particularly his wife, the hostility engendered by his failures, without ever seeking to understand its true causes. His boisterous drunken sprees were often the source of many tragic and comic barrio scenes. In El Hoyo there are many "houses where *compadres* get very drunk and where the police car is ofttimes sent to pacify noisy parties."[45] An unfortunate fall keeps Nacho Lopez from working but not from coming home drunk at dawn and serenading his wife Lola and his neighbors.[46] The man often took a mistress in order to restore his self-esteem and the respect of others. Juan Rubio, unable to satisfy his thirst for dignity and dominance either in his work as a farm laborer or in a family shaken by external forces, goes off in search of his friend Cirilo's young wife. When his world begins to crumble, it is important ". . . that he maintain his dignity as a man, that he be true to himself, that he satisfy his body of its needs—and his body needed more than tortillas."[47] Virility and dignity were the demands of machismo.

A woman was to bow down before her husband, resign herself to his infidelities and physical abuse, and accept her alienation. When Consuelo Rubio learns of Juan's affair, she uncharacteristically retaliates verbally, but she is quickly put back in her place by her husband:

> Enough! . . . I have had my fill of your whimpering and your back talk!
> You are thinking yourself an American woman—well, you are not one,
> and you should know your place. You have shelter, and you have food and
> clothing for you and the children. Be content! What I do outside the house
> is not your concern.[48]

The wife breaks down in tears; her daughters also cry but are careful not to
interfere, knowing that they are in a doubly inferior position, both as women
and as daughters:

> . . . because they were women, they wept for themselves and their destiny—
> their subservience to men. They were unable to condemn their father, and
> they knew that they could not completely sympathize with their mother,
> for too well they knew that hers had been a breach of discipline, and thus
> etiquette.[49]

The woman who dared to stray from the norms was swiftly punished by
the barrio, as the *corridos* showed earlier. A Mexican-American woman's position was ambiguous: apparently she had neither the desire nor the ability to
overcome her alienation within her own community; her resignation toward
her inferior status seemed masochistic; she cried out when her husband beat
her but seemed to see this punishment as a natural part of any love relationship.
The facetious short story by Suárez, "Las Comadres," shows this: Anastacia
Elizondo, a battered wife, finally decides to leave El Hoyo with her daughters.
Her flight is of short duration, however, and her new feminism turns out to be
less than profound. Forced to return to the barrio to arrange a hasty marriage
for her daughter, she returns to her own husband that night. She is greatly
surprised to learn that her dear Lazarillo has become indifferent to her, so much
so that he doesn't even bother to beat her. She redoubles her efforts in her
household chores in a vain attempt to regain his love. "A few weeks later, however, most of El Hoyo was awakened one night by wails, cries, and crashing
furniture. For a while it seemed as though somebody was being murdered."[50]
The following day,

> As she heard her comadre Lola's Nacho start her serenade a few win-
> dows away, Anastacia breathed deeply of El Hoyo's cool summer air and
> sighed dreamily. Then she gently scratched her own Lazarillo's shoulder
> and asked, "Are you awake, my love?"[51]

Those who love well, punish well; everything is back in order, the author
seems to conclude, with a wink at his cronies.

The disintegration of the Mexican immigrant family became more and more
common, caused by the increasingly frequent desertion of the father. The
mother was forced to assume his role while she waited for the eldest son to
take his place. Thus, after the departure of Juan, Consuelo Rubio, who earlier
showed signs of independence, rejoins the mainstream of Mexican mothers,
those moving figures in black shawls, keepers of the home and of traditional

values, who so inspired Anglo-American writers. Rechy evokes them in a tone fluctuating between irony and lyricism:

> Mexicans really love Mothers. Americans don't. I don't have a single American acquaintance whose mother faints everytime he comes home and again when he leaves. Mine does. The Mexican mother-love has nothing to do with sex, either. You can imagine an American wanting to make it with his mother. She is slick. She looks almost as young and bad as he does. But can you imagine making it with your mother when she wears a Black Shawl, and, even if she doesn't, if she acts all the time as if she is wearing One?[52]

The Community

The barrio is a state of mind, the inalienable possession of every Mexican-American. In order to bring it to life, I will proceed in a series of tableaux, since the preceding sections have described the barrio's framework. I will use an impressionistic presentation in the manner of Mario Suárez, who showed the human comedy of the barrio through a succession of "vignettes."[53] This technique will better showcase Suárez's undeniable talent.

Meet Señor Garza—barber, confidant, and philosopher all rolled into one, as much a bon vivant as the barber of Seville, but less wily and infinitely more generous. "Señor Garza" is not really a short story in the conventional sense, but a work midway between the portrait study and the "character," in the style of La Bruyère. It is quite possible that some unforgettable barrio barber of years past served as a model. The portrait of Señor Garza is admirably drawn. He is presented as a function of his shop, not only because he spends most of his time there, but because it is the gathering place for El Hoyo's residents. Through the shop, the relationships between its proprietor, other people, and the world are expressed. The spatiotemporal dimension of Garza's shop matters less than its human and metaphysical dimension: though located on the edge of the Tucson barrio, it becomes the barrio's vital center and almost its symbol. The shop's interior is barely touched upon; as in the description of the neighborhood, primacy is given to human beings (the barber, his assistants, clients, and friends) and not to objects:

> Garza's Barber Shop is more than razors, scissors, and hair. It is where men, disgruntled at the vice of the rest of the world, come to air their views. It is where they come to get things off their chests along with the hair off their heads and beard off their faces. Garza's Barber Shop is where everybody sooner or later goes or should. This does not mean that there are no other barber shops in El Hoyo. There are. But none seem quite to capture the atmosphere that Garza's does.[54]

The terms "philosophize," "philosophy," "philosopher," and "wisely" recur with meaningful frequency. Garza's fundamental characteristic is his philosophy; it gives his portrait its internal cohesion. It shapes the barber's attitude toward others and toward life: his liberalism toward his employees, his moderate zeal for his work, the serenity with which he slowly but surely builds his fortune; these attitudes explain his popularity in the barrio. Step by step, the author heads toward his triumphant conclusion, a revelation of the key to his character's philosophy: "Garza, a philosopher. Owner of Garza's Barber Shop. But the shop will never own Garza."[55] Just like the French moralist La Bruyère, Suárez finishes off his portrait with a concise turn of phrase that contains the ultimate truth about the character, the one that underlies the facts and acts by which the narrator has presented him to us. Señor Garza is a sage; he knows how to be rich without being materialistic. Suárez adds many curious and amusing details; he is not afraid of stretching the facts, of exaggerating the color: "He was born with so much hair that perhaps this is what prompted him to be a barber."[56] Repetition and "accumulation" are among his favorite techniques; here they are combined:

> When zoot suiters come in for a very slight trim, Garza, who is very versatile, puts on a bit of zoot talk and hepcats with the zootiest of them. When the boys that are not zoot suiters come in, he becomes, for the purposes of accommodating his clientele, just as big a snob as their individual personalities require. When necessity calls for a change in his character Garza can assume the proportions of a Greek, a Chinaman, a gypsy, a republican, a democrat, or if only his close friends are in the shop, plain Garza.[57]

Suárez does not confer the title of *maestro* ("master") on the barber since he values him less for his skill with the scissors than for his wisdom.[58] By contrast, Arnulfo Trejo's barber, who specializes in cutting hair to the exclusion of any other accomplishment, is promoted to the rank of *maistro*;[59] but how lackluster Arturo Ramírez, the master of Santa Monica, appears to us in comparison to Señor Garza! Trejo falls short of Suárez's mastery. Whenever a man is called a *maestro*—having reached a certain age—it means that he has fully mastered "whatever trade, art or folly he practices,"[60] Suárez explains. He commands the respect—indeed, the affection—of the barrio. In Suárez's brief narrative "Maestría," the principal character, Gonzalo Pereda, is an expert in the art of training fighting cocks. It relates the exploits of Killer, the invincible champion cock who is the equal of his trainer, and, at the end, describes a bitterly wept-over death that foreshadows the end of a world. For the author, the death symbolizes the progressive disappearance, since the war, of the *maestros* of the past; a hint of sadness shines through the sarcasm he heaps upon their inept successors:

> They say that the new generation of so-called shoemakers are nothing but repairers of cheap shoes in need of half soles. They say that the musicians are but accompanists who learned to play an instrument in ten lessons and thus take money under false pretenses. Even the thieves, they tell you,

are nothing but two-bit clips. The less said about other phases of *maestría*, they will add, the better.[61]

Let us proceed with our tour of the barrio. At the end of the day, Cuco Martinez prefers to go to a bar or to his friend Garza's barber shop than to go home to his wife, Emilia; this good-natured comrade forces himself, however, to play the model husband to appease his irascible brothers-in-law:

> Every night he hurried home from work because his two brothers-in-law did it and thought it *right*. The brothers-in-law believed that if a man got up very early in the morning and cooked his breakfast, it was *right*. . . . The brothers-in-law also believed that if a man worried about the price of household needs and discussed them with his wife it was *right*. But only to his two brothers-in-law. To Cuco, it was very boring.[62]

But one evening, unable to endure the routine any longer or to shake off his boredom, Cuco gives in to good fellowship and to his love for the bottle.

In another Suárez story, in an old barn or abandoned hovel lives a gang of winos, tramps who are perpetually hung over; these merry spiritual brothers of Steinbeck's *paisanos* work only enough to buy red wine at eighty-seven cents a gallon: "For food they prey on the neighbors' chickens. For love they seek out lonely but passionate divorcees."[63]

While on his way to visit a parishioner, Padre Ramon passes through the barrio; his presence is just as vital at family celebrations as at religious ceremonies. Here and there one can see "*comadres* sitting out in the sun combing their very long tresses or the ones of their younger daughters,"[64] or Loco-Chu, the barrio idiot with a passion for five-cent pieces, pestering the passersby.[65]

The bus passes by. Those getting off include Señora Alvedre, who goes to Mass daily to thank the Lord for her pretty home, its patio overflowing with flowers, that her sons built for her; old Florencia, who bemoans the indifference of her own two sons, whom she raised by the sweat of her brow; and Alfredito, a little shoeshine boy who is the sole support of his family. He has flashing eyes and black locks he constantly pushes back from his face.[66]

A common spirit, a similar lust for life, vibrates in these very different people. No one understands the deep-seated hedonism of his parishioners better than Padre Ramon, the former Father Raymond, who converts himself to their way of thinking in order better to convert them in turn. When he finds himself at the bedside of a dying young man terrified of death, he adeptly paints a verbal picture of the joys of Heaven. His description would relieve the apprehensions of any Mexican-American about the beyond:

> There the beer you love will flow, God permitting, in golden rivers. And wine in deep lakes and well fermented, not made in test tubes like some of the stuff one often buys around here. As for the dark-eyed girls you adore, surely they will be just as pretty and sweet in Heaven. . . .[67]

Padre Ramon tactfully approved only the most superficial aspects of this ethic of pleasure, which had a double edge. Since it assigned no intrinsic value to work, the ethic encouraged laziness and often drunkenness. Suárez did not fail to emphasize these two Mexican frailties, which he apparently accepted with a certain fatalism as inherent flaws in the people of his race: the husband of Lola Lopez, Anastacia Elizondo's *comadre*, is a perpetually hung-over good-for-nothing; the *compadres'* drinking bouts are ritual-like; the intemperence of Cuco Martinez causes domestic difficulties, and so forth.

No doubt, a form of hedonism creates problems for Mexican-Americans; on the other hand, the art of enjoying things and people, because it presupposes an indifference to materialism, constitutes a safeguard of their freedom. This was the lesson Suárez implicitly taught his Anglo-American readers, who tend to judge people according to a rigid work ethic, in terms of their success, and to evaluate this success in terms of quantity and not quality. "Garza's pet philosophy is that a man should not work too hard";[68] money "would never possess Garza." The wise old barber prefers to seek excuses for Lily-Boy's laziness and close his eyes to the absenteeism of Rodríguez, rather than lose his employees' friendship.

Garza is perhaps extreme, but he represents a profound sense of community. Hospitality was the rule in the barrio. Muro's short story "María Tepache" is an homage to Mexican generosity; the old grocerywoman welcomes a hobo, a passing drifter, into her home. Having just fed four others and nearly exhausted her supplies, she nonetheless offers him something to eat and a sack of food for the road: *tamales de dulce* ("sweet tamales"); *nopalitos* (edible prickly-pear pads); a bottle of *champurrado* (a mixture of liquors); and some *tortillas*. She says to him: "I have enough for today, perhaps tomorrow, and another day too. . . . After that, God will say."[69] A similar kindness and consideration for others characterizes the two barbers of El Hoyo and Santa Monica. Garza's shop is a veritable confessional, where everyone can count on an understanding ear:

> On most days, by five-thirty everybody has usually been in the shop
> for friendly reasons, commercial reasons, and even spiritual reasons. . . .
> There have been arguments. Fortunes made and lost. Women loved.[70]

Garza, a true "Saint Francis,"[71] was also the friend of the poor and the weak. When he catches Loco-Chu, the barrio idiot, making faces at his clients through the window, he never chases him away without first giving him a five-cent piece and an old magazine to resell for his own profit. Trejo's master barber gives his white clients a curious and meaningful lesson in antiracism after they express shock at seeing him cut the hair of Blacks. He pulls a handful of hair from the wastebasket and sorts it into little piles on the table according to color. Then, taking his scissors as if to perform a difficult surgical operation, he begins to shorten the tufts a bit, saying, with a hint of malice: "You see, these scissors don't know the difference between blond, brown, or black hair. Why this is such a good brand of scissors that they can even cut curly or straight hair."[72]

A place like no other, the barrio escapes definition. Suárez knew this better than anyone else. He tried in vain to capture its essence and lock it into three pages in his brief narrative "El Hoyo." The barrio is perhaps the "blood-well from which he springs,"[73] he concludes, the only place where Mexican-Americans feel alive in the fullest sense.

These works reflect a society radically different from the dominant society, but in no way hostile to it. The barber of El Hoyo is not at all similar to the protesting barber of Seville, who is indignant at not having a social status equal to his merits. Suárez takes pains to caution us against finding a belligerent spirit in the barrio:

> ... El Hoyo is not an outpost of a few families against the world. It fights for no causes except those which soothe its immediate angers. It laughs and cries with the same amount of passion in time of plenty and of want.[74]

In this respect, the role played by such publications as *Lulac News*[75] is significant. When Robert Felix Salazar published a polemic poem, "The Other Pioneers," on the exploits of the Spanish pioneers in the Southwest in the paper, he not only wanted to make his readers conscious of their Mexican cultural heritage, but also to elicit their pride in being Americans. A note reflecting the newspaper's orientation was added to the story, aimed at those who might have missed the author's real intention:

> Respect your citizenship and preserve it: honor your country, maintain its traditions in the spirit of its citizens and embody yourself into its culture and civilization.
> Study the past of your own and of the country to which you owe your allegiance, learn how to master with purity the two most essential languages—English and Spanish.[76]

Anglo-Americans are noticeably absent from the barrio, a world closed in upon itself; when they are mentioned, however, it is without surliness. Witness the short story by Juan Sedillo published just before the war, "Gentlemen of Rio en Medio."[77] The subject is familiar: an American company purchases land belonging to the leading citizen of a small New Mexico village. Although this type of transaction often turned out to the disadvantage of the landowner, here the financial broker displays remarkable generosity. Trejo's *maistro* of Santa Monica has overcome the bias he may have had against American tourists he had dealt with and allowed himself to be persuaded to emigrate to the United States; he apparently never regretted the decision.

These vignettes from the barrio provide a static, past-oriented vision of Mexican-Americans still immersed in their myths and resistant to assimilation. Does their fatalism work against change in their closed system? When he didn't dwell on universal themes, Fray Angélico Chávez, a military chaplain during the war, turned resolutely toward a time gone by. Rechy's novels are best appreciated on an existential level; unfortunately for this study, they lack an ethnic dimension. Alongside the opaque and brutal world of Rechy's *City of Night*, the sketches of El Hoyo may appear too clear and simple, their author's approach too traditional. However, Suárez's testimony is precious and his narrative talent undeniable. He observes the human comedy of the barrio with amused compassion, not unlike that of Bradbury; the latter, however, never goes beyond mere entertainment; a lover of the ludicrous and the exceptional, Bradbury dwells upon the most outrageous and colorful aspects of the Mexican quarter. Suárez, by contrast, perceptively observes things from within the barrio, his home place. Through its sounds and colors, he captures its human warmth without being insensitive to its humor. The essence of his art consists precisely of this reconciliation of verve and reserve, of compassion and objectivity.

Turning pocho *was a half-step toward turning American.*[1]

CHAPTER II

The Pocho's Dilemma

The barrio is not so closed a world that it can lock out history. For better or for worse, once they became Americanized, Mexicans were forced to live on "American time." Outside the barrio, they found themselves immersed in a different civilization, faced with a dilemma. Should they blend into the dominant society at the risk of giving up their culture, or remain faithful to it and stay on the periphery of the mainstream society? Was there a middle road? The foreign culture was alienating in two ways: first, it discriminated against Mexican-Americans, excluding and making them second-class citizens; second, through the trap of assimilation, it made them strangers to their own ethnic community and turned them into hybrids, or *pochos*. While Anglo-American writers stressed the dilemma, the first form of alienation, Mexican-American writers emphasized ambivalence, the second form of alienation. The Mexican-American writers, with their more intimate knowledge, went to the root of the problem, exposing the dangers posed by each solution. *Pachuquismo*, an unconditional refusal of any form of integration, led only to anarchy. Excessive assimilation, implying a categorical rejection of the original culture, was both simplistic and demeaning. Even a lesser degree of assimilation represented an unsatisfactory compromise between two antithetical systems of value. That was the dilemma of the *pocho*.

Because Suárez focused on the barrio, he dwelt upon the traditional side of Mexican-Americans, while Villarreal, who dealt with intrusions from the outside world, underscored the ambiguity of their situation. Neither dealt with the Mexican-American middle class, which was more or less cut off from its origins and already enjoying a certain affluence. The lower classes, closer to their sources, preserved the traditions. It was they who most felt the difficulties of integration and the dangers of assimilation.

Confronting an Exclusionary Society

Villarreal's novel *Pocho* is the story of a young Mexican-American, Richard Rubio. He is caught between the Anglo world in which he is destined to live but whose access remains difficult, and the familiar family environment he remains attached to but cannot avoid questioning. The action is set in Santa Clara, California, in the period between the two world wars, approximately 1920 to 1942. The hero's first contact with the dominant society, in school, gives the author the opportunity to denounce the chauvinistic teaching in general and the one-sided historical views presented by the textbooks in particular. For example, General Benedict Arnold, who defected to the British side during the American Revolution, was considered a traitor in the United States but a hero on the other side of the Atlantic.[2] Elsewhere, the author attacks linguistic chauvinism, which Philip Ortego would later call the Anglo's "lexocentric" attitude[3] and which most often manifests itself in a mockery of the Mexican-American accent. When the teacher in Santa Clara hears Richard pronounce "sundries" with a Spanish "u" ("soondries") she gently but laughingly corrects him; the child would never forgive her laughter and from that point on feels embarrassed whenever corrected by anyone. The word "sundries" would long haunt him.[4] The incident might well have had an inhibiting effect on the subsequent development of a student less gifted and stable than Richard.

A third point that Villarreal dwells upon excessively but is barely touched upon by Shulman in *The Square Trap* is the educational and occupational counseling of children in relation to their social class and ethnic group. Quite often the young Mexican-American is automatically counseled to attend a vocational school that will provide him with a trade and place him "in a position to be a good citizen."[5] If we add that, in contrast to regular schools, these institutions do not stress initiative or critical thinking, but rather respect for discipline and authority, consistency and conscientiousness in work, and, finally, conformism, one can understand the author's implications. As the son of immigrants of modest means, Richard can hardly look forward to anything but manual labor or boxing, the traditional path to social success among minority groups. As a conscientious student and insatiable reader, he has read the novels of Horatio Alger and identified with his heroes, who are invariably rewarded with success and riches for their labors. The boxing trainer tells him that his ethnic origin constitutes a serious handicap; he tells him, as he told the young Filipino Thomas Nakano, Richard's friend: "I'm giving ya the chance of your life. . . . It's the only way people of your nationality can get ahead. . . ." Then: "Mexicans don't get too much chance to amount to much. You wanna pick prunes the rest of your life?"[6] But young Richard no more wants to fight in the ring than he wants to become a farm worker like his father. In high school, the counselors try in vain to discourage him from going to college and to steer him toward such work as welding, mechanics, or sales. The counselor finally gives in to his persistence and makes an exception for him, a step she pays for dearly, the author adds bitterly, for "She'd been eating crow ever since."[7]

The problems of the farm worker occupied a secondary role in Mexican-American writings of the postwar period. The great era of the *corridos* on emigration and migration was past; the theme of the *braceros*, laborers officially imported by the American government beginning in 1942, was not so fruitful. Not until the Chicano movement did additional inspiring subjects emerge to give new impetus to the *corrido*. Villarreal, in a few pages of *Pocho*, evokes the Depression and what it meant to all workers, whatever their ethnic origin, and the role of the Communists in those years. In Santa Clara, as elsewhere throughout the country, an unemployed workers' council is created to deal with the government on behalf of the needy; committees are formed, but their efficiency is often hampered by lack of coordination, internal quarrels, and incompetent leadership. The Communists try to rally these disparate associations together in common cause. In a red barn in Santa Clara, converted into a meeting hall and sporting the party flag, a San Francisco delegate quickly wins over his audience by vilifying the capitalist government in Washington and advocating a hunger march on Sacramento. Juan Rubio, a regular at these assemblies, is there with his son Richard, who quivers in youthful enthusiasm. His father is less enthused (even during the troubled period of the Depression, relatively few Mexican-Americans joined the Communist party): "The boy and his father always sat with a group of Spanish men, because, as his father said, they were not the best people with whom to associate, but at least they spoke the language of Christians."[8] The next scene takes place in northern California, on the ranch of a Mr. Jamison. The farm workers refuse to pick pears for fifteen cents and demand an hourly wage of twenty-five cents. The owner (who was "a good man . . . , and no man who had ever worked for him could say otherwise"[9]) cites the latest decisions of the growers association and says he'll maintain the original rate. His daughter, a charming young lady who has often shown Richard the treasures of her personal library, begins to harangue the workers in an attempt to justify her father's seemingly arbitrary position. The scene inevitably degenerates into melodrama. But Villarreal gives both sides, the accusations of the Communist orator, who speaks for the "have-nots," and the entreaties of management. The owner's call for work and calm leaves the workers cold; they respond with a strike and with violence. A truck loaded with melons is quickly commandeered by the strikers, the driver unable or unwilling to stand in their way; later on, they attack a shipment of pears. The police intervene, armed with clubs; an old Mexican-American is struck on the head; his son retaliates, and blood begins to flow. Yet the following day work resumes at Mr. Jamison's ranch at fifteen cents an hour.

Villarreal does not dwell on the specific problems of the itinerant farm worker. Juan Rubio is only partially nomadic; he moves alone, though some-times accompanied by his son, in the limited area of northern California. In the few passages devoted to migrant workers, Villarreal stresses not their often deplorable living conditions but the uniquely Mexican atmosphere the workers create in their hastily improvised living quarters. Once workers of Mexican origin gather together around campfires and tents in California, "a small piece of Mexico"[10] materializes. This persistence of Mexican culture on American soil is one of the two focal points of the novel.

The *bracero* appeared in 1942, after the incidents recounted in *Pocho*. His story is told in the *corrido* "El Bracero," composed by a bar owner in San Francisco, probably during the 1940s. It is the only one I have been able to find on the subject:

Soy bracero mexicano;	[I am a Mexican laborer
he venido a trabajar	I have come to work
para esta nación hermana	For this sister nation
que me ha mandado llamar.	Which has sent for me.
A mi país piden brazos	They've asked my country for strong arms
para poder sustituir	In order to replace
a los que están en la lucha	Those who are in the war
sin temor de morir . . .[11]	Without fear of dying . . .]

The American government had made guarantees to the Mexican government of decent salaries and adequate working conditions for this imported labor force; that the provisions of the treaty were not observed is clearly evident from the sequel to this *corrido*, in which the author incites his comrades to be wary of the "gringos" and their crooked *tratos* ("deals").

Clandestine immigration continued. Rechy, who spent his youth in the bor-der town of El Paso, saw more than one wetback arrive by swimming or walk-ing across the Rio Grande. With large, flashy brushstrokes and pitiless sarcasm, he paints a picture of their hopes, their border crossings, their disappointment, and their sometimes tragic misadventures:

> Wasn't it natural, those wetbacks wanting to come to America?—Christ, they heard about sweet-tasting toothpaste. . . . And if sweet-tasting Ameri-can toothpaste ain't enough to make a man face the Border Patrol (as Bad as L.A. fuzz) and the excellent labor conditions in progressive Georgia, well man, what is? . . . I remember a dead bracero near the bank of the Rio Grande, face down, drowned in the shallow water around him, red, red, red. Officially, he had drowned and was found, of course, by the Border Patrol . . .[12]

The theme of the wetback's exploitation, hardly touched upon by Rechy, is totally absent from the *corrido* "Los Dos Mojados" [The two wetbacks],[13] writ-ten in the forties. Based upon an actual incident, it details a grudge fight in 1946 between two wetbacks in a Texas saloon, a hackneyed subject of the preceding decades. This *corrido* has the same structure as the older epics; the first stanza introduces the theme and the final stanza, the *despedida*, bids farewell.

The farm worker, whether migrant laborer, *bracero*, or *mojado*, remained marginal. Rechy and Villarreal, however, concentrated their attacks less upon the discrimination directed at the farm worker than upon the racism that victimized all people of Mexican origin. To Rechy, the problem always came back to the visceral hatred of the "Mexican," the "greaser," which was especially rampant in Texas:

> They used to yell, Mexicangreaser, Mexicangreaser, when I went to Lamar Grammar School, and I thought, well, yes, my mother did do a lot of frying but we never put any grease on our hair, and so it bothered me— if God was Mexican, as my mother said, why did He allow this?[14]

In Rechy's eyes, this hatred is pathological; for Texans, he sees it as a way of compensating for ". . . the full-scale really huge (consistent with everything Big in Texas—and Alaska won't change anything) Texan inferiority complex."[15] The prototype of the Texan is

> . . . the Texas rancher strutting across San Jacinto Plaza, all bones and legs, getting kicks from sitting, later, booted-feet propped getting a shine from the barefoot spik kid, tipping him 50 cents . . .[16]

The writer takes revenge in an outburst of sarcasm: "They don't really dislike Mexicans in Texas if they're maids and laborers."[17]

The ethnocentrism that Villarreal railed against manifested itself at all levels, among the young and the old, against Mexicans, Italians, Portuguese, and Japanese. The early Spanish conquerors and the later Anglo invaders held to a fundamental principle, that the quality of people is a function of the color of their skin. It is not by chance in *Pocho* that the hero's family name is Rubio, a Spanish word meaning "blond." Juan, the father, has light skin and gray-blue eyes, but his son inherits the dark skin, dark eyes, and prominent cheekbones of the Indian from his mother. The child is obsessed by his racial origins and has his parents explain over and over again the different strains in Mexican blood. His "obsession about the brown"[18] is such that this young "half-caste" ends up believing that the color white has an intrinsic value. For him, ". . . a white horse is the best horse that there is."[19] Mexicans are put into the same low category as Blacks; Zelda, a 15-year-old blond Anglo, shamelessly calls Consuelo Rubio a "sonuvabitchen black Messican" and Richard a "blackie."[20]

There are some hackneyed racist slurs in the novel, ideas that Anglos applied to the "dirty Mexican," the person who was still the "greaser" to most of them. Mrs. Madison fears that her daughter might become contaminated by a book lent to her by the young Mexican-American: "It's filthy . . . you might catch something from it! . . . a load of germs."[21] Americans feel a physical repulsion for Mexican food, especially for its two basic specialties, *tortillas* and chilebeans, which they contemptuously associate with Mexican-Americans' physical appearance. The word "chilebeans" is used as an insult.[22] The term *cholo* ("half-breed") was used by the Spaniards, or by Southwestern natives, to designate an immigrant.

Villarreal approached the problem of racism dispassionately and objectively. The passage on the arrest of Richard Rubio is significant; the police mistake Richard's group for a gang of *chucos* [*pachucos*], take the young men to the police station, and rough them up somewhat (they are even accused of raping a gringa). For the first time, Richard feels himself the victim of racial discrimination. However, the matter is finally straightened out. The police officer is favorably impressed by young Richard, just as the officer in Shulman's novel *The Square Trap* is impressed by its hero, even though he is a *pachuco*. Each of the policemen show compassion; with the exception of a few details, the two scenes are identical. Later on, Richard admits that his painful experience with the American police was "due more to the character of a handful of men than to the wide, almost organized attitude of a society. . . ."[23] The tone of the Mexican-American writer proved no more caustic than that of the Anglo-American.

Rejection and Attempts at Assimilation

How could Mexican-Americans make a place for themselves in a society that accepted them only as long as they were content with inferior status and with working as servants or manual laborers, and whose culture, so different from their own, both fascinated and confounded them? The *pachuco* wanted no part of either culture. His total rejection of the heritage of his ancestors and the values of the dominant culture placed him outside both his own ethnic community and the Anglo-American system. Postwar Anglo writers tried to understand and justify the revolt of these youths, whom they considered rather pathetic. The Chicano writers saw *pachuquismo* either as the source of their own sociopolitical protest movement or as a form of existentialism. But to the older generation, during the period of assimilation, the *pachuco* was nothing more than the *enfant terrible* of the barrio. Rechy depicted *pachuquismo* as a fascinating game, and Villarreal, as a difficult, irritating, and inevitable phase.

Rechy goes to the heart of southside El Paso, where *pachuquismo* was born during the 1930s. With a sense of complicity the author evokes the *pachucos* and then their successors, the *neo-pachucos*, though his personal rebellion took an entirely different form. With his usual savage abandon, he sets them boldly before us:

> They're black-haired. And tense. Mean and bad, with Conflict seeth-
> ing. . . . They used to call them boogies, marijuanos, the zoot-suits . . .
> and man, those tigers walked cool, long graceful bad strides, rhythmic as

hell, hands deep into pockets, shoulders hunched. Much heart. They really did wear and still sometimes do, those hats that Al Capp draws—and the chains, too, from the belt to the pockets in a long loop.

And sitting talking Mexican jive,* mano ["man"], under the El Paso streetlamps . . . outside the dingy 40-watt-bulb-lighted Southside grocery stores avoiding la jura,** the neo-Pachucos with dreamy junk eyes and their chicks in tight skirts and giant pompadours and revealing 1940-style sweaters hang in the steamy El Paso nights, hunched, mean and bad, plotting protest, unconscious of, though they carry it, the burden of the world, and additionally, the burden of Big Texas.[24]

To the author of Pocho, pachuquismo is a dead-end street; he emphasizes, with irritation, its ridiculous and juvenile aspects. The pachuco's style of dress is "unique to the point of being ludicrous";[25] the pants legs pegged at the ankles make Richard think of "some longforgotten pasha in the faraway past";[26] the entire outfit gives the wearer "the appearance of a strutting cock."[27] The girls wear jackets so long that they almost cover their very short skirts. The pachucos' language is unintelligible to anyone but themselves. In "their frantic desire to become different . . . to segregate themselves from both their cultures" they succeed in becoming "a lost race."[28]

Though he never fully joins, pachuquismo is decisive in the evolution of young Rubio. He quickly sees its limitations and pitfalls. He associates with the pachucos without becoming a part of the gang; he has trouble understanding their Spanish, which is not as good as his own; he is obliged to denigrate the "Whites" and avoid speaking English; against his will, he is dragged into grudge fights with another gang; he steadfastly refuses to touch marijuana. He observes his new friends with more condescension than sympathy. In his view, the pachucos are "defeated"[29] like his father, and pachuquismo is nothing more than escapism. It represents a stage he has to pass through before discovering his true identity.

In his own way, the vendido ["sell-out"] was also defeated, a person whose attempts at assimilation and social advancement were often doomed to failure. Amado Muro treats the vendido as a humorous subject. If he had been a true Mexican-American, he might have handled it more seriously. The humor of his short story "Cecilia Rosas" is on two levels. At the plot level, the hero-narrator, Amado Muro, fears that his ethnic origin may prevent him from winning the beautiful Cecilia Rosas, who affects being very American. At the author-narrator level, the humor lies in the fact that Chester Seltzer totally invented his Mexican identity as Amado Muro. This aspect, naturally, escapes the uninformed reader. The idea is ingenious and the hoax is the work of a consummate artist-practical joker. In the story, it's as if Amado Muro, because he is in love, wishes to become a sort of Chester Seltzer. In real life, Seltzer wished to become a sort of Muro. Quite sure of himself, the impostor adds one last daring touch to his fabrication. Let's examine more closely the story's details.

Cecilia Rosas is a salesgirl in an El Paso department store. She is young and very beautiful but she is less proud of her beauty than of the fact that she was born in El Paso and is more American than Mexican. She acts, dresses, and speaks like an American; she has even Anglicized her name to Cecile Rose. But to the other Mexican-American salesgirls she is "La Americana" (the American) or the "Gringa de Xochimilco."[30] Fifteen-year-old Amado Muro works on Saturday evenings in the same store. Cecilia's beauty fascinates him, and in his imagination he sees himself as worthy of her:

> The dreams I dreamed were imaginative masterpieces. . . . They transformed me from a colorless Mexican boy who put women's coats away into the debonair American, handsome, dashing and worldly, that I longed to be for her sake.[31]

His refusal to speak Spanish with his family creates a "real uproar"; his attitude is judged to be "unorthodox, if not scandalous"[32] in a neighborhood predominated by the Burciagas, the Rodríguezes, and the Castillos, all traditional families. When Amado turns up his nose at the traditional food of *sopa* ("soup"), *frijoles* ("beans"), *mondojo* ("tripe"), and *pozole* ("boiled corn"), he is sharply reprimanded by his uncle, who ranks him among "the renegade Mexicans who want to eat ham and eggs even though the Montes Packing Company turned out the best *chorizo* ("spiced sausage") this side of Toluca."[33] His sister Consuelo calls him a "gringo," "a Rio Grande Irishman," a "*bolillo*" ("Anglo"),[34] and "an American Mister." When she sarcastically suggests that he legally change his name to "Beloved Wall," the English translation of Amado Muro, the mother quickly squelches the idea: "If *Nuestro Señor* ["Our Lord"] had meant for Amadito to be an American he would have given him a name like Smeeth or Jonesy."[35] Convinced that the beautiful Cecilia likes him because she jokingly asks him to take her to the movies someday, Amado decides to serenade her. He even hires three mariachis, strolling musicians, to accompany his modest guitar but, because of his inexperience in the rites of love, he has them arrive at sundown rather than the early hours of the morning. One can imagine his dismay at finding a tall American in front of Cecilia's house, at the wheel of a beautiful car, and at seeing his beloved come out to join the handsome stranger without realizing that the serenade is for her and without granting him anything more than a condescending smile! The musicians end up playing for Cecilia's father. Amado has no choice other than to "go back to being a Mexican again" and to be content with a girl "as Mexican as *chicharrones* ["chitlins"]."[36]

In this masquerade of people trying to pass for something they are not, the author pokes fun at everyone. He ridicules those who are tempted by American civilization, from which he believes he personally has escaped by assuming a false identity. He secretly laughs at the reader he has deceived, but those who are aware of his identity are inclined to believe that Chester Seltzer-Amado Muro's own misrepresentation is just as illusory and naive as that of his two characters.

Assimilation continued; the barrio, little by little, opened itself up to progress and to Anglo civilization. Paradoxically, the Mexican minority owed some improvement in its living conditions to the United States' entry into World War II after Pearl Harbor; the war brought an increase in industrial production and new jobs. A relative prosperity resulted for many barrios, such as the one in Tucson, around which air bases and aircraft factories were built. According to Suárez, a "trickle" of money, which soon became a "river,"[37] finally arrived at El Hoyo, bringing with it many amenities of modern life. But money, by inevitably creating differences among people in a community, also changed their relationships. Little by little a middle class, which would soon desert the barrio, began to develop. In the banter with which Suárez denounces the baleful effects of Anglo civilization's supposed benefits, there is a veiled sadness: a gulf was created between those who had indoor plumbing and those who did not. The haves looked down on the unprogressive have-nots. "The spirit of comadreada underwent change"[38] and everyone was more or less touched by it: "the sickness even afflicted a few compadres."[39] The "strange metamorphosis"[40] experienced by the Rubio family, among others, manifested itself through a middle-class mentality and progressive abandonment of traditions. Richard himself does not remain impervious to change, whose consequences he deplores.

On the linguistic level, erosion took place. While the older generation, that of Juan Rubio and of the *maestros* evoked by Suárez, spoke English with a Spanish accent, the English of the younger generation, Richard's group, gave no hint of its ethnic origin. The *corridos*, a spontaneous expression of the lower classes, who were closer to their roots, became even rarer. Beyond the language, an entire system of values, personified by the *maestros* of the past, tended to disappear. Suárez's short story "Maestría" ends on a pessimistic note: "There are not so many *maestros* any more."[41] The time of manual labor and art for art's sake was over; the Southwest would henceforth live in the industrial era.

The dangers of assimilation appeared most obviously in the family. Assimilation attacked the fundamental family principle of male supremacy, upsetting family stability and causing severe problems. This is one of the major themes of Villarreal's novel; the book chronicles the slow and irreversible "metamorphosis" of an immigrant family. Juan no longer physically abuses his wife, as he had in Mexico. American law protects the wife and Consuelo knows it: "If your father ever put a hand on me—why, they would lock him up, that is all,"[42] she said to Richard. However, each of her attempts to shake off the marital yoke is firmly rebuffed. But Consuelo becomes more and more American and develops a self-assurance prejudicial to family harmony; contact with her Mexican and American neighbors, who are more liberated, permits her to see another conception of marriage and the family. She intervenes with greater frequency in the quarrels between Juan and the various children, who, in turn, take advantage of the parental discord. Richard is mature enough to grasp the seriousness of the matter; without approving, the young Mexican-American understands his mother's attitude:

> . . . a family could not survive when the woman desired to command, and
> he knew that his mother was like a starving child who had become glut-
> tonous when confronted with food. She had lived so long in the tradition
> of her country that she could not help herself now, and abused the privilege
> of equality afforded the women of her new country.[43]

She expresses her liberation through intentional slovenliness in her household
duties. The husband, now left to prepare his own breakfast, among other
tasks, deserts the couple's bedroom in reprisal. From that point on, Consuelo,
formerly the perfect housewife, considers her poorly kept house "a symbol of
her emancipation."[44]

Double Allegiance

Villarreal raises the problem of assimilation but offers no solution. The novel
remains ambiguous just as Richard Rubio, the problematic hero, is ambiguous,
"a product of two cultures,"[45] confronted with Anglo society and a Mexican
family. He is "a pocho,"[46] as he explains to Pilar Ramírez, a young girl recently arrived from Mexico who laughs at "his Spanish, which was California-
Mexican American Castilian."[47] Suspect to Mexicans, who considered them
pseudo-gringos,[48] pochos were also suspect to recent immigrants, who believed
"that they considered themselves too good for the barrio but were not, for some
reason, good enough for the Americans."[49] All things considered, the pocho, the
"faded one," was "uprooted."[50] While the more spectacular adventures of the
diehard pachuco could not fail to attract the Anglo writer, the pocho's dilemma,
more unobtrusive but no less profound or pathetic, was best described by
those who had experienced it. Caught between a respect for traditions and the
attraction of a new lifestyle, some Mexican-Americans made a choice in one
direction or the other, but most lived with this schizophrenia daily.

Amado Muro, the child in the short story "Sunday in Little Chihuahua,"
learns Longfellow at school and reads Mexican poets Antonio Plaza and Juan
de Dios Peza[51] at home. The ambivalence of Richard Rubio first appears in his
language; he constantly switches back and forth between English, his "vehicular" language, and Spanish, his "vernacular" language.[52] The first allows him
to communicate with the outside world and gradually becomes more concep-
tually satisfying; the second links him to his family and retains a more affective
character. The numerous exchanges between mother and child are significant.
For example, in Chapter 2, following the strike, they have a conversation in
Spanish (transcribed into English in the text), but as the discussion becomes
more complex, Richard's "thoughts suddenly switched into English." "Back
in Spanish,"[53] he returns to discussing a concrete subject, his future, the professional position that the Rubios, like so many Mexican immigrants, dream
of for their sons. Elsewhere, the switch from one language to another goes in
the reverse direction. When Mary Madison claims that her brother's snobbism

is caused by his plan to become a minister, Richard finds the idea so ridiculous that he impulsively cries out in Spanish: "Eso no lo será [That can't be]." [54] Later, angry at his mother's criticisms, he quite naturally swears in Spanish: "Mierda! Es pura mierda! [Shit! It's nothing but shit!]" [55]

It is especially within the family that young Richard, born of Mexican parents and raised in the United States, becomes most painfully conscious of his ambivalence. Outside the barrio, it is sometimes uncomfortable but rarely intolerable; thus, at elementary school, a teacher's sympathy allows him to think of himself, for a while, as just like the others; in the police station, he finds excuses for the police officer's racism. At home, the differences between the generations continue to widen. The parents have never really tried to integrate into the dominant society (Richard has given up trying to teach them English), but they have done everything to facilitate their son's entry. For example, Richard never accompanies his father in his seasonal migrations if he would miss school. His parents see Richard drift farther away each day; they no longer speak the same language, literally or figuratively: ". . . we cannot even talk to you in your own language," [56] Consuelo says to Richard, whose "own language" informs a way of thinking that is becoming increasingly foreign to her. Without denying his Mexican origins, the young man takes pride in his American citizenship and believes strongly that immigrants must adapt to their new environment. "If we live in this country, we must live like Americans," [57] declares Richard in a peremptory tone, provoking his father to retort: "You are an American with that black face? Just because your name is Rubio does not mean that you are really blond." [58] Juan's decision not to return to Mexico, as he wants to, makes Richard aware of a double allegiance—to the country of his ancestors and to the one of his citizenship:

> He realized that it would be difficult for him in that strange place, for although he was a product of two cultures, he was an American and felt a deep love for his home town and its surroundings. So when he was certain the family would remain, he was both elated and sad. Glad that he would be raised in America and sad for the loss of what to him would be a release from a life that was now dull routine. [59]

The United States is the immediate reality, while Mexico is a marvelous "elsewhere."

This theme of double allegiance is taken up in Américo Paredes' moving short story "The Hammon and the Beans." This brief narrative, part autobiography, part fiction, takes us back to the author's childhood in the Texas border town of Jonesville-on-the-Grande, the location of the Fort Jones garrison. The narrator recalls young Chonita, who died of malnutrition, and whose mother was a charwoman in his parents' home. The attention of the reader, however, is drawn to the miserable living conditions of the Mexican immigrants but to the fact that they are dependent upon two cultures: "Give me the hammon and the beans!" [60] little Chonita shouts each day as she looks through the windows of the mess hall at the soldiers eating. She cries out her ambiguous status (and that of the narrator): her American half (ham) lacks the necessary eggs[61] and her Mexican half (beans) is separated from the traditional *tortillas*.

Could *pochos* escape their dilemma? Richard is trapped inside himself and hasn't the slightest desire to escape; for him, the problem is strictly personal; it's not a collective issue. The search for his identity leads to exaggerated egocentrism and frenzied individualism, whose only purpose is to protect his doubly threatened self from outside influences. Nothing better defines Richard than this response to his mother, who has just asked him why he reads and studies so diligently if not to change the world and improve the lot of his ethnic brothers:

> "And I am supposed to educate my children so that they can change my way of living and they theirs, and so on? . . . I want to learn, and that is all. I do not want to be some thing. I do not care about making a lot of money. . . . I have to learn as much as I can, so that I can live . . . learn for *me*, for *myself*. . . ."[62]

His real mentor is an old Portuguese individualist, Joe Pete Manoel Alves, who does not pretend to be able to communicate his own experience and impose it upon others: ". . . a man must find out some things for himself, inside himself."[63] From his early youth, Richard rejects group activity: he plays alone, to the despair of his mother; his best friend, Ricky, is "an egotist of the worst species."[64] Marriage seems an alienating institution to him. His mistrust of all groups strengthens over the years:

> "Never—no, never—will I allow myself to become a part of a group —to become classified, to lose my individuality. . . . I will not become a follower, nor will I allow myself to become a leader, because I must be myself and accept for myself only that which I value, and not what is being valued by everyone else these days. . . ."[65]

He is swayed neither by the *pachucos* nor the Anglo police. During his arrest he withdraws from the former, but does not collaborate with the police under the false pretext of helping his people:

> "I'm no Jesus Christ. Let 'my people' take care of themselves."
> "You were defending them a while ago."
> "I was defending myself."[66]

He later refuses to identify with his ethnic group and is not seduced by the young Marxist militants and others who are anxious to win him over to the Mexican cause. Intellectually brilliant, Richard is forced to work in a steel mill to provide for the needs of his family, now without a father. The ideas of these militants

> . . . constituted a threat to his individuality, and his individuality was already in jeopardy. And it bothered him that they should always try to

find things in his life that could make him a martyr of some sort, and it pained him when they insisted he dedicate his life to the Mexican cause, because it was the same old story, and he was quite sure he did not really believe there was a Mexican cause—at least not in the world with which he was familiar.[67]

He rejects ancestral traditions for the same reasons that make him hostile to any political commitment; he considers them just so many constraints upon the individual. He deplores the fact that his mother is "locked up"[68] in an archaic female role; he slowly frees himself from the hold of religion and from the fear of sin, in particular. In order to be completely free, he has to leave his mother and cut the umbilical cord tying him to his Mexican past. World War II has erupted, and he enlists in the military. He does feel some remorse at abandoning a family dependent upon him, and his regret makes him a bit more sympathetic. However, he sees the military only as a temporary solution. The cynicism of his enlisting gives him a guilty conscience and softens the brashness of his act. The war is the only way for him to end a meaningless life and realize himself more fully:

> There was nothing to be done now except run away from the insidious tragedy of such an existence. And it came to him that it was all very wrong, somehow, that he should think of himself at this time. All very wrong that he should use the war, a thing he could not believe in, to serve his personal problem.[69]

The tone is quite different in a *corrido* of the period, "Los Veteranos de 1941" [The veterans of 1941]. The author, as a Texan and an American citizen, feels a sense of commitment; contrary to Richard Rubio, he believes he is "fulfilling a duty"[70] by fighting against Japan and Germany. He praises the courage of the Mexicans from Texas, sent forth under the flag by the "fine president of the United States":[71]

Que sepan los Alemanes	[The Germans must know
Que en la patria americana	That in the American homeland
hay valientes capitanes	There are valiant captains
de alma noble y soberana.	With noble and proud souls.
Que sepan que los texanos	They must know that we Texans
también sabemos morir, . . .	Also know how to die, . . .
Volveremos? no sabemos	Will we come back? We don't know
la suerte que nos espera;	The fate that awaits us;
tal vez allá moriremos	Perhaps we'll die over there
al pie de nuestra bandera.[72]	At the foot of our flag.]

Perhaps the war will give a true meaning to Richard's life, in a temporary and precarious way, but the demands of group life in the Army would doubtless weigh heavily upon this individual so enamored of independence.

The end of the novel is equivocal. The hero does not appear to have enlisted in the Army in order to assimilate rapidly and certainly. His departure, nonetheless, implies a radical break with his Mexican past; he leaves his family with the certitude that ". . . for him there would never be a coming back."[73] The book ends as he breaks away. The author evidently considers the integration of his *pocho* into American society a desirable eventuality. In the barrio of El Hoyo, some praise with equal fervor ". . . the beauty of Mexico and the comfort of the United States."[74]

Villarreal's *pocho* is not the Chicano of the years to come. Blinded by his ego, he sees no way out of his dilemma but to lock himself in "his protective shell of cynicism."[75] Though he believes he is preserving his identity, he actually risks losing it. Chicanos later overcame ambivalence through collective action; by losing themselves within the group they found their true identity. The apolitical, ahistorical attitude of the *pocho* is escapist; Richard Rubio, the future writer, would not be the spokesman for the Mexican minority. The very name Chicano represents a commitment.

Villarreal's novel does not radically question Anglo society any more than Suárez's short stories do. Both through its structure and its hero's nature, *Pocho* reflects Mexican-Americans' attempts at assimilation. It is in the mainstream of the traditional novel; it breaks no new ground; its form is not original. It is a profoundly individualistic novel, as is the author's second novel, *The Fifth Horseman*, published fifteen years later, in 1974. With the same insistence, it stresses the autonomy of the individual and the development of personality. (Villarreal's articles, however, reveal a more combative and committed writer.[76]) *Pocho* centers on the psychology and originality of the hero, a hero who denies the value of the group. The author pours his thoughts into an Anglo-American mold. For decades, Spanish had prevailed, and an original form, the *corrido*, was created to express the experience of the Mexican people on American soil. The literature after 1965 was marked by a radical change of form, which corresponded to a radical reevaluation of Mexican-Americans and their status in American society. But not a single innovation characterized the postwar transitional period: there was a perfect conformity with the dominant mode of expression. The "classic" writing of Villarreal, Suárez, and others (with the exception of Rechy, whose verbal abandon was a form of protest) testified to their implicit agreement with existing social structures.

During the period from World War II to the beginning of the Mexican protest movement, the assimilationist phase of Mexican-Americans, a new literary image took shape. An increasingly more objective vision of the Mexican-American appeared in works by Anglo writers, to the extent that traditional stereotypes began to fade away. Mexican-American writers gradually developed a perspective on themselves and on the society that they reflected; by becoming more critical, they also freed themselves from a "prefabricated" self-image; the new one had more depth. If these writers went back to their past, it was not to revive a myth but to find sustenance in the myth and go beyond it, for the discovery of the true self had to begin with the discovery of their heritage. It was in the barrio, the symbol of the past and the source of life, that the Chicano would be born. By a curious coincidence, the term Chicano, then lacking its current connotation, appeared for the first time, in 1947, in Suárez's short story "El Hoyo." *El hoyo* is the hole, the fertile womb, from which the Chicano would come. In 1972, Edward Simmen would define the Chicano as "an American of Mexican descent who attempts through peaceful, reasonable, and responsible means to correct the image of the Mexican-American and to improve the position of this minority in the American social structure."[77]

PART THREE
1965–1974

Chicanos Present
Their Own Image

If the word huelga ["strike"] has not yet appeared in an English language dictionary along with other Spanish words which have come into common usage in English, it surely will now. [1]

The Anglo-American Point of View

What America is, California is, with accents, in italics. [2]

Confronting the Chicano Phenomenon

Many Anglo-Americans espoused the Chicano cause, not only in their writings but by active participation in the protest movement; they belonged to la Raza as it was broadly defined by poet Abelardo Delgado, as a group open to all people of good will.[3] Eugene Nelson's detailed narrative of the first 100 days of the great Delano strike was published by the Farm Workers Press in 1966; it paints a particularly flattering portrait of César Chávez.[4] Nelson was accused of threatening the Rangers during a farm workers' strike in Texas in 1967 and was jailed in Rio Grande City. In *Forty Acres*, Father Mark Day describes the hectic years from 1967 to 1970, when he was the Catholic chaplain of César Chávez's National Farm Workers Association.[5] Sister Mary Prudence, B.V.M., wrote the poem "The Nun's Tale" after she participated in a workers' march on Sacramento; it bears witness to the support some Anglo members of the Catholic clergy gave to la Causa.[6] Sam Kushner's *Long Road to Delano*,[7] a study of the prolonged struggle of the Mexican-American laboring class, was acclaimed in Chicano literary circles. Anglos and Mexican-Americans also established a fruitful collaboration in letters and sociology; among the more tangible results was the publication of such anthologies as *Aztlán*, a joint work by dramatist Luis Valdez and sociologist Stan Steiner, the author of *La Raza*.[8] More generally, there was a renewed interest in Chicano history. In 1969, for example, Carey McWilliams's book *North from Mexico* was reprinted; it had aroused little enthusiasm when it first appeared in 1949.

But were the Anglo writers presenting a more accurate reflection of Mexican-American reality? In view of the increasingly intense opposition to modern and western values since the 1960s, one might have expected a revival of romanticism, a glorification of Mexican-Americans as capable of living life fully on the periphery of technology. But with the exception of two stories that returned to this myth, the new Anglo works did focus on Mexican-American reality, particularly on the phenomena of alienation and ethnic awakening. The new writers were more often people of action rather than literary types. The novel *Bracero* was the work of Eugene Nelson, an active member of the UFWOC (United Farm Workers of California) AFL-CIO; novelist Joseph Wambaugh, the author of *The New Centurions*, was a former Los Angeles policeman; the underworld of California's large urban centers was well known to Frank Bonham, author of *Cool Cat* and *Viva Chicano*, who was particularly interested in juvenile delinquency. In addition, these writers resituated Mexican-American reality into the larger context of American culture of the past few years. Ethnic communities were also caught up in the breakdown of western values. Anglo literature became less "folkloric" and Mexican-Americans lost some of their exoticism, which had previously given them a certain prestige but also contributed to their marginality. Writers setting out to demonstrate the general decay and bad faith of the dominant society made Chicanos the spokemen for their pessimism.

CHAPTER 12

One Last Beautiful Dream

By treating the theme of the alienation of older Mexican-Americans, still faithful to their ancestral values, Anglo writers vicariously relived a past obliterated by their own advanced industrial civilization. Two mythic short stories illustrate this point. Juan, the hero of Richard Dokey's short story "Sánchez," is a farm worker recently emigrated from Mexico to California; he resembles old Vidal Catanios in the Shulman novel, *The Square Trap*. Like Catanios's son, Juan's son Jesús (whose name evokes Mexican tradition) has adopted the American lifestyle and way of thinking. Any dialogue between father and son becomes impossible, as demonstrated by their last meeting, which occurs in the first part of the story. Juan takes Jesús in his old Ford to the cannery in Stockton. While the young man becomes ecstatic over the factory's machines, imposing size, and toilet facilities, his father sees only ugliness and filth. Jesús is interested in objects and the money they can provide (for example, some houses that have been torn down to make way for new subdivisions); Juan is concerned about people (such as those who were evicted to make way for the real estate development) and the quality of their lives (the new courthouse has no curtains). The second part of the story, the longer of the two, take us into the Sierra Nevada, a fairyland where the extraordinary love affair of Juan and Bellezza, Jesús's mother, took place long ago. Their love had allowed them to transcend their demeaning living conditions. Estranged from his son, separated by death from Bellezza, Juan has no reason to continue living in a world whose values he finds unacceptable. He sets fire to his house and disappears in the flames of his memories. "Juan Sánchez had simply gone home."[1] The author is swept along by his own evocation of a past transfigured by love and beauty, one that gives his tale a lyrical and quite moving character.

A short story by C. W. Gusewell, "Robert Melendez: Retrospect,"[2] takes up the theme of Mexican-Americans' attachment to tradition. Its hero is a painter of the 1940s who remains resolutely outside the expressionist movement. His excessively simple paintings—children's portraits—have little success. The situation of the day laborer, as we shall see, was just as problematical.

CHAPTER 13

Marginality and Difference

The Mexican Farm Worker

The Mexican worker was a pawn on the chessboard of American agribusiness, moved around or eliminated according to business needs.

The exploitation of the *bracero*, who served as a sort of "exchange currency" between the Mexican and American governments, was roundly denounced by Nelson, an unwavering supporter of Chávez and the *huelga* ("strike"), in his novel *Bracero*. This Anglo militant was familiar with the Chicano leader's struggle to put an end to the *bracero* program, a fight that Edmund Villaseñor emphasized in his novel *Macho!*[1] The dedication of *Bracero* set its tone; it was addressed

> To the real authors of this book, those hundreds of thousands of Mexicans who wrote it with their labor, their misery, and in some cases their lives while feeding without just compensation the millions of ignorant or ungrateful citizens of the United States.[2]

The epigraph, an adaptation of an Aztec poem, recalls the Indian component of Chicanos' cultural identity, of which they are particularly proud. The novel is the story of a deception. The young Mexican, Nacho, a native of Esperanza, a miserable little village with an ironically promising name, takes a long walk, on an empty stomach, through the burning deserts of the interior to Calexico, the threshold of the Promised Land—California. There, the would-be *bracero* enters the Kafkaesque world of Mexican bureaucracy, subject to the whims of American agribusiness and its constantly changing quota of laborers. After several weeks of doubt, he is finally declared acceptable, but first must take a series of humiliating tests: undressing, to detect venereal disease; washing; delousing. Finally, an X-ray scan detects a tubercular condition that will forever deny him access to the United States. Nacho turns back toward his village, which he will perhaps never reach; the book ends with the exhausted young Mexican lying on his *serape* (shoulder blanket) in the middle of the desert.

The hero of *Bracero*, then, will never become a *bracero*; but the author's ingenuity consists of giving the young Mexican, and the reader, a view of *braceros'* American experience through other characters. While making his way north, Nacho meets some Mexicans returning home; their miserable appearance shocks him. He realizes that a *corrido* he has heard many times before is correct: "I went to the United States in *huaraches* ["sandals"]. . . And I came back barefoot . . ."[3] A truck driver agrees to take him for five pesos as far as Empalme, Sonora, a *bracero* staging area. A man of forty who has spent half his life in American fields, the driver considers himself a veteran. His experience was negative at the beginning (working conditions in Texas were so harsh during a certain period that the Mexican government temporarily stopped sending laborers there), but had a positive conclusion. His last employer, a particularly humane Kansas grower, renewed his contract and gave him the opportunity to earn the money to buy his truck. Nacho later hears of the pitiful conditions in the work camps in the United States (for the Mexican government, overwhelmed by internal problems, this discontent directed at the neighboring country was an excellent diversion). At his last stop before the border, the young peasant has to deal with American anti-communism (the story is quite likely situated in the 1950s). For having taken part in a strike during a previous stay in the United States, another Mexican is accused of subversion by a representative of the American immigration service and brutally refused admission.

The book brings out the complicity between the Mexican and American governments. For example, when the "communist" tries to defend himself, he is immediately subdued by a Mexican soldier and beaten almost senseless. The *braceros* were exploited on both sides of the border; they were simply exchanging one form of subjugation for another. Twenty-five years separated the publication of Claud Garner's novel *Wetback* from that of *Bracero*, and the principal source of agricultural labor for the United States had not been exhausted. Nelson put the *bracero* program on trial; he saw it as nothing less than the institutionalized exploitation of the immigrant Mexican worker. In his novel, however, he does not allow himself the polemicism of his other writings; he depicts the inner distress of young Nacho without ever degenerating into the affectation that mars Garner's book and makes his hero less convincing.

The problems of the Chicano worker were brought out briefly in *California*, a semi-autobiographical cyclical novel by Leland Frederick Cooley; his perspective is radically different from Nelson's in *Bracero*. The author, descended through his great-grandmother from an old and perfectly integrated Hispanic-American family, presents California and its agricultural conflicts from a very American point of view. The book retraces the Americans' conquest and settlement of the former Mexican territory; above all else, it is the epic of the Yankee pioneers. Cooley spends little time on the golden age of the Californios, on the art of living that fascinated Anglos at the end of the nineteenth century. The author apparently intends his California to represent a perfect synthesis. His paternalistic view of the workers on the Los Nidos ranch is significant; the principal antagonist is César Chávez.

Nevertheless, the book brings up a burning issue: developers were buying up arable land, posing a threat to thousands of Mexican farm workers. In the book, the expropriated landowners, supported by Chávez and the unions, fiercely but vainly oppose the construction of the Micropolis 2000 development on the Los Nidos ranch. The hero, Howdy, the author's spokesman, advocates a radical solution; progressive mechanization would systematically reduce the labor force and, correspondingly, the worries of management; this would be the best way to circumvent Chávez. The businessman fears the latter's charisma, his impact on uneducated and poorly informed crowds, and considers him, wrongly, to be power-mad. The workers would lose if they listened to him, for ". . . in the end Chavez would be killing the patient to cure the ailment."[4] Cooley knew only too well that the defender of the *campesinos* had his detractors within the Mexican minority; in the novel, the characters who personify the antithetical points of view are the two Morales cousins, Carlos, the "good one," the author's spokesman, and Luis, the "bad one," a tool of Chávez. Carlos, who has become "middle class," believes acculturation possible for his ethnic brothers and ridicules the farm workers' union by reversing its acronym, UFWOC, to COWFU ("cow dung"). Luis is a man of bad faith; he knows that working conditions on the Los Nidos ranch are excellent; to organize the workers, he deliberately creates situations that would justify the establishment of a union.

California and *Bracero* represent two facets of the Anglo-American attitude toward the Mexican worker and the Chicano protest movement. Cooley-Howdy never addresses the severity of the problem, nor does he ever use the term "Chicano." A descendant of Anglo-Saxon pioneers, marked by the puritan ethic, he becomes indignant at seeing minorities shirk their jobs. The novel by union leader Nelson, in contrast, exposes the problems of the Mexican seasonal worker, whose labor, in part, made California's affluence possible.

The Emergence of the Chicano

The emergence of the Chicano was a new and positive aspect of Mexican-American reality that found its way into Anglo literature. Chicanos were proud of their ethnic and cultural heterogeneity, and were seeking to overcome their alienation through action. For outsiders, no matter how sensitive and sympathetic, these new attitudes presented difficulties, which Chicano critics were quick to point out. Activist Chicanos advocated measures that implied, to some degree, the destruction of the oppressive dominant society and, if necessary, of those who personified it. How did WASP writers view these subversive ideas? The two themes of ethnic consciousness and self-liberation are the focus of William Cox's novel *Chicano Cruz*; they are treated in a slightly bantering manner in the short novel by Frank Bonham, *Viva Chicano*, which addressed itself more to adolescents than adults; Joseph Wambaugh's novel *The New Centurions*, better known than the preceding works,[5] centers on the problem of identification.

The New Centurions delineates the psychological evolution of three young California policemen from 1960 to 1965: Serge Duran, an ambitious ex-Marine tries in vain to escape his Mexican identity; Gus Plebesly, a prostitution specialist, has doubts about his own manhood; the liberalism of Roy Fehler is tested during his first confrontation with Blacks. Serge Duran occupies center stage; he is the subject of the first chapter of each part of the book; the two following sections, respectively, are devoted to his comrades. In the epilogue, titled "Reunion," the three protagonists assess their five years together.

Serge (Sergio) passes for an Anglo: tall and freckled, he speaks broken Spanish with an English accent. He is even called a "gringo" by a young barrio hoodlum. He has deliberately cut himself off from his Mexican past: he has left the barrio in Chino for Los Angeles, refusing to return there after the death of his mother; he has broken away from the Catholicism of his childhood, dates only Anglo women, and prefers the Anglicized form of his first name. Because of his poor Spanish, his colleagues assume his mother was Anglo. He does not rectify the error, which releases him from the translation duties reserved for more authentic Chicanos. Despite his appearance, he is sent to the Hollenbeck barrio[6] in East Los Angeles, as all policemen of Mexican origin automatically are. He finds the poverty of the barrio repugnant and, at first, feels nothing but contemptuous pity for its inhabitants: "Those poor stupid Chicanos, he thought. Pitiful bastards."[7] But it is in Hollenbeck that he is converted; the Los Angeles barrio causes an emotional shock. Long-suppressed desires are brought to the surface: his growing appetite for Mexican food is significant. He confusedly experiences a feeling of security in the barrio, the same feeling that his very Mexican mother gave him so long ago. Initially, he requests a transfer to Hollywood but then insists upon returning to Hollenbeck. There, he has a fateful meeting with Mariana Paloma in a Mexican restaurant; the young girl with the face of a Spanish madonna slowly eclipses Paula, Serge's rich American girlfriend. Mariana has remained close to her origins; although she has learned English, she intends to impose the use of Spanish in her future household. She precipitates a crisis in this man who thought himself infinitely more American than Mexican. She makes him aware of his schizoid state: "If you can be a whole man by marrying your other one, then do it. Do something, Sergio. Find out what you must do,"[8] adding: "I want you, Sergio, but only if you are a complete man. I want Sergio Duran, a *complete* man. Do you understand?"[9] He does understand. In the final chapter, he announces his marriage to his colleagues and reveals his true background: "One hundred percent . . . I guess I'm probably more Mexican than anyone I know."[10] The book concludes with the "Santa María" Sergio murmurs over the body of Roy, who is shot during a gun battle. Since the story ends just after the Black riots in Watts, on the eve of events at the grape-pickers' strike in Delano, we have no idea how the newly converted policeman will react to the protest movement of his own ethnic group.

Sports enthusiast William Cox[11] set his novel *Chicano Cruz* in a familiar sports-world context. His young hero, Mando Cruz, temporarily abandons his studies and joins a baseball team with the aim of gaining financial independence and overcoming his alienation. This is the well-worn theme of athletics as the recourse of the minority group member. But the book brings out another path, extremism, personified by Mando's brother Ricky, a member of the Brown Berets. These two sons of an alleged alien were raised in a typically Mexican environment: "We had it rough in the *barrio*. But there was always the family. Somehow we stayed off relief. We ate a lot of fried beans."[12] The issue of identity is no more a problem for Mando than for Ricky; he has always felt himself a Chicano and affirmed his ethnic identity. The manager of the team unintentionally offends a Black player by calling him "boy." He doesn't know how to address the young Mexican-American. Mando tells him: "I was born in Los Angeles . . . You can call me 'Chicano' if you can't use my name."[13] Throughout the book, the author stresses the pride in being Chicano. At the end, the young champion receives the acclaim of the public, who christen him "Chicano Cruz." The nickname crowns his triumph.

The two brothers disagree on how Chicanos should overcome their alienation. Mando, obviously the author's spokesman, disapproves of the radicalism of the Brown Berets, who, like the Black Panthers, ". . . want everything overnight";[14] nor does he approve of the attitude of his rich uncle Luis, the turncoat "Mr. Cheapola," who sells out to the dominant society for "a few bucks." The problem is finding an intermediate position between these two extremes. Cox stresses the importance of education; Mando plans to resume his interrupted university studies and become a teacher to educate his ethnic brothers. In this respect, he places himself in a tradition that's reassuring to Anglos, a tradition also advocated by Adalberto Joel Acosta, the author of *Chicanos Can Make It*.[15] Acosta and Cox believe that Chicanos can succeed without either accepting all the values of the dominant society or denying their cultural heritage. But this nonviolent middle road is unsatisfactory, as Mando and his girlfriend Maria realize:

"Maybe we should remain with our own, Mando. My grandfather says we run to false idols, to foreign blood, that we are ashamed of our blood. I am not ashamed to be *mexicana*. But I am proud to be an American of the United States. Am I wrong, Mando?"

"You are right. . . . We must not think of ourselves otherwise. It is to be proud of heritage but aware of today."

"Ah, this is not easy, Mando."

"Nobody promised us it would be easy." [16]

In *Viva Chicano* by Frank Bonham, we find ourselves in East Los Angeles, or more precisely in Happy Valley, one of the run-down Mexican sections of the immense ghetto called Dogtown. Seventeen-year-old Keeny (Joaquín) Durán has spent a third of his life in reform schools. After six months on probation, two new charges are brought against him: he is accused first of having thrown his young brother through a window (the mother has incriminated her oldest son in order to get rid of him) and, second, of having put LSD in some orangeade sold at a fair (a false charge). Keeny is finally acquitted and placed in a home for young prison parolees. We will return later to the question of juvenile delinquency. Aside from this issue, the book treats—in a rather naive and unrealistic way—the emergence of ethnic consciousness in a teenager from East Los Angeles, one of the hotbeds of the Chicano revolt, and the way he internalizes the biases of his elders.

Keeny is in the midst of a crisis of "Mexicanism";[17] to him, only "brown is beautiful." The author is on target when he compares his hero to an Aztec prince, the glorious symbol of the Mexican past, whom the young Chicano is proud to resemble; he is also accurate when he depicts him as "a young [Spanish] grandee"[18] with an aristocratic bearing, thus evoking a prestigious heritage unmarked by the stigma of colonization. From his father, long since dead, Keeny inherited an unshakable pride in la Raza, a pride that has resisted demoralizing school propaganda:

> They'd call us things like Spanish-Americans and Latins—everything but Mexicans, so our feelings wouldn't be hurt. Man, I was *proud* of being a Mexican! My father taught me to be proud of *la raza*! And here the teachers were working six hours a day trying to knock it out of us.[19]

The young Chicano bears an ethnic tattoo not only on his right forearm but on his entire being: "He had eagles and serpents tattooed on his brain. He wouldn't settle for being an American citizen: No, no, *he* was a *Chicano!*"[20] But Keeny's sense of nationalism does not go far. He belongs to the gang known as the "Aztecs," but this group is "all talk and no action." His two theoretical mentors are the revolutionary, Zapata, the barrio idol, and Baker, the fatherly judge responsible for him. As if trying to capture Zapata's spirit, the young man steals a cardboard figure of the famous Mexican from the entrance to a theater. There follows an imaginary dialogue between Keeny and Zapata, who represents his alter ego. In this dialogue, Zapata seems oddly "co-opted" by the authorities. When Keeny flees after the two charges are filed against him, the Mexican revolutionary does not condemn the partiality of the law and of social institutions, or incite him to rebel. Instead, he advises him to turn himself in quietly to the judge.

The judge listens to the young man's complaints against the school system and advises him to take action: "So why don't you *Chicano* guys get involved in trying to clean the mess up? Get in the Brown Berets, things like that."[21] Baker's intentions should not be misinterpreted. He adds: "But don't forget one thing: Nobody's going to forgive you the mistakes you make today, just because you had an unhappy childhood. You're stuck with what you are, what you do."[22] And Bonham-Baker believes that the home for parolees, run by two liberal Anglo women, will solve the young Chicano's problems.

Three separate attitudes on the part of Anglo writers emerge: sympathy for Chicanos, difficulty in describing the details and true nature of *Chicanismo*, and reservations about the actions advocated by radical groups.

Bonham's good intentions should not be questioned. Sociologist Nick Vaca, though he criticizes *Viva Chicano* severely, recognizes it as "an impassioned plea for youth."[23]

As Vaca says clearly, the question is whether Anglo writers are qualified to speak on the Chicano experience. The inadequacies of Bonham's book underscore the need for an authentically Chicano literature, Vaca wrote, adding that despite its title

> . . . there is very little about it that is Chicano . . . in spite of the fact that the protagonist, Joaquin "Keeny" Duran, along with numerous other characters, have Chicano names, that the book contains a sprinkling of Spanish words and phrases with *bato loco* ["crazy guy"] being decidedly overused, that it is set in a *barrio* (Dogtown) in Los Angeles . . .[24]

And he adds: "If Joaquin were substituted by a protagonist of any other color or race the essential quality of the book would not have been altered."[25] Such a work cannot respond to the expectations of the Chicano public, for,

> Instead of feeling infused with the symbolic qualities of Chicanismo or of being exposed to those sometimes imperceptible clues that are distinctively Chicano, the reader comes away from this book with a feeling of having been entertained to a simplistic and naive narrative . . .[26]

Vaca's thoughts echo Delgado's. The latter declared that liberal Anglos, in spite of their sympathy for his people's cause, are "unable to share in feelings which only a Chicano can have. . . ."[27]

It is true that Wambaugh, Cox, and Bonham had difficulty in absorbing Mexican "color" and depicting a world so foreign to them. They wisely elected not to dwell on this subject. Anglo writers in general were less inclined to speak on Chicanos' return to their ethnic roots than on the assimilation of Mexican-Americans.

Anglo writers were also less bold. It was easy for them to espouse integration, which would satisfy their liberalism at no great risk since integration implied the neutralization of the foreign element. But they became fearful when Chicanos refused to be blended into the "melting pot" and questioned the ideal of homogeneity. Anglo-American writers could only offer prudent solutions that fell well short of those advocated by Chicano activists. To do otherwise would be to subvert themselves.

CHAPTER 14

Mexican-Americans Confront
the Debacle

Since the mid-1960s, Anglo literature has engaged in progressively sharper
questioning of Western culture. Juvenile delinquency and violence were seen
as the concrete manifestations of the crumbling of established values; in this
national shipwreck, the Chicano was a piece of flotsam like any other. American society was taking on water from all sides while refusing to see the causes,
but the Chicano, as the pessimistic spokesman for the Anglo-American writer,
perceived and denounced the roots of this decline.

East Los

In East Los, the Los Angeles barrio, the ills afflicting Western civilization
were brought to a head. Four of the five works treated below are situated there.

Hollenbeck, Dogtown, and the other lower-class brown, black, and white
sections had the same sorry look. The name of Happy Valley, as described in
Cool Cat, undoubtedly was the result of some malicious joke. Lined up along
narrow, unlit streets, the houses, really just tiny shacks with neither running
water nor electricity, were built out of packing crates, traffic signs, and spare
lumber; some of these dwellings, which resemble grocery boxes, sport such
slogans as "THIS SIDE UP" or "A GREAT NAME IN DOG FOODS."[1]
But the ugliness of Dogtown, this "city of dogs," is so foul that even black
humor cannot exorcise it.

Inside these shacks, families have generally broken down; Keeny's Anglo-
American stepfather, for example, is a swindler, and his hysterical mother

is devoid of any maternal feelings. The young Chicano's real family is the Aztecs gang. His delinquency is a direct and inevitable consequence of his environment: "I tried to be a straight arrow, didn't I?" Keeny reflects. "But man, how do you do it with a crazy mother, and neighbors down on you? Man, it's not possible."[2]

In Bonham's two novels about juvenile delinquency, *Viva Chicano* and *Cool Cat*, (the first is dedicated to Kenneth R. Cilch, a juvenile-court judge), the author denounces the decay common to both the Mexican barrio and the Black ghetto, a ". . . subculture of gangs interrelated like the Mafia";[3] ". . . anywhere you sliced the *barrio*, it bled trouble."[4] Drug addicts, car thieves, burglars, cop-baiters and killers emerge from the lowest social strata of East Los:

> Day and night they freaked about the black ghettos and the Mexican-American *barrios*. Hundreds of them didn't even go to school. They passed their time leaning against lamp posts, trying to decide what delinquent acts to perform next.[5]

To the "cool cat," whether brown, black, or white, who remained detached from the dominant culture, drugs represented escape, refusal, and violence. This last element, along with the problem of individual identity, is the focus of Wambaugh's novel *The New Centurions*; three men are confronted with a violent society. There is such a war raging among the gangs of Hollenbeck that young novice Serge Duran hopes to be transferred to Hollywood. During a bloody battle waged by *Los Gavilanes* and *Los Rojos* against the Junior Falcons and the Easystreeters, the Mexican-American policeman notices the sign CON SAFOS, the untranslatable gang signature, placed on a wall to indicate that what is written there should not be changed or plagiarized by the enemy.[6] In the last part of the book, the three new centurions are subjected to a much more depressing ordeal: the Black riots of Watts, a murderous explosion of long-supressed hatred.

The image of the barrio that Shulman and Barrett gave in the 1950s differs in two ways from the one presented by Bonham and Wambaugh. First, Shulman and Barrett depict a community, poverty-stricken, of course, but a relatively calm place hardly disturbed by the *pachucos*, who were, all things considered, rather harmless. Bonham and Wambaugh's image reflects the violent eruptions America has experienced since the mid-1960s. Second, while the earlier writers still believed that Anglo liberalism could combat the evils of discriminatory social and economic institutions, the later writers abandoned all hope in the face of what they saw as a nightmarish debacle for the United States.

The Bad Faith of the Dominant Society

Elia Kazan's novel *The Assassins* is not only the story of a trial, but the indictment of an entire nation.

An Air Force master sergeant of Mexican origin, Cesario Flores, somewhat infatuated with his oldest daughter, Juana, kills her hippie lover and a Black friend of theirs. Their friend, Michael, does everything in his power to avenge the murders, but a conspiracy is launched by the power structure, the Air Force, the law, and even the Mafia, to have Cesario, a model noncommissioned officer, pardoned. The novels of Stilwell (*Border City*, 1945), Barrett (*The Shadows of the Images*, 1954), and Mankiewicz (*Trial*, 1955) all centered upon legal matters, but in these the Mexican-American is inevitably the victim of traditional racial prejudice. In Kazan's book, he is co-opted by the Establishment.

Two incompatible worlds with opposing moral values confront one another in *The Assassins*. To the uninhibited and fraternal community of young drug users, which seduces Juana and even interests her father, American civilization is a failure. Michael, for instance, regrets not being Mexican—the Beat Kerouac's old dream. Juana's group considers the double murder unjustifiable homicide. But conformists, omnipresent in the work, make every effort to find excuses for Cesario: "This community—I mean the nation, not just the military—is not going to kill a man it has spent hundreds of thousands of dollars to train,"[7] Mr. Clifford, an executive in a chemical products factory, explains to his son Michael. To the public, which has been subtly manipulated, the affair takes on a new dimension, described in the novel's sarcastic conclusion. Here, the author, before ironically celebrating the air base in Tucson, Arizona, a symbol of American technological power, summarizes the plot: "Early the next year, an officer in the air force, retired, shot and killed a long hair who'd been running around with his daughter. Defense counsel did not think it necessary to plead temporary insanity."[8] Significantly, the crime is committed by a serviceman no longer on active duty, and thus does not compromise the Air Force's reputation; in addition, the defendant's ethnic background goes unmentioned.

The novelist apparently made his hero a Mexican-American for two reasons: his ethnic origin makes his act more plausible, since, as a member of a "Virgin Mary-oriented society,"[9] he is particularly concerned about his daughter's purity. And, conscious of his duties as a man, he refuses to join in the disgraceful game played by the authorities, who try to acquit him in spite of himself. He declares himself ready to accept the full consequences of his act.

Anglo society wants to absolve Cesario because its own survival is at stake. It wants to make him not a scapegoat but its official executioner. "This community is not going to let your man pay with his life for something every single one of them would have done,"[10] says Wheeler, an attorney, to Colonel Dowd, who cannot deny his subordinate's guilt. Even Michael, weary of pursuing the murderer, ends up admitting: "You can't blame him. He was trained to kill,"[11] while Gavin, the liberal attorney, urges him to persevere. Cesario has killed in cold blood, Gavin says, like all those bomber pilots, "relieved of the burden of conscience."[12] Like their airplanes, the pilots "are also automates, also programmed, the highest expression of a technological society. They know not what they do."[13]

This conflict is an absurd battle between two condemned groups: the dominant society, protecting the killer, is rotten and moribund; the lifestyle of the young drug users carries the seeds of its own destruction. The funeral ceremony they organize turns into a bacchanal, then degenerates into a violent brawl over a motorcycle.

The Chicano as Spokesman for Anglo Pessimism

Chicanos are co-opted in a different way in Wambaugh's *The New Centurions* and Bonham's *Viva Chicano*. Posited as lucid observers of the dominant society, they lament its obvious disintegration, thus becoming spokesmen for Anglo pessimism.

Wambaugh, a former policeman who advocates a hard line, reproaches his countrymen for their growing "softness."[14] In his view, the Watts riots sounded America's death knell by revealing the nation's inability to resolve its domestic problems. Through two Mexican-Americans, the author expresses his own preoccupations about his country's fate. In the book, on a warm summer evening in 1965, a Mexican-American working at a hamburger stand confides in Serge Duran, whose Chicano identity he is unaware of. Blacks are not afraid of Anglos, he says, the *gabachos* ["Anglos"] certainly have nothing to be envied. And he adds:

> I'm glad to live in your country, but only as a Mexican. Forgive me, señor, but I wouldn't be a gringo. And if your people continue to grow weak and corrupt I'll leave your comforts and return to Mexico because I don't wish to see your great nation fall.[15]

Sergio shares the man's pessimism. The Watts riots, a challenge hurled at the authorities and the Establishment, move him to forecast a bleak future: "This was the beginning, and the Anglos were neither strong enough nor realistic enough to stop it. They doubted everything, especially themselves. Perhaps they had lost the capacity to believe."[16] This is also the essence of the criticisms expressed by Chicano literature.

The young hero of *Viva Chicano* is also struck by the latent death of the world around him. In a bus, "everybody was sealed in his own little coffin."[17] With "its cargo of mummies,"[18] this East Los bus recalls the car loaded with "freeze-dried" tourists, against whom Adán, the protagonist of the Chicano short story "Un Hijo del Sol,"[19] vents his rage.

But Chicanos' questioning of the power structure was never pushed too far in Anglo literature. The writers did not show the luminous side of the face of the rebel, the exuberant savior of a moribund America. The Anglo writers' Chicano was irreversibly contaminated by Anglo defeatism.

We hate the agribusiness system that seeks to keep us enslaved, and we shall overcome and change it not by retaliation or bloodshed but by a determined non-violent struggle carried on by those masses of farm workers who intend to be free and human.

CÉSAR CHÁVEZ,
"Letter from Delano,"
Good Friday 1969

A Chicano is a Mexican-American with a non-Anglo image of himself.

RUBÉN SALAZAR.

La actitud occidental es enfermiza. Es moral. Gran aisladora, gran separadora, la moral parte en dos al hombre. Volver a la unidad de la visión en reconciliar cuerpo, alma y mundo.

O. PAZ,
"Corriente Alterna"

The Mexican–American
Point of View

> *Thus far*
> *The image of mi raza (of my people)*
> *Comes from gringo hands . . .*
> *Now must be the time to change,*
> *And with my forming hands, create my real self.*[1]
>   A. ARZATE

CHAPTER 15

The Chicano Movement: Sociopolitical and Literary Awareness

In 1965, Luis Valdez founded El Teatro Campesino in Delano, California, on the very spot where, for almost five years, the grape-pickers' strike organized by César Chávez would take place.[2] This theater gave the Chicano movement, which had been developing in the barrios of the Southwest for several years,[3] a decisive focus and for the first time drew the attention of the general public to the Mexican minority.

"Cesar is our first real Mexican American leader,"[4] wrote Valdez; to others he was "the long awaited 'Messiah' of the Mexican American." Although Chávez, like John the Baptist, denied being the true prophet and obstinately refused to become a leader,[5] this peaceful, almost timid man, seemingly indistinguishable from the average Mexican farm worker, galvanized the masses through his "personal magnetism"[6] and his faith, which he made the foundation of his nonviolent fight for social justice: ". . . tu sueño es contagioso, hermano / ya toda la nación sufre tu fiebre justiciera,"[7] exclaimed poet Abelardo Delgado.

Que tienes tú César Chávez	[What is it that you have, César Chávez
Que le has dado tú a la gente	What have you given to the people
Que los que andan agachados	That those who walk bent over
Ya levantaron la frente?[8]	Have now lifted their faces?]

This hero's unusual undertaking—the strike at Delano—naturally gave new impetus to the *corrido*. But his pacifism did not earn universal approval, as attested to by these sarcastic verses of Raúl Salinas, an active member of the Raza Unida party:

> Rich Dago Vineyards
> Chávez doing his pacifist thing
> "Lift that crate
> & pick them grapes"
> Stoop labor's awright—with God on your side
> Califa's gold not ours to spend, baby.[9]

A character in a play by Nepthalí De León remarks: "While America basks in plenty, our dear brown Saint starves with his brothers, sweats his life out for a contract that has chained them."[10]

Chávez's pacifism and his hostility toward the *bracero* program, whose cancellation he pushed for, made him unpopular in Mexico. Edmund Villaseñor's novel *Macho!* is the only work that presents the view of the nonstriking worker (this is the only original element in an otherwise mediocre book). The worker illegally crosses the border "*a la brava*," at the risk of his life, but finds that the strike denies earnings to him, and to his family back in Mexico. To the intrepid *norteño*, Chávez is a *pocho*, "not a macho"; he "talks softly, doesn't drink, preaches nonviolence, and has no women pulling at his pants but instead a lady, a female, as his second in charge. . . . He is ridiculed and despised."[11]

Zapata, Mahatma Gandhi, and Martin Luther King were Chávez's theoretical mentors and the Virgin of Guadalupe his source of inspiration. After one year, the strike had not won results. To restore the workers' morale, he organized a protest march on the capital of California, but he intended it to be essentially religious, as this *corrido* emphasizes:

> The seventeenth of March,
> First Thursday morning of Lent,
> Cesar walked from Delano,
> Taking with him his faith. . . .
>
> Now we reach Stockton.
> The mariachis sing to us:
> Long live Cesar Chavez
> And the Virgin who guides him.[12]

That march was, at the same time, "Peregrinación, Penitencia, Revolución" [Pilgrimage, penance, revolution].[13] Workers and sympathizers made their way toward the capitol in Sacramento, holding aloft the statue of the brown Virgin. Like the processions of the Penitentes in years gone by, their pilgrimage was an act of expiation; all hatred, desire for vengeance, and pettiness, which could stain the purity of their cause, were to be banished from their hearts.[14] The strike dragged on; the *campesinos* grew impatient and clamored for more vigorous action. To remind the workers of the pacifist nature of la Causa, Chávez conducted a penitent fast twenty-five days long, beginning on February 14, 1968. The Cause won a signal victory on July 29, 1970, when an agreement was reached between the growers and the United Farm Workers Organizing Committee (UFWOC) (a merger of the National Farm Workers Association [NFWA] and the Agricultural Workers Organizing Committee [AWOC] arranged by Chávez in 1966).

Delano became the symbol of oppression and of Chicano resistance; *Huelga!* ("strike"), the order sent out on September 16, 1965, by the Chávez union,[15] was an echo of the famous call for independence, *El Grito de Dolores* ("the cry of Dolores"), shouted out 150 years earlier by the Mexican monk, Miguel Hidalgo y Costilla. Delgado cried out with fervor:

> Say *huelga* over and over
> like an ave maría.
> huelga with joy
> for today the sixteen of September
> and July the fourth have gone to bed together.[16]

In the city barrios, the villages, and the camps, the *corridos* celebrated the strike at Delano:

Viva la huelga en el fil	[Long live the strike in the fields
Viva la Causa en la historia	Long live the Cause in our history
La Raza llena de gloria	La Raza has done itself proud
La victoria va cumplir. [17]	The victory will be won.]

This triumphal stanza recurs like a leitmotif throughout the *corrido* "Viva Huelga en General" [Long live the general strike]. In the two cantos he composed on the occasion of the third Delano march in September 1968, poet Roberto Vargas sets this demonstration by the Mexican minority within the context of the social protest movement sweeping the entire continent. He addresses the victims of capitalism and Yankee imperialism, whether brown or black. By linking the situation of Mexican farm workers in California to that of Blacks in the South, the author makes an implicit appeal to Blacks to make common cause with Chicanos.

In 1968, land-grant activist Tijerina contacted Black activists in California with a view toward forming a coalition. But relations between Blacks and Chicanos were tense; Chicanos tended to consider Blacks as "Black Anglos"; they resented the relatively higher status of Blacks. And despite their ethnocultural ties, no link was ever established between American Indians and Chicanos.

Let's return once more to Vargas's poem:

Ay Raza Vieja	[Ah! Ancient race
Raza nueva y orgullosa	New and Proud race]
Sun bronzed and arrogant	
Con el Espíritu de Che y Sandino	[With the spirit of Che and Sandino]
Con el ardor de Malcom X y Zapata	[With the ardor of Malcolm X and
Now Marching Against Exploitation	Zapata]

Now Marching Against Shit and
    Frustration
Now Marching Against the Bastard
    Grape
Grapes of Wrath / Grapes of Paradox
And bitter-sweet madness
Grapes of big white houses
That mold or destroy
the innocent lives of our children
Children that starve
while pigs feed off their backs
Children of brown eyes in Delano
Delano the epitome of America
Delano of César el santo . . .

Delano the Mississippi of California. . . .[18]

In Northern New Mexico, another Chicano was fighting to recover the old land grants. A zealous evangelist before he embraced the cause of dispossessed Hispanos, Reies López Tijerina applied the fanatical ardor to his new cause that he had to his old religious mission.[19] He spent an entire year (1958–59) in a Mexico City library studying treaties from the former Mexican Southwest. In 1963, he founded the Alianza Federal de Mercedes (a land grant confederation), which was later to become the Alianza Federal de los Pueblos (confederation of free states). He set up headquarters in the poverty-stricken county of Rio Arriba and set off in search of former property deeds held by old Hispanic families. Armed with these proofs, Tijerina made many unsuccessful attempts to deal with the governor. Finally, he tried to establish an autonomous state right in the middle of American territory, provoking an inevitable confrontation with the authorities;[20] on June 5, 1967, with a contingent from the Alianza, he attacked the courthouse in Tierra Amarilla, the county seat. Acquitted in December 1968, he found himself back in prison in June 1969; he serenely accepted his successive incarcerations, convinced that the true guilty party was Anglo imperialism.[21]

A charlatan to some, a dangerous dreamer to others, Robin Hood and Don Quixote rolled into one,[22] Tijerina was a hero to the disinherited populations of Rio Arriba County:

Salió el grupo de Valientes
de la Alianza Federal
todos con picos y palas
a enterrar a Satanás
diciendo, miren no más
que terrible funeral. . . .

Reies López Tijerina
Nunca se dió por vencido

[The band of valiant men
of the Alianza Federal sallied forth
each one armed with picks and shovels
to bury Satan
as they said: just look
at this terrible funeral. . . .]

[Reies López Tijerina
Refused to give in

con el diablo Satanás   to the devil Satan
y dijo el diablo "No más!   and the devil ended up saying "Enough!"
Aquí me doy por vencido."[23]   I surrender here.]

So sang Pedro Padilla in his *corrido* "Sepultura del Diablo Atrevido" [The tomb of the Daring Devil]. The conqueror of the Devil himself, Reies Tijerina or Rey Tigre [King Tiger], as he was nicknamed, became a legend. A more factual *corrido* by Rumel Fuentes emphasizes Tijerina's fight for recovery of the land and places him in the historical lineage of Zapata,[24] whose plans for land reform had made him the idol of Mexican peons. In a narrative by Philip Ortego, "The Coming of Zamora,"[25] the messiah whom the peasants of New Mexico were awaiting turns out to be Tijerina, who is venerated in the same manner as Zapata.

"Denver's Corky boxing lackey's ears back."[26] In Colorado, Rudolfo "Corky" Gonzales,[27] a militant activist and poet, fought against capitalist society with the same virile fury of the boxer that he had been in his youth. To him, art was a revolutionary act. He was more realistic than Tijerina and advocated more violent measures than Chávez did (perhaps he took umbrage at the latter's prestige). In March 1969, Corky rallied together fifteen hundred young people at the headquarters of the organization that he had created, the Cruzada Para la Justicia (crusade for justice). Members of this convention, the Chicano Youth Liberation Conference, drafted the landmark manifesto "El Espiritual Plan de Aztlán" [The spiritual plan of Aztlán].[28] The name resurrected the Aztecs' mythic kingdom; the document proclaimed nationalism as the only "common denominator" of all the composite elements of la Raza.

> Stifling
>   Crystal City
>   heat
> rouses Texas sleepers
>   the long siesta finally over
> at last, at long, long last
>
>   flames are fanned
> Conflagrating flames
>   of socio-political awareness.[29]

In the municipal elections of 1963, the Chicanos of Crystal City, Texas, won a crushing victory, their first ever. Located in southwest Texas, Crystal City, like most border towns, was preponderantly Mexican-American, but the Anglo minority held the power. Getting more equitable representation was primarily a matter of dragging the barrios out of political lethargy. Among those who worked at this task was José Angel Gutiérrez:[30]

> José Angel Gutiérrez: MAYO's fiery vocal cat
>   the world does not love energetic noise makers

or so says papa henry b. (the savior of San Anto)
who only saved himself.[31]

The position taken by Henry B. Gonzales, U.S. senator from Texas, on the issue of Mexican-American Youth Organization (MAYO) nationalism—he labeled it "reverse racism"[32]—was typical of the conservative wing of the Mexican minority. In 1970, Gutiérrez became the chairman of the elementary school board of Crystal City; the same year, he founded a third party[33] designed to serve Chicano interests, the Raza Unida party.[34] Poet-singer Rumel Fuentes acclaimed this new political group;[35] he stressed the gravity of Crystal City's school situation;[36] and he especially urged his listeners to unite and assume their political rights: "Y muy pronto veremos / El que no habla Dios no lo oye / Solo juntos venceremos." ["And we will soon see / God hears only those who speak up / Only united will we triumph."][37]

The same determination motivated young David Sánchez,[38] who, "impatient & enraged in East L.A. / dons a beret, its color symbolizing / Urgent Brown."[39] He mobilized young people;[40] the Brown Berets, like the Black Panthers, proudly emphasized the color of their skin in the struggle for their rights. Less violent than their Black counterparts, however, the young Chicanos set a triple goal for themselves: "to serve" their ethnic brothers, "to observe" the machinations of the Anglos, and "to protect" and guarantee the rights of Mexican-Americans, resorting to violence if necessary.[41]

Chávez, the apostle of nonviolence; Tijerina, the visionary; Corky, the militant-poet; Gutiérrez and Sánchez, the young lions of the Chicano movement; all five[42] figure in Raúl Salinas's poem "Los Caudillos" [The leaders]. But Mexican-Americans were divided; none of these men was able to attract the whole ethnic group's loyalty. The Zapata cult among young militant Chicano youths is revealing: for lack of a contemporary leader they could totally identify with, they resurrected a great figure from the past; their attachment to Zapata (often paired with Che Guevara) was more emotional than ideological. Sociologist George I. Sánchez had long lamented this absence of a leader, which he attributed to the deep-seated individualism of Mexican-Americans.[43] However, in the 1960s "Juan Tortilla" awakened from his long siesta and permanently abandoned his legendary apathy.[44] In its place was real sociopolitical awareness.

On the literary scene, a "renaissance" was taking place.[45] Efforts were made to free the Mexican-American from the stereotypical yoke and to forge a new image. With the writer as spokesman, Mexican-Americans became aware of their true identity. The writer fought alongside the worker; Valdez's Teatro Campesino treated the strike in Delano, while poet Jorge Gonzales, filled with hope, cried out: "guns and pens / *juntos venceremos* (together we will conquer)."[46]

Conscious of the need to publicize older Mexican-American works and those of the talented young Chicano writers, Octavio I. Romano-V., a professor of anthropology at the University of California at Berkeley, founded the publishing house Quinto Sol (this "fifth sun" was a reference to Aztec cosmogony). He also created the periodical *El Grito: A Journal of Contemporary Mexican-American Thought* in 1967, the date that Philip Ortego considers the beginning of "the Chicano Renaissance."[47] *El Grito*, recalling the shout of Father Miguel Hidalgo, the fomenter of Mexican independence, is indicative of the journal's content. In 1969, Quinto Sol brought out a collection of Chicano poems and short stories, *El Espejo—The Mirror*, the first of its kind. Since 1968, the struggle for "cultural expression and freedom," has continued on the university level, with "El Plan de Santa Barbara";[48] study centers were created to revitalize Mexican-American culture. A great number of anthologies appeared (some resulting from Anglo-Mexican collaboration). Theaters sprang up throughout the Southwest; a cultural center designed for farm workers opened in 1967 in Del Ray, California; in 1970, a few miles from McAllen, Texas, in the Rio Grande Valley, the Colegio Jacinto Treviño, taking its name from the border hero, became the first Chicano university. Soon after, another was created in Mercedes, Texas; Deganawidda-Quetzalcoatl, in Davis, California, had a dual Indian and Chicano origin.

Was this intellectual ferment truly a "renaissance" or simply a literary "awakening"? Valdez, for whom culture and the political act were intimately related, leaned toward the second term; he regretted that Mexican-Americans, unlike Blacks, had no long literary and artistic tradition to furnish relevant inspirational themes.[49] The Berkeley group rebelled against such terms as "awakening" and "emergence,"[50] which they believed led to the erroneous idea that the Mexican minority had never produced anything but folklore. There was a great difference between the contemporary and the earlier writers. The older Mexican-American poets and short-story writers were isolated; though they sometimes attacked the dominant society harshly and felt themselves to be marginal, they were a part of it in spite of themselves. They had no separate image of themselves. By contrast, Chicano writers had a will to define and assert themselves with respect to the Anglo world, a will conditioned by ethnic allegiance. "Chicanismo simply embodies an ancient truth: that man is never closer to his true self as when he is closer to his Community."[51]

The theme of identity recurs like an obsession throughout Chicano literature. Many writings are autobiographical: *The Autobiography of a Brown Buffalo* by Oscar Zeta Acosta, *Barrio Boy* by Ernesto Galarza, "Back to Bachimba" by Enrique Hank López, "The Week of the Life of Manuel Hernández" by Nick C. Vaca, and so forth. The title of the anthology *El Espejo* [The mirror] and its brief preface ["In order to know themselves and know who they are, some need only see their own reflection. . . ."[52]] reveal its perspective. The psychological and moral evolution of the young hero of Tomás Rivera's novel *. . . and the earth did not part* reflects the progress of an entire people.

Chicanos refused the image fashioned many decades ago by Anglo history, literature, and sociology, for to accept it would allow political and social manipulation by the Other. In his poem "Lazy Skin," José Montoya rejects the stereotype of the lazy Mexican, and for good reason:

Como	[As
Imagen primordial	The primordial image
De las épocas	From the most distant times
Más allá del pasado	Of the past]
Formulated by the Gaba	[Gaba(cho): white]
Who has used	
It to strap,	
Stifle and	
Almost convince	
Me.[53]	

History, that "great prostitute,"[54] gave a partial and distorted interpretation of the role played by Mexicans; indeed, as poet Sergio Elizondo cried out about the war between Texas and Mexico:

En placas blancas de mármol	[On white slabs of marble
nombres de Chicanos	names of Chicanos
desmienten que sólo había anglos.	belie that only anglos fought.
Mienten, mienten escritores de historias tejanas,	They lie, they lie the writers of Texas
no hay lugar donde no se vean huellas	history,
mexicanas.[55]	there is no place one cannot see traces of
	the Mexican.]

Literature and sociology perpetuated stereotypes that bore the stamp of Anglo ethnocentrism and romanticism. Thus, "the no-nonsense attitude of American politics merged with white racism to create the stereotype of the Mexican greaser,"[56] wrote Valdez. Romano dismantled the sociologists' favorite myths, one by one: the laziness of Mexicans asleep under the cactus, their fatalism, male machismo and female hyperpassivity, and so forth.[57] The primary objective of his literary review was to allow Chicanos to present a less negative image of themselves. Ricardo Sánchez debunked the work of one of the many Anglo sociologists who "proclaimed themselves specialists in the Chicano question":

> Stan Steiner . . . crucifies his subjects rather than suffer the stings of arrows himself. Steiner's myopic study of La Raza is more farcical than factual; more projection than observation . . . [58]

Advertising, which no longer dared exploit Blacks, shamelessly turned to their advantage Mexican and Indian stereotypes forged by sociology;[59] thus it was that the Frito-Lay Company created the Frito Bandito,[60] the little mustachioed Mexican bandit, armed with two rifles. Sánchez became indignant over this "caricature,"

> . . . frito bandito caricature
> bandied about nomenclature
>   as if that were our nature
>   to be of comic stature
> just because the gringo says so . . .[61]

(Note the assonance of "bandied"/"bandito," and the equally ironic repetition of the rhyme "-ture"). Anglo romanticism was just as prejudicial; Valdez justifiably took strong issue with the romanticizing of the Mexican bandit: this process neutralized the bandit by stripping him of his political dimension.[62]

Chicanos waged war against stereotypes through their own comic mode, the satirical farce. It was the perfect vehicle for the Teatro Campesino, as evidenced by *Los Vendidos* and *Los Bandidos*. These playlets both are set in stores that sell second-hand Mexican objects. The three most requested items—the Farm Worker, the Pachuco, and the Revolutionary—are on display. In *Los Bandidos*, the Farm Worker wears a sombrero, is dirty, eats beans, *tortillas*, and chile, lives in an old shack, and speaks no English; the Pachuco kills cops, wears dark glasses, has a shuffling gait, likes to fight and dance, gets arrested, lives on hamburgers, soft drinks, and drugs, has an inferiority complex, carries a knife, and earns his living by stealing; the Revolutionary drinks *tequila*, eats raw meat, smells like a horse. Manufactured in Mexico in 1910, he wears a serape and shouts "Viva Villa!"[63] In each of the plays, an assimilated Mexican-American woman enters a shop. In *Los Vendidos*, Miss Jimenez, secretary to the governor of California, is entrusted with finding "a Mexican type"[64] for the administration—personable, not too dark, and a hard worker. Sancho, the second-hand dealer, shows her a model that seems to fit her requirements:

> "This is our standard farm worker model. As you can see, in the words of our beloved Senator George Murphy, he is 'built close to the ground.' Also take special notice of his 4-ply Goodyear huaraches, made from the rain tire. This wide-brimmed sombrero is an added feature—keeps off the sun, rain and dust."[65]

Harry, the other second-hand dealer, touts the advertising advantages of his *revolucionario* to his client.

Anglos had an unhealthy need for scapegoats in order to feel themselves superior. Chicanos were demanding the right to be themselves—nothing more, nothing less—and that, to militant activist Lydia E. Aguirre, was the ultimate meaning of the Chicano movement. It was imperative, she wrote, to ". . . demand that others recognize our differentness . . . rather than make the Chicano suppress his chicanismo and adopt Anglo-Saxon ideals."[66] Valdez attacked the system that ". . . recognizes him as a Mexican, but only to the extent that he is 'American,' and which accepts Mexican culture only to the extent that it has been Americanized, sanitized, sterilized, and made safe for democracy . . ."[67]

From this point on, writers rejected second-hand images of the Chicano and imposed their own vision:

> I slap the clay,
> My clay,
> Upon the wheel and begin.
> And the clenched fist I use

To smash and crush the gringo's vision
Of what I should be . . .[68]

In these candid and unpolished verses, Arzate, a Los Angeles poet, expressed the task that Mexican-American literature was henceforth to undertake.

Political and social activism directly inspired some writers, while others, with a new awareness brought on by the struggle, glorified the uniqueness of their ethnic group. Most of their themes—the alienation of Mexican-Americans, their reaction to oppression, their dual allegiance—were not new, but they were treated differently or given more breadth. Linguistically, writers showed originality in an alternating use of English and Spanish, particularly in plays and in poetry. Chicanos were seen as victims of the assimilationist "melting pot." Through the repeated juxtaposition of English and Spanish, writers affirmed, in the name of cultural pluralism, the equality of both forms of expression; through often ingenious manipulation of the majority society's own language, they forged the perfect instrument for their subversive work.

Chicanos consider themselves both wholly American and the heirs of a foreign culture, as evidenced by their deliberate bilingualism. But their Spanish heritage, tainted by colonialism, has become less important to them than the ancient civilization of their Indian ancestors. Writers, for example, frequently refer to Aztec mythology and history. Often of brooding realism, sometimes bitter and sad, Chicano literature, nevertheless, is infused with strong currents of hope and vigor. At the crossroads of two worlds, Chicanos proclaim themselves the precursors of cosmic humankind, the biological and spiritual fusion of all races.

CHAPTER 16

Strangers in Their Own Land

Since the defeat of 1848, the American of Mexican descent has felt like a "stranger in his own land";[1] the sociopolitical fever that gripped the barrios in the sixties and seventies exacerbated this feeling of alienation. Literary works expressed such feelings boldly. But the land plunderings of the past, given new currency by Tijerina, proved less fruitful as a theme than the continued "cultural assassination"[2] that forced Chicanos to adopt the language and culture of the invaders in order to survive. The educational system, established by a "monolingual, monocultural, and colorless"[3] society, was an instrument of subjugation. Anglo capitalists, wresting away Mexican-American territory, victimized the *campesino*, who was condemned to wander from camp to camp.

Gringolandia

Colonized and dispossessed of their lands despite the Treaty of Guadalupe-Hidalgo, Mexicans became strangers in their own land: "La Raza came to this land over three-hundred years ago. . . . And now we walk the earth as aliens in the land of our fathers,"[4] Ortego lamented. To Chicanos, the Southwest forever remained *"Chicanolandia,"* where their ancestors had once lived in peace and from which, one day, gringos would be expelled. Fuentes's "Corrido de Aztlán" expresses, by turns, nostalgia for the past and hope:

Tierra famada
Donde mis padres vivieron en paz.

[Fabled land
Where my forefathers lived in peace.

Aquí trabajaban, amaban su tierra	Here they worked and loved their land
Pero vino un diablo	But a devil came
Y se las robó	And stole it from them
Malditos demonios vestidos de blanco.	Cursed devils dressed in white.
Ya llegó el día de justificar . . .[5]	The day of reckoning has come . . .]

In the name of the Chicano people, De León demanded the rights of first occupant, and ironically cast back at the gringos their ethnic slurs:

> Our ancestors were at Plymouth Rock long before the Gringo wetback landed. Stupid Gringos! Calling us wetbacks when they swam across thousands of miles to steal the land of our fathers.[6]

The memory of the Anglos' fraudulent acquisition of the former land grants persisted, revived by Tijerina's crusade in New Mexico. In his *corrido* dedicated to Tijerina, Rumel Fuentes ridicules those who seized Mexican land under the protection of the law:

Se esconden bajo su ley	[They hide behind their laws
Para hacer destrocidades	To commit their atrocities
Malditos rinches cobardes	Those damned, cowardly Rangers
Mandaderos del Gobierno	The errand boys of the government
Pero Dios tiene otra ley	But God has another law
Que los mandara al infierno.[7]	That will send them all to Hell.]

Philip Ortego's "The Coming of Zamora," more a narration of events than a short story, centers on Zamora, alias Tijerina. It traces his impossible undertaking step by step and outlines events at Tierra Amarilla, New Mexico, where the struggle for the recovery of the land grants was waged. Old Alarcón, seated on the steps of the courthouse where Zamora-Tijerina is being tried, reflects both the bitterness and the hope of the rural Hispanos. To them, Tijerina is a reincarnation of Zapata and his Alianza nothing less than another Plan of Ayala:[8] "*Hijos de la chingada*! [Sons of bitches!] He curses silently. They! They are the foreigners! the gringos! the poachers! But Zamora will show them!"[9] The prisoner appears and calmly disperses the crowd awaiting the verdict: if he loses the first hand of this game against the gringo government, he will surely win the next. Alarcón, now confident, returns home to await the coming of Zamora.

The skeptical author does not share the old peasant's optimism; like many Chicanos, he knows that Tijerina's battle was lost before it began:

> Alarcón is a philosopher; *he* sees the justice of his cause and he wonders why others don't. But Alarcón is a victim of the romantic fallacy: he believes that good eventually triumphs over evil. If he did not believe this, then he would not have joined so quixotic a cause. But he does not mistake a windmill for an adversary.[10]

A second colonization, this one economic, followed the first. The fraudulently acquired lands were taken over by Anglo-American capital; the formerly Mexican Southwest became *"gringolandia,"* [11] built up by Chicano labor. A more bitter alienation was added to the first. We will return to this issue later.

"My name ees Jorge Alesandro" [12]

The violation of Mexican culture, also protected under the terms of the Treaty of Guadalupe-Hidalgo, was tied to the theft of the land: "My land is lost / And stolen, / My culture has been raped," [13] shouted poet Rudolfo Gonzales. Chicano writers denounced the policy of acculturation undertaken during the preceding decades as an attempt at deculturation. Out of the "homogenizing" action of the "monolingual, monocultural, and colorless" society, which aroused the polemic verve of Armando Rendón, the new concept of cultural pluralism was born. [14] Hostile to this idea, the educational system held primary responsibility for the cultural schizophrenia of Mexican-Americans.

As a formidable instrument of uniformization, the schools had already been criticized by Villarreal. They now became the Chicano writer's favorite target. [15] Rendón saw Anglo educational policy as a "studied form of cultural genocide," [16] while Albert S. Herrera accused it of seeking "the eradication of the language and culture of the Mexican-American child." [17] Sánchez declared:

> and they strive
> to un-root us, cutting out our knowledge of our past
> building gringo stories in our minds from cradle to grave
> As if we never did exist outside the pale of their shadow. [18]

The urgent need for reform in the teaching of young Spanish-speaking children had long been felt; a *corrido* composed in memory of George I. Sánchez recalls the steps taken by this pioneer of bilingualism:

Desde los años del treinta	[Since the 1930s
George I. Sánchez protestaba	George I. Sánchez has been protesting
Que sistemas escolares	That school systems
A nuestra raza ignoraban.	Are ignoring our people.
Los chiquitos de la Raza	The youngsters of La Raza
Si se pueden educar	Can be educated
Pero tendremos que hablarles	But we'll have to speak to them
La idioma de su mamá. [19]	In their mother's language.]

Chicanos argued that their children should be entrusted to teachers who knew Spanish.

"A product of linguistic and cultural dichotomies," [20] the Mexican-American was truly stricken with "schizophrenia"; this term appeared repeatedly in many works.[21] Poet Elizondo gave this ambivalence a vivid representation: "Chicana el alma / Gringos los bolsillos" [Chicana my soul / Gringos in my pockets].[22]

This duality is found on the linguistic level in "binary phenomena,"[23] characterized by a seemingly arbitrary succession of English and Spanish terms that maintain their respective syntactical structures. This occurs nearly every time the two linguistic groups coexist. While such Jewish writers as Bellow and Roth are content to use a few Yiddish words here and there, for Chicano poets, the process is systematic. Their verses vibrate to the clash of two cultures, keeping the reader constantly on the alert. Here, for example, is the beginning of the Sánchez poem titled "Denver":

Denver loneliness,
Caught fragmented
Neath neon anomie . . .
Chicanismo rapped *en inglés*,
tatteredly worn
como jorongo engarrado . . .   [like a ripped poncho]
café where
mexican hamburgers
are gurgled down
con cerveza y con furia.[24]   [with beer and anger]

Denver was the American city where Corky resurrected the myth of Aztlán. In the following excerpt from the Alurista poem *"mis ojos hinchados"* [my swollen eyes], the amalgam of English and Spanish words reflects the author's distress:

Mis ojos   [My eyes]
   flooded with *lagrimas*   [tears
de bronce   of bronze]
melting on the cheek bones
of my concern
   rasgos indígenas   [Indian features]
the scars of history on my face
   and the veins of my body
that aches
   vomito sangre   [I spit up blood
y lloro libertad   and cry freedom]
   I do not ask for freedom
I am freedom.[25]

This cultural conflict is at the heart of Chicano literature; it is particularly brought to light, from differing perspectives, in two autobiographies and one novel. Without denying or minimizing this conflict, *Barrio Boy* by Ernesto Galarza and *Chicanos Can Make It* by Adalberto Joel Acosta demonstrate that it can be overcome and that social success is not unattainable. In Richard Vásquez's novel *Chicano*, by contrast, the balance sheet is negative. In spite of inevitable cultural evolution, which becomes stronger from one generation to the next, integration of Mexican-Americans remains problematical. Their chances are often compromised as soon as they enter school. The harmful consequences of a monolithic educational system are a major theme of the book.

Barrio Boy is, as the author states in his preface, "a true story of the acculturation of Little Ernie";[26] the first section evokes the little village of Jalcocotán in the Sierra de Nayarit, Mexico, where Galarza was born; the second, which recounts the "pilgrimages" of the family, gives a glimpse of the situation of the peons on the eve of the revolution. The following two sections are steeped in the Mexican atmosphere of the Sacramento barrio where the Galarzas finally settled after stops in Nogales and Tucson. With piquant and provocative details, the narrative brings out the traditional character of the colonia ("colony").

Little Ernie quickly perceives the existence of a world totally different from his own. It increasingly intrudes into the barrio, threatening its integrity. Little by little, the influence of the family gives way to that of the school; the child is initiated into another way of thinking. But conditions are particularly favorable:

> The school was not so much a melting-pot as a griddle where Miss Hopley and her helpers warmed knowledge into us and roasted racial hatreds out of us. At Lincoln, making us into Americans did not mean scrubbing away what made us originally foreign.[27]

What a contrast between these model teachers and Miss Russell, the elementary-school teacher in the bitter short story by C. G. Vélez, "So Farewell Hope, and with Hope, Farewell Fear." She is assigned the Mexican-American students weak in English, including young Ricardo: "She, dressed in somber gabardines, peered through steel-rimmed glasses at him as if he were a microbe under a microscope."[28] One day, she pulls his hair and banishes him to the corner for speaking the only language he knows. Ernie Galarza, by contrast, is soon able to handle both languages and help his monolingual compatriots. In the fifth and last part of the book, he is about to enter high school, something relatively rare for a young Mexican-American during the 1920s. One will not find in Galarza's book the bitterness which permeates Black Boy, in which Richard Wright evokes his own childhood.

The critic John Womack regrets that Galarza did not devote a section to his "rare career in redefining America."[29] It should not be regretted. Such a section would have taken us far from the sounds, colors, and odors of the barrio, which make the book picturesque and piquant.

Through the example of his own family, Adalberto Acosta argues that Chicanos can make a place for themselves in the Anglo world without denying their origins, provided that they make the effort:

> My father's thesis was very simple. We lived in the U.S.A., so it was up to us to adjust ourselves to American culture and laws if we wanted

to progress, and this could be done, he argued, while we remained good Mexicans.[30]

This unusual idea is a refrain throughout *Chicanos Can Make It*, making the book undeniably interesting. Unfortunately, the author never allows himself an occasional gratuitous anecdote, as Galarza does; never losing sight of his thesis, the author quickly degenerates into didacticism.

Like Galarza's book, Acosta's is the autobiography of a Mexican. Born in 1909, he and his family were forced by the revolution to emigrate; they ultimately settled in Miami, a little mining town in Arizona. After some initial difficulties, the Acostas rapidly assimilated. The father's role was pivotal. Upon their arrival, he refused to move into the Los Angeles barrio, fearing social immobility. As a member of the Mexican middle class, he was convinced that only a perfect command of English (which he spoke almost without accent) and the acquisition of certain intellectual tools would prevent his children from joining the herd of "burros" exploited by the Anglo system. He did not allow them to become discouraged by racist teachers; thus, when young Acosta's elementary-school teacher, bothered by the presence of a Mexican-American in her class, asked him to change his name to "something American,"[31] the father opposed her and the child remained Adalberto. By contrast, in the Vélez short story, when school administrators wish to enroll young Ricardo under the name of Richard, his father finally gives in to the arguments of his wife, that "he could do nothing if those with more education and learning demanded the change."[32] On the whole, Adalberto Acosta retained fond memories of his school years. His autobiography ends in 1970. He succeeded in striking a workable balance between two lifestyles and ways of thinking; he married a progressive Chicana, a professor of Spanish at the University of Nevada-Reno, to whom the book is dedicated. His work is incontestable proof that certain, if not all, Chicanos can "make it."

Richard Vásquez's *Chicano*, by contrast, ends on a note of failure. It was published in 1970, eleven years after *Pocho*, the first Mexican-American novel written in English. Denser and less ambiguous than the earlier book, this second novelized chronicle of a Mexican family covers four generations. The first two, born in the nineteenth century, are hindered by the cultural shock of their arrival in a foreign land; the third, which grew up during World War II, is tempted by assimilation; while the fourth, the generation of the 1960s, is characterized by the eruption of violence, an increase in juvenile delinquency, and ethnic awareness. This vast epic of the Mexican immigrant, while of undeniable documentary interest, unfortunately fails to avoid the pitfalls of melodrama and didacticism.

Forced into emigration by poverty and politics, the first generation leads just as miserable an existence north of the border, in a California barrio. They are "trapped":[33] they cannot integrate into the world of the *Americanos* and they have burned all their bridges behind them. "Either do the white man's work, or if you're a young girl, service him, or live like an animal in Mexico,"[34] sobs one of Hector Sandoval's daughters. The father drowns his sorrows in drink; the daughters, Hortensia and Jilda, become prostitutes in order to survive. Neftali, their brother, is the first to try seriously to establish roots in their new homeland. But he buys a lot in Rabbit Town (Irwindale), the only Mexican barrio at that time outside of Los Angeles, with the deliberate intention of isolating himself from the Anglo-American community. He becomes the *zanjero*, the municipal employee in charge of reservoirs and water canals. When this work becomes obsolete, he quietly goes back to packing oranges in the same factory where he used to work. Despite his many years in the United States, he cannot speak or even read English, so his granddaughter Mariana acts as his reader and translator. On his radio and television (his only concessions to American technology), he tunes in only to Spanish programs. He never applies for naturalization for fear he will have to reveal his illiteracy and, consequently, be deported; thus, legally, he remains a foreigner in the land that belonged to his ancestors. In their little Mexican island, Don Neftali and his wife, Doña Alicia, are not entirely sheltered from the outside world.

After World War II, this world does catch up with them through their children, Angelina and Pedro. They are raised in a bilingual and bicultural milieu, speaking Spanish at home and English at school. Through contact with young Anglos, they discover a system of values different from their own and experience a dilemma from which their parents were spared. At twenty-three, Angelina leaves for the barrio of East Los Angeles[35] after a confrontation with her father, who is angry that she speaks to her brother in a foreign language forbidden in his home. Angelina and Pedro make every effort to become integrated into white society. Intelligent and bilingual, "Angie" confidently adapts to her new life. Her Americanization, though sometimes naive, fulfills a need for emancipation. She rejects motherhood (her own mother had seven children) and opens up a taco stand. She marries Julio Salazar, whose own immigrant family was troubled by the disappearance of the father. "Julie" engages in the trafficking of wetbacks as a shortcut to assimilation and success, following the example of Johnny Rojas, a successful Mexican-American "who did things the gringo way."[36] Though he appears completely American, Julie remains fundamentally very Mexican in private life. The author interjects ironically:

> Angie was naive—or perhaps Americanized—enough to believe that, by God, if she could work and earn equally as well as (indeed, better than) Julie, she should enjoy equal rights so far as wanting to know where he spent his evenings and their money.[37]

The Americanization of Angie and Julie remains purely superficial.

The Army proves decisive in the life history of Pedro Sandoval, Angie's

brother. When he returns from the service, "Pete" considers the inhabitants
of Rabbit Town "Mexican hillbillies." [38] His military experience helps him to
find a lucrative job as a mason; unlike his father, who stayed away from workers' protests, he joins the American Federation of Labor, the Anglo-American
union. Later, he does not hesitate to leave the East Los Angeles barrio in hopes
of giving his own son a better chance for success. Pete's accent, however, be-
trays his Mexican origin. Although his English might sound "fairly good" [39]
to a non-Anglo such as Julio, the author often points out, with a hint of didacticism, Pete's phonetic errors: the lengthening of short vowels—Pete says
"spleet" instead of "split," "beach" instead of "bitch," "meester" instead of
"mister," "peek" instead of "pick"; the change of a fricative into a "t"—"shovel"
becomes "chawbull"; as for "sure," "the sh being an alien sound combination to
his native tongue, the word came out 'choor.' " [40] But Pete's "broken English" [41]
does not handicap either his work or his dealings with Anglos; like Angie, he
thinks of himself as assimilated.

But the educational failures of his son Samuel make him painfully aware of
the ambiguity of his family's situation—an issue dear to the author.[42] Vásquez
does not dwell on the education of Angelina, Pedro, or Mariana, Samuel's twin
sister, because these three people are sufficiently talented and well adjusted to
be taught in a foreign language. Of only average intelligence and immersed
in a Spanish environment since childhood, Samuel is handicapped from the
start of his schooling. The novelist does not automatically criticize the child's
Anglo teachers; he takes issue with the educational system itself. One teacher,
Mrs. Eva Weiner, is a woman of good will; she speaks Spanish, albeit with an
Anglo accent, and uses the children's native language when necessary. But she
does not lose sight of her obligation to teach English to her young Mexican
students; indeed,

> She opposed this rule—at least so far as youngsters of this age were con-
> cerned—but she had no choice but to comply. The board had run into too
> much criticism by graduating teen-agers unable to speak or read English.[43]

She prefers to keep the bilinguals with the others in order to avoid creating
too great a gulf between the two groups. Less concerned about this issue, Mrs.
Flanner, the teacher of the succeeding class, inconsiderately groups the students
according to their ability to speak English. While realizing that they have problems different from other children's, she does not understand that her essential
task is to prepare them to confront the outside world with confidence, which,
in the author's view, should be the basic function of schools for minorities.

The first teacher realizes that Samuel's scholastic difficulties are caused by a
lack of self-confidence, reinforced by repeated comparisons to his more gifted
twin sister. The next year, his feelings of inferiority grow when Mrs. Flanner
places him in the group of weak students. But the solidarity that automatically
develops among them is some compensation:

... the boys formed a sort of a clique, sticking together at recess time and during lunch hour. Their image of themselves was poor, and worsened as they began to take defensive pride in being intellectual failures and outcasts. ... A pattern was forming.[44]

It was the schools that spawned the East Los Angeles gangs. Seeing the danger, Pete decides to move to a white neighborhood to take his son away from that harmful environment. The discrimination that Pete encounters there, the harassment that his son is subjected to at the Anglo school, prove once and for all the futility of Pete's hopes for assimilation. In her harshness and racism, Miss Clark, Sammy's new teacher, resembles the fearsome Cora Dart of *Giant*; but while Dart makes only a brief appearance in Edna Ferber's novel, the Chicano writer dwells at length, with ferocious malice, on Miss Clark. She is destined to play a determining role in Sammy's disastrous career. Her previous teaching experience was in an East Los Angeles school where she had been sent as a disciplinary measure. Her cruelty inhibits Sammy; when he has to read aloud, in a class where he is the only one with accented English, he is so traumatized that he dreams of returning to the barrio school; there, at least, he did not feel like a foreigner. He has the same pronunciation difficulties as his father, but for him they produce an irreversible block:

> He saw the word "pick" rushing towards him in the sentence he was reading. He knew words containing the vowel as in "pick" were the ones most often seized upon by those who lampooned the Mexican. "Pee-eek," they always said, making their voices drop a little for the last half of the word. Sammy read the word, straining to avoid his natural pronunciation. It came out "peck." Again the teacher stopped him.
> "Say 'pick,' Sammy." Sammy was silent, eyes on the book.
> "You've got to at least try," the teacher said in a demanding tone. Sammy remained silent.
> "Now listen," she said, "one of the things you've got to learn is that when we say something, we mean it."[45]

Two ways of thinking, symbolized by the "you" and the "we," clash with one another. Samuel is once again made aware of this duality when he borrows a book from the school library. He realizes that its Anglo content is too foreign for him to identify with it.

The family returns to the East Los Angeles barrio. Samuel, the failure, would lead the same pathetic life there as the other failures of the Mexican ghetto. Of the entire clan, Mariana, the brilliant student whose English accent is practically perfect, is the most assimilable, but she considers herself more Mexican than American. Had she desired assimilation, however, it would have been refused her: hadn't she been rejected by David Stiver? This young Anglo, after impregnating her, demands that she undergo an abortion, which leads to her death. The novel ends, melodramatically, with the funeral of Mariana

Sandoval. The author seems to bury along with her all hopes of a resolution to this cultural conflict that is now more than one hundred years old.

The Barrio

While the barrio remained a spiritual haven, it also became a den of drugs and delinquency; its *vatos locos* ["crazy guys"] were even more disturbing and pathetic than the *pachucos* of the 1940s. By stressing the chaotic and marginal nature of the barrio, Chicano writers attacked the socioeconomic system at its root.

More than ever, for those unable or unwilling to integrate, the barrio became a spiritual haven for cultural identity:

> Neighborhood of my youth
> demolished, erased forever from
> the universe.
> You live on, captive, in the lonely
> Cellblocks of my mind. . . .
>
> i needed you then . . . identity . . . a sense of belonging.
> i need you now. . . .
>
> i respect your having been:
> My Loma of Austin
> My Rose Hill of Los Angeles . . .
>
> My Segundo of El Paso
> My westside of Denver . . .
>
> all Chicano neighborhoods that now exist and once existed;
> somewhere . . . someone remembers . . .[46]

In this long poem, "A Trip Through the Mind Jail," dedicated to Eldridge Cleaver and written in Leavenworth Prison, Raúl Salinas returns to his childhood in Austin. The short story by Suárez, "El Hoyo," emphasizes the common identity of the barrio inhabitants despite their diversity: each evening, those who spend the entire day in an alien society gather together once more.

Like the short stories of the preceding generation, Chicano poetry evoked, with tenderness and nostalgia, the cultural legacy of the barrio: its traditions, its fiestas, its women, its cuisine. In a long and majestic litany, Salinas, the poet-prisoner, parades before our eyes the multiple images of his native barrio, forever fixed in his memory; La Loma, in Austin, expanded to mythic proportions, becomes the symbol of "all the barrios of today and yesterday." Elizondo's Spanish plunges us into a world cut off from the outside:

Ahí en la esquina no falta la iglesia,
muy romana, siempre católica, seria.
Hay una panadería,
donde prietas siempre voluptuosas
van a comprar el pan,
a ver lo que hay que ver,
a decir lo que hay que decir.

Suave murmullo de palabras Chicanas
en ese español
de Raza, de chiles, de tacos, de tamal . . .[47]

[There on the corner you can't miss the
   church
very Roman, always Catholic, serious.
There's a bakery,
where dark, ever-voluptuous women
go to buy the bread,
to see what there is to see,
to say what there is to say.

Soft murmur of Chicano words
in that Spanish
of Raza, of chiles, of tacos, of tamal . . .]

Alurista's bilingualism reflects the Chicano's ambivalence toward the Mexican reality of the barrio:

en el barrio
—en las tardes de fuego
when the dusk prowls
   en la calle desierta
pues los jefes y jefas
   trabajan
—often late hours
after school
   we play canicas . . .[48]

[in the barrio
—in those fiery afternoons]

[in the deserted street
since fathers and mothers
   work]

[marbles]

In the poem "Nuestro barrio" [Our barrio],[49] Alurista presents his memories one by one: graffiti on faded walls, the past loves of Pedro and Virginia, Don José sweeping his sidewalk, the wilted flowers on the grave of the poet's grandfather. The central image of dustiness confers a tone of romantic sadness; death is at the heart of this barrio striken by inertia; the inhabitants are locked into solitude. This representation is completely untypical—the Mexican quarter is usually vibrant with sounds and life. It reflects the poet's sadness at the loss of a bygone era.

With a humor resembling Suárez's, "Zeta" (Oscar Zeta Acosta), in his short story "Perla Is a Pig," describes a humble Texas barrio, which for him reflects the human race. This is Nico:

> He wore a Levi jacket, Levi pants, and Lama boots. His brilliant black hair was immaculate. He wore a long mustachio, as did the Mexican cowboys in Texas from whom he had learned all there was to know of manhood. This same little man had also learned from his mother that no gentleman should be out in the streets without a pencil, a pad of paper, a comb and, at the very least, fifty cents on his person.[50]

A more troubling facet of the barrio tends to dominate Chicano literature: the underworld of the vatos locos, the drug addicts, the delinquents, and those who cannot integrate at all into American society. This seamy aspect of the barrio was like an open wound on the prestigious society that governed over it. In a succession of fourteen-syllable verses, Abelardo Delgado gives an overpowering definition of the modern urban barrio:

> I am that piece of land "la ciudad" [the city] is trying to hide
> I house "gente" [people] to whom the American dream has lied,
> in my corner stand the youth "morena" [brown] with no future. . . .
>
> I am the alma mater of lost "almas" [souls] and bodies, . . .
>
> "escupo" [I spit out] the sick, the delinquent, I am a hammock
> to the "prostituta" [prostitute], a cemetery to ambition,
> a corner to "talento" [talent], no exit just admission.
> "Yo soy el barrio" [I am the barrio], the slum, the ghetto, progress' sore
>   thumb.[51]

What emerges from the "voyage" of Salinas "through the jail of his mind" is the profoundly paradoxical nature of the barrio, at once a source of life and scene of often deadly violence. To the physical suffering, always present in the Mexican ghetto, was now added a progressively more serious moral breakdown. Vásquez places particular emphasis on this in the second part of his novel: crime and vice flourished in the barrios of East Los Angeles in the 1960s, posing a serious problem for educators.

The *vato loco* of today is a reincarnation of the *pachuco* of the thirties and forties; although the majority of writers used either term indiscriminately, the half-*pachuco* and half-Spanish term *vato* (*bato*) *loco* (crazy guy), began to predominate from the 1960s on. It designates a young man who no longer knows where he stands; it does not carry a pejorative connotation.

The *pachuco* of the 1940s continued to haunt the imagination of Chicano writers. Either his rebellious spirit and combativeness were highlighted (*pachuquismo* was more or less explicitly co-opted by the Chicano movement), or he was portrayed as the absurd man, who found in absurdity a way of asserting himself and existing. *Pachuquismo* thus became a form of existentialism. A poem by José Montoya, "Los Vatos," dwells at length on a bloody quarrel one summer day in 1948, and the studied nonchalance of the participants. Here, two of them are getting out of a "lowered" Chevrolet:

> . . . soothing long sleek hair,
> Hidden eyes squinting behind green tinted tea-timers.★
> In cat-like motions, bored and casual, they sauntered
> Then settled heavily on the car.[52]

Like Rechy a native of the El Chuco barrio of El Paso, Sánchez nostalgically evokes his anarchical and belligerent youth:

> Three *pachuquios* [little *pachucos*] with burning eyes—coal black—ducktail haircuts, jitty kind of walk (hands swaying to the *ritmo* [rhythm] of our bodies . . .) and the perceptible *coraje* [anger] that came from living in *el barrio del diablo* [devil's *barrio*] in east el paso. We were from the X-9 gang —*batos muy locos* [very hip guys]—so we thought, and the switch blades in our pockets gave us both security and a throbbing itch to go out assailing a non-caring world, and thus by our strongly proving ourselves, we would be able to redeem ourselves.[53]

Sánchez, writing in Soledad Prison, returns on several occasions to his inter-pretation of the meaning of *pachuquismo*, which he sees as the point of departure for the current Chicano movement. The *pachucos*, who could be recognized by the cross tattooed on their hands, were motivated by "a deep sense of respect and love for their families"[54] and were united in a common goal, "to protect the barrio from gringos."[55] Sánchez claims he never saw gringos cross the borders of the barrio during his youth. "Champing at the bit" in prison, Sánchez quite naturally tends to idealize the young rebels of the past; he does not mention their dissension or the terror caused by their excesses. In somewhat the same spirit, Javier Alva recalls, in his short narrative "The Sacred Spot,"[56] the fa-mous race riots of June 6, 1943, and the *pachucos'* resistance against the Los Angeles police. J. L. Navarro, in the surrealist style peculiar to him, evokes the same memorable day in the short story "Frankie's Last Wish." The brawl between *pachucos* and American sailors, resituated into the context of the Chris-tian Redemption and the Mexican Revolution, takes on noble overtones. As the young zoot-suiter Payaso tries to escape his pursuers, a series of visions flashes through his fevered imagination:

> *The Bleeding heart throbbing in the light of the flaming sun. He won't die.* The people waiting, watching. Can see them through the corner of my eyes. Across the street. *A cross. He won't die. Drink that wine that will kill him for three days. Somewhere else; elsewhere again.* Alive again. Closer. *Heart beating in anticipation of the knife.* Closer. Alive. *In Mexico. The desert heat. The sticky juice of the cactus.* In L.A. *In Mexico.* On Main Street.[57]

Then, he is confronted with the sailors:

> *Revolución! The horses. The dust. The sounds of rifles biting the wind with their lead . . . Libertad* [liberty], *came the cry, libertad! . . .*[58]

He falls in a hail of gunfire.

Romano, the anthropologist, hailed the *pachuco* as the "existential man"[59] who had purposely cut himself off from history; he rejected Mexican and American conventions, and, through his clothing, language, and behavior, created new values. Poet Tino Villanueva hailed the *pachuco* as a "precursor" of the nonconformists to come; his "baroque" behavior[60] and his "esthetics existential"[61] were a provocation, a way of fighting the Establishment. The *pachuco*'s rejection of the existing culture, his new vocabulary, implicitly made him a forerunner of the young, white activists of the 1950s and 1960s:

Ese!	[You there!]
within your will-to-be culture,	
incisive,	
aguzado,	[razor sharp]
clutching the accurate click	
first-warm flash of your *filero*	[knife]
(hardened equalizer gave you life,	
opened up counter-cultures U.S.A.).	
Precursor.	
Vato loco alivianado—a legend in your	[Stoned *vato loco*]
own time flaunting early Mod, sleazy,	
but rigid,	
with a message,	
in a movement of your own,	
in your gait sauntering,	
swaying,	
leaning the wrong way	
in assertion.[62]	

Other Chicanos saw the *pachuco*'s excesses, his arrogance, as a way of coping with a dead-end situation, which made him a hero of sorts. A poem by Montoya, "El Louie," written in memory of a legendary *pachuco* of the 1940s, is a funeral oration, delivered in a half-comic tone, with the exordium, reprised like a refrain, of "*Hoy enterraron al Louie*" (Today they buried Louie), and peroration.

His death was an insult	
porque no murio en accion—	[because he didn't die in action—
no lo mataron los vatos,	the *vatos* didn't kill him,
ni los gooks en Korea.	nor the gooks in Korea.]
He died alone in a rented	
room—perhaps like in a	
Bogard movie.	
The end was a cruel hoax.	
But his life had been	
remarkable.[63]	

The poem, studded with *pachuco* terms that heighten its insolence (*chale* and *nel*, "no"; *simon*, "yes"; *abusan*, "clever"; *vaisa*, "hand"; *trucha*, "knife") relates the "remarkable" career of the deceased—remarkable for its drinking bouts, amorous adventures, and flights into the imaginary. Louie liked to believe that he was Bogart or some other film actor.

Only the short story by Tomás Rivera, "On the Road to Texas: Pete Fonseca"[64] presents a negative view of *pachuquismo*—which caused some publication difficulties for its author.[65] The *pachuco* in the story is just a common tramp. A young stranger speaking the *pachuco* dialect arrives in a little Texas village in 1948. He gets married, pretends to want to settle there, then disappears with the family savings as mysteriously as he came.

Neither the clownlike nor the unsavory aspects of *pachuquismo* appeared in Anglo writings of the postwar period; eager to be objective and understanding, the Anglo writers justified the behavior of young Mexican-Americans by stressing their deep anguish. Furthermore, unfamiliar with the little incidents of life in the barrio, they did not have the background to fuel a comic or mock-heroic vision.

Los vatos took over where the *pachucos* had left off. They were distinguishable by their low-suspension cars, which earned their drivers the nickname of "lowriders"; their uniform generally included a pair of khaki-colored pants. Their cars harked back to the *pachuco* era; born in the barrios of Los Angeles, low-riding cars were an authentically Mexican-American invention.[66] Navarro specialized in the subject of *los vatos*; the author of the dozen short stories in *Blue Day on Main Street*, he was fascinated by these youths, whose aspirations and aversions he expressed with sympathy and talent. His style is in turn whimsical, realistic, and surrealistic, and never sinks into sentimentality or melodrama. His mock-heroic tone recalls Montoya's. His rebellious adolescents are both pathetic and engaging.

They appear again in his poem "To a Dead Lowrider." Navarro commemorates a certain Tito, a "lowriding ace," who dies in a confrontation with a white policeman. The wild and jerky verses, punctuated with Spanish, *pachuco*, and American slang, reproduce the frenetic movement that intoxicated the young lowrider:

He never had a care, that guy,
Balling and cruising and making love.
That was the trip with Tito.
On the corner he'd come around and
Say to us, "*Me gusta la mota cuando*   [I like some pot when
Traigo una burnena ruca! . . ."[67]   I'm out with a fine chick! . . ."]

Like their predecessors, the *vatos locos* formed gangs that reigned over the barrio, justifying more than ever Galarza's definition of barrio from the 1930s: "a neighborhood within a city containing an underground society of young males who regarded the area as their exclusive territory."[68] Navarro's short story "Weekend" recounts a liquor-store burglary by a gang of lowriders and the brutal intervention of the police. Through the words of one of his characters, the author denounces the attitude of the police, who never hesitate to shoot when there's trouble in the barrio: "If you're a Chicano, you're a dead man. . . ."[69] Forewarned is forearmed.

But the rebels' anarchical and eccentric behavior hid the bewilderment of adolescents caught between two cultures and searching for an identity in an increasingly absurd world. What's the use of fighting? a young lowrider asks himself in Navarro's story "Passing Time."[70] Mexican-Americans' problems were no more easily resolved than those of Blacks: the new laws that sought to change inequities had no force. While some people tried to bring about change, Navarro's hero preferred to run away.

Narcotics offered the *batos locos* the ideal escape. Drugs essentially were a phenomenon of the 1960s. Practically unknown to the first generations of the Sandoval family, in Vásquez's novel, for example, drug addiction afflicted the later generations in tragic proportions. Marijuana had long been used in the barrio,[71] but heroin trafficking increased, made easier by the proximity of the border. The addicts in the barrio had their own jargon. Marijuana was called *la lucas, la leña, la grifa,* or *la yesca,* depending on the region; an addict was called *un grifo* or *un yesco; chiva* or *carga* commonly designated heroin. The hip terms of Anglo addicts were also familiar: "cool," "man," "cat," "crazy," and so forth. The world of drugs was presented in various ways in Chicano literature. A brief narrative by Marcus Durán, "Retrato de un Bato Loco" [Portrait of a *bato loco*],[72] relates the last day in the life of a Los Angeles heroin addict. The author does not claim that his subject is a universal type, nor does he moralize; he simply states the facts without drawing conclusions. Navarro's technique is identical in his short story "Passing Time." Denny and a gang of idlers are killing time in East Los Angeles. One of them, a drug dealer, makes sure each one has his daily dose. The author, haunted by the harmful effects of urban life on youth, Chicano and otherwise, depicts drugs as a common, and unavoidable, phenomenon of the barrio; all his lowriders are drug-addicts. In "Frankie's Last Wish," he establishes an eloquent parallel between two scenes: on June 6, 1943, in Los Angeles, the young zoot-suiter Payaso dies heroically, while on the East Side, unaware of events on Main Street, ". . . two people lay fornicating in a dark corner of an old house."[73] Almost thirty years later, in April 1970, in East Los Angeles, Aron, the brother of the deceased Payaso, a young lowrider and heroin addict, kills one of his peers in a mean act of vengeance; a few steps away ". . . in the alley, two dogs were copulating near some trash cans."[74] Life and death, love and hatred pathetically coexist. The situation seems to have degenerated even more since the already distant era of the first barrio rebels.

Vásquez, the novelist, does not treat the barrio's rampant drug addiction as an isolated phenomenon; he links it to the discrimination of American society. The first part of *Chicano* ends with the scholastic failures of Samuel Sandoval; then the young boy begins the second phase of his life, under the influence of narcotics. The author sees the juvenile delinquency that plagues minorities as the direct consequence of irregular or inadequate education, and he stresses the heavy guilt of Anglo society. To further implicate it, he introduces David Stiver, a young sociology student inflamed with liberal ideas, who goes into the barrios of East Los Angeles to do research for his thesis and social-service work. His professor offers these instructions:

> If any of you reports back here that you've discovered the drop out problem is caused by the cultural barriers I'll personally brain you. We know all that. We want to know *what* in the cultural barrier is so insurmountable to the individual and *why*. It's complex.[75]

The Chicano writer puts Anglo liberalism on trial by portraying David Stiver as even weaker than young Sammy, the youngster he studies.

When Stiver contacts Sammy for the first time, the young Chicano has already had a brilliant career as a junkie and vagrant. He rejoined his gang in East Los Angeles, and began to skip school and smoke marijuana; then, on the advice of his principal, he took a job and enrolled in night school (education being compulsory to the age of eighteen). He worked for a swindler who sold stolen cars and who paid him in marijuana. Sammy and Celia, his young Chicana girlfriend, took drugs before making love to heighten their orgasms. Known to the narcotics squad, he found a new job taking clients to a Mexican abortionist who had set up shop in Los Angeles. He also became involved in heroin trafficking, with his uncle Julio Salazar. Sammy's story ends with his arrest in Tijuana.

David falls in love with Mariana, Sammy's sister, only to end up rejecting her because of her ethnic origin. She dies as a result of an abortion performed by her brother's employer. After her death, Stiver discovers a document that establishes the Spanish and middle-class descent of the Sandovals; he would not have been ashamed to marry the descendent of one of the old California families. The incident proves that racism can be used by anyone who wishes to avoid his responsibilities as a man.

The book ends with David rushing away from the cemetery in order not to miss a rehearsal for his graduation ceremony. His mission in the barrio might have been a failure on the human level but could be considered fruitful on the sociological level! In his thesis, he cannot deny that cultural barriers do, indeed, exist. He himself is living proof that Anglo society is in large measure responsible for making the barriers insurmountable: Mariana dies because of him and it is he who turns Sammy in to the police.

In addition to exposing Anglo liberalism's inability to solve the barrio's problems, the novel stresses the dangers of juvenile delinquency. This flaw in the dominant social system turned many young Chicanos into marginal people.

The barrio at the same time protects and imprisons. It is the alma mater of "lost souls and bodies" and restores a sense of identity. But a monolithic society also casts its failures into the barrio. It was dangerous for Chicanos to become locked in and "hidden": what can no longer be seen ceases to exist. The writer had a double role: to bring the people of the barrio to light and to give warning to Anglo society.

The Migration of the *Campesino*

Marginal to the dominant society, like the *bato loco*, the *campesino* also became a symbol of the Chicano of today. The term, which specifically means "peasant," was invested with the larger sense of "man of the soil" and "child of nature" by Anglos who were fascinated by primitivism. In the press and in Mexican-American literature, where it alternated with the word "migrant," it received limited acceptance as a substitute for "seasonal farm worker." The Teatro Campesino immortalized the *campesinos*, who figured in its plays both as actors and as characters. Two factors contributed to the new prominence of the *campesino*: the growth of agribusiness, Anglo agriculture raised to the level of an industry, and the politicization of the Mexican minority's intellectual elite. One must go back to the *corridos* of the past to find earlier images of itinerant *campesinos*, since they were all but absent from the Mexican-American literature in the postwar assimilationist era. A new preoccupation was the physical and moral problems of migrant children, not surprising in view of the interest shown in education and juvenile delinquency by Chicano writers and sociologists.

Campesinos were the subject of numerous poems and short stories, of a bilingual edition of a collection of stories in Spanish, . . . *Y no se lo tragó la tierra* / . . . *and the earth did not part* by Tomás Rivera,[76] a novel in English, *The Plum Plum Pickers* by Raymond Barrio,[77] and plays in the bilingual Chicano theater.

Three aspects were usually presented: the *campesinos'* migration, and the difficulties for both workers and their families. In its structure, Rivera's work reproduced the life-cycle of the itinerant workers; Barrio's experimental novel accentuated life in the camps and working conditions; the Teatro Campesino dramatized confrontations between Chicano farm workers and Anglo employers.

Rivera's book has a circular structure; its twelve stories represent both the year of a seasonal farm worker in Texas and the intellectual and moral evolution of the young hero-narrator. The latter, the anonymous "he" of the narrative, is introduced in the prologue, "The Lost Year." The epilogue is a sort of synthesis. The author-narrator explains how he transformed the cycle of painful years and the cycle of thoughts imprisoning his mind into a work of art:

> That year was lost to him. . . . He tried to figure out when it was that he had started to refer to that period as a year. He discovered that he was always thinking that he was thinking, and that he was trapped in this cycle.[78]

The unity of time is misleading; the year is less a chronological succession of events than a symbolic cycle. It begins in April in Texas, continues in the North during the summer beet harvest; the principal story, which gives the book its title and relates the hero's major crisis, is set in the dog days of summer; the tenth story takes place on Christmas Eve; and the epilogue is preceded by an anecdote that indicates that the year is over and everyone is back home. This year represents the inevitable cycle of years, the "year to year existence"[79] of migrant workers, a monotonous cycle punctuated by an inexorable sequence of events: the picking of fruits or vegetables on a Texas ranch, migration to the North, then the return home for more stoop labor, all in stifling heat. "You know that the only thing that we can look forward to is coming here every year. And as you yourself say, one does not rest until one dies,"[80] a child tells his mother.

Rivera stresses the repetitiveness of the seasonal worker's life. A worker reflects sadly in the truck that's taking him north:

> When we arrive, when we arrive. At this point, quite frankly, I'm tired of always arriving someplace. Arriving is the same as leaving because as soon as we arrive . . . well, quite frankly, I'm tired of always arriving. Maybe I should say when we don't arrive because that's the plain truth. We really never really arrive anywhere. [81]

In a moving, predominantly Spanish poem, "Que Hay Otra Voz" [Because there is another voice], Villanueva renders in existential terms the inner reality of these perpetual wanderers. He sees it as determined by two opposing forces: the *estar*, which corresponds to the transitory and itinerant nature of a life dictated by external circumstances, and the *ser*,[82] which represents an inner and permanent essence. This is expressed by the "other voice," one that insists upon speaking:

tú	[you
de los blue-jeans nuevos	in the new blue jeans
pareces	you seem
retoñar cada año como fuerza elemental,	to spring up again each year like a basic
temporal—arraigado entre el ser y el estar	temporal force
de un itinerario. Eres ganapán, estás aquí de	—caught between the *ser* and the *estar*
paso. [83]	of an itinerary. You're a day laborer, just
	passing through here.]

Through his twelve vignettes, Rivera gives us a global view of the *campesinos'* world without dwelling on their living or working conditions. As in the old *corridos* of the migration era, emphasis is placed on the journey: the trial it represents, its expenses, the uncertain future awaiting those who undertake it. The twelfth story, which bears the meaningful title "When We Arrive," features a truck, in the early hours of the morning, with its load of sleeping or meditative people. A succession of interior monologues reveals the passengers' preoccupations:

> First Passenger: "*The children must really get
> tired traveling up on their feet like that. Nothing to hold on to.*"[84]
> Second Passenger: "*My poor husband, he must be very
> tired by now, standing all the way.*"[85]
> Driver: "*When we arrive, and as soon as I parcel*

them out among the growers I'll head right back. Let each one look
out for his own skin." [86]

That the child is the first victim of this ambulatory life is one of the book's central ideas; it is introduced in the first story, "The Children Were Victims." Often hired for the harvest, youngsters suffered even more than adults from the harsh working conditions. Their limited productivity irritated the boss. In this story, the boss threatens a young cotton-picker who wants to stop a minute for a drink of water. Thinking to frighten the child with a rifle, he accidentally kills him.

> "I'm very thirsty, father. Will the boss be
> here soon?"
> "I think so. Can't you hold out any longer?"
> "Well, I don't know. I feel my throat very dry.
> Do you think he'll come soon? Shall I go to the
> water tank?"
> "No, wait a little longer. You heard what he
> said."
> "I know, he'll fire us if he catches us there, but
> I can't wait."
> "It's alright, everything will be alright. Keep on
> working. He'll be here any minute."
> "I guess that's all we can do. I hope I can hold
> up. Why doesn't this man let us bring our own
> water? Up north we . . ."
> "Because he's mean . . ."
> "But we could hide it under the seat, couldn't we?
> It's always better up north. . . . What if we
> pretend as if we're going to relieve ourselves
> near the water tank?" [87]

The spare and unsophisticated style, like that of children and humble people, prevails in the narratives and dialogues. Like Mexican novelist Juan Rulfo,[88] the Chicano writer makes every effort to recreate the *campesino's* language.

The moving simplicity of this dialogue recalls the scene between the mother and her child in Alurista's poem "allá ajuera"; "over there" is also forbidden to this little picker:

why?
   why am I here
wanna go play
      (*no mijo, tene que trabajar*)   [(no, my son, you have to work)
porque mamá   because, Mother,
     yo también   I also
yo quero   want
      (*no mijo, uste no puede*   (no, my son, you can't
         no debe)   you mustn't)

Mamá quero jugar	Mother, I want to play
quero vivir	I want to live
allá ajuera	outside there
(no mijo, allá ajuera no	(no, my son, not outside there, no
no con los ninos	not with the children
no con los del patrón)	not with the boss's children)
mamá, mamá, why?[89]	Mother, Mother, why?]

Caring for the children was a serious problem. If parents took them along to the fields, they were vulnerable to sunstroke; the boss might complain that the parents were taking time away from their work to look after the youngsters. Leaving them at home was even riskier. In Rivera's eighth story, the García children, left alone, die when their shack catches fire.

For school-age migrant children, education was intermittent and irregular. In the northern schools, there was no possibility of the bilingualism practiced so imperfectly in the Southwest. The preliminary delousing operation they were subjected to was only a prelude to a long series of humiliations: their linguistic difficulties made them a target of their gringo classmates, an ideal scapegoat; any minor misbehavior brought about immediate expulsion. The principal in Rivera's third story cavalierly justifies a hasty expulsion: "They could care less if I expel them . . . they need him in the fields."[90] The title of this story, which relates the narrator's brief education, is of eloquent succinctness: "It's Painful."

The itinerant worker usually inspired mistrust among the local population. In a brief narrative, "Saturday Belongs to the Palomía,"[91] Daniel Garza describes the invasion of his small Texas town each autumn by the *palomía*, a group of cotton-pickers from the Valley and from Mexico. Humiliations await the workers when they go off to town each Saturday; the restaurants and the barber shop discriminate against this marginal clientele, though they don't discriminate against local Chicanos. This idea is developed humorously in the short story "Everybody Knows Tobie."[92] The young narrator experiences two kinds of racism; first, the gringo barber, mistaking him for a cotton-picker, refuses him service; next, a Mexican laborer calls him a *pocho* ("bleached one"). The barber will not serve him until he proves that he is the brother of Tobie, the newspaper delivery boy, and, therefore, a regular city resident. In the tenth story, Rivera describes another typical case: a Mexican-American woman is wrongly accused of shoplifting.

Politics are intentionally absent from Rivera's work, which is set in the 1950s, before the spread of the Chicano movement. Though criticism is not his principal objective, his unsophisticated presentation contains a subtle denunciation of the scandalous treatment of farm workers. The author intends to show the inner evolution of the young Chicano narrator and the profoundly poignant drama taking place in the hearts of the migrants.

Barrio's technique is the opposite of Rivera's. Rivera's is an intimate work, whose simplicity of form reflects the thoughts and feelings of the characters.

Barrio's *The Plum Plum Pickers* is a novel of protest, in which individuals are re-situated into the context of social and economic institutions that either support or oppress them. His style is a combat weapon. The anonymity that contributes to the universality of Rivera's characters gives way in Barrio's work to thinly disguised names: Howlin Mad Nolan is Ronald Reagan, governor of California; Rat Barfy is his crony, George Murphy, the Republican senator; the State House Un-American Festivities Committee is, of course, the State House Un-American Activities Committee (the American Inquisition). *The Plum Plum Pickers* is a *roman à clefs*.

When Steinbeck's *The Grapes of Wrath* appeared in 1939, the Associated Farmers of California announced that it was preparing a "documented reply to Steinbeck's distortions of fact." It was to have been titled "Plums of Plenty,"[93] but was never published.

The Chicano plums of wrath, *The Plum Plum Pickers*, which appeared thirty years later, was a sort of challenge to the all-powerful Association of California Producers. The author lays his cards on the table immediately. "Bang bang. Crash":[94] a trash-can cover breaks down a garage door a few feet from the bed of Morton J. Quill, the manager of Western Grande, a fruit grove in Drawbridge, Santa Clara County. Through this character Anglo agribusiness is attacked. The company's profit-hungry owner, Turner, labor contractor Roberto Morales, and Quill reign as a sinister triumvirate over 10,000 Mexican-American farm workers transplanted from a Texas camp and hired for a summer's picking. Among them are Manuel and Lupe Gutierrez and their children.

Barrio's world caricatures capitalist society; it is divided into two classes, the "haves," who control the money and power in California, and the "have-nots," the agricultural laborers. The author manipulates the two key words of California capitalism, "agribusiness" and "dollar," playing with them as if they were marionettes, in the same way that the growers manipulate the workers:

> All the glands of agricombines owned by holding companies holding their regular hoard meetings, engendering still more agriblob conglomerates up and down the agricoats, the ups and downs of the greedy agridollar coasters had also to be computed . . .[95]

Barrio spreads the dollars around, using them here and there like a cheap, possibly fake coin. He plays on the similarity of the dollar sign and the letter "s":

> The only force that was stronger than the $un. Why worry, $enator? . . . $ $ $ $ The $enator from Drawbridge . . . wildly proclaimed $toop Over Play on Strawberry Day.[96]

In the minds of the pickers, all the words Barrio associates with the dollar are suspect: the sun, the detestable senator, the "stoop labor," the picking of strawberries, one of the most strenuous tasks of all.

The overabundance of the land is counterbalanced by the enormous amounts of work furnished by the laborers and their extreme destitution. The pickers are crushed by the multitudes of "plump, plump plums,"[97] symbols both of a wealth that belongs to others and the heavy labor that is the pickers' only share. The exuberant duality of the vocabulary corresponds to the dual connotation of this abundance; the text abounds in accumulations, repetitions, enumerations, anaphoras, alliterations (starting with the title). This is California:

> ... the richest, the greatest, the most productive chunk of rich earth in the world, this munificent cornucopian state pouring forth an unbelievable glut of gorgeous peaches, a blizzard of plums, a plethora of apricots, pears ... a bloat of tomatoes and ravishing radishes ...[98]

The richness of some presupposes the labor of others. Similarly, in the poems of Alurista, an affluent white American is fat with others' labor:

> we pang
>   but Mr. Jones is fat
> with money
> with our sweat
>   our blood
> why?[99]

We will run across Mr. Jones again later on. In Drawbridge, profits matter more than anything else. The labor contractor, Morales, even organizes a speed contest among the pickers. This internal competition system replaces the "pacer" used by other companies to regulate the work pace of the harvesters: "You were your own terrible boss. That was the cleverest part of the whole thing. The picker his own bone picker, his own willing built-in slave driver."[100] The zeal of these Stakhanovites of the harvest is poorly rewarded; even their meager pay of two cents per bucket is reduced.

In Barrio's prose, either commas are omitted and the reader runs out of breath trying to read the sentences without pause, like the picker filling the bucket with no respite, or they appear insistently in great quantity, chopping the sentences into little pieces, which cascade down like the fruit into the bucket. Or they punctuate the sentences just as the endlessly repeated tasks punctuate the daily lives of the workers: "Pick, hoe, till, weed, scratch, dig, cut, pack, and flex ..."[101]

The deprivation in which the Chicano laborers live contrasts flagrantly with the unseemly opulence of the gringos; the migrants, moved from one camp to the other depending upon the demands of the harvest, possess nothing. Cabin Number 9, where the Gutierrez family is crammed together, is a haven for cockroaches. No matter how miserable the workers' lodgings, the rent has to be paid on time, otherwise eviction followed, usually in the absence of the tenant. The family cabin, however, is relatively comfortable compared to the shack that temporarily houses Manuel, father of the family, a crack worker selected for the apricot harvest. Most of these shacks were run-down relics of the 1930s: "No refrigeration. . . . No food. No conveniences. No cleanliness. No quiet private kitchen. Above all, no privacy, no hiding, no place to rest alone in . . ."[102]

The world Barrio depicts is conditioned by the cult of the product, the obsessive concern for the fruit to be cultivated, picked, and marketed. It is overrun by the plums, just as the writing style is by the proliferation of words. Through a fair and ironic turnabout, it is the plums, and not the owner, who have the last word. Frustrated by a strike, Turner worries:

> But now, right now the main question was, how in hell was he going to find enough new prune pickers right away? . . . The plums sure didn't know. All they did was keep on ripening. Relentlessly.[103]

In this "universe of objects," human relationships are a function of the product. The tycoons, motivated only by the pursuit of maximum profit, consider other people mere production units serving their interests. Farm workers are judged by the number of plums they pick; they have no intrinsic human value. They are reduced to the level of insignificant work animals; living in veritable rabbit warrens, they are like chickens, "locked in a coop." Society in the Drawbridge camp is based not on dignity but on "rathood," a parody of the term "man-hood." Like "ant people,"[104] the workers hunch over the ground in a swarming mass of indistinguishable elements whose semi-invisibility absolves the Anglo employer of his own inhumanity. While the theme of abundance is the substance of the novel, it is through the animalistic vocabulary that Barrio reveals his furor.

The Plum Plum Pickers is not without its appealing aspects; its witty barbs are right on target; it has a few innovations of form, though the repetitions of the same terms end up wearying the reader. Its verbal inventiveness, however, does not salvage its inadequacies: the author barely succeeds in rising above the level of pure social protest; his characters are conditioned entirely by their economic environment. The caricature reflects a simplistic Manichaean vision of the world. Barrio's novel lacks the human dimension of *The Grapes of Wrath*.

The short stories and poems that emphasize the migrants' working conditions invariably contain the same elements that Rivera's and Barrio's books do: the sun, the rows of fruit or vegetables stretching out interminably, the foul-smelling insecticides, the curved and aching backs of the pickers.

The sun nearly causes a tragedy for Rivera's migrant family. The father and the youngest son are stricken by heat prostration and narrowly escape death; these incidents provoke a crisis for the young hero-narrator (story number six). In *The Plum Plum Pickers*, the sun, like "abundance," symbolizes both the California paradise and the exploitation of farm laborers. Excessive exposure to the sun often causes hallucinations, which serve as a pretext for poet José Montoya and writer Genaro González, an imaginative former migrant worker, to create a dreamlike vision of an ideal new world. Some visionary cottonpruners in the Montoya poem "Sunstruck While Chopping Cotton" flash a series of fantastic mental images, suggesting an eventual fusion of the Oriental and Occidental worlds:

> Not one but three Bothisattvas
> Suspended in a cloud of yellow dust
> Just above the rows of cotton
> Galloping comically on skeletal mounts
> Across the arid, sponge-like lust
> of a dessicated desert.
>
> They ride by, shouting in ruthless unison
> The name of Jesus, across the valley
> Halting not for an instant in their trek
> To the distant sea.
> The cool sea.[105]

In the Genaro González short story "El Hijo del Sol" [The son of the sun],[106] the revolt of Adán ["Adam"], a young cotton-picker dazed by the sun, is expressed through his final dream of death and rebirth. The lethal sun of the Rio Grande Valley explodes in the overwrought mind of the young hero, whose first name symbolizes and gives birth to the Aztec sun and the New Man.

Under the intense summer sun, the rows of fruits and vegetables stretch into infinity. Villanueva tries to capture the interminable length of the days in his poem "Day-Long Day:"

a family of sinews and backs,
row-trapped,
zig-zagging through Summer-long rows
of cotton: Lubbock by way of Wharton.
"*Está como si escupieran fuego,*" a mother   ["It's as if they're spitting fire,"]
   moans
in sweat-patched jeans,
stooping
with unbending dreams.[107]

The dream was the migrant worker's only inalienable possession, the sole means of escape.

Chicano writers finally mounted a unanimous protest against the use of insecticides, even more harmful than the rays of the sun. Airplanes dusted the crops and the pickers with nauseating clouds of chemicals, choking workers who already suffered from perpetually aching backs.

Other invariable elements in the sad litany of abuses were the employer and his despised henchman, the contractor of Mexican laborers. The Anglo producer and Don Coyote, the contractor, were ridiculed on stage, neutralized and reduced to harmless puppets by the Teatro Campesino.

Through the initiative of Valdez,[108] the Teatro Campesino was born in the grape fields of Delano in November 1965, two months after the start of the strike. It was a theater of militant amateurs; the farm workers, for whom it had been conceived, were themselves the actors, stagehands, and wardrobe keepers.[109] Just as the actors of the pastorals did, they improvised and kept the staging spare. There was no decor and hardly any wings; the actors' costumes were reduced to signs hung around the neck.

Valdez emphasized the militancy of the theater and its close ties to the Causa: "Linked by a cultural umbilical cord to the National Farm Workers Association, the Teatro lives in Delano as a part of the social movement."[110] The essence of the Teatro Campesino, as originally conceived, resided in ten- to fifteen-minute pieces called *actos*. These reflected the day-to-day experiences of the strikers. The first *actos*, staged in 1965, were "crude, vital, beautiful, powerful," and had "immediate, intense and cathartic" effects.[111] This orientation explains the choice of the term *acto*; "skit" was judged too lightweight and Anglo; "*cuadro*" (tableau), "*pasquín*" (lampoon), "*auto*" (mystery play), and "*entremés*" (interlude) were all suspected of intellectuality. The *actos* were both spectacle and action. Impregnated both with the popular humor of Cantinflas, the Mexican comic actor, and a Brechtian seriousness of purpose, they had a dual purpose: to entertain the workers and to restore their morale, which had been undermined by the length of the strike and its apparent ineffectiveness, and also to instruct by stressing the justness of their demands and their struggle. Entertainment, however, remained secondary. Valdez defined the goals this way: "Inspire the audience to social action. Illuminate specific points about social problems. Satirize the opposition. Show or hint at a solution. Express what people are feeling."[112]

But Valdez soon realized the need to establish some distance from the explosive events at Delano, and expanded his field of inquiry:

> . . . there is yet a need for independence for the following reasons: objectivity, artistic competence, survival. El Teatro Campesino was born in the Huelga [strike], but the very Huelga would have killed it, if we had not moved 60 miles to the north of Delano.[113]

From 1967 on, the Teatro Campesino treated subjects that went beyond the strike and the economic situation. Among them were the Vietnam war, the barrio, and racial discrimination. Gradually, the *acto* evolved into the *mito* ("myth"), which was more mystical.[114]

The impact of the *acto* depended on the degree of satirical exaggeration, so every effort was made to create caricatures of studied coarseness. The characters were extremely stylized, like those of the commedia dell'arte. Arlecchinos, Pantalones, and Brighellas gave way to other archetypes. In the *actos* dealing with the problems of the Delano workers, there were *esquiroles* ("scabs"), *contratistas* ("labor contractors"), *patroncitos* ("bosses"; the diminutive suffix *cito* is used sarcastically), and *huelguistas* ("strikers"). In those of more generalized scope, there were Johnny Pachuco, Juan Raza, Jorge el Chingón [Big George], and la Chicana. A simplistic Manichaeism reminiscent of the old morality plays pitted the good (Chicanos) against the bad (Anglos).

A marginal, "unbourgeois"[115] theater with rather rough expressionist techniques, the Teatro Campesino is related in many ways to the Free Southern Theater organized for black sharecroppers in the South, the Bread and Puppet Theater, the San Francisco Mime Troupe, and even the Free Street Theater of Chicago, although that group is less activist and is part subsidized. In its political commitments, the Teatro resembled the socialist agit-prop theater of the thirties and, more recently, the popular theater of immigrant workers in France, whose works are often created on the occasion of a strike or other conflict.[116] But El Teatro Campesino remains, above all, an authentic Chicano creation.

The Teatro Campesino is bilingual, the contrast between the two languages reflecting the conflict pitting Chicanos against Anglo society. Among the *actos* conceived and staged by Valdez in collaboration with the troupe, four pointedly denounce the double exploitation of the *campesinos* by the employer and the labor contractor. *Las Dos Caras del Patroncito* [The two faces of the boss][117] was performed in 1965 during the first months of the strike. It is one of the most humorous of the *actos*, using the most outrageous elements of farce. In addition to Charlie, an armed guard, there are two stock characters: the *esquirol*, a scab recruited in Texas or Mexico, and the *patrón* ("boss"). A *ranchero* explains to the *campesino* that the latter's job has a thousand and one advantages, such as free lodging and transportation, while, by contrast, he has many worries as a millionaire, such as the exorbitant cost of running his gigantic ranch, the expensive tastes of his blond wife, and so forth. At the rancher's suggestion, the two agree to reverse roles. The *patrón* exchanges his yellow mask, representing a bloated pig's face, his cigar, and his whip for the hat and pruning shears of the Mexican, who, getting into the game, uses the employer's own arguments against him (in perfect English):

> Farmworker: "Tough luck, son. You see this land, all
>   these vines? They're mine."
> Patroncito: "Just a damn minute here. The land,
>   the car, the house, hill, and the cherry on top
>   too? You're crazy! Where am I going to live?"
> Farmworker: "I got a nice, air-conditioned cabin
>   down in the labor camp. Free housing, free
>   transportation."
> Patroncito: "You're nuts! I can't live in those
>   shacks! They got rats, cockroaches. And those
>   trucks are unsafe. You want me to get killed?"[118]

The *patrón* has literally handed over the stick that beats him. His own employee has him thrashed by the guard; then, as the height of grotesqueness, the *patroncito* decamps, calling to Chávez for help and shouting ¡*huelga*!

In *Las Tres Uvas* [The three grapes], staged in 1967 in Santa Barbara, there are two *campesinos*—a scab and a striker—the boss, and the labor contractor. But the villain and dupe of this farce is not the Anglo employer but the Mexican labor recruiter, who is despised by the workers.[119]

La Quinta Temporada [The fifth season] and *Vietnam Campesino* [Rural Vietnam] have greater thematic richness. The first was performed during a strikers' meeting in Delano. Along with the usual trio of characters (*campesino*, boss, contractor), we find personifications of The Church, The Unions, La Raza, and the four seasons, as well as a fifth, a season of social justice in the future. While the boss and the contractor always stuff their pockets, in good years and bad, the farm worker is linked to the cycle of seasons. The worst, winter, is synonymous with hunger, illness, and humiliation.

> Winter: "I am Winter and I want money. Money for
>   gas, lights, telephone, rent." (He spots the
>   contractor and rushes over to him). "Money!"
> Don Coyote gives him his bonus. Winter bites the
> bone, finds it distasteful, throws it backstage
> over the flats. He whirls around towards the
> grower.
> Coyote: "Money!"
> Patron: (Remaining calm) "Will you take a check?"
> Winter: (Rushing over to him) "No, cash!"
> Patron: "Okay, here!" (Hands him a small wad of
>   bills) "Well, that's it for me. I'm off to Acapulco
>   'til next Spring." (Exits S.L.)
> Coyote: "And I'm off to Las Vegas." (Exits S.R.)
> Worker: "And I'm off to eat frijoles!"
> Winter nabs the farm worker as he tries to escape.
> Winter: "Ha, ha, Winter's got you! I want money.
>   Give me money."
> Worker: "I don't have any. I'm just a poor farm
>   worker."
> Winter: "Then suffer!" [120]

Vietnam Campesino [121] was presented in the church of Guadalupe in Delano, on Thanksgiving Day 1970, during a meeting held by strikers and members of the United Farm Workers Organizing Committee who were sympathetic to the Chávez cause. Along with the *campesinos* in this *acto*, we find the boss, Butt Anglo, a favorite target; Little Butt, the latter's son; Don Coyote; General Defense; The Draft; Dolores Huelga [Lady Strike]; and two Vietnamese. By projecting the drama of the *campesino* against the background of the war in Vietnam, Valdez incorporates into the usual framework of the *acto* some biting satire of the imperialistic aims of American capitalism. The complicity of the Pentagon (General Defense) and agribusiness (Butt Anglo) is the play's central plot. "You spray pesticides, and I bomb Vietnam," [122] the military man says cynically to the rancher, who furnishes recruits. The general repays the rancher by buying the produce harvested by strikebreakers. A direct parallel is established between the *campesinos* who work themselves to death in American fields and the great numbers of peasants dying in Vietnam. But the *acto* goes even further by linking the *campesino* in the American Southwest, a victim of pesticides, to the Vietnamese fieldworker exposed to napalm and bombs. The plot then intensifies, increasing in aggressiveness and scope; the tone escalates as the war in Vietnam does. The second of the five scenes is still pure slapstick: Little Butt amuses himself by spraying insecticide from his airplane on Don Coyote, who, stricken by temporary blindness, mistakes the boss for a *campesino* and brutalizes him. Then a Vietnamese peasant couple, followed by a Chicano father and mother, enter the stage. Showing the solidarity of the oppressed, the two couples identify with each other. Don Coyote personifies President Diem, whose every declaration is greeted by a loud "Chingao" from the Vietnamese, a swear word that sounds Asian but is actually Mexican-American ("son of a bitch"). The Chicanos recognize themselves in these poor Asians suspected of being communists; they all shake hands as a sign of peace in front of the embarrassed and furious general and grower. The war effort will now be intensified. This complicated *acto* lacks coherence; its didactic intention is the real link between the scenes.

One might criticize the Teatro Campesino for its excessive caricature, the marionette-like stiffness of its characters, and its overly systematic presentation of economic problems; Valdez was quite conscious of these failings. But it is more important to understand how and why his theater was born than to judge it according to our literary standards. The author relied upon simple and proven techniques that he knew would be effective with his unsophisticated public. To mobilize these people, he had to act quickly, taking the theater into the fields, using whatever means were available. "Don't say it: do it" was the motto of the Teatro Campesino.

CHAPTER 17

Enough! The Chicanos in a Rage

Dispossessed of their lands, cut off from their culture, shut out by the dominant society and the economic system on which it reposed, Mexican-Americans were strangers in their own land. How did they react to this alienation?

Mexican-Americans who tried to integrate into Anglo society, abandoning their ethnic group, were treated with contemptuous pity, ridiculed, or vilified by Chicano writers. By contrast, these writers heartily praised the ethnic and sociopolitical awareness arising among those called Chicanos (the term distinguished them from assimilated Mexican-Americans). This awareness began with a questioning of traditional ideas that were alienating, such as a conception of God and of religion that encouraged passivity, resignation, and fatalism; and a conception of women that trapped them in the pitfall of self-abnegation. Once liberated from these internal obstacles, Chicanos would be in a better position to emancipate themselves socially and politically. There were two divergent positions within the Mexican community on how to achieve this liberation. The proponents of nonviolence, such as the followers of Chávez, wanted to carry out a "peaceful revolution" of established society. The others advocated destruction of existing institutions; it was not in Vietnam that war should be waged, but on American soil. *¡BASTA YA!* ("enough")[1] was their battle cry. In the hands of these enraged Chicanos, art became a subversive act and an instrument of emancipation.

Don Coyote and the *Malinches*

The *vendidos*, the sell-outs, those who betray the race, appear in Chicano literature in the usual way: they are by turns ridiculous, repentant, and shameless. But resituated in the context of the Chicano movement, their attitude, like the *pachucos'*, takes on a new sociopolitical dimension.

Those who deny their origins in order to be accepted by white society are characterized as people who confuse tolerance with acceptance. The *regalados* ("given as a gift"), the term used by Sánchez to designate the *vendidos*, are "those who in trying to sell themselves have found no one to buy them . . ."[2] Tolerated but not accepted by Anglos, they never get their money's worth:

> A man sells out
> the minute he compromises
> with a different goal
> and needs not the criticism
> of his chicano brothers
> for he (the funny thing about selling out)
> pays for himself.
> Finally no chicano can sell himself
> for you see, he is too dumb,
> he has not arrived at a price
> or could it be he is too wise.[3]

From the other side of the grave, Montoya's more poignant, repentant *vendido* feels the moral censure of his ancestor who died fighting for the Mexican people. The poem chronicles the intensification of his vague sense of pain:

> Blunt, dull pain
> Like nothing
> But, oh, yes
> That lingers and
> Envelops my soul
>   Like sack-cloth . . .
>
> And he died for Villa
> That year of the
> Revolution / of pain
> So much
> Sweeter than
>   Mine.[4]

Of all the *vendidos*, none was better known, more hated, or more targeted in literature than Don Coyote, the recruiter of Mexican laborers. The Teatro Campesino ridiculed him; Barrio made him just as villainous, if not more so, than the owner and the guard at the Anglo-American camp. This is Morales:

> That shrewd, fat, energetic contratista [contractor], manipulator of mi-
> grating farm workers, that smiling middle man who promised to deliver so
> many hands to the moon at such and such a time at such and such an orchard
> at such and such a price, for such a small commission. A tiny percentage.
> Such a little slice. Silvery slavery . . . modernized.[5]

Edna Ferber, however caustic, was less sarcastic. Barrio, the Mexican–American who wrote *The Plum Plum Pickers*, saw the *coyote's* activities almost as a
betrayal of his own family.

The *vendido* played the Anglos' game just as real-life actor Leo Carrillo
did. In movies this Mexican-American played Mexicans who corresponded to
stereotypes held by white people. Mariana, the heroine of Vásquez's *Chicano*,
explains to young David that in Los Angeles Carrillo is considered the Chicano
"Uncle Tom."[6] Anyone who contributed to the perpetuation of the old stereotypes, reassuring prototypes of Mexicans, was dangerous. The two assimilated
Mexican-American secretaries in the *actos Los Vendidos* and *Los Bandidos* pur-
chased just such harmless Mexicans for the California governor.

The *vendido* not only betrayed the spirit of the Chicano movement (the
goals of capitalist society, to which the renegade in Delgado's poem "El Vendido" subscribes, have nothing in common with the aspirations of Mexican-
Americans) but could also hurt its expansion. To Rendón, the worst form
of betrayal was that of the *Malinches*, guilty, in their own way, of the same
duplicity as the Indian mistress of Cortés. Rendón, the activist author of the
Chicano Manifesto, criticized the harmful effects these renegades had on the Chicano movement. While the *vendidos* unknowingly impeded Chicano progress,
either out of fear or a longing for self-importance, the *Malinches* attacked their
own compatriots, spreading jealousy and dissension with the deliberate objective of hampering their advancement.[7] Rendón cites, among others, the farm
workers allegedly organized by Mexican-Americans, with the financial aid of
the agribusiness producers associations, to counter the activities of Chávez in
Delano, and Senator H. Gonzales, who called the nationalism of MAYO "reverse racism."

"God Is Beside You in the Picket Line"[8]

The *vendidos* and *Malinches* rejected ethnicity and the Chicano label, and
conspired with the oppressor. On the opposite side, Chicanos increasingly
accepted and asserted themselves socially and politically. This psychological
and moral evolution is at the heart of Rivera's work ". . . *y no se lo tragó la
tierra*" / . . . *and the earth did not part.*" As the years of his itinerant life pass
by, the child-narrator goes through several stages of consciousness; before he
can experience freedom he must reject, one by one, the obstacles posed by
tradition. He takes the first step the night that he ventures out alone and calls to

the Devil in vain (story number five). He ends up questioning the existence of this being so critical to the Mexican-American's religious universe. In a second decisive step, in the main story, he challenges God himself. The summer is at its hottest and the suffering of the workers at its zenith; the child holds the sun, then the earth, and finally God responsible for the misery, in particular for the sunstroke that almost kills two members of his family. He curses this God of the rich; when the earth does not part and swallow him up, he experiences the new and exalting feeling that he is "capable of doing or undoing whatever he chose" and that he "had completely detached himself from everything."[9] The migrants' son triumphs over the sun, the earth, and the master of the universe. A new life begins, symbolized by the dawn of a cool day breaking; but his victory is won only on the literary, not the political level.

The revolt of the young hero reflects the general unrest within the committed Mexican minority. But it was not the existence of God these activists questioned, but rather the prerogatives of the clergy. "I believe in God. But Not in Priests," poet-peasant Cleofas Vigil declared firmly.[10] Conservative, even racist, and in league with the powerful and the monied, the Catholic church no longer responded to Chicano aspirations. Sánchez spoke jeeringly of "*los rezos inútiles / de sacerdotes ciegos y racistas*" (the useless prayers / of blind and racist priests),[11] while Alurista implicitly reproached those who stood by impassively at the "massacre" of the minds; they were unworthy of "the nation under god."[12] The riches of the Church offered a flagrant contrast to the poverty of one of the poorest of all minorities:

> when we are born
>   we pay for birth
> when holy communion comes around
>   we pay
> get married
>   we pay and,
> finally,
>   the biggest *chingazo* ["rip-off"] comes . . .
> we have to pay for dying . . .[13]

The title of a poem by César López, "Católicos por la Raza" [Catholics for the race], is a reference to an association of the same name, created in Los Angeles by a group of militant Catholics to force the Church to bring itself closer to the Gospel. On Christmas Eve 1969, they demonstrated in front of Saint Basil's Cathedral to protest the racism and insensitivity of the Archdiocese of Los Angeles. On the whole, the Catholic church was indifferent and often hostile to the Chicano movement—for example, the bishops sided with the California producers during the strike. Rendón ranked the Church high on his list of the enemies of Chicanismo.[14] The time had come for the Church to repay its debt to its converts; the Indians had constructed the early missions and later churches in the Southwest were largely built by Mexican labor. Rendón wondered how and when the Church would assist, in its turn, those it had held "spiritually enslaved"[15] for generations. By its distant attitude, the Church lost some of its hold on the barrio to Protestant sects, which seemed closer to the Gospel and more aware of contemporary problems. For example, the Protestant clergy actively fought for the improvement of schools in East Los Angeles.

Chicanos also criticized the Church for being less concerned with justice than with submission to divine will, and for encouraging passivity and resignation among Mexicans, traits they were inclined toward through the fatalism inherited from the Aztecs. This idea is at the heart of Omar Salinas's poem "Robstown." The scene is a small Texas town in 1947; racial discrimination is still rampant. The central character is a Mexican-American mother. In the face of the humiliations her children are subjected to, she finds solace in reciting the rosary.[16] With somewhat contemptuous pity, the Chicano poet associates this resigned woman with the Llorona, the weeping mother of legend. Sánchez also blames the priests for the oppression of Mexican-Americans:

> la raza hurt,
> bent back—sacrificed
> to gringoismo—
> priests genuflecting
> to *pobreza* ["poverty"]
> lovers of destitution;
> priest jiving la raza,
> preaching
>   LOVE THY MASTER
>   OF THE BLUE-EYED HATRED . . .[17]

Chicanos had to free themselves from an alienating "spiritual slavery." A new brand of Christianity had to be established; "a new cross,"[18] as Delgado put it, would have to be erected. The inscription on the wall of the Filipinos' meeting hall, "God Is Beside You on the Picket Line," also reminded the Delano workers that God supported their cause. The "useless prayers" and sermons were over; the Church figured in the acto *La Quinta Temporada* [The fifth season] on the side of the unions. In Chapter 14 of his *Chicano Manifesto*, titled "New Strategies for the 1970s," Rendón gives primacy to action over sermonizing and calls for priests to follow the example of Mexican independence hero Father Hidalgo. A similar demand was expressed in Delgado's poem "The Chicano Manifesto":

> from the church we very piously ask
> less sermon and more delivery
> more priests to preach Christ's merciful justice,
> less alms and tokens in the name of charity
> and more pin pointment of the screwing going on.[19]

In his poem "A New Cross," addressed to the crucified Christ, Delgado says the humble wooden cross no longer inspires respect in the world; he beseeches Christ to exchange it for another. He gives some ironic suggestions: a cross made of three H-Bombs, or petrified dollar bills, or contraceptive pills; of solid gold or flowers; of psychedelic lights and sounds. He concludes:

> A wooden cross leaves us cold,
> Would you believe one
> With hot and cold running blood
> For war makers and soldiers?
> Personally, I prefer one twice as brilliant as the gun,
> Made of love, if you find it, buy that one.[20]

The poem recalls a short story by Black writer Langston Hughes, "On the Road." In the story, a Black jailed for vagrancy during the Depression has a dream; while he is wandering in the snow in search of shelter, door after door is closed to him, including the pastor's; even the door of the church is bolted. When he tries to force the church door open, the intruder damages the building, and it crumbles. Christ descends from the cross where he has been nailed for nearly two thousand years and thanks the man for freeing him. The framework of the traditional Church must first crumble for the "new cross" to be erected. But while some Blacks consider blackness an essential attribute of God—Hughes makes Christ a "Negro" in his poem "Christ in Alabama"— Chicanos do not try to contrast Christ with the white God of the Establishment by conferring a brown skin on him. God is love above all else, and the church, catholic in the true sense of the word, should be open to all, without distinction of race, culture, class, religion, or even conscience.[21] For Delgado, the Chicano movement was a new church.

The Chicana

Another pillar of Mexican tradition, the woman, also slowly took on a new look; the submissive and resigned spouse confined to a purely domestic role began to give way to the partner and comrade-in-arms.

Chicanas began to speak out; a special issue of *El Grito* (VII-1, September 1973), was devoted to them; in it, we find the variety of linguistic registers that characterizes all Chicano literature. The introduction was written by the most gifted of the women writers, Estela Portillo.[22] In an English handled with talent, she sets the tone for the volume: feminine and not feminist, psycho-philosophic and not political. The poetry of the woman, Chicana or otherwise, goes back to the same immemorial sources: the earth, creation, and life. Other women, though still few in number, denounced the particular exploitation they were victims of and affirmed the preeminence of their own liberation when told that the movement's class struggle was of greater importance: "When we talk of equality in the Mexican-American movement we better be talking about TOTAL equality, beginning right where it all starts, AT HOME . . ."[23] wrote journalist Enriqueta Vásquez. Mary Lou Espinosa stressed that women must achieve independence; she maintained that the new mother, *la madre de Aztlán*, would make a unique contribution to the Chicano movement:

> True woman's liberation must happen first
> in the mind of the woman . . .
>
> Socio-economic and political
> conditions can help
> the process of the woman's full
> assertion in the movement and
> in society, but the woman has first
> to want to make herself free.
>
> Woman's contribution is essential.
> A woman, a mother, knows life
> from within because of her function.
> Our society is sadly masculine oriented;
> it does not know life from within
> because men alone make it.[24]

This mental liberation, the fruit of a slow gestation period during which ancestral customs and ways of thinking are eliminated, was quite different from the wife's brief flight from her abusive husband in the Suárez short story "Las Comadres."

How did male writers react to this emancipation? Rendón, the unwavering proponent of change, was quite in favor of the advancement of women; in Chapter 10 of the *Chicano Manifesto*, titled "New Faith—Hope for Change," he largely bases his hopes on Chicanas. But his is the only feminist voice on the male side. The poets persisted in glorifying the traditional Mexican woman, evoking with emotion and passion the memory of a mother or other beloved woman. *La Jefita* ("little mother"), the mother in Montoya's poem of the same name,[25] is the very symbol of abnegation. She is a moving image from the past, as is Agustín Lira's mother. Lira represents her as a weeping woman:

> black shawled woman spreading truth,
> another night of prayers
> cadaver dead
> > et nominae
> > > et patrie
> > > > et filio sanctu
> > > > > amen.
> She will always be remembered that way
> someone died?

get the rosary
the bible and the black shawl,
she never got paid for her prayers
she was not a professional mourner
but she was there . . . praying,
she will always be remembered that way.[26]

Delgado celebrates what he sees as the basic nature of women in a poem whose form is based on traditional prosody. His idea is the antithesis of the model proposed by Mary Lou Espinosa; although in the avant-garde in other areas, Delgado remains fiercely loyal to an outmoded conception of women:

. . . her joy, her love, her endurance, is impressive
but the way she suffers almost without a tear
makes the *hembra chicana* ["Chicano woman"] divinely appear
makes her life fully mysterious and yet so clear.

Your critics whisper your life is dull, recluse,
deep down they envy your serene security,
you can give and take all with such maturity,
you can change pain to joy and lust to purity.[27]

Chicano, the novel by Vásquez, relates, as we have seen, the efforts of a Mexican immigrant family to adapt, then assimilate. Well aware of the tenacious hold of tradition, and with irreverent skepticism, the author traces the evolution of female behavior. No matter how liberated in the outside world, Minnie Sandoval and Angie Salazar (who both married just after World War II) are not liberated at home: they are not inwardly liberated. That they work and earn money is of no importance; often abused, they are slaves of their husbands. Angie, in her brash youth, leaves Rabbit Town and her family to live in East Los Angeles. In her marriage she does not even have the right to question her husband's mysterious late-night outings or how he spends money. By the fourth generation, Mariana's generation, the situation is different. Minnie Sandoval's daughter is a student, independent and aware of her rights; she keeps some distance from her family, goes out with the men of her choice, first with a rich Anglo, then, over her parents' objections, with a Chicano. Her personality wins over the Anglo graduate student David Stiver. But the book ends with Mariana's failure; she is a victim of her status as a Mexican–American woman and, simply, as a woman. Impregnated by David, she gives in to his entreaties to have an abortion, and dies.

Mariana assumes her ethnic condition as a Mexican-American; in another context, she would have made a perfect militant. "The contribution of the woman is essential," wrote Mary Lou Espinosa; it is particularly so to the Chicano movement. Indeed, hadn't the Virgin of Guadalupe begun to accompany the strikers on all their protest marches? "The Chicana is half the movement,"[28] declared Rendón, the optimist. If the Chicanas were still numerically inferior to the men, their commitment was at least equal. Like the woman in the poem by Gloria Pérez, some liked to compare themselves to Adelita, the heroine of a *corrido* of the revolution. Adelita was the symbol of Mexican women who accompanied the rebel army:

como la adelita	[like Adelita
siempre al lado	always at the
del guerrillero,	warrior's side,]
i'll live with you,	
i'll hunger with you,	
i'll bleed with you,	
and i'll die with you.[29]	

Certainly the best known among the female militants was Dolores Huerta, mother of seven and collaborator of Chávez; not by chance did the character of Huelga ("strike"), which figures in the two *actos La Quinta Temporada* and *Vietnam Campesino*, have Dolores for a first name. The movement permitted some Mexican-American women to break with tradition and defy male supremacy.

La Causa

"Chicano is an act of defiance," said journalist Rubén Salazar, who later was killed during a riot.[30] The Chicano began to speak out, for now another voice demanded to be heard, shouted poet Villanueva in his collection of poems *Hay Otra Voz* [There is another voice]. Mexican-Americans had come of age. Until recently, passive, well-mannered, humble, and ignorant children, good Americans who licked the hand that gave them crumbs to eat, Chicanos now refused to crawl. Like the student-poet Guadalupe de Saavedra, they let out *el grito*, the cry of independence that sealed their commitment.[31] Tension mounted in the barrio, the cradle of the Chicano renaissance. In the words of Delgado, the barrio defined itself as a dangerous powderkeg: "collectively I am a spirit 'que es' explosive."[32] His use of the Spanish words *que es* ("that is") underscores the real nature of the defiance intensifying in the barrio. The Chicano movement was the detonator:

es la causa, hermano, which has made me a	[it's the cause, brother]
new man. . . .	
this *causa, hermano,* is charcoaled abuse	
ready to burn. . . .	
es la causa de la raza an anthill upon your	
chest.[33]	

Like an obsessive leitmotif, "la causa" appears in the last verse of each of Delgado's seven quatrains. He returns several times to the latent threat of explosion, the result of an oppressive racial policy:

> stupid America, hear that chicano
> shouting curses on the street
> he is a poet
> without paper and pencil
> and since he cannot write
> he will explode.[34]

Mexican-Americans' deep-seated individualism prevented their revolt from unifying as it needed to; as an old proverb had it, *cada cabeza un mundo* ("each head a world unto itself"). Workers long remained distant from unionism, not because they were passive, but because they didn't see the need to join with others to make their demands known. Galarza ended his autobiography, *Barrio Boy*, with the failure of the labor movement; before World War II the author could still lament that "the only way to complain or protest was to leave." [35] He had done farm labor himself. Elected spokesman for his fellow workers, he went to the authorities in Sacramento to protest the inhuman conditions of the labor camp and to demand that an inspector visit. He returned with vague promises from the officials but with the conviction that unions were an absolute necessity. He was part of a massive, and sudden, layoff at the time that he was trying to organize his co-workers. Acosta, the author of *Chicanos Can Make It*, saw the lack of unions and political organizations, which particularly characterized the Mexican minority, as an obvious obstacle to advancement. They lacked a leader, as the inhabitants of the little town of Tierra Amarilla were aware, in the Ortego short story. These people anxiously await "The Coming of Zamora," who, they hope, will rally the people.[36]

Communism, which might have served as a unifying force, was more prevalent in the Black ghetto than in the barrio; membership in the party required a discipline repugnant to Mexican-Americans. Further, Chicano leaders preferred the movement to remain outside the Marxist orbit, as Luis Valdez told sociologist Stan Steiner in an interview:

> Marx and Hegel were Europeans. What have they got to say to us? . . . The Aztecs had a communal society before communism was ever heard of in Europe. I think Motecuhzoma has more to teach us than Marx. Our ideology is in this earth, this continent.[37]

The movement's great inspirational models were from the Americas: two Mexicans, Zapata (who promoted the Indian race and agrarian reform) and Villa (the revolutionary general); a Nicaraguan, Sandino (who led a rebellion against the United States), and an American, Malcolm X, the assassinated leader of the Black Muslims.

Mexican-Americans remained divided on strategies. Traditional barrio tactics died hard, as Estela Portillo demonstrated in her short story "Recast," which rapidly evokes the key events in the development of Mexican-American militancy. The era of the "serpents," of gangs divided among themselves, is succeeded by that of the "lions," whose nonviolent struggle, dictated by a common desire for justice, contrasts with the "wild" actions of the serpents. But many are now irritated by the slowness of nonviolent change, as Manolo notes when he returns from Vietnam. The impatient ones advocate a return to the serpents' old methods: "It was a pattern of centuries carved into the spirit. El Soldado still had his knife from the old days in a drawer at home." [38] It is in the name of an ideology that the two groups are confronting one another.

The stage of Chicano theater served as a platform for debates between the two sides. The Teatro Campesino staged a brief and didactic *acto*, *The Militants*, [39] in 1969. The scene is a debate, organized under the auspices of the University of California by Professor Bolillo (a nickname for Anglos). An opponent and a proponent of violence each try to demonstrate the effectiveness of his actions; each makes progressively more outlandish claims. One says that nonviolence is a delusion, that marching is not sufficient, that the Cause requires more than words. The other, a supporter of Chávez, denies that he is a pacifist and brings up the memory of the revolution. Finally, they begin hurling insults about whose clothes are more authentically Chicano. Violence has the last word: the two shoot each other to death. The ironic moral of the story is that violence, by creating a split within the militant minority, plays into the hands of the dominant society, against which it was originally directed. The professor, the White Man, leaves the stage wearing a victor's smile.

A play by Napthalí De León, *¡Chicanos! The Living and the Dead!* [40] has the same dialectic polarity. Without the slapstick that makes the Teatro Campesino's didactism palatable, the play presents a series of debates in English on the tactics to use to fight the Anglo oppressor. There is also a play within the play. It depicts a Chicano rally and revolves around two characters whose lives ended tragically, Che Guevara and Manuel (alias Rubén Salazar, the slain journalist). There is a dialogue of the dead in Hell, alternating with a conversation among the living, among a group of militant comrades, including Salazar's son Roberto. Manuel, the dreamer, a disciple of Chávez, espouses pacifism, faith, and love; Che, the revolutionary, refuses to identify with Christ or to speak in any language other than that of activism. The discussion is just as heated among the living; the resolute partisans of violence run into opposition from the moderates, including young Roberto. The moderates argue that hatred for the gringo is negative, that Chicanos must abandon simplistic Manichaeism and try instead to improve social conditions by first improving themselves. They resolve the problem of violence in favor of a conditional pacifism. Roberto remains resolutely deaf to his friends' urgings for revenge of his father's death, believing it more effective to manipulate the enemy covertly. But he does advocate violence in the case of legitimate self-defense; in the end, his position prevails. The dead, who silently witness the debates of the living, have the final word; Manuel is convinced that his son will never go beyond the stage of "philosophical rebellion;" [41] Che is not so positive. Referring to his own case, he argues that circumstances create the rebel; he concludes the play by accepting Roberto's suggestion and calls for a defensive war.

Play Number 9,[42] also by De León, evaluates the effectiveness of Mexican-American organizations. The play contrasts the assimilationist policy of the League of United Latin American Citizens (LULAC) and similar organizations to the radicalism of the Chicano movement but offers no solution. This time, it is not the dead who intrude upon the living, but rather a Greek mythological character. Prometheus, who stole fire from heaven to benefit humankind, also becomes the savior of the people of Aztlán. Juan, a young militant in the spiritual and political lineage of Roberto Salazar, expresses the Chicanos' grievances to Prometheus, whom Zeus has chained to a boulder in punishment for his theft. The Titan delivers a mysterious message to Juan, who returns to his comrades to recount his vision. He finds them spewing forth (in Spanish) their hatred for the gringo and their impatience with the half-measures taken during the last LULAC meeting. In the fourth and final act, a voice is heard in the wings; it is Prometheus himself revealing his message. Converted to *Chicanismo* by Juan, he has become aware of his own enslavement. He had almost begun to love his chains, but now understands that he must break them. It is something he alone can do. Likewise, Chicanos will one day be the instrument of their own liberation. This grandiloquent deus ex machina ending is the final blow to this play. Its mediocrity is not even redeemed by the structural refinement of *¡Chicanos! The Living and the Dead!*

Carlos Morton's *El Jardín* [The garden],[43] a more original play, presents a Chicano version of the fall of humanity. Based on the same dialectic of violence and nonviolence, it clearly favors the latter. After being driven from El Rancho Grande del Eden, Adán and Eva have lived on Earth for several centuries; they are now in Chicago. Adán, a guitarist and composer of traditional *corridos*, remains on the periphery of the revolutionary movement until a serpent, in the form of the quarrelsome Matón, an activist in dark glasses, beret, and zoot suit, comes to tempt him to join. Matón's depiction of the movement is initially repugnant to the peace-loving Adán; finally, by making him aware of social injustice and poverty, Matón convinces him to put his guitar to the service of the Causa. The scene is witnessed by God, who deplores not the end—social justice—but the means—the "quick solutions"[44] of Matón and those like him. Thus, despite Eva's objections, Adán is converted to militant activism and murder. But one day, as he is escorted by Death on a mission to the white section, he begins to waver. God quickly intervenes; He forgives Adán but not without first lecturing him:

> Adán, let it be known in history
> That la Raza are a peace loving people
> Who did not resort to foul violence
> To gain their freedom from oppression.[45]

The earthly paradise is not permanently closed to Adán; he goes to the Salinas Valley, where Chávez is waging his peaceful struggle against the Teamsters. From that moment, the picket line will be Adán's form of action.

Chávez attached a religious justification to the ideal of nonviolence; the poet Delgado, another mystic of the movement, saw nonviolence as the only means of reaching an understanding with Anglos and of achieving integration:

> . . . we want to let America know that she
> belongs to us as much as we belong to her
> by now we have learned to talk
> and want to be in good speaking terms
> with all that is America.[46]

As demanding as it is, Delgado's list of grievances in his "Chicano Manifesto" is never bitter. Nor is his poem "Stupid America," though a waspish impatience shines through the words:

> Stupid america, see that chicano
> with a big knife
> on his steady hand
> he doesn't want to knife you
> he wants to sit on a bench
> and carve christ figures
> but you won't let him.[47]

The supporters of nonviolence believed in the possibility of a "peaceful revolution" that would bring about change but not bloody destruction. The singer and activist Joan Baez said that it is violence that is "reactionary," since it represents "a reversion to a former pattern."[48] Brutality leads to nothing, as God said to Adán.

Huelga ("strike"), "the one Spanish word most English speakers know,"[49] was the only weapon of nonviolent Chicanos. *Huelga*, the magic word associated with Chávez, symbolized the protest of Chicano laborers and ironically gave their stereotypical "laziness and passivity" a positive connotation. It was their refusal to work and their passive resistance that finally triumphed over Anglo management. There were other strikes in the past, as anthropologist Romano has documented; they contradict the myth of Mexican-American docility perpetuated by historians and sociologists. Mexican-American history has been repeatedly punctuated with calls of ¡Basta! ("enough") and ¡Huelga![50] But the call of *Huelga* will forever evoke, not the strikes of the past, but the historic long strike at Delano.

This strike appears throughout Chicano literature. It was celebrated in *corridos*; it was at the very heart of the Teatro Campesino. The *acto Huelguistas* [The strikers],[51] performed in 1970, shows the confrontation between a *ranchero* and his striking workers; three *campesinos*, from Texas, Mexico, and the Philippines, along with two *campesinas*, represent the labor force. The workers jeer the *ranchero*, who decides to call in some strikebreakers. Don Coyote appears on the side of the employer; the final flight of these two amid the gibes of the workers is in the Teatro's slapstick tradition. The principal interest of this brief *acto* resides less in its banal, minimal action than in its contrapuntal structure. The famous *corrido* on the *Huelga*,[52] serving as a sort of plot line, is scattered throughout the *acto*. Parts of its stanzas are sung from time to time by one of the *campesinos*, while the refrain is sung on four occasions by the entire company. It concludes the play on an optimistic note.

Vietnam Campesino refers to a specific objective of the Delano strike, the banning of pesticides that are harmful to produce and pickers alike. Dolores Huelga, Lady Strike, appears in the *acto* and launches the lettuce boycott.

There are oblique references to the Chávez strike in the fictitious strike in Barrio's novel *The Plum Plum Pickers*. The plums of wrath, rotting in the sun, evoke only too clearly the grapes of wrath languishing on the vines of Delano. The author incorporated actual articles from the local press to give it a historical character.

In contrast to the Chávez strike, however, Barrio's fictional strike is violent and chaotic, which makes the novel explosive. Manuel responds to the foreman Morales's decision to deduct two cents from each bucket by dumping two containers full of fruit on the man's feet. His impulsive act recalls Adán's in the Genaro González short story "El Hijo del Sol" [The son of the sun]:

> Adán yanks off a yet-green cotton boll, an act tabooed by the pinche patrón [damned boss]. He fingers the boll-juicy flesh inside, unnatural in its pallor. Because of me, Adán reasons, it will never serve its purpose. Adán then shreds the compact fibers and then throws the ravaged, undeveloped cotton boll away.[53]

Quill, novice writer and camp guard at Drawbridge, receives a leaflet written as if with a goose-quill pen and signed Joaquín Murrieta. The book ends with the image of the "vigilante" of Drawbridge, swinging from the dark branch of the "Hangman's Tree," the camp's "justice tree."

The military intervention of the United States in Vietnam served as a catalyst for Chicano discontent; against this unjust war, which constituted a form of genocide, the militants raised a unanimous voice of protest.

Valdez denounced the inequities of the draft in *Vietnam Campesino*. In Scene 1, the general bemoans a lack of patriotism among Chicanos; the grower sarcastically suggests that he recruit a Mexican-American leader like César Chávez to persuade them to fight and die for American ideals. In Scene 3, death appears in the person of the recruiting agent; he exempts Little Butt, the boss's son, from the draft, but swoops down on a young *campesino* who is fleeing. The Teatro Campesino, an advocate of nonviolence, was indignant at a war that was ravaging the innocent civilian population of Vietnam. Death, the narrator of *El Soldado Razo* [The Chicano GI],[54] intimates that the young Chicano soldier will never return from Vietnam; in his last letter to his parents, the "private soldier" describes the massacres perpetrated in the name of anti-communism.

Under the pretext of waging a struggle against communism and liberating an oppressed people, the United States was actually pursuing an imperialist policy in Vietnam. Chicanos refused to serve as cannon fodder for American profiteers, for "materialist capitalists who are getting rich off the blood of Aztlán,"[55] as De León put it. For Sánchez, the imperialist battle in Vietnam recalled only too well a similar war in the past century, which snatched away from Mexico the territories north of the Rio Grande:

> patriotism rising like flag
> over viet nam
>   like it did in san jacinto
> holy holey wars
> holy holey wars strafing our people down.[56]

A sense of solidarity developed between Chicano activists and Vietnamese patriots. But while Valdez saw the handshake exchanged by the *campesinos* of the United States and those of Vietnam as a sign of ardently desired peace, Sánchez interpreted this solidarity more broadly in terms of a militant Third World consciousness, of an internationale of half-castes.[57]

Chicano activists agreed that their struggle to eliminate social ills had to be fought on American soil; the conflict in far-off Asia tended to obscure problems at home. The young Vietnam veteran of Estela Portillo's short story "Recast," furious at being forced to serve the interests of those he called tyrannosaurs, feels a mounting rage. At the end of a virulent essay, Sánchez calls for the fight here and now: ". . . we must prepare to fight our war here in the barrios, campos y valles [fields and valleys]—not in Asia. This then is where we shall either bring about a change or die fighting for an ideal."[58] *Vietnam Campesino* ends on the same warlike note: "The fight is here, Raza! En Aztlán."[59]

To some Chicanos, "decolonization" could only come through violence. The will to destroy was made explicit in the poetry of Rodolfo Gonzales, Alurista, and Sánchez; in his essays, Sánchez tried to conceptualize and justify the violence he advocated.

To Gonzales, "there are no revolutions without poets";[60] the extremist leader was also the poet of the Chicano revolution. His book *I Am Joaquín—Yo Soy Joaquín*[61] is a roiling epic of the Mexican-American people, symbolically designated by a name that evokes the violence of the legendary *bandido* Joaquín Murrieta. The long, tumultuous poem begins with the fall of the Aztec Empire and the beginnings of Spanish colonization and ends with the full ferment of the Chicano movement. The dual Spanish and Indian origin of the Mexican-American leads Joaquín to identify, in turn, with the oppressor and the oppressed. A second theme, his ancestors' bloody fight against tyranny, is described in terms that express the idea of survival by violence: "blood," "to bleed," and "bloody"; "to kill" and its synonyms; "to last," "to survive." History justifies the poet's own political position. In the preamble, Joaquín denounces his alienation:

> I am Joaquín,
> lost in a world of confusion,

> caught up in the whirl of a gringo society,
> confused by the rules,
> scorned by attitudes,
> suppressed by manipulation,
> and destroyed by modern society.[62]

In turning to the past, he finds the revolutionary fervor and faith he needs to wage his own battle. Aztec, Mexican, and Mexican-American history abounds in heroic and bloody deeds, which the poet takes pleasure in relating: Cortés wiping out the empire of Cuautémoc; Mexicans wresting independence from Spain in 1821 through force of arms; the revolution and its murderous vendettas; finally, the desperate resistance of rebels like Joaquín Murrieta:

> I rode the mountains of San Joaquín.
> I rode east and north
>   as far as the Rocky Mountains,
>   and
> all men feared the guns of
>   Joaquín Murrieta
> I killed those men who dared
>   to steal my mine
>   who raped and killed
>   my love
>   my wife.
> Then
> I killed to stay alive.[63]

The second part of the poem, devoted to the present, sings of Joaquín's hopes. The rumblings of the revolution could already be heard. The Chicano would survive oppression and annihilation as had his Indian ancestors in the past:

> I refuse to be absorbed,
>   I am Joaquín. . . .
>
>   I SHALL ENDURE!
>   I WILL ENDURE![64]

Alurista stressed the urgency and necessity of the fight, even if it had to be bathed in blood. The poem "when raza?" which opens *Floricanto en Aztlán*, is structured around two words: "today" and "tomorrow"; the present is the only temporal element that, from that point on, should govern the actions of the Chicano people:

when raza
when . . .
yesterday's gone
and
mañana
mañana doesn't come

for he who waits
no morrow . . .

our tomorrow *es hoy*	[is today
ahorita	now
que VIVA LA RAZA	long live la Raza
mi gente	my people]
our people to freedom	
when?	
now, *ahorita define tu mañana hoy.*[65]	[now, define your tomorrow today.]

The struggle against the oppressor cannot be postponed. The poet attacks the castrating and puerile "Anglo father of the world" for his "*voluntariosa actitud* [selfish attitude] / experimental and inhuman—the stench / of his unclean diapers."[66] Alurista denounces the sordid cruelty and insensitivity of the person he calls in turn "Mr. Jones," "the man," and, more rarely, "the gringo," and calls for murder if necessary. *Sudor* ("sweat") and *sangre* ("blood"), symbols of Mexican-American exploitation, demand another "blood," that of the oppressor:

. . . *ya basta*!	[enough!]
the sweat of our passiveness	
no more	
if blood be shed	
the man will sweat!	
with the blood	
of his guilt	
his ignorance	
let him	
bleed	
to death	
his own making.[67]	

Canto y grito mi liberación [I sing and shout my freedom], a poem by Sánchez, is the cry of a man who has "a million angers"[68] in his heart. He has an inordinate hatred of himself and the gringo, who, by preventing him from accepting himself, has made him a schizophrenic. A prisoner of a hatred compounded by successive incarcerations, the writer attempts to liberate himself by singing and shouting: "I was born into the cauldron of self-hate. . . . / . . . i was encloistered in a prison of inculcated hates."[69] The violence of his cry recalls poet Allen Ginsberg's prolonged "howl." Sánchez spews out his hatred for the racist and Nazi Anglo "Amerika" (the Germanic spelling has a specific connotation), which he distinguishes from "*las américas*," the Spanish-speaking parts of the American continents or America before the arrival of the gringo. Alurista sometimes uses this pejorative "k," as does Richard Mora in his collection of poems *The Black Sun*.[70]

Sánchez condemns the United States' ethnic policy, which he considers nothing less than "genocide." He cautions all those who do not meet its racial standards against "the vitriol of this genocidally manic nation,"[71] which is based on "a system bent on cruel oppression, repression and human suppression."[72] Its spirit, if not its procedures, only too clearly evoke Aryan theories: "repression in the Southwest took on the Hitlerian garments of racist, genocidic madness,"[73] he writes in "Desmadrazgo" [Uprooting]. This long essay traces the vicissitudes of the Mexican-American, a citizen of the "Useless States of Amerika";[74] in it, one can see the declarations of a somewhat unstable train of thought.

In face of the "genocidal and racist madness" of the dominant society, Sánchez advocates changing it radically or destroying it outright. He brandishes this second solution about with sadistic joy throughout the work. The only answer to violence is violence itself:

> i say
> that even if blood must be spilled
> that we might all
> achieve human-ness
> spill it now . . .[75]

The poem "smile out the revolu" is literally incendiary:

. . . smile out the revolu,
burn now your anguished hurt,

crush now our desecrators
chingue su madre the u.s.a.   [screw your mother]

burn *cabrones enraviados,*   [raging sons of bitches]
burn *las calles de amerika.*[76]   [streets of America]

The poet makes his stance even more explicit by harking back to *pachuquismo,* to which he adds a tremendously increased explosive charge:

> Discontent, lethargy, hate, turbulent twinges of revenge, a driving energy to fire at the world, a million drives and furies: these make up the new zoot suit of the revolutionary.[77]

While the lions of the movement were demanding recognition of their rights through peaceful means, the serpents, weary of protesting, wanted to use any means possible to establish Chicano power. "We shall create our own Chicano society,"[78] wrote Sánchez, without revealing his strategy. The nationalistic idea of creating a Chicano nation between the United States and Mexico was greeted skeptically by Rendón;[79] it was highly unlikely that Washington would ever accept such a compromise. The movement's violent wing was still in the agitation stage, not yet in the revolutionary stage, and farther still from the stage of the ideal society.

Art: A Subversive Act

In which writing styles did the struggle express itself? "Chicano Theater must be revolutionary in technique as well as content" declared Valdez.[80] Through its techniques, the Teatro Campesino negated "bourgeois" theater. Committed to a cause, it placed immediate impact before aesthetic concerns. Created by the common people and addressed to them, it sought to "educate" them, to make them aware of their exploitation and of the need for social change.[81] Its work was more subtly subversive than the agit-prop theater of the 1930s or the contemporary "guerilla" theater, which resembled political demonstrations, and from which the Teatro Campesino kept its distance.

In prose, Barrio, a graphic artist sensitive to the effects of printed words on a page, initiated such typographical innovations as scribblings streaking certain pages with black ink; columns of words; irregular spaces between words; and an absence of capital letters in some passages. These techniques sometimes reduced his novel to the level of a comic strip, but they also underscored specifically the confusion reigning in the camp he was writing about and, more generally, the absurdity of society.

The militant poets dismantled traditional verse, freeing it from the metric constraints of a single rhythm.

The spare stagings of the Teatro Campesino, Barrio's flights of fancy, and the breakdown of verse forms challenged traditional standards and the society that had established them. Subversion continued at the level of writing style.

A problem of expression arose for the "colonized" writer, who knew that "to speak a language is to embrace a world, a culture."[82] To speak French was, for the black writer Frantz Fanon of Martinique, to wear a white mask; similarly, to speak English was, for the Chicano, to subscribe to capitalist ideology. Black Americans, forced to use the language of whites, corrupted it so adroitly that whites were caught in their own trap; within the "major language" Blacks created a "minor literature."[83] Some Chicano writers—those who remained within the system in order to destroy it—did the same thing. They manipulated the enemy's language, exploiting its vocabulary and syntax, and turned it effectively against the enemy. Caustic and buffoonlike, Barrio undermined the official language by ridiculing it; with the joy and furor of the iconoclast, he attacked American civilization through its own language, which became an instrument of destruction. Sánchez, the poet, used English to create a combat language full of subversive metaphors.[84] He wanted both to raise a scandal and to exorcise his wrath; his force of expression rather than his logic carried conviction; he knew how to use just the right slogan to incite the masses in the barrio. The militant poet's cries recalled the explosive outbursts in which Black writer LeRoi Jones shouted out his hatred of white America and his desire to destroy it.

Unlike Black Americans, Chicanos had two modes of expression. The exclusive use of Spanish, however, was not in itself subversive. Novelist Tomás

Rivera and poet Sergio Elizondo wrote in their native language because they felt more at ease in it; their Spanish could not be perceived as a threat by an English-speaking reader.

It was entirely different with bilingualism, which Chicano writers used as a weapon. When they inserted Spanish words into an English sentence, they undermined the Anglos' language. By scattering the functions and attributes of English, they took a measure of authority away from the language of the "Anglo father of the world."

Bilingualism was practically absent in the Chicano novel; by contrast, it functioned quite effectively in poetry and in the theater, where it embodied the confrontation between two classes, *campesinos* and Anglo growers. It was part of a struggle waged against Americanism along two parallel fronts, linguistic and socioeconomic. Chicano writers dismantled the language of the Anglos and, along with it, the culture for which it served as the vehicle. By rising up against the language of the majority, Chicano writers sought to destroy the destructive dependency relationship Mexican-Americans had with Anglos. This effort threatened existing social institutions.

While William Burroughs, through his "cut-up" technique, tried to upset the system by eliminating words and expressions of the official language, the Chicano writer left them intact but interposed Spanish terms between them, thus breaking up the normal flow of the sentence. The chaos of the resulting sentences reflected the destabilization of the established society that was advocated by militants. Thus, bilingualism literally was a revolutionary writing style.

To challenge the language of the "father" was also, for Chicanos, to affirm their "otherness" and their true identity.

CHAPTER 18

I Am Joaquín / *Yo Soy Joaquín*: Chicanos Affirm Their Identity

One goal of the struggle was for Chicanos to be accepted as they were, as people of mixed Indian and Spanish origin and as Americans, citizens of the United States. In contrast to the *pochos* of preceding decades, distressed by their double allegiance and still searching for their identity, Chicanos knew who they were. They affirmed their duality with assurance, pride, and defiance.

To the question posed by the Mexican-American of the assimilationist era —"What am I?"—the Chicano answered, "I am." These two words recurred with meaningful insistence in the literature of the 1970s. For example, they appear in the title of the poem by Rodolfo Gonzales, *I Am Joaquín / Yo Soy Joaquín*, then as a leitmotif throughout this "journey back through history."[1] In the beautiful poem "Words of Yohamatack to His Son," José Nájera tries to capture the essence of the Chicano people through a series of images. It is based upon a counterpoint between the phrases "I am" and "they asked" or "they say," "they" being the Anglos:

> I am the ship!
> I am the sea!
> i'm the wine that turned to vinegar,
> i'm the one who can't be free.
>
> They asked me who I am,
>   where I'm going.
> They asked me where I've been,
>   and what have I done.

> They say that they don't want me around.
> They say that I am nobody,
>> but they're wrong.
>
> I am the power!
> I am the strength!
> i'm the river that failed to flow.
> i'm the seed that didn't grow.

The final stanza triumphantly proclaims the uniqueness of the Chicano:

> with my head high and back straight
> I walk down the road and whisper back to them,
> I'm the one you'll never be.[2]

The resolute "I am . . ." of Oscar Zeta Acosta, at the end of his *Autobiography of a Brown Buffalo*, sealed his commitment, at which he arrived only after a long period of wandering and an overpowering ethnic awakening: "I am neither a Mexican nor an American. I am neither a Catholic nor a Protestant. I am a Chicano by ancestry and a Brown Buffalo by choice."[3] The firm and provocative "Yo soy . . ." of the Chicano recalls the border hero's declaration of identity before squaring off against the Rangers; but while the border hero's declaration was shouted in defiance, the Chicano's was the culmination of a long, complex process of maturation.

The Children of the "Sacred Whore"

The Chicano movement conferred the stamp of nobility on the crossing of Spanish and Indian bloodlines, which Anglos considered degrading. It established the existence of la Raza,[4] a sort of ethnic and cultural brotherhood that has become a symbol of unity for the Chicano people, but has also obliged them to make common cause with all the peoples of the Americas, to whom they are linked by a common language, Indo-Hispanic heritage, and history (all have experienced Spanish colonization and Yankee imperialism). La Raza is more than just a principal figure of Chicano literature; it is its soul and confers upon it a rich, warm color. The term "bronze," often used to describe the brown race, heightens the splendor of this "alloy." Alurista speaks of the bronze *raza* as if it were a most beloved woman, to whom the poet imagines himself forever united through the bonds of matrimony:

> . . . today i marry la Raza
>> —*hasta que la muerte nos separe*   [until death do us part]
> she's waited long
>> now

—before the altar
she weeps
and i rejoice
our children
la Raza, *madre de mis hijos*   [la Raza, mother of my children
  morena virgen   dark virgin
bendita suerte   blessed good fortune
  —*hasta que la muerte nos separe* . . .[5]   —until death do us part . . .]

La Raza is present in Acosta's acerbic autobiography in his image of brown buffalos threatened with extinction. Their color is used less for its warmth than for its political tie-in with the Brown Berets and Brown Power, as the author insists on several occasions: "unless we band together, we brown buffalos will become extinct. And I do not want to live in a world without brown buffalos."[6]

If "*¡Basta Ya!*" was the militants' war cry, "*¡Viva la Raza!*" was their rallying cry. La Raza as a unifying factor and a stake of the struggle was particularly evident in the plays of De León and the *actos* of the Teatro Campesino. In the *acto* entitled *No Saco Nada de la Escuela* [I get nothing out of school], three classes of students, belonging to different ethnic groups, must recite their ABCs. These curious alphabets resemble a profession of faith to their racial heritages. In elementary school, Francisco, the little Chicano who knows no English, refuses to speak. In high school, he has become bolder: "A is for amor, como amor de mi Raza [love, as in love of my Raza]. . . . B is for barrio como where the Raza lives. And C is carnalismo ["brotherhood"]."[7] At the university, his ABCs amplify his way of thinking more specifically:

> A is for advanced, as the advanced culture of Indigenous American Aztlán. B is for Bronze, as the advanced culture of Indigenous American Aztlán which brought Bronze civilization to the Western Hemisphere. And C is for Century, as the advanced culture of Indigenous American Aztlán which brought Bronze civilization to the Western Hemisphere and which, moreover, will create el nuevo hombre [the new man] in the twenty-first century, El Chicano. Give me my diploma.[8]

La Raza expands the Chicano cause to the dimensions of the Hispanic-American continent. The shouts of *¡Viva la Raza!* in Chicano theater alternate with *vivas* acclaiming the Mexican revolution, a decisive event in the history of la Raza. At the end of his epic poem, Gonzales celebrates la Raza, the common denominator of all Latin American peoples:

La Raza!
  Mejicano!
    Español!
      Latino!
        Hispano!
          Chicano!

> or whatever I call myself
> > I look the same
> > I feel the same
> > I cry
> > > and
> > sing the same.[9]

Mexican–American literary production can be resituated in the broader context of Latin American literature; similarities in theme, point of view, and mode of expression can be detected.

Carlos Morton meshed the Biblical story of Eve with the Mexican story of Cortés and his Indian mistress, Malinche, in his satirical play *El Jardín* [The garden]. The serpent says to Eva:

> . . . your name will be Malinche and you will betray the Aztec people, tu raza! you will interpret for the bearded ones and divulge all our secrets and you will even mate with their leader, Hernán Cortés, and the first of a bastard race will be born in Méjico.[10]

The Mexican was born of this union between a Spanish father and an Indian mother. The image of the noble and victorious *conquistador*, fiercely defended by the great Hispanic-American families of the past, was gradually replaced by that of the castrating father; the *conquistador* had become the oppressive tyrant. The image of the mother also underwent modification, but in a positive direction. Malinche, long thought of as a traitor who helped the conqueror in his colonization through her knowledge of the Maya and Aztec languages, became instead the symbol of the oppressed Indian people, "the ravished mother, exposed to the outside world, torn apart by the Conquest." [11] Now, with no sense of shame, Chicanos proclaimed themselves *los hijos de la Chingada* ("the children of the Sacred Whore"), even though the nickname Malinche, given to Mexican-Americans who sell out their brothers, remains a caustic reminder of the treachery of "the first Mexican-American," [12] Malinche, alias Doña Marina. The expression *los hijos de la Chingada*, introduced by Octavio Paz in his study of Mexicans, *The Labyrinth of Solitude*, is often used by Chicanos in speaking of themselves. In a sense, another mother figure, the Virgin of Guadalupe, redeemed Malinche's "original sin," just as the Virgin Mary made up for Eve's fall. Corresponding to the heavenly Virgin of Guadalupe was the earthly resolute woman in the black shawl, the admirable, long-suffering foundation of the family. Of her Mary Lou Espinosa could say: "From the Indian comes strong mother figure / From Spanish comes dominant father figure." [13]

The dual ethnic descent of Chicanos forced them to identify, in a pride tinged with bitterness, both with the Spanish oppressor and the oppressed Indian. The long poem by Gonzales, "a mirror of [the] greatness and [the] weakness" [14] of the half-caste, stresses this ambiguity:

I am the sword and flame of Cortés
                    the despot.
                    And
I am the eagle and serpent of
                    the Aztec civilization.
I owned the land as far as the eye
Could see under the crown of Spain,
and I toiled on my earth
and gave my Indian sweat and blood
                    for the Spanish master . . .

I was both tyrant and slave.[15]

By overlooking some aspects of Spanish history, Javier Alva, in his short story "The Sacred Spot," could consider this complex origin an advantage of which his young zoot-suiter could be proud:

> And within the skin of these same brown hands there flowed the blood of the Aztec and the Spaniard and the Moor and the Toltec, the Iberian Christian and the Sephardic Jew. These hands were Felipe and his history.[16]

If Chicanos took pride in the Spanish people who conquered the Moors, they rejected these same Spaniards as colonizers of the New World. They were never able, however, to deny their ties of kinship.

Chicano writers indicted the *conquistadores* and their successors with the same sarcastic verve, if not with the same bitterness, that they did the gringos. They sided with the oppressed Indian; as Philip Ortego noted, the Chicano Renaissance situated itself outside the Hispanic tradition and harked back to the Indian past,[17] echoing the indigenist movement in Mexico of the 1920s and 1930s. Militants emphasized their "Indianness": while the flag of New Mexico displayed the sun of the Pueblo Indians on a background of red and gold, the Spanish colors, the Chicano standard was a reproduction of the Aztecs' banner, a black eagle on a red background. Zapata, symbol of the return to the indigenous past, became the object of a veritable cult.

In literature, this "Indianism" was manifested in a resurgence of Aztec myths and a renewed appreciation of everything Indian. Writers repeatedly alluded to the Indians' past grandeur and their beliefs, which had been eclipsed by colonization and Roman Catholicism.

Writers also ruminated on the humiliations of their history, especially the fall, in 1521, of Cuauhtémoc, the last Aztec emperor and nephew of the great Moctezuma; the destruction of Tenochtitlán, upon whose ruins Cortés built Mexico City; and the exploitation of the native population. The arrival of Cortés in the year Ce-Acatl, 1519,[18] and its baleful consequences are presented facetiously in the *acto La Conquista de Mexico* [The conquest of Mexico]. A fatal mistake costs the Aztecs their empire; they believed that the *Conquistador*, this "bearded coyote,"[19] is an incarnation of Quetzalcoatl, god-king of the Toltecs, he of the white skin and long white beard, who is returning to the throne after 500 years of exile. Banished from Mexico by Tezcatlipoca, the dark god of the night sky, the radiant Quetzalcoatl, the "plumed serpent," inventor of arts and sciences, was to return on the waves of the Atlantic Ocean.

The stage is dominated by an Aztec calendar, the *Piedra del Sol* ("Stone of the Sun"), set against a red canvas backdrop; the sun image in the center of the stone narrates the *acto* in English. Moctezuma appears. His power has been undermined by the quarrels between the various tribes of his kingdom; his authority holds sway only within the inner circle, on matters of minor importance. Afflicted with migraine headaches, he imperiously demands chocolate, peanuts, and wine—ten bottles of Thunderbird—and calls for a Westinghouse electric blanket. The announcement of the arrival of the *Conquistador* from the East arouses great consternation at the court. Cortés-Quetzalcoatl and the *gachupines*, the Spaniards accompanying him, immediately undertake their colonization. Brother Bartolo performs a series of rapid baptisms; Cortés takes Malinche for himself; he rallies the dissident tribes against Moctezuma by dangling the monarch's gold before them. The *Conquistador* shouts, "We are gathered here on this . . . Ask not what Cortez can do for Mexico, ask what Mexico can do for . . . yes, I got it, My fellow Americans,"[20] parodying successively Lincoln's Gettysburg Address and John F. Kennedy's inaugural speech.[21] The emperor's nephew begins to have doubts about Cortés's divinity; despite the nephew's warnings, Moctezuma welcomes the white god, who then stabs him on the temple steps.

Cuauhtémoc ascends the throne and runs the *gachupines* out of Mexico, but his victory is short-lived; the Spaniards destroy Tenochtitlán in 1521 and hang Cuauhtémoc, the last Aztec emperor. The facts in the *acto* are faithful to history but Valdez adds his own spice. For example, one of the *conquistadores*, Pedro de Alvarado, nicknamed "Pete," behaves and speaks in a fashion so typically Yankee (he calls one Aztec a "spic" and a "greaser") that one of the natives shouts: "Yankee Go Home!" By linking Spanish colonization and Anglo-American imperialism, the author emphasizes the double oppression that successively victimized the American of Mexican descent. The *acto* also draws a lesson from history: it was disunion within la Raza that gave the white men their strength and, ironically, made them as powerful as gods.

Varying forms of violence were used by the Spaniard against the native. The blood flowed during the Conquest. Ricardo Mora rebelled against

> . . . the screams of human victims
> sacrificed to the gods of rape
> and the desolation
> and the flaming swords in the bands of
> conquistadores . . .[22]

Miguel Méndez evokes the bloody extermination of the Yaquis in the late nineteenth century in his poetic short story "Tata Casehua" [Father Casehua].

The splendid Sonoran Desert is the background for the drama. At center stage stands the imposing tomb of Manuel Casehua, the last Indian emperor and symbol of the grandeur and decline of the Yaquis. The author contrasts the nobility of the Indians to the cruelty of the *yoris*, the whites. A mother and her young son are walking across the desert; a dialogue begins between the boy, who has been struck by the emperor's monument and its epitaph, and the now-deceased Casehua, who exists in the child's fevered imagination. The mother tries in vain to calm him: "Go to sleep my son; go to sleep, for the malignant *yori* will eat children who do not go to sleep early." [23] The Yaqui emperor does not try to lure the child to him in death; instead, he drives him back toward water and life, far from the deadly sands that have buried this tragedy of the Mexican Northwest: "Sand, sand, waves of sand, whirlwinds of sand, hurricanes of sand, formidable sand of oblivion that buries everything." [24]

The Spaniards baptized the Indians in order to exploit them all the better.[25] Valdez, in his Conquest *acto*, denounced the policy of eradicating Indian beliefs, as practiced by the Franciscans. Carlos Morton condemned the use of Christianity for the purposes of colonization. In Morton's play *El Jardín* [The garden], the serpent mocks Eva, who lives in the glory of Paradise "worshipping the Gabacho [white] God who will one day come with the soldados de España to land on our shores with the promises of a new world under the domain of Jesu-Cristo and El Rey de España." [26] Nothing better illustrates Mexicans' distrust of religion imported from Europe than their Mexicanization of the Virgin of Estremadura, a Spanish cult that symbolized both Hispanic Christianity and the evangelization of the New World.[27] The Indians co-opted the European virgin by fusing her with Tonantzín, Aztec goddess of the earth and fertility.[28] Indeed, on the very site of the apparitions of the Virgin of Guadalupe on Tepeyac hill, near Mexico City, there was originally a temple dedicated to the Aztec Earth-Mother. Some people have rashly attributed a Nahuatl origin to the term "Guadalupe"; formed from *coatl* ("serpent") and *alopeuh* ("who walks on"), it purportedly means "the one who crushed the serpent." The Aztec divinity, indeed, was represented crushing the snake. Chicano writers adopted this doubtful etymology of the word for their [29] own purposes and emphasized the indigenous nature of the Virgin of Guadalupe del Tepeyac. Poet Leonardo Elías, who wrote behind prison bars, invoked the Virgin, his "beautiful Aztec mother." [30] Among the figures with whom Gonzales's Joaquín identified were "the Virgin of Guadalupe / Tonantzín, Aztec goddess, too." [31] Alurista compared the cheeks of his beloved to fragrant flowers, which resembled "las de Tonantzín / on the lap of Juan Diego." [32]

But this fusion of two divinities remained purely literary. To the masses in the barrios of the American Southwest, the Virgin of Guadalupe was, above all, the symbol of la Raza. Alurista compared the birth of the Raza to the nativity of Jesus Christ; he hailed this "bronze-hued fruit" from the womb of the "bronze virgin." [33] To Delgado, *"mamá lupe"* was the spiritual mother of the *mestizos*: "you labored in pain at tepeyac hill / to give soul birth to a race of strong will . . ."[34] Just as Mexican nationalism had crystallized around the Virgin of Guadalupe, so did la Raza's militant rally around her. By making the Mexican Virgin Mary the patron saint of the *mestizos* and the figurehead of their struggle for freedom, Chicanos placed themselves in the mainstream of the Mexican indigenist movement.

Chicano literature proudly emphasized the distant and fabled origins of the Mexican people, whose emblem was the sun. In the poem "Saga de Aztlán," dedicated to Gonzales, Ramón Emiliano has the Mexican calendar begin in the year *Ce-Tochli*, the year 50 of our era:

> In the dusk, as evening shadows
> Creep across the inland valleys,
> Listen to our song of yesteryear,
> Of our people in their dawning.
> Let me now evoke dead memories
> And burn copal to gods long gone.[35]

The nomadic tribes of the North, the Chichimecas, who later called themselves the Aztecs, founded the legendary city of Aztlán along the shore of a lake:

> Here they built their first new village,
> Here grew the city called Aztlán,
> Place of the flowering azcahuitl,
> City of cranes, the great Aztlán.[36]

In the year *Ce-Tecpatl*, 1064, the high priest Huitzilton (later elevated to a god under the name of Huitzilopochtli) orders the Aztecs to begin a journey, a migration to the south. After almost three hundred years of wandering, in the year *Ome-Calli*, 1325, they settle in a desolate area where they see the sign promised by their god: an eagle perched on a cactus devouring a serpent. There they build their capital, Tenochtitlán (the place of the hard-fruited Barbary fig tree).

The Aztecs were truly the "people of the sun";[37] their supreme god, Huitzilopochtli, personified the sun at its zenith, the dazzling midday sun, the conqueror of the night. He had power over life and death; he was a father and benefactor but also a cannibal who required human flesh and blood, an ambivalence echoed in Chicano literature. The "Aztec sun" to the *campesino* is at once the symbol of fertility and of hard labor. For the Chicano, *un hijo del Sol* ("son of the Sun"), it had a third meaning, which we will consider in our final chapter. For the Aztecs there was no obligation more sacred than the offering of a human heart to Huitzilopochtli; from this death the life essential to the universe was born.[38] This is the principal idea of De León's epic poem "Of Bronze the Sacrifice." Tenochtitlán sacrifices its own blood to give life to Quetzalcoatl:

Oh Tenochtitlán!
Cradle of the Gods
Cradle of Bronze warriors . . .

The maiden
the sweet sacrificial flower
weeps and sings of her deep pain.[39]

In the theater, the Aztec solar myth was placed in a modern context, as in the Valdez play *Bernabé: A Drama of Modern Chicano Mythology*. (This work is not an *acto* based upon current social issues but a *mito* ["myth"] of a more mystical nature.) The action takes place in the San Joaquin Valley. Bernabé, a poor *campesino*, is the barrio idiot. He lives with his mother, a tyrannical old woman who makes every effort to suppress his sexuality: he is still a virgin at the age of thirty-one. An attempt to couple with Consuelo, the local prostitute, ends in a bloody fight with a cousin. Howling like a madman, Bernabé flees into the moonlit countryside. The play then turns supernatural. The Sun appears in all its magnificence and Bernabé asks him for the Earth. The Moon then comes out, in the form of a *pachuco*, to protect his sister, the Earth. The Sun consents to the marriage of the Earth and the *campesino* if he will sacrifice his heart to the Sun. ". . . life is death and death is life,"[40] he explains to Bernabé, who accepts death in order to live. The Sun first kills the man, then revives him. He makes the Earth a virgin once more before giving her to the *campesino* as a wife.

I have been unable, unfortunately, to secure a complete text of Jorge Huerta's play *El Renacimiento* [The rebirth] *de Huitzilopochtli*, which is apparently unpublished. The brief excerpt reproduced in the issue of *El Grito* devoted to Chicano theater,[41] however, permits us to imagine how this theme might be developed: the rebirth of the Sun god symbolizes, in all likelihood, the rebirth of the Chicanos. In the prologue, the narrator evokes the birth of Huitzilopochtli; on stage, his mother, Coatlicue, goddess of the earth, dresses and speaks like a Chicana. The poetry of Alurista is permeated with the light of the Aztec sun, Tonatiuh; the sun is present at the birth of Tenochtitlán in the poem "*El recuerdo de mis grillos*" [The memory of my shackles]:

—*el aguila*   [the eagle]
devouring a snake
    staring at the sun
        perched
on a cactus . . .[42]

From its heights, the pyramid of Teotihuacan, erected to the glory of the sun, looks down upon the poet's "moongloom dreams" and reduces to nothingness the "dreams that are as melancholy as the moon."[43]

Chicano pride in their Aztec descent permits Omar Salina's *bato loco* to sublimate his low social status:

Drunk
   lonely
      bespectacled
   the sky
   opens my veins
     like rain
clouds go berserk
        around me
my Mexican ancestors
      chew my fingernails
I am an Aztec angel
     offspring
   of a woman
      who was beautiful.[44]

It is not his Spanish father but his Indian mother who makes this "Aztec Angels" gang member proud. In his story "The Sacred Spot," Javier Alva enhances the image of the young zoot-suiter by giving him the designation "plumed serpent,"[45] the same one accorded to the god-king Quetzalcoatl. Delgado and Alurista invoke not only the Aztecs, Mexicans of the central plateau, but also the Mayas, Mexicans of the South, just two of the many tribes within the immense Aztec empire. In "Cactus Fruit," Delgado writes:

We are not deaf, nor dumb, we are maya, we are alert,
we are la raza experiencing a new birth. . . .

we are maya, we are cactus fruit soaking up the rain.[46]

To Alurista, the offensive imitation of Anglo-American models is over—the Chicanos have rediscovered their own people:

and we've played cowboys
—as opposed to indians
when ancestors of *mis charros abuelos*　　　　　[my Charro grandfathers
indios fueron　　　　　　　　　　　　　　　　were Indians
   de la meseta central　　　　　　　　　　　　from the central plateau]
and of the humid jungles of yucatan
   nuestros Mayas.[47]　　　　　　　　　　　　　[our Mayas.]

Perhaps nothing better illustrates the prestige of the indigenous past than the prize awarded in 1972 by Quinto Sol to Rudolfo A. Anaya for his novel *Bless Me, Ultima*. The author was honored for reaching into the depths of his people's "collective unconscious" and re-creating their myths and legends.[48] His book, written in English, evokes a society that, even after World War II, still reposes on ancestral values and conceptions of the universe. The action of this novel, which resembles a tale, takes place in a little village in northern New Mexico,

El Puerto de la Luna, whose residents live under the symbol of the moon goddess and the protection of the brown Virgin of Guadalupe. A *curandera* ("healer"), Ultima la Grande, has quasi-magic powers that fascinate the young hero–narrator, Antonio.

She becomes even more impressive to the child the day she tells him that she uses the medicinal plants of the Aztec and Maya tribes of the distant past and even those of the Moors. The novelist evokes the myth of the *Llorona* (Cihualcoatl), who shares the Devil's power to terrify children, and also the myth of the Golden Carp, the lord of the waters who one day emerged from the depths to reign once more. All this is related in a simple and unsophisticated style that aptly expresses the wonder of childhood and the natural intimacy of the ancients with the cosmos.

Chicano Bilingualism

A Spaniard in language and civilization, an Indian in blood and heart,[49] fate made the Mexican of the Southwest an American:

Por mi madre yo soy mexicano,	[On my mother's side I'm Mexican
Por destino soy americano . . .	Fate made me an American
Dos idiomas y paises	Two languages, two countries
Dos culturas tengo yo.[50]	Two cultures have I.]

sang Rumel Fuentes in his *corrido* "Mexico Americano." *Mestizos* demanded, with insistence and without shame, their rightful status as Americans: "*Yo soy Chicano, tengo color / Americano pero con honor . . .*" [I'm Chicano, my skin is colored / I'm American and proud of it . . .][51] wrote Juanita Domínguez, a militant of the Crusade for Justice, in her poem "Yo Soy Chicano," sung to the martial air "Soy la Rielera" [I am the ingot mold], a *corrido* of the Mexican Revolution. In their respective manifestoes, Rendón and Delgado demanded that the Chicano be recognized as a first-class citizen of the United States, for "He is a built-in foundation stone of this country,"[52] as Rendón declared. ". . . we want to let America know that she belongs to us as much as we belong in turn to her,"[53] Delgado maintained. The more aggressive Sánchez was exasperated by Anglo racism:

> What, if anything, must we do
> to prove that we too are worthy?
> must we prove
> that we are more american
> (which we are!) and
> that therefore
> we need not suffer?[54]

The Mexican-American was at the confluence of three civilizations; to the extent that he became "consciously tricultural" he would become the "new Chicano" whose "emergence" Guillermo Fuenfrios had acclaimed.[55] Rendón was bent on situating the Mexican-American as "a mezcla [mixture] of Mexican Indian, Spanish, and the North American—yes, even the Anglo-dominated society is his to absorb into himself."[56] But Chicanos are bilingual and not trilingual; they speak only the languages of the Spanish and American invaders: "My father is an Indian from the mountains of Durango. Although I cannot speak his language . . . you see, Spanish is the language of our conquerors. English is the language of our conquerors . . . ,"[57] lamented Oscar Z. Acosta. Many yearned for an indigenous language, in particular for Nahuatl, which remains, however, known only to a select few (Romano and his team of researchers).[58]

Chicanos' bilingualism is a double-edged sword:

. . . es que ya no soy niño: soy hombre.	[. . . A child no more: I am a man.
Mexicoamericano porque hablando nací,	Mexican-American, for I was born
lengua de la Raza.	speaking
Americano por estas otras costumbres	the language of la Raza.
de esta gente.	American from these other ways
Tengo dos palabras, español e inglés,	of these other people.
a veces bien, a veces mal,	I have two words, Spanish and English,
pero dos, ay se va, pues. [59]	good at times, at times not,
	but two, for better or for worse.]

They know that a command of two languages makes them superior to Americans. "Big deal! You call yourself a teacher? I can communicate in two languages. You can only communicate in one. Who's the teacher, Teach?"[60] young Francisco in the Valdez *acto* mockingly answers a teacher who wants him expelled from high school.

A symbol of their cultural schizophrenia and revolt against the Establishment, Chicanos' bilingualism was also a way to assert loudly that they were Americans of Mexican descent. But to what extent were English, their "vehicular" language, and Spanish, their "vernacular" language, used respectively? Did certain words bear the stamp of one culture or another? Was there a method in the mixture? No. As an example, let's turn to the mixture of English and Spanish words which forms the usual pattern in the poems of Alurista[61] and Sánchez.

There is no school of Chicano poetry. Not a single writer, to my knowledge, has clearly explained the collage of his or her writing, the how and why of the constant switching from one linguistic code to another. In his introduction to the special poetry issue of *El Grito*, Herminio Ríos declares that the switches themselves are a source of poetry; he recognizes, however, that the social context often intrudes in the choice of linguistic vehicle.[62] To Sánchez, bilingualism, as the spontaneous expression of the Mexican–American's duality, cannot be subjected to precise rules; like Ríos, he emphasizes its poetic potential:

> People viewing the universe with dual perspectives, and words some-how fumble out, tumble and pirouette on the hills, valleys, and plateaus of our minds . . . it is poetic, the merging of languages, thoughts, feelings, and observations so that one asks, what time is it, carnal, for i have tantas cosas que hacer [so many things to do] that it is espantoso [dreadful] at times, and we understand . . . and our ears reverberate.[63]

Elsewhere, speaking more passionately than theoretically, Sánchez maintains a dichotomy between the two languages:

> . . . and I tell you, brothers, that it hurts to hear my raza gabbing in English or asking for Chicano poetry written in the language of the gringo . . . and there are certain things that I cannot translate, for I feel my soul burst forth in cantos inspired by the Chicano spirit . . . and my whole being demands that the truth of our brotherhood be written with the blood of passion . . .[64]

Thus the things of the heart can be and should be expressed only in Spanish. Does this mean that anything less intimate may be expressed in either language? A lexical inventory of Alurista and Sánchez reveals that the following word-themes are expressed in Spanish: *alma* ["soul"], *carnal* ["brother"], *carnalismo* ["brotherhood"], *hermandad* ["brotherhood"], *amor* ["love"], *sol* ["sun"], *la pirámide del sol* ["the pyramid of the sun"], *solar* ["solar"], *calor* ["heat"], *cálida* ["hot"], *caliente* ["warm"], *ardor* ["fieriness"], *vida* ["life"], *gritar* ["to shout"], *grito* ["shout"], *desmadrazgo* ["rootlessness"], *revolución* ["revolution"], *ya basta* ["enough!"], *nosotros* ["us," "we"]. Also in Spanish are expressions with affective connotations: *mi alma* ["my soul"], *mi raza* ["my people"], *nuestra raza* ["our people"], *mi gente* ["my people"]. Other recurring key words are in English: "ashes," "chains," "desert," "dust," "frigid," "idiocy," "plastic." Without pretending to enunciate any absolute rules, we may note two points: first, an important verse in Spanish is sometimes set apart from the rest, as if to stress an antithesis in the poet's mind; second, the social context is important to the extent that word-themes referring to Chicanos usually appear in Spanish, while those referring to Anglos are in English.

In the following passage taken from the Alurista poem "what's happening. . . , " the first verse is in Spanish and glorifies la Raza. The following verses, in English, denigrate the American.

el aguila de nuestro orgullo   [the eagle of our pride]
    is now settled on the cactus of your
      apathy
devouring
    the serpent of inhumanities
that crawled viciously in your amérika.[65]

In the Sánchez poem "migrant lament," the worker's lament, largely expressed in the language of the oppressor, ends on a melodious note in Spanish, expressing a hope for universal brotherhood:

una	[a worldwide social work]
obra social	
mundial . . .[66]	

The verse "canto y grito mi liberación" recurs like a leitmotif throughout the Sánchez essay "Dichotomies . . ."

The Alurista poem "in the barrio sopla el viento" can serve as an example of the impact of social context on choice of language:

In the barrio *sopla el viento*	[the wind blows]
the stench	
of the cannery permeates	
the air	
and *mi gente* breathes	[my people]
the secretions	
of cancerous system	
suicidal infection	
drags *mi gente*	[my people
a la siembra inmunda	to the disgusting planting fields]
and to the frigid factory	
to spray our open wounds	
de yugo opresivo	[from the oppressive,
esclavizante	enslaving yoke
la pestilencia	the pestilence]
of its diseased skeleton	
and the dust	
our breath	
sweeps	
and whistles	
our alienated pride.[67]	

Two worlds are in conflict here: the barrio and the American cannery. The first is evoked through the Spanish expression "*mi gente*," the second through a series of negative English terms suggesting disease and death: "diseased skeleton," "stench," "secretions / of cancerous system," "suicidal infection." The verse "to spray on our open wounds" also refers to the pesticides dreaded by farm workers. The word "frigid," which describes the cannery, contrasts with the emotional warmth embodied in the possessive pronoun modifying "*gente*." To the subtle infiltration ("permeates") of the death-carrying germs and the whistling of the dust, the author contrasts the blowing of the wind, which generally carries life along with it ("*sopla el viento*"). The phrase "in the," in the first verse, marks the intrusion of the Anglo world into the poet's native barrio.

This initial notion of aggression is repeated and amplified by a second series of oppositions, which contrast with "*mi gente,*" who are "dragged" toward death and who breathe polluted air. The theme of alienation is expressed by the final verse in English.

Up to this point in our explication, the respective uses of the two codes appear to be well-founded; but a few terms pose problems. How can we justify the Spanish of "*siembra inmunda,*" "*yugo opresivo / esclavisante / la pestilencia,*" symbols of American agribusiness, or the English of "pride," which has always characterized Mexican-Americans? Does the conception of life evoked by the planting season suffice to explain the use of Spanish? If so, what are we to say about "*inmunda*" and "*pestilencia*"? In the case of "*yugo opresivo / esclavizante,*" is the use of Spanish justified because the line concerns a turning inward, the psychological yoke experienced in the Chicano's innermost being? Is "pride" Anglicized to better express the Mexican-American's alienation, and thus give the poem a pessimistic conclusion? (Compare this vocabulary with Alurista's use of the Spanish *orgullo* ("pride") in "what's happening . . . ," which celebrates Chicano pride.)

These examples demonstrate that we should not postulate overly rigid rules. In any case, the words have a life of their own, as Sánchez says, fumbling, tumbling, and pirouetting from the pens of Chicano writers.

In general, the choice of language depends upon the verse's internal harmony. The traditional Anglo-American verse of five strong measures disappears in favor of verse free of all metric constraints. Sánchez sometimes uses the harmonic possibilities of alliteration: "to die day by day,"[68] " 'neath neon anomie."[69] On occasion, Alurista's rhymes follow the model of Spanish consonance and assonance. The golden rule coincides with Verlaine's "Art Poétique": "music above all else." For the Chicano poet, there was no better school for this music than the barrio.

The Chicanos' bilingualism demonstrates that they have been influenced but not absorbed by Anglo-American civilization. It manifests their refusal to dissolve into the melting-pot and their finally established identity, whose uniqueness and complexity is expressed by the term "Chicano," "as difficult to define as 'soul.' "[70] It is broader than "la Raza" but more limited than "Mexican-American":

> Chicano is a beautiful word. Chicano describes a beautiful people. Chicano has a power of its own. Chicano is a unique confluence of histories, cultures, languages, and traditions.[71]

CHAPTER 19

The Children of the Sun: Chicanos as Precursors of a New World

Chicano literature is distinguishable from earlier Mexican–American works by its tone; it expresses with more recrimination the minority's alienation and exasperation. It also differentiates itself by its color; it no longer bears the fair complexion of the Spaniard, as in the colonial era, nor the neutral one of the *pocho* during the assimilationist period; it is brown and unashamedly so. Its message is also different; through its critique of Anglo-American society, it challenges all of Western civilization and proposes, with a somewhat juvenile sense of triumph, a radically different world.

Aztlán

This kingdom the Chicanos dreamed of is the legendary Aztlán, the Aztecs' place of origin, the "NortherN mYthical land" celebrated by Alurista[1] and others. Unable to recapture the lands of their distant ancestors through force of arms, Chicanos reconquered them in their imagination. Chicanos made modern uses of this ancient myth; "El Plan Espiritual," drafted in 1969 in Santa Barbara, advocated the reconquest of the Aztec kingdom, the expulsion of the *gabacho* ["Anglo"] usurper and exploiter, and the founding of a *mestizo* nation north of the Rio Grande. This politically unachievable plan of liberation had a spiritual side; it provided for a radical reorganization of institutions and the establishment of a society based upon love and brotherhood. In his play *¡Chicanos! The Living and the Dead!*, which examines violence and nonviolence, De León demonstrates how the myth could be exploited. Some used it to justify the use of force: "We are a great people, sons and daughters of Aztec kings and Spanish noblemen—who will push the Gringo out of Aztlán, our land! Our home!"[2] But for De León the reality of Aztlán was different: "It is the land and state of mind that we Chicanos give our new-found freedom to think for ourselves,"[3] explains young Juan, the author's spokesman, to Prometheus in *Play Number 9*. Aztlán was less a geographical and historical reality than a spiritual one: "We are part of the land, but we need not seek a geographic center for our Aztlán; it lies within ourselves. . . . We are Aztlán and Aztlán is us,"[4] declares Rendón at the beginning of his *Chicano Manifesto*. He emphasizes that the resurgence of the myth corresponded to a need for spiritual regrouping: "Ties much more profound than even language, birthplace, or culture bind us together—Aztlán represents that unifying force of our nonmaterial heritage."[5] The exhortations to build Aztlán, to come together in Aztlán, stand out like guideposts in the literature. This key word, like "la Raza," is often set off in capital letters, as in this poem by Mora:

Carnales,   [Brothers]
Tell me when you are ready
    for the rebirth
    for the dream of AZTLAN!
Carnales, tell me![6]

Valdez appealed to the *campesinos* to fight not in Vietnam but in the Southwest, in order to establish, not an El Dorado corrupted by gold and the dollar, but a new kingdom based upon love and brotherhood. It is toward this "promised land,"[7] that the pilgrim in Aristeo Brito, Jr.'s poem "El Peregrino" [The Pilgrim] journeys. At the end of this spiritual migration, in the twenty-first century, the Chicano would emerge as the initiator of a new order, the one whose coming Rendón acclaims at the end of his manifesto: "Chicano is a prophecy of a new day and a new world."[8]

The Pyramid of the Sun

Huitzilopochtli, god of the sun, drove the moon and the stars from Chicano literature; this eminently solar, diurnal and luminous literature does not focus on the deepest recesses of the heart and the universe, nor on the darkness of night. Rather, like the pyramid of Teotihuacan, it reaches up toward the sun. Unlike Aztec literature, weighed down by the dark shadow of death, it has no room for the bittersweet charm of melancholy. Unlike disillusioned Western literature, which reflects the "disenchantment of our culture with culture itself,"[9] Chicano literature is characterized by hope, as Herminio Ríos stresses in his preface to Rolando Hinojosa's story collection *Estampas del valle y otras obras* [Portraits of the valley and other works].[10] It blithely ignores existential anguish; Sartrian nausea was not part of the Chicano make-up. Only one short story, by the intellectual Nick Vaca, "The Week of the Life of Manuel Hernandez,"[11] stands out for its Kierkegaardian overtones in the midst of a literature marked by an exuberant will to live. It retraces the anguished spiritual itinerary of a man who, since his youth, has searched in vain for a meaning to life; living in Europe, he can no more escape the beast gnawing within him than he could in American farm fields in years gone by. Another beautiful and moving Vaca story, "Martín,"[12] about a Chicano child with the bloated stomach of the malnourished, offers a dark image of the barrio, one untouched by even the most feeble ray of light.

Elsewhere in Chicano literature, the Aztec sun always succeeds in breaking through the darkness. Barrio's *campesino*, bending over his plums in *The Plum Plum Pickers* has only to lift his head and the same sun that is scorching his back shines with the light of hope. Unlike poetry in general, Chicano poetry shows more interest in the day than the night; it seems to be trying to avoid being swept away by a morbid and decadent brand of romanticism. Thus, in the middle of Alurista's poem "Unexpectedly," which begins on a surprisingly funereal note (the author laments the "cultural assassination" of his people), there is a break, after which the solar poet pursues his usual course:

Y corrí hacia el sol	[And I ran toward the sun,
el de mis padres	the one of my forefathers]
the one that printed	
on the *sarape*	[shoulder blanket]
fantastic colors	
through the prism	
—*la pirámide del sol* . . .[13]	[—the pyramid of the sun . . .]

The principal star in Aztec cosmogony, the sun, dominates Chicano literature; the basic element of its symbology, the sun illuminates with particular brilliance its ultimate message, the affirmation of life over death. For the Aztecs, the East, kingdom of the rising sun, was the symbol of fertility, youth, triumph, and resurrection. Fire and light characterized the South, which evoked the sun at its zenith. The North, land of the nocturnal god Tezcatlicopa, represented darkness, cold, drought, war, and death. The West, land of the setting sun, was synonymous with old age, decline, and death. Transposed into the Chicano dialectic, this diagram gives rise to two contrasting structures: in opposition to the Western, particularly the Anglo-American, world, symbolized by the West and the North, it established a world of the East and the South, illuminated by a youthful and triumphant sun. Beyond its usual criticism of American capitalism, Chicano literature challenges the foundations of Western civilization, just as the Anglo-American romantics of the past did. We find the same oppositions in their world views: on one hand, a repressive society based on the puritan ethic and oriented toward profit and competition, and, on the other hand, a society with neither inhibitions nor constraints. But while the Anglo-American writers were content to stress nostalgically the contrast between the economic aspects of their own culture and the aesthetic aspects of the old Hispanic culture, Chicano writers emphasized the malaise of Western civilization—a world dominated by plastic and condemned to death—and proposed an alternative—a flourishing world characterized by the human and the fertile. The advanced industrial revolution had sickened and alienated humankind; only a genuine cultural revolution could restore life and freedom, and establish a humanistic, non-materialistic society based upon love and brotherhood.

American civilization, "that great gringoría / poisoned by gases and allergies,"[14] carries within itself the seeds of its own demise; it is homogenizing and sterilizing. Alurista's poetry figuratively conveys two antithetical universes, one positive and one negative. The negative elements evoke death, disease, aridity, lack of color, insipidity: to convey them, Alurista uses such words and images as the North, cold, snow, darkness; emaciated, skeleton, cancerous, pestilence, poison; dust, desert, weeds; gray or neutral colors; plastic, concrete buildings, absence of flowers. In the Genaro González short story "Un Hijo del Sol," American tourists are compared to mummies. The young hero, Adam, furious at their intrusion into the barrio, throws a rock at their car:

> . . . a gust of cold, sterile air escapes from within. . . . Too lifeless, too unlike the surrounding heat he knew. The withered mummies inside startle from their death, the opened tomb vomits a cold foreign air unto the torrid barrio streets. Las viejitas [the little old women]—caked putrid faces, sexless . . .[15]

Rendón congratulates himself for rallying to the Chicano movement in time: "I owe my life to my Chicano people. They rescued me from the Anglo kiss of death, the monolingual, monocultural, and colorless gringo society."[16] Virility, as glorified long ago by "that *pobre viejo* [poor old man] Walt Whitman," aroused sarcasm from Montoya, for it was in vain that the Anglo poet

Imposed his virile image
Upon an impotent people . . .

Land emasculating itself,
Dejando droppings of   [Leaving]
Asphalt and reinforced concrete.[17]

Industrialization and commercialization pushed to the extreme had created this cold, lifeless universe for which "plastic" was the perfect symbol. In his poem "Camino de perfección" [Road to perfection], Elizondo ironically describes that road that opens up at birth for everyone destined to live in America: a baby is born "with a plastic spoon in his mouth"; he is fed artificial milk from plastic bottles; he lies in a "plastic crib"; and so forth. Later, he goes on a honeymoon to a "city completely of glass and plastic"; he prefers music coming from a plastic radio to the natural song of the insects, which, he says, bothers him at night; the poem ends on a note of thanks to the "God of Plastic."[18] Americans themselves have become "plastic people,"[19] trapped in the material itself. Delgado believes that America "suffers from having neglected to spiritualize its material kingdom"; by contrast, Chicanismo represents a "very healthy phenomenon."[20] "America is a beast,"[21] shouts De León, while Valdez declares: "there is no poetry about the United States."[22] Americans have lost something vital, like the man of legend who, having made a pact with the Devil, loses his shadow and is forever after held in contempt by his fellow man:[23]

the man has lost his shadow	
y la de nuestros padres nos protege	[and the one of our forefathers protects
he's lost it	us]
forever	
in his humanity.[24]	

Because Alurista's "man," that is to say, gringo, has no shadow, "he knows not that he's alive."[25] He has sold his soul to Mammon and irrevocably given up his freedom.

Chicanismo sees itself as a spiritual renaissance, and its literature is full of the symbols of Adam and the dawn, closely tied to the sun symbol. Carlos Morton's allegorical drama *El Jardín* ends with a vision of Adam and Eve, prototypes of a new race, leaving the garden in the radiant brightness of the rising sun under the complicitous gaze of God. A sort of half-comic, half-lyrical epic, Alurista's play *Dawn* examines the destiny of Chicanos and their ancestors in the light of Aztec mythology. In the first of its three acts, "The Hunt," the stage is dominated by the tree of life. A couple, Quetzalcoatl and Cihuacoatl, appears. Their benevolent influence is negated by the evil deeds of Tezcatlipoca, god of darkness and war, and by Huitzilopochtli, god of the sun, who thirsts for human sacrifice. In addition to these two sons, Coatlicue has fathered two bastards, Pepsicoatl and Cocacoatl, Alurista's inventions, who symbolize Spanish oppression, economic imperialism, and Anglo–American "genocide" and "biocide."[26] These two are tried in the second act, before a court presided over by Huehuetéotl, the god of fire. Both Mexican and Chicano witnesses testify. The tree of life once again predominates in the third act; Cocacoatl (who has already killed Pepsicoatl accidentally) dies while giving birth to twins, the man and woman of the future. The sun rises; the date is August 16 of the year *ce-acatl* 1987; "nine hells / of fifty-two years,"[27] during which the evil couple has reigned, have passed since the arrival of Cortés in Mexico in 1519. The Council of the Elders sings while a group of children dance:

> let the young boy
> be the lord of dawn
> and the young girl
> be the lady of dawn

let the morning star
guide them
to be servants
of the tree of life.[28]

In the González story "Un Hijo del Sol," Adam suddenly realizes his true identity after a fight with some young gringos: ". . . somewhere in time an angry comet flares, a sleeping mountain erupts, an Aztec sun explodes in birth."[29] A new child of the sun has been born.

Life explodes on every page of this literature. Spanish words spring up in the English sentences like wildflowers in the midst of a desert. Chicano theater is, according to Luis Valdez, "first a reaffirmation of life,"[30] unlike American commercial productions, which are "so antiseptic," "antibiotic." "The characters and life situations emerging from our little teatros are too real, too full of sudor, sangre [sweat, blood], and body smells to be boxed in,"[31] explains Valdez. The colors, the scents, the sounds, the body heat, the earth, and the sun, which the writers use abundantly in their descriptions and images, are indications of a sensual and physical world. At the positive pole of Alurista's poetic universe are the sun and its attributes: blood, fire, and flames; red; seeds, fertilizer, lava, fruits and flowers; the blowing of the wind; the barrio. The "new machismo"[32] acclaimed by Sánchez is less a glorification of the Chicano male's virility than of all Chicanos' vitality in the face of a sterilizing society that robotizes and institutionalizes people. *Machismo* is no longer an attribute of men alone; it is "in the womb of our mother machismo"[33] that Aztlán's sons and daughters are formed.

El corazón ("the heart") also gives this literature a warmth all its own. But the sexual exuberance of Mexican-Americans (which makes them, along with Blacks, the envy of Anglo-Americans) is stressed less than love and *carnalismo*, the sense of ethnic brotherhood that has always characterized human relations in the barrio. According to De León, a qualitative change in relationships and social institutions will be required to preserve ". . . a sense of human kindness, a universal respect for life and emotions that the world has seemingly forgotten. Amerika cannot understand this. . . ."[34] "Amerika," the America of genocide and biocide, is resolutely insensitive to this point. The main theme of Anaya's novel *Bless Me, Ultima* is the love and respect that transcend individual relationships. Poet Richard Mora recounts his journey through the depths of poverty, crime, and prison, in the dim light of *The Black Sun*,[35] but this somber adventure ends, as Mora triumphantly observes, in a ". . . spiritual ascent from the depth of a brotherhood of evil, to the thin atmosphere of a brotherhood of love."[36] The instinctive tendency toward life wins out over the inclination toward death; love triumphs over hate, for people can truly escape from alienation only through the heart.

Chicanos hurl their youth, vigor, and impassioned sense of brotherhood like a challenge at a senile and mechanistic world: ". . . the nopal is old but we are the fruit, the youth,"[37] Delgado cries out proudly. Behind the bars of his prison cell, Sánchez sings and shouts his deliverance: "we are free in soul—indian-spanish soul." [38]

The prisoner in the two-act play by Francisco O. Burruel, *The Dialogue of Cuco Rocha*, bemuses his white jailer with his serene assurance; throughout his fifteen years of incarceration, he is comforted by the certainty that one day "people will no longer be slaves to suggestion or be programmed to the ways and philosophy of one system." [39] Alurista's profession of faith would one day make him famous: ". . . i do not ask for freedom / i am freedom." [40]

To Alurista, the Chicano, a liberating Orpheus buoyed by "*herencia solar*" (solar heritage), [41] has a new mission: to show the alienated Anglo the way to a new humanism, to open the eyes of the "blind man":

> so that he too
>   may
> be free
>   of chains and rules
> of inhuman statutes, routines. [42]

Alurista constantly reiterates the Chicanos' role as redeemer; it is their task: "*palpitante realidad y ardiente* [moving, burning reality] / to burn the weed and brighten the garden / of amérika." [43] La Raza is "*fertil abono del desierto*," the rich fertilizer of the desert, [44] and so forth. Sánchez believes it "urgent" that la Raza reveal its nature and be recognized, for it alone is "the crucible of humanness." [45] The two poets had unshakable faith in the redemptive power of the Chicano people.

Chicano literature focuses on the omnipresent sun. In Alurista, this ascendant verticality is suggested by the tree of life, and by the eagle and the butterfly, whose proud, free flight contrasts with the reptilian crawl of the gringo serpent. [46] The ultimate image of ascendancy, the pyramid of the sun, "the pyramid of joy," [47] dominates the poetry, symbolizing the triumph of life over death, of day over night, of brotherhood over racism. The poet goes forth, conscious of his role and confident in the future:

> my shadow
>   walking down with me
> to light my path
>   —the sun
>   —on the pyramid. [48]

The Cosmic Race

The new Adam, whose birth is hailed in the literature, is called to a lofty destiny. In the Chicano version of Genesis, the creation of the brown race required smaller doses of sun and time than either the white or the Black. This foreshadowed the inevitable synthesis of all races into one, according to

Rendón. As half-castes, at the midpoint between whites and Blacks, at the confluence of three cultures, Chicanos are the prototype of universal humans, the precursors of "the cosmic race" whose advent was predicted in 1925 by José Vasconcelos: "the definitive race, the race of synthesis, entirely complete, made up of the spirit and blood of all peoples, and, consequently, more capable of achieving true brotherhood and a truly universal vision."[49] Sánchez adapts this concept for his own purposes, crying out prophetically:

> mestizo, son of providence
>   merging indio with hispano,
> beginning of the cosmic process,
> universal man precursor,
> that, my brothers, is my vision . . .[50]

Writers stressed the pluralism of Mexican-Americans, the only people, perhaps, with the exception of the Hawaiians, "with a more legitimate claim to universality."[51] Anthropologist Octavio Romano took exception to the Hegelian bipolarity of American political thought, which created a rigid dichotomy between the rational and the mystical, the colonizers and the colonized, the Third World and "white" America. These dualistic schematic perceptions led to the monolithic treatment of entire populations, without the slightest consideration for their actual pluralistic nature.[52] Chicanos promoted instead a new notion, that multi-ethnic nations should cultivate differences, rather than try to eliminate them, and view them as a source of enrichment. "It is one thing to homogenize milk; it is quite another thing to homogenize the citizenry,"[53] writer-professor Sabine T. Ulibarrí declares ironically in an article on the cultural heritage of the Southwest. Alurista compares the complexity of the American of Mexican origin to the many colors of his poncho: ". . . el sarape de mi personalidad comes in fantastic colors . . ."[54]

The biological and cultural plurality of Chicanos made them a vital link between the two Americas. It was incumbent upon them to steer United States policy toward more open relations with the Latin American world. In a chapter of his *Chicano Manifesto* titled "The Chicano of the Americas," Rendón, ever the polemicist, praises the Chicanos' unifying role in the Americas and hails them as "the prototype of the citizen of the Americas"[55] of the twenty-first century; indeed, Chicanos personify the acculturation process that the other peoples of the American continents will have to undergo to arrive at mutual understanding. Walt Whitman prophetically stressed the importance of the Hispanic contribution to the development of North America; he saw the materialistic period of the United States as only a first phase, adding:

> To that composite American identity of the future, Spanish character will supply some of the most needed parts. No stock shows a grander historic retrospect, grander in religiousness and loyalty, or for patriotism, courage, decorum, gravity and honor.[56]

More than just mediators between the two hemispheres, members of la
Raza, the mixed-blood race, considered themselves members of all races, the
center of a cosmic circle. Alurista sees them as a symbol of the totality of the
universe:

. . . *la esencia de mi Raza es fundamental*
basic
    to the chromatic wheel of humanity
    free to compound in secondary colors
retaining the basic texture
our woolen skin of color bronze.[57]
	[. . . the essence of my Raza is
	fundamental]

To Eve, who sees this same multi-colored wheel in a dream in Morton's play
El Jardín, God explains that it is

> . . . the circle of racial harmonia singing together down the road of the
> future and we are the people who must set an example to all of the others
> because we are the hub, the center of that wheel. La Raza is in the middle
> of black and white, ves? [see?][58]

Chicanos considered themselves nothing less than the point of convergence of
two ways of life, of two contradictory worlds, of the East and the West. This
syncretism, more confusedly desired and perceived than coherently expressed,
surfaces, here and there, in a sporadic remark or image. Delgado fervently
advocates the fusion of beliefs:

> "And the flock shall be one . . ."
>
> . . . with buddhism crossed up
> With christianity.[59]

Montoya's "Sunstruck While Chopping Cotton," a poem in which three
Bothisattvas and Jesus appear simultaneously to a cotton-picker overcome by
the sun, suggests a common vision of the world.[60] "*Buddha is just as much God
as Christ,*"[61] concludes the gravedigger in the Navarro short story "Somewhere
Sometime." "I am Aztec prince and Christian Christ,"[62] shouts Joaquín in
the long Corky Gonzales poem, putting an end to his long litany of disparate identities with this synthesizing view of himself. Valdez turned toward
Asian theater. Estela Portillo's drama *Morality Play*[63] is an intellectual potpourri
in which she tries to synthesize Greek and Judeo-Christian thought by in-
voking great figures from various historical periods and civilizations: Homer,
Plato, Faith, Hope, and Charity of Christianity, Napoleon, Tolstoy, Kierke-
gaard, Freud, Russell. But these ideas of syncretism remained rather nebu-
lous. The "cosmic race" was nothing more than la Raza magnified to universal
dimensions.
    Chicano literature vibrates with the heady optimism of people convinced of

the justness of their cause, of their newly established identity, of their ethnic mix, the foundation for the people of tomorrow. Sánchez exults:

> WE ARE UNIVERSAL MAN,
> a spectral rivulet,
> multi-hued and beautiful—
> WE ARE LA RAZA
> the cradle of civilization
> the crucible of true humanity
> yesterday, today, & tomorrow
> MESTIZO HUMAN-NESS.[64]

Chicano literature is born of self-discovery; as Salazar said, "the Chicano is a Mexican-American with a non-Anglo image of himself,"[65] an image wiped clean of the stereotypes of the past. Unlike their ancestors, Chicanos have removed their masks, revealing themselves in confrontation with their oppressors.[66] This self-discovery has taken place in two ways: through a return to their roots, and through their struggle with an intolerable present. While conscious of their specifically Mexican characteristics, which they in no way think of denying, Chicanos intend not only to assume their rightful place in a rapidly changing world but also to lead it. Their literary works represent a synthesis of past and present.

This literature is still at a stage that requires a political orientation, with the writers feeling a sense of responsibility toward their ethnic group. As a result, content is more important than form: one has only to compare the contemporary Chicano novel to the Anglo-American and Black avant-garde novel to confirm that the concern for realism far outweighs any aesthetic considerations in Chicano works.

Chicano literature's true originality is to be found in its bilingualism, which represents the problematic and ambiguous reality of the Chicanos' world better than any considerations of form. Bilingualism has four functions: first, it expresses the experience of Chicanos as "outsiders" and reflects their unique cultural situation. Unlike any other ethnic group, Mexican-Americans live near their country of origin and have a long history in the United States. The "split" language of Chicano writers reflects their schizophrenia, their "dual conscience." Second, to the extent that bilingualism is a break with established speech patterns, it is in itself a subversive act. It represents the Chicanos' revolt against repressive institutions, not only against the Anglo-American language, but also against the capitalist and imperialist ideology for which it serves as a vehicle. Third, bilingualism permits Chicanos to affirm their double identity, their heterogeneity. If they live within the barrio, they also work outside it; they can no more deny belonging to the American nation than they can deny their Spanish and Indian heritage. English is the vehicular language to which they have more or less adapted; but their vernacular language, Spanish, remains charged with affective connotations and cultural references. The myths of the Chicanos are not those that haunt the Anglo-American psyche; they were born in the distant time of their Indian ancestors. Thus, bilingualism raises the principle of cultural pluralism. Fourth and finally, the Spanish words that writers sprinkle throughout their sentences are like sunlight and life breaking through darkness and death. They offer a different culture in opposition to the official one, a culture based on new relationships, on brotherhood. Bilingualism represents, above all, a challenge. Is it also a dead end? Only time will tell.

Conclusion

During the early period of the Mexican-American War and immigration, and during the later era of assimilation, Mexican-Americans were portrayed in similar ways in Anglo and in Mexican-American literary works. During the third period, of Chicanismo, there was a sharp divergence in the images drawn by Anglo and Chicano writers.

For a long time, Mexicans in the conquered territories and those who came during the increasing waves of legal and illegal immigration remained outsiders, forgotten and invisible. Anglo-Americans did not see Mexican-Americans as they really were but rather as they wished them to be. Blinded by their ethnocentric belief in Anglo superiority or by their romantic nostalgia for a golden age, Anglo writers made these marginal people static creatures, oriented either toward a pastoral era or a period of decline. Writers yoked them into stereotypes; as "greasers" or "noble savages," Mexican-Americans became either a convenient scapegoat or a model for the Other. By the turn of the twentieth century, however, a true concern for objectivity appeared; by the eve of World War II, the yoke of the stereotype began to loosen.

Mexican-Americans also provided a double image of themselves. Their folklore and neoclassic poetry stressed their attachment to traditional thinking and presented an outmoded and static view of Mexican-Americans. These works tended to justify the state of literary inferiority they were relegated to by Anglo writers; indeed, everything seems to indicate that Mexican-Americans unconsciously accepted the image of themselves formulated by the Anglos. But the early *romances* inspired by the war and especially the *corridos* written toward the end of the nineteenth century offered a dynamic and living view of

Mexican-Americans. In these works, the first instruments of protest, Mexican-Americans began to make themselves "seen." The writers' Spanish was the symbol of their estrangement and marginality; the ironic use they sometimes made of English was a form of revolt. It also represented an initial attempt at self-definition.

The period from the Mexican-American War to World War II was marked by the clash of two cultures, but the postwar assimilationist phase was dominated by an attempt at fusion. Manifest Destiny was followed by Anglo liberalism. In Anglo literature, where romanticism still persisted, traditional stereotypes crumbled under the impact of social activism. On the Mexican-American side, the past, symbolized by the traditions of the barrio, still held a place of honor, but the dilemma of the *pocho*'s integration into the dominant society was profoundly felt. Writers portrayed this problem poignantly but without acrimony; in general, acceptance dominated this time period. For the first time, the problem of identity was raised, if not resolved. The English language, which Mexican-American writers handled masterfully, became a means of making themselves heard and "seen" by the majority; not only was it proof of their acculturation, it showed their acceptance of literary styles valued by the dominant society. The lyrical period of the *romances* and *corridos* coincided with an unacceptable world that only poetry and song could transcend. It was followed by an age of prose.

After 1965, a break occurred. Anglo-American writers' criticism of their technological culture was sincere, but—at least in the case of the writers studied in this book—they never went so far as to suggest a radical change of institutions. No matter how liberal or lucid, the Anglo writers offered suggestions that fell short of Chicano objectives. The image these writers presented of Chicanos was relatively conservative and cautious; the most radical characters in their books were militant integrationists.

The Anglo-Americans' attitude toward Mexican-Americans, Indians, and Blacks offers both interesting similarities and differences. During the first phase, in which they conceived of the Others in unrealistic terms, according to either the flattering or pejorative image that they held of themselves, according to the need to justify their superiority or to overcome their own deficiencies, they saw Mexican-Americans as "greasers" and "*dons*" and Indians as blood-thirsty killers or noble savages (in the novels by Cooper, the former is found among the Iroquois and the latter among the Mohicans). Portrayals of Blacks varied between two stereotypes: on one hand, the kindly servant or clown (as in the literature of the colonial era and the novels of the South prior to the Civil War), and on the other, the primitive man and rebel, enamored of individual freedom (as in "Benito Cereno" and *Moby Dick* by Melville and *The Narrative of Arthur Gordon Pym* by Poe). As we have seen, however, the exploitation of Mexican laborers has aroused the sympathy of certain Anglo-American writers since the end of the nineteenth century. During the same era, reacting to the violation of Indian treaties, Helen Hunt Jackson wrote a report, *A Century of*

Dishonor,[1] which was sent at her own expense to every member of Congress. As a result of the ineffectiveness of this act, she turned to literature and wrote a novel, *Ramona*, which was intended primarily as an indictment of the deceit and cruelty of the American government.

The era of illusion was followed by one of suspicion; the Anglo-American began to question himself. Liberal laws that favored the oppressed minorities were passed. On the literary level, while a romantic view of Indians, Mexican-Americans, and Blacks persisted (in the eyes of the Beatnik, the Black represented the pariah, par excellence), the exploitation of these minorities provoked a strong reaction from Anglo-American writers. By means of his character Crooks in *Of Mice and Men*, Steinbeck denounced, although briefly, the discrimination to which Blacks were subjected. Faulkner's position was more complex, divided between a Southern conception of Blacks and a sense of guilt toward them, which is particularly evident in the fourth part of his short story "The Bear." In this same story, moreover, while extolling the primitive values of the Indians, the author protested against the way these first colonized peoples were dispossessed of their lands.

The era of lost illusions following the 1960s sounded the death knell for the West. While the minorities were fighting for their freedom and, turning away from a moribund world, were rediscovering their ancestral values, Anglo-Americans embraced those in contact with the sources of true life: the Hippies no longer tended to identify with the Blacks, as had the Beatniks, but with the Indians. Others (Mailer, in particular) pinned their hopes on Blacks; it was Blacks, not Mexican-Americans, whom they saw as the eventual saviors of America. Century-old suspicions? Cultural differences? Without a doubt. If the Blacks' power provoked fear, it also commanded admiration; Americans of Mexican origin continued, implicitly at least, to provoke mistrust, if not contempt.

The mold into which Mexican-Americans had been poured began to crumble; the Chicanos' joyful return to their ethnicity was coupled with their desire to break away from the values of the dominant society. Their literature was no longer naive and timid, as it had been in the early period; it was no longer good-natured, as in the assimilationist period; it was no longer burdened by the defeatism and pessimism of Anglo literature. It was strong, diurnal, and exuberant; its "cosmic man" of the future triumphantly challenged the declining "Western man."

Chicanos once more made poetry the instrument of their protest, but there is little of the troubadours of old in the militant poets of today fighting for the liberation of their ethnic brothers. The prose works, currently lagging behind the poetry, nonetheless continue on their upward trajectory.

Chicano literature has faced a problem posed to all nationalistic literatures. As early as the 1950s, the Black writers James Baldwin and Ralph Ellison noted the limitations of the writer whose source of inspiration is purely racial. Born, for all practical purposes, in 1965 with the strike in Delano, Chicano literature subsequently was forced to throw off the yoke of nationalism in order to reach full development. Valdez, for example, quickly saw the need to remove the Teatro Campesino from the site of the strike and to give it a more mystical orientation. Rivera and Anaya, who certainly do not have the stature of a Baldwin or an Ellison, have demonstrated that Chicano literature can liberate itself from its political context. In general, however, it is still in the militant stage.

Every nationalistic literature is also confronted by the problem of linguistic vehicle. Black writers succeeded in introducing a "minor" language into the "major" language; Chicano literature's principal originality continues to be its bilingualism. In this respect, it sets itself apart from all other Spanish-language literatures. The Quinto Sol publishing house "has scrupulously avoided publishing Latin-Americans and Spaniards under the banner of Chicano or Mexican-American literature."[2] Bilingualism represents, perhaps, the only way Chicano literature can avoid becoming what Herminio Ríos has called "an unwelcome appendage to Anglo-American literature."[3]

To what extent, however, can it be said that bilingualism is not actually a limitation? If only on the level of popularization. . . . It is still too soon to tell what the future of Chicano literature will be.

Notes

Introduction

1. P. Galindo, "The Mexican American Devil's Dictionary," vol. 1, *El Grito: A Journal of Contemporary Mexican American Thought* 6 (1973): 48–49.

2. Cortés set the example by taking an Indian mistress, Malinche, who was known among the Spaniards as Doña Marina. She is considered the mother of the *mestizos*. José Vasconcelos writes, *"La colonización española creó mestizaje; esto señala su carácter, fija su responsabilidad y define su porvenir. El Inglés siguió cruzándose sólo con el blanco y exterminó al indígena; lo sigue exterminando en la sorda lucha económica, mas eficaz que la conquista armada. Esto prueba su limitación y es el indicio de su decadencia."* (*La raza cósmica*, chap. 1, "El mestizaje," *Obras completas* [Mexico City: Mexicanos Unidos, 1958] 2: 918–19). The percentage of full-blooded Spaniards remains small to this day.

3. Nuevo México comprised the current states of New Mexico and Arizona.

4. A French expedition led by La Salle descended the Mississippi in 1682, then attempted to establish a colony at its mouth; during the second half of the eighteenth century, the Spanish, fearful of Russian and English ambitions along the Pacific Coast, rushed to colonize California.

5. Wayne Moquin and Charles Van Doren, eds., *A Documentary History of the Mexican Americans* (New York: Praeger, 1971) 1.

6. In California, there were only twenty *ranchos* before 1821. Between 1821 and 1846, Mexican governors gave out more than 630 land grants, some to newly arrived Americans. In 1846, at the outset of the war, most of the Sacramento Valley was composed of ranches ranging from 1,800 to 40,000 hectares. See Stan Steiner, *La Raza: The Mexican-Americans* (New York: Harper, 1970) 61–62.

7. See Tom Lea, *The King Ranch*, 2 vols. (Boston: Little, 1957) 1: 113–14: "The hacienda work developed a picturesque and unprecedented type of New World herdsman: the vaquero. . . . The Mexican vaqueros became the prototypes who furnished the ready-made tools, the range techniques, even the lingo, from which sprang the cowboy

of song and story. The Mexican haciendas provided the primal outlines for the pattern which produced the later Cattle Kingdom of the American West."

8. From 1826 on, American hunters settled in California; according to Hubert Howe Bancroft (*History of California*, 7 vols. [San Francisco, 1886–90] 3: 402), in 1835 the territory had 300 Americans, some of whom had Mexican mothers. William Becknell opened the Santa Fe commercial trail in 1822. Such later merchants as Charles Bent and James Magoffin became linked to Mexican families. See Matt S. Meier and Feliciano Rivera, *The Chicanos: A History of Mexican Americans* (New York: Hill, 1972) 32.

9. In the *New York Morning News* of 5 Jan. 1846, this same John O'Sullivan (who had used the expression "Manifest Destiny" regarding the annexation of Texas in "Annexation," *Democratic Review* 17 [1845]: 5) writes on the subject of the United States' claim to Oregon: "And that claim is by the right of our Manifest Destiny to overspread and to possess the whole of the continent which Providence has given us for the development of the great experiment of liberty and federated self-government entrusted to us." Reported by Albert K. Weinberg, *Manifest Destiny: A Study of Nationalist Expansionism in American History* (Baltimore: Johns Hopkins UP, 1935) 145.

10. See Richard Henry Dana, *Two Years Before the Mast* (1840; New York: Macmillan, 1915).

11. Former Franciscan mission of San Antonio.

12. The territory of present-day Arizona, California, New Mexico, Utah, Nevada, and half of Colorado.

13. *Treaties and Other International Acts of the United States of America* (Washington, 1937) 5: 207–36: "The Mexicans who, in the territories aforesaid, shall not preserve the character of citizens of the Mexican Republic, conformably with what is stipulated in the preceding article, shall be incorporated into the Union of the United States and be admitted, at the proper time (to be judged of by the Congress of the United States) to the enjoyment of all rights of citizens of the United States according to the principles of the Constitution; and in the mean time shall be maintained and protected in the free enjoyment of their liberty and property, and secured in the free exercise of their religion without restriction."

14. Carey McWilliams, *Brothers Under the Skin*, 3rd rev. ed. (Boston: Little, 1964) 119: "Historically Mexicans have never emigrated to the Southwest; they have simply moved 'North from Mexico.' " In 1942, Nelson Rockefeller appointed Williams, a sociologist, to head the new Spanish-Speaking Peoples' Division of the Office of Inter-American Affairs, one of whose tasks was to fight discrimination against Mexican-Americans.

15. In 1930, the number of people "of Mexican race" was calculated at two million; in 1940, the number of "Spanish-Speaking" people was tallied; in 1950 and 1960 the number of "Spanish-surnamed" people (more than five million) was calculated. In 1970, the census figure was about seven million, making Spanish-surnamed the nation's third-largest minority; there were 2,059,671 in Texas; 3,101,589 in California; 407,286 in New Mexico. On the subject of the inaccuracies of a census based upon surnames, see: Texas Institute for Educational Development, *The Chicano Almanac* (Austin: Futura, 1973). This census was contested since it primarily took into account only Mexican-American families with Spanish names, living in the Southwest, and speaking Spanish and not English. Mexican-American and Puerto Rican pressure groups, led by Bert Corona, then spokesman for MAPA [Mexican-American Political Association] unsuccessfully tried to have the U.S. census postponed and its forms modified. See Armando B. Rendón, *Chicano Manifesto: The History and Aspirations of the Second Largest Minority in America* (New York: Collier, 1972) 38–41.

16. See also Part I, chap. 1, "Ethnocentrism."

17. Herewith the definition given by L. V. Berrey and M. Van den Bark, comps., *The American Thesaurus of Slang*, 2nd ed. (New York: Crowell, 1967) 348: "Anyone of Latin stock, loosely applied to any foreigner of dark complexion, especially of the laboring class." The tendency of "Latins" to pronounce the English verb "speak" as "spik" is the origin of this nickname.

18. John Womack, Jr., "Who are the Chicanos?" *New York Review of Books* 31 Aug. 1972: 12.

19. In Arizona, whose history linked it closely to the neighboring state of Sonora, the term "Mexican" was adopted uniformly without a pejorative connotation.

20. Luis Valdez and Stan Steiner, eds., *Aztlán: An Anthology of Mexican American Literature* (New York: Knopf, 1972) xiv.

21. See Edward Simmen, "Chicano: Origin and Meaning," *Pain and Promise: The Chicano Today* (New York: NAL, 1972) 54.

22. See Eliu Carranza, "The Gorkase Mirror," *The Chicanos: Mexican American Voices*, ed. Edward Ludwig and James Santibañez (Baltimore: Penguin, 1971) 227.

23. See Simmen, *Pain and Promise* 77, note 3.

24. But in a Mexican publication by M. Quiros Martínez, *La educación pública en el Distrito Norte de la Baja California* (Mexicali, Jan. 1928) [no page reference], the word *chicano* is mentioned for the first time, as a synonym for *Mexicano*.

25. Manuel Gamio, *Mexican Immigration to the United States: A Study of Human Migration and Adjustment* (Chicago: U of Chicago P, 1930) 129: "The attitude of the Mexicans who are American citizens towards the immigrants is a curious one. . . . They call these recent immigrants cholos or chicamos." The word also appears spelled with an *m* in Carey McWilliams, *North From Mexico: The Spanish-Speaking People of the United States* (Philadelphia: Lippincott, 1949) 209.

26. Ernesto Galarza, *Barrio Boy* (New York: Ballantine, 1972) 196.

27. Womack 12.

28. Mario Suárez, "El Hoyo," *Arizona Quarterly* 3 (1947): 112.

29. Political party founded in 1970 in Crystal City, Texas, by José Angel Gutiérrez.

30. In the introduction by Herminio Ríos to the bilingual edition of the Tomás Rivera novel, ". . . *y no se lo tragó la tierra*" (Berkeley: Quinto Sol, 1971) viii, xiv, the Spanish sentence *"El punto inicial de la literatura chicana es el año 1848"* is translated into English as: "1848 is the beginning point of Mexican American literature."

31. A series of equivalents stressed by Philip D. Ortego in a letter dated 26 May 1970; reported by Simmen, *Pain and Promise* 54.

32. Carranza 233: "a minority within a minority."

33. As noted by Pierre Dommergues, "Les Chicanos ou la fierté retrouvée," *Monde Diplomatique* Apr. 1974: 16.

34. The reference is to the short story "Señor Garza" by Mario Suárez, *Arizona Quarterly* 3 (1947): 115–21.

35. See Luis Dávila, "On the Nature of Chicano Literature: En los extremos del Laberinto," Spanish Section 3, Michigan Modern Language Association Convention, Detroit, 1971, p. 1: ". . . the bicultural Mexican-American writer of yesteryear often found himself in awkward relation to the supposedly monolithic cultures of the United States and Mexico. For this reason he virtually did not exist."

36. According to Steiner (*La Raza* 57), the records of Santa Fe were destroyed between 1869 and 1871 on the order of Governor William A. Pike. Some books probably suffered a similar fate.

37. To cite only the better-known ones, the two weeklies *El Clamor Público: Independiente y Literario*, Francisco P. Ramírez, ed., Los Angeles, 1855–59 (?) and *La Gaceta*, José Azaga, ed., Santa Barbara, Calif., 1880–81 (?); the biweekly *El Nuevo Mundo*, J. M. Vigil, ed., San Francisco 1864–67 (?).

38. Steiner, *La Raza* 219–20: "The culture of the Chicano is voiced. It is voiced in the *corridos* of exodus, the chronicles of spoken history, Pachuco legends and *cholo* tales of ghettos, *posadas*, the old, remembered church plays . . . cantina love lyrics and aphorisms. . . ."

39. In the issue of *El Grito* devoted to Mexican-American works in the years following the 1848 defeat, Octavio Romano refutes Edward Simmen (*The Chicano: From Caricature to Self-Portrait* [New York: NAL, 1971] 24–25), who denies the existence of any Mexican-American literature prior to 1947: "Should the Simmen thesis prevail, then all Chicano thought, creativity, poetry and literature will be permanently entombed in that sterile academic cemetery called folklore" (*El Grito* 5 [Fall 1971]: 8).

40. This first journal having suspended publication, Romano founded another, *El Grito del Sol*.

41. This is the case of León Calvillo-Ponce at the end of the nineteenth century and Gabriel de la Riva in the 1920s.

42. Herminio Ríos and Lupe Castillo are compiling a bibliography of all Mexican-American newspapers published since 1848. A first section, 1848–1942, has been completed. See *El Grito* 3 (Summer 1970): 18–24.

Part One. The Conquered

1. "Who am I?" *Pain and Promise: The Chicano Today*, ed. Edward Simmen (New York: NAL, 1972) 40.

2. See Josiah Royce, *California: From the Conquest in 1846 to the Second Vigilance Committee in San Francisco* (Boston, 1886) 35; Hubert H. Bancroft, *History of California*, 7 vols. (San Francisco, 1886–90) 3: 402.

3. See Stan Steiner, *La Raza: The Mexican Americans* (New York: Harper, 1970) 27–39.

4. George W. B. Evans, *Mexican Gold Trail: The Journal of a 49er* (San Marino, Calif.: Huntington Library, 1945); Alonzo Delano, *Life on the Plains and Among the Diggings* (New York, 1854); William Lewis Manly, *Death Valley in '49* (San Jose, 1894); Louise Amelia Knapp Clappe (Smith), *The Shirley Letters from the California Mines, 1851–1852* (New York: Knopf, 1949), originally published in installments in the *Pioneer Magazine of San Francisco* of 1854 and 1855.

5. The Beadle Collection of Dime Novels was donated to the New York Public Library by Frank P. O'Brien in 1922. Consult the *Bulletin of the New York Public Library*, July 1922.

6. On 10 May 1869 construction was completed on the transcontinental railroad. It had been carried out jointly by the Union Pacific and the Central Pacific railroads.

7. Leonard Pitt, *The Decline of the Californios: A Social History of the Spanish-Speaking Californians, 1846–1890* (Berkeley: U of California P, 1966) 284.

8. Hubert H. Bancroft, "The War as an American Plot," *The Mexican American War: Was It Manifest Destiny?* ed. Ramón Ruiz (New York: Holt, 1963) 85–94.

9. Royce, *California* [no page reference].

10. Franklin Walker, *A Literary History of Southern California*, Berkeley: U of California P, 1950) 106.

11. Walker 124. Helen Hunt Jackson made three trips to California, in 1872, 1881, and 1883, spending a total of eleven months there. In 1881, she published *A Century of Dishonor* on the Indians, then, in 1884, *Ramona* on Spanish-speaking Californians.

12. Gertrude Atherton, *Los Cerritos* (1890; Ridgewood, N.J.: Gregg, 1968) 134.

13. Atherton, *Los Cerritos* 201–02.

14. Atherton, *Los Cerritos* 124.

15. Walker 152.

16. Walker 118 (chap. 3, "Cultural Hydroponics"). Plants cultivated this way have their roots in an artificial environment of nutritive liquid, not in the soil.

17. *Los Pastores* consists of several religious plays; reported by Sister Joseph Marie, "The Role of the Church and the Folk in the Development of the Early Drama in New Mexico," diss., U of Pennsylvania, 1948, 9.

18. Variable spellings: Murieta, Murietta, Murrieta. See Walter Noble Burns, *The Robin Hood of El Dorado: The Saga of Joaquin Murrieta, Famous Outlaw of California's Age of Gold* (New York: Grosset, 1932) 3n.

19. Gertrude Atherton was born in San Francisco in 1857. After her marriage she lived in Fair Oaks, California (since renamed Atherton), near Menlo Park.

20. Charles Warren Stoddard, born in Rochester, New York, arrived in California in 1855, at the age of 12. Mary Hunter-Austin arrived in Southern California with her parents during the wave of prosperity of the 1880s.

21. A monthly founded in June 1894 by Charles Dwight Willard, renamed *Out West* in 1902 by Lummis; ceased publication in 1910.

22. It is not a matter of Mexican nationality but rather Mexican culture. I will use the term in this sense often in this study.

23. See Walker, chap. 6, "The Middle Nordic Period." Walker uses the classification of Phil T. Hanna, *Libros Californios; or, Five Feet of California Books* (Los Angeles: Zeitlin, 1931) 5, according to which the late nineteenth century and early twentieth centuries were a middle-class period during which women, in particular, devoted themselves to literature.

24. Refers to Louise Amelia Knapp Clappe, author of *The Shirley Letters*.

25. Carey McWilliams, *Brothers Under the Skin*, 3rd rev. ed. (Boston: Little, 1964) 113. Chapter 3, "The Forgotten Mexican" 113–39, is devoted to the Mexicans.

26. Among others, Julian Samora, *La Raza: Forgotten Americans* (Notre Dame, Ind.: Notre Dame UP, 1966).

27. McWilliams 113.

28. See Edward Simmen, ed., *The Chicano: From Caricature to Self-Portrait* (New York: NAL, 1971) 20.

29. See Henry B. Parkes, *Histoire du Mexique*, trans. C. Delavaud, rev. ed. (Paris: Payot, 1971) 333. These incidents of 1912 and 1913 led President Wilson to embargo the sale of munitions to Mexico.

30. Matt Meier and Feliciano Rivera, *The Chicanos: A History of Mexican Americans* (New York: Hill, 1972) 132: "One reason for this suspicion was the revelation in March 1917 of the German offer of an alliance with Mexico against the United States. The proposals of the famous Zimmermann Note, intercepted by the Allies, promised Mexico that, in exchange for Mexican support of the Central Powers, lands lost to the United States by the Treaty of Guadalupe Hidalgo would be returned after the defeat of the

United States." See also John Higham, *Strangers in the Land: Patterns of American Nativism, 1860–1925* (New Brunswick, N.J.: Rutgers UP, 1955) 207.

31. Higham 264.

32. Lothrop Stoddard, *The Rising Tide of Color: Against White World-Supremacy* (New York: Scribner's, 1920) 132–33.

33. Gertrude Atherton, *The Splendid Idle Forties: Stories of Old California* (New York: Macmillan, 1902). Originally published as *Before the Gringo Came*, 1894.

34. It is impossible to give an exhaustive list of studies examining the mysterious hold Joaquín Murrieta still maintains on people's minds. According to Meier and Rivera (*Chicanos* 81–82), "There were many Joaquins so accursed, but Californians tended to blend them all into one image and credited Joaquin Murieta with every crime committed in the state." On highway robbery in California, see Franklin Walker, *San Francisco's Literary Frontier* (New York: Knopf, 1939) 49. Ranger and man of letters Horace Bell devotes all of chap. 4 to bandits and describes Murrieta's death in *On the Old West Coast: Being Further Reminiscences of a Ranger* (New York: Morrow, 1930), 1st edition.

35. See Américo Paredes, *With His Pistol in His Hand: A Border Ballad and Its Hero* (Austin: U of Texas P, 1958) 23–24.

36. Crying "Remember the Alamo!" Texans, haunted by the memory of the Alamo massacre (6 March 1836), defeated the Mexicans at San Jacinto (21 April 1836). The Texans were under the command of Sam Houston.

37. Armando Valdez, "Insurrection in New Mexico, the Land of Enchantment," *Voices: Readings from El Grito: A Journal of Contemporary Mexican Thought, 1967–1971*, ed. Octavio Romano (Berkeley: Quinto Sol, 1971) 109: "The manner in which the Anglo legal system was introduced into this territory and its impact upon the indigenous population is historically paralleled only by the introduction of Christianity into this same region several centuries earlier. Both of these doctrines were equally unsolicited and equally forced upon their unsuspecting beneficiaries by equally fervent 'missionaries' of a conquering political order."

38. Meier and Rivera 56: "Manifest Destiny was a peculiarly Anglo-American version of the chosen race theory."

39. Higham 5.

40. See also Part I, chap. 1, "Ethnocentrism."

41. This dichotomy was to prove long lasting. In 1881, Horace Bell noted: "The Author wishes to say that in using the word *Mexican* he does not mean the native California rancheros, who generally cooperated with the authorities in the suppression of outlawry and contributed largely to the support of the Rangers" (*Reminiscences of a Ranger; or, Early Times in Southern California* [1881; Santa Barbara: Hebberd, 1927] 102). Placed within quotation marks, this word carries a pejorative connotation in this book.

42. Title of the novel by Charles F. Lummis, *Flowers of Our Lost Romance* (Boston: Houghton, 1929).

43. Lummis xiv: "The dour spirit of the Puritans made their taming of New England as unromantic as such a brave adventure could be. They despised Romance, as John Alden and Priscilla are about the one pathetic little flower of their century. The Spaniard, on the other hand, kept his childhood, his ideals and imagination and love of mystery and adventure, his chivalry and his warm humanity. He wasn't ashamed to show that he had feelings. It is no wonder that the discovery and the taming of the New World by such spirits has given us four centuries of uninterrupted and infinitely varied Romance."

44. Cecil Robinson, *With the Ears of Strangers: The Mexican in American Literature* (Tucson: U of Arizona P, 1963) 151.

Chapter 1. Ethnocentrism

1. Luis Valdez and Stan Steiner, eds., *Aztlán: An Anthology of Mexican American Literature* (New York: Knopf, 1972) xxvi.

2. Refers to the novels of Texas published before the annexation (rather mediocre works in the spirit of the Dime Novels).

3. Jeremiah Clemens, *Bernard Lile, an Historical Romance* (Philadelphia, 1856) 214.

4. Willa Cather, "The Dance at Chevalier's," [1900] *Early Stories*, ed. Mildred Bennett (New York: Dodd, 1957) 219.

5. A Mexican dish of corn and chopped meat, seasoned with red pepper and other spices, wrapped in corn husks and steamed.

6. O. Henry, "Tamales," *The Complete Works of O. Henry* (Garden City, N.Y.: Garden City Publ., 1937) 1042.

7. See Duncan Emrich, *It's an Old Wild West Custom* (New York: Vanguard, 1949) 168–69.

8. Important commercial artery linking Independence, Mo., to Santa Fe; it was important from 1822 to about 1880.

9. See Carey McWilliams, *North From Mexico: The Spanish-Speaking People of the United States* (Philadelphia: Lippincott, 1949), chap. 7, "Gringos and Greasers" 115–32.

10. Encountered only once, and with an explanatory note, in *Arizona Nights*, a novel by Stewart E. White (New York: McClure, 1907) 282, note 1.

11. Regarding the term "greaser," Pitt, in his glossary of ethnic terms, writes: "It is as abusive a term as 'nigger.' Probably derives from U.S. Army camps in the Mexican War, but native-born Californians and neophyte Indians turned it around and applied it to dishevelled looking Yankee fortyniners" (Leonard Pitt, *The Decline of the Californios: A Social History of the Spanish-Speaking Californians, 1846–1890* [Berkeley: U of California P, 1966] 309).

12. See McWilliams 75: "The absence of local self-government and the presence of a population that was seven-eighths illiterate in 1850, predisposed the Anglo-Americans to form an extremely negative opinion of the Mexican lower classes who constituted nine-tenths of the population."

13. John W. DeForest, *Overland* (New York, 1871) 3.

14. J. O. Borthwick, *Three Years in California* (Edinburgh, 1857) 75.

15. John Russell Bartlett, *Personal Narrative of Explorations and Incidents in Texas, New Mexico, California, Sonora, and Chihuahua*, 2 vols. (New York, 1854) 1: 38.

16. Sidney Lanier, "San Antonio de Bexar," *Retrospects and Prospects* (New York, 1899) 85.

17. S. S. Hall, *The Rough Riders; or, Sharp Eye, The Seminole Scourge: A Tale of the Chapparal* (New York, 1883) 4.

18. Edward Willet, *The Canyon King; or, A Price on His Head: A Tale of the Wahsatch Range* (New York, 1885).

19. Joseph Badger, *Big George, The Giant of the Gulch; or, The Five Outlaw Brothers* (New York, 1880) 10.

20. O. Henry 1040.

21. Badger, *Big George* 10.

22. Badger, *Big George* 10.

23. S. S. Hall, *Dandy Dave and His Horse White Stocking; or, Ducats or Death* (New York, 1884) 5.

24. S. S. Hall, *The Black Bravo; or, The Tonkaway's Triumph: A Romance of the Frio Ranch* (New York, 1882) 9.

25. "Roy Bean, Law West of the Pecos," *A Treasury of American Folklore*, ed. B. A. Botkin (New York: Crown, 1944) 136.

26. Botkin 147–50.

27. Frederick Law Olmsted, *A Journey through Texas; or, A Saddle Trip on the Southwestern Frontier* (New York, 1857) 149.

28. Lieut. Henry L. Boone (pseud.), *Yankee Jim, the Horse Runner: A Tale of Love and Hate in Southern California* (New York, 1867).

29. Patrick Romanell, *Making of the Mexican Mind: A Study in Recent Mexican Thought* (Lincoln: U of Nebraska P, 1952) 21. On this epic sense of life, he writes: "The substance of the tragic is not, as the traditional theory of tragedy maintains, the conflict between good and evil. Such is, in fact, the polarity of the epic situation. For the epic hero looks upon the very obstacles he encounters in his ventures as evils to overcome."

30. Francis Parkman, *The Oregon Trail* (1849; Garden City, N.Y.: Garden City Publ., 1948) 263.

31. Alfred Lewis, *Wolfville Days* (London: Isbister, 1902) 181.

32. Harvey Fergusson, *The Blood of the Conquerors*, in *Followers of the Sun: A Trilogy of the Santa Fe Trail* (New York: Knopf, 1942) 210; includes *Wolf Song*, 1927; *In Those Days*, 1929; and *The Blood of the Conquerors*, 1921 (published in that order).

33. Hall, *The Rough Riders* 10.

34. S. S. Hall, *The Merciless Marauders; or, Chaparall Carl's Revenge* (New York, 1884) 14.

35. Joseph Badger, *Joaquin the Saddle King: A Romance of Murieta's First Fight* (New York, 1881); *Joaquin the Terrible: The True Story of the Three Bitter Blows that Changed an Honest Man to a Merciless Demon* (New York, 1881); and *The Pirate of Placers; or, Joaquin's Death Hunt* (New York, 1882). John R. Ridge attempts objectivity in *The Life and Adventures of Joaquin Murieta, the Celebrated California Bandit*, 3rd ed. rev. and augmented (1854; San Francisco, 1871).

36. Bartlett 1: 192.

37. Botkin 355.

38. John Frank Dobie cites, among others, Texas Ranger Jim Gillett, who writes: "It is a strange fact, but one without question, that no wild animal or bird of prey will touch the body of a Mexican. These corpses had lain on the ground nearly two weeks and were untouched. If they had been the bodies of Indians, Negroes or Americans, the coyotes, buzzards and crows would have attacked them the first day and night" (*The Voice of the Coyote* [Lincoln: U of Nebraska P, 1961] 124–25).

39. Botkin 335.

40. Alonzo Delano, *Life on the Plains and Among the Diggings* (New York, 1854) 341.

41. William Davis, *El Gringo; or, New Mexico and Her People* (New York, 1857) 183.

42. Refers to the social revolution lasting 12 years after the fall of Santa Anna in 1855. The Revolution of Ayutla (1854–55) was followed by the War of the Reform (1858–62).

The War of Independence began on 16 September 1810. Mexican independence dates back to 1821.

43. O. Henry 1040.

44. Walter Prescott Webb writes: "Without disparagement, it may be said that there is a cruel streak in the Mexican nature. . . . This cruelty may be a heritage from the Spanish of the Inquisition; it may, and doubtless should, be attributed partly to the Indian blood" (*The Texas Rangers* [Boston: Houghton, 1935] 14).

45. See Irving Babbitt, *Spanish Character and Other Essays* (Boston: Houghton, 1940) 8. Norris stresses this taste for blood and Mexican-Americans' passion for cockfights in *The Octopus* (New York: Doubleday, 1904) 141–42.

46. William Davis, *El Gringo; or, New Mexico and Her People* (New York, 1857) 86.

47. "Billy the Kid," *American Ballads and Folk Songs*, ed. John Lomax and Alan Lomax (New York: Macmillan, 1953) 136. The expression "a man for breakfast" was common as there were many instances of "settling a score" up until 1930. See Emrich 130.

48. See Américo Paredes, *With His Pistol in His Hand* (Austin: U of Texas P, 1958) 18: "The records of frontier life after 1848 are full of instances of cruelty and inhumanity. But by far the majority of the acts of cruelty are ascribed by American writers themselves to men of their own race. The victims, on the other hand, were very often Mexicans. There is always the implication that it was 'defensive cruelty,' or that the Mexicans were being punished for their inhumanity to Texans at the Alamo, Mier, and Goliad."

49. Bartlett 1: 322.

50. Paredes 28: "The Borderer's belief that all Rangers are shooters-in-the-back is one of the same stuff as the Texan belief that all Mexicans are back-stabbers."

51. Hall, *The Merciless Marauders* 2, 5, 14: "villainous-looking," "serpent-eyed"; *The Rough Riders* 4, 10: "snake-like eyes," "snake eyes."

52. Davis 219.

53. John W. Audubon, *Audubon's Western Journals, 1849–1850: Being the MS. Record of a Trip from New York to Texas and an Overland Journey Through Mexico and Arizona to the Gold-Fields of California* (Cleveland: Clark, 1906) 103. The famous ornithologist's son.

54. Delano 341.

55. Lewis, *Wolfville Days* 147.

56. Paredes 80: "Heroization"; "Here's to the Ranger!" *Cowboy Songs and Other Frontier Ballads*, ed. John Lomax (New York: Macmillan, 1910) 354–55.

57. See Harvey Fergusson, *Rio Grande* (New York: Knopf, 1933) 253–54.

58. Parkman 260: "They disappeared as they saw us approach. . . ."

59. Bartlett 1: 488.

60. "Juan Murray," Lomax 277.

61. See Davis 220–21: "Their ancestors were governed in this matter by the standard of morality that prevailed in Southern Europe and along the shores of the Mediterranean, where morals were never deemed as essential to respectability and good standing in society. . . ."

62. Davis 231.

63. Davis 223.

64. See George W. B. Evans, *Mexican Gold Trail: The Journal of a 49er* (San Marino, Calif.: Huntington Library, 1945) 221, note 13: "Monte, or 'Mexican Monte,' was a banking game in which the players bet against the banker and his funds. The Mexicans

who were most adept at gambling preferred it to all other games because they considered the player's chances to be more equal and the banker to have less opportunity for cheating. See Hubert Howe Bancroft, *California Inter Pocula* (1888) chap. XXIII."

65. See Davis 229.

66. J. Ross Browne, *Crusoe's Island: A Ramble in the Footsteps of Alexander Selkirk, with Sketches of Adventures in California and Washoe* (New York, 1864) 177.

67. Parkman 260.

68. Browne 177, 223.

69. Bartlett 1: 40.

70. Evans 109–10.

71. This "truism" is illustrated by an H. L. Boone character: "Alberto returned to Santa Perona in high spirits but took little interest in his rancho, looking languidly on the new shed, and on the cattle. . . . 'Es muchissimo travajo,' he remarked and thought to himself, 'Caramba I love not work,' but did not say so; it was sufficiently evident" (*Yankee Jim* 33).

72. Martin Offenbacher, "Konfession und Soziale Schichtung: Eine Studie über die wirtschaftliche Lage der Katholiken und Protestanten in Baden," *Volkswirtschaftliche Abhandlungen der badischen Hochschule* (Tübingen: n.p., 1901) 4: Part 5, 58. Reported by Max Weber, *The Protestant Ethic and the Spirit of Capitalism*, trans. from the German [*Die protestantische Ethik und der Geist des Kapitalismus*] by T. Parsons (New York: Scribner's, 1958) 40–41.

73. Davis 225.

74. This refers not to the Spanish Virgin of Estremadura, who appeared to a shepherd in the Guadalupe Mountains of Spain around 1322, but to the Virgin who appeared in 1531 on Mount Tepeyac near Mexico City to the Indian shepherd Juan Diego, recently converted by the Franciscans, and appeared also to Juan de Zumárraga, the archbishop of Mexico City. The building of the first stone basilica of Our Lady of Guadalupe del Tepeyac began in 1609. Cortés and many of his followers were from Estremadura, which explains why the images of these two Virgins bear the same name.

75. Fergusson, *The Blood of the Conquerors* 100–01.

76. See William H. Prescott, *History of the Conquest of Mexico, with a Preliminary View of the Ancient Mexican Civilization and the Life of the Conqueror, Hernando Cortés*, 3 vols. (New York, 1843) 3: 362: "The mind, occupied with forms, thinks little of substance. In a worship that is addressed too exclusively to the senses it is often the case, that morality becomes divorced from religion; and the measure of righteousness is determined by the creed rather than by the conduct."

77. O. Henry 1042.

78. Davis 189.

79. Boone 18.

80. Boone 50.

81. Alfred Lewis, *The Throwback: A Romance of the Southwest* (London: Cassel, 1907) 342.

82. Bartlett 1: 43.

83. Pitt 186.

84. Hall, *The Black Bravo* 29.

85. Lewis, *The Throwback* 274. Note also this remark by Davis: "They . . . lack the stability of character and soundness of intellect that give such vast superiority to the Anglo-Saxon race over every other people" (*El Gringo* 217).

86. Octavio Romano, ed., *Voices: Readings from* El Grito: A Journal of Contemporary Mexican-American Thought, *1967–1971* (Berkeley: Quinto Sol, 1971) Part 1, "Stereotypes and the Distortion of History" 26–73.

87. McWilliams 132.

88. R. V. Padilla, "A Critique of Pittian History," *El Grito* 6 (Fall 1972): 21.

89. See Herminio Ríos, introduction, *Voices*, ed. Octavio Romano, 8: "It is interesting to note that the negative stereotypes of the Mexican American were not created by the social scientists, but by such chauvinistic and ethnocentric Anglo-American mountain men as James Ohio Pattie (*The Personal Narrative of James O. Pattie of Kentucky*) and the obtuse jingoist newspaperman George Wilkins Kendall (*Narrative of the Texas Santa Fe Expedition*), and countless 'poets' and 'novelists' whose literary defecations were the distillate of U.S. expansionist philosophies."

90. See Francisco A. Ríos, "The Mexican in Fact, Fiction and Folklore," *Voices*, ed. Octavio Romano 59–73.

91. F. Ríos, *Voices*, ed. Octavio Romano 67.

92. Octavio Romano, "Goodbye Revolution—Hello Slum," *El Espejo—The Mirror: Selected Mexican-American Literature*, ed. Octavio Romano (Berkeley, Quinto Sol, 1969) 81.

93. Nick Vaca, "The Mexican-American in the Social Sciences," *El Grito* 4 (Fall 1970): 45.

94. See Octavio Romano, "The Anthropology and Sociology of the Mexican-Americans: The Distortion of Mexican-American History," *El Grito* 2 (Fall 1968): 13–26.

95. Romano, "The Anthropology" 16.

96. Romano, "The Anthropology" 17.

97. Vaca 45.

98. Romano, "The Anthropology" 23.

99. On the term "gringo," see McWilliams 115–32. He claims a song, "Green Grow the Rushes, O!" sung in 1846 by the Yankees as they crossed into Mexico, is the origin of the word. *The New English Dictionary* of 1884 sees a deformation of the Spanish word *griego* ("Greek"), a nickname Mexicans called foreigners, especially Americans. The Spanish expression *hablar en gringo* ("to speak in *gringo*") may relate to the American expression "It's all Greek to me." Another possible explanation: during the war with Mexico, Yankee soldiers wore green jackets, "green coats," which became "gringos" in the speech of Mexicans. In these early days, "gringo" did not have the pejorative connotation of "greaser."

A Chicano, José Angel Gutiérrez, founder of the La Raza Unida party in Texas, defines "gringo" as: "an attitude. Blacks have called it racism or honky. In South America or in the Far East it is called 'yankee imperialism.' It's the whole paternalistic, ethnocentric, xenophobic attitude" (reported by Clarke Newlon, *Famous Mexican-Americans* [New York: Dodd, 1972] 177–78).

100. Horace Bell, *Reminiscences of a Ranger; or, Early Times in Southern California* (1881; Santa Barbara: Hebbard, 1927) 49.

Chapter 2. Romanticism

1. Spanish proverb reported by Franklin Walker, *A Literary History of Southern California* (Berkeley: U of California P, 1950) 197.

2. Gertrude Atherton, *The Californians* (London, 1898) 22.

3. Charles Lummis, *The Land of Poco Tiempo* (London, 1893) 3.

4. Gertrude Atherton, *The Splendid Idle Forties: Stories of Old California* (New York: Macmillan, 1902) 220–21. *Reboso*: a small cape or shawl.

5. Atherton, *The Californians* 22.

6. Atherton, *The Californians* 150: "California is faultless; it is civilization that has spoilt her."

7. See Wayne Moquin and Charles Van Doren, eds., "The Spanish Land Grant Question in New Mexico," *A Documentary History of the Mexican Americans* (New York: Praeger, 1971) 452–63.

8. Mary (Stewart) Daggett, *Mariposilla* (Chicago, 1895) 206.

9. Frank Norris, *The Octopus* (1901; Boston: Houghton, 1958) (Book I, chap. 6) 146.

10. Daggett 32–33.

11. Atherton, *The Californians* 215–16.

12. Helen Hunt Jackson, *Ramona* (Boston, 1884) 41.

13. Marah Ellis Ryan, *For the Soul of Rafael*, 11th ed. (Chicago: McClurg, 1914).

14. Daggett 250.

15. Daggett 94.

16. Hunt Jackson, *Ramona* 41.

17. Atherton, *The Californians* 40.

18. Atherton, *The Californians* 112.

19. Hunt Jackson, *Ramona* 99.

20. Harvey Fergusson, *In Those Days, Followers of the Sun: A Trilogy of the Santa Fe Trail* (New York: Knopf, 1942) 21.

21. Hunt Jackson, *Ramona* 30.

22. Charles Lummis, "Bravo's Day Off," *The King of the Broncos and Other Stories of New Mexico* (London, 1897) 140.

23. Robert Herrick, *Waste* (New York: Harcourt, 1924) 423.

24. J. Ross Browne, *Crusoe's Island: A Ramble in the Footsteps of Alexander Selkirk, with Sketches of Adventure in California and Washoe* (New York, 1864) 227.

25. Gertrude Atherton, *Los Cerritos: A Romance of the Modern Time* (New York, 1890).

26. Mary Austin, "The Little Town of the Grapevines," *The Land of Little Rain* (Boston: Houghton, 1903) 263.

27. Charles Lummis, "Pablo Apodaca's Bear," *A New Mexico David and Other Stories and Sketches of the Southwest* (New York, 1891) 71.

28. Atherton, *Los Cerritos* 176.

29. George Emery, "The Water-Witch," *The Chicano*, ed. Edward Simmen (New York: NAL, 1971) 36, 37.

30. Robinson Jeffers, *Cawdor and Other Poems* (1928; New York: Random, 1934) 129.

31. Willa Cather, *The Song of the Lark* (Boston: Houghton, 1915) 44.

32. Lummis, "Bravo's Day Off" 143.

33. Willa Cather, *Death Comes for the Archbishop* (1927; New York: Knopf, 1966) 259.

34. Atherton, *Los Cerritos* 176.

35. Daggett 227.

36. Jeffers, *Cawdor* 129.

37. Horace Bell, *Reminiscences of a Ranger; or, Early Times in Southern California* (Santa Barbara: Hebbard, 1927) 240.

38. Atherton, "A Ramble with Eulogia," *The Splendid Idle Forties* 231.

39. Cather, *Death Comes for the Archbishop* 206–07.

40. Willa Cather, *The Professor's House* (New York: Knopf, 1925).

41. Herrick 418.

42. Daggett 35.

43. Norris, *The Octopus* (Book I, chap. 1) 15.

44. Austin, *The Land of Little Rain* 267.

45. Atherton, *The Californians* 10.

46. Atherton, "A Ramble with Eulogia" 220–21.

47. Norris, *The Octopus* vii.

48. Lummis, *The Land of Poco Tiempo* 3.

49. Atherton, *The Californians* 157.

50. Atherton, *The Californians* 169.

51. Grace Ellery Channing, "The Basket of Anita," *The Sister of a Saint and Other Stories* (Chicago, 1895) 234.

52. Fergusson, *In Those Days* 201–02.

53. Atherton, *The Californians* 29.

54. Atherton, *The Californians* 138.

55. Atherton, "A Ramble with Eulogia" 214–15.

56. Atherton, *Los Cerritos* 162.

57. Atherton, *Los Cerritos* 163.

58. Charles Lummis, "My Spanish Cigarette," *A Bronco Pegasus* (Boston: Houghton, 1928) 89.

59. "Box S" represents the distinctive brand of the ranch's cattle. Possibly, the letter S was inside a square or a rectangle; perhaps the S followed a square. The brand often designates the ranch itself.

60. See Edward Larocque Tinker, *The Horsemen of the Americas and the Literature They Inspired*, 2nd rev. ed. (Austin: U of Texas P, 1967) 118–19.

61. See Américo Paredes, *Estados Unidos, Mexico y el Machismo* (Austin: U of Texas P, 1967) reprinted from *Journal of Inter-American Studies* 9 (Jan. 1967): 66.

62. Joaquin Miller, "Vaquero," *Complete Poetical Works of J. Miller* (San Francisco, 1897) 166. The poem first appeared under the title "El Vaquero" in *Overland Monthly* 10 (Feb. 1873): 279.

63. Refers to the poem "Joaquin," published in *Joaquin et al.* (Portland, Ore., 1869). The same poem, revised and augmented, appeared as the "Californian," in [Miller] *Song of the Sierras* (London, 1871).

64. Frederic Remington, *Pony Tracks: Sketches of Pioneer Life* (Norman: U of Oklahoma P, 1961).

65. Mark Twain, *Roughing It* (Hartford, 1888) 178.

66. Bret Harte, "The Devotion of Enríquez" Simmen 48–71.

67. Robinson Jeffers, "Roan Stallion," *The Selected Poetry of Robinson Jeffers* (New York: Random, 1937) 141–57.

68. Fergusson, *In Those Days* 56.

69. Fergusson, *In Those Days* 39–41.

70. Fergusson, *In Those Days* 63.

71. Eugene Rhodes, "Pasó por Aquí," *Once in the Saddle and Pasó por Aquí* (Boston: Houghton, 1927) 159.

72. Atherton, "The Ears of Twenty Americans," *The Splendid Idle Forties* 82.

73. Atherton, *Los Cerritos* 58.

74. Carey McWilliams, *North From Mexico: The Spanish-Speaking People of the United States* (Philadelphia: Lippincott, 1949) 72.

75. Atherton, "The Ears of Twenty Americans" 59.

76. The Franciscans were re-established in New Mexico in 1897, thanks to Monsignor Lamy. Beginning in 1909, they took over many missions. On the California missions and Father Junípero [Serra], see Helen Hunt Jackson, *Glimpses of Three Coasts* (Boston, 1886) 30–77.

77. Charles Stoddard, *In the Footprints of the Padres* (San Francisco: Robertson, 1902).

78. Norris, *The Octopus* (Book I, chap. 1) 34.

79. The author never specifically mentioned the mission of Santa Barbara. She called it "the Franciscan monastery" (chap. 4) then the "college" (chap. 25); in reality, it was neither. See Carlyle C. Davis and William A. Alderson, *The True Story of* Ramona (New York: Dodge, 1914) 140.

80. Hunt Jackson, *Ramona* 50.

81. Carey McWilliams, *Southern California Country: An Island on the Land* (New York: Duell, Sloan and Pearce, 1946) chap. 4, p. 75: ". . . the story extolled the Franciscans in the most extravagant manner and placed the entire onus of mistreatment of the Indians upon the noisy and vulgar gringos."

82. According to Davis and Alderson (*The True Story of* Ramona 145), the author transformed the name of a real monk Zalvidea, into Salvierderra. "She sought a name bearing significance. She had only to take the Spanish verbs *salvar*, to save, and *dar*, to give, and create the name she desired. Dropping the *r* from *salvar*, and combining the root with the subjunctive imperfect of the irregular verb *dar*, which is *dierra*, produces *salva dierra*, thus signifying giving salvation." In real life, this priest was probably Padre Francisco de Jesús Sánchez of the mission of Santa Barbara (Davis and Alderson 132–33).

83. Daggett 249.

84. Atherton, *The Californians* 337.

85. Daggett 85.

86. Leonard Pitt, *The Decline of the Californios: A Social History of the Spanish-Speaking Californians, 1846–1890* (Berkeley: U of California P, 1966) 289.

87. Cecil Robinson, *With the Ears of Strangers: The Mexican in American Literature* (Tucson: U of Arizona P, 1963) 151.

88. Daggett 87.

89. Franklin Walker, *A Literary History of Southern California* (Berkeley: U of California P, 1950) 196.

90. Mary Austin, *Earth Horizon* (Boston: Houghton, 1932) 186. This book, intended as an indictment of government policies toward the Indians, owed its success to its romantic image of the Hispanic-Americans of California rather than the problem she wished to make known.

91. Austin 186.

92. Walker 171.

93. Robinson 67.

94. McWilliams, *North From Mexico* 36.

95. Matt Meier and Feliciano Rivera, *The Chicanos: A History of Mexican Americans* (New York: Hill, 1972) 46.

96. McWilliams, "The Growth of a Legend" 76.

97. John H. Allen, *Southwest* (Philadelphia: Lippincott, 1952) 39.

98. On the bandits Joaquín Murrieta and Tiburcio Vásquez, Luis Valdez writes: "History dismissed them as bandits; asinine romanticized accounts of their 'exploits' have totally distorted the underlying political significance of their rebellion" (Luis

Valdez and Stan Steiner, eds., *Aztlán: An Anthology of Mexican American Literature* [New York: Knopf, 1972] xxvii).

99. R. Padilla, "A Critique of Pittian History," *El Grito* 6 (Fall 1972): 3–44.

100. Ozzie G. Simmons, "The Mutual Images and Expectations of Anglo-Americans and Mexican-Americans," *Pain and Promise: The Chicano Today*, ed. Edward Simmen (New York: NAL, 1972) 112.

101. McWilliams, "The Growth of a Legend" 83.

102. Ruth Tuck, *Not With the Fist: Mexican-Americans in a Southwest City* (New York: Harcourt, 1946) 16–17.

103. See McWilliams, *North From Mexico* 36.

104. Tuck 19.

Chapter 3. Realism

1. Leonard Pitt, *The Decline of the Californios: A Social History of the Spanish-Speaking Californians, 1846–1890* (Berkeley: U of California P, 1966) 269.

2. See Henry Steele Commager, *The American Mind: An Interpretation of American Thought and Character Since the 1880s* (New Haven: Yale UP, 1950) 41–54.

3. Hamlin Garland, "Delmar of Pima" [1902], *The Chicano: From Caricature to Self-Portrait*, ed. Edward Simmen (New York: NAL, 1971) 74.

4. See the documentary book by Fabiola Cabeza de Baca, *We Fed Them Cactus* (Albuquerque: U of New Mexico P, 1954). The Baca family possessed a million sheep on the Llano Estacado in New Mexico in the nineteenth century. The rivalry between cattle ranchers and sheep raisers led to the Lincoln County (N. Mex.) War (1876–78). The sheep raisers were the losers.

5. However, Spanish speakers in New Mexico, like the entire Mexican minority, have always voted massively (95 percent) for the Democratic party until recent years. Finding the Democrats' social reforms inadequate, in the state's gubernatorial election of 1966, 90 percent of Mexican-American voters supported Republican David Cargo, who won.

6. A term used in New Mexico and Texas to designate the descendants of the early Spanish settlers.

7. Jack London, "The Mexican" [1911], Simmen 89–112.

8. Willa Cather, *Death Comes for the Archbishop* (New York: Knopf, 1927).

9. Stephen Crane, "The Bride Comes to Yellow Sky," *McClure's Magazine* 10 (Feb. 1898): 377–84; "Moonlight on the Snow," *Frank Leslie's Popular Monthly* 49 (April 1900): 606–18.

10. Fergusson explains himself in the introduction of his trilogy: "It seems appropriate, too, that the central figure of this last story should be a Mexican. In each of the others the contact between the races is part of the drama but the viewpoint is nearly always that of the conquering Yankee. Here, at the end, is the story of the beaten, of a great condition gone to seed and fallen back to the ground" (Harvey Fergusson, *Followers of the Sun: A Trilogy of the Santa Fe Trail* [New York: Knopf, 1942] xii).

11. See Simmen 48–71.

12. Bret Harte, "The Passing of Enríquez," *The Writings of Bret Harte* (Boston: Houghton, 1900) 16: 71–107.

13. Harte, "The Passing of Enríquez" 100.

14. Harvey Fergusson, *The Blood of the Conquerors*, in *Followers of the Sun* 51.

15. See Wayne Moquin and Charles Van Doren, eds., *A Documentary History of the Mexican Americans* (New York: Praeger, 1971) 285–95. Father Lamy was apostolic vicar of Cincinnati before being sent to New Mexico in 1850. Father Joseph P. Machebeuf (Father Vaillant in the novel) accompanied him west.

16. Cather, *Death Comes for the Archbishop* 9.

17. Father Antonio José Martínez was one of the most fascinating figures of Mexican life in the nineteenth-century Southwest. He enjoyed great prestige and played an important political role in the Taos region, rallying dissidents about him. Hostile to the Americans, whose arrival was eroding the clergy's power in New Mexico, he instigated the Indian rebellion of 1847, which ended in bloodshed. He also took charge of the rebellious church. He was director of a fine school and founded the first newspaper, *El Crepúsculo*. See Harvey Fergusson's documentary work, *Rio Grande* (New York: Knopf, 1933) 239; on the uncordial dealings with J.-B. Lamy, see Matt Meier and Feliciano Rivera, *The Chicanos: A History of Mexican Americans* (New York: Hill, 1972) 52–53.

18. Cather, *Death Comes for the Archbishop* 148–49.

19. See John Russell Bartlett, *Personal Narrative of Explorations and Incidents in Texas, New Mexico, California, Sonora and Chihuahua* (New York, 1854) 1: 213–14; William H. Brewer, *Up and Down California in 1860–1864: The Journal of William H. Brewer, Professor of Agriculture in the Sheffield Scientific School from 1864 to 1903*, 1st ed. (New Haven: Yale UP, 1930) 292–93.

20. Horace Bell, *Reminiscences of a Ranger; or, Early Times in Southern California* (Santa Barbara: Hebberd, 1927) 474, 482.

21. Frederick Olmsted, *A Journey Through Texas; or, A Saddle-Trip on the Southwestern Frontier* (New York, 1857) 163: "The Mexicans were treated for a while after annexation like a conquered people. Ignorant of their rights, and of the new language, they allowed themselves to be imposed upon by the new comers, who seized their lands and property without shadow of claim. . . ."

22. Garland 73.

23. Robert Herrick, *Waste* (New York: Harcourt, 1924) 429.

24. London 111.

25. Stephen Crane, "Moonlight on the Snow," *The Complete Short Stories and Sketches of Stephen Crane* (Garden City, N.Y.: Doubleday, 1963) 712.

26. Crane, "The Bride Comes to Yellow Sky," *Complete Short Stories* 386.

27. Crane, "The Bride" 387.

28. London 89.

29. Certain lodges continue to this day in isolated areas of New Mexico. On this religious sect, see Fergusson, *Rio Grande* 76–77; Charles Lummis, *The Land of Poco Tiempo* (London, 1893) 24.

30. Anthony Ganilh, *Mexico versus Texas* (Philadelphia, 1838) 79.

31. Josiah Gregg, *Commerce of the Prairies; or, The Journal of a Santa Fe Trader, During Eight Expeditions Across the Great Western Prairies and a Residence of Nearly Nine Years in Northern Mexico*, 2 vols. (Philadelphia, 1851) 1: 260.

32. See also Cather, *Death Comes for the Archbishop* 148–49.

33. Fergusson, *The Blood of the Conquerors* 139. *Bailes*: dances.

34. London 112.

35. Garland 83.

36. Harte 48.

37. Fergusson, *Followers of the Sun* vii–viii: "I have become a realist, at least in thought and intention."

38. Josiah Royce, *California: From the Conquest in 1846 to the Second Vigilance Committee in San Francisco* (Boston, 1886) 345.

39. Knapp Clappe writes: "Resentment against 'foreigners' was almost a universal phenomenon in the California diggings. Many experienced Mexican gold miners arrived early at the Sierra placers. . . . To many of the Yankees, and to most of the narrow-minded 'pikes,' from Missouri (and other midwestern areas), a man who could not speak English was a monstrosity. Ignorance, prejudice, and bigotry soon commenced their work throughout the diggings" (Louise Knapp Clappe, *The Shirley Letters from the California Mines, 1851–1852* [New York: Knopf, 1949] 142).

40. A cowboy strike in the Texas Panhandle in 1883, instigated by a Juan Gómez, the first Mexican-American strike; a strike by beet-pickers in Ventura, Calif., in 1903; in the Arizona copper mines in 1917, and so forth.

41. R. V. Padilla, "A Critique of Pittian History," *El Grito* 6 (Fall 1972): 11.

42. The word is to be taken in Sartre's sense of "transfer on the level of the unreal."

43. Fergusson, *In Those Days,* in *Followers of the Sun* 237.

1930–1940: The Yoke of the Stereotype Loosens

1. John Steinbeck, *Tortilla Flat,* 2nd ed. (New York: Modern Library, 1937) 1.

2. Madison Grant and Charles S. Davidson, eds., *The Alien in Our Midst; or, "Selling Our Birthright for a Mess of Pottage"* (New York: Galton, 1930). These articles are directed principally against Mexican immigrants.

3. See Matt Meier and Feliciano Rivera: "Anti-Mexican feelings were widespread and overt throughout the Southwest in the 1930's; signs reading 'Only White Labor Employed' and 'No Niggers, Mexicans, or Dogs Allowed,' were evidences of the feelings and attitudes of that time . . ." (*The Chicanos* [New York: Hill, 1972] 154).

4. Frank Harris, *My Reminiscences as a Cowboy* (New York: Boni, 1930) 68.

Chapter 4. Admiration for a Different People

1. Frank Norris, *The Octopus* (New York: Doubleday, 1904) (Book I, chap. 1) 16.

2. Paul Horgan, *No Quarter Given* (New York: Harper, 1935).

3. Paul Horgan, "The End of an Occupation," *Figures in a Landscape* (New York: Harper, 1940) 261: "It is a sad thing that Hollywood should compose the epitaph for this charming and unpredictable race. But Hollywood is so utterly contemporary that its authority cannot be denied."

4. Paul Horgan, *The Return of the Weed* (New York: Harper, 1936) 66–81.

5. Maurice G. Fulton and Paul Horgan, eds., *New Mexico's Own Chronicle: Three Races in the Writings of Four Hundred Years* (Dallas: Banks, 1937). In the first section, "The New Beside the Old," a passage by Harvey Fergusson, taken from *Rio Grande* (New York: Knopf, 1933), is titled by the editors "Old Town and New," pp. 335–38.

6. Philip Stevenson, "The Shepherd," *Southwest Review* 16 (Oct. 1930): 65–74.

7. Calvin Ross, *Sky Determines: An Interpretation of the Southwest* (Albuquerque: U of New Mexico P, 1965) x. Refers to the preface of the 1934 edition, reproduced in the 1965 edition.

8. John Steinbeck, *The Pastures of Heaven* (New York: Viking, 1932). The fourth and seventh sections deal with two Mexican-American families.

9. John Steinbeck, *The Long Valley* (New York: Viking, 1938). From this collection of short stories, we will study "Flight," 45–70, and "The Red Pony," 203–79.

10. John Steinbeck, *Tortilla Flat* (New York: Modern Library, 1937) 10.

11. Mary Austin, "The Politeness of Cuesta la Plata," *One-Smoke Stories* (Boston: Houghton, 1934) 160–69.

12. Richard Summers, *Dark Madonna* (Caldwell, Idaho: Caxton, 1937).

13. Ernest Hemingway, "The Gambler, the Nun, and the Radio" [1933], *The First Forty-Nine Stories* (London: Cape, 1939) 388–404.

14. Early in the Depression there were massive repatriations to Mexico. Employment priority was given to American workers.

15. Steinbeck, *Tortilla Flat* 11.

16. Steinbeck, *Tortilla Flat* 11.

17. Steinbeck, *Tortilla Flat* 17.

18. Steinbeck, *Tortilla Flat* 1.

19. Steinbeck, *Tortilla Flat* 9.

20. Steinbeck, *Tortilla Flat* 10.

21. Steinbeck, *Tortilla Flat* 26.

22. Steinbeck, *The Pastures of Heaven* 53.

23. Paul Horgan, *Main Line West* (New York: Harper, 1936) 288.

24. William Saroyan, "The Mexicans," *Little Children* (London: Faber, 1937) 170.

25. Steinbeck, *The Pastures of Heaven* 129.

26. Horgan, *No Quarter Given* 70.

27. Steinbeck, *Tortilla Flat* 144.

28. *Tortilla Flat* had many problems in Hollywood. Ten years after its publication, Steinbeck wrote a scenario called "A Medal for Benny" with the collaboration of Jack Wagner and Frank Butler (J. Gassner and D. Nichols, eds., *Best Film Plays—1945* [New York: Crown, 1946]).

29. Steinbeck, *Tortilla Flat* 1.

30. Steinbeck, *Tortilla Flat* 3.

31. Francisco Ríos, "The Mexican in Fact, Fiction, and Folklore," *Voices of Aztlán*, ed. Dorothy Harth and Lewis Baldwin (New York: NAL, 1974) 63.

32. Letter from Steinbeck to his literary agents at Modern Library, winter 1934. Reported by Peter Lisca, *The Wide World of John Steinbeck* (New Brunswick, N.J.: Rutgers UP, 1958) 82.

33. Steinbeck, *Tortilla Flat* 9.

34. See also Austin 160–69.

35. Horgan, *No Quarter Given* 70.

36. See John H. Allen, *Southwest* (Philadelphia: Lippincott, 1952) 39.

37. John H. Allen, *Song to Randado* (Dallas: Kaleidograph, 1935) 9. Randado is a city in South Texas near the border.

38. Ernest Hemingway, *Men Without Women* (New York: Scribner's, 1927). A collection of short stories.

39. Steinbeck, "Flight" [no page reference].

40. Steinbeck, "Flight" 49.

41. Steinbeck, "Flight" 54.

42. Hemingway, "The Gambler" 401.

43. Hemingway, "The Gambler" 400.

44. On Mexican-American characters in the first works by Mexican-Americans, Luis Valdez writes: "Some are sketched, some are fully drawn, but they are all intimately real, a far cry from the racist stereotypes of the John Steinbeck past" (*Aztlán: An Anthology of Mexican American Literature*, ed. Luis Valdez and Stan Steiner [New York: Knopf, 1972] xxx).

Chapter 5. The Defenders of the Oppressed

1. Wetback: a Mexican who swims across the Rio Grande clandestinely at night and enters the United States illegally. Such migrants earn starvation wages and are constantly threatened with deportation; frequently, they are deported then return in the same way.

2. Paul Horgan, "The Surgeon and the Nun," *The Chicano*, ed. Edward Simmen (New York: NAL, 1971) 121–38. This short story is also in Horgan's collection *Figures in a Landscape* (New York: Harper, 1940) 135–56. In a section titled "Two Energies," the author praises the work of German nuns in the Southwest.

3. The Pecos River begins in New Mexico and crosses West Texas before flowing into the Rio Grande.

4. William Saroyan, "With a Hey Nonny Nonny," Simmen 115–20.

5. John McGinnis, "The Tomato Can," *Southwest Review* 16 (1931): 507–16.

6. Saroyan 116.

7. Horgan 121.

8. Horgan 123.

9. McGinnis 511.

10. McGinnis 515.

11. Carey McWilliams, *North From Mexico: The Spanish-Speaking People of the United States* (Philadelphia: Lippincott, 1949) 193.

12. "*But McWilliams did not count on either the semantic genius, or the frontier-expansionist mentality of the social scientists who later came west to rewrite history*—to merge the myth of the docile Mexican with that of the fatalistic and non-goal oriented Mexican-American . . ." (Octavio Romano, "The Anthropology and Sociology of the Mexican-Americans: The Distortion of Mexican-American History," *El Grito* 2 [Fall 1968]: 25).

13. Saroyan 117.

14. John Dos Passos on a Mexican restaurant in Los Angeles: "Everybody talked Mexico. Madero had started his revolution. The fall of Díaz was expected any day. All over the peons were taking to the hills driving the rich científicos off their ranches. Anarchist propaganda was spreading among the town workers . . ." (*The 42nd Parallel* [1930; New York: Washington Square, 1961] 136–37).

15. Mexican unions unaffiliated with either the C.I.O or the A.F.L. were powerless. When Mexican-Americans launched a strike, Anglo workers responded with hostility. Clinging to the stereotype of Mexican submissiveness, the Anglos saw their demands as an expression of animosity toward whites.

16. Saroyan 120.

17. Saroyan 116.
18. Saroyan 115.
19. Saroyan 116.
20. Philip Stevenson, "At the Crossroads," *Folk-Say: A Regional Miscellany*, ed. B. A. Botkin (Norman: U of Oklahoma P, 1931) 70–82.
21. Saroyan 118.

The Mexican-American Point of View: Early Modes of Expression

1. Translated and published in *El Grito: A Journal of Contemporary Mexican-American Thought* 5 (Fall 1971): 17.
2. Harris Newmark, *Sixty Years in Southern California, 1853–1913* (New York: Knicker Bocker, 1916) 156.
3. Josiah Royce, *California: From the Conquest in 1846 to the Second Vigilance Committee in San Francisco* (Boston, 1886) 30–31.
4. Alfred Lewis, *The Throwback: A Romance of the Southwest* (London: Cassel, 1907) 342: The *guitarrero* "sang a song in exaltation of the Prof, which for hyperbole was never matched or mated throughout the Southwest."
5. Harvey Fergusson, *In Those Days*, in *Followers of the Sun* (New York: Knopf, 1942) 68: "Juan Gutiérrez brought out his home-made guitar and strummed and sang short ditties and long ballads. All of them in minor keys and sadly told stories of romantic and disappointed love."
6. Gertrude Atherton, "The Ears of Twenty Americans," *The Splendid Idle Forties: Stories of Old California* (New York: Macmillan, 1902) 122: "The play began with the announcement by Gabriel of the birth of the Saviour, and exhortations to repair the manger. On the road came the temptation of Lucifer; the archangel appeared once more; a violent altercation ensued in which all took part, and finally the prince of darkness was routed. Songs and fanciful by-play, brief sermons, music, gay and solemn, diversified the strange performance."
7. I include folklore, which long was the principal means of expression of Mexican-Americans. But, since its themes are often repeated, I will discuss only its most significant poems, plays, and stories.
8. J. Frank Dobie was born on a Texas ranch in 1888 and became a professor at the University of Texas at Austin.
9. Founded in 1916 in Austin, Texas.
10. Octavio Romano, Introduction, *El Grito* 5 (Fall 1971): 7–8: "In his introduction to his book he categorically states that until recently, '. . . *neither the upper-class Mexican American nor the lower class laborer has produced literature: the former is not inclined; the latter is not equipped.*' This incredibly inaccurate statement can only be interpreted as a blatant, unmitigated and totally inexcusable case of professional incompetence. . . . Should the Simmen thesis prevail, then all Chicano thought, creativity, poetry, and literature will be permanently entombed in that sterile academic cemetery called folklore."
11. Franklin Walker writes: "In *Two Years Before the Mast* (1840; New York: Macmillan, 1915), Richard Henry Dana described a Spanish-Californian society whose members were little more likely to create a distinctive literature than the Indians, who lived

on acorns and dried grasshoppers. The Spaniards in California had not developed a frontier; they had merely held it for fear that someone else would get it" (*San Francisco's Literary Frontier* [New York: Knopf, 1939] 17).

12. See Royce 30–31: "The Californians had, of course, little opportunity for cultivation, and they had generally few intellectual ambitions. But like the Southern peoples of European blood generally, they had a great deal of natural quickness of wit, and in their written work often expressed themselves with ease and force." Royce describes the women as: "fascinating conversers, even when not at all educated" (p. 33).

13. Twenty newspapers, mostly weeklies, were published in Los Angeles alone between 1848 and 1930; eighteen in San Francisco.

14. Aurelio Gallardo, *Leyendas y Romances: Ensayos Poéticos* (San Francisco, 1868) 7: "*Publicar un libro tan lejos de la patria, una collection de poesías eróticas y descriptivas, en un país en donde tan poco florecen las letras españolas, parecerá a muchos una empresa casi temeraria . . .*"

15. The Huntington Library, San Marino, Calif., has a collection of these newspapers.

16. Gallardo, *Leyendas y Romances*.

17. Gallardo, *Adah; o, El Amor de un Angel* (Mexico City: Paz, 1900).

18. Miguel A. Otero, *My Life on the Frontier, 1864–1882*, 1st ed. (New York: Pioneers, 1935); *My Life on the Frontier, 1882–1897*, 1st ed. (Albuquerque: U of New Mexico P, 1939); *My Nine Years as Governor of the Territory of New Mexico, 1897–1906*, 1st ed. (Albuquerque: U of New Mexico P, 1940); *The Real Billy the Kid: With New Light on the Lincoln County War* (New York: Wilson, 1936).

19. Jovita González, "Among My People," *Tone the Bell Easy*, ed. J. Frank Dobie, Publications of the Texas Folklore Society 10 (Austin, 1932) 99–108.

20. LULAC is the League of United Latin American Citizens, founded in Texas in 1929. *Lulac News*, an English-language monthly, was also founded in 1929.

21. The first play performed on American soil was *Los Moros y Los Cristianos* (The Moors and the Christians), a religious piece directed by Juan de Oñate in 1598. The religious folkloric theater of the Mexicans remained unknown to Anglos until 1889, when Miss Honora de Busk attended, in San Rafael, N. Mex., a performance of *Los Pastores* (The shepherds). She obtained the script. Two years later, Capt. John G. Bourke saw this same pastoral in Rio Grande City, Texas. Bourke reported that most of the actors, who could neither read nor write, memorized their parts by listening to the "producer," a shoemaker, repeat the text line by line. Bourke later asked the shoemaker to write out the script. Two years later, he saw the play once more in San Antonio, took photographs of the actors, recorded the songs, and submitted all his documents to the American Folklore Society. The two texts gathered by de Busk and Bourke were published and translated by M. R. Cole as *Los Pastores: A Mexican Play of the Nativity*, Memoir 9 of the American Folklore Society (Boston: Houghton, 1907). *Los Pastores* is still performed today, but the original text has been modified by the Catholic church, which was concerned by its tone, more often pagan and comic than religious. This play is performed between the Feast of Guadalupe, December 12, and the Feast of the Three Kings, January 6.

22. See Ruth (Barker) Laughlin, *Caballeros* (New York: Appleton, 1931) 241: "As the years brought freckled Strangers into the Land of Poco Tiempo history became homemade drama. There is a sly, humorous slant to such plays as 'La Lluvia de los Ingleses,'

'The Showers of the English Men' and the burlesque of the coming of the Americans."

Américo Paredes finds unusual the term "Ingleses" to designate the Americans and wonders if her reference was actually to the play *Los Tejanos* (see Aurelio M. Espinosa, "Los Tejanos: A New Mexico Spanish Folk Play in the Middle Nineteenth Century," *New Mexico Quarterly* 13 (1943): 299–308). This play takes place in 1846, after the independence of Texas, and relates a Texan punitive expedition in New Mexico (Paredes personal interviews, Austin, August 1975).

23. The *décima* came from Mexico during the colonization period. It generally contained four stanzas of ten lines each (whence its name) and a refrain; it was most often sung and almost never printed.

24. See Américo Paredes, *With His Pistol in His Hand: A Border Ballad and Its Hero* (Austin: U of Texas P, 1958) 1: "*Corrido*, the Mexicans call their narrative folk songs, especially those of epic themes, taking the name from *correr*, which means 'to run' or 'to flow,' for the *corrido* tells a story simply and swiftly, without embellishments."

25. Próspero Baca, "Alfonso Sedillos y su perro Fido," reported by Arthur L. Campa in *Spanish Folk-Poetry in New Mexico* (Albuquerque: U of New Mexico P, 1946) 113.

26. Andrellita Baca de Martínez, "Inundación de Bernalillo," Campa 108–09.

27. "Different from the songs so far quoted, which are autobiographical in character and express the attitude of the writer with the directness of the lyric, is that type of Mexican song commonly known as the 'corrido.' It may be well to confine the term 'corrido,' or 'ballad,' to the songs which tell a story. The 'corridos' are, of all the songs collected, nearest to the human-interest story of the popular newspaper. Like the human-interest story, they express the interests and attitudes of the people. The heroes of the 'corridos' are types that catch the popular imagination. Swaggering bandits who boldly defy all the rest of the world, brave men foully assassinated, or men who 'kill for love'" (Manuel Gamio, *Mexican Immigration to the United States: A Study of Human Migration and Adjustment* [Chicago: U of Chicago P, 1930] 96).

28. The *cuando* is a *corrido* characterized by the repetition of the word *cuando* ("when") at the end of each stanza.

29. As in "El Toro Moro" (The purple bull), collected and translated by Frank Goodwyn, *Texas Folk and Folklore*, ed. Mody Boatwright, Wilson M. Hudson, and Allen Maxwell, Publications of the Texas Folklore Society 26 (Dallas: Southern Methodist UP, 1954) 150:

Y con ésta me despido	And with these words I say farewell
Y sin dilación ninguna	With no further delay
El que compuso estos versos	The one who wrote these verses
Se llama Miguel de la Luna.	Is named Miguel de la Luna.

30. Aurelio Espinosa, "Romancero Nuevomejicano," *Revue Hispanique* 33-84 (1915): 446–560; 40-97 (1917): 215–27; 41-100 (1917): 678–80.

31. Manuel Gamio, "The Songs of the Immigrant," *Mexican Immigration to the United States: A Study of Human Migration and Adjustment* (Chicago: U of Chicago P, 1930) 84–107; Paul S. Taylor, *Mexican Labor in the United States: Bethlehem, Pennsylvania* (Berkeley: U of California P, 1931) 2: viii–ix; P. Taylor, *Mexican Labor in the United States: Chicago and the Calumet Region* (Berkeley: U of California P, 1932) 2: vi–vii; P. Taylor, *An American-Mexican Frontier: Nueces County, Texas* (Chapel Hill: U of North Carolina P, 1934) 144–46.

32. J. Frank Dobie, "Versos of the Texas Vaqueros," *Happy Hunting Grounds*, Publications of the Texas Folklore Society 4 (Dallas: Southern Methodist UP, 1925) 20–43; Frank Goodwyn, "Folklore of the King Ranch Mexicans," *Southwestern Lore*, ed. J. Frank Dobie, Publications of the Texas Folklore Society 9 (Dallas: Southwest, 1931) 48–62.

33. Collected in the Texas Folklore Archive, at the University of Texas-Austin.

Chapter 6. Mexicans Take Refuge in Their Myths

1. Juan B. Hijar y Jaro, "Que el cielo os de la Dicha" (En el álbum de las Señoritas A.), *El Nuevo Mundo* (San Francisco) 19 July 1864; reprinted in *El Grito* 5 (Fall 1971): 29.

2. *El Grito* 5: 28, 29. Hijar y Jaro was born in Mexico at the beginning of the nineteenth century; after studying medicine at the University of Guadalajara, he settled in San Francisco, where he wrote and practiced medicine.

3. *El Grito* 5: 30.

4. J. M. Vigil, "El Amor y La Amistad" (A mi querido amigo E.S.D. Sotero Prieto), *El Nuevo Mundo* 26 July 1864; reprinted in *El Grito* 5: 27: "*la amargura de un destino despiadado,*" "*en una playa extranjera,*" "*insensible suelo.*"

5. Aurelio L. Gallardo, *Leyendas y Romances: Ensayos Poéticos* (San Francisco, 1868) 7: "*los que viven en la amargura del destierro y diseminados sobre estas playas extranjeras . . .*"

6. Gallardo, *Leyendas y Romances* 7–8: "*. . . es necesario que se encuentra en las patéticas narraciones de mi propia historia, mucho concerniente a esa patria lejana y bendita; mucho de sus tradiciones y costumbres nacionales . . . la dulce paz de la casa paterna y esa pompa sublime de la creencia cristiana . . .*"

7. José Elías González, "A C . . . V . . ." *El Clamor Público* (Los Angeles) 12 Jan. 1856; reprinted in *El Grito* 5: 26.

8. F. N. Gutiérrez, "A una Hermosa," *La Gaceta* (Santa Barbara, Calif.) 24 April 1880; reprinted in *El Grito* 5: 32.

9. Collected by Arthur L. Campa in *Spanish Folk-Poetry in New Mexico* (Albuquerque: U of New Mexico P, 1946) 22.

10. See Octavio Paz, *El laberinto de la soledad* (Mexico City: Cuadernos Americanos, 1950) 41: "*. . . es revelador como el carácter combativo del erotismo se acentúa entre nosotros y se encona. . . . Nosotros concebimos el amor como conquista y como lucha.*"

11. "Los Amados," collected by Aurora Lucero-White [Lea] in *Literary Folklore of the Hispanic Southwest* (San Antonio: Naylor, 1953) 137.

12. See the poem recited by Próspero Baca, in Campa 99.

13. "Jesús Cadena," collected by Manuel Gamio in *Mexican Immigration to the United States: A Study of Human Migration and Adjustment* (Chicago: U of Chicago P, 1930) 99.

14. "Frank Cadena," Gamio 102.

15. José E. Gutiérrez, "Qué Más Quieres Tú," *La Gaceta* (Santa Barbara) 11 Oct. 1879; reprinted in *El Grito* 5: 31: "*. . . diosa aquí entre las bellas.*"

16. F. Ramírez [1854]; reprinted in *El Grito* 5: 22–23: "*Angel de amor,*" "*ninfa encantadora,*" "*objeto idolatrado.*"

17. José González, *El Grito* 5: 26.

18. J. E. Gutiérrez, *El Grito* 5: 31.

19. Gallardo, "Lágrimas y Perfumes," *Leyendas y Romances* [no page reference].

20. Campa 183: "The sadness of the soul of the Mexican people is its inseparable

companion, its older sister, austere, fiery at times, tragic upon occasions" (trans. from Santana Vásquez, *Historia de la Canción Mexicana* [Mexico City: Talleres Gráficos, 1931] 3: 21).

21. Collected by Aurora Lucero-White [Lea], *The Folklore of New Mexico* (Santa Fe: Setton Village, 1941) 1: 13.

22. See Aurelio Espinosa, *Romancero de Nuevo Méjico* (Madrid: Consejo Superior, 1953) 110–11. For another variant, see Campa 89–90. In 1949, Carey McWilliams wrote that "El Vaquero Nicolas" was still very popular in New Mexico (*North From Mexico* [Philadelphia: Lippincott, 1949] 96).

23. Consult *El Trovado Mexicano (La Colección Más Completa de Canciones Populares)* (San Antonio: Quiroga, n.d.) and *El Ruiseñor Mexicano* (Colección de Canciones Populares) (San Antonio: Lozano, 1924).

24. "El Abandonado," collected and translated by John Lomax and Alan Lomax, eds., *American Ballads and Folksongs* (New York: Macmillan, 1935) 364–66.

25. Aurelio Gallardo, *Adah; o, El Amor de un Angel* (Mexico City: Paz, 1900) 8: "*El dolor y la resignación son hermanos.*"

26. Gallardo, *Leyendas y Romances* 241.

27. Ramírez, "A Mi María Antonia" [1854]; reprinted in *El Grito* 5: 23.

28. "Elegía a la Memoria de Doña María Ignacia Alvarado de Pico," *El Clamor Público* (Los Angeles) 31 July 1855; reprinted in *El Grito* 5: 24.

29. Ramírez, "A Mi María Antonia" 23: "*en indolente calma.*"

30. "A M . . ." *El Clamor Público* (Los Angeles) 30 Nov. 1855.

31. Andrellita Baca de Martínez, "Inundación de Bernalillo," Campa 109.

32. "Elegía a la Memoria" 24.

33. English version of the French translation from the Nahuatl by Jacques Soustelle, *La Vie quotidienne des Aztèques à la veille de la Conquête espagnole* (Paris: Hachette, 1955) 273:

> O amis, cette terre nous est seulement prêtée.
> Il faudra abandonner les beaux poèmes,
> Il faudra abandonner les belles fleurs.
> C'est pourquoi je suis triste en chantant pour le soleil . . .

34. Próspero Baca, "San Lorenzo," Campa 115. The *matachines* is a Spanish dance that represents the struggle between Christians and Moors.

35. Princess Malinche, given in marriage to Cortés by her father, Montezuma, the Aztec emperor, falls under the influence of El Toro, the spirit of malevolence. At the instigation of Cortés, she persuades her father to desert his people. The grandfather, El Abuelo, pleads the cause of his people to Malinche; he is killed by El Toro. The grandfather returns from the land of the Ancients and changes the heart of Malinche, who brings Montezuma back to his people. See Sister Joseph Marie, "The Role of the Church and the Folk in the Development of the Early Drama in New Mexico," diss., U of Pennsylvania, 1948, 101–03.

36. "Corrido de José Apodaca," *Literatura Chicana: Texto y Contexto. Chicano Literature: Text and Context*, ed. Antonia Castañeda Shular, Tomás Ybarra-Frausto, and Joseph Sommers (Englewood Cliffs, N.J.: Prentice, 1972) 177–78. *Palme*: a sculpted and colored stick with three branches.

37. Próspero Baca 115.

38. "Despedida de un Norteño," collected and translated by Paul Taylor in *Puro Mexicano*, ed. J. Frank Dobie, Publications of the Texas Folklore Society 12 (Austin:

n.p., 1935) 222. This *corrido* is part of a collection compiled by Taylor and titled "Songs of the Mexican Migration" (*Puro Mexicano* 222–43).

39. "Vida, Proceso, y Muerte de Aurelio Pompa," collected and translated by Margaret Redfield in Shular 21.

40. J. M. Espinosa, *Spanish Folk-Tales from New Mexico*, Memoirs of the American Folk-Lore Society 30 (New York: Stechert, 1937) 10–12, 93.

41. "The Guadalupana Vine," *Texas Folk and Folklore*, ed. Mody Boatright, Wilson Hudson, and Allen Maxwell, Publications of the Texas Folklore Society (Dallas: Southern Methodist UP, 1954) 23–24. This remedy is still used in South Texas to treat wounds.

42. Jovita González, "Among My People," *Tone the Bell Easy*, ed. J. Frank Dobie, Publications of the Texas Folklore Society 10 (Austin, 1932) 100.

43. Nina Otero, "Count La Cerda's Treasure," *Old Spain in Our Southwest* (New York: Harcourt, 1936) 134.

44. Wilson M. Hudson, "To Whom God Wishes to Give He Will Give," *Texas Folk and Folklore*, ed. M. Boatright et al. 46.

45. *The Healer of Los Olmos and Other Mexican Lore*, ed. Mody Boatright, Publications of the Texas Folklore Society 24 (Dallas: Southern Methodist UP, 1951) 90 + .

46. In the Spanish chronicles, La Llorona weepingly predicts the fall of the Aztec Empire; in a contemporary Mexican story, she is Malinche, no longer traitorous but rather betrayed by Cortés.

47. In "La Llorona in Southern Arizona," *Western Folklore* 7 (1948): 272–77, Betty Leddy cites forty-two versions.

48. "Mexican Folklore from Austin, Texas," *Healer of Los Olmos*, ed. Mody Boatright 74.

49. Soladad Pérez, "The Weeping Woman," *Healer of Los Olmos*, ed. Mody Boatright [no page reference].

50. Her other aspect is that of the *Chingada*, the woman who gives birth after being violated. La Llorona is celebrated on 10 May, Mothers' Day.

51. Alurista, "Must Be the Season of the Witch," *El Espejo—The Mirror: Selected Mexican-American Literature*, ed. Octavio Romano (Berkeley: Quinto Sol, 1969) 176. The poem ends:

Must be the season of the witch
La bruja llora   [The witch cries
Sus hijos sufren, sin ella.   Her children suffer without her.]

52. Herminio Ríos explains: "If for one poet it is painful to tear himself away from Mexico, and his soul remains in its Mexican cradle, '*Y dije adiós a mis benditos lares*' [I bid adieu to my blessed home], the Chicano of 1974 openly declares his independence. And if Juan B. Hijar y Haro was to wave '*el pabellón de las estrellas*' [the Stars and Stripes], his Chicano descendants would not necessarily embrace it 100 years later. . . . The romantic plaint of Juan B. Hijar y Haro echoes the theme of '*el destierro*,' the escape of the romantic" (*El Grito* 7 [Mar.–May 1974]: 6).

53. Hijar y Jaro, *El Grito* 5: 29.

54. Sergio Elizondo, "Padres, Hijos; Ayer, Hoy," *Perros y antiperros* (Berkeley: Quinto Sol, 1972) 30. *Apá*: shortened form of *Papá*.

55. Espinosa, "El Burro y el Coyote," *Spanish Folk-Tales* 184.

Chapter 7. Mexican-Americans Confront the Present

1. "Canción Inglés," collected by Arthur L. Campa, *Spanish Folk-Poetry in New Mexico* (Albuquerque: U of New Mexico P, 1946) 214.

2. *El Clamor Público* (Los Angeles) 2 Aug. 1856, 2: "*Todos están convencidos de que California está perdido para todos los hispano-americanos; y aquí en Los Angeles, por causa de la última revolución* [?] *si antes pedían favores ahora pedirán de rodillas justicia y libertad para ejercer su industria.*" On F. Ramírez, see Leonard Pitt, *The Decline of the Californios: A Social History of the Spanish-Speaking Californians, 1846–1890* (Berkeley: U of California P, 1966), (chap. 9, "El Clamor Público: Sentiments of Treason,") 181–94.

3. *El Clamor Público* (Los Angeles) 26 Apr. 1856, 1: "*Son extranjeros en su proprio país. No tienen ninguna voz en este senado, exceptuando, la que ahora tan débilmente está hablando a su favor* . . . *Se nos debería mostrar una poca de consideración* . . . *estamos obligados a pagar contribuciones que ascienden a más de un millón de pesos, y para pagarlos nos hemos visto compelidos a vender nuestra propiedad personal y parte de nuestros terrenos* . . . *después de sufrir todas estas injusticias, y sobrellevado toda clase de injurias, ahora hallamos a una legislatura hambienta por quitarnos hasta el último centavo, simplemente porque los squatters son más numerosos que los nativos de California.*"

4. Santiago de la Hoz, "Sinfonía de Combate," *Literatura Chicana: Texto y Contexto. Chicano Literature: Text and Context*, ed. Antonia Shular (Englewood Cliffs, N.J.: Prentice, 1972) 26. The poem was published in Los Angeles in 1904 in the *cuadernillo* (five-sheet booklet) *El Cancionero Libertario* and sold in the Librería Mexicana, San Fernando Street.

5. In his first proclamation, 30 Sept. 1859, Cortina declared: ". . . our personal enemies shall not possess our lands until they have fattened it with their gore" (Thirty-Sixth Congress, First Session, "Difficulties on Southwestern Frontier," *House Executive Document No. 52*, (serial set number 1,050) 70–72). In his second proclamation, 25 Nov. 1863, he exposed the grievances of Mexican-Americans (*House Document* 79–82). Reported by Walter Prescott Webb, *The Texas Rangers: A Century of Frontier Defense* (Boston: Houghton, 1935) 175–93.

6. Reported by Américo Paredes, *With His Pistol in His Hand: A Border Ballad and Its Hero* (Austin: U of Texas P, 1958) 204.

7. After the fall of Díaz in 1910, there was political agitation in Texas. Early in 1915 some Mexican-American ranch owners in the valley, including Aniceto Pizaña, drew up the San Diego Plan in San Diego, Texas. It called for a general uprising on 20 Feb. and for the independence of Texas, New Mexico, Arizona, California, and Colorado, which would become an autonomous republic, later to be annexed by Mexico. Six other states—Oklahoma, Kansas, Nebraska, South Dakota, Wyoming, and Utah—would then be conquered. Blacks could form their own republic; Indians would regain their former lands in exchange for their support. All Anglo males over age sixteen were to be killed. Some ranches were burned, and their owners fled into towns and even into Mexico. A German plot was suspected, but this movement actually was encouraged by Mexican revolutionaries. See William M. Hager, "The Plan of San Diego: Unrest on the Texas Border in 1915," *Arizona and the West* 5 (1963): 331; Sixty-Sixth Congress, Second Session, "Mexican Affairs," *Senate Document 285* 1205–07.

8. See J. Frank Dobie, ed., *Happy Hunting Grounds*, Publications of the Texas Folklore Society 4 (Dallas: Southern Methodist UP, 1925) 35–38. In 1900, Encarnación García

killed another Mexican; he was killed by the sheriff of Cameron Country, Montalgo, who himself was killed ten years later by the García family.

9. Collected by Américo Paredes, Texas Folklore Archive, U of Texas-Austin P 42-7, P 8-5.

10. Paredes, *With His Pistol* 247.

11. These are the most significant stanzas of the longest variant, No. X, collected and translated by Paredes in *With His Pistol* 154–58, which also contains other variants. "El Corrido de Gregorio Cortez," sung by Los Trovadores Regionales, is in the Library of Congress, Vocalion Record number SA 2838351. [Trans. note: the English version here is taken directly from Paredes.]

12. "El General Cortina," Texas Folklore Archive, "Ese General Cortinas" P 21-7.

13. The *"yo soy . . ."* is found in the play *Los Comanches*, which depicts the battles of New Mexico pioneers against the Indians in the late eighteenth century. See Aurelio M. Espinosa, ed., *"Los Comanches*: A Spanish Heroic Play of 1780," *Bulletin of the University of New Mexico* 1 (1942): 35.

14. The Mexican *corridos* generally contain the expression *en su caballo* ("on horseback"), or even *en su caballo melado* ("on his honey-colored horse"). See "El Corrido de José Mosqueda," collected by John Lomax and Alan Lomax in Brownsville, Texas, in 1939, transcribed by Paredes, *Western Folklore* 17 (1958): 155–56.

15. "Corrido de Joaquín Murrieta," Shular 66.

16. "El General Cortina." Cortina(s) headed a group of about 400 men; the Rangers pursued him into Mexico, then were ordered to return across the border. He later became a brigadier general in the Mexican army, then governor of Tamaulipas. He amassed a considerable fortune and continued to encourage raids into Texas territory. Unfortunately, we possess only a few fragments of this *corrido*, so popular at the end of the nineteenth century, and these thanks to Paredes.

17. See "Jacinto Treviño," Texas Folklore Archive P 37-2.

18. "Ignacio Treviño," Texas Folklore Archive P 4-3.

19. "Ignacio Treviño," Texas Folklore Archive P 4-3. Here *me llamo* is the equivalent of *yo soy.*

20. See "El Corrido de Mariano Resendez," Texas Folklore Archive P 1-2, P 1-3, P 15-4, P 39-1.

21. "Corrido de Laredo," Texas Folklore Archive P 38-2.

22. "Corrido de Laredo," Texas Folklore Archive P 38-2.

23. "Corrido de Laredo," Texas Folklore Archive P 38-2.

24. "El Contrabando del Paso," collected and translated by B. McNeil, *Texas Folk and Folklore*, ed. Mody Boatright, Wilson Hudson, and Allen Maxwell, Publications of the Texas Folklore Society 26 (Dallas: Southern Methodist UP, 1954) 154.

25. At the turn of the twentieth century, the Rio Grande changed its course downstream from El Paso to the advantage of the United States, which, however, did not claim the area. It became a no-man's-land called Cordova's Island or El Charco Seco, the scene of confrontations between smugglers and police during Prohibition. The expression *andar en el Charco Seco* came to mean "getting involved in smuggling."

26. The King Ranch, which contained about 500,000 hectares, or more than a million acres, extended along the Gulf of Mexico some seventy miles north of the mouth of the Rio Grande. It contained five subdivisions: Norias (the largest and southernmost), Tordilla, Encino, Santa Gertrudes, and Laureles. The land between the Nueces River

and the Rio Grande was often the scene of raids, the most memorable of which, before this one, took place in 1875. See L. Morris, "The Mexican Raid of 1875 on Corpus Christi," *Quarterly* (Texas State Historical Association), 4 (1900): 128+; *Frontier Times* (Bandera, Tex.) 2 (1925): 44–47. There is no trace of the verses that undoubtedly were composed on this subject.

27. "Versos de los Bandidos," annotated and translated by Dobie in Boatright 145.

28. "Los Sediciosos," Texas Folklore Archive P 4-2.

29. "Versos de los Bandidos," Boatright 145; *dao* instead of *dado* (apocopated form).

30. "Versos de los Bandidos," Boatright 145, 146; *valiente, teme morir*.

31. "Los Sediciosos," Texas Folklore Archive P 4-2.

32. "Los Sediciosos," Texas Folklore Archive P 4-2; *abrochándose un zapato*.

33. "Los Sediciosos," Texas Folklore Archive P 4-2.

34. "Los Sediciosos," Texas Folklore Archive P 4-2.

35. "Los Sediciosos," Texas Folklore Archive P 4-2; *ha manchado el pabellón*.

36. See the ballad collected by W. A. Settle, Jr., ed., *Jesse James Was His Name; or, Fact and Fiction Concerning the Careers of the Notorious James Brothers of Missouri* (Columbia: U of Missouri P, 1966) 173–74. José Mosqueda, a Mexican bandit, derailed and robbed an American train in 1891. See Américo Paredes, "El Corrido de José Mosqueda as an Example of Pattern in the Ballad," *Western Folklore* 17 (1958): 154–62.

37. "Los Sediciosos," Texas Folklore Archive P 4-2.

38. "José Lozano," collected by Manuel Gamio, *Mexican Immigration to the United States: A Study of Human Migration and Adjustment* (Chicago: U of Chicago P, 1930) 101: *su estatura gigante, combatiendo era un león, . . . como hombre pacífico tenía buen corazón.*

39. "José Lozano," Gamio, *Mexican Immigration* 101.

40. "Reunión de Los Vaqueros," collected by Aurora Lucero-White [Lea], ed., *Literary Folklore of the Hispanic Southwest* (San Antonio: Naylor, 1953) 136.

41. "Reunión de Los Vaqueros," Lucero-White [Lea] 136.

42. "El Toro Moro," collected and translated by Frank Goodwyn, in Boatright 147. Another variant is reported by Goodwyn in "Folklore of the King Ranch Mexicans," *Southwestern Lore*, ed. J. Frank Dobie, Publications of the Texas Folklore Society 9 (Dallas: Southwest, 1931) 60–62.

43. "El Revilión," Campa 111. *Revilión*: storm (New Mexico term).

44. "La Canción del Rancho de los Olmos," collected and translated by Dobie, *Happy Hunting Grounds* 40. Cameron: one of the ranches in the Los Olmos domain.

45. "Corrido de Kiansis," collected and translated by B. McNeil, in Boatright 151. The variant collected by Paredes (Texas Folklore Archive P 2-2) relates only the death of the *vaquero*.

46. "Corrido de Kiansis," collected and translated by Paul Taylor, in Shular 211.

47. "Corrido de Kiansis," Shular 210.

48. Manuel Gamio, *The Mexican Immigrant: His Life Story* (Chicago: U of Chicago P, 1931) 149.

49. See W. F. Adams, *Ireland and Irish Emigration to the New World From 1815 to the Famine* (New Haven: Yale UP, 1932) 207–08.

50. "Despedida de un Norteño," *Puro Mexicano*, ed. J. Frank Dobie, Publications of the Texas Folklore Society 12 (Austin, 1935) 222.

51. "Despedida de un Norteño," *Puro Mexicano*, ed. J. F. Dobie 223.

52. "Defensa de los Norteños," collected and translated by Paul Taylor in Shular 235. *Patotas*: literally, big feet, a pejorative term for Americans.

53. "Defensa de los Norteños," Shular 233; *pura necesidad.*
54. "Defensa de los Norteños," Shular 234.
55. "Defensa de los Norteños," Shular 234.
56. "Los Deportados," collected and translated by Paul Taylor, in Shular 232.
57. "Vida, Proceso, y Muerte de Aurelio Pompa," Shular 21.
58. "Deportados," collected and translated by Paul Taylor, in Boatright 156.
59. "La Pensilvania," collected by Américo Paredes, in Texas Folklore Archive P 4–5. Another variant is reported by Taylor under the title "Corrido Pensilvanio" (Paul Taylor, *Mexican Labor in the U.S.: Bethlehem, Pennsylvania* [Berkeley: U of California P, 1931] 2: viii–ix).
60. "Los Inmigrantes," collected by Gamio, *Mexican Immigration* 84.
61. "Corrido de Texas," collected and translated by Paul Taylor, in Boatright 158.
62. "Corrido de Robeston," collected and translated by Paul Taylor, *An American-Mexican Frontier: Nueces County, Texas* (Chapel Hill: U of North Carolina P, 1934) 145.
63. "Los Betabeleros," collected by Gamio and translated by Margaret Redfield, in Gamio, *Mexican Immigration* 86–87.
64. "El Enganchado," collected and translated by Paul Taylor, in Taylor, *Mexican Labor in the United States: Chicago and the Calumet Region* (Berkeley: U of California P, 1932) 2: vi. The term *enganchado* means "hooked."
65. "Los Betabeleros," Gamio, *Mexican Immigration* 87.
66. See "Deportados," Boatright 157.
67. "Los Inmigrantes," Gamio, *Mexican Immigration* 86.
68. "Los Inmigrantes," Gamio, *Mexican Immigration* 85.
69. "Los Reenganchados en Kansas," collected and translated by B. McNeil, in Shular 223.
70. "Efectos de la Crisis," collected and translated by Paul Taylor, in *Puro Mexicano,* ed. J. F. Dobie 232–33.
71. "Corrido de la emigración," in *Puro Mexicano,* ed. J. F. Dobie, 234–35.
72. "Deportados," Boatright 156.
73. "Los Deportados," Shular 233.
74. "Defensa de los Norteños," Shular 234.
75. "Vida, Proceso, y Muerte de Aurelio Pompa," Shular 21.
76. "Deportados," Boatright 155.
77. "Los Inmigrantes," Gamio, *Mexican Immigration* 86.
78. "El Enganchado," Taylor, *Mexican Labor: Chicago* vii: "*puro inglis,*" "*regüenos pa'l charleston,*" "*casi encueradas,*" "*pintada como piñata,*" "*esa tonteada,*" "*fader*": deformation of "father"; "*estor*": deformation of "the store"; Michoacán: a state in Mexico.
79. "El Rancho donde yo nací," Gamio, *Mexican Immigration* 88–89.
80. "El Ferrocarril," Gamio, *Mexican Immigration* 93.
81. "El Renegado," Gamio, *Mexican Immigration* 93–94.
82. "El Padre del Charro Vargas," Gamio, *Mexican Immigration* 95.
83. "Las Pelonas," Gamio, *Mexican Immigration* 89; *metate*: stone utensil for grinding of cacao beans and corn.
84. "La Vida Moderna," Texas Folklore Archive P 2–9.
85. "La Vida Moderna," Texas Folklore Archive P 2–9; "*leonas.*"
86. "La Guerra Mundial," Campa 107.
87. "La Guerra Mundial," Campa 109–10.
88. See also chap. 8, "Mexican Slapstick."

89. "Los Mexicanos Que Hablan Inglés," Texas Folklore Archive P 13-4.

90. "Los Mexicanos," Texas Folklore Archive P 13-4; *real*: 12.5 U.S. cents. Compare this with another version collected by Campa, "Canción Inglés" (see note 1 above).

91. Campa 214; *pochis*: the correct form of the plural is *pochos*. This may be as a hybrid form, midway between *pochos* and what would be the word with an English plural: *poches*.

92. In the poem "A una niña de ese país," collected by A. M. Espinosa, *Romancero de Nuevo Méjico* (Madrid: Consejo Superior, 1953) 264.

93. "Viva México," Texas Folklore Archive P 43-2.

94. "Corrido Pensilvanio," collected by Taylor, *Mexican Labor: Bethlehem* ix: "*los que ya saben inglear.*"

95. See the short story "El mejicano que creía que sabía hablar inglés" [The Mexican who thought he could speak English], collected in Manassa, Colorado, reported by Juan B. Rael, *Cuentos Españoles de Colorado y Nuevo Méjico*, 2 vols. (Stanford: Stanford UP, 1957) 2: (no. 433) 537. The author explains: "In all cases, the stories were transcribed verbatim and the narrator's archaic and sometimes incorrect Spanish was retained" (p. 7).

96. "El Tonto" [The idiot], Rael (no. 51) 119–20.

97. "El Paisano," Rael 537. The three stories "El mejicano que creía que sabía hablar inglés," "El Tonto," and "El Paisano" were also collected by A. M. Espinosa, *Cuentos Populares Españoles* (Madrid: Consejo Superior, 1947) nos. 23, 24, 51.

98. "La Americanita," collected by A. M. Espinosa in *Romancero de Nuevo Méjico* 264.

99. "La Americanita," Espinosa, *Romancero* 264.

100. "La Americanita," Espinosa, *Romancero* 264.

101. "Los Americanos," Espinosa, *Romancero* 249.

102. "Los Americanos," Espinosa, *Romancero* 250.

103. "Sinfonía de Combate," Shular 26.

104. Ralph Ellison, "The Blues," *New York Review of Books* 6 Feb. 1964: 5–7.

105. "La de la 'Nagua Azul' " [The girl in the blue skirt], collected by Gamio, in *Mexican Immigration* 90.

106. Rumel Fuentes, "Corridos de Rumel," *El Grito* 6 (1973): 9; ". . . a sort of 'emotional escape valve.' "

Part Two. The Invisible but Invincible Minority

1. This may be translated as "The invisible but invincible minority." National Education Association, Department of Rural Education, *Report of the N.E.A.-Tucson Survey of the Teaching of Spanish to the Spanish-Speaking* (Washington, D.C.: National Education Association, 1966) (no page reference). An objective of this commission was bilingualism in the schools.

2. Charles Goldfinch, "Juan N. Cortina 1824–1892: A Re-Appraisal," M.A. thesis, U of Chicago, 1949.

3. Mexican-Americans distinguished themselves by numerous acts of heroism, in particular, at Bataan in the Philippines, where the New Mexico National Guard was stationed when war broke out. On the attitude of Mexican-American soldiers, see Raúl Morín, *Among the Valiant: Mexican-Americans in World War II and Korea* (Alhambra, Calif: Borden, 1963).

4. These riots, also called the Pachuco Riots, took place in Los Angeles and were provoked by two incidents. The first was the "Sleepy Lagoon" case. A young Mexican-American was found dead in August 1942, and seventeen *pachucos* were found guilty of his murder; some were sentenced to life imprisonment. (Two years later the sentence, found to be unjust, was revoked.) The year 1943 was marked by clashes between *pachucos* and American sailors stationed in San Pedro and San Diego, who spent their leave time with young Mexican-American women in Los Angeles. Their rivalry degenerated into a conflict when several sailors were beaten in the Mexican barrio. In June, the Navy, supported by the police, made a punitive expedition against the *pachucos* of East Los Angeles.

5. Refers to Beatrice Griffith, whose short story "In the Flow of Time" (*Common Ground* 9 [1948]: 13–20) relates the incidents of June 1943.

6. Octavio Paz, *El laberinto de la soledad* (Mexico City: Fondo de Cultura, 1959) 14: "*A través de un dandismo grotesco y de una conducta anárquica, señalan no tanto la injusticia o incapacidad de una sociedad que no ha logrado asimilarlos, como su voluntad personal de seguir siendo distintos.*"

7. On the *pachuco* dialect, its origins, and its influence on young Mexican-Americans, see the interesting study by George C. Barker, *Pachuco: An American-Spanish Argot and Its Social Functions in Tucson, Arizona* (1950; Tucson: U of Arizona P, 1970), a study containing a glossary of terms and a list of a *pochismos* specific to Tucson. See also Beatrice Griffith, "The Pachuco Patois," *Common Ground* 7 (1947): 77–84.

8. Octavio Paz reports that when he arrived in the United States in 1943, there were more than one million people of Mexican ancestry in Los Angeles alone (Paz 12).

9. Paz 13: "*No reivindican su raza ni la nacionalidad de sus ante-pasados. A pesar de que su actitud revela una obstinada y casi fanática voluntad de ser, esa voluntad no afirma nada concreto sino la decisión-ambigua como se verá—de no ser como los otros que los rodean. El 'pachuco' no quiere volver a su origen mexicano; tampoco—al menos en aparencia—desea fundirse a la vida norteamericana.*"

10. The *bracero* program ended in 1964. See Rachel Ertel, Geneviève Fabre, and Elise Marienstras, *En Marge: Les Minorités aux Etats-Unis* (Paris: Maspero, 1971) 207–08.

11. The Immigration and Nationality Act of 1952 outlawed the importation, transportation, and sheltering of illegal immigrants. Roundups were carried out in the barrios. In 1953, 875,000 "wetbacks" were apprehended; in 1954, 1,035,282. See Rudolfo Acuña, *A Mexican American Chronicle* (New York: American Book Co., 1971) 127.

12. See Carey McWilliams, *North From Mexico: The Spanish-Speaking People of the United States*, 2nd ed. (New York: Greenwood, 1969) 145: "Without attempting to fix an arbitrary date it can be said that the Spanish-Speaking began to develop a new political awareness and self-consciousness as a minority in the wake of World War II and more noticeably, since the early 1950's when the Negro Civil Rights movement began to emerge."

13. José Antonio Villarreal, *Pocho* (Garden City, N.Y.: Doubleday, 1959).

Chapter 8. Flight Into the Past

1. William Faulkner, *Go Down Moses* (1942; Harmondsworth, Eng.: Penguin, 1970).

2. Jack Kerouac, *On the Road* (1957; Harmondsworth, Eng.: Penguin, 1972). Two years before the novel was published, parts of chaps. 12 and 13 of Book 1 appeared as

"The Mexican Girl," *Paris Review* 11 (1955): 9–32. The California episode was part of the fourth journey and serves as a conclusion to Book 1. This was the reason the episode was lengthened. It was the only section published separately.

3. Quoted from Robert Granat's short story, "To Endure," *The Chicano: From Caricature to Self-Portrait*, ed. Edward Simmen (New York: NAL, 1971) 228–35. The story appeared in *New Mexico Quarterly* 28 (1958): 46–53; it was reprinted in *Prize Stories 1960: The O. Henry Awards*.

4. John Steinbeck, *The Pastures of Heaven* (New York: Viking, 1932); Steinbeck, *The Long Valley* (New York: Viking, 1938).

5. Oliver LaFarge, *Behind the Mountains* (Boston: Houghton, 1956) 151.

6. Robert Bright, *The Life and Death of Little Jo* (Garden City, N.Y.: Doubleday, 1944).

7. Frank Waters, *People of the Valley* (Chicago: Swallow, 1941) 29.

8. Waters 266.

9. Helen Stevens, "The Black Shawl," *Southwest Review* 32 (1947): 295–300.

10. Agnes Morley Cleaveland, *No Life for a Lady* (Boston: Houghton, 1941) 117.

11. Roy Rosen, "Music for the Night," *Southwest Review* 38 (1953): 113.

12. Stevens 297.

13. LaFarge 151.

14. LaFarge 152.

15. Rosen 104.

16. Rosen 104.

17. Alvin Gordon, *Inherit the Earth: Stories from Mexican Ranch Life* (Tucson: U of Arizona P, 1963).

18. LaFarge's *Behind the Mountains* appeared in installments in the *New Yorker* from 1951 to 1954, with the exception of chaps. 4, 7, and 10; the other sections were slightly reworked for the book's publication. It was the only work to treat this subject, even though the author's wife belonged to a great Hispanic-American family. LaFarge is better known for his works on Indians; his novel *Laughing Boy* earned him the Pulitzer Prize in 1929.

19. LaFarge 103.

20. Harvey Fergusson, *The Conquest of Don Pedro* (New York: William Morrow, 1954); Paul Horgan, *The Common Heart* (New York: Harper, 1942); Jane Barry, *A Shadow of Eagles* (Garden City, N.Y.: Doubleday, 1964).

21. One of the greatest Hispanic-American families, descended from Alvar Núñez Cabeza de Vaca, a sixteenth-century Spanish explorer.

22. LaFarge 123.

23. In his introduction to the sociological study by Oscar Lewis, *Five Families* (New York: Basic Books, 1959) ix, LaFarge writes: "All of the families in this book consist of people whose culture is what we usually call 'in transition,' meaning that it is going to hell in a handbasket before the onslaught of the Age of Technology."

24. Conrad Richter, *The Lady* (New York: Knopf, 1957).

25. Waters 9.

26. Rosen 103.

27. Rosen 103.

28. *Le Monde* (Paris), 5 April 1974: 15.

29. Walter van Tilburg Clark, *The Ox-Bow Incident* (New York: Readers Club, 1942)

233–34. The Chicano critic F. A. Ríos points out the survival of this stereotype, citing this novel specifically ("The Mexican in Fact, Fiction, and Folklore," *Voices of Aztlán: Chicano Literature of Today*, ed. Dorothy Harth and Lewis Baldwin [New York: NAL, 1974] 63).

30. Waters 239.

31. See also note 3 above.

32. Granat, "To Endure," Simmen 235.

33. Waters 13. Faulkner used images from nature to describe Mollie, the Black mother in *Go Down Moses* 83.

34. Kerouac 95: "The old man was yelling. But the sad, fat brown mother prevailed, as she always does among the great fellahin peoples of the world. . . ."

35. Florence Crannel Means, *Teresita of the Valley* (Boston: Houghton, 1943).

36. Faulkner 129.

37. Kerouac uses the term of Oswald Spengler, who classifies people into three categories: primitive peoples, peoples of culture, and "fellah" peoples. The fellah is basic, neither cultured, nor civilized, nor primitive, the "ahistoric" eternal peasant (*Le Déclin de l'Occident*, trans. M. Tazerout [Paris: Gallimard, 1948] 2: 145 +). In Kerouac, the fellah is the original and primitive man, whom neither civilization nor culture has cut off from the sources of life.

38. John Steinbeck, *Travels with Charley: In Search of America* (New York: Viking, 1962).

39. John Steinbeck, *The Wayward Bus* (New York: Viking, 1947).

40. Steinbeck, *Wayward Bus* 242.

41. Kerouac 93.

42. Kerouac 93.

43. Steinbeck, *Travels with Charley* 201.

44. See Peter Lisca: "Steinbeck's novels and stories often contain groves, willow thickets by a river, and caves which figure prominently in the action. . . . For George and Lennie, as for other Steinbeck heroes, coming to a cave or thicket by a river symbolizes a retreat from the world to primeval innocence" (*The Wide World of John Steinbeck* [New Brunswick, N.J.: Rutgers UP, 1958] 135).

45. Steinbeck, *Wayward Bus* 264.

46. Steinbeck, *Wayward Bus* 245.

47. Fergusson (*The Conquest of Don Pedro*) and Horgan (*The Common Heart*) remained faithful to New Mexico. The principal interest of their works resides in their depiction of the disappearance of the great Hispanic-American families of the past.

48. Cited in Steinbeck, *Travels with Charley* 202.

49. Steinbeck, *Travels with Charley* 198.

50. Kerouac 88.

51. Kerouac 89.

52. Kerouac 255–56.

53. Steinbeck, *Travels with Charley* 200.

54. Steinbeck, *Wayward Bus* 35.

55. Frank Goodwyn, *The Black Bull* (Garden City, N.Y.: Doubleday, 1958) 141.

56. Fergusson 106.

57. See Arthur L. Campa: "In Spanish, even grammatically, the future is of little importance. In the last decade the future subjunctive has disappeared; the future tense is

formed with the *present* of the auxiliary, and we continue to use the present to express a future!" ("Mañana is Today," *Southwesterners Write*, ed. T. M. Pearce and A. P. Thomason [Albuquerque: U of New Mexico P, 1946] 296).

58. Kerouac 90.

59. Kerouac 90–91.

60. Kerouac 88.

61. Kerouac 90.

62. Kerouac 88.

63. Kerouac 89.

64. Lisca 233: "the damned, those in Purgatory and the saved or elect."

65. Steinbeck, *Wayward Bus* 141.

66. Steinbeck, *Wayward Bus* 6.

67. Steinbeck, *Wayward Bus* 222.

68. Steinbeck, *Wayward Bus* 266–67.

69. Fergusson 115–16.

70. Fergusson 56–57.

71. Horgan 284.

72. Goodwyn 142.

73. Kerouac 169.

74. Kerouac 79.

75. Kerouac 284.

76. Steinbeck, *Travels with Charley* 199.

77. Beaumarchais, *Le Barbier de Séville*, act 1, scene 2.

78. See the brief short story by Ray Bradbury, "I See You Never," (*The Golden Apples of the Sun* [London: Transworld, 1956] 89–92). The drama of repatriation, about a Mexican who has come to work in Los Angeles with a temporary visa, is treated as a playful light opera. After thirty months of happily sharing the same house, the man and his landlady realize emotionally at the moment of his departure that they will never see one another again.

79. Ray Bradbury, "The Little Mice," *The Day It Rained Forever* (London: Hart-Davis, 1959) 196.

80. Bradbury, "The Little Mice" 195.

81. As in Bradbury's *Farenheit 451*, for example. It is often through Mexicans from Mexico that the author criticizes the Anglo mentality ("Sun and Shadow," *The Golden Apples of the Sun* 141–50), or capitalism ("And the Rock Cried Out," *The Day It Rained Forever* 218–44).

82. Frank Goodwyn, *The Magic of Limping John* (New York: Farrar, 1944).

83. Larry Harris, "Mex," *The Fantastic Universe Omnibus*, ed. H. S. Santesson (Englewood Cliffs, N.J.: Prentice, 1960) 157.

84. Alice Marriott, "El Zopilote," *Southwest Review* 32 (1947): 284.

85. Bradbury, "The Wonderful Ice Cream Suit," *The Day It Rained Forever* 49.

86. Bradbury, "Ice Cream Suit" 63.

87. Bradbury, "Ice Cream Suit" 63.

88. Bradbury, "En la Noche," *The Golden Apples of the Sun* 136–41.

89. William E. Barrett, "Señor Payroll," Simmen 159–63.

90. Granat, "Sánchez and the Vibora," Simmen 218. Quetzalcoatl was the Toltec god of air and water, represented by a serpent who wore the plumage of the quetzal, a bird of the Guatemala highlands held sacred by the Mayas. His priests opposed human

sacrifices. In later legends he had white skin and a long white beard, and came to Mexico from the East by sea. The legend linked the fall of the Toltecs with the departure of this god.

91. Granat, "Sánchez," Simmen 218.

92. Granat, "Sánchez," Simmen 220.

93. *Cabrón*: a Spanish swear word with no exact equivalent in English; *sanamagán*: phonic transposition of "son of a gun."

94. Granat, "Sánchez," Simmen 224.

95. Kerouac 94.

96. LaFarge vi.

97. Kerouac 91.

98. LaFarge 3.

Chapter 9. The Barrio: Refuge and Trap

1. Sylvan Karchmer, "A Fistful of Alamo Heroes," *The Chicano*, ed. Edward Simmen (New York: NAL, 1971) 167. The story first appeared in the *University of Kansas City Review* Summer 1950.

2. The term "peon-lover" is based upon "nigger-lover."

3. Karchmer 167.

4. Edna Ferber, *Giant* (New York: Grosset, 1952) 160.

5. In another novel of the same period, *Ice Palace* (1958), Ferber describes the fabulous riches of the Anglos who exploit the resources of Alaska; she commiserates with the impoverished Eskimos.

6. While the novel centers upon the great size of Texas, the film *Giant* (written by Ferber, directed by George Stevens and performed by nonconformist actors such as James Dean), stresses social problems.

7. To cite only a few: "It reads like broad caricature of new quick money; I can't imagine even Texans will like it. It has money-snob appeal for the masses, but for this reader, it created frank distaste." (*Kirkus Reviews* 15 July 1952). "*Giant* will be joyfully received in forty-seven states and avidly though angrily read in Texas. . . ." (*Saturday Review* 27 Sept. 1952). "Some years ago, Edna Ferber wrote a book about a very tiny group of very rich Texans. Her description was accurate, so far as my knowledge extends, but the emphasis was one of disparagement. And instantly the book was attacked by Texans of all groups, classes and professions." (John Steinbeck, *Travels with Charley: In Search of America* [New York: Viking, 1962] 227–28).

8. See also note 1 above.

9. Ferber 333.

10. Ferber 10.

11. Ferber 217–18.

12. Don Mankiewicz, *Trial* (New York: Harper, 1955) 8.

13. The exclusive use of English in the schools was coupled for a long time with a systematic denigration of Spanish; Mexican schoolchildren were often physically punished for speaking their native language. Not until the 1960s and 1970s was the value of bilingualism in education recognized. W. H. Cooke explains educational policy toward Mexican-Americans: "The characteristics of all Mexican-Americans have been set in the minds of most citizens by the descriptions of these early peasants who spoke a foreign

tongue and lived unto themselves in ways that seemed uninviting and even squalid. It did not look like discrimination twenty-five years ago to furnish these people with a school and a teacher or two. The building did not have to be much better than their homes. The teacher might have been just anybody who would go 'down there'; no results were to be expected" ("The Segregation of Mexican-American School Children in Southern California," *A Documentary History of the Mexican Americans*, ed. Wayne Moquin and Charles Van Doren [New York: Praeger, 1971] 423). The article first appeared in *School and Society* 5 June 1948: 418.

14. In August 1947, the educational segregation of Mexican-American children was declared illegal in California (Westminster School Case); and in June 1948 in Texas (Delgado Case).

15. Ferber 154–55.

16. Ferber 155.

17. Ferber 156. Oliver LaFarge speaks in the same terms about the teacher of his wife Consuelo: "She was a mean woman, who brought to Las Vegas all of a lower-middle-class Middle Westerner's resentment of and hostility toward the exotic characteristics of the Spanish Southwest . . ." (*Behind the Mountains* [Boston: Houghton, 1951] [no page reference]).

18. William E. Barrett, *The Shadows of the Images* (Kingswood, Eng.: Heinemann, 1954) 164.

19. Ferber 28.

20. Ferber 201.

21. John H. Allen, *Southwest* (Philadelphia: Lippincott, 1952).

22. Ferber 159.

23. Ferber 159.

24. Ferber 277.

25. See Carey McWilliams: "California farm industrialists have always justified their employment of alien labor on the ground that with particular reference to the Mexican, migratory labor left the State after the harvest season and, therefore, presented no social problem. The fable of the Mexican as a 'homing pigeon' has, however, been eloquently refuted by the records" (*Factories in the Field: The Story of Migratory Farm Labor in California* [Boston: Little, 1939] 148).

26. Barrett 62.

27. Barrett 107.

28. The supporters of Zapata fought for social and agrarian reform. After the Mexican Revolution (1910–17), there were internal struggles between revolutionaries led by Zapata and reactionaries who favored social order. The *federales* were a formidable police force.

29. Irving Shulman, *The Square Trap* (Boston: Little, 1953) 106.

30. Shulman 107.

31. See John Steinbeck, *Their Blood Is Strong* (San Francisco: Lubin, 1938); McWilliams (*Factories in the Fields* 298), mentions a study on these camps carried out by the Resettlement Administration. In it, the producers made their views known: "1. They wanted the camps . . . to be located on *private property*; 2. They insisted that the facilities of the camp be as meager as possible so as to emphasize the transient nature of the shelter . . . ; 3. They demanded that the supervisor of each camp should be under the control of a local committee of growers; and, 4. that the camps be strictly regulated so as to prevent the spread of subversive ideas. . . ."

32. This term is rare but has the advantage of being accurate. Only those who swim

across the Rio Grande to get to Texas should be called "wetbacks." All other illegal immigrants are "border-jumpers."

33. Ferber 269.

34. Ferber 318.

35. Claud Garner, *Wetback* (New York: Coward-McCann, 1947) 63–64.

36. Ferber 222. A coyote is a small, clever animal that feeds on carrion; by extension, in the Mexican idiom, it is a shady businessman who acts as a go-between. Here it's a man who smuggles in foreign workers (in Spanish *coyote* = labor contractor).

37. James K. Bowman, "El Patrón," Simmen 176.

38. Ferber 224.

39. Ferber 318–19.

40. Ferber 317.

41. Garner 59. On repatriation, see Abraham Hoffman, *Unwanted Mexican Americans in the Great Depression: Repatriation Pressures, 1929–1939* (Tucson: U of Arizona P, 1974) 166–69.

42. See Arturo Madrid-Barela, "Alambristas, Braceros, Mojados, Norteños: Aliens in Aztlán, An Interpretative Essay," *Aztlán: International Journal of Chicano Studies Research* 6 (1975): 27–42.

43. Bowman, "El Patrón," Simmen 175.

44. Bowman, "El Patrón," Simmen 179.

45. Barrett 129 + ; *El socorrido*: public welfare program.

46. Beatrice Griffith, "In the Flow of Time," *Best American Short Stories of 1949*, ed. Martha Foley (Boston: Houghton, 1949) 110: "The police were standing along the sides holding their night sticks, looking pleased about the whole thing."

47. Hart Stilwell, *Border City* (Garden City, N.Y.: Doubleday, 1945).

48. In 1931, a group of young, unemployed Blacks from Scottsboro, Ala., were condemned to death for raping two white prostitutes. The Communist newspaper, the *Daily Worker*, succeeded in making the case known throughout the world. Several years later, the case was reopened and the prisoners still living were released.

49. Ferber 120.

50. Ferber 146.

51. Francis Parkman, *The Oregon Trail* (Garden City, N.Y.: Garden City Publ., 1948) 260: "They disappeared as they saw us approach."

52. Jack London, "The Mexican," Simmen 91: "He gave no confidences. He repelled all probing."

53. Ferber 109.

54. Octavio Paz, *El laberinto de la soledad* (Mexico City: Cuadernos Americanos, 1950) 18: "*La existencia de un sentimiento de real o supuesta inferioridad frente al mundo podría explicar, parcialmente al menos, la reserva con que el mexicano se presenta ante los demás y la violencia inesperada con que las fuerzas reprimidas rompen esa máscara impasible.*"

55. Helen Stevens, "The Black Shawl," *Southwest Review* 32 (1947): 300.

56. Shulman 107.

57. Ferber 220.

58. See also note 82 below.

59. Barrett 203.

60. Shulman 103.

61. Shulman 9. Olvera Street: a short, tourist-oriented street in Los Angeles with many Mexican shops and restaurants.

62. Shulman 374.

63. Karchmer 166.

64. Norman Mailer, *The Naked and the Dead* (New York: NAL, 1948) 55.

65. Mailer 114.

66. Griffith, "In the Flow of Time," Foley 115.

67. Griffith, "In the Flow of Time," Foley 114.

68. Ferber 414.

69. Ferber 415.

70. Griffith, "In the Flow of Time," Foley 116.

71. Beatrice Griffith, "American Me," *Literatura Chicana: Texto y contexto. Chicano Literature: Text and Context*, ed. Antonia Shular (Englewood Cliffs, N.J.: Prentice, 1972) 254.

72. Shulman 358.

73. Shulman 32.

74. Shulman 15. Paz compares this style of dress to the baroque, eccentric clothing worn by young Frenchmen at the end of the occupation. He sees the French styles as a form of resistance to Germanic order and also as an indirect imitation of the *pachuco* style (*El laberinto* 16–17, note 3).

75. Shulman 13.

76. Shulman 133. Ferber uses only one example, in the language affected by young Angel Obregón, whom she does not present as a *pachuco*. The author used the word *güisa* ("girl"), probably without distinguishing it from the *pochismos* (Anglicized Spanish) that preceded it: "He did not speak of an automobile as a coche but as a carro. A battery was not an acumulador but a bateria. A truck was Hispanicized as a troca. A girl was a güisa—a chick." (*Giant* 384).

77. In Shulman, it has an adjectival value: "la raza kids" (*The Square Trap* 97).

78. Shulman 45.

79. Ferber 424–25. Among these organizations are the League of United Latin American Citizens (founded in Texas in 1929); Club Latino Americano de Long Beach y Signal Hill (Calif., 1933); and Pan American Student Forum of Texas (Texas, 1943).

80. Barrett 161.

81. Barrett 256.

82. On the activities of the American Communist party and its role during the Depression, see E. Browder, "The American Communist Party in the Thirties," *As We Saw the Thirties*, ed. Rita J. Simon (Urbana: U of Illinois P, 1967) 216–53. During the Depression, the Communists also exploited the discontent of Mexican-American workers, but they recruited more Blacks than Mexican-Americans as members. Later on, the Chicano movement clearly set forth its distinctions from Communist ideology.

83. Also nicknamed Tío Taco, Tío Tomás. Chicano militants also use the term "coconut," meaning brown on the outside and white on the inside.

84. Ferber 221.

85. Ferber 221.

86. Richard C. Brown, "Mr. Iscariot," Simmen 203–13.

87. Shulman 26.

88. Brown, "Mr. Iscariot," Simmen 209.

89. Norman D. Humphrey believes that immigration to the United States created problems for the Mexican family that would not have existed had they remained in Mexico ("The Changing Structure of the Detroit Mexican Family," *American Sociological Review* 9 [1944]: 622–26).

90. Allen 145.
91. Ferber 384–85.
92. Shulman 93.
93. Ferber 385.
94. Shulman 108.
95. Shulman 9–10.

The Mexican-American Point of View: The First Literary Spokesmen

1. P. Galindo, "The Mexican-American Devil's Dictionary," *El Grito* 6 (1973): 42.

2. *Mario Suárez*, a migrant worker who became professor of romance languages at the University of Texas.

Arnulfo D. Trejo, a graduate of the University of Arizona, was assistant librarian at Long Beach State College and later served as professor of library science at the University of Arizona.

José Antonio Villarreal, born in California to a family of migrant workers, graduated in 1950 from the University of California after four years in the navy. He wrote a novel, *Pocho*, articles for newspapers and literary journals, then a second novel, *The Fifth Horseman* (1974).

Ernesto Galarza, born in Mexico in 1905, spent his youth in the barrio of Sacramento, Calif. He recounted his family's immigration in *Barrio Boy* (1971). He is a graduate of Columbia University. During the 1930s, he tried unsuccessfully to found a union in the Imperial Valley. In 1940, he became director of the Division of Labor and Social Information but resigned in 1946 to protest U.S. policy in Latin America. Very active within the National Agricultural Workers Union (N.A.W.U.), he worked to end the *bracero* program, which was canceled in 1964; he is the guiding force of the Southwest Council of La Raza.

3. Philip Ortego, "The Chicano Renaissance," *Social Casework* 52 (1971): 303.

4. John Rechy, "Mardi-Gras," *Evergreen Review* 2 (1958): 60–70; idem, "Fl Paso del Norte," *Evergreen Review* 2 (1958): 127–40.

5. Fray Angélico Chávez (Manuel), *Eleven Lady-Lyrics and Other Poems* (Paterson, N.J.: St. Anthony, 1945). Philip Ortego writes: ". . . Fray Angélico Chávez points to the fact that the Mexican-American could (and did) write poetry about and engendered by the same universal themes which motivated Anglo-American poets" ("Backgrounds of Mexican-American Literature," diss., U of New Mexico, 1971, 204).

6. See Elroy Bode, "The Making of a Legend," *Texas Observer* 30 March 1973: 1–5. The story of Chester Seltzer-Amado Muro is a curious one. Not wanting his future to depend upon his father, the publisher of the *Cleveland Press*, he left for the Southwest, where he took the family name of his Mexican wife. He was a born rebel: in 1942, when he was 27 years old, he declared himself a conscientious objector and refused to do his military service, which earned him three years in prison. Later, his opposition to the Vietnam War reportedly cost him his position at the *San Diego Union*; he wrote stories about "hoboes": "Road Buddy" (1966), "Night Train to Fort Worth" (1967), "Hobo Jungle" (1970), among others. He died in 1971. Ortego was the first to uncover Amado Muro's true identity. In his article on Chicano literature, John Womack, Jr., writes: "The funniest, brightest, most moving, accomplished and prolific Mexican American writer used to be Amado Muro, a veritable Isaac Babel of the Southwest. . . . But Muro

was really an Anglo, Chester Seltzer, and is now dead." In a footnote, Womack cites Ortego as the source of his information ("Who Are the Chicanos?" *New York Review of Books* 31 Aug. 1972: 17).

7. Seltzer-Muro's fictional biography is found in an anthology edited by Edward Ludwig and James Santibañez, *The Chicanos: Mexican American Voices* (Baltimore: Penguin, 1971) 276–77: "Amado Muro is a first generation Mexican American who was born in Parral, Chihuahua, Mexico, and came to El Paso, Texas, with his parents, at the age of nine.

"He has lived most of his life in El Paso, where he has worked at a number of jobs, one of the most recent being that of laborer on the Pacific Fruit Express ice docks.

"His avocation is writing stories and sketches, mostly of old Mexico, where he recalls his grandfather's making a living by playing his Ramírez guitar and singing revolutionary ballads such as 'The Wet Buzzard' and 'The Three Bald-Headed Women.' "

8. Ortego himself took Amado Jesús Muro for a Mexican American in "The Chicano Renaissance" 303. In his anthology *The Chicano: From Caricature to Self-Portrait* (New York: NAL, 1971) editor Edward Simmen ranks Muro among the Mexican-American writers. Muro himself took pleasure in the confusion; in his autobiographical short story "Cecilia Rosas," he appears as a young Mexican-American who wishes to pass for an American to win the heart of the beautiful Cecilia Rosas (Simmen 279–91).

Chapter 10. In the Traditional Framework of the Barrio

1. Mario Suárez, "Mexican Heaven," *Arizona Quarterly* 6 (1950): 314.
2. Suárez, "El Hoyo," *Aztlán: An Anthology of Mexican American Literature*, ed. Luis Valdez and Stan Steiner (New York: Knopf, 1972) 155.
3. Suárez, "El Hoyo" 155.
4. Suárez, "Southside Run," *Arizona Quarterly* 4 (1948): 365.
5. Suárez, "Southside Run" 365.
6. Amado Muro, "Cecilia Rosas," *The Chicano: From Caricature to Self-Portrait*, ed. Edward Simmen (New York: NAL, 1971) 286.
7. John Rechy, "El Paso del Norte," *Evergreen Review* 2 (1958): 130.
8. Suárez, "Southside Run" 366.
9. Suárez, "El Hoyo" 155.
10. Suárez, "El Hoyo" 157.
11. Amado Muro, "Sunday in Little Chihuahua," *Voices of Aztlán: Chicano Literature of Today*, ed. Dorothy Harth and Lewis Baldwin (New York: NAL, 1974) 16–23.
12. Rechy, "El Paso del Norte," *Evergreen Review* 127. D.F. means Distrito Federal.
13. Suárez, "Kid Zopilote," *Arizona Quarterly* 3 (1947): 132.
14. Suárez, "Kid Zopilote" 137.
15. Collected by Arthur L. Campa, *Spanish Folk-Poetry in New Mexico* (Albuquerque, U of New Mexico P, 1946) 216.
16. Suárez, "Mexican Heaven" 310.
17. Suárez, "Mexican Heaven" 311.
18. Suárez, "El Hoyo" 156.
19. José Antonio Villarreal, *Pocho* (Garden City, N.Y.: Doubleday, 1970) 28.
20. Muro, "Cecilia Rosas" 286.
21. John Rechy, *City of Night* (New York: Grove, 1964) 11.

22. Rechy, "El Paso del Norte," *Literatura Chicana: Texto y contexto. Chicano Literature: Text and Context*, ed. Antonia Shular et al. (Englewood Cliffs, N.J.: Prentice, 1972) 162.

23. John Rechy, "Mardi-Gras," *Evergreen Review* 2 (1958): 69.

24. Villarreal 29.

25. Rechy, "El Paso del Norte," Shular 163.

26. Rechy, "El Paso del Norte," Shular 164.

27. Rechy, "El Paso del Norte," *Evergreen Review* 135.

28. Muro, "María Tepache," Simmen 128.

29. Fray Angélico Chávez, *New Mexico Triptych* (Paterson, N.J.: St. Anthony, 1940) 59–76.

30. Rechy, "El Paso del Norte," Shular 162.

31. Rechy, "El Paso del Norte," Shular 159.

32. Chávez, "The Penitente Thief," *New Mexico Triptych* 28. Chávez returns to this idea in another short story, "The Fiddler and the Angelito," *Southwest Review* 32 (1947): 242–44. It used to be thought that innocent children became *angelitos* ("little angels") the day they died, while adults' sins justified the necessity, indeed the cruelty, of the *penitente* ceremonies.

33. Suárez, "El Hoyo" 155.

34. Villarreal 131.

35. Muro, "María Tepache" 127, 128, 131.

36. Amado Muro, "Going to Market," *Arizona Quarterly* 18 (1962): 209.

37. María Elvira Bermúdez, *La Vida Familiar del Mexicano* (Mexico City: Robredo, 1955) 98.

38. See Miguel Montiel, "The Social Science Myth of the Mexican American Family," *Voices of Aztlán*, ed. Dorothy Harth and Lewis Baldwin, 40–47. "The myth of the Mexican family has been created because of certain questionable assumptions that have dominated Mexican and Mexican American family studies. First and foremost is the concept social scientists have regarding *machismo*, as supposedly the underlying cause of Mexican and Mexican-American problems. Secondly, it follows that this formulation is inherently incapable of defining normal behavior and thus automatically labels all Mexican and Mexican-American people as sick—*only in the degree of sickness do they vary*" (p. 46). This criticism is directed at such Anglo-American sociologists as William Madsen, *The Mexican-American of South Texas* (New York: Holt, 1964) 48; R. G. Hayden, "Spanish-Americans of the Southwest: Life Style Patterns and Their Implications," *Welfare in Review* 4 (April 1966): 20; Celia S. Heller, *Mexican American Youth: Forgotten Youth at the Crossroads* (New York: Random, 1966) 34.

39. Villarreal 92.

40. Villarreal 94.

41. Villarreal 131.

42. Villarreal 96.

43. Mario Suárez, "Cuco Goes to a Party," *Arizona Quarterly* 3 (1947): 121–27.

44. Muro, "Sunday in Little Chihuahua" 19.

45. Suárez, "Southside Run" 367. The *padrino* ("godfather") and *madrina* ("godmother") of a child automatically become the *compadre* or *comadre*, or friends, of the parents. Two men may also confer upon one another the honorary title of *compadre* in an excess of emotion, especially when inebriated.

46. Suárez, "Las Comadres," Valdez 158.

47. Villarreal 135.

48. Villarreal 91.

49. Villarreal 92–93.

50. Suárez, "Las Comadres" 163.

51. Suárez, "Las Comadres" 163.

52. Rechy, "El Paso del Norte," *Evergreen Review* 134.

53. John Womack, Jr., calls Suárez's narratives "good vignettes of Tucson's barrio" ("Who Are the Chicanos?" *New York Review of Books* 31 Aug. 1972: 17).

54. Suárez, "Señor Garza," Simmen 268.

55. Suárez, "Señor Garza" 273.

56. Suárez, "Señor Garza" 271.

57. Suárez, "Señor Garza" 269.

58. In "Cuco Goes to a Party" 124, Suárez says that Garza "has always been a good barber and better philosopher."

59. Arnulfo Trejo, "Maistro," *Arizona Quarterly* 16 (1960): 352–56. *Maistro*: dialectical form of the Spanish *maestro*.

60. Suárez, "Maestría," Shular 169.

61. Suárez, "Maestría," Shular 173.

62. Suárez, "Cuco Goes to a Party" 121.

63. Suárez, "Mexican Heaven" 312.

64. Suárez, "Southside Run" 367.

65. Suárez, "Loco-Chu," *Arizona Quarterly* 3 (1947): 128–30.

66. Suárez, "Southside Run" 372–73.

67. Suárez, "Mexican Heaven" 314.

68. Suárez, "Señor Garza" 269.

69. Muro, "María Tepache" 131.

70. Suárez, "Señor Garza" 270.

71. Suárez, "Señor Garza" 268.

72. Trejo 356.

73. Suárez, "El Hoyo" 157.

74. Suárez, "El Hoyo" 157.

75. A monthly, published in English in Phoenix, Ariz., beginning in 1929. It takes its name from the League of United Latin American Citizens, founded in the same year in Texas.

76. *Lulac News* July 1939: 32.

77. Juan Sedillo, "Gentleman of Rio en Medio," *New Mexico Quarterly* 9 (1939): 181–83.

Chapter 11. The Pocho's Dilemma

1. Ernesto Galarza, *Barrio Boy* (New York: Ballantine, 1972) 203.

2. José Antonio Villarreal, *Pocho* (1959; Garden City, N.Y.: Doubleday, 1970) 71.

3. See Philip Ortego, "Moctezuma's Children," *Voices of Aztlán: Chicano Literature of Today*, ed. Dorothy Harth and Lewis Baldwin (New York: NAL, 1974) 122: "For many lexocentric Anglo-Americans this settles the question, the logic being that once a Spanish-speaking child is forbidden the use of Spanish he will then speak fluent idiomatic English like all other Americans. The truth is that the disadvantages are more the product of a thoroughly lexocentric (linguistically chauvinistic) society than they are real. . . ."

4. Villarreal 34.

5. Villarreal 108.

6. Villarreal 106–07.

7. Villarreal 108.

8. Villarreal 48–49.

9. Villarreal 52.

10. Villarreal 43.

11. *Aztlán: International Journal of Chicano Studies Research* 6 (1975): 104.

12. John Rechy, "El Paso del Norte," *Evergreen Review* 2 (1958): 129. Rechy does not give *bracero* the specific meaning it has had since 1942 but rather its general sense of "laborer."

13. Texas Folklore Archive, U of Texas-Austin, P 14-1; composed by Nicanor Torres; collected by A. Paredes in August 1954 in Brownsville, Texas.

14. Rechy 129.

15. Rechy 129.

16. Rechy 129.

17. Rechy 129.

18. Villarreal 97.

19. Villarreal 97.

20. Villarreal 68.

21. Villarreal 77.

22. Villarreal 41–42: ". . . then he told Richard to get the hell away from there, cholo, because they did not want any chilebeans hanging around . . . he started saying things to him to make everybody laugh like 'why don't you go home and eat some tortillas.'"

23. Villarreal 151.

24. Rechy 130. Jive: the speech of the Swing enthusiasts; *la jura* ("the police") is a genuinely *pachuco* term, probably derived from *jurar* ("to take an oath"), as are *la chota* (origin unknown) and *la placa* (inspired by the badges worn by police officers). *Los changos* ("monkeys") and *los cochinos* ("pigs") are more generally Hispanic-American terms.

25. Villarreal 150.

26. Villarreal 150.

27. Villarreal 150.

28. Villarreal 149.

29. Villarreal 149.

30. Amado Muro, "Cecilia Rosas," *The Chicano: From Caricature to Self-Portrait*, ed. Edward Simmen (New York: NAL, 1971) 280.

31. Muro 281.

32. Muro 287.

33. Muro 287–88. Toluca: capital of the state of México.

34. Muro 288.

35. Muro 288.

36. Muro 290.

37. Mario Suárez, "Las Comadres," *Aztlán: An Anthology of Mexican American Literature*, ed. Luis Valdez and Stan Steiner (New York: Knopf, 1972) 159.

38. Suárez, "Las Comadres" 159.

39. Suárez, "Las Comadres" 159.

40. Villarreal 132.

41. Mario Suárez, "Maestría," *Arizona Quarterly* 4 (1948): 373.

42. Villarreal 93.

43. Villarreal 134.

44. Villarreal 135.

45. Villarreal 129.

46. Villarreal 165.

47. Villarreal 165.

48. See Enrique H. López, "Back to Bachimba," *Horizon* 9 (Winter 1967): 81: "Pocho is ordinarily a derogatory term in Mexico (to define it succinctly, a *pocho* is a Mexican slob who has pretensions of being a gringo sonofabitch). . . ."

49. Galarza 202.

50. López 81.

51. I have been unable to find any biographical information on Antonio Plaza. Suárez calls him "the immortal Antonio Plaza" ("Señor Garza," Simmen 270). He apparently was a poet, probably in the nineteenth century; his *Book of Poetry*, popular for decades, was published in Mexico City by a firm whose name has been lost. Juan de Dios Peza was born in Mexico City in 1852; he is primarily known for his poems. See Carlos González Peña, *Historia de la literatura mexicana* (Mexico City: Porrúa, 1966) 193–95.

52. Henri Gobard's terminology, described in "De la véhicularité de la langue anglaise," *Langues Modernes* (Jan. 1972).

53. Villarreal 62.

54. Villarreal 75.

55. Villarreal 95.

56. Villarreal 61.

57. Villarreal 133.

58. Villarreal 133.

59. Villarreal 129.

60. Américo Paredes, "The Hammon and the Beans," Simmen 276.

61. "Ham and Eggs" is a symbol of Anglo civilization for the Mexican-American, and a passkey for Juan Rubio, whose knowledge of English upon arriving in the United States was limited to these two words. He tells his son, who wishes to live like an American: "And next you will tell me that those are not tortillas you are eating but bread, and those are not beans but *hahm an' ecks*" (Villarreal 133).

62. Villarreal 63–64.

63. Villarreal 85.

64. Villarreal 109.

65. Villarreal 152–53.

66. Villarreal 162.

67. Villarreal 175.

68. Villarreal 95.

69. Villarreal 186.

70. "Los Veteranos de 1941," Texas Folklore Archive P 44-3: "*cumplir un deber.*"

71. "Los Veteranos" P 44-3: ". . . *el lindo presidente de los Estados Unidos.*"

72. "Los Veteranos" P 44-3. The entry of Mexico into the war on the side of the United States on 28 May 1942 inspired numerous Mexican *corridos*, among others, the "Corrido de los Japoneses" (Texas Folklore Archive [no reference number]). One finds there the same combative ardor, the same patriotic fervor, the same sense of duty, as in its Texas counterpart.

73. Villarreal 187.

74. Suárez, "Señor Garza," Simmen 270.

75. Villarreal 164.

76. Among others: "Mexican Americans in Upheaval," *Los Angeles Times West Magazine* 18 Sept. 1966: 21–30; "Mexican Americans and the Leadership Crisis," *Los Angeles Times West Magazine* 25 Sept. 1966: 44–50.

77. Edward Simmen, "Chicano: Origin and Meaning," *Pain and Promise: The Chicano Today*, ed. Edward Simmen (New York: NAL, 1972) 56.

Part Three. Chicanos Present Their Own Image

1. Eugene Nelson, "Huelga: New Goals for Labor," *The Nation* 5 June 1967: 724. The grape pickers' strike in Delano, Calif., launched by César Chávez, lasted from 1965 to 1970 and unleashed the Chicano protest movement. For details, see chapter 15.

2. Farnsworth Crowder, quoted by Curt Gentry, *The Last Days of the Late, Great State of California* (New York: Ballantine, 1968) [no page reference].

3. Abelardo Delgado, *Chicano: 25 Pieces of a Chicano Mind* (Denver: Barrio, 1971) 4: "Some mistake chicanismo in that it is so exclusive when actually we are the opposite, including our cuban and puerto rican brothers and even a few anglos whose tequilic hearts are in the right place and who, unable to share in feelings which only a chicano can have, conform themselves with sharing our dreams and our causa."

4. Eugene Nelson, *Huelga: The First Hundred Days of the Great Delano Grape Strike* (Delano, Calif.: Farm Workers Press, 1966) 51.

5. Mark Day, *Forty Acres: César Chávez and the Farm Workers* (New York: Praeger, 1971).

6. Edward Ludwig and James Santibañez, eds., *The Chicanos: Mexican American Voices* (Baltimore: Penguin, 1971) 113–14.

7. Sam Kushner, *Long Road to Delano* (New York: International Publ., 1975). Albert Camarillo (*Aztlán: International Journal of Chicano Studies Research* 6 [1975]: 463–65) congratulates the author for situating his narrative in a historical perspective, while reproaching him for emphasizing the importance of the first socialist-communist Anglo unions, to the detriment of the first Mexican-American workers' organizations. Camarillo praises the following authors for their understanding attitude toward Chávez and the strike: John Gregory Dunne (*Delano* [New York: Farrar, 1971]), Peter Mathiessen (*Sal Si Puedes* [New York: Dell, 1969]), Mark Day (*Forty Acres* [New York: Praeger, 1971]), and Joan London and Henry Anderson (*So Shall Ye Reap* [New York: Crowell, 1971]).

8. Stan Steiner, *La Raza: The Mexican-Americans* (New York: Harper, 1970).

Chapter 12. One Last Beautiful Dream

1. Richard Dokey, "Sánchez," *The Chicano: From Caricature to Self-Portrait*, ed. Edward Simmen (New York: NAL, 1971) 267.

2. C. W. Gusewelle, "Robert Melendez: Retrospect," *Texas Quarterly* 11 (1968): 155–67.

Chapter 13. Marginality and Difference

1. Edward Villaseñor, *Macho!* (New York: Bantam, 1973). See also chapter 15.
2. Eugene Nelson, *The Bracero* (Berkeley: Thorp Springs, 1972).
3. Nelson 102.
4. Leland Frederick Cooley, *California* (New York: Avon, 1973) 520.
5. A film of the same title, based on the book, was made in 1972.
6. In East Los Angeles, near Chavez Ravine.
7. Joseph Wambaugh, *The New Centurions* (New York: Dell, 1972) 45.
8. Wambaugh 308.
9. Wambaugh 309.
10. Wambaugh 352.
11. With the exception of a few detective and western novels, Cox's books deal with sports.
12. William Cox, *Chicano Cruz* (New York: Bantam, 1972) 91.
13. Cox 22.
14. Cox 2.
15. Adalberto Acosta, *Chicanos Can Make It* (New York: Vantage, 1971). See also below, chapter 18, "Chicano Bilingualism" sec.
16. Cox 105.
17. Frank Bonham, *Viva Chicano* (New York: Dell, 1970) 34.
18. Bonham 8.
19. Bonham 119.
20. Bonham 34.
21. Bonham 120.
22. Bonham 120.
23. Nick Vaca, rev. of *Viva Chicano*, by Frank Bonham, *El Grito* 3 (1970): 32.
24. Vaca 32.
25. Vaca 32.
26. Vaca 32.
27. Abelardo Delgado, *Chicano: 25 Pieces of a Chicano Mind* (Denver: Barrio, 1971) 4.

Chapter 14. Mexican-Americans Confront the Debacle

1. Frank Bonham, *Cool Cat* (New York: Dell, 1971) 54.
2. Bonham, *Viva Chicano* (New York: Dell, 1970) 27.
3. Bonham, *Viva Chicano* 98.
4. Bonham, *Viva Chicano* 42.
5. Bonham, *Viva Chicano* 31–32.
6. CON SAFOS (which became "Can't Score" in Chicago) is probably derived from the Spanish nautical term *Zafo* ("free and clear"). Young Chicanos, anxious to make known the meaning of their revolt, gave the term another meaning. The editors of the literary review *Con Safos* explain that this title expresses Chicanos' rejection of their American identity and affirms the moral and aesthetic values of the barrio.
7. Elia Kazan, *The Assassins* (Greenwich: Fawcett, 1973) 170.
8. Kazan 382.
9. Kazan 171.

10. Kazan 107.

11. Kazan 317.

12. Kazan 292.

13. Kazan 293.

14. Joseph Wambaugh, *The New Centurions* (Boston: Little, 1970) 324.

15. Wambaugh 325.

16. Wambaugh 327.

17. Bonham, *Viva Chicano* 36.

18. Bonham, *Viva Chicano* 36.

19. See also Genaro González, "Un Hijo del Sol," *The Chicano: From Caricature to Self-Portrait*, ed. Edward Simmen (New York: NAL, 1971) 310.

Chapter 15. The Chicano Movement

1. Edward Simmen, ed., *Pain and Promise: The Chicano Today* (New York: NAL, 1972) 122.

2. Since a detailed study of the strike and the Chicano movement is not within the scope of this work, the interested reader should consult the bibliography on the matter. César Estrada Chávez was born in 1927 near Yuma, Ariz., of parents who were farmers. Ruined by the Depression, they moved to California in 1937 and settled in the San José barrio of Sal Si Puedes ("Get Out If You Can"), one of the poorest in the state. At seventeen, César enlisted in the Navy and spent two years (1944–45) in the Pacific. An itinerant farm worker at nineteen, he joined the National Agricultural Workers Union; in 1948, he married Helen Fabela, whose father had been a colonel in Villa's army. In 1958, he became general director of the Community Service Organization (C.S.O.), then resigned in 1962 because it refused to allow him to begin a farm workers' union. He then founded his National Farm Workers Association, which had 1,700 members by 1965.

3. It is difficult to establish a date for the start of the Chicano movement. According to Alfredo Cuellar, the decisive impetus was given during conferences held at Loyola University in Los Angeles during the summer of 1966. See Philip Ortego, ed., *We Are Chicanos: An Anthology of Mexican-American Literature* (New York: Washington Square, 1973) 110–11.

4. Luis Valdez, "The Tale of La Raza," *Ramparts* 5 July 1966: 41.

5. Luis A. Solís-Garza, "César Chávez: The Chicano Messiah?" *Pain and Promise*, ed. Edward Simmen 298: "the long awaited 'Messiah' of the Mexican American."

6. Eugene Nelson, *Huelga: The First Hundred Days of the Great Delano Grape Strike* (Delano, Calif.: Farm Workers Press, 1966) 51.

7. Abelardo Delgado, *Chicano: 25 Pieces of a Chicano Mind* (Denver: Barrio, 1971) 19.

8. Rumel Fuentes, "Corrido de César Chávez," *El Grito* 6 (1973): 18.

9. Raúl Salinas, "Los Caudillos" [The leaders], *We Are Chicanos*, ed. Philip Ortego 193. "Dago" = Italian. Refers to the Di Giorgio Fruit Corporation.

10. Nephtalí de León, *!Chicanos! The Living and the Dead!* in *Five Plays* (Denver: Totinem, 1972) 62.

11. Edmund Villaseñor, *Macho!* (New York: Bantam, 1973) 227.

12. English translation of a *corrido* on César Chávez, in Stan Steiner, *La Raza: The Mexican-Americans* (New York: Harper, 1970) 315.

13. Title of the passage in which Chávez elaborates on the march from Delano to Sacramento ("Peregrinación, penitencia, revolución," undated mimeograph reprinted in *Aztlán: An Anthology of Mexican American Literature*, ed. Luis Valdez and Stan Steiner [New York: Knopf, 1972] 385–86.)

14. *Aztlán*, ed. Luis Valdez and Stan Steiner 386: "The penitential process is also in the blood of the Mexican-American, and the Delano march will therefore be one of penance—public penance for the sin of the strikers, their own personal sins as well as their yielding perhaps to feelings of hatred and revenge in the strike itself. They hope by the march to set themselves at peace with the Lord, so that the justice of their cause will be purified of all lesser motivation."

15. On 16 Sept., Chávez's N.F.W.A. decided to take part in the strike called on the 8 Sept. by the Agricultural Workers Organizing Committee (A.W.O.C.), largely made up of Filipinos.

16. Delgado 7.

17. "Viva Huelga en General," *Literatura Chicana: Texto y contexto. Chicano Literature: Text and Context*, ed. Antonia Shular (Englewood Cliffs, N.J.: Prentice, 1972) 71.

18. "*Homeaje a la tercera marcha de Delano; manifestación contra la uva gorda y blanca, Domingo 8 de Septiembre, 1968, San Francisco, Califas.*" "Segundo Canto," Shular 55–56. Augusto Sandino (1893–1934), was a Nicaraguan general who led the guerilla war against the American occupation troops. He died a victim of assassination.

19. Reies López Tijerina, an unusual man who could go for three days with neither food nor sleep, was born in Texas in 1926, into a family of migrant workers. He claimed his grandfather was killed by gringos and stripped of his lands and that his mother's family owned part of the King Ranch. Originally a Catholic, at eighteen he was converted to fundamentalism and joined the Assembly of God Institute at Ysleta de Sur, Texas. He became a preacher, traveling around the United States with his wife and six children. Later, he turned to politics and reverted to the Catholicism of his youth and of his followers.

20. In Oct. 1966, the members of the Alliance occupied a part of Carson National Forest and proclaimed the Republic of San Joaquín del Rio de Chama.

21. See a letter he wrote in August 1968 in the prison of Santa Fe, particularly its conclusion: "Because I know WE ARE RIGHT, I have no regrets as I sit in my jail cell. . . . While others are free, building their personal empires, I am in jail for defending and fighting for the rights of my people. Only my Indo-Hispano people have influenced me to be what I am. I am what I am, for my brothers" (*We Are Chicanos*, ed. Philip Ortego 98).

22. See Norma P. Herring, "Reies López Tijerina: Don Quixote in New Mexico," *Pain and Promise*, ed. Edward Simmen 286–96.

23. Shular 69–70.

24. Rumel Fuentes, "El Corrido de Reies López Tijerina," *El Grito* 6 (1973): 38–39.

25. Philip Ortego, "The Coming of Zamora," *The Chicano*, ed. Edward Simmen 292–98.

26. Salinas, "Los Caudillos," *We Are Chicanos*, ed. Philip Ortego 194.

27. "Corky" Gonzales was born in 1929 in Denver, to a family of farm workers. After finishing high school, he became an amateur featherweight boxing champion. Through politics, he made a place for himself in the Anglo world. In 1965, he per-

manently turned his back on that world and embraced the Chicano cause. In 1968, he joined Tijerina in the Poor People's March on Washington.

28. See *Aztlán*, ed. Luis Valdez and Stan Steiner 404–06.

29. Salinas, "Los Caudillos," *We Are Chicanos*, ed. Philip Ortego 193.

30. Gutiérrez was born in Crystal City in 1945. He earned a degree in political science at Saint Mary's University, San Antonio. The subject of his thesis was "La Raza and Revolution." He currently teaches at the University of Texas-Austin and works in Crystal City for the Colorado Migrant Council.

31. Salinas, "Los Caudillos," *We Are Chicanos*, ed. Philip Ortego 194.

32. *Aztlán*, ed. Luis Valdez and Stan Steiner 311–18.

33. Similar attempts in Mathis, Tex. (1965), and in New Mexico (1966) had failed. On this subject, see Armando B. Rendón, *Chicano Manifesto: The History and Aspirations of the Second Largest Minority in America* (New York: Collier, 1972) 241–75.

34. Particularly active in four south Texas counties.

35. Rumel Fuentes, "Partido La Raza Unida," *El Grito* 6 (1973): 28.

36. Rumel Fuentes, "Walk out en Crystal City," *El Grito* 6 (1973): 24.

37. Rumel Fuentes, "Política en los barrios," *El Grito* 6 (1973): 26.

38. Chairman of the Mayor's Advisory Youth Council of Los Angeles.

39. Salinas, "Los Caudillos," *We Are Chicanos*, ed. Philip Ortego 193.

40. Besides the Brown Berets, a group founded in 1967 in East Los Angeles that spread throughout the Southwest and beyond, there were other less well known youth organizations, such as La Junta and Los Comancheros del Norte, in the mountain villages of New Mexico, and various student groups, such as Mexican American Youth Organization (M.A.Y.O.), Movimiento Estudiantil Chicano de la Raza (M.E.C.H.A.).

41. On the platform of the Brown Berets, see *Aztlán*, ed. Luis Valdez and Stan Steiner 303–05.

42. Chávez, Tijerina, Corky Gonzales and Gutiérrez were the four dominant leaders of the Chicano movement, the Four Horsemen, as they were called by Matt Meier and Feliciano Rivera (*The Chicanos: A History of Mexican Americans* [New York: Hill, 1972] 259–80).

43. George I. Sánchez, "The Default of Leadership" 3, a mimeographed copy of a speech delivered at the Fourth Regional Conference, Southwest Council on Education of the Spanish-Speaking People, Albuquerque, January 23–25, 1950.

44. John R. Martínez, "Leadership and Politics," *La Raza: Forgotten Americans*, ed. Julian Samora (Notre Dame, Ind.: Notre Dame UP, 1966) 52.

45. This expression was used by Philip Ortego in his essay "The Chicano Renaissance," *Social Casework* 52 (1971): 294–307.

46. Jorge Gonzales, "*a delano*" [To Delano], *Voices of Aztlán: Chicano Literature of Today*, ed. Dorothy Harth and Lewis Baldwin (New York: NAL, 1974) 183.

47. In the introduction to *Canto y grito mi liberación* by Ricardo Sánchez (Garden City, N.Y.: Anchor, 1973) 19, he wrote: "Needless to say, the Quinto Sol writers of *El Grito* were leading the way for what has since come to be known as 'the Chicano renaissance.' And Chicano literary production since 1967 has indeed been a renaissance in every sense of the word."

48. Excerpt from the English translation of "El Plan de Santa Barbara," in Shular 85.

49. See the interview by Stan Steiner with Luis Valdez, "The Cultural Schizophrenia of Luis Valdez," *Vogue Magazine* 15 March 1969: 143: "The Blacks have a tradition in the arts that is as old as the country. Theater, poetry, novels, essays, paintings, music—they have been expressing what they felt for a long time. Black liberation is predicated on ideas that have gone before.

"We don't have that. . . . There is no *chicano* leader who has yet put his finger on our problem because we have lacked the poets, novelists, and essayists that prefigure the appearance of such a leader of leaders."

50. Romano writes: "If an individual Chicano accepts this externally imposed image of himself, then clearly he can do no more than hope that someday he will 'awake' or 'emerge' as if out of a cocoon. And if that same Chicano hopes for such an 'awakening' then, *claro que sí*, he has accepted the notion of the Mexican sleeping under the cactus for his own self-image. He is now programmed to believe that Chicanos have no history other than a long and tedious siesta! *¡Qué relajo!*" (*El Grito* 5 [Fall 1971]: 6). He returns to this idea later: "Quinto Sol Publications has never taken the position of 'helping to develop talent,' or 'helping Chicanos to find an identity,' and other such glib slogans (emerging, awakening, stirring . . .) which basically tell Chicanos that in the beginning they are nothing, and the vacuum must be filled. On the contrary, it is the position of Quinto Sol that both talent and identity already exist and have always existed in the Chicano community" (*El Grito* 5 [Summer 1972]: 3–4).

51. "El Plan de Santa Barbara" (translation), Shular 85.

52. "*Para conocerse, para saber quienes son, a algunos les basta con ver su reflejo. . . .*"

53. José Montoya, "Lazy Skin," *El Espejo—The Mirror: Selected Mexican-American Literature*, ed. Octavio Romano (Berkeley: Quinto Sol, 1969) 183. *Gabacho* refers to the white man.

54. Octavio Romano, "Goodbye Revolution," *El Espejo*, ed. Octavio Romano 82.

55. Sergio Elizondo, "Pastourelle," *Perros y antiperros: Una épica chicana*, trans. G. Segade (Berkeley: Quinto Sol, 1972) 22.

56. *Aztlán*, ed. Luis Valdez and Stan Steiner xxv–xxvi.

57. See Octavio Romano, "The Anthropology and Sociology of the Mexican-Americans: The Distortion of Mexican-American History," *El Grito* 2 (Fall 1968): 13–26.

58. Sánchez, "Desmadrazgo," *Canto y grito* 31.

59. See Thomas M. Martínez, "Advertising and Racism: The Case of the Mexican-American," Harth and Baldwin 48–58.

60. See the list of best-known ads given by Armando Rendón (*Chicano Manifesto* [New York: Collier, 1972] 50), for example, the Arrid commercial: we see a Mexican bandit putting deodorant under his arms while a voice says, "if it works for him, it will work all the better for you," an allusion to the bandit's nauseating body odor. Frito-Lay was sued for defamation by the Mexican American Anti-Defamation Committee, the Involvement of Mexican Americans in Gainful Endeavors, of San Antonio, Tex., and the Council to Advance and Restore the Image of the Spanish Speaking and Mexican American of Los Angeles. The company was ordered to cease airing its commercial by August 1970.

61. Sánchez, "Juan," *Canto y grito* 89.

62. See also chap. 2, note 98.

63. An excerpt has been published in *The Chicanos: Mexican American Voices*, ed. Edward Ludwig and James Santibañez (Baltimore: Penguin, 1971) 145. *Bandidos*: a nickname given by Anglos to Mexican revolutionaries.

64. Luis Valdez, *Los Vendidos, Actos: El Teatro Campesino* (San Juan Bautista, Calif.: Cucaracha, 1971) 36.

65. Valdez, *Actos* 37.

66. Lydia R. Aguirre, "The Meaning of the Chicano Movement," *We Are Chicanos*, ed. Philip Ortego 124.

67. *Aztlán*, ed. Luis Valdez and Stan Steiner xxxiii.

68. A. Arzate, *Pain and Promise*, ed. Edward Simmen 123.

Chapter 16. Strangers in Their Own Land

1. Title of the book written by Rubén Salazar, a journalist for the *Los Angeles Times*, on the Mexican minority (U.S. Commission on Civil Rights, *A Stranger in One's Land* [Washington, D.C.: GPO, 1970]).

2. Alurista, "Unexpectedly," *Floricanto en Aztlán* (Los Angeles: Chicano Studies Center, UCLA, 1971) 30.

3. Armando Rendón, *Chicano Manifesto: The History and Aspirations of the Second Largest Minority in America* (New York: Collier, 1972) 325.

4. Philip Ortego, "The Coming of Zamora," *The Chicano: From Caricature to Self-Portrait*, ed. Edward Simmen (New York: NAL, 1971) 294.

5. Rumel Fuentes, "Corrido de Aztlán," *El Grito* 6 (1973): 36.

6. Nephtalí de León, *¡Chicanos! The Living and the Dead!* in *Five Plays* (Denver: Totinem, 1972) 49.

7. Rumel Fuentes, "Corrido de Reies López Tijerina," *El Grito* 6 (1973): 40. *Destrocidades*: probably a deformation of *atrocidades*.

8. Zapata's plan for agrarian reform (28 Nov. 1911).

9. Ortego, "The Coming of Zamora," Simmen 294.

10. Ortego, "The Coming of Zamora," Simmen 295.

11. According to Ricardo Sánchez, "The latest invaders of Aztlán, in their racist onslaughts on the Chicano, managed to dispossess the Chicano. Chicano lands became gringolandia. Under the force of gun and whip. Chicano labor built up the huge agricultural combines of the Southwest for the foreign invader with the blue eyes and the quick, silvery tongues that promised much and delivered neo-colonialism and slavery" ("Desmadrazgo," *Canto y grito mi liberación* [El Paso: Mictla, 1971] 33).

12. Richard Vásquez, *Chicano* (Garden City, N.Y.: Doubleday, 1970) 173.

13. Rodolfo Gonzales, *I Am Joaquín—Yo Soy Joaquín* (New York: Bantam, 1972) 66.

14. According to Ortego, " 'Cultural pluralism' depends upon the wisdom and magnanimity of the dominant group, a wisdom and magnanimity which has been conspicuously absent from Anglo-America judged in terms of its record with American Indians, Blacks, and Mexican-Americans" (Introduction, Sánchez, *Canto y grito* 20).

15. Edward Ludwig and James Santibañez, eds., *The Chicanos: Mexican American Voices* (Baltimore: Penguin, 1971), "Education, a Way In or Out" 157–211.

16. Rendón 192.

17. Albert S. Herrera, "The Mexican-American in Two Cultures," Ludwig and Santibañez 250.

18. Sánchez, "Juan," *Canto y grito* 89.

19. Rumel Fuentes, "El Corrido de George I. Sánchez," *El Grito* 6 (1973): 30.

20. Sánchez, "Desmadrazgo," *Canto y grito* 32.

21. Among others, Luis Valdez: "Our Cultural Schizophrenia has led us to action . . ." ("The Tale of La Raza," *Ramparts* 5 July 1966: 41).

22. Sergio Elizondo, "Mis Cuentos," *Perros y antiperros: Una epica chicana*, trans. G. Segade (Berkeley: Quinto Sol, 1972) 18.

23. Philip Ortego, "The Chicano Renaissance," *Social Casework* 52 (1971): 306.

24. Sánchez, "Denver," *Canto y grito* 93.

25. Alurista, "mis ojos hinchados," *El Espejo—The Mirror: Selected Mexican-American Literature*, ed. Octavio Romano (Berkeley: Quinto Sol, 1972) 172.

26. Ernesto Galarza, *Barrio Boy* (New York: Ballantine, 1972) 2.

27. Galarza 207.

28. C. G. Vélez, "So Farewell Hope," *El Espejo*, ed. Octavio Romano 129.

29. John Womack, Jr., "Who Are the Chicanos?" *New York Review of Books* 31 Aug. 1972: 18: "This is the only disappointment in the book, that it does not go on for another couple of volumes to recount its author's rare career in redefining America."

30. Adalberto Joel Acosta, *Chicanos Can Make It* (New York: Vantage, 1971) 207.

31. Acosta 137.

32. Vélez, "So Farewell Hope," *El Espejo*, ed. Octavio Romano 129.

33. Vásquez 54.

34. Vásquez 54.

35. "East Los" is the largest barrio in the United States; a few miles east of the city limits of Los Angeles, it is part of Los Angeles County. Its official population, mainly Mexican-American, was 110,000 in 1975. See Earl C. Gottschalk, Jr., "A Place Apart: Chicano 'Barrio' of Los Angeles Has Joy, Despair," *Wall Street Journal* 8 Aug. 1975: 1; 7 percent of male residents are farm workers.

36. Vásquez 107.

37. Vásquez 117–18.

38. Vásquez 78.

39. Vásquez 129.

40. Vásquez 152.

41. Vásquez 151.

42. See Richard Vásquez, "Chicano Studies: Sensitivity for Two Cultures," Ludwig and Santibañez 205–11.

43. Vásquez, *Chicano* 173.

44. Vásquez, *Chicano* 176.

45. Vásquez, *Chicano* 201–02.

46. Raúl Salinas, "A Trip Through the Mind Jail," *We Are Chicanos: An Anthology of Mexican-American Literature*, ed. Philip Ortego (New York: Washington Square, 1973) 195, 200.

47. Elizondo, "Del Nueces al Bravo," *Perros* 44.

48. Alurista, "En el barrio," *Floricanto* 36.

49. Alurista, "En el barrio," *Floricanto* 87.

50. Oscar Acosta, "Perla is a Pig," *Voices of Aztlán: Chicano Literature of Today*, ed. Dorothy Harth and Lewis Baldwin (New York: NAL, 1974) 29.

51. Abelardo Delgado, "El Barrio," *Chicano: 25 Pieces of a Chicano Mind* (Denver: Barrio, 1971) 20.

52. José Montoya, "Los Vatos," *El Espejo*, ed. Octavio Romano 186. "Tea-timers" are sunglasses. "Tea" is slang for marijuana; dark glasses can hide eyes reddened by use of the drug.

53. Sánchez, "it was in," *Canto y grito* 103.

54. Sánchez, "Desmadrazgo," *Canto y grito* 34.

55. Sánchez, "Desmadrazgo," *Canto y grito* 35.

56. Javier Alva, "The Sacred Spot," *Aztlán: An Anthology of Mexican American Literature*, ed. Luis Valdez and Stan Steiner (New York: Knopf, 1972) 170–73.

57. J. L. Navarro, "Frankie's Last Wish," *Blue Day on Main Street and Other Short Stories* (Berkeley: Quinto Sol, 1973) 81.

58. Navarro 82.

59. Octavio Romano, "The Historical and Intellectual Presence of the Mexican-Americans," *El Grito* 2 (Winter 1969): 40.

60. Tino Villanueva, "Pachuco Remembered, " *Hay Otra Voz Poems (1968–1971)* (Staten Island, N.Y.: Mensaje, 1972) 40.

61. Villanueva 41.

62. Villanueva 40.

63. José Montoya, "El Louie," Valdez and Steiner 333, 336–37.

64. Valdez and Steiner 146–54.

65. Reported by Tomás Rivera during an interview at the University of Texas–San Antonio, August 1975.

66. See Luis Javier Rodríguez: "Lowriding is our way of cruising on the boulevards. We lower our cars, or get lifts, so we can dance down the road. . . . The Black kids also have shorts, as these cars are called. Many of the Jewish kids ride low too. But it is a Chicano creation that sprang from the barrios of L.A., since the days of the Pachucos" ("Expresiones de mi Barrio/Barrio Expressions," *El Grito* 6 [Summer 1973]: 23).

67. Navarro, "To A Dead Lowrider," Valdez and Steiner 338.

68. Galarza 264.

69. Navarro, *Blue Day* 54.

70. Navarro, "Passing Time," Valdez and Steiner 163–70.

71. Samuel R. Alvidrez ("Drug Use Trends in California," Harth and Baldwin 150) declares that the use of marijuana is less widespread among Mexican-American youths than among young whites.

72. Marcus Durán, "Retrato de un Bato Loco," *Con Safos* 2 (1970): 22–23.

73. Navarro, *Blue Day* 82–83.

74. Navarro, *Blue Day* 91.

75. Vásquez, *Chicano* 236.

76. Tomás Rivera's novel " . . . *y no se lo tragó la tierra*" was published by Quinto Sol in August 1971; it was translated into English by Herminio Ríos in collaboration with the author and Octavio Romano. It won the Quinto Sol literary prize in 1970. Rivera describes his language problem this way: "I had published some of my writings before but they were in English and didn't reach into my subconscious mind because English is a learned experience with me. But when I learned that Quinto Sol accepted the manuscripts in Spanish, it liberated me. I knew that for the first time, I could express myself exactly as I wanted" (*Los Angeles Times* 28 Jan. 1973: 66). Rivera was born in Crystal City, Tex., in 1935. He is a professor of romance languages at the University of Texas–San Antonio and a former editor of *El Grito*. He has published other short stories and poems (see bibliography).

77. Raymond Barrio, *The Plum Plum Pickers* (New York: Harper, 1969) 60. A veteran of the Second World War, Barrio went to Yale, the University of California–Berkeley, and the Art Center College of Los Angeles; he has taught at Ventura Junior College and the University of California–Santa Barbara. A resident of Santa Clara County, Calif., he has published articles in art journals and was for a time art critic for the *Palo*

Alto Times. His works include short stories, novels, and essays: *The Big Picture* (1967), *Experiments in Modern Art* (1968), *Selections from "Walden"* (1968), *Prism* (1968), *Art: Seen* (1968), and *The Fisherman's Dwarf* (1968).

78. Rivera 1.

79. Octavio Romano, "A Rosary," *El Espejo*, ed. Octavio Romano 109.

80. Rivera 68: "You know that the only thing that we can expect is to come back here each year. And as you yourself say, there is no rest until one is dead."

81. Rivera 152.

82. In Spanish there are two forms of the verb "to be": "*estar*" indicates relative or temporary conditions with regard to time and space; "*ser*" indicates absolute being.

83. Villanueva 36.

84. Rivera 149.

85. Rivera 151.

86. Rivera 152.

87. Rivera 6–7.

88. Juan Rulfo, author of *Pedro Páramo y El Llano en llamas, Novelas* (Barcelona: Planeta, 1969).

89. Alurista, *Floricanto* 83.

90. Rivera 25.

91. Daniel Garza, "Saturday Belongs to the Palomía," Ludwig and Santibañez 25–30.

92. Daniel Garza, "Everybody Knows Tobie," *We Are Chicanos*, ed. Philip Ortego 301–10.

93. Warren French, ed., *A Companion to* The Grapes of Wrath (New York: Viking, 1963) 133–34.

94. Barrio 1.

95. Barrio 113.

96. Barrio 151.

97. Barrio 123.

98. Barrio 49.

99. Alurista, "la caneria y el sol," *Floricanto* 3.

100. Barrio 58.

101. Barrio 99.

102. Barrio 155.

103. Barrio 201.

104. Barrio 113.

105. José Montoya, "Sunstruck While Chopping Cotton," *El Espejo*, ed. Octavio Romano 182.

106. Genaro González, "El Hijo del Sol," Simmen 308–16.

107. Villanueva 38.

108. Many later theaters followed the model of the Teatro Campesino. The best known are Teatro Urbano (San Jose), Teatro de los Actos (Oakland), Teatro Bilingüe (El Paso), Teatro Frontera (San Diego), Teatro Popular de la Vida y la Muerte (Los Angeles), and Teatro Aztlán (San Fernando, Calif.).

109. Among the farm workers who contributed to the early success of the Teatro were Agustín Lira, a songwriter and guitarist; Errol Franklin, an Indian originally from Cheyenne, Wyo.; Felipe Cantú, a gifted comic; and Gilbert Rubio.

110. Luis Valdez, "El Teatro Campesino—Its Beginnings," *Ramparts*, 5 July 1966: 55. The Teatro Campesino collaborated for two years throughout the Southwest with the

N.F.W.A., for example, following the 1966 march to Sacramento organized by Chávez. In 1967, the group toured the country; in 1968, a production won an Obie; in 1969, the Teatro participated in the International Dramatic Festival in Nancy, France.

111. Luis Valdez, "The Actos," *Actos: El Teatro Campesino* (San Juan Bautista, Calif.: Cucaracha, 1971) 5.

112. Valdez, *Actos* 6.

113. Valdez, "Notes on Chicano Theater," *Actos* 4. In Sept. 1967, the troup settled in Del Ray, Calif., where a cultural center was created for the farm workers.

114. Valdez, *Actos* 5: "Our rejection of white western European (gavacho) proscenium theater makes the birth of new Chicano forms necessary—thus, los actos y los mitos; one through the eyes of man; the other, through the eyes of God."

115. Valdez, "El Teatro Campesino," *Aztlán*, ed. Luiz Valdez and Stan Steiner 360.

116. *Le Monde* (Paris) 3 July 1975: 15.

117. Valdez, *Actos* 9–19.

118. Valdez, *Actos* 17.

119. See excerpt in Ludwig and Santibañez 143.

120. Valdez, *Actos* 27–28.

121. Valdez, *Actos* 104–30.

122. Valdez, *Actos* 129.

Chapter 17. Enough! The Chicanos in a Rage

1. *¡Basta Ya!* was also the name of a newspaper founded during the "Los Siete" affair, in which seven young Latinos of the Mission District in San Francisco were unjustly arrested for robbery on 1 May 1969 and acquitted on 7 Nov. 1969.

2. Ricardo Sánchez, "Stream," *Canto y grito mi liberación* (El Paso: Mictla, 1971) 73.

3. Abelardo Delgado, "El Vendido," *Chicano: 25 Pieces of a Chicano Mind* (Denver: Barrio, 1971) 33.

4. José Montoya, "El Vendido," *El Espejo—The Mirror: Selected Mexican-American Literature*, ed. Octavio Romano (Berkeley: Quinto Sol, 1969) 181.

5. Raymond Barrio, *The Plum Plum Pickers* (New York: Harper, 1969) 54.

6. Richard Vásquez, *Chicano* (Garden City, N.Y.: Doubleday, 1970) 275: "An actor who acted just like the white man told him to act, who acted out the white man's image of a Mexican exactly like the white man wanted to think about Mexicans. In Watts they call a guy like Leo Carrillo an Uncle Tom."

7. Armando Rendón, *Chicano Manifesto: The History and Aspirations of the Second Largest Minority in America* (New York: Collier, 1972) 96–97.

8. See below, p. 250.

9. Tomás Rivera "*. . . y no se lo tragó la tierra* (Berkeley: Quinto Sol, 1971) 70: "*capaz de hacer y deshacer cualquier cosa que él quisiera; Le parecía que se había separado de todo.*"

10. Cleofas Vigil, "I Believe in God. But Not in Priests," *Aztlán: An Anthology of Mexican-American Literature*, ed. Luis Valdez and Stan Steiner (New York: Knopf, 1972) 383.

11. Sánchez, "Stream," *Canto y grito* 73.

12. Alurista, "With liberty and justice for all," *Floricanto en Aztlán* (Los Angeles: Chicano Studies Center, UCLA, 1971) 29.

13. C. López, "Católicos por la Raza," *Voices of Aztlán: Chicano Literature of Today,*

ed. Dorothy Harth and Lewis Baldwin (New York, NAL, 1974) 185.

14. Rendón 93.

15. Rendón 297.

16. Omar Salinas, "Robstown," Harth and Baldwin 189.

17. Sánchez, "Migrant Lament," *Canto y grito* 91.

18. Delgado, "A New Cross," *Aztlán*, ed. Luis Valdez and Stan Steiner 396–97.

19. Delgado, "The Chicano Manifesto," *Chicano: 25 Pieces* 35.

20. Delgado, "A New Cross," *Aztlán*, ed. Luis Valdez and Stan Steiner 397.

21. Delgado, "The Organizer," *Aztlán*, ed. Luis Valdez and Stan Steiner 395–96.

22. Estela Portillo is the author of plays (*Morality Play, The Day of the Swallows*) and short stories (*Rain of Scorpions* [Berkeley: Tonatiuh, 1975]).

23. Enriqueta Vásquez, "The Woman of La Raza," *Aztlán*, ed. Luis Valdez and Stan Steiner 278. The article first appeared in *El Grito del Norte* 6 July 1969.

24. Mary Lou Espinosa, "La Madre de Aztlán," *Aztlán*, ed. Luis Valdez and Stan Steiner 279–80. The poem first appeared in *El Grito del Norte* 24 Dec. 1969.

25. José Montoya, "La jefita," Romano 188–89.

26. Agustín Lira, "Cruz," *Aztlán*, ed. Luis Valdez and Stan Steiner 270.

27. Delgado, "La Hembra," *Chicano: 25 Pieces* 11.

28. Rendón 183.

29. Gloria Pérez, "Mi Hombre," Harth and Baldwin 184.

30. A journalist for the *Los Angeles Times*, Salazar was reporting on the National Chicano Moratorium, held on 29 Aug. 1970, to protest the war in Vietnam. He was killed in the ensuing riot.

31. Guadalupe de Saavedra, "El Grito," *Aztlán*, ed. Luis Valdez and Stan Steiner 289–91.

32. Delgado, "El Barrio," *Chicano: 25 Pieces* 20.

33. Delgado, "La Causa," *Chicano: 25 Pieces* 12.

34. Delgado, "Stupid America," *Chicano: 25 Pieces* 32.

35. Ernest Galarza, *Barrio Boy* (New York: Ballantine, 1972) 259.

36. Philip Ortego, "The Coming of Zamora," *The Chicano: From Caricature to Self-Portrait*, ed. Edward Simmen (New York: NAL, 1971) 292–98.

37. Luis Valdez, interview, *La Raza: The Mexican-Americans*, ed. Stan Steiner (New York: Harper, 1970) 89–90.

38. Estela Portillo, "Recast," *Rain of Scorpions and Other Writings* (Berkeley: Tonatiuh, 1975) 75.

39. Luis Valdez, *Actos: El Teatro Campesino* (San Juan Bautista, Calif.: Cucaracha, 1971) 96–98.

40. Nephtalí de León, *Five Plays* (Denver: Totinem, 1972) 44–89.

41. De León 88.

42. De León 92–129.

43. Carlos Morton, *El Jardín*, in *El Grito* 7 (June–Aug. 1974): 7–37.

44. Morton 29.

45. Morton 36.

46. Delgado, "The Chicano Manifesto," *Chicano: 25 Pieces* 35.

47. Delgado, "Stupid America," *Chicano: 25 Pieces* 32.

48. Joan Baez [Harris], "Thoughts on a Sunday Afternoon," *The Chicanos: Mexican American Voices*, ed. Edward Ludwig and James Santibañez (Baltimore: Penguin, 1971) 259.

49. P. Galindo, "The Mexican American Devil's Dictionary," *El Grito* 6 (1973): 46.

50. Octavio Romano, "Goodbye Revolution—Hello Slum," *El Espejo*, ed. Octavio Romano 82.

51. Valdez, *Actos* 100–03.

52. See Delgado, *Chicano: 25 Pieces* 7.

53. Genaro González, "El Hijo del Sol," Ludwig and Santibañez 312.

54. Valdez, *Actos* 132–45.

55. De León, *¡Chicanos! The Living and the Dead!* in *Five Plays* 49.

56. Sánchez, "Juan," *Canto y grito* 88.

57. Sánchez, "Desmadrazgo," *Canto y grito* 38: "We, los mestizos del mundo tercero [third world], are aware that we are not alone in our struggle against the desmadrazgo of the Useless States of Amerika."

58. Sánchez, "Desmadrazgo," *Canto y grito* 38.

59. Valdez, *Actos* 130.

60. Rodolfo Gonzales, *I Am Joaquín—Yo Soy Joaquín* (New York: Bantam, 1972) 1.

61. First published in 1967 by the Crusade for Justice, Denver. Translated into Spanish by the author.

62. Gonzales 6.

63. Gonzales 44.

64. Gonzales 100.

65. Alurista, "when, raza," *Floricanto* 1.

66. Alurista, "El buho sabio de mi aldea," *Floricanto* 21.

67. Alurista, "The man has lost his shadow," *Floricanto* 4.

68. Sánchez, "Stream," *Canto y grito* 78.

69. Sánchez, "EXISTIR ES . . . an experiment in writing in and around a few songs from the barrio . . ." *Canto y grito* 152.

70. Ricardo Mora, *The Black Sun* (Lubbock: Trucha, 1973).

71. Sánchez, "Desmadrazgo," *Canto y grito* 36.

72. Sánchez, "Stream," *Canto y grito* 75.

73. Sánchez, "Desmadrazgo," *Canto y grito* 35.

74. Sánchez, "Desmadrazgo," *Canto y grito* 38.

75. Sánchez, "This of Being the Soul / Voice of My Own Consciousness Is Too Much (Petersburg, Virginny)," *Canto y grito* 64.

76. Sánchez, "smile out the revolu," *Canto y grito* 139.

77. Sánchez, *Canto y grito* 37.

78. Sánchez, *Canto y grito* 37.

79. Rendón 309.

80. Valdez, "Notes on Chicano Theater," *Actos* 2.

81. Valdez, *Actos* 2.

82. Frantz Fanon, *Peau Noire, masques blancs* (Paris: Seuil, 1952) 32.

83. Expressions used by Gilles Deleuze and Félix Guattari in their study *Kafka: pour une littérature mineure* (Paris: Minuit, 1975) 29–50.

84. These sample metaphors are from Sánchez, *Canto y grito*: "hydra-headed racism" (p. 39), "the mandible spewed out honey madness of racist resin in amerika" (p. 75), "thy master of blue-eyed hatred" (p. 91).

Chapter 18. I Am Joaquín / *Yo Soy Joaquín*

1. Rodolfo Gonzales, *I Am Joaquín—Yo Soy Joaquín* (New York: Bantam, 1972) 1.
2. José Nájera, "Words of Yohamateah to His Son," *El Grito* 5 (Fall 1971): 60.
3. Oscar Z. Acosta, *The Autobiography of a Brown Buffalo* (San Francisco: Straight Arrow, 1972) 199.
4. Philosopher José Vasconcelos developed the somewhat racist connotation of this term. In his book *La Raza Cósmica* (Barcelona: Agencia Mundial, 1925), he stresses that Spanish-speaking nations must confront the power of the United States; he contrasts Hispanic to Anglo values, sees weakness in the American tendency toward racial homogeneity, and predicts the triumph of the "cosmic race," the peoples of mixed blood.
5. Alurista, "bendita suerte," *Floricanto en Aztlán* (Los Angeles: Chicano Studies Center, UCLA, 1971) 70.
6. Acosta 199.
7. Luis Valdez, *No Saco Nada de la Escuela*, in *Actos: El Teatro Campesino* (San Juan Bautista, Calif.: Cucaracha, 1971) 80.
8. Valdez, *Actos* 90.
9. Gonzales 98.
10. Carlos Morton, *El Jardín*, in *El Grito* 7 (June–Aug. 1974): 13.
11. Octavio Paz, in the preface to the book by Jacques Lafaye, *Quetzalcoatl et Guadalupe: La Formation de la conscience nationale au Mexique (1531–1813)*, trans. Françoise-Marie Rosset (Paris: Gallimard, 1974) xxv.
12. Luis Valdez, *La Conquista de Mexico*, in *Actos* 58.
13. Mary Lou Espinosa, "La Madre de Aztlán," *Aztlán: An Anthology of Mexican American Literature*, ed. Luis Valdez and Stan Steiner (New York: Knopf, 1972) 279.
14. Gonzales 1.
15. Gonzales 16, 19.
16. Javier Alva, "The Sacred Spot," *Aztlán*, ed. Luis Valdez and Stan Steiner 71.
17. Philip Ortego, "The Chicano Renaissance," *Social Casework* 52 (1971): 307: "The Chicano Renaissance came into being not in relation to the traditional past but rather in the wake of growing awareness by Mexican Americans of their Indian, not Hispanic, identity."
18. On the Aztec year, see Jacques Soustelle, *La Vie quotidienne des Aztèques à la veille de la conquête espagnole* (Paris: Hachette, 1955) 294–95. For the Aztecs, each year had characteristics related to a cardinal point: for example, Acatl, "East," symbolized fertility and abundance. Cortés's defeat of Mexico in 1521 took place during a Calli ("West") year, whose sign evoked the setting of the sun, decline, and death. The last Mexican emperor was named Cuauhtemotzin, the "descending eagle," that is, the "setting sun."
19. Valdez, *Actos* 55.
20. Valdez, *Actos* 62.
21. The actual historical text is: "We are met on a great battlefield of that war."
22. Ricardo Mora, *The Black Sun* (Lubbock: Trucha, 1973) 45.
23. Miguel Méndez, "Tata Casehua," *El Espejo—The Mirror: Selected Mexican-American Literature*, ed. Octavio Romano (Berkeley: Quinto Sol, 1969) 54.
24. Méndez, "Tata Casehua," Romano 57.
25. Wayne Moquin and Charles Van Doren (*A Documentary History of the Mexican Americans* [New York: Praeger, 1971] 25–31) cite, under the title "A Condemnation of Spain's Indian Policy," an excerpt from *Brevíssima Relación de la Destruyción de las Indias Occidentales* (1541–42) by Bartolomé de las Casas.

26. Morton 13.

27. After 1600, the feast day of the Mexican Guadalupe was moved from 8 Sept., the feast of the Spanish Guadalupe of Estremadura, to 12 Dec., the current date. The Spanish image was also replaced by an indigenous one, in order to differentiate the Mexican Virgin completely from the original one. Only the name remained the same. In 1737, the Virgin of Tepeyac, was proclaimed the patron saint of Mexico. On this subject, see J. Lafaye, *Quetzalcoatl et Guadalupe* 282–362.

28. A major divinity of the Aztecs, Tonantzín, whose name means "Our Mother," was often identified with the goddess Cihuacoatl, "the woman [wife?] of the Serpent."

29. See *Aztlán*, ed. Luis Valdez and Stan Steiner 265. Although the meaning and origin of this name are still debated, there is general agreement that it contains the Arabic radical *guad* (*oued*, "river"); according to Lafaye 290, the suffix *upe* means "deeply embanked," an interpretation corroborated by the configuration of the location. *Al* is an Arabic article.

30. Leonardo Elías, "Aztec Mother," *Voices of Aztlán: Chicano Literature of Today*, ed. Dorothy Harth and Lewis Baldwin (New York: NAL, 1974) 177.

31. Gonzales 42.

32. Alurista, "La carne de tus labios," *Floricanto* 41.

33. Alurista, "Fruto de bronce," *Floricanto* 53.

34. Abelardo Delgado, "Mamá Lupe," *Chicano: 25 Pieces of a Chicano Mind* (Denver: Barrio, 1971) 27.

35. Ramón Emiliano, "Saga de Aztlán," *Grito del Sol* 1 (Jan.–Mar. 1976): 14.

36. Emiliano 16.

37. Title of the study by Alfonso Caso, *El Pueblo del Sol* (Mexico City: Fondo de Cultura, 1953).

38. According to Soustelle (p. 124), the sacrifice was a "cosmic duty," since the primary function of people was to nourish all the gods of the universe. Thus the strange "war of the flowers" was carried on in the midst of the Mexican peace; its purpose was to take prisoners for sacrifice. (See A. Caso, *El Teocalli de la Guerra Sagrada* [Mexico City: n.p., 1927]; cited by Soustelle 294, note 18.)

39. Nephtalí de León, "Of Bronze the Sacrifice," *We Are Chicanos: An Anthology of Mexican-American Literature*, ed. Philip Ortego (New York: Washington Square, 1973) 157.

40. Luis Valdez, *Bernabé*, in *Aztlán*, ed. Luis Valdez and Stan Steiner 373.

41. Jorge Huerta, *El Renacimiento de Huitzilopochtli*, in *El Grito* 7 (June–Aug. 1974): 4.

42. Alurista, "El recuerdo de mis grillos," *Floricanto* 68.

43. Alurista, "Moonglow dreams," *Floricanto* 72.

44. Omar Salinas, "Aztec Angel," *We Are Chicanos*, ed. Philip Ortego 165.

45. Alva, "The Sacred Spot," *Aztlán*, ed. Luis Valdez and Stan Steiner 171.

46. Delgado, "Cactus fruit," *Chicano: 25 Pieces* 16.

47. Alurista, "We've played cowboys," *Floricanto* 23.

48. In the introduction to Anaya's *Bless Me, Ultima* (Berkeley: Quinto Sol, 1972) ix, H. Ríos and O. Romano write: "Rudolfo Anaya further draws from our collective experience and our collective subconscious to recreate, in his own individual way, our objective realities, our myths, our legends, hopes, dreams and frustrations."

49. José Vasconcelos, *La Raza Cósmica* 917.

50. Rumel Fuentes, "Mexico Americano," *El Grito* 6 (1973): 16.

51. Juanita Domínguez, "Yo Soy Chicano," in Armando Rendón, *Chicano Manifesto* (New York: Collier, 1972) 182.

52. Domínguez, in Rendón 35.

53. See also Delgado, "The Chicano Manifesto," *Chicano: 25 Pieces* 35.

54. Ricardo Sánchez, "Something or other," *Canto y grito mi liberación* (El Paso: Mictla, 1971) 51.

55. Guillermo Fuenfrios, "The Emergence of the New Chicano," *Aztlán*, ed. Luis Valdez and Stan Steiner 285.

56. Rendón 13.

57. Acosta 198.

58. The Spanish spoken by the Mexicans and the Chicanos has felt an Aztec influence —for example, the repeated use of the diminutive, *lueguito, ahorita*. Ramón Emiliano has cataloged Nahuatl terms still used today, such as *piscar* or *pixcar*, derived from *pixka* ("to harvest"); *gachupín*, derived from *kaktzopin*, made up of *kaktli* ("shoe") + *tzopina* ("to hit"). *Gachupín* thus means he who kicks people with the point of his shoe. This name was given to Spaniards, particularly government officials ("Nahuatlan Elements in Chicano Speech," *Grito del Sol* 4 [1976]: 89–108).

59. Sergio Elizondo, "Chicanos," *Perros y antiperros* (Berkeley: Quinto Sol, 1972) 24.

60. Luis Valdez, *Actos* 81.

61. Alurista even describes his style as "tetralingual," a mixture of Spanish, English, Black, and Spanish slang. Reported by Frank Sotomayor, "An Explosion of Chicano Literary Merit," *Los Angeles Times* 28 Jan. 1973: 66.

62. Herminio Ríos, Introduction, *El Grito* 7 (Mar.–May 1974): 7: "Code switching in Chicano poetry is a reflection of everyday speech in which the social situation determines, to a large extent, the frequency and location within the sentence where the changes from one system to another will occur. Code switching can achieve great poetic force. This force is created by the juxtaposition of two linguistic systems. Psychologically the reader expects linguistic continuity in one system. The violent switch into another system gives power to the poetic expression. . . ."

63. Sánchez, "Dichotomies . . ." *Canto y grito* 155.

64. Sánchez, "Stream," *Canto y grito* 81–82: ". . . *Y les digo, carnales, que duele al oír mi raza periquiar en inglés o que ellos pidan poesía chicana escrita en el idioma del gringo . . . y no puedo traducir ciertas cosas, pues siento mi alma brotar cantos del espíritu chicano . . . y mi ser demanda la verdad de nuestro carnalismo escrita con sangre apasionada . . .*" *Periquiar* is a deformation of "*periquear*".

65. Alurista, "what's happening . . . , " *Floricanto* 19.

66. Sánchez, "migrant lament," *Canto y grito* 92.

67. Alurista, "in the barrio sopla el viento," *Floricanto* 16.

68. Sánchez, "Reo Eterno," *Canto y grito* 43.

69. Sánchez, "Denver," *Canto y grito* 93.

70. Lydia R. Aguirre, "The Meaning of the Chicano Movement," *We Are Chicanos*, ed. Philip Ortego 122.

71. Rendón 325.

Chapter 19. The Children of the Sun

1. Alurista, "Poem in Lieu of Preface," *Aztlán: An Anthology of Mexican American Literature*, ed. Luis Valdez and Stan Steiner (New York: Knopf, 1972) 332–33.

2. Nephtalí de León, *Five Plays* (Denver: Totinem, 1972) 49.

3. De León, *Play Number 9*, in *Five Plays* 108.

4. Armando Rendón, *Chicano Manifesto: The History and Aspirations of the Second Largest Minority in America* (New York: Collier, 1972) 16.

5. Rendón 10.

6. Ricardo Mora, *The Black Sun* (Lubbock: Trucha, 1973) 63.

7. Aristeo Brito, "El Peregrino," *Voices of Aztlán: Chicano Literature of Today*, ed. Dorothy Harth and Lewis Baldwin (New York: NAL, 1974) 199.

8. Rendón 325.

9. Lionel Trilling, *Beyond Culture* (New York: Viking, 1965) 3.

10. Rolando R. Hinojosa, *Estampas del valle y otras obras—Sketches of the Valley and Other Works* (Berkeley: Quinto Sol, 1973).

11. Nick C. Vaca, "The Week of the Life of Manuel Hernandez," *The Chicano: From Caricature to Self-Portrait*, ed. Edward Simmen (New York: NAL, 1971) 299–307.

12. Nick C. Vaca, "Martín," *El Grito* 1 (Fall 1967): 25–31.

13. Alurista, *Floricanto en Aztlán* (Los Angeles: Chicano Studies Center, UCLA, 1971) 30.

14. Sergio Elizondo, "Flor," *Perros y antiperros: Una épica chicana* (Berkeley: Quinto Sol, 1972) 48.

15. Genaro González, "Un Hijo del Sol," Simmen 310.

16. Rendón 324–25.

17. José Montoya, "Pobre Viejo Walt Whitman," *El Espejo—The Mirror: Selected Mexican-American Literature*, ed. Octavio Romano (Berkeley: Quinto Sol, 1969) 180.

18. Elizondo, *Perros y antiperros: "con cuchara de plástico en la boca: En cuna de plástico"* and *"un pueblo de vidrio y plástico"* (p. 70); *"Dios de Plástico"* (p. 74).

19. Gallo Kirach, "Tecatos," Harth and Baldwin 185.

20. Abelardo Delgado, *Chicano: 25 Pieces of a Chicano Mind* (Denver: Barrio, 1971) 4.

21. De León, *Five Plays* 58.

22. Luis Valdez, "The Tale of La Raza," *Ramparts* 5 July 1966: 41.

23. The loss of a shadow suggests a crime or pact with the Devil; see Adalbert von Chamisso, *Peter Schlemihls Wundersame Geschichte* (1814). According to some popular traditions, the shadow is a guardian angel.

24. Alurista, "The man has lost his shadow," *Floricanto* 4.

25. Alurista, "hombre ciego," *Floricanto* 6.

26. Alurista, *Dawn*, in *El Grito* 7 (June–Aug. 1974): 62.

27. Alurista, *Dawn* 81. The Mexican "century" was composed of fifty-two years. Nine was considered an ill-fated number.

28. Alurista, *Dawn* 82–83.

29. González, "Un Hijo del Sol," Simmen 316.

30. Luis Valdez, "Notes on Chicano Theater," Valdez and Steiner 354.

31. Valdez, "Chicano Theater," Valdez and Steiner 354–55.

32. Ricardo Sánchez, "migrant lament," *Canto y grito mi liberación* (El Paso: Mictla, 1971) 91.

33. Kirach, "Tecatos," Harth and Baldwin 184.

34. De León, *Five Plays* 9.

35. Negative or black valorization of the sun. This refers not to Quetzalcoatl but to Uitzilopochtli, the warlike man-eating sun, also a god of darkness.

36. Mora vii.

37. Delgado, "Cactus Fruit," *Chicano: 25 Pieces* 16.

38. Sánchez, "Juan," *Canto y grito* 90.

39. Francisco O. Burruel, *The Dialogue of Cuco Rocha, El Grito* 3 (Summer 1970): 42.

40. Alurista, "mis ojos hinchados," *Floricanto* 40.

41. Alurista, "chicano heart," *Floricanto* 9.

42. Alurista, "hombre ciego," *Floricanto* 6.

43. Alurista, "chicano heart," *Floricanto* 9.

44. Alurista, "to be fathers once again," *Floricanto* 65.

45. Sánchez, "it is urgent," *Canto y grito* 131.

46. Alurista, "la cucaracha," "what's happening . . . ," etc., *Floricanto* 7, 19.

47. Alurista, "chicano infante," *Floricanto* 54.

48. Alurista, "Sacred robe," *Floricanto* 57.

49. José Vasconcelos, *La Raza Cósmica*, in *Obras Completas* (Mexico City: Libreros Mexicanos Unidos, 1958) 922: ". . . *la raza definitiva, la raza síntesis o raza integral, hecha con el genio y con la sangre de todos los pueblos y, por lo mismo, más capaz de verdadera fraternidad y de visión realmente universal.*"

50. Sánchez, "Vision," *We Are Chicanos: An Anthology of Mexican-American Literature*, ed. Philip Ortego (New York: Washington Square, 1973) 207.

51. G. Fuenfrios, "The Emergence of the New Chicano," *Aztlán*, ed. Luis Valdez and Stan Steiner 284.

52. Introduction, *Voices of Aztlán*, ed. Dorothy Harth and Lewis Baldwin 21.

53. Sabine R. Ulibarrí, "Cultural Heritage of the Southwest," Ortego 15.

54. Alurista, "el sarape de mi personalidad," *Floricanto* 10.

55. Rendón 313.

56. Walt Whitman, "November Boughs," *The Works of Walt Whitman*, 2 vols. (New York: Funk & Wagnalls, 1968) 2: 402–03.

57. Alurista, "el sarape de mi personalidad," *Floricanto* 10.

58. Carlos Morton, *El Jardín*, in *El Grito* 7 (June–Aug. 1974): 33.

59. Delgado, "The organizer," Valdez and Steiner 395.

60. See José Montoya, "Sunstruck While Chopping Cotton," *El Espejo*, ed. Octavio Romano 182.

61. J. L. Navarro, "Somewhere, Sometime," *Blue Day on Main Street and Other Short Stories* (Berkeley: Quinto Sol, 1973) 94.

62. Rodolfo Gonzales, *I Am Joaquín—Yo Soy Joaquín* (New York: Bantam, 1972) 100.

63. Estela Portillo, *Morality Play, El Grito* 7 (Sept. 1973): 7–21 (excerpts).

64. Sánchez, "It is urgent," *Canto y grito* 131.

65. Rubén Salazar, quoted by Lydia R. Aguirre, "The Meaning of the Chicano Movement," Ortego 122.

66. Eliu Carranza, "The Gorkase Mirror," Simmen 231.

Conclusion

1. Helen Hunt Jackson, *A Century of Dishonor* (New York, 1881).

2. Octavio Romano and Herminio Ríos, "Quinto Sol and Chicano Publications," *El Grito* 5 (Summer 1972): 4.

3. Herminio Ríos, "Introductory Comments," *El Grito* 5 (Fall 1971): 9.

Bibliography

Since this field of American literature has been neglected until recently, the bibliography cannot be exhaustive. Certain manuscripts dating from the nineteenth and early twentieth centuries are still not accessible; one day, I hope, they will be published.

The bibliography includes only the most important books and articles. In selecting sociological and historical works, in particular, I have been guided by a desire to simplify and to reserve as much space as possible for Mexican-American authors.

In cases of multiple works by the same author, I have employed the following sequence of entries: individual as author, as editor, as co-editor, and as author of publications in journals, publications in anthologies, and unpublished works. In the section dealing with Chicano poems and short stories, when there is more than one work by the same author in a journal or anthology, the name of the publication is followed by an alphabetical list of the poems or short stories. Journals are listed chronologically by issue followed by an alphabetical list of poems or short stories.

Outline of the Bibliography

Part One. Bibliographic Sources
  1. General bibliographies and Mexican-American literary bibliographies
  2. Southwestern literary journals
  3. Mexican-American journals and newspapers
Part Two. Literary Criticism, History, and Sociology
  1. Literary and philosophical works
  2. Books and articles on Mexican-American literature
  3. Historical works
      A. On the United States
      B. On the Southwest
      C. On the Chicano movement

    4. Works on Mexico
    5. Sociological works
        A. Customs of the Southwest
        B. The Mexican minority
            (1) In general
            (2) The Mexican character
            (3) Assimilation and acculturation
            (4) Immigration and working conditions
Part Three. Anglo-American Authors
    1. Before 1940
    2. From 1940 to the present
Part Four. Mexican-American Authors
    1. Anthologies
    2. Poems
    3. Short stories
    4. Novels
    5. Plays
    6. Autobiographies
Part Five. Folklore

Part One. Bibliographic Sources

1. General bibliographies and Mexican-American literary bibliographies

Barrios, Ernie. *Bibliografía de Aztlán: An Annotated Chicano Bibliography*. San Diego: San Diego State College, 1971.

The Beadle Collection of Dime Novels. Donated to the New York Public Library by F. P. O'Brien; New York, 1922.

Bibliografía de Aztlán: An Annotated Chicano Bibliography. San Diego: Centro de Estudios Chicanos, 1972.

Bibliografía de Materiales Tocante al Chicano. San Jose State College Library, 1971.

Campa, Arthur L. "A Bibliography of Spanish Folklore in New Mexico." *Bulletin of the University of New Mexico* 2 (1930).

Chicano Bibliography. University of Utah Libraries, 1971.

Cumberland, Charles C. "The United States–Mexico Border: A Selective Guide to the Literature of the Region." *Rural Sociology* 25 (1960): 90–102.

Cumins, Ella Sterling. *The Story of the Files: A Review of Californian Writers and Literature*. San Francisco: World's Fair Commission of California, 1893.

Dengler, Nadine. *Bibliography of Spanish, Mexican, Puerto Rican Culture in the United States*. Denver: Denver Public Library, 1968.

Dobie, J. Frank. *Guide to Life and Literature of the Southwest*. Dallas: Southern Methodist UP, 1952.

Fodell, Beverly. *Cesar Chavez and the United Farm Workers: A Selective Bibliography*. Detroit: Wayne State UP, 1974.

Grismer, Raymond, ed. *A Reference Index to Twelve Thousand Spanish American Authors*. New York: Wilson, 1939.

Guzmán, Ralph. *Revised Bibliography: With a Bibliographical Essay*. Advance Report no. 3, Mexican American Study Project. Los Angeles: UCLA, 1967.

Hanna, Philip Townsend. *Libros Californianos; or, Five Feet of California Books*. Los Angeles: Zeitlin, 1931.

Haywood, Charles. *A Bibliography of North American Folklore and Folksong*. Vol. 1. New York: Greenberg, 1951. Rev. ed.; New York: Dover, 1961.

Hinkel, Charles E., ed. *Biographies of California Authors and Indexes of California Literature*. 2 vols. Oakland: Alameda County Library, 1942.

Inter-Agency Committee on Mexican-American Affairs. *A Guide to Materials Relating to Persons of Mexican Heritage in the United States*. Washington, 1969.

Major, Mabel, Rebecca Smith, and T. M. Pearce, eds. *Southwest Heritage: A Literary History with Bibliography*. Albuquerque: U of New Mexico P, 1938.

Meier, Matt S., and Feliciano Rivera. *A Selective Bibliography for the Study of Mexican American History*. San Jose: San Jose State College, 1971.

Nogales, Luis, ed. *The Mexican American: A Selected and Annotated Bibliography*. 2nd ed. Stanford: Stanford UP, 1971.

Pearce, T. M., and A. P. Thomason, eds. *Southwesterners Write*. Albuquerque: U of New Mexico P, 1946.

Pino, Frank. *Mexican-Americans: A Research Bibliography*. 2 vols. East Lansing: Latin American Studies Center, Michigan State U, 1974.

Saunders, Lyle. *Spanish-Speaking Americans in the United States: A Selected Bibliography*. New York: Bureau for Intercultural Education, 1944.

———, comp. *A Guide to Materials Bearing on Cultural Relations in New Mexico*. Albuquerque: U of New Mexico P, 1944.

Simmons, Merle E. *A Bibliography of the Romance and Related Forms in Spanish America*. Bloomington: Indiana UP, 1963.

Sonnichsen, C. L., ed. *The Southwest in Life and Literature: A Pageant in Seven Parts*. New York: Devin, 1962.

Tully, Marjorie F., and Juan B. Rael, comps. *An Annotated Bibliography of Spanish Folklore in New Mexico and Southern Colorado*. University of New Mexico Publications in Language and Literature. Albuquerque: U of New Mexico P, 1950.

The Zamorano 80: A Selection of Distinguished California Books. Los Angeles: Zamorano Club, 1945.

2. Southwestern literary journals

Arizona Quarterly. Tucson: U of Arizona P. Vol. 1: 1945.

Frontier Times. Bandera, Tex. Monthly; vol. 1: 1923.

Hispanic Review. Philadelphia: U of Pennsylvania P. Bilingual quarterly; vol. 1: 1933.

Land of Sunshine. Los Angeles: 1894–1902; later published with the title *Out West*, 1902–10, then merged with *Overland Monthly*.

New Mexico Quarterly. Albuquerque: U of New Mexico P. Vol. 1: 1931.

Publications of the Texas Folklore Society. Austin/Dallas. Vol. 1: 1916.

Southwest Review. Quarterly founded as *Texas Review* by the University of Texas in June 1915. Transferred to Southern Methodist University in August 1924.

Texas Observer. Austin. Biweekly; vol. 1: 1906.

Texas Quarterly. Austin: U of Texas P. Vol 1: 1958.

Western Folklore. Berkeley: U of California P. Vol. 1: 1947. Called *California Folklore Quarterly* from 1942 to 1947.

3. Mexican-American journals and newspapers

It would be tedious to list all Mexican-American newspapers published since 1848. An initial list of 195 newspapers (1848–1942) has been published by *El Grito: A Journal of Contemporary Mexican-American Thought* 3 (Summer 1970): 17–24, and a second one of 185 newspapers (1881–1951) appeared in the same journal (Summer 1972): 40–47. I will mention only journals and newspapers of truly literary interest.

El Clamor Público: Independiente y Literario. Francisco P. Ramírez, ed. Los Angeles: 1855–59 (?). Spanish-language weekly.

La Gaceta. José Azaga, ed. Santa Barbara: 1880–81 (?). Spanish-language weekly.

Lulac News. Phoenix. English-language monthly; vol. 1: 1929.

El Nuevo Mundo. J. M. Vigil, ed. San Francisco: 1864–67 (?). Spanish-language biweekly.

La Prensa. San Antonio: 1913–42. Spanish-language daily.

The following list of contemporary publications is far from complete; selections are based on their relation to this study. Those marked by an asterisk are referred to often in the text.

Alianza. Tucson. Spanish-language monthly; vol. 1: 1907.

★*Aztlán: Chicano Journal of the Social Sciences and Arts.* Los Angeles: UCLA P. Bilingual, semiannual; vol. 1: 1970. Became *Aztlán: International Journal of Chicano Studies Research* with vol. 6.

Basta Ya. San Francisco. Bilingual, irregular; vol. 1: 1969.

La Causa. Compton, Calif.: National Beret Association. Bilingual, irregular; vol. 1: 1969.

Chicano Quarterly Review. New Haven: Yale UP. English language; vol. 1: 1975.

★*Con Safos: Reflections on Life in the Barrio.* Los Angeles. Bilingual, irregular; vol 1: 1968.

El Gallo. Denver. English-language monthly; vol. 1: 1967.

★*El Grito: A Journal of Contemporary Mexican-American Thought.* Berkeley: Quinto Sol. Bilingual quarterly; 1967–74.

El Grito del Norte. Española, N.Mex. Bilingual, irregular; vol. 1: 1968.

★*Grito del Sol: A Chicano Quarterly.* Berkeley: Tonatiuh. Bilingual; vol. 1: 1976.

El Hispano. Sacramento. Bilingual weekly; vol. 1: 1969.

Inside Eastside. Los Angeles. English-language bimonthly; vol. 1: 1967.

★*Journal of Mexican American History.* Santa Barbara. English-language annual; vol. 1: 1970.

★*Journal of Mexican American Studies.* Anaheim, Calif. English-language quarterly; vol. 1: 1970.

Lado. Chicago. Bilingual, irregular; vol. 1: 1967.

La Luz: National Review of La Raza. Denver. Bilingual monthly; vol. 1: 1972.

El Machete. Los Angeles: Los Angeles City College. Bilingual, irregular; vol. 1: 1968.

Magazin. San Antonio. Bilingual monthly; vol. 1: 1971.

★*El Malcriado.* Delano, Calif.: U.F.W.O.C. Bilingual monthly; vol. 1: 1966.

El Papel. Albuquerque, N.Mex. Bilingual, irregular; vol. 1: 1969.

El Pocho Che. Berkeley. Bilingual quarterly; vol. 1: 1969.

La Raza. Los Angeles. Bilingual, irregular; vol. 1: 1969.

Regeneración. Los Angeles. Bilingual, irregular; vol. 1: 1970.

★*Revista Chicano-Riqueña.* Gary: Northwest Indiana U. Bilingual, irregular; vol. 1: 1973.

★*Tejidos.* Austin: U of Texas P. Bilingual, irregular; vol. 1: 1974.

La Verdad. San Diego. Bilingual monthly; vol. 1: 1969.

La Verdad. Crystal City, Tex. Spanish-language monthly; vol. 1: 1970.

La Vox Mexicana. Wantoma, Wis. Bilingual, irregular; vol. 1: 1965.
El Zapatista. Pueblo, Colo. Bilingual, biweekly; vol. 1: 1970.

Part Two. Literary Criticism, History, and Sociology

1. *Literary and philosophical works*

Allport, Gordon W. *The Nature of Prejudice*. Garden City, N.Y.: Doubleday, 1954.

Babbitt, Irving. *Spanish Character and Other Essays*. Boston: Houghton, 1940.

Bentley, Harold W. *A Dictionary of Spanish Terms in English with Special Reference to the American Southwest*. New York: Columbia UP, 1932.

Commager, Henry Steele. *The American Mind: An Interpretation of American Thought and Character since the 1880s*. New Haven: Yale UP, 1950.

Fergusson, Edna. *Our Southwest*. 1940. New York: Knopf, 1952.

Fishman, Joshua A. *Sociolinguistics: A Brief Introduction*. Rowley, Mass.: Newbury, 1970.

Fulton, Maurice Garland, and Paul Horgan, eds. *New Mexico's Own Chronicle: Three Races in the Writings of Four Hundred Years*. Dallas: Banks, 1937.

González Peña, Carlos. *Historia de la literatura mexicana*. Mexico City: Porrúa, 1966.

Johannsen, Albert. *The House of Beadle & Adams and Its Dime and Nickel Novels: The Story of a Vanished Literature*. 2 vols. Norman: U of Oklahoma P, 1950.

Marcuse, Herbert. *Eros and Civilization: A Philosophical Inquiry into Freud*. Boston: Beacon, 1955.

Northrup, F.S.C. *The Meeting of East and West: An Inquiry Concerning World Understanding*. New York: Macmillan, 1947.

Paredes, Raymund. "The Image of the Mexican in American Literature." Diss. U of Texas-Austin, 1973.

Pearce, T. M. "On Regionalism in the Southwest." *New Mexico Quarterly* 1 (1931): 197.

Persons, Stow. *American Minds: A History of Ideas*. New York: Holt, 1958.

Ríos, Francisco Armando. "The Mexican in Fact, Fiction and Folklore." *Voices: Readings from El Grito*. Ed. Octavio Romano. Berkeley: Quinto Sol, 1971. 59–73.

Robinson, Cecil. *With the Ears of Strangers: The Mexican in American Literature*. Tucson: U of Arizona P, 1963.

Romanell, Patrick. *Making of the Mexican Mind: A Study in Recent Mexican Thought*. Lincoln: U of Nebraska P, 1952.

Ross, Calvin. *Sky Determines: An Interpretation of the Southwest*. Albuquerque: U of New Mexico P, 1965.

Rulfo, Juan. *Pedro Páramo y El llano en llamas*. In *Novelas*. Barcelona: Planeta, 1969.

Simmons, Ozzie G. "The Mutual Images and Expectations of Anglo-Americans and Mexican-Americans." *Daedalus* 90 (1961): 286–89.

Spengler, Oswald. *Le Déclin de l'Occident*. 2 vols. Trans. M. Tazerout. Paris: Gallimard, 1948. Trans. of *Der Untergang des Abendlands*.

Tinker, Edward Larocque. *The Horsemen of the Americas and the Literature They Inspired*. 2nd rev. ed. Austin: U of Texas P, 1967.

Trilling, Lionel. *Beyond Culture*. New York: Viking, 1965.

Vasconcelos, José. *Obras Completas*. Vol. 2. Mexico City: Mexicanos Unidos, 1958.

Walker, Franklin. *A Literary History of Southern California*. Berkeley: U of California P, 1950.

———. *San Francisco's Literary Frontier*. New York: Knopf, 1939.

Weber, Max. *The Protestant Ethic and the Spirit of Capitalism*. Trans. T. Parsons. New York: Scribner's, 1958. Trans. of *Die protestantische Ethik und der Geist des Kapitalismus*.

2. *Books and articles on Mexican-American literature*

Dávila, Luis. "On the Nature of Chicano Literature: En los Extremos del Laberinto." Spanish Section 3, Michigan Modern Language Association Convention. Detroit, 1971.
―――. "Chicano Fantasy Through a Glass Darkly." 16th Convention of the Instituto Internacional de Literatura Iberoamericana. East Lansing: Michigan State U, 30 Aug. 1973.
Hancock, Joel. "The Emergence of Chicano Poetry: A Survey of Sources, Themes and Techniques." *Arizona Quarterly* 29 (1973): 57–73.
Hinojosa, Rolando. "Mexican-American Literature: Towards an Identification." *Books Abroad: An International Literary Quarterly* 49 (1975): 422–30.
Huerta, Jorge A. "Contemporary Chicano Theatre." *Aztlán: Chicano Journal of the Social Sciences and the Arts* 2 (Fall 1971): 66–71.
Leal, Luis. "Mexican-American Literature: Historical Perspective." *Revista Chicano-Riqueña* 1 (1973): 32–44.
Ortego, Philip D. "Backgrounds of Mexican-American Literature." Diss. U of New Mexico, 1971.
―――. "The Chicano Renaissance." *Social Casework* 52 (1971): 294–307.
―――. "Mexican American Literature." *The Nation* Sept. 1969: 258–59.
Rivera, Tomás. "Chicano Literature: Fiesta of the Living." *Books Abroad* 49 (1975): 439–52.
―――. "Into the Labyrinth: The Chicano in Literature." Conference on Chicano Literature. Edinburgh, Tex., Panamerican U, 7–8 Oct. 1971.
Sotomayor, Frank. "An Explosion of Chicano Literary Merit." *Los Angeles Times* 28 Jan. 1973: 1+.
Tatum, Charles M. "Contemporary Chicano Prose Fiction: A Chronicle of Misery." *Latin American Literary Review* 1 (1972): 7–17.
―――. "Contemporary Chicano Prose Fiction: Its Ties to Mexican Literature." *Books Abroad* 49 (1975): 431–38.

3. *Historical works*

A. *On the United States*

Billington, Ray Allen. *The Protestant Crusade, 1800–1860: A Study of the Origins of American Nativism*. New York: Macmillan, 1938.
Higham, John. *Strangers in the Land: Patterns of American Nativism, 1860–1925*. New Brunswick, N.J.: Rutgers UP, 1955.
Hofstadter, Richard, William Miller, and Daniel Aaron. *The American Republic*. 2 vols. Englewood Cliffs, N.J.: Prentice, 1959.
Jaulin, Robert. *La Paix Blanche: Introduction à l'Ethnocide*. Collection "Combats." Paris: Seuil, 1970.
Ruiz, Ramón, ed. *The Mexican War: Was It Manifest Destiny?* New York: Holt, 1963.
Weinberg, Albert K. *Manifest Destiny: A Study of Nationalist Expansionism in American History*. Baltimore: Johns Hopkins UP, 1935.

B. On the Southwest

Acuña, Rudolfo. *A Mexican American Chronicle*. New York: American Book Co., 1971.

———. *Occupied America: The Chicano's Struggle Towards Liberation*. San Francisco: Canfield, 1972.

Arnold, Elliott. *The Time of the Gringo*. New York: Knopf, 1953.

Atherton, Gertrude. *California: An Intimate History*. New York: Harper, 1914.

Bancroft, Hubert Howe. *History of Arizona and New Mexico*. San Francisco, 1889.

———. *History of California*. 7 vols. San Francisco, 1886–90.

———. *History of the North Mexican States and Texas*. 2 vols. San Francisco, 1884–89.

Barker, Eugene C. *Mexico and Texas*. Austin: U of Texas P, 1934.

Burns, Walter Noble. *The Robin Hood of El Dorado: The Saga of Joaquin Murrieta, Famous Outlaw of California's Age of Gold*. New York: Grosset, 1932.

Canales, José T. *Juan N. Cortina Presents His Motion for a New Trial*. San Antonio: Artes Gráficas, 1951.

Cleland, Robert G. *The Cattle on a Thousand Hills: Southern California, 1850–1880*. San Marino, Calif: Huntington Library, 1941.

———. *From Wilderness to Empire: A History of California*. 1944. New York: Knopf, 1959. Rev. ed. of the combined *From Wilderness to Empire (1542–1900)* and *California in Our Time (1900–40)*.

Clendenen, Clarence C. *Blood on the Border: The United States Army and the Mexican Irregulars*. London: Macmillan, 1969.

Dumke, Glenn S. *The Boom of the Eighties in Southern California*. San Marino, Calif.: Huntington Library, 1944.

Ganilh, Anthony. *Mexico versus Texas*. Philadelphia, 1838.

Gentry, Curt. *The Last Days of the Late, Great State of California*. New York: Ballantine, 1968.

Goldfinch, Charles W. "Juan N. Cortina, 1824–1892: A Re-Appraisal." M.A. Thesis, U of Chicago, 1949.

Hager, William M. "The Plan of San Diego: Unrest on the Texas Border in 1915." *Arizona and the West* 5 (1963): 327–36.

Jackson, Helen Hunt. *Glimpses of California and the Missions*. Boston: Little, 1919.

———. *Glimpses of Three Coasts*. Boston, 1886.

Lummis, Charles F. *The Spanish Pioneers and the California Missions*. Rev. ed. Chicago: McClurg, 1929.

Moore, Joan W. *Mexican-Americans: Problems and Prospects*. Madison: U of Wisconsin P, 1967.

Moquin, Wayne, and Charles Van Doren, eds. *A Documentary History of the Mexican Americans*. New York: Praeger, 1971.

Nava, Julian. *Mexican-Americans: Past, Present, and Future*. Millbrae, Calif.: American Book Co., 1969.

Padilla, R. V. "A Critique of Pittian History." *El Grito* 6 (Fall 1972): 3–44.

Pitt, Leonard. *The Decline of the Californios: A Social History of the Spanish-Speaking Californians, 1846–1890*. Berkeley: U of California P, 1966.

Ridge, John R. *The Life and Adventures of Joaquin Murrieta, the Celebrated California Bandit*. 3rd ed. 1854. San Francisco, 1871.

Royce, Josiah. *California: From the Conquest in 1846 to the Second Vigilance Committee in San Francisco*. Boston, 1886.

Van Dyke, Theodore Strong. *Millionaires of a Day: An Inside History of the Great California "Boom."* New York, 1890.

Webb, Walter Prescott. *The Texas Rangers: A Century of Frontier Defense.* Boston: Houghton, 1935.

C. On the Chicano movement

Blawis, Patricia Bell. *Tijerina and the Land Grants: Mexican Americans in Their Struggle for Their Heritage.* New York: International Publ., 1971.

Bongartz, Roy. "No Mere Sombrero: The Chicano Rebellion." *The Nation* 3 Mar. 1969: 271–74.

Carney, Francis. "The Progress of César Chávez." *New York Review of Books* 13 Nov. 1975: 39–42.

Castro, Tony. *Chicano Power.* New York: Dutton, 1974.

———. "Chicano Proves Term of Controversy." *Dallas Morning News* 26 Feb. 1973: D-1.

Chávez, César. "The Organizer's Tale." *Ramparts* 5 July 1966: 43–50.

Day, Mark. *Forty Acres: César Chávez and the Farm Workers.* New York: Praeger, 1971.

Delgado, Abelardo. *The Chicano Movement: Some Not Too Objective Observations.* Denver: Totinem, July 1971.

Dommergues, Pierre. "Les Chicanos ou la fierté retrouvée." *Monde Diplomatique* Apr. 1974: 16–20.

Dunne, John Gregory. *Delano.* 1967. New York: Farrar, 1971.

Gardner, Richard. *¡Grito! Reies Tijerina and the New Mexico Land Grant War of 1967.* New York: Bobbs, 1970.

Kushner, Sam. *Long Road to Delano.* New York: International Publ., 1975.

Levy, Jacques E. *César Chávez: Autobiography of La Causa.* New York: Norton, 1975.

"The Little Strike That Grew to La Causa." *Time* 4 July 1969: 12–17.

London, Joan, and Henry Anderson. *So Shall Ye Reap: The Story of César Chávez and the Farm Workers' Movement.* New York: Crowell, 1971.

Maddern Pitrone, Jean. *Chávez: Man of the Migrants. A Plea for Social Justice.* New York: Pyramid, 1971.

Mathiessen, Peter. *Sal Si Puedes: César Chávez and the New American Revolution.* New York: Dell, 1969.

———. "Organizer: Profile of César Chávez." *New Yorker* 21 and 28 June 1969.

Meier, Matt S., and Feliciano Rivera. *The Chicanos: A History of Mexican Americans.* New York: Hill, 1972.

———. *Readings on la Raza: The Twentieth Century.* New York: Hill, 1974.

Nabokov, Peter. *Tijerina and the Courthouse Raid.* Albuquerque: U of New Mexico P, 1969.

Nelson, Eugene. *Huelga: The First Hundred Days of the Great Delano Grape Strike.* Delano, Calif.: Farm Workers Press, 1966.

———. "Huelga: New Goals for Labor." *The Nation* 5 June 1967: 724–25.

Newlon, Clarke. *Famous Mexican Americans.* New York: Dodd, 1972.

Rendón, Armando B. *Chicano Manifesto: The History and Aspirations of the Second Largest Minority in America.* New York: Collier, 1972.

———. "How Much Longer the Long Road?" *Civil Rights Digest* 1 (1968): 34–44.

———. "La Raza Today Not Mañana." *Civil Rights Digest* 1 (1968): 7–17.

Shockley, John Staples. *Chicano Revolt in a Texas Town*. Notre Dame, Ind.: Notre Dame UP, 1974.

Taylor, Ronald B. *Chávez and the Farm Workers*. Boston: Beacon, 1975.

Valdez, Luis. "The Tale of La Raza." *Ramparts* 5 July 1966: 40–43.

Villarreal, José Antonio. "Mexican Americans and the Leadership Crisis." *Los Angeles Times West Magazine* 25 Sept. 1966: 44–50.

———. "Mexican-Americans in Upheaval." *Los Angeles Times West Magazine* 18 Sept. 1966: 21–30.

4. Works on Mexico

Azuela, Mariano. *Los de abajo: Novela de la revolución mexicana*. Mexico City: Fondo de Cultura, 1958.

Bermúdez, María Elvira. *La vida familiar del mexicano*. Mexico City: Robredo, 1955.

Caso, Alfonso. *El pueblo del sol*. Mexico City: Fondo de Cultura, 1953.

———. *La religión de los Aztecas*. Mexico City: Fondo de Cultura, 1936.

Caso, Antonio. *El problema de México y la ideología nacional*. Mexico City: Libro-Mexico, 1955.

Cumberland, Charles C. "Mexican Revolutionary Movements from Texas, 1906–1912." *Southwestern Historical Quarterly* 52 (1948–49): 301–24.

Lafaye, Jacques. *Quetzalcoatl et Guadalupe: La Formation de la conscience nationale au Mexique (1531–1813)*. Trans. by Françoise-Marie Rosset. Paris: Gallimard, 1974.

León-Portilla, Miguel. *Los antiguos: Mexicanos a través de sus crónicas y cantares*. Mexico City: Fondo de Cultura, 1961.

Lewis, Oscar. *Five Families*. New York: Basic, 1959.

Paredes, Américo. *Estados Unidos, Mexico y el machismo*. Austin: U of Texas P, 1967.

Parkes, Henry Bamford. *Histoire du Mexique*. Trans. by C. Delavaud of *A History of Mexico*. Rev. ed. Paris: Payot, 1971.

Paz, Octavio. *El laberinto de la soledad*. Mexico City: Fondo de Cultura, 1959.

Prescott, William H. *History of the Conquest of Mexico, with a Preliminary View of the Ancient Mexican Civilization and the Life of the Conqueror, Hernando Cortés*. 3 vols. New York: 1843.

Ramos, Samuel. *Profile of Man and Culture in Mexico*. Trans. by P. G. Earle of *El perfil del hombre*. Austin: U of Texas P, 1962.

Santiago, Ramírez. *El Mexicano: Psicología de sus motivaciones*. Mexico City: Pax, 1959.

Sejourne, Laurette. *La Pensée des anciens Mexicains*. Paris: Maspero, 1966.

Soustelle, Jacques. *La Pensée cosmologique des anciens Mexicains*. Paris: Hermann, 1940.

———. *La Vie quotidienne des Aztèques à la veille de la conquête espagnole*. Paris: Hachette, 1955.

Vaillant, George. *The Aztecs of Mexico*. New York: Doubleday, 1941.

Vasconcelos, José. *La raza cósmica*. Barcelona: Agencia Mundial, 1925. Reprinted in his *Obras Completas*. Mexico City: Libreros Mexicanos Unidos, 1958.

Vásquez, Santana. *Historia de la canción mexicana*. Mexico City: Talleres Gráficos, 1931.

Yañez, Agustín. *The Edge of the Storm*. Trans. by Ethel Brinton of *Al filo del agua*. Austin: U of Texas P, 1963.

5. *Sociological works*

A. *Customs of the Southwest*

Arias, Ronald. "The Barrio." *Agenda* 2 (1966): 15–20.

Atherton, Gertrude. *Golden Gate Country*. American Folkways Collection. New York: Duell, 1945.

Brenner, Anita. *Idols Behind Altars*. New York: Harcourt, 1929.

Cabeza de Baca, Fabiola. *We Fed Them Cactus*. Albuquerque: U of New Mexico P, 1954.

Emrich, Duncan. *It's an Old Wild West Custom*. New York: Vanguard, 1949.

Fergusson, Harvey. *Rio Grande*. New York: Knopf, 1933.

Garth, Thomas R., and E. Candor. "Musical Talent of Mexicans." *American Journal of Psychology* 1 (1926): 183–87.

Hurt, Wesley R., Jr. "Spanish American Superstitions." *El Palacio* 47 (1940): 193–201.

Kiev, Ari. *Curanderismo: Mexican-American Folk Psychiatry*. New York: Free, 1968.

Laughlin, Ruth (Barker). *Caballeros*. New York: Appleton, 1931.

Lea, Tom. *The King Ranch*. 2 vols. Boston: Little, 1957.

Lummis, Charles F. *Flowers of Our Lost Romance*. Boston: Houghton, 1929.

———. *The Land of Poco Tiempo*. London, 1893.

McWilliams, Carey. *Southern California Country: An Island on the Land*. New York: Duell, Sloan and Pearce, 1946.

Rojas, Arnold R. *The Vaquero*. Charlotte, N.C.: McNally, 1964.

Scott, Florence Johnson. "Customs and Superstitions Among Texas Mexicans." *Publications* 2 (1923): 75–85.

Waugh, Julia Nott. *The Silver Cradle*. Austin: U of Texas P, 1955.

Winters, Alan. "Peonage in the Southwest." *Fourth International* 14 (Mar. 1953): 43–49; (May 1953): 74–78.

B. *The Mexican minority*

(1) *In general*

Browder, E. "The American Communist Party in the Thirties." *As We Saw the Thirties*. Ed. Rita J. Simon. Urbana: U of Illinois P, 1967.

De la Garza, Rudolf, and John Womack, Jr. "An Exchange on the Chicanos." *New York Review of Books* 19 Apr. 1973: 41–42.

Emiliano, Ramón. "Nahuatlan Elements in Chicano Speech." *Grito del Sol* 4 (Oct.-Dec. 1976): 89–108.

Ertel, Rachel, Geneviève Fabre, and Elise Marienstras. *En Marge: Les Minorités aux Etats-Unis*. Paris: Maspero, 1971.

Fergusson, Erna. *New Mexico: A Pageant of Three Peoples*. New York: Knopf, 1955.

———. "The New New Mexican." *New Mexico Quarterly Review* 19 (1949): 417–26.

Frank, Waldo. *Our America*. New York: Boni, 1919.

Galarza, Ernesto, Herman Gallegos, and Julian Samora. *Mexican-Americans in the Southwest*. Santa Barbara: McNally, 1969.

Galindo, P. "The Mexican-American Devil's Dictionary." *El Grito* 6 (1973): 41–53.

Glazer, Nathan, and P. Moynihan. *Beyond the Melting Pot*. Cambridge: MIT P, 1963.

González, Nancie L. *The Spanish Americans of New Mexico: A Heritage of Pride*. Albuquerque: U of New Mexico P, 1969.

Grebler, Leo, Joan W. Moore, and Ralph C. Guzmán. *The Mexican-American People, the Nation's Second Largest Minority*. New York: Free, 1970.

Griffith, Beatrice. *American Me*. Boston: Houghton, 1948.

Handlin, Oscar. *The Uprooted*. New York: Grosset, 1951.

McWilliams, Carey. *Brothers Under the Skin*. 3rd rev. ed. Boston: Little, 1964.

———. *The Mexican in America*. New York: Columbia UP, 1968.

———. *North From Mexico: The Spanish-Speaking People of the United States*. Philadelphia: Lippincott, 1949. New York: Greenwood, 1969.

———. "America's Disadvantaged Minorities: Mexican-Americans." *Journal of Negro Education* 20 (1951): 301–09.

———. "The Forgotten Mexican." *Common Ground* (1943): 65–78.

———. "The Mexican Problem." *Common Ground* (1948): 3–17.

Madsen, William. *The Mexican-Americans of South Texas*. New York: Holt, 1964.

"The Mexican-Americans, Their Plight and Struggles." *Political Affairs* 28 (1949): 71–80. Resolutions adopted at the 14th National Convention of the American Communist Party, 3 Aug. 1948.

Prado, E. L. "Sinarquism in the United States." *New Republic* 26 July 1943: 97–102.

Samora, Julian, ed. *La Raza: Forgotten Americans*. Notre Dame: Notre Dame UP, 1966.

Sánchez, George I. *Forgotten People: A Study of New Mexicans*. 1940. Albuquerque: Horn, 1967.

Saunders, Lyle. "The Social History of Spanish-Speaking People in Southwestern United States Since 1846." Fourth Regional Conference, Southwest Council on Education of Spanish-Speaking People. Albuquerque, 23–25 Jan. 1950.

Simmen, Edward, ed. *Pain and Promise: The Chicano Today*. New York: NAL, 1972.

Steiner, Stan. *La Raza: The Mexican-Americans*. New York: Harper, 1970.

Tuck, Ruth. *Not With the Fist: Mexican-Americans in a Southwest City*. New York: Harcourt, 1946.

Vaca, Nick C. "The Mexican American in the Social Sciences: 1912–1970; Part I: 1912–1935." *El Grito* 3 (1970): 3–24.

(2) The Mexican character

Campa, Arthur L. "Mañana Is Today." *New Mexico Quarterly* 9 (1939): 3–8.

Gamio, Manuel. "Static and Dynamic Values in the Indigenous Past of America." *Hispanic American Historical Review* 23 (1930): 386–93.

Hewes, G. W. "Mexicans in Search of the 'Mexican': Notes on Mexican National Character Studies." *American Journal of Economics and Sociology* 2 (1954).

Humphrey, Norman D. "The Stereotype and the Social Types of Mexican-American Youth." *Journal of Social Psychology* 22 (1945): 69–78.

Landazuri, Elena. "Why We Are Different." *Survey* 52 (1924): 159–60.

Marston, H. D. "Mexican Traits." *Survey* 44 (1920): 562–64.

Reiss, Winold. "Draughtsmanship and Racial Types: Mexican Character Studies." *Arts and Decoration* 15 (1921): 28–29.

Werlin, Joseph Sidney. "Mexican Opinion of Us." *South Atlantic Quarterly* 43 (1944): 233–47.

(3) Assimilation and acculturation

Aragón, Roberto, and José Aragón. "Needed: A Chicano Voting Rights Act Now." *Regeneración* 1 (1970): 7.

"Authentic Pachuco." *Time* 10 July 1944: 72.

Barker, George C. *Pachuco: An American-Spanish Argot and Its Social Functions in Tucson, Arizona.* 1950. Tucson: U of Arizona P, 1970.

Bode, Elroy. "The Making of a Legend." *Texas Observer* 30 Mar. 1973: 1–5.

Bogardus, Emory S. "Second Generation Mexicans." *Sociology and Social Research* 13 (1929): 276–83.

Braddy, H. "Pachucos and Their Argot." *Southern Folk-Lore Quarterly* 24 (1960): 255–71.

Carranza, Eliu. *Pensamientos on los Chicanos: A Cultural Revolution.* Berkeley: California Book Co., 1969.

Dworkin, Gary Anthony. "Stereotypes and Self-Images Held by Native-Born and Foreign-Born Mexican-Americans." *Sociology and Social Research* 49 (1965): 214–24.

Garrison, George P. *Texas: A Contest of Civilizations.* Boston: Houghton, 1903.

Grant, Madison, and Charles Stewart Davison, eds. *The Alien in Our Midst; or, "Selling Our Birthright for a Mess of Pottage."* New York: Galton, 1930.

Griffith, Beatrice. "The Pachuco Patois." *Common Ground* 7 (1947): 77–84.

———. "Viva Roybal—Viva America." *Common Ground* 10 (1949): 61–70.

Heller, Celia S. *Mexican-American Youth: Forgotten at the Crossroads.* New York: Random, 1966.

Humphrey, Norman D. "The Changing Structure of the Detroit Mexican Family." *American Sociological Review* 9 (1944): 622–26.

Jones, Robert C. "Ethnic Family Patterns: The Mexican Family in the United States." *American Journal of Sociology* 53 (1947–48): 450–60.

López y Rivas, Gilberto. *The Chicanos: Life and Struggles of the Mexican Minority in the United States.* New York: Monthly Review, 1974.

McWilliams, Carey. "Is Your Name Gonzales?" *The Nation* Mar. 1947: 302–04.

———. "Los Angeles Pachuco Gangs." *New Republic* 18 Jan. 1943: 76–77.

———. "Zoot-Suit Riots." *New Republic* 21 June 1943: 818–20.

Manuel, H. T. "The Educational Problem Presented by the Spanish-Speaking Child of the Southwest." *School and Society* 11 (1934): 692–95.

Martínez, Paul G. "Teaching English to Spanish-Speaking Americans in New Mexico." *New Mexico School Review* 13 (1933): 22–23.

Morales, Armando. *Ando Sangrando (I Am Bleeding): A Study of American-Mexican Police Conflict.* La Puente, Calif.: Perspectiva, 1972.

Morín, Raúl. *Among the Valiant: Mexican-Americans in World War II and Korea.* Alhambra, Calif.: Borden, 1963.

Ortego, Philip D. "The Education of Mexican Americans." *The Chicanos: Mexican-American Voices.* Ed. Edward Ludwig and James Santibañez. Baltimore: Penguin, 1971.

"Pachuco: Secret Language." *Science Digest* Oct. 1950: 47–48.

Paredes, Américo. "Texas' Third Man: The Texas Mexican." *Race* 3 (May 1963): 49–58.

Pinkney, A. "Prejudice Toward Mexican and Negro Americans: A Comparison." *Phylon* 24 (1963): 353–59.

"Pocho's Progress: Nation's Second Largest Disadvantaged Minority." *Time* 28 Apr. 1967: 24–25.

Rechy, John. "Jim Crow Wears a Sombrero." *The Nation* 10 Oct. 1959: 210–13.

Romano-V., Octavio I. "The Anthropology and Sociology of the Mexican-Americans: The Distortion of Mexican-American History." *El Grito* 2 (Fall 1968): 13–25.

———. "Donship in a Mexican-American Community in Texas." *American Anthropologist* 62 (1960): 966–76.

———. "The Historical and Intellectual Presence of Mexican-Americans." *El Grito* 2 (Winter 1969): 32–45.

Sánchez, George I. "New Mexicans and Acculturation." *New Mexico Quarterly Review* 11 (1941): 61–68.

———. "Pachucos in the Making." *Common Ground* 4 (1943): 13–20.

———. "The Default of Leadership." Fourth Regional Conference, Southwest Council on Education of Spanish-Speaking People. Albuquerque, 23–25 Jan. 1950. Mimeographed.

Saunders, Lyle. *Cultural Difference and Medical Care: The Case of the Spanish-Speaking People of the Southwest*. New York: Russell Sage, 1954.

Sommers, Vita S. "The Impact of Dual Cultural Membership on Identity." *Psychiatry* 27 (1964): 332–44.

Stoddard, Lothrop. *The Rising Tide of Color: Against White World-Supremacy*. New York: Scribner's, 1920.

Turner, Ralph H., and Samuel J. Surace. "Zoot-Suiters and Mexicans: Symbols in Crowd Behavior." *American Journal of Sociology* 62 (1956): 14–20.

West, Guy A. "Race Attitudes Among Teachers in the Southwest." *Journal of Abnormal and Social Psychology* 21 (1936): 331–37.

"What Is a Chicano? Difficulty in the Subject Heading." *Wilson Library Bulletin* 46 (1972): 492–93.

Womack, John Jr. "Who Are the Chicanos?" *New York Review of Books* 31 Aug. 1972: 12–18.

Woodbridge, H. C. "Mexico and U.S. Racism: How Mexicans View Our Treatment of Minorities." *Commonweal* 22 June 1945: 234–37.

(4) Immigration and working conditions

Caldwell, Erskine. *Around About America*. New York: Farrar, 1963.

Galarza, Ernesto. *Merchants of Labor: The Mexican Bracero Story: An Account of the Managed Migration of Mexican Farm Workers in California, 1942–1960*. Charlotte, N.C.: McNally, 1964.

———. *Spiders in the House and Workers in the Field*. South Bend: Notre Dame UP, 1970.

———. *Strangers in Our Fields*. U.S. Section, Joint United States-Mexico Trade Union Committee. Washington, 1956.

———. "Big Farm Strike: A Report on the Labor Dispute at the Di Giorgio's." *Commonweal* 48 (1948): 178–82.

———. "Program for Action." *Common Ground* 10 (Summer 1949): 27–38.

———. "They Work for Pennies." *American Federationist* 59 (Apr. 1952): 10–13.

———. "Without Benefit of Lobby." *Survey* 1 May 1931: 181.

Gamio, Manuel. *The Mexican Immigrant: His Life Story*. Chicago: U of Chicago P, 1931.

———. *Mexican Immigration to the United States: A Study of Human Migration and Adjustment*. Chicago: U of Chicago P, 1930.

Gómez, David F. *Somos Chicanos: Strangers in Our Own Land*. Boston: Beacon, 1973.

Grebler, Leo. *Mexican Immigration to the United States*. Mexican–American Study Project. Advance Report 2. Division of Research, Graduate School of Business Administration, UCLA, 1966.

Hoffman, Abraham. *Unwanted Mexican Americans in the Great Depression: Repatriation Pressures, 1929–1939*. Tucson: U of Arizona P, 1974.

McWilliams, Carey. *Factories in the Field: The Story of Migratory Farm Labor in California*. Boston: Little, 1939.

————. "California and the Wetback." *Common Ground* 10 (Summer 1949): 15–20.

Madrid-Barela, Arturo. "Alambristas, Braceros, Mojados, Norteños: Aliens in Aztlán, an Interpretive Essay." *Aztlán* 6 (1975): 27–42.

Mangan, Frank J. *Bordertown*. El Paso: Hertzog, 1964.

Steinbeck, John. *Their Blood Is Strong*. San Francisco: Lubin Society, 1938.

Stilwell, Hart. "The Wetback Tide." *Common Ground* 10 (Summer 1949): 27–38.

Taylor, Paul S. *An American-Mexican Frontier: Nueces County, Texas*. Chapel Hill: U of North Carolina P, 1934.

————. *Mexican Labor in the United States*. 6 vols. Berkeley: U of California P, 1928–34.

Taylor, Ronald B. *Sweat-Shops in the Sun: Child Labor on the Farm*. Boston: Beacon, 1973.

Part Three. Anglo-American Authors

For reasons of convenience, Anglo-American literary works are divided into two groups, the year 1940 roughly marking the beginning of a new era.

1. Before 1940

Allen, John Houghton. *Song to Randalo*. Dallas: Kaleidograph, 1935.

Atherton, Gertrude. *The Californians*. London, 1898.

————. *Los Cerritos: A Romance of the Modern Time*. New York, 1890. Ridgewood, N.J.: Gregg, 1968.

————. *The Splendid Idle Forties: Stories of Old California*. New York: Macmillan, 1902. Original title: *Before the Gringo Came*, 1894.

Audubon, John W. *Audubon's Western Journals, 1849–1850: Being the Ms. Record of a Trip from New York to Texas and an Overland Journey Through Mexico and Arizona to the Gold-Fields of California*. Cleveland: Clark, 1906.

Austin, Mary. *Earth Horizon*. Boston: Houghton, 1932.

————. *The Land of Journey's Ending*. New York: Century, 1924.

————. *The Land of Little Rain*. Boston: Houghton, 1903.

————. *Mother of Felipe and Other Early Stories*. Comp. F. Walker. San Francisco: Book Club, 1950.

————. *One-Smoke Stories*. Boston: Houghton, 1934.

Badger, Joseph E. *Big George, the Giant of the Gulch: or, The Five Outlaw Brothers*. New York, 1880. Beadle's Dime Novel Collection, New York Public Library no. 88.

————. *Joaquin, the Saddle King: A Romance of Murieta's First Fight*. New York, 1881. Beadle's Dime Novel Collection no. 154.

————. *Joaquin the Terrible: The True History of the Three Bitter Blows That Changed an*

Honest Man to a Merciless Demon. New York, 1881. Beadle's Dime Novel Collection no. 165.

————. *The Pirate of the Placers; or, Joaquin's Death Hunt.* New York, 1882. Beadle's Dime Novel Collection no. 201.

————. *The Rustler Detective: or, The Bounding Buck from Buffalo Wallow.* New York, 1887. Beadle's Dime Novel Collection no. 450.

Bartlett, John Russell. *Personal Narrative of Explorations and Incidents in Texas, New Mexico, California, Sonora and Chihuahua.* 2 vols. New York, 1854.

Bell, (Major) Horace. *On the Old West Coast: Being Further Reminiscences of a Ranger.* New York: Morrow, 1930. Begun in 1881, published posthumously.

————. *Reminiscences of a Ranger; or, Early Times in Southern California.* 1881. Santa Barbara: Hebbard, 1927.

Boone, Henry L. (pseud. of Henry Llewellyn Williams). *Yankee Jim, the Horse-Runner: A Tale of Love and Hate in Southern California.* New York, 1867. Beadle's Dime Novel Collection no. 71.

Borthwick, J. D. *Three Years in California.* Edinburgh, 1857.

Brewer, William H. *Up and Down California in 1860–1864: The Journal of William H. Brewer, Professor of Agriculture in the Sheffield Scientific School from 1864 to 1903.* 1st ed. New Haven: Yale UP, 1930.

Browne, J. Ross. *Adventures in the Apache Country: A Tour Through Arizona and Sonora, with Notes on the Silver Regions of Nevada.* New York, 1869.

————. *Crusoe's Island: A Ramble in the Footsteps of Alexander Selkirk, with Sketches of Adventure in California and Washoe.* New York, 1864.

Cather, Willa Sibert. "The Dance at Chevalier's." [1900] *Early Stories.* Ed. Mildred R. Bennett. New York: Dodd, 1957. 217–29. This short story, written under the pseudonym Henry Nicklemann, first appeared in the magazine *The Library,* 28 Apr. 1900.

————. *Death Comes for the Archbishop.* New York: Knopf, 1927.

————. *The Professor's House.* New York: Knopf, 1925.

————. *The Song of the Lark.* Boston: Houghton, 1915.

Channing, Grace Ellery (Stetson). *The Sister of a Saint and Other Stories.* Chicago, 1895.

Clappe, Louise Amelia Knapp (Smith). *The Shirley Letters from the California Mines, 1851–1852.* New York: Knopf, 1949. Originally published in installments in the *Pioneer Magazine of San Francisco* in 1854–55.

Clemens, Jeremiah. *Bernard Lile, an Historical Romance.* Philadelphia, 1856.

Crane, Stephen. *The Complete Short Stories and Sketches of Stephen Crane.* Garden City, N.Y.: Doubleday, 1963.

————. "A Man and Some Others." *Century Magazine* 53 (1897): 601–07.

Daggett, Mary (Stewart). *Mariposilla.* Chicago, 1895.

Dana, Richard Henry. *Two Years Before the Mast.* 1840. New York: Macmillan, 1915.

Davis, Carlyle C., and William A. Alderson. *The True Story of Ramona.* New York: Dodge, 1914. A critical work on the novel by Helen Hunt Jackson.

Davis, William Watts Hart. *El Gringo; or, New Mexico and Her People.* New York, 1857.

Deforest, John William. *Overland.* New York, 1871.

Delano, Alonzo. *Life on the Plains and Among the Diggings.* New York, 1854.

Dos Passos, John. *The 42nd Parallel.* New York: Harper, 1930.

Ellis, Edward Silvester. *Irona; or, Life on the Old Southwest Border.* New York, 1861. Beadle's American Library no. 35.

Emery, George. "The Water-Witch." *The Chicano*. Ed. Edward Simmen. New York: NAL, 1971. Originally published in *Overland Monthly* 3 (1869): 94–96.

Evans, George W. B. *Mexican Gold Trail: The Journal of a 49er*. 1st ed. San Marino, Calif.: Huntington Library, 1945.

Fergusson, Harvey. *Followers of the Sun: A Trilogy of the Santa Fe Trail*. New York: Knopf, 1942. Includes: *Wolfsong*, 1927; *In Those Days*, 1929; *The Blood of the Conquerors*, 1921 (published in that order).

Garland, Hamlin. "Delmar of Pima." *McClure's Magazine* Feb. 1902: 340–48.

Giddings, Luther. *Sketches of the Campaign in Northern Mexico*. New York, 1853.

Gregg, Josiah. *Commerce of the Prairies: Or, The Journal of a Santa Fe Trader, During Eight Expeditions Across the Great Western Prairies and a Residence of Nearly Nine Years in Northern Mexico*. 2 vols. Philadelphia, 1851.

Hall, (Major) S. S. *The Black Bravo: or, The Tonkaway's Triumph: A Romance of the Frio Ranch*. New York, 1882. Beadle's Dime Novel Collection no. 186.

———. *The Crooked Three: or, The Black Hearts of the Guadalupe*. New York, 1883. Beadle's Dime Novel Collection no. 264.

———. *Dandy Dave, and His Horse White Stocking: or, Ducats or Death*. New York, 1884. Beadle's Dime Novel Collection no. 287.

———. *Double Dan, the Dastard: or, The Pirates of the Pecos*. New York, 1883. Beadle's Dime Novel Collection no. 256.

———. *Kit Carson, Jr., the Crack Shot of the West: A Romance of the Lone Star State*. New York, 1877. Frank Starr's New York Library, no. 3.

———. *The Merciless Marauders: or, Chaparral Carl's Revenge*. New York, 1884. Beadle's Dime Novel Collection no. 282.

———. *The Rough Riders: or, Sharp Eye, the Seminole Scourge: A Tale of the Chaparral*. New York, 1883. Beadle's Dime Novel Collection no. 250.

Harris, Frank. *My Reminiscences as a Cowboy*. New York: Boni, 1930.

Harte, Bret. "The Devotion of Enríquez." *The Chicano: From Caricature to Self-Portrait*. Ed. Edward Simmen. New York: NAL, 1971. 48–71. First published in *Century Magazine*, Nov. 1895.

———. "The Passing of Enríquez." *The Writings of Bret Harte*. Boston: Houghton, 1900. 16: 71–107.

Hemingway, Ernest. "Give Us a Prescription, Doctor." *Scribner's Magazine* 93 (Apr. 1933): 272–78. Included by the author in his short-story collection *Winner Take Nothing* (New York: Scribner's, 1933) under its current title "The Gambler, the Nun and the Radio."

———. *Men Without Women*. New York: Scribner's, 1927.

Henderson, Stanley. *Karaibo; or, The Outlaw's Fate*. New York: 1886. Beadle's Dime Novel Collection no. 100.

Henry, O. (pseud. of William Sidney Porter). *The Complete Works of O. Henry*. New York, 1899. Garden City, N.Y.: Garden City Publ., 1937.

Herrick, Robert. *Waste*. New York: Harcourt, 1924.

Horgan, Paul. *Main Line West*. New York: Harper, 1936.

———. *No Quarter Given*. New York: Harper, 1935.

———. *The Return of the Weed*. New York: Harper, 1936.

Jackson, Helen Hunt. *Ramona*. Boston, 1884.

Jeffers, Robinson. *Cawdor and Other Poems*. New York: Random, 1934.

———. *The Selected Poetry of Robinson Jeffers*. New York: Random, 1937.

————. *Women at Point Sur*. New York: Random, 1935.

Kendall, George Wilkens. *Narrative of the Texan Santa Fe Expedition*. London, 1847. Chicago: Lakeside, 1929.

Lanier, Sidney. "San Antonio de Bexar." *Retrospects and Prospects: Descriptive and Historical Essays*. New York: 1899. 34–93. This essay first appeared in *Southern Magazine*, 1873.

Lewis, Alfred Henry. *The Throwback: A Romance of the Southwest*. London: Cassel, 1907.

————. *Wolfville*. New York, 1897.

————. *Wolfville Days*. London: Isbister, 1902.

London, Jack. "The Mexican." *The Chicano: From Caricature to Self-Portrait*. Ed. Edward Simmen. New York: NAL, 1971. 89–112. First published in *The Saturday Evening Post*, 1911.

Lummis, Charles F. *A Bronco Pegasus*. Boston: Houghton, 1928.

————. *The Enchanted Burro: Stories of New Mexico and South America*. Chicago, 1897.

————. *The King of the Broncos and Other Stories of New Mexico*. London, 1897.

————. *A New Mexico David and Other Stories and Sketches of the Southwest*. New York, 1891.

McGinnis, John. "The Tomato Can." *Southwest Review* 16 (1931): 507–16.

Magoon, (Lieut.) Jas. *The Life of Major Gen. John C. Fremont*. London, 1862.

Manly, William Lewis. *Death Valley in '49*. San Jose, 1894.

Means, Florence Crannel. *Pepita's Adventures in Friendship: A Play for Juniors About Mexicans in the United States*. New York: Friendship, 1929.

Means, Florence Crannel, and Harriet Louise Fullen. *Rafael and Consuelo: Stories and Studies About Mexicans in the United States for Primary Children*. New York: Friendship, 1929.

Miller, Cincinnatus Hiner [Joaquin]. *The Complete Poetical Works*. San Francisco, 1897.

————. *Joaquin et al*. Portland, Ore., 1869.

————. *Songs of the Sierras*. London, 1871.

Newmark, Harris. *Sixty Years in Southern California, 1853–1913*. New York: Knicker Bocker, 1916. Rev. ed. 1930.

Norris, Frank. *The Octopus*. New York: Doubleday, 1901.

Olmsted, Frederick Law. *A Journey Through Texas; or, A Saddle-Trip on the Southwestern Frontier*. New York, 1857.

Parkman, Francis. *The Oregon Trail*. Garden City, N.Y.: Garden City Publ., 1948. Originally published in 1849 as *The California and Oregon Trail*.

Pattie, James O. *The Personal Narrative of James O. Pattie of Kentucky, During an Expedition from Saint-Louis, Through the Vast Regions Between That Place and the Pacific Ocean, and Thence Back Through the City of Mexico to Veracruz, During Journeyings of Six Years; in Which He and His Father Who Accompanied Him, Suffered Unheard of Hardships and Dangers; Had Various Conflicts with the Indians, and Were Made Captives, in Which Captivity His Father Died, Together With a Description of the Country, and the Various Nations Through Which They Passed*. First published in Cincinnati, 1831. Republished by Timothy Flint with the collaboration of M. M. Quaife. Chicago: Lakeside, 1930.

Remington, Frederic. *Pony Tracks: Sketches of Pioneer Life*. New York, 1895.

Rhodes, Eugene Manlove. *Once in the Saddle and Pasó por Aquí*. Boston: Houghton, 1927.

Richter, Conrad. "Smoke Over the Prairie." *Early Americana and Other Stories*. New York: Knopf, 1936. 38–83.

Ryan, Marah Ellis. *For the Soul of Rafael*. 11th ed. 1906. Chicago: McClurg, 1914.

Saroyan, William. "The Mexicans." *Little Children*. London: Faber, 1937. 163–72.

————. "With a Hey Nonny Nonny." *Inhale and Exhale*. New York: Random, 1936. 211–16.

Steinbeck, John. *The Long Valley*. New York: Viking, 1938.

————. *The Pastures of Heaven*. New York: Viking, 1932.

————. *Tortilla Flat*. New York: Modern Library, 1937.

Sterling, George. "Father Coyote." *Beyond the Breakers and Other Poems*. San Francisco: Robertson, 1914. 132–33.

Stevenson, Philip E. "At the Crossroads." *Folk-Say: A Regional Miscellany*. Ed. B. A. Botkin. Norman: U of Oklahoma P, 1931. 70–82.

————. "The Shepherd." *Southwest Review* 16 (1930): 65–74.

Stoddard, Charles W. *In the Footprints of the Padres*. San Francisco: Robertson, 1902.

Summers, Richard. *Dark Madonna*. Caldwell, Idaho: Caxton, 1937.

Twain, Mark (pseud. of Samuel Langhorne Clemens). *Roughing It*. 1888. Hartford: American, 1972.

Warne, Philip S. *Black-Hoss Ben: or, Tiger Dick's Lone Hand: A Tale of Wild Ranch Life*. New York, 1884. Beadle's Dime Novel Collection no. 280.

White, Stewart Edward. *Arizona Nights*. New York: McClure, 1907.

Willett, Edward. *The Canyon King: or, A Price on His Head: A Tale of the Wahsatch Range*. New York, 1885. Beadle's Dime Novel Collection no. 368.

2. From 1940 to the present

Allen, John Houghton. *Southwest*. Philadelphia: Lippincott, 1952.

Barrett, William E. *The Shadows of the Images*. Kingswood, Eng.: Heinemann, 1954.

————. "Señor Payroll." *Southwest Review* 28 (1943): 17–20.

Barry, Jane. *A Shadow of Eagles*. Garden City, N.Y.: Doubleday, 1964.

Bonham, Frank. *Cool Cat*. New York: Dell, 1971.

————. *Viva Chicano*. New York: Dell, 1970.

Bowman, James K. "El Patrón." *New Campus Writing*. Ed. Nolan Miller. Vol. 2. New York: Putnam, 1957. 50–56.

Bradbury, Ray. "I See You Never," "En la Noche." *The Golden Apples of the Sun*. London: Transworld, 1956. 89–92, 136–41.

————. "The Wonderful Ice Cream Suit," "The Little Mice." *The Day It Rained Forever*. London: Hart-Davis, 1959. 38–64, 193–98.

Bright, Robert. *The Life and Death of Little Jo*. Garden City, N.Y.: Doubleday, 1944.

Brown, Richard G. "Mr. Iscariot." *Literary Review* 6 (1963): 441–51.

Clark, Walter van Tilburg. *The Oxbow Incident*. New York: Random, 1940.

Cleaveland, Agnes Morley. *No Life for a Lady*. Boston: Houghton, 1941.

Cooley, Leland Frederick. *California*. New York: Avon, 1973.

Cox, William. *Chicano Cruz*. New York: Bantam, 1972.

Dokey, Richard. "Sánchez." *Southwest Review* 42 (1967): 354–67.

Ferber, Edna. *Giant*. New York: Grosset, 1952.

Fergusson, Harvey. *The Conquest of Don Pedro*. New York: William Morrow, 1954.

Garner, Claud. *Wetback*. New York: Coward, 1947.

Goodwyn, Frank. *The Black Bull*. Garden City, N.Y.: Doubleday, 1958.

————. *The Magic of Limping John*. New York: Farrar, 1944.

Gordon, Alvin. *Inherit the Earth: Stories from Mexican Ranch Life*. Tucson: U of Arizona P, 1963.

Granat, Robert. "Sánchez and the Víbora: A New Mexican Tale." *Texas Quarterly* 7 (1964): 128–38.

————. "To Endure." *New Mexico Quarterly* 28 (1958): 46–53.

Griffith, Beatrice. "In the Flow of Time." *Common Ground* 9 (1948): 13–20. Reprinted in *Best American Short Stories of 1949*, Ed. Martha Foley. Boston: Houghton, 1949. 106–16.

Gusewelle, C. W. "Robert Melendez: Retrospect." *Texas Quarterly* 11 (1968): 155–67.

Harris, Larry. "Mex." *The Fantastic Universe Omnibus*. Ed. Hans Stefan Santesson. Englewood Cliffs, N.J.: Prentice, 1960. 157–59.

Horgan, Paul. *The Common Heart*. New York: Harper, 1942.

————. *Figures in a Landscape*. New York: Harper, 1940.

Karchmer, Sylvan. "A Fistful of Alamo Heroes." *The Chicano: From Caricature to Self-Portrait*. Ed. Edward Simmen. New York: NAL, 1971. 164–71. The story also appeared in *Twenty-One Texas Short Stories*. Ed. William Perry. Austin: U of Texas P, 1954.

Kazan, Elia. *The Assassins*. New York: Stein, 1972. Greenwich, Conn.: Fawcett, 1973.

Kerouac, Jack. *On the Road*. New York: Viking, 1955.

————. "The Mexican Girl." *Paris Review* 11 (1955): 9–32.

LaFarge, Oliver. *Behind the Mountains*. Boston: Houghton, 1951.

Lisca, Peter. *The Wide World of John Steinbeck*. New Brunswick, N.J.: Rutgers UP, 1958.

Mailer, Norman. *The Naked and the Dead*. New York: NAL, 1948.

Mankiewicz, Don M. *Trial*. New York: Harper, 1955.

Marriott, Alice. "El Zopilote." *Southwest Review* 32 (1947): 284–90.

Means, Florence Crannel. *Teresita of the Valley*. Boston: Houghton, 1943.

Nelson, Eugene. *The Bracero*. Berkeley: Thorp Springs, 1972.

Richter, Conrad. *The Lady*. New York: Knopf, 1957.

Rosen, Roy. "Music for the Night." *Southwest Review* 38 (1953): 102–14.

Seale, George. "Dilemma, Mi Amigo." *Texas Quarterly* 9 (1966): 111–24.

Shulman, Irving. *The Square Trap*. Boston: Little, 1953.

Steinbeck, John. *Travels With Charley: In Search of America*. New York: Viking, 1962.

————. *The Wayward Bus*. New York: Viking, 1947.

Stevens, Helen. "The Black Shawl." *Southwest Review* 32 (1947): 295–300.

Stilwell, Hart. *Border City*. Garden City, N.Y.: Doubleday, 1945.

Wambaugh, Joseph. *The New Centurions*. Boston: Little, 1970. New York: Dell, 1972.

Waters, Frank. *People of the Valley*. Chicago: Swallow, 1941.

Part Four. Mexican-American Authors

A bibliography of Chicano theater, prose works, and poetry was established in 1972–73, thanks to the National Endowment for the Humanities; it appeared in *El Grito* 7 (Dec. 1973): 3 +. The list here includes only the most outstanding short stories and poems. Some works were published before the Chicano period.

1. Anthologies

Alurista (Alberto Urista), ed. *El Ombligo de Aztlán*. San Diego: Centro de Estudios Chicanos, 1971.

Chávez, Albert. *Yearnings: Mexican-American Literature*. West Haven, Conn.: Pendulum, 1972.

Flores, Joseph. *Songs and Dreams: Mexican-American Literature*. West Haven, Conn.: Pendulum, 1972.

Gross, Theodore L., ed. *A Nation of Nations: Ethnic Literature in America*. New York: Free, 1971.

Harth, Dorothy E., and Lewis M. Baldwin, eds. *Voices of Aztlán: Chicano Literature of Today*. New York: NAL, 1974.

Ludwig, Edward, and James Santibañez, eds. *The Chicanos: Mexican American Voices*. Baltimore: Penguin, 1971.

Ortego, Philip D., ed. *We Are Chicanos: An Anthology of Mexican-American Literature*. New York: Washington Square, 1973.

Paredes, Américo, and Raymund Paredes. *Mexican-American Authors*. Boston: Houghton, 1972.

Pearce, T. M., and Telfair Hendon, eds. *America in the Southwest: A Regional Anthology*. Albuquerque: U of New Mexico P, 1933.

Perry, G. Sessions, ed. *Roundup Time: A Collection of South-Western Writing*. New York: Whittlesey, 1943.

Romano-V., Octavio I., ed. *El Espejo—The Mirror: Selected Mexican-American Literature*. Berkeley: Quinto Sol, 1969. Rev. ed. 1972.

———. *Voices: Readings from El Grito: A Journal of Contemporary Mexican-American Thought, 1967–71*. Berkeley: Quinto Sol, 1971.

Salinas, Luis O., and Lillian Faderman, eds. *From the Barrio: A Chicano Anthology*. San Francisco: Canfield, 1973.

Shular, Antonia Castañeda, Tomás Ybarra-Frausto, and Joseph Sommers. *Literatura chicana: Texto y contexto. Chicano Literature: Text and Context*. Englewood Cliffs, N.J.: Prentice, 1972.

Simmen, Edward, ed. *The Chicano: From Caricature to Self-Portrait*. New York: NAL, 1971.

Valdez, Luis, and Stan Steiner, eds. *Aztlán: An Anthology of Mexican American Literature*. New York: Knopf, 1972.

2. Poems

Alurista (Alberto Urista). *Floricanto en Aztlán*. Los Angeles: Chicano Studies Center, UCLA, 1971.

———. "Poem in Lieu of Preface." *Aztlán: An Anthology of Mexican American Literature*. Ed. Luis Valdez and Stan Steiner. New York: Knopf, 1972. 332–33.

———. "War, Power, Peace, a Letter to Tizoc." *El Malcriado* 15 Nov. 1970. 8–9.

———, ed. *El Ombligo de Aztlán*. San Diego: Centro de Estudios Chicanos, 1971 [n. pag.]. "Bronze Rape," "Day and Fire," "En las montañas," "Face Your Fears, Carnal," "Got To Be on Time," "Me retiro con mis sueños," "Urban Prison."

———. *El Espejo—The Mirror: Selected Mexican-American Literature*. Ed. Octavio Romano-V. Berkeley: Quinto Sol, 1969. "Can This Really Be the End?" 178, "Cantos de ranas viejas" 173, "Grietas paredes" 174, "I Found a Picture" 177, "I've Been Conditioned" 176, "Mis ojos hinchados" 172, "Must Be the Season of the Witch" 176, "Nuestro barrio" 175, "Unexpectedly: My Night Gloom Came" 177.

———. *Papel Chicano* (Houston) 1 June 1972: "Chicano infante," "En la mesa," "In the barrio sopla el viento," "El pan nuestro" 8–9.

———. *El Pocho Che* (Berkeley) I-2 (1969). "Offering of Man to God" 34, "The People Bronzed in the Sun" 33.

————. *La Verdad* (San Diego) May 1970: "El carnalismo nos une" 9; Feb. 1969: "La cucaracha," "Have You Seen the cucaracha?" 7, "We've Played Cowboys," "Wheat Paper Cucarachas" 6; March 1969: "En el barrio," "I Know What Awaits Me" 3.

Alvarez, Jorge. *El Grito: A Journal of Contemporary Mexican-American Thought* 3 (Winter 1970): "Autobiography in Maize" 44, "Mi Papá—Fourth Canto" 42, "Old Man Bumming Some Heaven" 46, "On What I Know about the Delano Grape Strike," "Reminiscence No. 729" 45; 5 (Fall 1971): "The Affairs of State As Seen from Any College U.S.A." 62–63, "On the Natural Death of Federico García Lorca" 64, "The War on Poverty: The Only One We Waited for" 64–66.

Chávez, Fray Angélico (Manuel). *Eleven Lady-Lyrics and Other Poems.* Paterson, N.J.: St. Anthony, 1945.

Delgado, Abelardo. *Chicano: 25 Pieces of a Chicano Mind.* Denver: Barrio, 1971.

Elizondo, Sergio. *Perros y antiperros: Una épica chicana.* Trans. G. Segade. Berkeley: Quinto Sol, 1972.

Emiliano, Ramón. "Saga de Aztlán." *Grito del Sol* 1 (Jan.–Mar. 1976): 14.

Estupinián. *El Espejo—The Mirror: Selected Mexican-American Literature.* Ed. Octavio Romano. Berkeley: Quinto Sol, 1969. "Al abrir 'Les Fleurs du Mal'" 194, "Colors" 196, "Contrapunto" 202, "Dead Resident of a Western City" 198, "En la calle" 201, "En mi barrio" 195, "Ira furor brevis est. . . ." 199, "Markets" 198, "On the Portrait Scene from *Hernani* by Victor Hugo" 200, "Paisaje surrealístico" 197, "Sonido del teponaztle" 197, "III" 195, "Ubi sunt profesores?" 196.

Fuentes, Rumel. *El Grito* 6 (1973): "Corrido de César Chávez" 7–8, "Partido La Raza Unida" 27–28, "Walk Out en Crystal City" 23–24.

Gallardo, Aurelio Luis. *Leyendas y Romances: Ensayos Poéticos.* San Francisco, 1868.

Gómez-Quiñones, Juan. *5th and Grande Vista (Poems, 1960–1973).* Staten Island, N.Y.: Mensaje, 1974.

Gonzales, Rodolfo (Corky). *I Am Joaquín—Yo Soy Joaquín.* Delano, Calif.: Farm Workers Press, 1967. New York: Bantam, 1972.

Montoya, José Ernesto. *El sol y los de abajo.* San Francisco: Pocho Che, 1972.

————. "El Louie" *Aztlán.* Ed. Luis Valdez and Stan Steiner. New York: Knopf, 1972. 333–37.

————. *El Espejo—The Mirror: Selected Mexican-American Literature.* Ed. Octavio Romano. Berkeley: Quinto Sol, 1969. "La cantinera de Stockton" 192, "In a Pink Bubblegum World" 184, "La jefita" 188–89, "Lazy Skin" 183, "Pobre viejo Walt Whitman" 180, "Resonant Valley" 190–91, "Sunstruck While Chopping Cotton" 182–83, "Los vatos" 186–87, "El Vendido" 181.

Mora, Ricardo. *The Black Sun.* Lubbock: Trucha, 1973.

Nájera, José. "Words of Yohamateah to His Son." *El Grito* 5 (Fall 1971): 59–60.

Navarro, José Antonio. "Saltillo Mountain." *Lulac News* Sept. 1940: 23.

Pérez, Raymundo (Tigre). *Free, Free at Last.* S. 1., 1970.

————. *Phases.* Corpus Christi, Tex.: Tercer Sol, 1971.

Ponce, Miguel. *El Espejo* Ed. Octavio Romano. Berkeley: Quinto Sol, 1969. "A Conversation Held at a Party at Noah's" 169, "Lament" 168, "Night Rider" 168, "Three Faces" 170.

————. *El Grito* 2 (Winter 1969): "Assim Ontologicus," "Liliana by the Sea" 73, "Lucubrations, Presuntuosos" 74–77, "Tenochtitlán" 71–72; 3 (Winter 1970): "Aaron, a Birth" 49, "After My Father" 47, "Canción a la comida mexicana" 48.

Rivera, Tomás. *Always and Other Poems.* Sisterdale, Tex.: Sisterdale, 1973.

————. *El Grito* 3 (Fall 1969): "De niño, de joven, de viejo" 62–63, "Hide the Old People" 59, "Me lo enterraron" 57, "M'ijo no mira nada," "Odio" 60, "The Rooster Crows en Iowa y en Texas" 58, "Siempre el domingo" 61.

Romano-V., Octavio I. *El Grito* 4 (Winter 1971): "Plegaria" 62–63, "Por el estilo" 66, "Un teléfono" 64–65, "Yo no perdí nada" 66.

Salazar, Robert F. "The Other Pioneers." *Lulac News* July 1939: 32.

Salinas, Luis Omar. *Crazy Gypsy*. Fresno: Origines Publ., U de Aztlán, 1970.

Sánchez, Richard. *Canto y grito mi liberación*. El Paso: Mictla, 1971. Garden City, N.Y.: Anchor, 1973.

————. *Obras*. Pembroke, N.C.: Quetzal-Vihio, 1971.

————. *El Grito* 3 (Winter 1970): "Duelos" 30–31, "Mind Shopping" 34, "Mi única manera de vivir" 32, "Time: An Eclipse" 28.

Valdez, Luis. "There Is No Poetry About the U.S." *La Voz de Joaquín*. Albuquerque: U of New Mexico P, 1970.

Villanueva, Tino. *Hay Otra Voz Poems (1968–1971)*. Staten Island, N.Y.: Mensaje, 1972.

3. Short stories

Chávez, Fray Angélico. *New Mexico Triptych*. Paterson, N.J.: St. Anthony, 1940.

————. "The Fiddler and the Angelito." *Southwest Review* 32 (1947): 242–44.

Durán, Marcus. "Retrato de un bato loco." *Con Safos* 2 (1970).

Espinosa, Rudy. *El Grito* 2 (Winter 1969): "Little Eagle and the Rainbow" 78–80; 4 (Winter 1971): "La casita" 54–57, "Mono" 38–41; 5 (1972): "Mamá" 57.

Hinojosa-S., Rolando R. *Estampas del valle y otras obras—Sketches of the Valley and Other Works*. Berkeley: Quinto Sol, 1973.

Mendoza, Durango. "Summer Water and Shirley." *Prairie Schooner* Fall 1966: 219–28.

————. *The Chicanos: Mexican American Voices*. Ed. Edward Ludwig and James Santibañez. Baltimore: Penguin, 1971. "The Passing" 59–64, "The Woman in the Green House" 53–68.

Muro, Amada (pseud. for Chester Seltzer). *Arizona Quarterly* 18 (1962): "Going to Market" 209–16; 20 (1964): "Chihuahua Capirotada" 142–46; 24 (1968): "Mala Torres" 163–68; 25 (1969): "María Tepache" 343–47.

————. *New Mexico Quarterly* 34 (1964): "Cecilia Rosas" 353–64; 35 (1965): "Sunday in Little Chihuahua" 223–30.

Navarro, J. L. *Blue Day on Main Street and Other Short Stories*. Berkeley: Quinto Sol, 1973.

————. "Passing Time." *Aztlán: An Anthology of Mexican American Literature*. Ed. Luis Valdez and Stan Steiner. New York: Knopf, 1972. 163–70.

————. "Tamale Leopard." *El Grito* 3 (Summer 1970): 46–55.

Ortego, Philip D. "The Coming of Zamora." *El Grito* 1 (1968): 12–17.

Paredes, Américo. "The Hammon and the Beans." *Texas Observer* 55 (1963): 11–12.

Portillo, Estela. *Rain of Scorpions and Other Writings*. Berkeley: Tonatiuh, 1975.

Rechy, John. *Evergreen Review* 2 (Fall 1958): "Mardi-Gras" 60–70, "El Paso del Norte" 127–40.

Rivera, Tomás. "On the Road to Texas: Pete Fonseca." Trans. Victoria Ortiz. *Aztlán: An Anthology of Mexican American Literature*. Ed. Luis Valdez and Stan Steiner. New York: Knopf, 1972. 146–54.

————. *El Grito* 5 (1972): "Eva y Daniel" 18–21, Trans. ("Eva and Daniel") 22–25.

Romano-V., Octavio I. *El Espejo—The Mirror: Selected Mexican-American Literature*. Ed.

Octavio Romano. Berkeley: Quinto Sol, 1969. "Mosaico mexicano" 83–103, "A Rosary for Doña Marina" 104–22.

———. *El Grito* 1 (Winter 1968): "Goodbye Revolution—Hello Slum" 8–14; 5 (Fall 1971): "Strings for a Holiday" 45–54.

Sedillo, Juan A. "Gentlemen of Rio en Medio." *New Mexico Quarterly* 9 (1939): 181–83.

Suárez, Mario. *Arizona Quarterly* 3 (1947): "Cuco Goes to a Party" 121–27, "El Hoyo" 112–15, "Kid Zopilote" 130–37, "Loco Chu" 128–30, "Señor Garza" 115–21; 4 (1948): "Maestría" 368–73, "Southside Run" 362–68; 6 (1950): "Mexican Heaven" 310–15.

———. *Con Safos* I–3 (1969): "Las Comadres" 38–40; I–8 (1972): "Los Coyotes" 43–46.

Torres, José Acosta. *Cachito mío*. Berkeley: Quinto Sol, 1973.

Trejo, Arnulfo. "Maistro." *Arizona Quarterly* 16 (1960): 352–56.

Ulibarrí, Sabine R. *Tierra Amarilla: Stories of New Mexico*. Trans. Thelma Campbell Nason. Albuquerque: U of New Mexico P, 1971.

Vaca, Nick C. "Martín." *El Grito* 1 (Fall 1967): 25–31.

———. *El Espejo—The Mirror: Selected Mexican-American Literature*. Ed. Octavio Romano. Berkeley: Quito Sol, 1969. "The Purchase" 144–49, "The Visit" 150–60, "The Week of the Life of Manuel Hernández" 136–43.

4. Novels

Anaya, Rudolfo. A. *Bless Me, Ultima*. Berkeley: Quinto Sol, 1972.

Barrio, Raymond. *The Plum Plum Pickers*. New York: Harper, 1969.

Gallardo, Aurelio Luis. *Adah; o, El Amor de un Angel*. Mexico City: Paz, 1900.

Rechy, John. *City of Night*. New York: Grove, 1964.

———. *Numbers*. New York: Grove, 1967.

Rivera, Tomás. *". . . y no se lo tragó la tierra."* Trans. into English *(". . . and the earth did not part")* by H. Ríos in collaboration with the author and O. Romano-V. Berkeley: Quinto Sol, 1971.

Salas, Floyd. *Tattoo the Wicked Cross*. New York: Grove, 1967.

Vásquez, Richard. *Chicano*. Garden City, N.Y.: Doubleday, 1970.

Villarreal, José Antonio. *Pocho*. 1959. Garden City, N.Y.: Doubleday, 1970.

Villaseñor, Edmund. *Macho!* New York: Bantam, 1973.

5. Plays

Burruel, Francisco O. *The Dialogue of Cuco Rocha*. El Grito 3 (Summer 1970): 37–45.

Chávez, Mauro. *The Last Day of Class*. El Grito 4 (1971): 48–63.

De León, Nephtalí. *Five Plays*. Denver: Totinem, 1972.

Portillo, Estela. *The Day of the Swallows*. El Grito 3 (Summer 1970): 4–47.

Romano-V., Octavio I. *Mugre de la canción*. El Grito 3 (Summer 1970): 50–55.

Valdez, Luis. *Actos: El Teatro Campesino*. San Juan Bautista, Calif.: Cucaracha, 1971.

———. *Bernabé: A Drama of Modern Chicano Mythology*. Unpublished. An excerpt appears in *Aztlán: An Anthology of Mexican American Literature* Ed. Luis Valdez and Stan Steiner. New York: Knopf, 1972. 364–76.

Articles on Chicano theater

Bagby, Beth. "El Teatro Campesino. Interviews with Luis Valdez." *Tulane Drama Review* 11 (1967): 70–80.

Drake, Sylvie. "El Teatro Campesino: Keeping the Revolution on Stage." *Performing Arts* Sept. 1970: 56–62.

"Guerilla Drama: Productions of the San Francisco Mime Groups, Bread and Puppet Theater, and California's Teatro Campesino." *Time* 18 Oct. 1968: 72.

"New Grapes: El Teatro Campesino Performs for Migrant Farmworkers." *Newsweek* 31 July 1967: 79.

Steiner, Stan. "The Cultural Schizophrenia of Luis Valdez." *Vogue* 15 Mar. 1969: 112–13.

"Teatro Campesino." *New Yorker* 19 Aug. 1967: 23–25.

"El Teatro Campesino to Perform." *San Francisco Chronicle* 12 Feb. 1971: 45.

Valdez, Luis. "El Teatro Campesino—Its Beginnings." *Ramparts* July 1966: 50–56. Reprinted in *Aztlán*, ed. Luiz Valdez and Stan Steiner.

6. Autobiographies

Acosta, Adalberto Joel. *Chicanos Can Make It*. New York: Vantage, 1971.

Acosta, Oscar Zeta. *The Autobiography of a Brown Buffalo*. San Francisco: Straight Arrow, 1972.

Galarza, Ernesto. *Barrio Boy*. New York: Ballantine, 1972.

López, Enrique Hank. "Back to Bachimba." *Horizon* 9 (1967): 80–83.

Otero, Miguel Antonio. *My Life on the Frontier, 1864–1882*. 1st ed. New York: Pioneers, 1935.

———. *My Life on the Frontier, 1882–1897*. 1st ed. Albuquerque: U of New Mexico P, 1939.

———. *My Nine Years as Governor of the Territory of New Mexico, 1897–1906*. 1st ed. Albuquerque: U of New Mexico P, 1940.

Part Five. Folklore

Antología del Saber Popular: A Selection of Various Genres of Mexican Folklore Across the Border. Aztlán Publications, Monograph 2. Los Angeles: Chicano Studies Center, UCLA, 1971.

Applegate, Frank G. *Native Tales of New Mexico*. Philadelphia: Lippincott, 1932.

———. "New Mexican Sketches." *Yale Review* 21 (1932): 376–92.

Austin, Mary. "Folk Plays in the Southwest." *Theatre Arts Monthly* 17 (1933): 599–606.

———. "The Folk Story in America." *South Atlantic Quarterly* 33 (1934): 10–19.

———. "Native Drama in Our Southwest." *The Nation* 20 Apr. 1927: 437–40.

———. "New Mexico Folk Poetry." *El Palacio* 30 Nov. 1919: 146–50.

———. "Sources of Poetic Influence in the Southwest." *Poetry* 3 Dec. 1933: 152–63.

Boatwright, Mody C., ed. *The Healer of Los Olmos and Other Mexican Lore*. Publications of the Texas Folklore Society 24. Dallas: Southern Methodist UP, 1951.

———, ed. *Mexican Border Ballads and Other Lore*. Publications of the Texas Folklore Society 21. Austin: n.p., 1946.

Boatwright, Mody C., Wilson M. Hudson, and Allen Maxwell, eds. *Mesquite and Willows*. Publications of the Texas Folklore Society 27. Dallas: Southern Methodist UP, 1957.

———, eds. *Texas Folk and Folklore*. Publications of the Texas Folklore Society 26. Dallas: Southern Methodist UP, 1954.

Botkin, B. A., ed. *Folk-Say: A Regional Miscellany*. Norman: U of Oklahoma P, 1930.

———. *A Treasury of American Folklore*. New York: Crown, 1944.

Campa, Arthur L. *Spanish Folk-Poetry in New Mexico*. Albuquerque: U of New Mexico P, 1946.

———. *Spanish Religious Folklore in the Spanish Southwest*. Albuquerque: U of New Mexico P, 1934.

———. *Spanish Religious Folktheatre in the Spanish Southwest*. Albuquerque: U of New Mexico P, 1934.

———. "Spanish Traditional Tales in the Southwest." *Western Folklore* 6 (1947): 322–34.

———. "Today's Troubadours." *New Mexico Quarterly* 14 (1936): 16+.

Cole, M. R., ed. *Los Pastores: A Mexican Play of the Nativity*. Trans., intro., and notes by M. R. Cole. Boston: Houghton, 1931.

Curtis, F. S., Jr. "Spanish Folk-Poetry in the Southwest." *Southwest Review* 10 (1925): 68–73.

Dobie, John Frank. *Coronado's Children: Tales of Lost Mines and Buried Treasures of the Southwest*. Dallas: Southwest, 1930.

———. *The Flavor of Texas*. Dallas: Dealy, 1936.

———. "El [*sic*] Canción del Rancho de los Olmos." *Journal of American Folklore* 36 (1923): 192–95.

———. "The Mexican Corrido: Its Rise and Fall." *Madstones and Twisters*. Ed. M. Boatwright, M. H. Wilson, and A. Maxwell. Publications of the Texas Folklore Society 28. Dallas: Southern Methodist UP, 1958.

———. "The Mexican Vaquero of the Texas Border." *Southwestern Social Science Quarterly* 8 (1927–28): 15–26.

———. *The Mustangs*. New York: Bantam, 1954.

———. *A Vaquero of the Brush Country*. Boston: Little, 1952.

———. *The Voice of the Coyote*. Boston: Little, 1949. Lincoln: U of Nebraska P, 1961.

———, ed. *Happy Hunting Grounds*. Publications of the Texas Folklore Society 4. Dallas: Southern Methodist UP, 1925.

———, ed. *Man, Bird and Beast*. Publications of the Texas Folklore Society 8. Austin: n.p., 1930.

———, ed. *Puro Mexicano*. Publications of the Texas Folklore Society 12. Austin: n.p., 1935.

———, ed. *Southwestern Lore*. Publications of the Texas Folklore Society 9. Dallas: Southwest, 1931.

———, ed. *Tone the Bell Easy*. Publications of the Texas Folklore Society 10. Austin: n.p., 1932.

Dobie, John Frank, and Mody C. Boatwright, eds. *Straight Texas*. Publications of the Texas Folklore Society 13. Austin: n.p., 1937.

Dorson, Richard M. *American Folklore*. Chicago: U of Chicago P, 1959.

———. *Buying the Wind: Folklore in the United States*. Chicago: U of Chicago P, 1964.

Espinosa, Aurelio M., ed. "*Los Comanches*: A Spanish Heroic Play of 1780." *Bulletin of the University of New Mexico* 1 (1942).

———, ed. *Cuentos Populares Españoles*. 3 vols. Madrid: Consejo Superior, 1947.

———, ed. "The Field of Spanish Folklore in America." *Southern Folklore Quarterly* 5 (1941): 29–35.

———, ed. *Romancero de Nuevo Méjico*. Madrid: Consejo Superior, 1953.

———, ed. "Romancero Nuevomejicano." *Revue Hispanique* 33–84 (1915): 446–560; 40–97 (1917): 215–27; 41–100 (1917): 678–80.

Espinosa, José Manuel. *Spanish Folk-Tales from New Mexico*. Memoirs of the American Folk-Lore Society 30. New York: Stechert, 1937.

González, Jovita. "Among My People." *Tone the Bell Easy*. Ed. J. F. Dobie. Publications of the Texas Folklore Society 10. Austin: n.p., 1932. 99–108.

———. "Folklore of the Texas-Mexican Vaquero." *Texas and Southwestern Lore*. Ed. J. F. Dobie. Publications of the Texas Folklore Society 6. Austin: n.p., 1927. 7–22.

———. "Tales and Songs of the Texas-Mexicans." *Man, Bird and Beast*. Ed. J. F. Dobie. Publications of the Texas Folklore Society 8. Austin: n.p., 1930. 86–116.

Goodwyn, Frank. *The Devil in Texas*. Dallas: Dealy, 1936.

———. "Folklore of the King Ranch Mexicans." *Southwestern Lore*. Ed. J. F. Dobie. Publications of the Texas Folklore Society 9. Dallas: Southwest, 1931. 48–62.

Joseph Marie, Sister. "The Role of the Church and the Folk in the Development of the Early Drama in New Mexico." Diss. U of Pennsylvania, 1948.

Lomax, John A. *Cowboy Songs and Other Frontier Ballads*. New York: Macmillan, 1910.

Lomax, John A., and Alan Lomax, eds. *American Ballads and Folksongs*. New York: Macmillan, 1934.

Lucero-White [Lea], Aurora, ed. *The Folklore of New Mexico*. Vol. 1. Santa Fe: Seton Village, 1941.

———. *Literary Folklore of the Hispanic Southwest*. San Antonio: Naylor, 1953.

Otero, Nina. *Old Spain in Our Southwest*. New York: Harcourt, 1936.

Paredes, Américo. *With His Pistol in His Hand: A Border Ballad and Its Hero*. Austin: U of Texas P, 1958.

———. " 'El Corrido de José Mosqueda' as an Example of Pattern in the Ballad." *Western Folklore* 17 (1958): 154–62.

Rael, Juan B. *Cuentos españoles de Colorado y de Nuevo Méjico*. 2 vols. Stanford: Stanford UP, 1957.

———. "Cuentos españoles de Colorado y de Nuevo Méjico." *Journal of American Folklore* 52 (1939): 227–323; 55 (1942): 1–93.

Settle, W. A., Jr. *Jesse James Was His Name; or, Fact and Fiction Concerning the Careers of the Notorious James Brothers of Missouri*. Columbia: U of Missouri P, 1966.

Vásquez, Santana. *Historia de la canción mexicana*. Mexico City: Talleres Gráficos, 1931.

Texas Folklore Archive. Austin: U of Texas.

Index

Acculturation. *See* Assimilation
Acosta, Adalberto J., 197, 220, 221, 222, 255
Acosta, Oscar Zeta, 213, 227, 267, 268, 277
Adah; o, El Amor de un Angel, 76
Addis, Yda, 5
Agribusiness, 62, 193, 194, 234, 238, 245, 265, 279
Aguirre, Lydia E., 215
Alienation: and Anglo society, 171; and bilingualism, 280; and Mexican-Americans, 141, 246; and *pachucos,* 111
The Alien in Our Midst, 51
"Allá aguera," 236
Allen, John Houghton, 38, 59, 134, 150
Alurista (Alberto Urista): on Aztlán, 281; on the barrio, 227; on bilingualism, 278, 279, 280; on the cosmic race, 285–86, 289; on cultural conflict, 220, 284; on cultural pluralism, 288; on ethnic roots, 272, 275; on freedom, 287; on the *gringo,* 285; on migrant labor, 236, 239; on political activism, 261–62; on *la Raza,* 267; on redemption, 287; on the *vendido,* 249
Alva, Javier, 229, 270, 275
"Los Amados," 74
"La Americanita," 103
"American Me," 130, 145
"Los Americanos," 103
Anaya, Rudolfo, 275, 286, 290
Applegate, Frank, 68
Arzate, A., 216
The Assassins, 202–4

Assimilation: into Anglo culture, xiii, xvi, xvii, 54, 69, 100, 111, 112, 126–27, 130, 141, 148, 150, 154, 157, 169, 172, 184, 216, 219; assimilationist period, xvii, 112, 158, 184, 234, 266, 281, 293; of the barrio, 171, 178, 184, 196, 200, 221, 222, 223, 225, 253, 293; through boxing, 142–43, 172; into Indian culture, x; of the middle class, 111, 179, 257; through the military, 143–45, 183, 223–24
Atherton, Gertrude: on artistic sensitivity, 35; on communality, 29; on courtship, 7; on feminine sensuality, 33; on hedonism, 31; literary role of, 6; on materialism, 5; on the theatre, 67; on value systems, 26, 28, 30
Audubon, John W., 4, 18
Austin, Mary: on nature, 24, 54; on politeness, 58; on *Ramona,* 37; on Spanish dress, 5; on value systems, 28, 31
The Autobiography of a Brown Buffalo, 213, 267
Aztecs: in Chicano literature, 260–61, 270–76, 285–86; in Chicano movement, 81, 153; communal aspects of, 255; folklore tales of, 70, 81; history of, ix; mythology of, 79, 80, 211, 212, 216
Aztlán, 211, 217, 219, 220, 252, 257, 260, 268, 273, 281–82, 286

Baca, Próspero, 70, 71, 78
Baca family, 311 n. 4
"Back to Bachimba," 213
Badger, Joseph, 13, 14, 16
Baez (Harris), Joan, 258

Los Bandidos, 215, 248

Barrett, William: on the barrio, 202; on discrimination, 130; on injustice, 139, 140, 203; on the *jefe político*, 142, 148; on labor exploitation, 135; on the *paisano*, 124, 125, 126; on political activism, 147; on social mobility, 143; on social status, 132, 133, 138

Barrio, Raymond: biog. note on, 249 n. 77; on the *coyote*, 247; on labor strikes, 259; literary expression of, 237, 264; on migrant labor, 234, 238–39, 240; on the sun, 283

Barrio Boy, 153, 213, 220, 221, 255

Barrios: communal aspects of, 112, 120, 121, 125, 154, 156, 164–70, 176, 202, 221, 226; description of, 118, 155–56, 227, 279; drugs in, 226–27; ferment in, 111, 112, 117–18, 128, 137, 139, 146, 196, 228, 231; illegal aliens in, 112; militancy in, xiii, xv, 207, 217, 254; political aspects of, 102, 140, 148, 211, 255; as refuge/trap, 131–32, 142, 143, 144, 145, 151, 153, 162, 164, 169, 171, 196, 222, 233; religion/supernatural in, 158–59, 160–62, 250, 272

Bartlett, John Russell: on the barrio, 12; on biological determinism, 16; on land expropriations, 44; on laziness, 20; on the term "Mexican," 15; on missions, 22; on thievery, 19; on treachery, 18

"The Basket of Anita," 32

"The Bear," 295

Behind the Mountains, 114, 115, 127, 128, 131

Bell, Maj. Horace, 23, 30–31, 44

Bernabé: A Drama of Modern Chicano Mythology, 274

"Los Betabeleros," 95

The Black Bull, 119, 123

Blacks: ethnicity of, xvi, 104, 110, 113, 117, 118, 129, 131, 141, 149, 197, 202, 204, 209, 288, 295; exploitation of, 134; generational conflict of, 149; ghettoes and, 123, 132; literature of, 213, 251, 264, 290, 295–96; marginality of, 129; perseverance of, 116; sociopolitical aspects of, 8, 17, 19, 45, 95, 115, 132, 133, 134, 139, 147, 175, 196, 197, 209, 212, 214, 232, 255

"The Black Shawl," 114, 141

The Black Sun, 262, 271, 282, 286

Bless Me, Ultima, 275, 286

The Blood of the Conquerors, 16, 41, 43, 45, 47

Blue Day on Main Street, 231, 232

Bonham, Frank, 190, 196, 198–200, 202, 204

Boone, Henry J., 4, 21, 28

Border City, 130, 139, 203

Borthwick, J. O., 12

Bowman, James K., 138, 141

"The Box S Roundup," 33

Bracero, 190, 193, 194, 195

"El Bracero," 174

Braceros. *See* Immigration

"Bravo's Day Off," 27–28

Bradbury, Ray, 124, 125, 126, 170

Brewer, William, 8, 44

Brito, Aristeo, 282

Brown, Richard G., 148–49

Brown Berets (Brown Power), xv, 197, 212, 268, 345 n. 40

Browne, J. Ross, 4, 19, 20

Burruel, Francisco, 287

"Cactus Fruit," 275

California, 194, 195

The Californians, 24, 26, 32, 33, 37, 43

"Camino de perfección," 284

Campesinos, 113, 114–17, 124, 126, 130, 208, 217, 234–37, 243–44, 258, 265. *See also* Migrant farm workers; Primitivism

"La Canción del Rancho de los Olmos," 91

Canto y grito mi liberación, 262

Cather, Willa: on Catholicism, 41, 42, 44, 47; on cultural conflict, 44; on generosity, 29; on "greaser," 11; on musicality, 36; on primitivism, 28; on values, 17, 29, 30

Catholicism: Anglo view of, 6, 19, 20–21, 36, 43–44, 122–23; in the barrio, 154, 159; and Chicano movement, 189; Chicano rejection of, 196, 249–50; rites of, 36; and the supernatural, 77–80, 159

"Católicos por la Raza," 249

"Cecilia Rosas," 156, 158, 177–78

A Century of Dishonor, 294

Los Cerritos, 5, 28, 29, 33, 35

Channing, Grace Ellery, 5, 32

Chávez, (Fray) Angélico, 154, 160, 161

Chávez, César, 189, 193, 195, 205, 207–9, 210, 211, 212, 243, 244, 246, 248, 254, 257–58, 259, 343 n. 2

Chicano, 219, 220–21, 222–25, 232–33, 248, 253

Chicano Cruz, 196, 197

Chicano Manifesto, xii, 212, 217, 219, 248, 250, 252, 263, 277, 280, 282, 284, 288

"The Chicano Manifesto," 250, 258

"The Chicano Renaissance," 153, 154, 212, 213

Chicanos: Chicanas, 251–52; definition of, xii, xiv, xv, 156, 280, 282, 285, 299 n. 24, 341 n. 3; emergence of, 196–200, 246, 247; literary renaissance of, 214, 246; pessimism of, 201–4; protest movement of, xiii, 189, 190, 212, 249–51, 263, 343 n. 3

¡Chicanos! The Living and the Dead! 256, 257

Chicanos Can Make It, 197, 220, 222

"The Children Were Victims," 236

"Christ in Alabama," 251

City of Night, 153, 170

El Clamor Público, 67, 69, 77, 82

Clappe, Louisa Knapp (Dame Shirley), 3, 6, 48

Cleaveland, Agnes Morley, 114

Clemens, Jeremiah, 11, 22
"Las Comadres," 163, 164, 252
"The Coming of Zamora," 211, 217, 218, 255
The Common Heart, 115, 122
Communism, 129, 140, 142, 147, 173, 182, 194, 245, 255, 259, 334 n. 82, 341 n. 7
Conflict, cultural: in barrio, 131; in border *corrido*, 99–104; in Chicano literature, 220; post-1848, 42–43; in schools, 221
The Conquest of Don Pedro, 120, 122, 131
La Conquista de México, 270
"El Contrabando del Paso," 87
Cool Cat, 190, 201, 202
Cooley, Leland Frederick, 194–95
"El Corrido de Aztlán," 217
"El Corrido de Gregorio Cortez," 84, 90
"El Corrido de Kiansis," 92, 94
"El Corrido de la Emigración," 97
"El Corrido de la Pennsylvania," 92, 94
"El Corrido de Laredo," 87
"El Corrido de los Japoneses," 340 n. 72
"El Corrido de Macario Romero," 75
"El Corrido de Robestown," 95
"El Corrido de Texas," 95
"El Corrido Pennsylvanio," 102
Corridos: of border conflict, 83–90, 93, 99; of deportation, 98–99; of emigration, 93–95; as emotional safety-valve, 104–5; form of, 84, 318 n. 27; of immigration, 71, 90, 94–99; of migration, 94–95, 173; origin of, xvi, 70–71
Cortina, Juan Nepomuceno, 85–86, 322 n. 5, 323 n. 16
Cosmic race, 216, 241, 267, 287–91, 295
Cox, William, 197–98
Coyote. *See Vendido*
Crane, Stephen, 6, 42, 46

Daggett, (Mrs.) Charles Stewart, 5, 24, 25, 26, 30
"The Dance at Chevalier's," 11, 17
Dark Madonna, 54, 56, 58
Davis, William, 4, 17, 19, 20, 21
Dawn, 285
Day, Father Mark, 189
"Day Long Day," 241
"The Dead Man's Child," 29
Death, concept of, 75–77, 117, 124–25
Death Comes for the Archbishop, 29, 30, 41, 42, 44, 47
The Decline of the Californios, 4, 12, 22, 40
"Defensa de los Norteños," 93
DeForest, John William, 12, 13, 14, 15
Delano, Alonso, 3, 17, 18, 48
Delano (Calif.) strike, xvii, 189, 197, 207–9, 210, 212, 242, 244, 245, 248, 250, 258–59, 295, 341 n. 1
De León, Nepthalí: on Anglo society, 285; on Aztlán, 218, 281–82; on César Chávez, 208;

on conscription, 260; on ethnic roots, 273; on political activism, 256–57; on qualities of the heart, 286; on *la Raza*, 268
Delgado, Abelardo: on Anglo society, 284; on the barrio, 228; on brotherhood, 287; on César Chávez, 207; on Chicano experience, 199, 254–55; on Delano strike, 209; on discrimination, 276; on ethnic roots, 272, 275; on pacifism, 258; on religion, 250–51, 289; on the *vendido*, 248; on women, 253
"Delmar of Pima," 41, 45, 48, 64, 148
"Denver," 220
"Deportados," 94, 98, 99
"Desmadrazgo," 263
"The Devotion of Enríquez," 34, 42, 48
The Dialogue of Cuco Rocha, 287
"Dichotomies," 279
Dime Novels, 4, 5, 8, 13, 15, 18
Discrimination: in housing, 131–32; before the law, 97, 131, 139–41, 171, 181; in schools, 131, 132–33, 145, 172, 217, 218, 224–25, 237; in the workplace, 112, 131, 134, 174. *See also* Ethnocentrism; Nativism
Dobie, Frank, 17, 67, 69, 71
Dokey, Richard, 191
Domínguez, Juanita, 276
Las Dos Caras del Patroncito, 243
"Los Dos Mojados," 174
Durán, Marcus, 232

"Efectos de la Crisis," 97
Elizondo, Sergio, 81, 214, 220, 226, 265, 284
Emery, George, 28
Emiliano, Ramón, 273
Emrich, Duncan, 11
"El Enganchado," 96, 99
"El Paso del Norte," 153
"En la Noche," 125
El Espejo—The Mirror, 213
Espinosa, Aurelio, 68, 71
Espinosa, José M., 68, 79
Espinosa, Mary Lou, 252, 253
Estampas del valle y otras obras, 282
Ethnocentrism (racism): in Anglo writers, 12–16, 22; in the barrio, 139; toward foreigners, 175; toward the "greaser," 8, 11, 17, 22, 27, 175; of police, 181; reverse racism, 212; stereotypes of, 23, 214, 293. *See also* Discrimination; Nativism
Evans, George, 3, 24, 109
"Everybody Knows Tobie," 237

Families: 162, 337 n. 38; assimilation in, 179–82; generational conflict in, 100, 111, 149–51, 191, 222–23; traditions of, xvi, 59, 135–36, 162–64, 179
Ferber, Edna: on discrimination, 144; on generational conflict, 150; on labor, 135, 137,

Ferber, Edna (*continued*)
    148; on protest, 146; on segregation, 131,
    133, 134; on *vaqueros*, 134
Fergusson, Harvey: on biological determin-
    ism, 16, 48; on Catholicism, 21; on cultural
    conflict, 42; on duality, 41; on ethnic pride,
    27; on hedonism, 32, 35, 119; on land expro-
    priations, 45; on music, 67; on the *penitentes*,
    47; on sexuality, 122
"El Ferrocarril," 100
Figures in a Landscape, 53
"A Fistful of Alamo Heroes," 129
"Flight," 54, 58, 162
Floricanto en Aztlán, 261
Folklore: forms of, 67–71, 73, 79, 190; *La
    Llorona*, 80, 250, 276; oral tradition, xvi,
    xvii; and the supernatural, 159; tales, 67, 70,
    79, 80, 102
For the Soul of Rafael, 26
Forty Acres, 189
"Frankie's Last Wish," 229, 232
Fuentes, Rumel, 212, 217, 218, 276

La Gaceta, 69
Galarza, Ernesto, xiv, 153, 213, 220–21, 231,
    255, 335 n. 1
Gallardo, Aurelio, 68, 72, 76
"The Gambler, the Nun and the Radio," 54,
    55, 58, 60
Gamio, Manuel, xiv, 70
Ganilh, Anthony, 47
Garland, Hamlin, 6, 9, 40, 45, 46
Garner, Claud, 130, 136
Garza, Daniel, 237
"Gentlemen of Rio en Medio," 169
Giant, 129, 131, 133, 134, 135, 137, 142, 144,
    146, 148, 150, 225
Gonzales, Rodolfo (Corky): biog. note on,
    344 n. 27; on the term "Chicano," xiii; on
    justice, 211; on land expropriation, 219; on
    political activism, 260–61; on *la Raza*, 268;
    on religion, 289
González, Genaro, 204, 241, 284, 286
González, Jorge, 212
González, Jovita, 68, 79
"Goodbye Revolution—Hello Slum," 22, 214,
    258
Goodwyn, Frank, 68, 71, 119, 128
Granat, Robert, 117, 126, 127
Grant, Madison, 51
Grapes of Wrath, 54, 63, 238
Greaser: Anglo view of, 8; origin of term,
    11–12; skin color of, xii, xiii; stereotype of,
    18–20, 175, 214; unpejorative connotation
    of, 42. *See also* Ethnocentrism
Gregg, Josiah, 47
Griffith, Beatrice, 130, 136, 144, 145
Gringo: gringoism, 23, 30, 38, 40, 45, 65, 116,

176, 218, 219, 250, 260; hatred of, 89, 93, 98,
    99, 102, 174, 180, 196, 204, 207, 214, 215,
    217–18, 219, 220, 223, 229, 237, 250, 256,
    262, 278, 281, 285, 286, 287; origin of term,
    23, 307 n. 99
Guadalupe, Virgin of: as Aztec Tonantzín,
    272; in Chicano movement, 79, 208, 253;
    as mother figure, 269; origin of term, 272,
    306 n. 74, 355 n. 27; as patron saint, 20, 57,
    78–79, 160, 162, 203; as tie to homeland, 93,
    160
Guadalupe Hidalgo, Treaty of, xii, 217, 219
"La Guerra Mundial," 101
Gutiérrez, José Angel, 211–12, 345 n. 30

Hall, Maj. Sam S., 4, 13, 16, 18
"The Hammon and the Beans," 181
Harris, Frank, 52
Harte, Bret, 6, 7, 34, 42, 48
Hay Otra Voz, 254
Heart, qualities of, 28–30, 56, 57, 120, 125,
    168, 286
Hedonism: lack of inhibitions, 8, 19–20,
    75–76, 258; lust for life, 30–32, 119–20, 122,
    168; sexuality and, 35, 56–57, 75–76, 123,
    286
Hemingway, Ernest, 55, 58–61
Henry, O. (William Sidney Porter), 11, 13, 16,
    21
Herrera, Albert, 219
Herrick, Robert, 7, 30, 45
"Un Hijo del Sol," 204, 241, 259, 284, 286
Horgan, Paul: on Catholicism, 122; His-
    panophilia of, 53–54; on labor, 62, 63; on
    the *paisano*, 57, 58; on qualities of the heart,
    56
"El Hoyo," xiv, 155–56, 158, 161, 169, 185, 226
Huelguistas, 258
Huerta, Jorge, 274
Hughes, Langston, 251
"Hunchback Madonna," 160

I Am Joaquín / Yo Soy Joaquín, 219, 260, 266,
    269, 270, 272, 289
"Ignacio Treviño," 86
Immigrants: Anglo, x–xi; deportation of, 97,
    98, 99, 135, 137–38, 223; exploitation of,
    97–98, 135, 138; families of, 164; illegal, 62,
    63, 96, 112, 134, 135–39, 147, 174–75, 193,
    194, 315 n. 1; legal (and *braceros*), 97, 111–12,
    134, 135–39, 147, 174, 175, 194–95, 208, 293;
    in literature, xvi; from Mexico, xii, 6, 62;
    and Rangers, 137
Inherit the Earth, 115
"Los Inmigrantes," 95
Integration. *See* Assimilation
"In the barrio sopla el viento," 279
"In the Flow of Time," 110, 130, 139, 144, 145

In the Footprints of the Padres, 36
In Those Days, 27, 34
"It's Painful," 237

Jackson, Helen Hunt, 5, 6, 24, 37, 38, 44
El Jardín, 257, 269, 272, 285, 289
Jeffers, Robinson, 7, 24, 28, 34
"La Jefita," 252
"José Lozano," 90

Karchmer, Sylvan, 129, 131, 143
Kazan, Elia, 202–4
Kerouac, Jack: on the mother, 117; on mysticism, 113, 118, 121; on primitivism, 119, 120, 127, 128; on sexuality, 123
"Kid Zopilote," 157
King Ranch, 323 n. 26

The Labyrinth of Solitude, 74, 111, 141, 269
The Lady, 116
La Farge, Oliver, 114, 115, 127
Lamy, Fr. Jean-Baptiste, 44
Land Grants: expropriation of, 45; landed families and, 31; pre-1848, x, 3, 25; Tijerina movement and, 209–11, 217–18
The Land of Sunshine, 5
Language: barrier, 43, 102–3, 131, 132, 135, 224; bilingualism, xvii, 70, 112, 214, 216, 219, 224, 227, 234, 237, 243, 265, 276, 297, 331 n. 13, 356 n. 62; conflict, 35, 41, 43, 48, 65, 101, 102–3, 239, 277; erosion of, 101, 179–81; florid, 21; Nahuatl influence on, 356 n. 58; *pachuco*, 111; *pochismo*, 127; satirical, 102–3
Lanier, Sidney, 12
La Salle, Sieur de, 297 n. 4
"Lazy Skin," 213
Lewis, Alfred, 16, 17, 21
Lira, Augustín, 252
"The Little Mice," 124
La Llorona, 80, 321 n. 46
La Lluvia de los Ingleses, 69
"Loco-Chu," 167
London, Jack, 6, 7, 42, 45, 46, 48
Long Road to Delano, 189
The Long Valley, 54, 114
López, César, 249
"El Louie," 230
Love, concept of, 67, 73–76, 121, 122, 123
Lulac News, 69, 169
Lummis, Charles F.: on ethnic pride, 27, 28; on hedonism, 31; Hispanophilia of, 5; on primitivism, 28; on virility, 33; on women, 33

McGinnis, John, 63
Machismo. *See* Virility
Macho! 193, 208

McWilliams, Carey, 7–8, 12, 22, 23, 36, 38, 39, 64, 112, 134, 135, 189, 298 n. 14
"Maestría," 166
The Magic of Limping John, 125
Magoon, James, 4
Mailer, Norman, 130, 144, 145
Main Line West, 56
Malinche, Malentzín, 78, 269, 297 n. 2
Manifest Destiny, xi, 3, 8, 9, 295
Mankiewicz, Don, 132, 139, 140
Manly, W. L., 3
"Mardi Gras," 153
"María Tepache," 160, 162, 168
Mariposilla, 24, 25, 26, 36, 37
Marriott, Alice, 124–25
"Martín," 283
Martínez, Fr. Antonio José, 44, 313 n. 17
"Los Matachines," 77
Méndez, Miguel, 271–72
Mestizos: acceptance of, 39, 42; in colonial era, ix–x; pride in, 269, 272–73, 276–77, 287–88, 289; rejection of, xiii, 12, 15–17, 20, 26, 27, 38, 175, 403
"Mex," 124
"The Mexican," 42, 46, 48, 141
Mexican Gold Trail, 109
"Mexican Heaven," 157, 160, 167
"Los Mexicanos que Hablan Inglés," 101
"The Mexicans," 56
Mexico: independence of, xii, 17, 158, 209, 213, 261; political situation of, xv, 71; provinces of, xi; 1910 revolution in, 6, 9, 17, 46, 64, 65, 81, 135, 155, 158, 161, 174, 215, 221, 222, 247, 255, 315 n. 14; war with U.S., xi, 3, 8, 17, 22, 67, 105, 214, 260
"Mexico Americano," 276
Migrant farm workers: *braceros*, 193–95; and *coyotes*, 135, 147, 148, 245, 247; in Depression, 62; exploitation of, 82, 98–99, 111–12, 130, 134, 135, 136, 194, 237–45, 247; generational conflict of, 150, 172, 191; itinerant life of, 234–37; living and working conditions of, 62, 134, 135, 136, 148, 174, 195, 234, 255; strikes of, 64, 207, 208, 248, 258; as writers, 153
"Migrant Lament," 279
The Militants, 256
Miller, Cincinnatus Hiner (Joaquin), 5, 24, 34
"Mis ojos hinchados," 220
"Mr. Iscariot," 149
Montoya, José: on cultural conflict, 282; on migrant labor, 241; on *pachuquismo*, 228, 230; on religion, 289; on self-abnegation, 252; on stereotypes, 213–14; on the *vendido*, 247
"Moonlight on the Snow," 42, 46
Mora, Richard, 271, 282, 286
Morality Play, 289
Los Moros y los Cristianos, 317 n. 21

Morton, Carlos, 257, 267–68, 272, 285
Mosqueda, José, 89
Muro, Amado (Chester Seltzer), 154, 156, 168, 177–78, 336 n. 6
Murrieta, Joaquín, 5, 7, 13, 16, 34, 38, 46, 69, 86, 260, 261, 302 n. 34, 310 n. 98
"Music for the Night," 114, 116

Nájera, José, 266
The Naked and the Dead, 130, 144
Navarro, J. L., 229, 231, 232, 289
Nativism, 6, 8. See also Discrimination; Ethnocentrism
Nelson, Eugene, 189, 190, 193–94, 195
The New Centurions, 190, 196, 202, 204
"A New Cross," 251
A New Mexico David, 33
New Mexico Triptych, 160
No Quarter Given, 53, 57, 58
Norris, Frank, 25, 31, 36
North from Mexico, 189
No Saco Nada de la Escuela, 268, 277
"Nuestro Barrio," 227
El Nuevo Mundo, 69
"The Nun's Tale," 189

The Octopus, 36
"Of Bronze the Sacrifice," 273
Of Mice and Men, 295
Olmsted, Frederick Law, 15, 44
"On the Paystreak," 34
On the Road, 113, 117, 118, 119, 120, 121, 123, 128
"On the Road," 251
"On the Road to Texas: Pete Fonseca," 231
The Oregon Trail, 16, 19, 20, 141
Ortego, Philip D.: on Aztlán, 217; on the term "Chicano," xiv; on ethnic roots, 270; on land grants, 211, 218; on political activism, 255
Otero, Miguel A., 69
"The Other Pioneers," 169
Overland, 12, 13, 15
The Ox-Bow Incident, 117

"Pablo Apodaca's Bear," 33
Pachuco riots, 110
Pachucos: alienation of, 131, 145, 157, 171, 229, 263; definition of, 111; dialect of, 11, 127, 146, 177, 230, 231, 327 n. 7; dress of, 110, 139, 146, 177; and escapism, 177; as existential men, 176, 228–30; origins of, 111; rejected by the barrio, 156, 176; stereotype of, 215; and vatos locos, 226
Padilla, Pedro, 211
"El Padre del Charro Vargas," 100
Paisanos, 55–58, 60, 61, 113–14, 116, 118, 119, 126, 167. See also Campesinos; Primitivism

Paredes, Américo, 67, 71, 84, 181
Parkman, Francis, 4, 15, 16, 20
"El Paso del Norte," 153, 156, 159, 160, 165, 174, 175, 177
"The Passing of Enríquez," 42
"Passing Time," 232
Pastorals, 5
Los Pastores, 67, 69, 301 n. 17, 317 n. 21
The Pastures of Heaven, 54, 56, 114
"El Patrón," 138
Pattie, James O., 22
Paz, Octavio, 110, 111, 141, 205, 269
"Las Pelonas," 100
Penitentes (Hermanos), 44, 46–47, 65, 114, 161
"The Penitent Thief," 161
People of the Valley, 114, 116
"El Peregrino," 282
Pérez, Gloria, 254
"Perla Is a Pig," 227
"Un Picnic," 101
Pitt, Leonard, 38
Pizaña, Aniceto, 88, 89
Play Number 9, 256, 282
Plaza, Antonio, 180
The Plum Plum Pickers, 237–40, 248, 259, 283
Pocho, 112, 153, 158, 159, 162, 163, 172–74, 175, 177, 179, 181, 182, 184, 222
Pochos: and assimilation, 154, 171, 180, 184, 237, 281, 294, 340 n.48; dialect of, 102, 127, 181; and double allegiance, 181, 266; and education, 172
"The Politeness of Cuesta la Plata," 54, 58
Portillo (Tramblay), Estella, 251, 255, 260, 289
Primitivism, 17, 28, 30, 55, 113, 115, 118, 119, 123–24, 125, 126, 128, 234. See also Campesinos; Paisanos
The Professor's House, 30

"Que Hay Otra Voz," 235
Quetzalcoatl, xiv, 125, 126, 270, 273, 275, 285, 330 n. 90
La Quinta Temporada, 244, 250, 254

"A Ramble with Eulogia," 30
Ramírez, Francisco P., 67, 69, 77, 82
Ramona, 24, 26, 36, 37, 38, 39, 195
"El Rancho Donde Yo Nací," 100
Rangers: in border conflicts, 7, 8, 13, 18, 104, 218; in corridos, 84, 85, 86, 88, 89, 90; and illegal aliens, 136, 137; in literature, 34
La Raza: and term "Chicano," 20, 131, 261, 262, 267, 280; as cosmic race, 257, 268, 287–90; definition of, 189; and education, 219; exploitation of, 250; language of, 227, 277; origins of, 217, 269–70, 272, 275; politicization of, 146, 147, 209, 211, 212; pride in, 198; traditional values of, 150
La Raza (book), x, xv, xvi, 255

"Recast," 255, 260
Rechy, John: on the barrio, 156, 157; on discrimination, 175; on the family, 160; on *pachucos*, 176–77; on religion, 159, 160, 161
"El Recuerdo de mis grillos," 274
"The Red Pony," 54, 55, 57
"Los Reenganchados a Kansas," 97
Remington, Frederic, 34
"El Renacimiento de Huitzilopochtli," 274
Rendón, Armando: on Aztlán, 282; on Catholicism, 249–50; on cosmic race, 287, 288; on cultural conflict, 284; on cultural schizophrenia, 276; on discrimination, 219; on the *mestizo*, 277; on the *vendido*, 248; on women's emancipation, 252, 253
"El Renegado," 100
"Retrato de un Bato Loco," 232
"Reunión de los Vaqueros," 90
Rhodes, Eugene Manlove, 5, 7
Richter, Conrad, 116
The Rising Tide of Color, 6
Rivera, Tomás: on identification, 213; literary expression of, 264–65, 296; on migrant labor, 234–36, 237, 240; on *pachuquismo*, 231
"Roan Stallion," 34
"Robert Meléndez: Retrospect," 192
"Robstown," 250
Romano, Octavio, xvi, 64, 68, 214, 229, 255, 258, 288
Romanticism: of bandits, 46; in border *corrido*, 90; decline of, 51, 66; in Dime Novels, 4; and escapism, 73, 81, 109; of *machismo*, 60; in post-1848 writers, 9, 24, 25, 27, 37, 47, 48, 73, 113; stereotypes, 48, 49, 61, 109–10, 127, 214, 215, 294
Rosen, Roy, 114, 116
Ross, Calvin, 54
Royce, Josiah, 3, 4, 48, 67, 68
Ryan, Marah Elliis, 5, 26, 37

Sacramento Valley, 297 n. 6
"The Sacred Spot," 229, 270, 275
"Saga de Aztlán," 273
Salazar, Robert Felix, 169
Salinas, Omar, 250, 274
Salinas, Raúl, 208, 212, 226–28
Sánchez, David, 212
"Sánchez," 191–92
Sánchez, Ricardo: on bilingualism, 278–80; on Catholicism, 249, 250; on cosmic race, 288, 290; on cultural conflict, 219, 220; on cultural schizophrenia, 262; on literary expression, 264; on *pachuquismo*, 229; on redemption, 287; on repression, 262–63; on stereotypes, 214; on the *vendido*, 247; on Vietnam, 260, 261; on virility, 286
"Sánchez and the Víbora," 101, 126
Saroyan, William, 56, 62, 63, 64–65

"Saturday Belongs to the Palomía," 237
Schizophrenia, cultural, 40, 145, 180–85, 219, 262, 277
"Los Sediciosos," 87, 88
Sedillo, Juan, 169
Seltzer, Chester. *See* Muro, Amado
"Señor Garza," xv, 165–67, 168, 184, 299 n. 34
"Señor Payroll," 126
"Sepultura del Diablo," 211
The Shadows of the Images, 130, 133, 135, 138, 139, 143, 147, 148, 203
"The Shepherd," 54
Shock, cultural, xi, xvi, 40, 41, 71, 72, 99, 131, 150, 171, 181, 220, 222, 226, 294
Shulman, Irving: on cultural schizophrenia, 145–46; on the family, 130; on generational conflict, 150–51; on migrant labor, 135; on social mobility, 143; on the *vendido*, 148
Simmen, Edward, xiv, xv, 6, 68, 154, 185
Simmons, Ozzie, 38
Sky Determines, 54
"Smile out the revolu," 263
"So Farewell Hope and with Hope, Farewell Fear," 221
El Soldado Razo, 259
"Somewhere, Sometime," 289
The Song of the Lark, 28, 36
"Southside Run," 155, 156, 163, 167
Southwest, 38
The Spendid Idle Forties, 7, 24, 30, 33, 36
The Square Trap, 130, 134, 135, 141, 142, 145, 146, 148, 149, 151, 172, 176, 191
Steinbeck, John: on discrimination, 295; on escapism, 54; on the *paisano*, 55–56, 57–58, 60–61; on primitivism, 119–29; on virility, 58
Stereotypes: in advertising, 214; in Anglo writers, xi, xvii, 22–23, 38, 49; in early Mexican American writers, 73; questioning of, 52; in realistic writers, 61; rejection of, 213–15
Stevens, Helen, 114, 141
Stevenson, Philip, 54, 65
Stilwell, Hart, 130, 134, 203
Stoddard, Charles W., 5
Stoddard, Lathrop, 6
Strikes, 49, 64–65, 258–59. *See also* Delano strike
"Stupid America," 258
Suárez, Mario: on assimilation, 147, 179; on the barrio, 156, 165–66, 169; biog. note on, 335 n. 2; on Catholicism, 158, 159, 160–61; on the term "Chicano," xiv; on hedonism, 167–68; on *pachucos*, 157; on women's emancipation, 164
Summers, Richard, 54, 55, 58
Sun: Aztec, 133, 212, 241, 271, 273–74, 281, 282–83, 285, 286, 287; in migrant labor,

Sun (continued)
240–41; negative value of, 63, 216, 240–41, 249, 273, 286; positive value of, 24, 240, 273, 291
"Sunday in Little Chihuahua," 156, 163, 180
"Sunstruck While Chopping Cotton," 241, 289
"Surgeon and the Nun," 62

"Tamales," 11, 14
"Tata Casehua," 271
"Tears and Perfume," 75
Teatro Campesino, 69, 207, 212, 215, 234, 242–45, 247, 256, 258, 259, 264, 268. See also Valdez, Luis
Texas Romances, 22
Tijerina, Reies López, 209–11, 212, 217, 218, 344 n. 19
"To a Dead Lowrider," 231
"To Endure," 117, 126
"The Tomato Can," 62, 63
"El Toro Moro," 91, 318 n. 2
Tortilla Flat, 54, 55, 56, 57, 58, 61, 109, 113, 119, 120, 123, 125
Travels with Charley, 118, 119, 123
Trejo, Arnulfo, 166, 168, 169, 335 n. 2
Las Tres Uvas, 244
Trial, 130, 132, 139, 202
"A Trip Through the Mind Jail," 226
Tuck, Ruth, 38–39
Two Years Before the Mast, 68

Ulibarrí, Sabine, 288
"Unexpectedly," 283

Vaca, Nick, 22, 23, 199, 213, 283
Valdez, Luis: on Anglo society, 285; on assimilation, 215; on Aztec cosmogeny, 274; on bilingualism, 277; on the term "Chicano," xiii; on the Chicano movement, 207, 212; on conscription, 259; on the "greaser," 214; on literature, 213, 264, 286, 296; on Marxism, 255; on migrant labor, 241–45; on the Spanish conquest, 271, 292. See also Teatro Campesino
Van Tilburg Clark, Walter, 117
"El Vaquero," 76
Vaqueros: in border corridos, 71, 90–93; dress of, 5, 35, 36, 90; exploitation of, 134; in folklore, 70, 79; as prototype of cowboy, xi; realistic view of, 38; romantic view of, 28, 73, 78; stereotype of, 20, 61; strikes of, 313 n. 40; virility of, 82, 91, 92
Vargas, Roberto, 298
Vásquez, Enriqueta, 252
Vásquez, Richard, xiv, 220–21, 228, 232–33
Vásquez, Tiburcio, 310 n. 98

Vato (bato) loco, 226, 227, 228, 230, 232–33, 274–75
"Los Vatos," 228
Vélez, C. G., 221
"El Vendido," 248
Vendido: condemnation of, 148–49; as coyote, 147, 241, 247; definition of, 147, 247; failure of, 177–78; as jefe político, 147–48; as malinche, 248
Los Vendidos, 215, 248
"Versos de los Bandidos," 87, 88
"Versos del Rancho de las Norias," 88
"Los Veteranos de 1941," 183
"Vida, Proceso y Muerte de Aurelio Pompa," 79
"La Vida y Aventura de Joaquín Murrieta," 69, 97
La Vie quotidienne des Aztèques, 77, 270, 273
Vietnam, 245, 256, 259–60, 282
Vietnam Campesino, 244–45, 254, 259, 260
Vigil, Cleofas, 249
Villanueva, Tino, 229–30, 235, 241, 254
Villarreal, José Antonio: on assimilation, 154, 171, 179; on barrio wife, 162; biog. note on, 335 n. 2; on Communism, 173, 182; on cultural schizophrenia, 180–81; on discrimination, 172, 175–76; on the Mexican Revolution, 158; on religion, 159
Villaseñor, Edmund, 193, 208
"Vine of Guadalupe," 79
Virgin of Guadalupe. See Guadalupe, Virgin of
Virility: effect on family, 162–64; in romanticism, 32–35; sexuality and, 122–23; as stoicism, 56–61
Viva Chicano, 190, 196, 198, 199, 202, 204
"Viva Huelga en General," 209

Walker, Franklin, 37
Wambaugh, Joseph, 190, 196–97, 202, 204
Waste, 27, 30, 45
"The Wasteland," 51
Waters, Frank, 114, 116
The Wayward Bus, 118, 119, 121
"Weekend," 231
"The Week of the Life of Manuel Hernández," 213, 283
Wetback, 130, 136, 137, 194
Wetbacks. See Immigrants
"What's happenin . . . ," 278
"When raza?" 261
Williams, Henry Llewellyn, 15
"With a Hey Nonny Nonny," 62, 64, 65
With His Pistol in His Hand, 7, 18, 70, 83, 84, 85
Wolfville Days, 18
Woman, Mexican-American: as the Chicana, 222, 243, 251–54, 274; courtship role

of, 74–75; as earth mother, 28, 30, 117; emancipation of, 99, 101, 122, 157, 180, 223; endurance of, 126; as love/sex object, 32–34, 35, 73–75; as mother, 59, 80–81, 126, 149, 165, 188, 253; as primitive woman, 29; sensuality of, 34, 122; as wife, 162, 163, 164
"The Wonderful Ice Cream Suit," 125
"Words of Yohamatack to His Son," 266

Yankee Jim, 21

. . . Y no se lo tragó la tierra, 213, 234–37, 248–49
"Yo Soy Chicano," 276

Zapata, Emiliano, 135, 158, 198, 208, 209, 211, 212, 218, 255, 270, 332
Zimmerman Note, 301 n. 30
Zootsuiters, xiv, 157, 166, 176, 229, 232, 257, 270, 275. See also Pachucos
Zoot Suit Riots, 110, 144, 327 n. 4
"El Zopilote," 125

About the Author

MARCIENNE ROCARD was born in Paris in 1931. She completed her undergraduate studies at the Sorbonne, earning B.A. degrees in German and English. In 1963, she received a Master's Degree in French from the University of California at Los Angeles. Professor Rocard earned the French *agrégation* in 1970 and received a doctorate from the University of Lyon II in 1978. She has taught French, English, and German language courses in France, Switzerland, Canada, and the United States. In 1971, she joined the faculty of the University of Toulouse–Le Mirail, where she has taught English and courses in American and Canadian literature. In 1981, she spent the spring semester at Ohio University as a Fulbright exchange professor. In addition to *Les Fils du soleil*, Professor Rocard has published numerous articles and book reviews in the fields of Canadian and Chicano literature.

About the Translator

EDWARD GUILLÉN BROWN, JR., was born in the south Texas border town of Del Rio in 1933. He was raised in a bilingual-bicultural family and spent his formative years in East Los Angeles, California. He taught both French and Spanish at Garden Grove (Calif.) High School and West Texas State University, and currently teaches French at the University of Arizona. In 1968 he earned a doctorate in French, with a minor in Spanish, from the University of Arizona. He specializes in the study of contemporary theater and has published articles on the Teatro Campesino de Aztlán and on Spanish-born "French" dramatist Fernando Arrabal. He is at work on an annotated bibliography of the works of Arrabal. He has also written on foreign-language pedagogy and has served as acting head of the Department of French and Italian, and as associate dean of the College of Liberal Arts at the University of Arizona.